Bradley L. Jones

SAMS

# Teach Yourself C# in 21 Days

Techmedia
Munish Plaza, 20 Ansari Road, Darya Ganj, New Delhi-110002

***FIRST INDIAN EDITION 2001***

***REPRINTED 2002***

Distributors:

**MICRO BOOK CENTRE**
2, City Centre, CG Road,
Near Swastic Char Rasta,
**AHMEDABAD-380009** Phone: 6421611

**COMPUTER BOOK CENTRE**
12, Shrungar Shopping Centre, M.G. Road,
**BANGALORE-560001** Phone: 5587923, 5584641

**MICRO BOOKS**
Shanti Niketan Building, 8, Camac Street,
**KOLKATTA-700017** Phone: 2826518, 2826519

**BUSINESS PROMOTION BUREAU**
8/1, Ritchie Street, Mount Road,
**CHENNAI-600002** Phone: 8534796, 8550491

**DECCAN AGENCIES**
4-3-329, Bank Street,
**HYDERABAD-400001** Phone: 4756400, 4756967

**MICRO MEDIA**
Shop No. 5, Mahendra Chambers, 150 D.N. Road,
Next to Capital Cinema V.T. (C.S.T.) Station,
**MUMBAI-400001** Ph.: 2078296, 2078297, 2002732

**BPB PUBLICATIONS**
B-14, Connaught Place, **NEW DELHI-110001**
Phone: 3325760, 3723393, 3737742

**INFO TECH**
G-2, Sidhartha Building, 96 Nehru Place,
**NEW DELHI-110019**
Phone: 6438245, 6415092, 6234208

**INFO TECH**
Shop No. 2, F-38, South Extension Part-1
**NEW DELHI-110049**
Phone: 4691288, 4641941

**INFO TECH**
B-11, Vardhman Plaza, Sector-16,
Electronics Nagar, **NOIDA-201301**
Phone: 914-512329, 515917, 515918

**BPB BOOK CENTRE**
376, Old Lajpat Rai Market,
**DELHI-110006 PHONE**: 3861747

Original ISBN 0-672-32072-1



Composed in AGramond and MCP digital by Macmillan Computer Publishing.



*Printed in India by arrangement with*
**Macmillan Computer Publishing, USA.**

**Price : Rs. 297/-**

ISBN 81-7635-579-8

Published by G.C. Jain for Techmedia, Munish Plaza, 20 Ansari Road,
Darya Ganj, New Delhi-110 002 and Printed by KWALITY OFFSET PRINTING PRESS.

# Contents at a Glance

# Contents

# Origin of the C# Name

I asked Tony Goodhew, C# Product Manager, how Microsoft came up with C# as a final name for their new language. The following is his answer:

Ok it's a bit like making sausages—You like the end product but don't really want to see the process...

We started with around 150 names and worked with all the internal teams to create a list of the top 20 names. From there I locked Anders Hejlsberg, Scott Wiltamuth, Joe Nalewabau and myself in a room until we came up with a list of 7 names. We then sent those off to legal for international trademark searches. Based on their feedback we created an ordered list of the names (in the order on which we liked them) and had Paul Maritz, Jim Allchin, Todd Neelson, David Vascovitch and Bill Gates select the one they liked. They agreed with us that C# was the best name and we went forward and trademarked our Visual C# name.

The basic criterion for the name was to show its C/C++ heritage so that is the common thread the first 150 names had.

This entire process took about 8 months.

Tony G

# About the Author

**Bradley L. Jones** is the site manager for a number of high-profile developer sites—including `CodeGuru.com`, `Developer.com`, and `Javascripts.com`—and an executive editor of internet.com's EarthWeb channel. Bradley has been working with C# longer than most developers, because he was invited to Microsoft prior to the official beta release. Bradley's background includes experience developing in C, C++, PowerBuilder, SQL Server, and numerous other tools and technologies. Additionally, he is an internationally best-selling author who wrote the original 21 Days book: *Sams Teach Yourself C in 21 Days*.

# Dedication

*This book is dedicated to my wife, Melissa.*

# Acknowledgments

Although I create the structure and write the words, I don't create a book like this on my own. There were many people whose contributions helped to make this a much better book.

First, however, let me thank my wife and family for being patient and understanding while I set the normal flow of life aside in order to focus on writing this book.

I'd also like to give my personal thanks to Mattias Sjögren. Mattias proved to be one of the best technical editors that I have had review one of my books. His suggestions and corrections to this book truly brought it to a higher level of quality. I'd also like to thank Andy Beaster who's remained calm even though chapters of this book were being passed thirteen different ways all at once. In the end, Andy pulled the material together and ensured that all was perfect for the final product. Neil Rowe, Kevin Howard, Brad Shannon, Nancy Albright, and others also spent large amounts of time focused on making this the best book possible. They deserve to be acknowledged as well.

On a different note, this book would have been impossible to do without the support of a number of people at Microsoft. Over the last several years I have gained help from too many people to list all of them. A number of people on the C# team—such as Nick Hodapp, Tony Goodhew, and Eric Gunnerson—helped provide information on C# in addition to answering many of my questions.

Because this book provides the chance to publicly acknowledge people, I'd also like to thank a number of other people at Microsoft for their help over the last several years—either on this book or on many other projects. This includes Brad Goldberg, Rob Howard, Jeff Ressler, Scott Guthrie, Megan Stuhlberg, Connie Sullivan, Dee Dee Walsh, Dennis Bye, Bob Gaines, Robert/Bob Green, David Lazar, Greg Leake, Lizzie Parker, Charles Sterling, Susan Warren, and lots of others.

I'd like to thank you, the reader. There are a number of books on C# that you could have bought or could use. I appreciate you giving me the chance to teach you C#.

Finally, thanks go to Bob, who seems to always be blue.

# Tell Us What You Think!

As the reader of this book, *you* are our most important critic and commentator. We value your opinion and want to know what we're doing right, what we could do better, what areas you'd like to see us publish in, and any other words of wisdom you're willing to pass our way.

As an Associate Publisher for Sams, I welcome your comments. You can fax, e-mail, or write me directly to let me know what you did or didn't like about this book—as well as what we can do to make our books stronger.

*Please note that I cannot help you with technical problems related to the topic of this book, and that due to the high volume of mail I receive, I might not be able to reply to every message.*

When you write, please be sure to include this book's title and author as well as your name and phone or fax number. I will carefully review your comments and share them with the author and editors who worked on the book.


Fax: 317-581-4770

E-mail: `feedback@samspublishing.com`

Mail: Jeff Koch, Associate Publisher
Sams Publishing
201 West 103rd Street
Indianapolis, IN 46290 USA

# Introduction

Welcome to *Sams Teach Yourself C# in 21 Days*. As you can guess from the title of this book, I have written this book with the expectation that you will spend 21 days learning the C# programming language. The book is divided into 21 lessons that can each be accomplished in a couple of hours or a single evening. If you dedicate 2 to 3 hours for 21 days, you should easily be able to work through this book. This doesn't have to be sequential evenings—nor does it even have to be evenings.

Each lesson can be read in an hour or two. Some will take longer to read, some less time. If you expect to learn C# by just reading, you will be greatly disappointed. Rather, you should expect to spend half your time reading and the other half of the time entering the code from the chapters, doing the quizzes, and trying out the exercises. That might sound like a lot, but you can do each lesson in an evening if you try.

The quizzes and exercises are part of the 21-day series, designed to help you confirm your understanding of that day's material. After reading a day's lesson, you should be able to answer all the quiz questions. If you can't, you many need to review parts of that lesson.

The exercises present you with a chance to apply what you've learned. The exercises will generally focus on understanding code, identifying common code problems, or writing code based on the day's lesson.

Answers to the quizzes and most of the exercises are provided in Appendix A, "Answers." Try to come up with the answers on your own before jumping to the appendix!

There are several other features you will notice when reading this book. You'll find Tips, Notes, and Caution boxes throughout the book. Tips provide useful suggestions. Notes provide additional information you might find interesting. Cautions alert you to a common problem or issue you might encounter.

A special element of this series of books is the Q&A section at the end of each day. The Q&A section provides questions—along with the answers—you might have while reading that day's lesson. These questions might involve peripheral topics to the chapter.

## Assumptions I've Made

I've made a few assumptions about you. I've assumed that you have a C# compiler and the .NET runtime environment. Although you can read this book without them, you will have a harder time fully understanding what is being presented.

I've assumed that you are a beginning-level programmer. If you are not, you will still gain a lot from this book; however, you might find that in some areas you will progress slower than you'd like.

This book does not assume that you are using Visual C# or the Visual Studio .NET development environment. Many books assume you are using these tools from Microsoft. I do not make that assumption here. You can use Microsoft's tools or you can use a number of other tools. You'll learn more about this within the book.

# Web Site Support

No one is perfect—especially me. Combine this with a programming language that is relatively new, and you can expect problems to crop up.

This book has been reviewed by a number of people. In addition to my reviews of the book, there have been technical and development reviews of the book. Even with all the reviews, errors still happen. In case a problem did sneak through, errata for this book can be found on a number of Web sites. The publisher's web site is located at `http://www.samspublishing.com/`

Additionally, I have created a site specifically for the support of this book:

`www.TeachYourselfCSharp.com`

I will post errata at this location.

# Source Code

I believe that the best way to learn a programming language is to type the code and see it run. For that reason, I don't expect CDs to be included with beginning-level books. I also understand, however, that my beliefs are not the same as everyone else's. For that reason, I have included the source code for this book on the `www.TeachYourselfCSharp.com` Web site.

This book is for learning. You can use the source code contained within it. You can adapt it. You can extend it. You can give it to your Mom. Learn from it. Use it. By purchasing this book, you gain the right to use this code any way you see fit, with one exception. You can't repurpose this code for a C# tutorial.

## Getting Started

I applaud your efforts in reading the Introduction; however, you're most likely more interested in learning about C#. "Week One at a Glance" gives you an overview of what you can expect in your first week of C#.

# WEEK 1

# At a Glance

Welcome to *Sams Teach Yourself C# in 21 Days*. If you are unsure what you need to know to get the most out of this book, you should review the Introduction. The Introduction will also explain the elements used within this book.

You are getting ready to start the first of three weeks of lessons that will help you gain a solid foundation for writing C# programs. Starting with Day 1, "Getting Started with C#," you will be entering C# programs. You will also learn how a C# program is created.

On Day 2, "Understanding C# Programs," you will learn how C# fits into the Microsoft .NET framework. You will also be taught about the fundamental principles of an object-oriented language.

Days 3, "Storing Information," 4, "Working with Operators," and 5, "Control Statements," will teach you the core programming concepts required for C# programming. This includes the concepts surrounding storing and manipulating data, as well as how to control program flow.

Days 6, "Classes," and 7, "Class Methods and Member Functions," cover classes and class methods. Classes are a core concept to object-oriented programming and therefore a core concept to C# programming.

By the end of the first week, you will have learned many of the foundational concepts for C# programming. You'll find that by the time you review this first week, you will have the tools and knowledge to build basic C# programs on your own.

# WEEK 1

# DAY 1

# Getting Started with C#

Welcome to *Sams Teach Yourself C# in 21 Days!* In today's lesson you begin the process of becoming a proficient C# programmer. Today you

- Learn why C# is a great programming language to use
- Discover the steps in the Program Development Cycle
- Understand how to write, compile, and run your first C# program
- Explore error messages generated by the compiler and linker
- Review the types of applications that can be created with C#

## What Is C#?

It would be unusual if you bought this book without knowing what C# is. It would not, however, be unusual if you didn't know a lot about the language. Released to the public in June 2000, C#—pronounced See Sharp—has not been around for very long.

C# is a new language created by Microsoft and submitted to the ECMA for standardization. This new language was created by a team of people at Microsoft led by Anders Hejlsberg. Interestingly, Hejlsberg is a Microsoft

Distinguished Engineer who has created other products and languages, including Borland Turbo C++ and Borland Delphi. With C#, he focused on taking what was right about existing languages and adding improvements to make something better.

C# is a powerful and flexible programming language. Like all programming languages, it can be used to create a variety of applications. Your potential with C# is limited only by your imagination. The language does not place constraints on what you can do. C# has already been used for projects as diverse as dynamic Web sites, development tools, and even compilers.

C# was created as an object-oriented programming (OOP) language. Other programming languages include object-oriented features, but very few are fully object-oriented. Later in today's lesson you will understand how C# compares to some of these other programming languages. You'll also learn what types of applications can be created. On Day 2, "Understanding C# Programming," you will learn what it means to use an object-oriented language.

## Why C#?

Many people believed that there was no need for a new programming language. Java, C++, Perl, Microsoft Visual Basic, and other existing languages were believed to offer all the functionality needed.

C# is a language derived from C and C++, but it was created from the ground up. Microsoft started with what worked in C and C++ and included new features that would make these languages easier to use. Many of these features are very similar to what can be found in Java. Ultimately, Microsoft had a number of objectives when building the language. These objectives can be summarized in the claims Microsoft makes about C#:

- C# is simple.
- C# is modern.
- C# is object-oriented.

In addition to Microsoft's reasons, there are other reasons to use C#:

- C# is powerful and flexible.
- C# is a language of few words.
- C# is modular.
- C# will be popular.

1

**Caution** The following section contains a lot of technical terms. Don't worry about understanding these. Most of them don't matter to C# programmers. The ones that do matter will be explained later in this book.

## C# Is Simple

C# removes some of the complexities and pitfalls of languages such as Java and C++, including the removal of macros, templates, multiple inheritance, and virtual base classes. These are all areas that cause either confusion or potential problems for C++ developers. If you are learning C# as your first language, rest assured—these are topics you won't have to spend time learning!

C# is simple because it is based on C and C++. If you are familiar with C and C++—or even Java—you will find C# very familiar in many aspects. Statements, expressions, operators, and other functions are taken directly from C and C++, but improvements make the language simpler. Some of the improvements include eliminating redundancies. Other areas of improvement include additional syntax changes. For example, C++ has three operators for working with members: ::, ., and ->. Knowing when to use each of these three symbols can be very confusing in C++. In C#, these are all replaced with a single symbol—the "dot" operator. For newer programmers, this and many other features eliminate a lot of confusion.

**Note** If you have used Java and you believe it is simple, you will find C# to be simple. Most people don't believe that Java is simple. C# is, however, easier than Java and C++.

## C# Is Modern

What makes a modern language? Features such as exception handling, garbage collection, extensible data types, and code security are features that are expected in a modern language. C# contains all of these. If you are a new programmer, you might be asking what all these complicated-sounding features are. By the end of your twenty-one days, you will understand how they all apply to your C# programming!

**Note** Pointers are an integral part of C and C++. They are also the most confusing part of the languages. C# removes much of the complexity and trouble caused by pointers. In C#, automatic garbage collection and type safety are an integral part of the language. If you are not familiar with the concepts of pointers, garbage collection, and type safety, don't worry. These are all explained in later lessons.

## C# Is Object-Oriented

**New Term** The keys to an object-oriented language are encapsulation, inheritance, and polymorphism. C# supports all of these. *Encapsulation* is the placing of functionality into a single package. *Inheritance* is a structured way of extending existing code and functionality into new programs and packages. *Polymorphism* is the capability of adapting to what needs to be done. Detailed explanations of each of these terms and a more detailed description of object orientation are provided in Day 2's lesson. Additionally, these topics are covered in greater detail throughout this book.

## C# Is Powerful and Flexible

As mentioned before, with C# you are limited only by your imagination. The language places no constraints on what can be done. C# can be used for projects as diverse as creating word processors, graphics, spreadsheets, and even compilers for other languages.

## C# Is a Language of Few Words

**New Term** C# is a language that uses a limited number of words. C# contains only a handful of terms, called *keywords,* which serve as the base on which the language's functionality is built. Table 1.1 lists the C# keywords. A majority of these keywords are used to describe information. You might think that a language with more keywords would be more powerful. This isn't true. As you program with C#, you will find that it can be used to do any task.

**Table 1.1** The C# Keywords

| | | | | |
|---|---|---|---|---|
| abstract | as | base | bool | break |
| byte | case | catch | char | checked |
| class | const | continue | decimal | default |
| delegate | do | double | else | enum |
| event | explicit | extern | false | finally |
| fixed | float | for | foreach | goto |
| if | implicit | in | int | interface |
| internal | is | lock | long | namespace |
| new | null | object | operator | out |
| override | params | private | protected | public |

**TABLE 1.1** continued

| | | | | |
|---|---|---|---|---|
| readonly | ref | return | sbyte | sealed |
| short | sizeof | stackalloc | static | string |
| struct | switch | this | throw | true |
| try | typeof | uint | ulong | unchecked |
| unsafe | ushort | using | virtual | void |
| while | | | | |

> **Note** There are a few other words used in C# programs. While not keywords, they should be treated as though they were. Specifically, get, set, and value.

## C# Is Modular

**NEW TERM** C# code can (and should) be written in chunks called *classes*, which contain routines called *member methods*. These classes and methods can be reused in other applications or programs. By passing pieces of information to the classes and methods, you can create useful, reusable code.

> **Note** On Day 2, you learn about classes, and on Day 6, "Classes," you learn how to start creating your own.

## C# Will Be Popular

C# is one of the newest programming languages. At the time this book was written, it was unknown as to what the popularity of C# would be, but it is a good bet that this will become a very popular language for a number of reasons. One of the key reasons is Microsoft and the promises of .NET.

Microsoft wants C# to be popular. Although a company cannot make a product be popular, it can help. Not long ago, Microsoft suffered the abysmal failure of the Microsoft Bob operating system. Although Microsoft wanted Bob to be popular, it failed.

C# stands a better chance of success than Microsoft Bob. I don't know whether people at Microsoft actually used Bob in their daily jobs. C#, however, *is* being used by Microsoft. Many of its products have already had portions rewritten in C#. By using it, Microsoft helps validate the capabilities of C# to meet the needs of programmers.

Microsoft .NET is another reason why C# stands a chance to succeed. .NET is a change in the way the creation and implementation of applications is done. Although virtually any programming language can be used with .NET, C# is proving to be the language of choice. Tomorrow's lesson includes a section that explains the high points of .NET.

C# will also be popular for all the features mentioned earlier: simplicity, object-orientation, modularity, flexibility, and conciseness.

# C# Versus Other Programming Languages

You might have heard about Visual Basic, C++, and Java. Perhaps you're wondering what the differences are between C# and these other programming languages. You might also be wondering whether you should be teaching yourself one of these three languages instead of C#.

**Note**

The top questions on Internet discussion forums related to .NET are

- What is the difference between Java and C#?
- Isn't C# just a Java clone?
- What is the difference between C# and C++?
- Which should I learn, Visual Basic .NET or C#?

Microsoft says that C# brings the power of C++ with the ease of Visual Basic. C# does bring a lot of power, but is it as easy as Visual Basic? It might not be as easy as Visual Basic 6, but it is as easy as Visual Basic .NET (version 7), which was rewritten from the ground up. The end result is that Visual Basic is really no easier than programming C#. In fact, you can actually write many programs with less code using C#.

Although C# removes some of the features of C++ that cause programmers a lot of grief, no power or functionality was really lost. Some of the programming errors that are easy to create in C++ can be totally avoided in C#. This can save you hours or even days in finishing your programs. You'll understand more about the differences from C++ as you cover topics throughout this book.

Another language that has gotten lots of attention is Java. Java, like C++ and C#, is based on C. If you decide to learn Java later, you will find that a lot of what you learn about C# can be applied.

You might also have heard of the C programming language. Many people wonder if they should learn C before learning C#, C++, or Java. Simply put, there is absolutely no need to learn C first.

Enough about whys and wherefores. You most likely bought this book so you could learn to use the C# language to create your own programs. The following sections explore the steps involved in creating a program. You then walk through the creation of a simple program from start to finish.

# Preparing to Program

You should take certain steps when you're solving a problem. First, you must define the problem. If you don't know what the problem is, you can't find a solution! After you know what the problem is, you can devise a plan to fix it. When you have a plan, you can usually implement it. After the plan is implemented, you must test the results to see whether the problem is solved. This same logic can be applied to many other areas, including programming.

When creating a program in C# (or in any language), you should follow a similar sequence of steps:

1. Determine the objective(s) of the program.
2. Determine the methods you want to use in writing the program.
3. Create the program to solve the problem.
4. Run the program to see the results.

An example of an objective (see step 1) might be to write a word processor or database program. A much simpler objective is to display your name on the screen. If you don't have an objective, you won't be able to write an effective program.

The second step is to determine the method you want to use to write the program. Do you need a computer program to solve the problem? What information needs to be tracked? What formulas will be used? During this step, you should try to determine what will be needed and in what order the solution should be implemented.

As an example, assume that someone asks you to write a program to determine the area inside a circle. Step 1 is complete, because you know your objective: Determine the area inside a circle. Step 2 is to determine what you need to know to ascertain the area. In this example, assume that the user of the program will provide the radius of the circle. Knowing this, you can apply the formula $\pi r^2$ to obtain the answer. Now you have the pieces you need, so you can continue to steps 3 and 4, which are called the Program Development Cycle.

# The Program Development Cycle

The Program Development Cycle has its own steps. In the first step, you use an editor to create a file containing your source code. In the second step, you compile the source code to create an intermediate file called either an executable file or a library file. The third step is to run the program to see whether it works as originally planned.

## Creating the Source Code

**New Term** *Source code* is a series of statements or commands that are used to instruct the computer to perform your desired tasks. As mentioned, the first step in the Program Development Cycle is to enter source code into an editor. For example, here is a line of C# source code:

```
System.Console.WriteLine("Hello, Mom!");
```

This statement instructs the computer to display the message `Hello, Mom!` onscreen. (For now, don't worry about how this statement works.)

### Using an Editor

**New Term** An *editor* is a program that can be used to enter and save source code. There are a number of editors that can be used with C#. Some are made specifically for C#, and others are not.

At the time this book was written, there were only a few editors created for C#; however, as time goes on, there will be many more. Microsoft has added C# capabilities to its Visual Studio product which includes Visual C#. This is the most predominant editor available. If you don't have Visual Studio .NET, however, you can still do C# programming.

There are also other editors available for C#. Like Visual Studio.NET, many of these enable you to do all the steps of the development cycle without leaving the editor. More importantly, most of these color-code the text you enter. This makes it much easier to find possible mistakes. Many editors will even help you by given you information on what you need to enter and giving you a robust help system.

If you don't have a C# editor, don't fret. Most computer systems include a program that can be used as an editor. If you're using Microsoft Windows, you can use either Notepad or WordPad as your editor. If you're using a Linux or UNIX system, you can use such editors as ed, ex, edit, emacs, or vi.

Most word processors use special codes to format their documents. Other programs can't read these codes correctly. Many word processors—such as WordPerfect, Microsoft Word, and WordPad—are capable of saving source files in a text-based form. When you want to save a word processor's file as a text file, select the text option when saving.

**Note** To find alternative editors, you can check computer stores or computer mail-order catalogs. Another place to look is in the ads in computer programming magazines. The following are a few editors that were available at the time this book was written:

1

- **CodeWrite.** CodeWright is an editor that provides special support for ASP, XML, HTML, C#, Perl, Python, and more. It is located at `www.premia.com`.
- **EditPlus.** EditPlus is an Internet-ready text editor, HTML editor, and programmer's editor for Windows. Although it can serve as a good replacement for Notepad, it also offers many powerful features for Web page authors and programmers, including the color-coding of code. It is located at `www.editplus.com`.
- **JEdit.** JEdit is an Open-Source editor for Java; however, it can be used for C#. It includes the capability of color-coding the code. It is located at `http://jedit.sourceforge.net`.
- **Poorman IDE by Duncan Chen.** Poorman provides a syntax-highlighted editor for both C# and Visual Basic.NET. It also enables you to run the compiler and capture the console output so you don't need to leave the Poorman IDE. Poorman is located at `www.geocities.com/duncanchen/poormanide.htm`.
- **SharpDevelop by Mike Krüger.** SharpDevelop is a free editor for C# projects on Microsoft's NET platform. It is an Open-Source Editor (GPL), so you can download both source code and executables from `www.icsharpcode.net`.

## Naming Your Source Files

When you save a source file, you must give it a name that describes what the program does. In addition, when you save C# program source files, give the file a .cs extension. Although you could give your source file any name and extension, .cs is recognized as the appropriate extension to use.

# Executing a C# Program

Before digging into the Program Development Cycle, it is important to understand a little bit about how a C# program executes. C# programs are different from programs you could create with other programming languages.

**NEW TERM** C# programs are created to run on the Common Language Runtime (CLR). This means that if you create a C# executable program and try to run it on a machine that doesn't have the CLR or a compatible runtime, it won't execute. *Executable* means that the program can be run, or executed, by your computer.

The benefit of creating programs for a runtime environment is portability. In older languages such as C and C++, if you wanted to create a program that could run on different platforms or operating systems, you had to compile different executable programs. For example, if you wrote a C application and you wanted to run it on a Linux machine and a Windows machine, you would have to create two executable programs—one on a Linux machine and one on a Windows machine. With C#, you create only one executable program, and it runs on either machine.

**New Term** If you want your program to execute as fast as possible, you want to create a true executable. A computer requires digital, or *binary,* instructions in what is called *machine language*. A program must be translated from source code to machine language. A program called a *compiler* performs this translation. The compiler takes your source code file as input and produces a disk file containing the machine language instructions that correspond to your source code statements. With programs such as C and C++, the compiler creates a file that can be executed with no further effort.

With C#, you use a compiler that does not produce machine language. Instead it produces an Intermediate Language (IL) file. Because this isn't directly executable by the computer, you need something more to happen to translate or further compile the program for the computer. The CLR or a compatible C# runtime does this final compile just as it is needed.

One of the first things the CLR does with an IL file is a final compile of the program. In this process, the CLR converts the code from the portable, IL code to a language (machine language) that the computer can understand and run. The CLR actually compiles only the parts of the program that are being used. This saves time. Additionally, after a portion of your IL file has been given a true compile on a machine, it never needs to be compiled again, because the final compiled portion of the program is saved and used the next time that portion of the program is executed.

> **Note** Because the runtime needs to compile the IL file, it takes a little more time to run a program the first time than it does to run a fully compiled language such as C++. After the first time a program is completely executed, the time difference disappears because the fully compiled version will be used from that point.

> **Note** The last minute compiling of a C# program is called Just In Time compiling or *jitting*.

1

## Compiling C# Source Code

To create the IL file, you use the C# compiler. You typically use the csc command to run the compiler, followed by the name of the source file. For example, to compile a source file called radius.cs, you type the following at the command line:

```
csc radius.cs
```

If you're using a graphical development environment, compiling is even simpler. In most graphical environments, you can compile a program by selecting the compile icon or selecting the appropriate option from the menu. After the code is compiled, selecting the run icon or selecting the appropriate option from the menus executes the program. You should check your compiler's manuals for specifics on compiling and running a program.

**NEW TERM** After you compile, you have an IL file. If you look at a list of the files in the directory or folder in which you compiled, you should find a new file that has the same name as your source file, but with an .exe (rather than a .cs) extension. The file with the .exe extension is your "compiled" program (called an *assembly*). This program is ready to run on the CLR. The assembly file contains all the information that the common runtime needs to know to execute the program.

Figure 1.1 shows the progression from source code to executable.

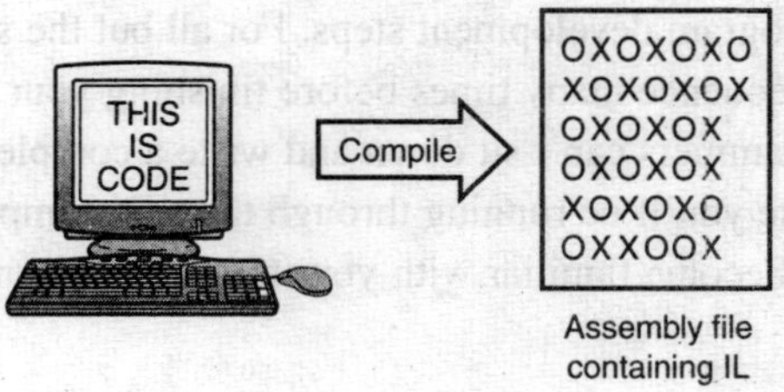


**FIGURE 1.1.**
*The C# source code that you write is converted to Intermediate Language (IL) code by the compiler.*

> **Note**
> In general, two types of deliverables are created as C# programs—executables and libraries. For the two weeks of this book you focus on executables, which are EXE files. You can also use C# for other types of programming, including scripting on ASP.NET pages. You learn about libraries in the third week.

## Completing the Development Cycle

After your program is a compiled IL file, you can run it by entering its name at the command-line prompt or just as you would run any other program.

If you run the program and receive results different from what you thought you would, you need to go back to the first step of the development process. You must identify what caused the problem and correct it in the source code. When you make a change to the source code, you need to recompile the program to create a corrected version of the executable file. You keep following this cycle until you get the program to execute exactly as you intended.

**The C# Development Cycle**

**Step 1** Use an editor to write your source code. C# source code files are usually given the .cs extension (for example, a_program.cs, database.cs, and so on).

**Step 2** Compile the program using a C# compiler. If the compiler doesn't find any errors in the program, it produces an assembly file with the extension .exe or .dll. For example, myprog.cs compiles to myprog.exe by default. If the compiler finds errors, it reports them. You must return to step 1 to make corrections in your source code.

**Step 3** Execute the program on a machine with a C# runtime, such as the Common Language Runtime. You should test to determine whether your program functions properly. If not, start again with step 1 and make modifications and additions to your source code.

Figure 1.2 shows the program development steps. For all but the simplest programs, you might go through this sequence many times before finishing your program. Even the most experienced programmers can't sit down and write a complete, error-free program in just one step! Because you'll be running through the edit-compile-test cycle many times, it's important to become familiar with your tools: the editor, compiler, and runtime environment.

# Your First C# Program

You're probably eager to try your first program in C#. To help you become familiar with your compiler, Listing 1.1 contains a quick program for you to work through. You might not understand everything at this point, but you should get a feel for the process of writing, compiling, and running a real C# program.

This demonstration uses a program named hello.cs, which does nothing more than display the words `Hello, World!` on the screen. This program is the traditional program used to introduce people to programming. It is also a good one for you to use to learn. The source code for hello.cs is in Listing 1.1. When you type this listing, don't include the line numbers on the left or the colons.

**FIGURE 1.2.**

*The steps involved in C# program development.*

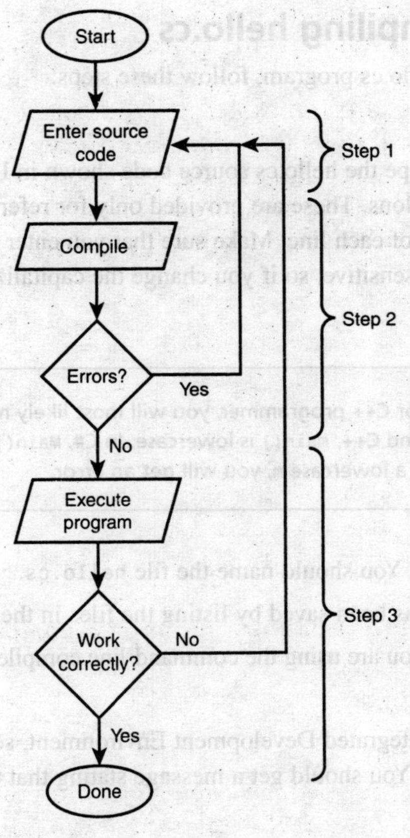


**LISTING 1.1** hello.cs

```
class Hello
{
    static void Main()
    {
        System.Console.WriteLine("Hello, World!");
    }
}
```

Be sure that you have installed your compiler as specified in the installation instructions provided with the software. When your compiler and editor are ready, follow the steps in the next section to enter, compile, and execute hello.cs.

## Entering and Compiling hello.cs

To enter and compile the hello.cs program, follow these steps:

1. Start your editor.
2. Use the keyboard to type the hello.cs source code shown in Listing 1.1. Don't enter the line numbers or colons. These are provided only for reference within this book. Press Enter at the end of each line. Make sure that you enter the code using the same case. C# is case sensitive, so if you change the capitalization, you will get errors.

> **Caution**
>
> If you are a C or C++ programmer, you will most likely make a common mistake. In C and C++, `main()` is lowercase. In C#, `Main()` has a capital `M`. In C#, if you type a lowercase `m`, you will get an error.

3. Save the source code. You should name the file `hello.cs`.
4. Verify that hello.cs has been saved by listing the files in the directory or folder.
5. Compile hello.cs. If you are using the command-line compiler, enter the following:

   ```
   csc hello.cs
   ```

   If you are using an Integrated Development Environment, select the appropriate icon or menu option. You should get a message stating that there were no errors or warnings.
6. Check the compiler messages. If you receive no errors or warnings, everything should be okay.

   If you made an error typing the program, the compiler will catch it and display an error message. For example, if you misspelled the word `Console` as Consol, you would see a message similar to the following:

   ```
   hello.cs(5,7): error CS0117: 'System' does not contain a definition for
   'Consol'
   ```
7. Go back to step 2 if this or any other error message is displayed. Open the hello.cs file in your editor. Compare your file's contents carefully with Listing 1.1, make any necessary corrections, and continue with step 3.
8. Your first C# program should now be compiled and ready to run. If you display a directory listing of all files named hello (with any extension), you should see the following:

   ```
   hello.cs, the source code file you created with your editor
   hello.exe, the executable program created when you compiled hello.cs
   ```

9. To *execute*, or run, hello.exe, enter `hello` at the command line. The message `Hello, World!` is displayed onscreen.

> **Note**
>
> If you run the hello program by double-clicking in Microsoft's Windows Explorer, you might not see the results. This program runs in a command-line window. When you double-click in Windows Explorer, the program opens a command-line window, runs the program, and—because the program is done—closes the window. This can happen so fast that it doesn't seem that anything happens. It is better to open a command-line window, change to the directory containing the program, and then run the program from the command line.

Congratulations! You have just entered, compiled, and run your first C# program. Admittedly, hello.cs is a simple program that doesn't do anything useful, but it's a start. In fact, most of today's expert programmers started learning in this same way—by compiling a "hello world" program.

## Understanding Compilation Errors

A compilation error occurs when the compiler finds something in the source code that it can't compile. A misspelling, typographical error, or any of a dozen other things can cause the compiler to choke. Fortunately, modern compilers don't just choke; they tell you what they're choking on and where the problem is. This makes it easier to find and correct errors in your source code.

This point can be illustrated by introducing a deliberate error into the hello.cs program you entered earlier. If you worked through that example (and you should have), you now have a copy of hello.cs on your disk. Using your editor, move the cursor to the end of line 5 and erase the terminating semicolon. hello.cs should now look like Listing 1.2.

**LISTING 1.2** hello.cs with an Error

```
1: class Hello
2: {
3:     static void Main()
4:     {
5:         System.Console.WriteLine("Hello, World!")
6:     }
7: }
```

Next, save the file. You're now ready to compile it. Do so by entering the command for your compiler. Remember, the command-line command is

```
csc hello.cs
```

Because of the error you introduced, the compilation is not completed. Rather, the compiler displays a message similar to the following:

```
hello.cs(5,48): error CS1002: ; expected
```

Looking at this line, you can see that it has three parts:

| | |
|---|---|
| `hello.cs` | The name of the file where the error was found |
| `(5,48):` | The line number and position where the error was noticed: line 5, position 8 |
| `error CS1002: ; expected` | A description of the error |

This message is quite informative, telling you that when the compiler made it to the 48th character of line 5 of hello.cs, the compiler expected to find a semicolon but didn't. Although the compiler is very clever about detecting and localizing errors, it's no Einstein. Using your knowledge of the C# language, you must interpret the compiler's messages and determine the actual location of any errors that are reported. They are often found on the line reported by the compiler, but if not, they are almost always on the preceding line. You might have a bit of trouble finding errors at first, but you should soon get better at it.

Before leaving this topic, take a look at another example of a compilation error. Load hello.cs into your editor again and make the following changes:

1. Replace the semicolon at the end of line 5.
2. Delete the double quotation mark just before the word `Hello`.

Save the file to disk and compile the program again. This time, the compiler should display an error message similar to the following:

```
hello.cs(5,32): error CS1010: Newline in constant
```

The error message finds the location of the error correctly, locating it in line 5. The error messages found the error at location 32 on line 5. This location is the location of the first quote for the text to be displayed. This error message missed the point that there was a quotation mark missing from the code. In this case, the compiler took its best guess at the problem. Although it was close to the area of the problem, it was not perfect.

**Tip** If the compiler reports multiple errors, and you can find only one, fix that error and recompile. You might find that your single correction is all that's needed, and the program will compile without errors.

### Understanding Logic Errors

There is one other type of error you might get: logic errors. Logic errors are not errors you can blame on the code or the compiler; they are errors that can be blamed only on you. It is possible to create a program with perfect C# code that still contains an error. For example, suppose you want to calculate the area of a circle by multiplying 2 multiplied by the value of PI multiplied by the radius:

Area = $2\pi r$

You can enter this formula into your program, compile, and execute. You will get an answer. The C# program could be written syntactically correct; however, every time you run this program, you will get a wrong answer. The logic is wrong. This formula will never give you the area of a circle; it gives you its circumference. You should have used the formula $\pi r^2$!

No matter how good a compiler is, it will never be able to find logic errors. You have to find these on your own by reviewing your code and by running your programs.

## Types of C# Programs

Before ending today's lessons, it is worth knowing what types of applications you can create with C#. There are a number of types you can build:

- **Console applications.** Console applications run from the command line. Throughout this book you will create console applications, which are primarily character- or text-based and therefore remain relatively simple to understand.
- **Windows applications.** You can also create Windows applications that take advantage of the graphical user interface (GUI) provided by Microsoft Windows.
- **Web Services.** Web services are routines that can be called across the Web.
- **Web Form / ASP.NET applications.** ASP.NET applications are executed on a Web server and generate dynamic Web pages.

In addition to these types of applications, C# can be used to do a lot of other things, including creating libraries, creating controls, and more.

# Summary

At the beginning of today's lesson you learned what C# has to offer, including its power, its flexibility, and its object orientation. You also learned that C# is considered simple and modern.

Today you explored the various steps involved in writing a C# program—the process known as program development. You should have a clear grasp of the edit-compile-test cycle before continuing.

Errors are an unavoidable part of program development. Your C# compiler detects errors in your source code and displays an error message, giving both the nature and the location of the error. Using this information, you can edit your source code to correct the error. Remember, however, that the compiler can't always accurately report the nature and location of an error. Sometimes you need to use your knowledge of C# to track down exactly what is causing a given error message.

# Q&A

**Q Will a C# program run on any machine?**

**A** No. A C# program will run only on machines that have the Common Language Runtime (CLR) installed. If you copy the executable program to a machine that does not contain the CLR, you get an error. On versions of Windows without the CLR, you usually are told that a DLL file is missing.

**Q If I want to give people a program I wrote, which files do I need to give them?**

**A** One of the nice things about C# is that it is a compiled language. This means that after the source code is compiled, you have an executable program. If you want to give the hello program to all your friends with computers, you can. You give them the executable program, hello.exe. They don't need the source file, hello.cs, and they don't need to own a C# compiler. They do need to use a computer system that has a C# runtime, such as the Common Language Runtime from Microsoft.

**Q After I create an executable file, do I need to keep the source file (.cs)?**

**A** If you get rid of the source file, you have no easy way to make changes to the program in the future, so you should keep this file.

Most integrated development environments create files in addition to the source file (.cs) and the executable file. As long as you keep the source file (.cs), you can almost always re-create the other files. If your program uses external resources, such as images and forms, you also need to keep those files in case you need to make changes and re-create the executable.

1

**Q If my compiler came with an editor, do I have to use it?**

**A** Definitely not. You can use any editor, as long as it saves the source code in text format. If the compiler came with an editor, you should try to use it. If you like a different editor better, use it. I use an editor that I purchased separately, even though all my compilers have their own editors. The editors that come with compilers are getting better. Some of them automatically format your C# code. Others color-code different parts of your source file to make it easier to find errors.

**Q Can I ignore warning messages?**

**A** Some warning messages don't affect how the program runs, and some do. If the compiler gives you a warning message, it's a signal that something isn't right. Most compilers let you set the warning level. By setting the warning level, you can get only the most serious warnings, or you can get all the warnings, including the most minute. Some compilers even offer various levels between. In your programs, you should look at each warning and make a determination. It's always best to try to write all your programs with absolutely no warnings or errors. (With an error, your compiler won't create the executable file.)

# Workshop

The Workshop provides quiz questions to help you solidify your understanding of the material covered and exercises to provide you with experience in using what you've learned. Try to understand the quiz and exercise answers before continuing to the day's lesson. Answers are provided in Appendix A, "Answers."

## Quiz

1. Give three reasons why C# is a great choice of programming language.
2. What do IL and CLR stand for?
3. What are the steps in the Program Development Cycle?
4. What command do you need to enter to compile a program called my_prog.cs with your compiler?
5. What extension should you use for your C# source files?
6. Is filename.txt a valid name for a C# source file?
5. If you execute a program that you have compiled and it doesn't work as you expected, what should you do?
8. What is machine language?

9. On what line did the following error most likely occur?

   `my_prog.cs(35,6): error CS1010: Newline in constant`

10. Near what column did the following error most likely occur?

    `my_prog.cs(35,6): error CS1010: Newline in constant`

## Exercises

1. Use your text editor to look at the EXE file created by Listing 1.1. Does the EXE file look like the source file? (Don't save this file when you exit the editor.)
2. Enter the following program and compile it. (Don't include the line numbers or colons.) What does this program do?

```
// circle.cs - Using variables and literals
// This program calculates some circle stuff.
//-----------------------------------------------

using System;

class variables
{
    public static void Main()
    {
        //Declare variables

        int radius = 4;
        const double PI = 3.14159;
        double circum, area;

        //Do calculations

        area = PI * radius * radius;
        circum = 2 * PI * radius;

        //Print the results

        Console.WriteLine("Radius = {0}, PI = {1}", radius, PI );
        Console.WriteLine("The area is {0}", area);
        Console.WriteLine("The circumference is {0}", circum);
    }
}
```

3. Enter and compile the following program. What does this program do?

```
class AClass
{
   static void Main()
   {
      int x,y;
      for ( x = 0; x < 10; x++, System.Console.Write( "\n" ) )
```

```
 7:            for ( y = 0; y < 10; y++ )
 8:                System.Console.Write( "X" );
 9:        }
10:    }
```

4. **BUG BUSTER:** The following program has a problem. Enter it in your editor and compile it. Which lines generate error messages?

```
1:  class Hello
2:  {
3:     static void Main()
4:     {
5:        System.Console.WriteLine(Keep Looking!);
6:        System.Console.WriteLine(You'll find it!);
7:     }
8:  }
```

5. Make the following change to the program in exercise 3. Recompile and rerun this program. What does the program do now?

```
8:                System.Console.Write( "{0}",  (char) 1 );
```

# WEEK 1

# DAY 2

# Understanding C# Programs

In addition to understanding the basic composition of a program, you also need to understand the structure of creating a C# program. Today you

- Learn about the parts of a C# application
- Understand C# statements and expressions
- Discover the facts about object-oriented programming
- Examine encapsulation, polymorphism, inheritance, and reuse
- Display basic information in your programs

## C# Applications

The first part of today's lesson focuses on a simple C# application. Using Listing 2.1, you will gain an understanding of some of the key parts of a C# application.

**LISTING 2.1** app.cs—Example C# Application

```
// app.cs - A sample C# application
// Don't worry about understanding everything in
// this listing. You'll learn all about it later!
//-----------------------------------------------

using System;

class sample
{
    public static void Main()
    {
        //Declare variables

        int radius = 4;
        const double PI = 3.14159;
        double area;

        //Do calculation

        area = PI * radius * radius;

        //Print the results

        Console.WriteLine("Radius = {0}, PI = {1}", radius, PI );
        Console.WriteLine("The area is {0}", area);
    }
}
```

You should enter this listing into your editor and then use your compiler to create the program. You can save the program as `app.cs`. When compiling the program, you enter the following at the command prompt:

```
csc app.cs
```

Alternatively, if you are using a visual editor, you should be able to select a compiler from the menu options.

**Caution**

Remember, you don't enter the line numbers or the colons when you are entering the listing above. The line numbers are to help discuss the listing in the lessons.

When you run the program, you get the following output:

OUTPUT
```
Radius = 4, PI = 3.14159
The area is 50.3344
```

As you can see, the output from this listing is pretty straightforward. The value of a radius and the value of `PI` are displayed. The area of a circle based on these two values is then displayed.

In the following sections you are going to learn about some of the different parts of this program. Don't worry about understanding everything. In the lessons presented on later days, you will be revisiting this information in much greater detail. The purpose of the following sections is to give you a first look.

## Comments

The first four lines of Listing 2.1 are comments. Comments are used to enter information in your program that can be ignored by the compiler. Why would you want to enter information that the compiler will ignore? There are a number of reasons.

Comments are often used to provide descriptive information about your listing—for example, identification information. Additionally, by entering comments, you can document what a listing is expected to do. Even though you might be the only one to use a listing, it is still a good idea to put in information about what the program does and how it does it. Although you know what the listing does now—because you just wrote it—you might not be able to remember later what you were thinking. If you give your listing to others, the comments will help them understand what the code was intended to do. Comments can also be used to provide revision history of a listing.

The main thing to understand about comments is that they are for programmers using the listing. The compiler actually ignores them. In C#, there are three types of comments you can use:

- One-line comments
- Multiline comments
- Documentation comments

**Tip**

Comments are removed by the compiler. Because they are removed, there is no penalty for having them in your program listings. If in doubt, you should include a comment.

## One-Line Comments

Listing 2.1 uses one-line comments in each of lines 1 through 4. Lines 12, 18, and 22 also contain one-line comments. One-line comments have the following format:

```
// comment text
```

The two slashes indicate that a comment is beginning. From that point to the end of the current line, everything is treated as a comment.

A one-line comment does not have to start at the beginning of the line. You can actually have C# code on the line before the comments; however, after the two forward slashes, the rest of the line is a comment.

## Multiline Comments

Listing 2.1 does not contain any multiline comments, but there are times when you want a comment to go across multiple lines. In this case you can either start each line with the double forward slash (as in lines 1 to 4 of the listing), or you can use multiline comments.

Multiline comments are created with a starting and ending token. To start a multiline comment, you enter a forward slash followed by an asterisk:

```
/*
```

Everything after that token is a comment until you enter the ending token. The ending token is an asterisk followed by a forward slash:

```
*/
```

The following is a comment:

```
/* this is a comment */
```

The following is also a comment:

```
/* this is
a comment that
is on
a number of
lines */
```

You can also enter this comment as the following:

```
// this is
// a comment that
// is on
// a number of
// lines
```

The advantage of using multiline comments is that you can “comment out” a section of a code listing by simply adding the `/*` and `*/`. Anything that appears between the `/*` and the `*/` is ignored by the compiler as a comment.

**Caution**

> You cannot nest multiline comments. This means that you cannot place one multiline comment inside of another. For example, the following is an error:
>
> ```
> /* Beginning of a comment...
>    /* with another comment nested */
> */
> ```



## Documentation Comments

C# has a special type of comment that enables you to create external documentation automatically.

These comments are identified with three slashes instead of the two used for single-line comments. These comments also use Extensible Markup Language (XML) style tags. XML is a standard used to mark up data. Although any valid XML tag can be used, common tags used for C# include `<c>`, `<code>`, `<example>`, `<exception>`, `<list>`, `<para>`, `<param>`, `<paramref>`, `<permission>`, `<remarks>`, `<returns>`, `<see>`, `<seealso>`, `<summary>`, and `<value>`.

These comments are placed in your code listings. Listing 2.2 shows an example of these comments being used. You can compile this listing as you have earlier listings. See Day 1, “Getting Started with C#,” if you need a refresher.

**LISTING 2.2** xmlapp.cs—Using XML Comments

```
// xmlapp.cs - A sample C# application using XML
//             documentation
//-----------------------------------------------

/// <summary>
/// This is a summary describing the class.</summary>
/// <remarks>
/// This is a longer comment that can be used to describe
/// the class. </remarks>
class myApp
{
   /// <summary>
   /// The entry point for the application.
   /// </summary>
   /// <param name="args"> A list of command line arguments</param>
    public static void Main(string[] args)
```

**LISTING 2.2** continued

```
    {
        System.Console.WriteLine("An XML Documented Program");
    }
}
```

When you compile and execute this listing, you get the following output:

**OUTPUT**

```
An XML Documented Program
```

To get the XML documentation, you must compile this listing differently from what you have seen before. To get the XML documentation, add the `/doc` parameter when you compile at the command line. If you are compiling at the command line, you enter

```
csc /doc:xmlfile xmlapp.cs
```

When you compile, you get the same output as before when you run the program. The difference is that you also get a file called `xmlfile` that contains documentation in XML. You can replace `xmlfile` with any name you'd like to give your XML file. For Listing 2.2, the XML file is

```
<?xml version="1.0"?>
<doc>
    <assembly>
        <name>xmlapp</name>
    </assembly>
    <members>
        <member name="T:myApp">
            <summary>
            This is a summary describing the class.</summary>
            <remarks>
            This is a longer comment that can be used to describe
            the class. </remarks>
        </member>
        <member name="M:myApp.Main(System.String[])">
            <summary>
            The entry point for the application.
            </summary>
            <param name="args"> A list of command line arguments</param>
        </member>
    </members>
</doc>
```

**Note**

It is beyond the scope of this book to cover XML and XML files.

**Note** If you are using a tool such as Visual Studio.NET, you need to check the documentation or help system to learn how to generate the XML documentation. Even if you are using such a tool, you should still be able to compile your programs from the command line.

2

# Basic Parts of a C# Application

A programming language is composed of a bunch of words combined. A computer program is the formatting and use of these words in an organized manner. The parts of a C# language include the following:

- Whitespace
- C# keywords
- Literals
- Identifiers

## Whitespace

**NEW TERM** If you look at Listing 2.1, you can see that it has been formatted so that the code lines up and is relatively easy to read. The blank spaces put into a listing are called *whitespace*. The basis of this term is that on white paper, you wouldn't see the spaces. Whitespace can consist of spaces, tabs, line feeds, and carriage returns.

The compiler almost always ignores whitespace. Because of this, you can add as many spaces, tabs, or line feeds as you want. For example, consider line 14 from Listing 2.1:

```
int radius = 4;
```

This is a well-formatted line with a single space between items. This line could have had additional spaces:

```
int        radius        =        4        ;
```

This line with extra spaces executes the same way as the original. In fact, when the program is run through the C# compiler, the extra whitespace is removed. You could also format this code across multiple lines:

```
int
radius
=
4
;
```

Although this is not very readable, it still works.

Because whitespace is ignored in general usage, you should make liberal use of it to help format your code and make it readable.

The exception to the compiler ignoring whitespace has to do with the use of text within quotation marks. When you use text within double quotes, whitespace is important because the text is to be used exactly as presented. Text has been used within quotation marks with the listings you have seen so far. In Listing 2.1, lines 24 and 25 contain text within double quotes. This text is written exactly as it is presented between the quotation marks.

**Tip**

Use whitespace to make your code easier to read.

## C# Keywords

Recall from Day 1 that keywords are specific terms that have special meaning and therefore make up a language. The C# language has a number of keywords, which are listed in Table 1.1.

These keywords have a specific meaning when you program in C#. You will learn the meaning of these as you work through this book. Because all these words have a special meaning, they are reserved. You cannot use them for your own use. If you compare the words in Table 2.1 to Listing 2.1 or any of the other listings in this book, you will see that much of the listing is composed of keywords.

**Note**

Appendix B, "C# Keywords," contains short definitions for each of the C# keywords.

## Literals

**NEW TERM** *Literals* are straightforward hard-coded values. They are literally what they are! For example, the numbers 4 and 3.14159 are both literals. Additionally, the text within double quotes is literal text. In tomorrow's lesson, you will learn more details on literals and their use.

### Identifiers

**NEW TERM** In addition to C# keywords and literals, you have other words that are used within C# programs. These words are considered *identifiers*. In Listing 2.1 there are a number of identifiers, including `System` in line 6; `sample` in line 8; `radius` in line 14; `PI` in line 15; `area` in line 16; and `PI`, `radius`, and `area` in line 22.

2

## Structure of a C# Application

Words and phrases are used to make sentences and sentences are used to make paragraphs. In the same way, whitespace, keywords, literals, and identifiers are combined to make expressions and statements. These in turn are combined to make a program.

### C# Expressions and Statements

**NEW TERM** *Expressions* are like phrases. They are snippets of code made up of keywords. For example, the following are simple expressions:

```
PI = 3.14159
```

```
PI * radius * radius
```

*Statements* are like sentences. They complete a single thought. A statement generally ends with a punctuation character—a semicolon (`;`). In Listing 2.1, lines 14, 15, and 16 are examples of statements.

### The Empty Statement

One general statement deserves special mention: the empty statement. As you learned previously, statements generally end with a semicolon. You can actually put a semicolon on a line by itself. This is a statement that does nothing. Because there are no expressions to execute, the statement is considered an empty statement.

You might be wondering why you would want to include a statement that does nothing. Although this might not seem like something you would do, by the time you finish this book, you will find that an empty statement is valuable. You explore one of the most prevalent uses of an empty statement on Day 5, "Control Statements."

## Analysis of Listing 2.1

**ANALYSIS** It is worth taking a closer look at Listing 2.1 now that you've learned of some of the many concepts. The following sections review each line of Listing 2.1.

## Lines 1–4—Comments

As you already learned, lines 1–4 contain comments that will be ignored by the compiler. These are for you and anyone who reviews the source code.

## Lines 5, 7, 13, 17, 21, and 23—Whitespace

Line 5 is blank. You learned that a blank line is simply whitespace that will be ignored by the compiler. This line is included to make the listing easier to read. Lines 7, 13, 17, 21, and 23 are also blank. You can remove these lines from your source file and there will be no difference in how your program runs.

## Line 6—The `using` Statement

Line 6 is a statement that contains the keyword `using` and a literal `System`. As with most statements, this ends with a semicolon. The `using` keyword is used to condense the amount of typing you need to do in your listing. Generally, the `using` keyword is used with namespaces. Namespaces and details on the `using` keyword are covered in some detail on Day 6, "Classes."

## Line 8—Class Declaration

C# is an object-oriented programming {OOP} language. Object-oriented languages use classes to declare objects. This program defines a class called `sample`. You will understand classes by the time you complete this book, and will get an overview of classes later in today's lesson. The C# details concerning classes start on Day 6.

## Lines 9, 11, 26, and 27—Punctuation Characters

Line 9 contains an opening braces that is paired with a closing brace in line 27. Line 11 has an opening brace that is paired with the closing one in line 26. These sets of braces contain and organize blocks of code. As you learn about different commands over the next four days, you will see how these braces are used.

## Line 10—`Main()`

**NEW TERM** The computer needs to know where to start executing a program. C# programs start executing with the `Main()` function, as in line 10. A *function* is a grouping of code that can be executed by calling the function's name. You'll learn the details about functions on Day 7, "Class Methods and Member Functions." The `Main()` function is special because it is used as a starting point.

**Caution** The case of your code—whether letters are capitalized—is critical in C# applications. `Main()` has only the *M* capitalized. C++ and C programmers need to be aware that `main()`—in lowercase—does not work for C#.

2

### Lines 14, 15, and 16—Declarations

Lines 14, 15, and 16 contain statements used to create identifiers that will store information. These identifiers are used later to do calculations. Line 14 declares an identifier to store the value of a radius. The literal `4` is assigned to this identifier. Line 15 creates an identifier to store the value of PI. This identifier, `PI`, is filled with the literal value of `3.14159`. Line 16 declares an identifier that is not given any value.

### Line 20—The Assignment Statement

Line 20 contains a simple statement that multiplies the identifier `PI` by the radius twice. The result of this expression is then assigned to the identifier `area`.

### Lines 24 and 25—Calling Functions

Lines 24 and 25 are the most complex expressions in this listing. These two lines call a predefined routine that prints information to the console (screen). You will learn about these predefined functions later in today's lesson.

## Object-Oriented Programming (OOP)

As mentioned earlier, C# is considered an object-oriented language. To take full advantage of C#, you should understand the concepts of object-oriented languages. The following sections present an overview about objects and what makes a language object-oriented. You will learn how these concepts are applied to C# as you work through the rest of this book.

### Object-Oriented Concepts

What makes a language object-oriented? The most obvious answer is that the language uses objects! This, however, doesn't tell you much. Recall from Day 1 that there are three concepts generally associated with object-oriented languages:

- Encapsulation
- Polymorphism
- Inheritance

There is a fourth concept that is expected as a result of using an object-oriented language: reuse.

## Encapsulation

Encapsulation is the concept of making "packages" that contain everything you need. With object-oriented programming, this means that you could create an object (or package) such as a circle that would do everything that you would want to do with a circle. This includes keeping track of everything about the circle, such as the radius and center point. It also means knowing how to do the functionality of a circle, such as calculating its radius and possibly knowing how to draw it.

By encapsulating a circle, you allow the user to be oblivious to how the circle works. You only need to know how to interact with the circle. This provides a shield to the inner workings of the circle. Why should users care how information about a circle is stored internally? As long as they can get the circle to do what they want, they shouldn't.

## Polymorphism

Polymorphism is the capability of assuming many forms. This can be applied to two areas of object-oriented programming (if not more). First, it means you can call an object or a routine in many different ways and still get the same result. Using a circle as an example, you might want to call a circle object to get its area. You can do this by using three points or by using a single point and the radius. Either way, you would expect to get the same results. In a procedure language such as C, you need two routines with two different names to address these two methods of getting the area. In C#, you still have two routines; however, you can give them the same name. Any programs you or others write will simply call the circle routine and pass your information. The circle program automatically determines which of the two routines to use. Based on the information passed, the correct routine will be used. Users calling the routine don't need to worry about which routine to use. They just call the routine.

Polymorphism is also the ability to work with multiple forms. You will learn more about this form of polymorphism on Day 11, "Inheritance."

## Inheritance

Inheritance is the most complicated of the object-oriented concepts. Having a circle is nice, but what if a sphere would be nicer? A sphere is just a special kind of circle. It has all the characteristics of a circle with a third dimension added. You could say that a sphere is a special kind of circle that takes on all the properties of a circle and then adds a little more. By using the circle to create your sphere, your sphere can inherit all the properties of the circle. The capability of inheriting these properties is a characteristic of inheritance.

2

### Reuse

One of the key reasons an object-oriented language is used is the concept of reuse. When you create a class, you can reuse it to create lots of objects. By using inheritance and some of the features described previously, you can create routines that can be used again in a number of programs and in a number of ways. By encapsulating functionality, you can create routines that have been tested and proven to work. This means you won't have to test the details of how the functionality works, only that you are using it correctly. This makes reusing these routines quick and easy.

## Objects and Classes

**NEW TERM** Now that you understand the concepts of an object-oriented language, it is important to understand the difference between a class and an object. A *class* is a definition for an item that will be created. The actual item that will be created is an *object*. Simply put, classes are definitions used to create objects.

An analogy often used to describe classes is a cookie cutter. A cookie cutter defines a cookie shape. It isn't a cookie, and it isn't edible. It is simply a construct that can be used to create shaped cookies over and over. When you use the cookie cutter to create cookies, you know that each cookie is going to look the same. You also know that you can use the cookie cutter to create lots and lots of cookies.

As with a cookie cutter, a class can be used to create lots of objects. For example, you can have a circle class that can be used to create a number of circles. If you create a drawing program to draw circles, you could have one circle class and lots of circle objects. You could make each circle in the snowman an object; however, you would need only one class to define all of them.

You also can have a number of other classes, including a name class, a card class, an application class, a point class, a circle class, an address class, a snowman class (that can use the circle class), and more.

> **Note** Classes and objects are covered again in more detail starting on Day 6. Today's information gives you an overview of the object-oriented concepts.

# Displaying Basic Information

To help you have a little more fun early in this book, let's look at two routines that you can use to display information. When you understand these two routines, you will be able to display some basic information.

The two routines that you will be seeing used throughout this book to display basic information are

- `System.Console.WriteLine()`
- `System.Console.Write()`

These routines print information to the screen. Both print information in the same manner, with only one small difference. The `WriteLine()` routine writes information to a new line. The `Write()` routine does not start a new line when information is written.

The information you are going to display on the screen is written between the parentheses. If you are printing text, you include the text between the parentheses and within double quotes. For example, the following prints the text "Hello World":

```
System.Console.WriteLine("Hello World");
```

**Note** You used this routine on Day 1.

This prints `Hello World` on the screen. The following examples illustrate other text being printed:

```
System.Console.WriteLine("This is a line of text");
System.Console.WriteLine("This is a second line of text");
```

If you execute these consecutively, you see the following displayed:

```
This is a line of text
This is a second line of text
```

Now consider the following two lines. If these execute consecutively, what do you see printed?

```
System.Console.WriteLine("Hello ");
System.Console.WriteLine("World!");
```

If you guessed that these would print

```
Hello World!
```

you are not correct! Those lines print the following:

```
Hello
World!
```

Notice that each word is on a separate line. If you execute the two lines using the `Write()` routine instead, you get the results you want:

```
Hello World!
```

As you can see, the difference between the two routines is that `WriteLine()` automatically goes to a new line after he text is displayed, whereas `Write()` does not. Listing 2.3 shows the two routines in action.



**LISTING 2.3** display.cs—Using `WriteLine()` and `Write()`.

```
 1:  // display.cs - printing with WriteLine and Write
 2:  //-----------------------------------------------
 3:
 4:  class display
 5:  {
 6:     public static void Main()
 7:     {
 8:          System.Console.WriteLine("First WriteLine Line");
 9:          System.Console.WriteLine("Second WriteLine Line");
10:
11:          System.Console.Write("First Write Line");
12:          System.Console.Write("Second Write Line");
13:
14:          // Passing parameters
15:          System.Console.WriteLine("\nWriteLine: Parameter = {0}", 123 );
16:
17:          System.Console.Write("Write: Parameter = {0}", 456);
18:     }
19:  }
```

Remember that to compile this listing from the command line, you enter the following:

```
csc display.cs
```

If you are using an integrated development tool, you can select the compile option.

**OUTPUT**

```
First WriteLine Line
Second WriteLine Line
First Write LineSecond Write Line
WriteLine: Parameter = 123
Write: Parameter = 456
```

**ANALYSIS** This listing uses the `System.Console.WriteLine()` routine on lines 8 and 9 to print two pieces of text. You can see from the output that each of these print on a separate line. Lines 11 and 12 show the `System.Console.Write()`routine. These two lines print on the same line. There is not a return line feed after printing. Lines 15 and 17 show each of these routines with the use of a parameter.

## Printing Additional Information

In addition to printing text between quotation marks, you can also pass values to be printed within the text. Consider the following example:

```
System.Console.WriteLine("The following is a number: {0}", 456);
```

This prints

```
The following is a number: 456
```

As you can see, the `{0}` gets replaced with the value that follows the quoted text. The format is

```
System.Console.WriteLine("Text", value);
```

where *`Text`* is almost any text you want to display. The `{0}` is a placeholder for a value. The braces indicate that this is a placeholder. The `0` is an indicator for using the first item following the quotation marks. A comma separates the text from the value to be placed in the placeholder.

You can have more than one placeholder in a printout. Each placeholder is given the next sequential number. To print two values, use the following:

```
System.Console.Write("Value 1 is {0} and value 2 is {1}", 123, "Brad");
```

This prints

```
Value 1 is 123 and value 2 is Brad
```

You will learn more about using these routines throughout this book.

**Caution** The first placeholder is numbered `0` and not `1`.

**Note** You can also see some weird text in line 15 of Listing 2.3. The `\n` on this line is not a mistake. This is an indicator that a newline should be started before printing the information that follows. You will learn more about this on Day 3, "Storing Information with Variables."

# Summary

Today's lesson continued to help build a foundation that will be used to teach you C#. Today you learned about some of the basic parts of a C# application. You learned that comments help make your programs easier to understand.

You also learned about the basic parts of a C# application, including whitespace, C# keywords, literals, and identifiers. Looking at an application, you saw how these parts are combined to create a complete listing. This included seeing a special identifier used as a starting point in an application—`Main()`.

After you examined a listing, you explored an overview of object-oriented programming, including the concepts of encapsulation, polymorphism, inheritance, and reuse.

Today's lesson concluded with some basic information on using the `System.Console.WriteLine()` and `System.Console.Write()` routines. You learned that these two routines are used to print information to the screen (console).

# Q&A

**Q What is the difference between component-based and object-oriented?**

**A** C# has been referred to as component-based by some people. Component-based development can be considered an extension of object-oriented programming. A component is simply a standalone piece of code that performs a specific task. Component-based programming consists of creating lots of these standalone components that can be reused. You then link them to build applications.

**Q What other languages are considered object-oriented?**

**A** Other languages that are considered object-oriented include C++, Java, and SmallTalk. Microsoft's Visual Basic.NET can also be used for object-oriented programming. There are other languages, but these are the most popular.

**Q What is composition? Is it an object-oriented term?**

**A** Many people confuse inheritance with composition, but they are different. With composition, one object is used within another object. Figure 2.1 is a composition of many circles. This is different from the sphere in the previous example. The sphere is not composed of a circle; it is an extension of the circle. To summarize the difference between composition and inheritance: Composition occurs when one class (object) has another within it. Inheritance occurs when one class (object) is an expansion of another.

**FIGURE 2.1**

*A snowman made of circles.*

# Workshop

The Workshop provides quiz questions to help you solidify your understanding of the material covered and exercises to provide you with experience in using what you've learned. Try to understand the quiz and exercise answers before continuing to the next day's lesson. Answers are provided in Appendix A, "Answers."

## Quiz

1. What are the three types of comments you can use in a C# program?
2. How are each of the three types of comments entered into a C# program?
3. What impact does whitespace have on a C# program?
4. Which of the following are C# keywords?

   `field, cast, as, object, throw, baseball, catch, football, fumble, basketball`
5. What is a literal?
6. Which is true:

   Expressions are made up of statements.

   Statements are made up of expressions.

   Expressions and statements have nothing to do with each other.
7. What is an empty statement?
8. What are the key concepts of object-oriented programming?

9. What is the difference between `WriteLine()` and `Write()`?
10. What is used as a placeholder when printing a value with `WriteLine()` or `Write()`?

## Exercises

1. Enter and compile the following program (listit.cs). Remember, you don't enter the line numbers.

```
// ListIT.cs - program to print a listing with line numbers
//-----------------------------------------------------------

using System;
using System.IO;

class ListIT
{
    public static void Main(string[] args)
    {
      try
      {

        int ctr=0;
        if (args.Length <= 0 )
        {
           Console.WriteLine("Format: ListIT filename");
           return;
        }
        else
        {
           FileStream f = new FileStream(args[0], FileMode.Open);
           try
           {
              StreamReader t = new StreamReader(f);
              string line;
              while ((line = t.ReadLine()) != null)
              {
                 ctr++;
                 Console.WriteLine("{0}:  {1}", ctr, line);
              }
              f.Close();
           }
           finally
           {
              f.Close();
           }
        }
      }
      catch (System.IO.FileNotFoundException)
      {
```

```
                    Console.WriteLine ("ListIT could not find the file {0}", args[0]);
                }

            catch (Exception e)
            {
                Console.WriteLine("Exception: {0}\n\n", e);
            }
        }
}
```

2. Run the program entered in exercise 1. What happens when you run this program? Run this program a second time. This time enter the following at the command line:

   ```
   listit listit.cs
   ```

   What happens this time?

3. Enter, compile, and run the following program. What does it do?

   ```
   // ex0203.cs - Exercise 3 for Day 2
   //-----------------------------------------------

   class Exercise2
   {
       public static void Main()
       {
           int x = 0;

           for( x = 1; x <= 10; x++ )
           {
               System.Console.Write("{0:D3} ", x);
           }
       }
   }
   ```

4. **BUG BUSTER:** The following program has a problem. Enter it in your editor and compile it. Which lines generate error messages?

   ```
    1: // bugbust.cs
    2: //-----------------------------------------------
    3:
    4: class bugbust
    5: {
    6:     public static void Main()
    7:     {
    8:         System.Console.WriteLine("\nA fun number is {1}", 123 );
    9:     }
   10: }
   ```

5. Write the line of code that prints your name on the screen.

# WEEK 1

# DAY 3

# Storing Information with Variables

When you start writing programs, you are going to quickly find that you need to keep track of different types of information. This might be the tracking of your clients' names, the amounts of money in your bank accounts, or the ages of your favorite movie stars. To keep track of this information, your computer programs need a way to store the values. Today you

- Learn what is a variable
- Discover how to create variable names in C#
- Use different types of numeric variables
- Evaluate the differences and similarities between character and numeric values
- See how to declare and initialize variables

# Variables

A *variable* is a named data storage location in your computer's memory. By using a variable's name in your program, you are, in effect, referring to the information stored there. For example, you could create a variable called `my_variable` that holds a number. You would be able to store different numbers in the `my_variable` variable.

You could also create variables to store information other than a simple number. You could create a variable called `BankAccount` to store a bank account number, a variable called `email` to store an email address, or a variable called `address` to store a person's mailing address. Regardless of what type of information will be stored, a variable is used to obtain its value.

## Variable Names

To use variables in your C# programs, you must know how to create variable names. In C#, variable names must adhere to the following rules:

- The name can contain letters, digits, and the underscore character (_).
- The first character of the name must be a letter. The underscore is also a legal first character, but its use is not recommended at the beginning of a name. An underscore is often used with special commands, and it's sometimes hard to read.
- Case matters (that is, upper- and lowercase letters). C# is case-sensitive; thus, the names `count` and `Count` refer to two different variables.
- C# keywords can't be used as variable names. Recall that a keyword is a word that is part of the C# language. (A complete list of the C# keywords can be found in Appendix B, "C# Keywords.")

The following list contains some examples of valid and invalid C# variable names:

| *Variable Name* | *Legality* |
|---|---|
| `Percent` | Legal |
| `y2x5__w7h3` | Legal |
| `yearly_cost` | Legal |
| `_2010_tax` | Legal, but not advised |
| `checking#account` | Illegal; contains the illegal character # |
| `double` | Illegal; is a C keyword |
| `9byte` | Illegal; first character is a digit |

Because C# is case-sensitive, the names `percent`, `PERCENT`, and `Percent` are considered three different variables. C# programmers commonly use only lowercase letters in variable names, although this isn't required. Often, programmers use mixed case as well. Using all-uppercase letters is usually reserved for the names of constants (which are covered later today).

Variables can have any name that fits the rules listed previously. For example, a program that calculates the area of a circle could store the value of the radius in a variable named `radius`. The variable name helps make its usage clear. You could also have created a variable named `x` or even `billy_gates`; it doesn't matter. Such a variable name, however, wouldn't be nearly as clear to someone else looking at the source code. Although it might take a little more time to type descriptive variable names, the improvements in program clarity make it worthwhile.



Many naming conventions are used for variable names created from multiple words. Consider the variable name `circle_radius`. Using an underscore to separate words in a variable name makes it easy to interpret. Another style is called *Pascal notation* Instead of using spaces, the first letter of each word is capitalized. Instead of `circle_radius`, the variable would be named `CircleRadius`. Yet another notation that is growing in popularity is *Camel notation.* Camel notation is like Pascal notation, except the first letter of the variable name is also lower case. A special form of Camel notation is called Hungarian notation. With Hungarian notation, you also include information in the name of the variable—such as whether it is numeric, has a decimal value, or is text—that helps to identify the type of information being stored. The underscore is used in this book because it's easier for most people to read. You should decide which style you want to adopt.

| Do | Don't |
|---|---|
| **DO** use variable names that are descriptive.<br>**DO** adopt and stick with a style for naming your variables. | **DON'T** name your variables with all capital letters unnecessarily. |

**Note** C# supports a Unicode character set, which means that letters from any language can be stored and used. You can also use any Unicode character to name your variables.

# Using Variables

Before you can use a variable in a C# program, you must declare it. A variable declaration tells the compiler the name of the variable and the type of information the variable will be used to store. If your program attempts to use a variable that hasn't been declared, the compiler will generate an error message.

Declaring a variable also enables the computer to set aside memory for it. By identifying the specific type of information that will be stored in a variable, you gain the best performance and avoid wasting memory.

## Declaring a Variable

A variable declaration has the following form:

```
typename varname;
```

*typename* specifies the variable type. In the following sections you will learn about the types of variables that are available in C#. *varname* is the name of the variable. To declare a variable that can hold a standard numeric integer, you use the following line of code:

```
int my_number;
```

The name of the variable declared is `my_number`. The data type of the variable is `int`. As you will learn in the following section, the type `int` is used to declare integer variables, which is perfect for this example!

You can also declare multiple variables of the same type on one line by separating the variable names with commas. This enables you to be more concise in your listings. Consider the following line:

```
int count, number, start;
```

This line declares three variables: `count`, `number`, and `start`. Each of these variables is type `int`, which is for integers.

**Note** Although declaring multiple variables on the same line can be more concise, I don't recommend that you always do this. There are times when it is easier to read and follow your code by using multiple declarations. There will be no noticeable performance loss by doing separate declarations.

## Assigning Values to Variables

Now that you know how to declare a variable it is important to learn how to store values. After all, the purpose of a variable is to store information!

The format for storing information in a variable is

```
varname = value;
```

You have already seen that *varname* is the name of the variable. *value* is the value that will be stored in the variable. For example, to store the number 5 in the variable, `my_variable`, you enter the following:

```
my_variable = 5;
```

To change the value, you simply reassign a new value:



```
my_variable = 1010;
```

Listing 3.1 illustrates assigning values to a variable. It also shows that you can overwrite a value.

**LISTING 3.1** var_values.cs—Assigning Values to a Variable

```
// var_values.cs - A listing to assign and print the value
//                 of a variable
//---------------------------------------------------------

using System;

class var_values
{
   public static void Main()
   {
      // declare my_variable
      int my_variable;

      // assign a value to my_variable
      my_variable = 5;
      Console.WriteLine("\nmy_variable contains the value {0}",
      ➥my_variable);

      // assign a new value to my_variable
      my_variable = 1010;
      Console.WriteLine("\nmy_variable contains the value {0}",
      ➥my_variable);
   }
}
```

**Output**

```
my_variable contains the value 5

my_variable contains the value 1010
```

**Analysis** Enter this listing into your editor, compile it, and execute it. If you need a refresher on how to do this, refer to Day 1, "Getting Started with C#." The first three lines of this listing are comments. Lines 11, 14, and 18 also contain comments. Remember that comments provide information; the compiler will ignore them. Line 5 includes the `System` namespace which you need to do things such as writing information. Line 7 declares the class that will be your program (`var_values`). Line 9 declares the entry point for your program, the `Main()` function. Remember, `Main()` has to be capitalized or you'll get an error!

Line 12 is the beginning point of today's lesson. Line 12 declares a variable called `my_variable` of type integer (`int`). After this line has executed, the computer knows that a variable called `my_variable` exists and it enables you to use it. In line 15 you use this variable and assign the value of `5` to `my_variable`. In line 16 you use `Console.WriteLine` to display the value of `my_variable`. As you can see in the output, the value `5`—which was assigned in line 15—is displayed. In line 19 you change the value of `my_variable` from `5` to `1010`. You see that this new assignment worked because the call to `Console.WriteLine` in line 20 prints the new value `1010` instead of `5`.

After you assign the value `1010` to `my_variable` in line 19, the value of `5` is gone. From that point, the program no longer knows that `5` ever existed.

**Note** You must declare a variable before you can use it. A variable can, however, be declared at almost any place within a listing.

## Setting Initial Values in Variables

You might be wondering whether you can assign a value to a variable at the same time you declare it. Yes, you definitely can. In fact, it is good practice to make sure you always initialize a variable at the time you declare it. To initialize `my_variable` to the value of `8` when you declare it, you combine what you've done before:

```
int my_variable = 8;
```

Any variable can be initialized when being declared using the following structure:

```
typename varname = value;
```

You can also declare multiple variables on the same line and assign values to each of them:

```
int my_variable = 8, your_variable  = 1000;
```

This line declares two integer variables called `my_variable` and `your_variable`. `my_variable` is assigned the value of `8` and `your_variable` is assigned `1000`. Notice that these declarations are separated by a comma and that the statement ends with the standard semicolon. Listing 3.2 shows this statement in action.



**LISTING 3.2** multi_variables.cs—Assigning More than One Variable

```
 1:  // multi_variables.cs
 2:  // A listing to assign values to more than one variable.
 3:  //-----------------------------------------------------
 4:
 5:  using System;
 6:
 7:  class multi_variables
 8:  {
 9:      public static void Main()
10:      {
11:          // declare the variables
12:          int my_variable = 8, your_variable = 1000;
13:
14:          // print the original value of my_variable
15:          Console.WriteLine("my_variable was assigned the value {0},
             ➥my_variable);
16:
17:          // assign a value to my_variable
18:          my_variable = 5;
19:
20:          // print their values
21:          Console.WriteLine("\nmy_variable contains the value {0}",
             ➥my_variable);
22:          Console.WriteLine("\nyour_variable contains the value {0}",
             ➥your_variable);
23:      }
24:  }
```

**OUTPUT**

```
my_variable was assigned the value 8

my_variable contains the value 5

your_variable contains the value 1000
```

**ANALYSIS** This listing declares and initializes two variables on line 12. The variable. `my_variable`, is initialized to the value of `8` and the variable, `your_variable`, is initialized to the value of `1000`. Line 15 prints the value of `my_variable` so you can see what it contains. Looking at the output, you see that it contains the value 8, which was just assigned.

In line 18, the value of `5` is assigned to `my_variable`. Lines 21 and 22 print the final values of the two variables. The value of `my_variable` is printed as `5`. The original value of `8` is gone forever! `your_variable` still contains its original value of `1000`.

## Using Uninitialized Variables

What happens if you try to use a variable without initializing it? Consider the following:

```
int blank_variable;
Console.WriteLine("\nmy_variable contains the value {0}", blank_variable);
```

In this snippet of code, `blank_variable` is printed in the second line. What is the value of `blank_variable`? This variable was declared in the first line, but it was not initialized to any value. You'll never know what the value of `blank_variable` is because the compiler will not create the program. Listing 3.3 proves this.

**LISTING 3.3** `blank.cs`—Using an Uninitialized Variable

```
// blank.cs - Using unassigned variables.
// This listing causes an error!!
//-----------------------------------------------------

using System;

class blank
{
    public static void Main()
    {
        int blank_variable;

        Console.WriteLine("\nmy_variable contains the value {0}",
➥blank_variable);
    }
}
```

**ANALYSIS** This program will not compile. Rather, the compiler will give you the following error:

```
blank.cs(13,67): error CS0165: Use of unassigned local variable 'blank_variable'
```

C# will not let you use an uninitialized variable.

> **Note** In other languages, such as C and C++, this listing would compile. The value printed for the `blank_variable` in these other languages would be garbage. C# prevents this type of error from occurring.

# Understanding Your Computer's Memory

If you already know how a computer's memory operates, you can skip this section. If you're not sure, read on. This information is helpful to understanding programming.

What is your computer's RAM used for? It has several uses, but only data storage need concern you as a programmer. Data is the information with which your C# program works. Whether your program is maintaining a contact list, monitoring the stock market, keeping a budget, or tracking the price of snickerdoodles, the information (names, stock prices, expense amounts, or prices) is kept within variables in your computer's RAM when it is being used by your running program.

A computer uses random access memory (RAM) to store information while it is operating. RAM is located in integrated circuits, or chips, inside your computer. RAM is volatile, which means that it is erased and replaced with new information as often as needed. Being volatile also means that RAM "remembers" only while the computer is turned on and loses its information when you turn the computer off.



A *byte* is the fundamental unit of computer data storage. Each computer has a certain amount of RAM installed. The amount of RAM in a system is usually specified in megabytes (MB), such as 32MB, 64MB, 128MB or more. One megabyte of memory is 1,024 kilobytes (KB). One kilobyte of memory consists of 1,024 bytes. Thus, a system with 8MB of memory actually has 8×1,024KB, or 8,192KB of RAM. This is 8,192KB×1,024 bytes for a total of 8,388,608 bytes of RAM. Table 3.1 provides you with an idea of how many bytes it takes to store certain kinds of data.

**TABLE 3.1** Minimum Memory Space Generally Required to Store Data

| *Data* | *Bytes Required* |
|---|---|
| The letter x | 2 |
| The number 500 | 2 |
| The number 241.105 | 4 |
| The phrase *Teach Yourself C#* | 34 |
| One typewritten page | Approximately 4,000 |

The RAM in your computer is organized sequentially, one byte following another. Each byte of memory has a unique address by which it is identified—an address that also distinguishes it from all other bytes in memory. Addresses are assigned to memory locations in order, starting at 0 and increasing to the system limit. For now, you don't need to worry about addresses; it's all handled automatically.

Now that you understand a little about the nuts and bolts of memory storage, you can get back to C# programming and how C# uses memory to store information.

# C# Data Types

You know how to declare, initialize, and change the values of variables; it is important that you know the data types you can use. You learned earlier that you have to declare the data type when you declare a variable. You've seen that the `int` keyword declares variables that can hold integers. An integer is simply a whole number that doesn't contain a fractional or decimal portion. The variables you've declared to this point hold only integers. What if you want to store other types of data, such as decimals or characters?

# Numeric Variable Types

C# provides several different types of numeric variables. You need different types of variables, because different numeric values have varying memory storage requirements and differ in the ease with which certain mathematical operations can be performed on them. Small integers (for example, 1, 199, and –8) require less memory to store, and your computer can perform mathematical operations (addition, multiplication, and so on) with such numbers very quickly. In contrast, large integers and values with decimal points require more storage space and more time for mathematical operations. By using the appropriate variable types, you ensure that your program runs as efficiently as possible.

The following sections break the different numeric data types into four categories:

- Integral
- Floating-point
- Decimal
- Boolean

Earlier in today's lesson, you learned that variables are stored in memory. Additionally, you learned that different types of information required different amounts of memory. The amount of memory used to store a variable is based on its data type. Listing 3.4 is a program that contains code beyond what you know right now; however, it provides you with the amount of information needed to store some of the different C# data types.

**NEW TERM** You must include extra information for the compiler when you compile this listing. This extra information, referred to as a *flag* to the compiler, can be included on the command line. Specifically, you need to add the `/unsafe` flag as shown:

```
csc /unsafe sizes.cs
```

If you are using an integrated development environment, you need to set the `unsafe` option as instructed by its documentation.

**LISTING 3.4** `sizes.cs`—**Memory Requirements for Data Types**

```
// sizes.cs--Program to tell the size of the C# variable types
//----------------------------------------------------------

using System;

class sizes
{
   unsafe public static void Main()
   {
       Console.WriteLine( "\nA byte      is {0} byte(s)", sizeof( byte ));
       Console.WriteLine( "An sbyte    is {0} byte(s)", sizeof( sbyte ));
       Console.WriteLine( "A char      is {0} byte(s)", sizeof( char ));
       Console.WriteLine( "\nA short    is {0} byte(s)", sizeof( short ));
       Console.WriteLine( "An ushort   is {0} byte(s)", sizeof( ushort ));
       Console.WriteLine( "\nAn int     is {0} byte(s)", sizeof( int ));
       Console.WriteLine( "An uint     is {0} byte(s)", sizeof( uint ));
       Console.WriteLine( "\nA long     is {0} byte(s)", sizeof( long ));
       Console.WriteLine( "An ulong    is {0} byte(s)", sizeof( ulong ));
       Console.WriteLine( "\nA float    is {0} byte(s)", sizeof( float ));
       Console.WriteLine( "A double    is {0} byte(s)", sizeof( double ));
       Console.WriteLine( "\nA decimal  is {0} byte(s)", sizeof( decimal ));
       Console.WriteLine( "\nA boolean  is {0} byte(s)", sizeof( bool ));
   }
}
```

**OUTPUT**

```
A byte      is 1 byte(s)
An sbyte    is 1 byte(s)
A char      is 2 byte(s)

A short     is 2 byte(s)
An ushort   is 2 byte(s)

An int      is 4 byte(s)
An uint     is 4 byte(s)

A long      is 8 byte(s)
An ulong    is 8 byte(s)

A float     is 4 byte(s)
A double    is 8 byte(s)

A decimal   is 16 byte(s)

A boolean   is 1 byte(s)
```

**ANALYSIS** Although you haven't learned all the data types yet, I believed it valuable to present this listing here. As you go through the following sections, refer to this listing and its output.

This listing uses a C# keyword called `sizeof`. The `sizeof` keyword tells you the size of a variable. In this listing, `sizeof` is used to show the size of the different data types. For example, to determine the size of an `int`, you can use:

```
sizeof(int)
```

If you had declared a variable called `x`, you could determine its size—which would actually be the size of its data type—by using the following code:

```
sizeof(x)
```

Looking at the output of Listing 3.4, you see that you have been given the number of bytes that are required to store each of the C# data types. For an `int`, you need 4 bytes of storage. For a `short` you need 2. The amount of memory used determines how big or small a number can be that is stored. You'll learn more about this in the following sections.

The `sizeof` keyword is not one that you will use very often; however, it is useful for illustrating the points in today's lesson. The `sizeof` keyword taps into memory to determine the size of the variable or data type. With C#, you avoid tapping directly into memory. In line 8, an extra keyword is added—`unsafe`. If you don't include the `unsafe` keyword, you get an error when you compile this program. For now, understand that the reason `unsafe` is added is because the `sizeof` keyword works directly with memory.

**Caution**

> The C# keyword `sizeof` can be used; however, you should generally avoid it. The `sizeof` keyword sometimes accesses memory directly to find out the size. Accessing memory directly is something to be avoided in pure C# programs.

## Integral Data Types

Until this point, you have been using one of the integral data types—`int`. Integral data types store integers. Recall that an integer is basically any numeric value that does not include a decimal or a fractional value. The numbers 1, 1,000, 56 trillion, and –534 are integral values.

C# provides nine integral data types, including the following:

- Integers (`int` and `uint`)
- Shorts (`short` and `ushort`)

- Longs (`long` and `ulong`)
- Bytes (`byte` and `sbyte`)
- Characters (`char`)

## Integers

As you saw in Listing 3.4, an integer is stored in 4 bytes of memory. This includes both the `int` and `uint` data types. The `int` data type has been used in many of the programs you have seen so far. Although you might not have known it, this data type cannot store just any number. Rather, it can store any signed whole number that can be represented in 4 bytes or 32 bits—any number between –2,147,483,648 and 2,147,483,647.



A variable of type `int` is signed, which means it can be positive or negative. Technically, 4 bytes can hold a number as big as 4,294,967,295; however, when you take away one of the 32 bits to keep track of positive or negative, you can go only to 2,147,483,647. You can, however, also go to –2,147,483,648.

> **As you learned earlier, information is stored in units called bytes. A byte is actually composed of 8 bits. A *bit* is the most basic unit of storage in a computer. A bit can have one of two values—0 or 1. Using bits and the binary math system, you can store numbers in multiple bits. In Appendix C, "Working with Number Systems," you can learn the details of binary math.**

If you want to use a type `int` to go higher, you can make it unsigned. An unsigned number can only be positive. The benefit should be obvious. The `uint` data type declares an unsigned integer. The net result is that a `uint` can store a value from 0 to 4,294,967,295.

What happens if you try to store a number that is too big? What about storing a number with a decimal point into an `int` or `uint`? What happens if you try to store a negative number into an `uint`? Listing 3.5 answers all three questions.

**LISTING 3.5** `int_conv.cs`—Doing Bad Things

```
// int_conv.cs
// storing bad values. Program generates errors and won't compile.
//----------------------------------------------------------------

using System;

class int_conv
{
   public static void Main()
```

**LISTING 3.5** continued

```
10:     {
11:         int val1, val2;     // declare two integers
12:         uint pos_val;       // declare an unsigned int
13:
14:         val1 = 1.5;
15:         val2 = 9876543210;
16:         pos_val = -123;
17:
18:         Console.WriteLine( "val1 is {0}", val1);
19:         Console.WriteLine( "val2 is {0}", val2);
20:         Console.WriteLine( "pos_val is {0}", pos_val);
21:     }
22: }
```

**OUTPUT**

```
int_conv.cs(14,15): error CS0029: Cannot implicitly convert type
➥'double' to 'int'
int_conv.cs(15,15): error CS0029: Cannot implicitly convert type 'long'
➥to 'int'
int_conv.cs(16,18): error CS0031: Constant value '-123' cannot be
➥converted to a 'uint'
```

**Caution** This program gives compiler errors.

**ANALYSIS** This program will not compile. As you can see, the compiler catches all three problems that were questioned. In line 14 you try to put a number with a decimal point into an integer. In line 15 you try to put a number that is too big into an integer. Remember, the highest number that can go into an `int` is 2,147,483,647. Finally, in line 16, you try to put a negative number into an unsigned integer (`uint`). As the output shows, the compiler catches each of these errors and prevents the program from being created.

## Shorts

The `int` and `uint` data types used 4 bytes of memory for each variable declared. There are a number of times when you don't need to store numbers that are that big. For example, you don't need big numbers to keep track of the day of the week (numbers 1 to 7), to store a person's age, or to track the temperature to bake a cake.

When you want to store a whole number and you want to save some memory, you can use `short` and `ushort`. A `short`, like an `int`, stores a whole number. Unlike an `int`, it is only 2 bytes instead of 4. If you look at the output from Listing 3.4, you see that `sizeof` returned 2 bytes for both `short` and `ushort`. If you are storing both positive and negative numbers, you'll want to use `short`. If you are storing only positive and you want to use the extra room, you'll want to use `ushort`. The values that can be stored in a `short` are from –32,768 to 32,767. If you use a `ushort`, you can store whole numbers from 0 to 65535.

## Longs

If `int` and `uint` are not big enough for what you want to store, there is another data type to use—`long`. As with `short` and `int`, there is also an unsigned version of the `long` data type called `ulong`. Looking at the output from Listing 3.4, you can see that `long` and `ulong` each use 8 bytes of memory. This gives them the capability of storing very large numbers. A `long` can store numbers from –9,223,372,036,854,775,808 to 9,223,372,036,854,775,807. An `ulong` can store a number from 0 to 18,446,744,073,709,551,615.

## Bytes

As you have seen, you can store whole numbers in data types that take 2, 4, or 8 bytes of memory. For those times when your needs are very small, you can store a whole number in a single byte. To keep things simple, the data type that uses a single byte of memory for storage is called a `byte`! As with the previous integers, there is both a signed version, `sbyte`, and an unsigned version, `byte`. A `sbyte` can store a number from –128 to 127. An unsigned byte can store a number from 0 to 255.

## Characters

In addition to numbers, you will often want to store characters. Characters are letters, such as *A*, *B*, or *C*, or even extended characters such as the smiley face. Additional characters that you might want to store are characters such as $, %, or *. You might even want to store foreign characters.

A computer does not recognize characters. It can recognize only numbers. To get around this, all characters are stored as numeric values. To make sure that everyone uses the same values, a standard was created called Unicode. Within Unicode, each character and symbol is represented by a single whole number. This is why the character data type is considered an integral type.

To know that numbers should be used as characters, you use the data type `char`. A `char` is a number stored in 2 bytes of memory that is interpreted as a character. Listing 3.6 presents a program that uses `char` values.

**LISTING 3.6** chars.cs—Working with Characters

```
// chars.cs
// A listing to print out a number of characters and their numbers
//-----------------------------------------------------------------

using System;

class chars
{
   public static void Main()
   {
      int ctr;
      char ch;

      Console.WriteLine("\nNumber   Value\n");

      for( ctr = 60; ctr <= 95; ctr = ctr + 1)
      {
         ch = (char) ctr;
         Console.WriteLine( "{0} is {1}", ctr, ch);
      }
   }
}
```

**OUTPUT**

```
Number   Value

60 is <
61 is =
62 is >
63 is ?
64 is @
65 is A
66 is B
67 is C
68 is D
69 is E
70 is F
71 is G
72 is H
73 is I
74 is J
75 is K
76 is L
77 is M
78 is N
79 is O
80 is P
81 is Q
82 is R
83 is S
```

```
84 is T
85 is U
86 is V
87 is W
88 is X
89 is Y
90 is Z
91 is [
92 is \
93 is ]
94 is ^
95 is _
```

**Analysis** This listing displays a range of numeric values and their character equivalents. In line 11 an integer is declared called `ctr`. This variable is used to cycle through a number of integers. Line 12 declares a character variable called `ch`. Line 14 prints headings for the information that will be displayed.

Line 16 contains something new. For now, don't worry about fully understanding this line of code. On Day 5, "Control Statements," you learn all the glorious details. For now know that this line sets the value of `ctr` to `60`. It then runs lines 18 and 19 before adding `1` to the value of `ctr`. It keeps doing this until `ctr` is no longer less than or equal to `95`. The end result is that lines 18 and 19 are run using the `ctr` with the value of `60`, then `61`, then `62`, and on and on until `ctr` is `95`.

Line 18 sets the value of `ctr` (first `60`) and places it into the character variable, `ch`. Because `ctr` is an integer, you have to tell the computer to convert the integer to a character, which the `(char)` statement does. You'll learn more about this later.

Line 19 prints the values stored in `ctr` and `ch`. As you can see, the integer `ctr` prints as a number. The value of `ch`, however, does not print as a number; it prints as a character. As you can see from the output of this listing, the character `A` is represented by the value `65`. The value of `66` is the same as the character `B`.

**Note**

A computer actually recognizes only 1s and 0s (within bits). It recognizes these as on or off values (or positive charges versus negative charges). A binary number system is one that uses 1s and 0s to represent its numbers. Appendix C explains the binary number system.

### Character Literals

How can you assign a character to a `char` variable? You place the character between single quotes. For example, to assign the letter a to the variable `my_char`, you use the following:

```
my_char = 'a';
```

In addition to assigning regular characters, there are also several extended characters you will most likely want to use. You have actually been using one extended character in a number of your listings. The `\n` that you've been using in your listings is an extended character. This prints a newline character. Table 3.2 contains some of the most common characters you might want to use. Listing 3.7 shows some of these special characters in action.

**TABLE 3.2** Extended Characters

| *Characters* | *Meaning* |
|---|---|
| `\b` | Backspace |
| `\n` | Newline |
| `\t` | Horizontal tab |
| `\\` | Backslash |
| `\'` | Single quote |
| `\"` | Double quote |

**Note**

The extended characters in Table 3.2 are often called *escape characters* because the slash "escapes" from the regular text and indicates that the following character is special (or extended).

**LISTING 3.7** chars_table.cs—The Special Characters

```
// chars_table.cs
//-----------------------------------------------

using System;

class chars_table
{
    public static void Main()
    {
        char ch1 = 'Z';
        char ch2 = 'x';

        Console.WriteLine("This is the first line of text");
        Console.WriteLine("\n\n\nSkipped three lines");
        Console.WriteLine("one\ttwo\tthree <-tabbed");
        Console.WriteLine(" A quote: \' \ndouble quote: \"");
        Console.WriteLine("\n ch1 = {0}  ch2 = {1}", ch1, ch2);
    }
}
```

**OUTPUT**

```
This is the first line of text



Skipped three lines
one     two     three <-tabbed
 A quote: '
double quote: "

 ch1 = Z   ch2 = x
```

**ANALYSIS** This listing illustrates two concepts. First, in line 10 and 11 you see how a character can be assigned to a variable of type `char`. It is as simple as including the character in single quotes. In lines 13 to 17, you see how to use the extended characters. There is nothing special about line 13. Line 14 prints three newlines followed by some text. Line 15 prints `one`, `two`, and `three`, separated by tabs. Line 16 displays a single quote and a double quote. Notice that there are two double quotes in a row at the end of this line. Finally, line 17 prints the values of `ch1` and `ch2`.



## Floating Point

Not all numbers are whole numbers. For those times when you need to use numbers that might have decimals, you need to use different data types. As with storing whole numbers, there are different data types you can use, depending on the size of the numbers you are using and the amount of memory you want to use. The two primary types are `float` and `double`.

### `float`

A `float` is a data type for storing numbers with decimal places. For example, in calculating the circumference or area of a circle, you often end up with a result that is not a whole number. Any time you need to store a number such as 1.23 or 3.1459, you need a nonintegral data type.

The `float` data type stores numbers in 4 bytes of memory. As such, it can store a number from approximately $1.5\times10^{-45}$ to $3.4\times10^{38}$.

**Note** $10^{38}$ is equivalent to 10×10, 37 times. The result is 1 followed by 38 zeros, or 100,000,000,000,000,000,000,000,000,000,000,000,000. $10^{-45}$ is 10÷10, 44 times. The result is 44 zeros between a decimal point and a 1, or .000000000000000000000000000000000000000000001.

**Caution**

A `float` can retain only about 7 digits of precision, which means it is not uncommon for a `float` to be off by a fraction. For example, subtracting 9.90 from 10.00 might result in a number different from .10. It might result in a number closer to .099999999. Generally such rounding errors are not noticeable.

### `double`

Variables of type `double` are stored in 8 bytes of memory. This means they can be much bigger than a `float`. A `double` can generally be from $5.0\times10^{-324}$ to $1.7\times10^{308}$. The precision of a `double` is generally from 15 to 16 digits.

**Note**

C# supports the 4-byte precision (32 bits) and 8-byte precision (64 bits) of the IEEE 754 format, so certain mathematical functions return specific values. If you divide a number by 0, the result is infinity (either positive or negative). If you divide 0 by 0, you get a *Not-a-Number* value. Finally, 0 can be both positive and negative. For more on this, check your C# documentation.

## Decimal

C# provides another data type that can be used to store special decimal numbers. This is the `decimal` data type. This data type was created for storing numbers with greater precision. When you store numbers in a `float` or `double`, you can get rounding errors. For example, storing the result of subtracting 9.90 from 10.00 in a `double` could result in the string `0.099999999999999645` instead of `.10`. If this math is done with `decimal` values, the `.10` is stored.

**Tip**

If you are calculating monetary values or doing financial calculations where precision is important, you should use a `decimal` instead of a `float` or a `double`.

A `decimal` number uses 16 bytes to store numbers. Unlike the other data types, there is not an unsigned version of `decimal`. A `decimal` variable can store a number from $1.0\times10^{-28}$ to approximately $7.9\times10^{28}$. It can do this while maintaining precision to 28 places.

## Boolean

The last of the simple data types is the Boolean. Sometimes you need to know whether something is on or off, true or false, yes or no. Boolean numbers are generally set to one of two values: 0 or 1.

C# has a Boolean data type called a `bool`. As you can see in Listing 3.4, a `bool` is stored in 1 byte of memory. The value of a `bool` is either `true` or `false`, which are C# keywords. This means you can actually store `true` and `false` in a data type of `bool`.

> **Caution**
> "Yes," "no," "on," and "off" are not keywords in C#. This means you cannot set a Boolean variable to these values. Instead, you must use `true` or `false`.

## Checking Versus Unchecking

Earlier in today's lesson you learned that if you put a number that is too big into a variable, an error is produced. There are times when you might not want an error produced. In those cases, you can have the compiler avoid checking the code. This is done with the `unchecked` keyword. Listing 3.8 illustrates this.

**LISTING 3.8** unchecked.cs—Marking Code as Unchecked

```
// unchecked.cs
//-----------------------------------------------

using System;

class sizes
{
   public static void Main()
   {
      int val1 = 2147483647;
      int val2;

      unchecked
      {
         val2 = val1 + 1;
      }

      Console.WriteLine( "val1 is {0}", val1);
      Console.WriteLine( "val2 is {0}", val2);
   }
}
```

**OUTPUT**

```
val1 is 2147483647
val2 is -2147483648
```

**ANALYSIS** This listing uses `unchecked` in line 13. The brackets on line 14 and 16 enclose the area to be unchecked. When you compile this listing, you do not get any errors. When you run the listing, you get what might seem like a weird result. The number `2,147,483,647` is the largest number that a signed `int` variable can hold. As you see in line 10, this maximum value has been assigned to `var1`. In line 15, the unchecked line, 1 is added to what is already the largest value `var1` can hold. Because this line is unchecked, the program continues to operate. The result is that the value stored in `var1` rolls to the most negative number.

This operation is similar to the way an odometer works in a car. When the mileage gets to the maximum, such as 999,999, adding 1 more mile (or kilometer) sets the odometer to 000,000. It isn't a new car with no miles, it is simply a car that no longer has a valid value on its odometer. Rather than rolling to 0, a variable is going to roll to the lowest value it can store. In this listing, that value is `-2,147,483,648`.

Change line 13 to the following and recompile and run the listing:

```
13:    checked
```

The program compiled, but will it run? Executing the program causes an error. If you are asked to run your debugger, you'll want to say no. The error you get will be similar to the following:

```
Exception occurred: System.OverflowException: An exception of type
➥System.OverflowException was thrown.
   at sizes.Main()
```

On later days, you'll see how to deal with this error in your program. For now, you should keep in mind that if you believe there is a chance to put an invalid value into a variable, you should force checking to occur.

## Data Types Simpler than .NET

The C# data types covered so far are considered simple data types. The simple data types are `sbyte`, `byte`, `short`, `ushort`, `int`, `uint`, `long`, `ulong`, `char`, `float`, `double`, `bool`, and `decimal`. On Day 1 and Day 2, "Understanding C# Programs," you learned that C# programs execute on the Common Language Runtime (CLR). Each of these data types corresponds directly to a data type that the CLR uses. Each of these types is considered simple because there is a direct relationship to the types available in the CLR and thus in the .NET Framework. Table 3.3 presents the .NET equivalent of the C# data types.

**TABLE 3.3** C# and .NET Data Types

| *C# Data Type* | *.NET Data Type* |
|---|---|
| sbyte | System.SByte |
| byte | System.Byte |
| short | System.Int16 |
| ushort | System.UInt16 |
| int | System.Int32 |
| uint | System.UInt32 |
| long | System.Int64 |
| ulong | System.UInt64 |
| char | System.Char |
| float | System.Single |
| double | System.Double |
| bool | System.Boolean |
| decimal | System.Decimal |

If you want to declare an integer using the .NET equivalent declaration—even though there is no good reason to do so—you use the following:

```
System.Int32 my_variable = 5;
```

As you can see, `System.Int32` is much more complicated than simply using `int`. Listing 3.9 shows the use of the .NET data types.

**LISTING 3.9** net_vars.cs—Using the .NET Data Types

```
// net_vars
// Using a .NET data declaration
//-----------------------------------------------

using System;

class net_vars
{
     public static void Main()
     {

          System.Int32 my_variable = 4;
          System.Double PI = 3.1459;

```

**LISTING 3.9** continued

```
15:         Console.WriteLine("\nmy_variable is {0}", my_variable );
16:         Console.WriteLine("\nPI is {0}", PI );
17:     }
18: }
```

**OUTPUT**

```
my_variable is 4

PI is 3.1459
```

**ANALYSIS** Lines 12 and 13 declare an `int` and a `double`. Lines 15 and 16 print these values. This listing operates like those you've seen earlier, except it uses the .NET data types.

In your C# programs, you should use the simple data types rather than the .NET types. All the functionality that the .NET types have is available to you in the simpler commands that C# provides. You should, however, understand that the simple C# data types translate to .NET equivalents. You'll find that all other programming languages that work with the Microsoft .NET types also have data types that translate to these .NET types.

> **Note**
>
> The *Common Type System* (CTS) is a set of rules that data types within the CLR must adhere to. The simple data types within C# adhere to these rules, as do the .NET data types. If a language follows the CTS in creating its data types, the data created and stored should be compatible with other programming languages that also follow the CTS.

# Literals Versus Variables

**NEW TERM** In the examples you've looked at so far, you have seen a lot of numbers and values used that were not variables. Often, you will want to type a number or value into your source code. A *literal value* stands on its own within the source code. For example, in the following lines of code, the number `10` and the value `"Bob is a fish"` are literal values. As you can see, literal values can be put into variables.

```
int x = 10;

myStringValue = "Bob is a fish";
```

## Numeric Literals

In many of the examples, you have used numeric literals. By default, a numeric literal is either an `int` or a `double`. It is an `int` if it is a whole number, and it is a `double` if it is a floating-point number. For example, consider the following:

```
nbr = 100;
```

In this example, `100` is a numeric literal. By default, it is considered to be of type `int`, regardless of what data type the `nbr` variable is. Now consider the following:

```
nbr = 99.9;
```

In this example, `99.9` is also a numeric literal; however, it is of type `double` by default. Again, this is regardless of the data type that `nbr` is. This is true even though `99.9` could be stored in a type `float`. In the following line of code, is `100.` an `int` or a `double`?

```
x = 100.;
```

This is a tough one. If you guessed `int`, you are wrong. Because there is a decimal included with the `100`, it is a `double`.



### Integer Literal Defaults

When you use an integer value, it is put into an `int`, `uint`, `long`, or `ulong` depending on its size. If it will fit in an `int` or `uint`, it will be. If not, it will be put into a `long` or `ulong`. If you want to specify the data type of the literal, you can use a suffix on the literal. For example, to use the number 10 as a literal `long` value(signed or unsigned), you write it like the following:

```
10L;
```

You can make an unsigned value by using a `u` or a `U`. If you want an unsigned literal `long` value, you can combine the two suffixes: `ul`.

**Note**

> The Microsoft C# compiler gives you a warning if you use a lowercase *l* to declare a `long` value literal. The compiler provides this warning to help you be aware that it is easy to mistake a lowercase *l* with the number 1.

### Floating-Point Literal Defaults

As stated earlier, by default, a decimal value literal is a `double`. To declare a literal that is of type `float`, you include an `f` or `F` after the number. For example, to assign the number 4.4 to a `float` variable, `my_float`, you use the following:

```
my_float = 4.4f;
```

To declare a literal of type decimal, you use a suffix of `m` or `M`. For example, the following line declares `my_decimal` to be equal to the decimal number `1.32`.

```
my_decimal = 1.32m;
```

## Boolean Literals (`true` and `false`)

Boolean literals have already been covered. The values `true` and `false` are literal. They also happen to be keywords.

## String Literals

When you put characters together, they make words, phrases, and sentences. In programming parlance, a group of characters is called a *string*. A string can be identified because it is contained between a set of double quotes. You have actually been using strings in the examples so far. For example, the `Console.WriteLine` routine uses a string. A string literal is any set of characters between double quotes. The following are examples of strings:

```
"Hello, World!"

"My Name is Bradley"

"1234567890"
```

Because these numbers are between quotation marks, the last example is treated as a string literal rather than as a numeric literal.

> **Note** You can use any of the special characters from Table 3.3 inside a string.

# Constants

In addition to using literals, there are times when you want to put a value in a variable and freeze it. For example, if you declare a variable called `PI` and you set it to `3.1459`, you want it to stay `3.1459`. There is no reason to change it. Additionally, you want to prevent people from changing it.

To declare a variable to hold a constant value, you use the `const` keyword. For example, to declare `PI` as stated, you use the following:

```
const float PI = 3.1459;
```

You can use `PI` in a program; however, you will never be able to change its value. The `const` keyword freezes its contents. You can use the `const` keyword on any variable of any data type.

**Tip**

To help make it easy to identify constants, you can enter their names in all capital letters. This makes it easy to identify the fact that the variable is a constant.

# Reference Types

To this point, you have seen a number of different data types. C# offers two primary ways of storing information: by value (`byval`) and by reference (`byref`). The basic data types that you have learned about store information by value.

When a variable stores information by value, the variable contains the actual information. For example, when you store `123` in an integer variable called `x`, the value of `x` is `123`. The variable `x` actually contains the value `123`.

Storing information by reference is a little more complicated. If a variable stores by reference, rather than storing the information in itself, it stores the location of the information. In other words, it stores a reference to the information. For example, if `x` is a "by reference" variable, it contains information on where the value `123` is located. It does not store the value `123`. Figure 3.1 illustrates the difference.

**FIGURE 3.1**
*By reference versus by value.*

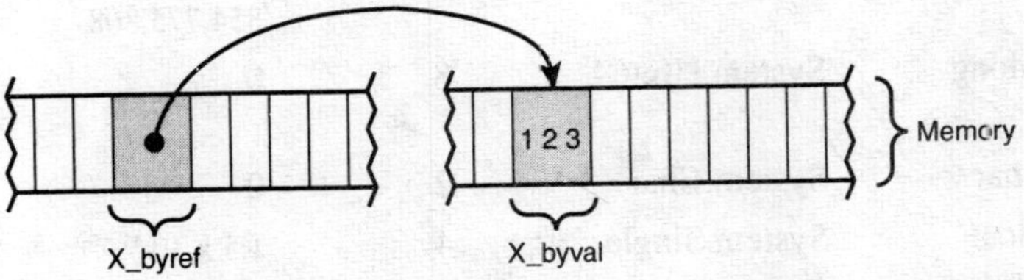


The data types used by C# that store by reference are

- Classes
- Strings
- Interfaces
- Arrays
- Delegates

Each of these data types is covered in detail throughout the rest of this book.

# Summary

In today's lesson, you learned how the computer stores information. You focused on the data types that store data by value, including `int`, `uint`, `long`, `ulong`, `bool`, `char`, `short`, `ushort`, `float`, `double`, `decimal`, `byte`, and `ubyte`. In addition to learning about the data types, you learned how to name and create variables. You also learned the basics of setting values in these variables, including the use of literals. Table 3.4 lists the data types and information about them.

**TABLE 3.4** C# Data Types

| *C# Data Type* | *NET Data Type* | *Size in Bytes* | *Low Value* | *High Value* |
|---|---|---|---|---|
| sbyte | System.Sbyte | 1 | -128 | 127 |
| byte | System.Byte | 1 | 0 | 255 |
| short | System.Int16 | 2 | -32,768 | 32,767 |
| ushort | System.UInt16 | 2 | 0 | 65,535 |
| int | System.Int32 | 4 | -2,147,483,648 | 2,147,483,647 |
| uint | System.UInt32 | 4 | 0 | 4,294,967,295 |
| long | System.Int64 | 8 | -9,223,372,036,854,775,808 | 9,223,372,036,854,775,807 |
| ulong | System.UInt64 | 8 | 0 | 18,446,744,073 709,551,615 |
| char | System.Char | 2 | 0 | 65,535 |
| float | System.Single | 4 | $1.5 \times 10^{-45}$ | $3.4 \times 10^{38}$ |
| double | System.Double | 8 | $5.0 \times 10^{-324}$ | $1.7 \times 1010^{308}$ |
| bool | System.Boolean | 1 | false (0) | true (1) |
| decimal | System.Decimal | 16 | $1.0 \times 10^{-28}$ | approx. $7.9 \times 10^{28}$ |

# Q&A

**Q Why shouldn't all numbers be declared as the larger data types instead of the smaller data types?**

**A** Although it might seem logical to use the larger data types, this would not be efficient. You should not use any more system resources (memory) than you need.

**Q What happens if you assign a negative number to an unsigned variable?**

**A** You get an error by the compiler saying you can't assign a negative number to an unsigned variable if you do this with a literal. If you do a calculation that causes an unsigned variable to go below 0, you get erroneous data. On later days, you will learn how to check for these erroneous values.

**Q A `decimal` value is more precise than a `float` or a `double` value. What happens with rounding when you convert from these different data types?**

**A** When converting from a `float`, `double`, or `decimal` to one of the whole number variable types, the value is rounded. If a number is too big to fit into the variable, an error occurs.

When a `double` is converted to a `float` that is too big or too small, the value is represented as infinity or 0, respectively.

When a value is converted from a `float` or `double` to a `decimal`, the value is rounded. This rounding occurs after 28 decimal places and occurs only if necessary. If the value being converted is too small to be represented as a `decimal`, the new value is set to `0`. If the value is too large to store in the `decimal`, an error occurs.

For conversions from `decimal` to `float` or `double`, the value is rounded to the nearest value the `float` or `double` can hold. Remember, a `decimal` has better precision than a `float` or a `double`. This precision is lost in the conversion.

**Q What other languages adhere to the Common Type System (CTS) in the Common Language Runtime (CLR)?**

**A** Microsoft Visual Basic.Net (version 7) and Microsoft Visual C++.NET (version 7) both support the CTS. Additionally there are versions of a number of other languages that are ported to the CTS. These include Python, COBOL, Perl, Java, and more. Check out the Microsoft Web site for additional languages.

3

# Workshop

The Workshop provides quiz questions to help you solidify your understanding of the material covered and exercises to provide you with experience in using what you've learned. Try to understand the quiz and exercise answers before continuing to the next day's lesson. Answers are provided in Appendix A, "Answers."

## Quiz

1. What are the by value data types available in C#?
2. What is the difference between a signed and unsigned variable?
3. What is the smallest data type you can use to store the number 55?
4. What is the biggest number that a type `short` variable can hold?
5. What numeric value is the character *B*?

6. How many bits in a byte?
7. What literal values can be assigned to a Boolean variable?
8. Name three of the reference data types.
9. Which floating-point data type has the best precision?
10. What .NET data type is equivalent to the C# `int` data type?

## Exercises

1. Change the range of values in Listing 3.6 to print the lowercase letters.
2. Write the line of code that declares a variable named `xyz` of type `float` and assign the value of `123.456` to it.
3. Which of the following variable names are valid?

   a) `X`

   b) `PI`

   c) `12months`

   d) `sizeof`

   e) `nine`
4. **BUG BUSTER:** The following program has a problem. Enter it in your editor and compile it. Which lines generate error messages?

```
1:  //Bug Buster
2:  //--------------------------------------------------------------
3:  using System;
4:
5:  class variables
6:  {
7:      public static void Main()
8:      {
9:          double my_double;
10:         decimal my_decimal;
11:
12:         my_double = 3.14;
13:         my_decimal = 3.14;
14:
15:         Console.WriteLine("\nMy Double:  {0}", my_double);
16:         Console.WriteLine("\nMy Decimal: {0}", my_decimal);
17:
18:     }
19: }
```

5. **ON YOUR OWN:** Write a program that declares two variables of each data type and assigns the values `10` and `1.879` to each variable.

WEEK 1

# DAY 4

# Working with Operators

Now that you know how to store information in variables, you'll want to do something with that data. Most likely you'll want to manipulate the data by making changes to it. For example, you might want to use the radius of a circle to find the area of the circle. Today you

- Discover the types and categories of operators available in C#
- Manipulate information using the different operators
- Change program flow using the `if` command
- Understand which operators have precedence over others
- Explore bitwise operations—if you're brave enough

## Types of Operators

Operators are used to manipulate information. You have actually used a number of operators in the programming examples on previous days. Operators are used to perform operations such as addition, multiplication, comparison, and more.

Operators can be broken into a number of categories:

- The Basic assignment operator
- Mathematical/arithmetic operators
- Relational operators
- The Conditional operator
- Other operators (type, size)

Each of these categories and the operators within them are covered in detail in today's lessons. In addition to these categories, it is also important to understand the structure of operator statements. There are three types of operator structures:

- Unary
- Binary
- Ternary

## Unary Operator Types

Unary operators are operators that impact a single variable. For example, to have a negative 1, you type

```
-1
```

If you have a variable called `x`, you change the value to a negative by using

```
-x
```

The negative requires only one variable, so it is unary. The format of a unary variable will be one of the following depending on the specific operator:

`[`*`operator`*`][`*`variable`*`]`

or

`[`*`variable`*`][`*`operator`*`]`

## Binary Operator Types

Whereas unary uses only one variable, binary operator types work with two variables. For example, the addition operator is used to add two values together. The format of the binary operator types is

`[`*`variable1`*`][`*`operator`*`][`*`variable2`*`]`

Examples of binary operations in action are

```
5 + 4
```

```
3 - 2
100.4 - 92348.67
```

You will find that most of the operators fall into the binary operator type.

## Ternary Operator Types

Ternary operators are the most complex operator types to work with. As the name implies, this type of operator works on three variables. C# has only one true ternary operator, the conditional operator. You will learn about it later today. For now, know that ternary operators work with three variables.

# Punctuators

Before jumping into the different categories and the specific operators within C#, it is important to understand about punctuators. Punctuators are a special form of operator that helps you format your code, do multiple operations at once, and simply signal information to the compiler. The punctuators that you need to know about are

- **Semicolon** :. The primary use of the semicolon is to end each C# statement. A semicolon is also used with a couple of the C# statements that control program flow. You will learn about the use of the semicolon with the control statements on Day 5,"Control Statements."
- **Comma** ,. The comma is used to stack multiple commands on the same line. You saw the comma in use on Day 3, "Storing Information with Variables," in a number of the examples. The most common time to use the comma is when declaring multiple variables of the same type:

  ```
  int var1, var2, var3;
  ```
- **Parentheses** (). Parentheses are used in multiple places. You will see later in today's lesson, that you can use parentheses to force the order of execution. Additionally, parentheses are used with functions.
- **Braces** {}. Braces are used to group pieces of code. You have seen braces used to encompass classes in many of the examples. You should also have noticed that braces are always used in pairs.

Punctuators operate the same way punctuation within a sentence operates. For example, you end a sentence with a period or another form of punctuation. In C#, you end a "line" of code with a semicolon or other punctuator. Line is in quotation marks because a line of code might actually take up multiple lines in a source listing. As you learned on Day 2, "Understanding C# Programs," whitespace and newlines are ignored.

**Note**

You will find that you can also use braces within the routines you create to block off code. The code put between two braces, along with the braces, is called a *block*.

## The Basic Assignment Operator

The first operator that you need to know about is the basic assignment operator. which is an equal sign (=). You've seen this operator already in a number of the examples in earlier lessons.

The basic assignment operator is used to assign values. For example, to assign the value 142 to the variable x, you type

```
x = 142;
```

This compiler takes the value that is on the right side of the assignment operator and places it in the variable on the left side. Consider the following:

```
x = y = 123;
```

This might look a little weird; however, it is legal C# code. The value on the right of the equal sign is evaluated. In this case, the far right is 123, which is placed into the variable y. Then the value of y is placed into the variable x. The end result is that both x and y equal 123.

**Caution**

You cannot do operations on the left side of an assignment operator. For example, you can't do

```
1 + x = y;
```

nor can you put literals or constants on the left side of an assignment operator.

## Mathematical/Arithmetic Operators

Now that you are aware of the punctuators, it is time to jump into the operators. Among the most commonly used operators are the mathematical operators. All the basic math functions are available within C#, including addition, subtraction, multiplication, division, and modulus. Additionally, there are compound operators that make doing some of these operations even more concise.

> **Note**
> The modulus operator is also known as the *remaindering operator*.

## Adding and Subtracting

The additive operators within C# are used for addition and subtraction. For addition, the plus operator (+) is used. For subtraction, the minus (-) operator is used. The general format of using these variables is

```
NewVal = Val1 + Val2;

NewVal2 = Val1 - Val2;
```

In the first statement, `Val2` is being added to `Val1` and the result is placed in `NewVal`. When this command is done, `Val1` and `Val2` remain unchanged. Any preexisting values in `NewVal` are overwritten with the result.

For the subtraction statement, `Val2` is subtracted from `Val1` and the result is placed in `NewVal2`. Again, `Val1` and `Val2` remain unchanged, and the value in `NewVal2` is overwritten with the result.

`Val1` and `Val2` can be any of the value data types, constants, or a literal. You should note that `NewVal` must be a variable; however, it can be the same variable as `Val1` or `Val2`. For example, the following is legal as long as `Var1` is a variable:

```
Var1 = Var1 - Var2;
```

In this example, the value in `Var2` is subtracted from the value in `Var1`. The result is placed into `Var1`, thus overwriting the previous value that `Var1` held. The following example is also valid:

```
Var1 = Var1 - Var1;
```

In this example, the value of `Var1` is subtracted from the value of `Var1`. Because these values are the same, the result is `0`. This `0` value is then placed into `Var1` overwriting any previous value.

If you want to double a value, you enter the following:

```
Var1 = Var1 + Var1;
```

`Var1` is added to itself and the result is placed back into `Var1`. The end result is that you double the value in `Var1`.

## Multiplicative Operators

An easier way to double the value of a variable is to multiply it by two. There are three multiplicative operators commonly used in C#.

### Multiplying

The first multiplicative operator is the multiplier (or times) operator, which is an asterisk (*). To multiply two values, you use the following format:

```
NewVal = Val1 * Val2;
```

For example, to double the value in `Val1` and place it back into itself (as seen with the last addition example), you can enter the following:

```
Val1 = Val1 * 2;
```

This is the same as

```
Val1 = 2 * Val2;
```

### Dividing

To do division, you use the divisor operator, which is a forward slash (/):

```
NewVal = Val1 / Val2;
```

This example divides `Val1` by `Val2` and places the result in `NewVal`. To divide 2 by 3, you write the following:

```
answer = 2 / 3;
```

### Working with Remainders

There are times when doing division that you want only the remainder. For example, I know that 3 will go into 4 one time; however, I also would like to know that I have 1 remaining. You can get this remainder using the remaindering (also called modulus) operator, which is the percentage sign (%).For example, to get the remainder of 4 divided by 3, you enter:

```
Val = 4 % 3;
```

The result is that `Val` is 1.

Consider another example that is near and dear to my heart. You have 3 pies that can be cut into 6 pieces, and 13 people each want pie. How many pieces of pie are left over? To solve this, you first determine how many pieces of pie you have:

```
PiecesOfPie = 3 * 6;  // three pies times six pieces
```

The value of `PiecesOfPie` should be obvious to you—`18`. Now to determine how many pieces are left, you use the modulus operator:

```
PiecesForMe = PiecesOfPie % 13;
```

This sets the value of `PiecesForMe` to `18 Mod 13`, which is 5. Listing 4.1 verifies this.

**LISTING 4.1** pie.cs—Number of Pieces of Pie for Me

```
 1:  // pie.cs - Using the modulus operators
 2:  //-----------------------------------------------
 3:  class pie
 4:  {
 5:     static void Main()
 6:     {
 7:        int PiecesForMe = 0;
 8:        int PiecesOfPie = 0;
 9:
10:        PiecesOfPie = 3 * 6;
11:
12:        PiecesForMe =  PiecesOfPie % 13;
13:
14:        System.Console.WriteLine("Pieces Of Pie = {0}", PiecesOfPie);
15:        System.Console.WriteLine("Pieces For Me = {0}", PiecesForMe);
16:     }
17:  }
```

**OUTPUT**

```
Pieces Of Pie = 18
Pieces For Me = 5
```

**ANALYSIS** Listing 4.1 presents the use of the multiplication and modulus operators. Line 10 illustrates the multiplication operator using the same formula as shown earlier. Line 12 then uses the modulus operator. As you can see from the information printed in lines 14 and 15, the results are as expected.

## Compound Arithmetic Assignment Operators

Earlier in today's lesson, you learned about the basic assignment operator. There are also other assignment operators, the compound assignment operators (see Table 4.1).

**TABLE 4.1** Compound Arithmetic Assignment Operators

| *Operator* | *Description* | *Non-Compound Equivalent* |
|---|---|---|
| `+=` | `x += 4` | `x = x + 4` |
| `-=` | `x -= 4` | `x = x - 4` |
| `*=` | `x *= 4` | `x = x * 4` |

**TABLE 4.1** continued

| *Operator* | *Description* | *Non-Compound Equivalent* |
|---|---|---|
| `/=` | `x /= 4` | `x = x / 4` |
| `%=` | `x %= 4` | `x = x % 4` |

The compound operators provide a concise method for performing a math operation and assigning it to a value. If you want to increase a value by 5, you use the following:

```
x = x + 5;
```

or you can use the compound operator:

```
x += 5;
```

As you can see, the compound operator is much more concise.

> **Tip** Although the compound operators are more concise, they are not always the easiest to understand in code. If you use the compound operators, make sure that what you are doing is clear or remember to comment your code.

## Doing Unary Math

All the arithmetic operators you have seen so far have been binary. Each has required two values to operate. There are also a number of unary operators that work with just one value or variable. The unary arithmetic operators are the increment operator (++) and the decrement operator (--).

These operators add 1 to the value or subtract 1 from the value of a variable. The following example:

```
++x;
```

adds 1 to x. It is the same as saying

```
x = x + 1;
```

Additionally, the following:

```
--x;
```

subtracts 1 from x. It is the same as saying

```
x = x - 1;
```

Listing 4.2 shows the increment and decrement operators in action.

**Tip**

> The increment and decrement operators are handy when you need to step through a lot of values one-by-one.

**LISTING 4.2** count.cs—Using the Increment and Decrement Operators

```
 1:  // count.cs - Using the increment/decrement operators
 2:  //----------------------------------------------------
 3:
 4:  class count
 5:  {
 6:     static void Main()
 7:     {
 8:        int Val1 = 0;
 9:        int Val2 = 0;
10:
11:        System.Console.WriteLine("Val1 = {0}  Val2 = {1}", Val1, Val2);
12:
13:        ++Val1;
14:        --Val2;
15:
16:        System.Console.WriteLine("Val1 = {0}  Val2 = {1}", Val1, Val2);
17:
18:        ++Val1;
19:        --Val2;
20:
21:        System.Console.WriteLine("Val1 = {0}  Val2 = {1}", Val1, Val2);
22:     }
23:  }
```



**OUTPUT**

```
Val1 = 0  Val2 = 0
Val1 = 1  Val2 = -1
Val1 = 2  Val2 = -2
```

**ANALYSIS** This listing doesn't do anything spectacular; however, it does illustrate the increment and decrement operators. As you can see in lines 8 and 9, two variables are initialized to `0`. Line 11 prints this so that you can see they are actually `0`. Lines 13 and 14 then increment and decrement each of the variables. Line 16 prints these values so you can see that the actions occurred. Lines 18 to 21 repeat this process.

### Using Pre- and Post-Increment Operators

The increment and decrement operators have a unique feature that causes problems for a lot of newer programmers. Assume that the value of `x` is `10`. Look at the following line of code:

```
y = ++x;
```

After this statement executes, what will the values of x and y be? You should be able to guess that the value of x will be 11 after it executes. The value of y will also be 11. Now consider the following line of code. Again consider the value of x to start at 10.

```
y = x++;
```

After this statement executes, what will the values of x and y be? If you said they would both be 11 again, you are wrong! After this line of code executes, x will be 11; however, y will be 10. Confused?

It is simple. The increment operator can operate as a pre-increment operator or a post-increment operator. If it operates as a pre-increment operator, the value is incremented before everything else. If it operates as a post-increment operator, it happens after everything else. How do you know if it is pre or post? Easy. If it is before the variable, ++x, it is pre. If it is after the variable, x++, it is post. The same is true of the decrement operator. Listing 4.3 illustrates the pre and post operations of the increment and decrement operators.

**LISTING 4.3** prepost.cs—Using the Increment and Decrement Unary Operators

```
// prepost.cs - Using pre- versus post-increment operators
//----------------------------------------------------

class prepost
{
    static void Main()
    {
        int Val1 = 0;
        int Val2 = 0;

        System.Console.WriteLine("Val1 = {0}  Val2 = {1}", Val1, Val2);

        System.Console.WriteLine("Val1 (Pre) = {0}  Val2 = (Post) {1}",
              ++Val1, Val2++);

        System.Console.WriteLine("Val1 (Pre) = {0}  Val2 = (Post) {1}",
              ++Val1, Val2++);

        System.Console.WriteLine("Val1 (Pre) = {0}  Val2 = (Post) {1}",
              ++Val1, Val2++);
    }
}
```

**OUTPUT**

```
Val1 = 0 Val2 = 0
Val1 (Pre) = 1  Val2 = (Post) 0
Val1 (Pre) = 2  Val2 = (Post) 1
Val1 (Pre) = 3  Val2 = (Post) 2
```

**ANALYSIS** It is important to understand what is happening in Listing 4.3. In lines 8 and 9, two variables are again being initialized to 0. These values are printed in line 11. As you can see from the output, the result is that `Val1` and `Val2` equal 0. Line 13, which continues to line 14, prints the values of these two variables again. The values printed, though, are `++Val1` and `Val2++`. As you can see, the pre-increment operator is being used on `Val1` and the post-increment operator is being used on `Val2`. The results can be seen in the output. Val1 is incremented by 1 and then printed. `Val2` is printed and then incremented by 1. Lines 16 and 19 repeat these same operations two more times.

| Do | DON'T |
|---|---|
| **DO** use the compound operators to make your math routines concise. | **DON'T** confuse the post-increment and pre-increment operators. Remember the pre-increment adds prior to the variable, and the post-increment adds after. |

# Relational Operators

Questions are a part of life. In addition to asking questions, it is often important to compare things. In programming, you will compare values and then execute code based on the answer. The relational operators are used to compare two values.

With the relational operators, you determine the relationship between two values. The relational operators are listed in Table 4.2.

**TABLE 4.2** Relational Operators

| *Operator* | *Description* |
|---|---|
| > | Greater than |
| < | Less than |
| == | Equal to |
| != | Not equal to |
| >= | Greater than or equal to |
| <= | Less than or equal to |

When making comparisons with relational operators, you get one of two results: true or false. Consider the following comparisons made with the relational operators:

5 < 10    5 is less than 10, so this is true

5 > 10    5 is not greater than 10, so this is false

5 == 10 5 does not equal 10, so this is false

5 != 10 5 does not equal 10, so this is true

As you can see, each of these results is either true or false. Knowing that you can check the relationship of values should be great for programming. The question is, how do you use these relations?

## The `if` Statement

The value of relational operators is that they can be used to make decisions. These decisions are used to change the flow of the execution of your program. The `if` keyword can be used with the relational operators to change the program flow.

The `if` keyword is used to compare two values. The standard format of the `if` command is

```
if( val1 [operator] val2)
    statement(s);
```

Where *operator* is one of the relational operators; `val1` and `val2` are variables, constants, or literals; and *statement(s)* is a single statement or a block containing multiple statements. Remember a block is one or more statements between brackets.

If the comparison of `val1` to `val2` is true, the statements are executed. If the comparison of `val1` to `val2` is false, the statements are skipped. Figure 4.1 illustrates how the `if` command works.

**FIGURE 4.1**

*The* `if` *command.*

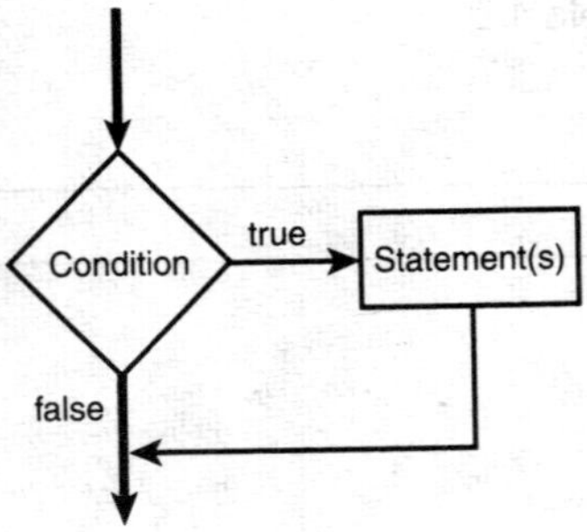


Applying this to an example helps make this clear. Listing 4.4 presents simple usage of the `if` command.

**LISTING 4.4** iftest.cs—Using the `if` Command

```
// iftest.cs- The if statement
//----------------------------------------------------

```

**LISTING 4.4** continued

```
 4: class iftest
 5: {
 6:    static void Main()
 7:    {
 8:       int Val1 = 1;
 9:       int Val2 = 0;
10:
11:       System.Console.WriteLine("Getting ready to do the if...");
12:
13:       if (Val1 == Val2)
14:       {
15:          System.Console.WriteLine("If condition was true");
16:       }
17:       System.Console.WriteLine("Done with the if statement");
18:    }
19: }
```

**OUTPUT**

```
Getting ready to do the if...
Done with the if statement
```

**ANALYSIS** This listing uses the `if` statement in line 13 to compare two values to see whether they are equal. If they are, it prints line 15. If not, line 15 is skipped. Because the values assigned to `Val1` and `Val2` in lines 8 and 9 are not equal, the `if` condition fails and line 15 is not printed.

Change line 13 to

```
if (Val1 != Val2)
```

Rerun the listing. This time, because `Val1` does not equal `Val2`, the `if` condition evaluates to `true`. The following is the output:

```
Getting ready to do the if...
If condition was true
Done with the if statement
```

**Caution**

There is not a semicolon at the end of the first line of the `if` command. For example, the following is incorrect:

```
if( x != x);
{
     // Statements to do when the if evaluates to true (which will
never happen)
}
```

x should always equal x, so `x != x` will be false and the line `// Statements to do when the if evaluates to true...` should never execute. Because there is a semicolon at the end of the first line, the `if` statement is ended. This means that the next statement *after* the if statement will be executed—the line `//Statements to do when the if evaluates to true....` This line will always execute regardless of whether the `if` evaluates to `true` or, as in this case, to `false`. Make sure you don't make the mistake of including a semicolon at the end of the first line of an `if` statement.

# Conditional Logical Operators

The world is rarely a simple place. In many cases you will want to do more than one comparison to determine whether a block of code should be executed. For example, you might want to execute some code if a person is a female and at least 21 years old. To do this, you execute an `if` statement within another `if` statement. The following pseudocode illustrates this:

```
if( sex == female )
{
    if( age >= 21)
    {
        // The person is a female that is 21 years old or older.
    }
}
```

There is an easier way to accomplish this—by using a conditional logical operator.

The conditional logical operators enable you to do multiple comparisons with relational operators. The two conditional logical operators that you will use are the AND operator (&&) and the OR operator (||).

## The Conditional AND Operator

There are times when you want to verify that a number of conditions are all met. The previous example was one such case. The logical AND operator (&&) enables you to verify that all conditions are met. You can rewrite the previous example as follows:

```
If( sex == female && age >= 21)
{
    // This person is a female that is 21 years old or older.
}
```

You can actually place more than two relationships within a single `if` statement. Regardless of the number of comparisons, the comparisons on each side of the AND (&&) must be true. For example:

```
if( x < 5 && y < 10 && z > 10)
{
   // statements
}
```

The `statements` line is reached only if all three conditions are met. If any of the three conditions in the `if` statements are false, the statements are skipped.

## The Conditional OR Operator

There are also times when you do not want all the conditions to be true: instead, you need only one of a number of conditions to be true. For example, you want might want to execute some code if the day of week is Saturday or Sunday. In these cases, you use the logical OR operator (`||`). The following illustrates this with pseudocode:

```
if( day equals sunday OR day equals saturday )
{
    // do statements
}
```

In this example, the statements are executed if the day equals either `sunday` or `saturday`. Only one of these conditions needs to be true for the statements to be executed. Listing 4.5 presents both the logical AND and OR in action.



**LISTING 4.5** and.cs—Using the Logical AND and OR

```
// and.cs- Using the conditional AND and OR
//-----------------------------------------------

class andclass
{
   static void Main()
   {
      int  day = 1;
      char sex = 'f';

      System.Console.WriteLine("Starting tests... (day:{0}, sex:{1})",
                               day, sex );

      if ( day >= 1 && day <=7 )       //day from 1 to 7?
      {
        System.Console.WriteLine("Day is from 1 to 7");
      }
      if (sex == 'm' || sex == 'f' )  // Male or female?
      {
         System.Console.WriteLine("Sex is male or female.");
      }

      System.Console.WriteLine("Done with the checks.");
```

**LISTING 4.5** continued

```
24:     }
25: }
```

**OUTPUT**

```
Starting tests... (day:1, sex:f)
Day is from 1 to 7
Sex is male or female.
Done with the checks.
```

**ANALYSIS** This listing illustrates both the `&&` and `||` operators. In line 14 you can see the AND operator (`&&`) in action. For this `if` statement to evaluate to `true`, the `day` must be greater than or equal to `1` as well as less than or equal to `7`. If the `day` is 1, 2, 3, 4, 5, 6, or 7, the `if` condition evaluates to `true` and line 16 prints. Any other number results in the `if` statement evaluating to `false, and line 16 will be skipped.`

Line 18 shows the OR (`||`) operator in action. Here, if the value in `sex` is equal to the character `'m'` or the character `'f'`, line 20 is printed; otherwise, line 20 is skipped.

**Caution**

Be careful with the `if` condition in line 18. This checks for the characters `'m'` and `'f'`. Notice these are lowercase values, which are not the same as the uppercase values. If you set `sex` equal to `'F'` or `'M'` in line 9, the `if` statement in line 18 would still fail.

Change the values in lines 8 and 9 and rerun the listing. You'll see that you get different output results based on the values you select. For example, change lines 8 and 9 to the following:

```
8:          int  day = 9;
9:          char sex = 'x';
```

Here are the results of rerunning the program:

**OUTPUT**

```
Starting tests... (day:9, sex:x)
Done with the checks.
```

There are also times when you will want to use the AND (`&&`) and the OR (`||`) commands together. For example, you might want to execute code if a person is 21 and is either a male or female. This can be accomplished by using the AND and OR statements together. You must be careful when doing this, though. An AND operator expects the values on both sides of it to be true. An OR statement expects one or the other value to be true. For the previous example, you might be tempted to enter the following:

```
if( age >= 21 AND gender == male OR gender == FEMALE)
    // statement
```

This will not accomplish what you want. If the person is 21 or older and a female, the statement will not execute. The AND portion will result in being `false`. To overcome this problem, you can force how the statements are evaluated using the parenthesis punctuator. To accomplish the desired results, you would change the previous example to

```
if( age >= 21 AND (gender == male OR gender == female))
    // statement
```

The execution always starts with the innermost parenthesis. In this case, the statement `(gender == male OR gender == female)` is evaluated first. Because this uses OR, this portion of the statement will evaluate to `true` if either side is true. If this is true, the AND will compare the age value to see whether the age is greater than or equal to `21`. If this proves to be true as well, the statement will execute.

**Tip**

Use parentheses to make sure that you get code to execute in the order you want.

| Do | Don't |
|---|---|
| **DO** use parentheses to make complex math and relational operations easier to understand. | **DON'T** confuse the assignment operator (=) with the relational equals operator (==). |

4

## Logical Bitwise Operators

There are three other logical operators that you might want to use: the logical bitwise operators. Although the use of bitwise operations is beyond the scope of this book, I've included a section near the end of today's lesson called "For Those Brave Enough." This section explains bitwise operations, the three logical bitwise operators, and the bitwise shift operators.

The bitwise operators obtain their name from the fact that they operate on bits. A bit is a single storage location that stores either an on or off value (equated to 0 or 1). In the section at the end of today's lesson, you learn how the bitwise operators can be used to manipulate these bits.

## Type Operators

As you begin working with classes and interfaces later in this book, you will have need for the type operators. Without understanding interfaces and classes, it is hard to fully understand these operators. For now, be aware that there are a number of operators that you will need later. These type operators are

- `typeof`
- `is`
- `as`

# The `sizeof` Operator

You have already seen the `sizeof` operator. This `sizeof` operator is used to determine the size of a value. You saw the `sizeof` operator in action on Day 3.

**Caution**

> Because the `sizeof` operator manipulates memory directly, avoid its use if possible.

# The Conditional Operator

There is one ternary operator in C#, the conditional operator. The conditional operator has the following format:

```
Condition ? if_true_statement : if_false_statement;
```

As you can see, there are three parts to this operation, with two symbols used to separate them. The first part of the command is a condition. This is just like the conditions you created earlier for the `if` statement. This can be any condition that results in either `true` or `false`.

After the condition is a question mark. The question mark separates the condition from the first of two statements. The first of the two statements executes if the condition is true. The second statement is separated from the first with a colon and is executed if the condition is false. Listing 4.6 presents the conditional operator in action.

The conditional operator is used to create concise code. If you have a simple `if` statement that evaluates to doing a simple true and simple false statement, the conditional operator can be used. Otherwise, you should avoid the use of the conditional operator. Because it is just a shortcut version of an `if` statement, you should just stick with using the `if` statement itself. Most people reviewing your code will find the `if` statement easier to read and understand.

**LISTING 4.6** cond.cs—The Conditional Operator in Action

```
 1:  // cond.cs - The conditional operator
 2:  //----------------------------------------------------
 3:
 4:  class cond
 5:  {
 6:     static void Main()
 7:     {
 8:        int Val1 = 1;
 9:        int Val2 = 0;
10:        int result;
11:
12:        result = (Val1 == Val2) ? 1 : 0;
13:
14:        System.Console.WriteLine("The result is {0}", result);
15:     }
16:  }
```

**OUTPUT**

```
The result is 0
```

**ANALYSIS** This listing is very simple. In line 12, the conditional operator is executed and the result is placed in the variable, `result`. Line 14 then prints this value. In this case, the conditional operator is checking to see whether the value in `Val1` is equal to the value in `Val2`. Because 1 is not equal to 0, the false result of the conditional is set. Modify line 8 so that `Val2` is set equal to `1` and then rerun this listing. You will see that because 1 is equal to 1, the result will be `1` instead of `0`.

**Caution**

> The conditional operator provides a shortcut for implementing an `if` statement. Although it is more concise, it is not always the easiest for to understand. When using the conditional operator, you should verify that you are not making your code harder to understand.

# Understanding Operator Precedence

You've learned about a lot of different operators in today's lessons. Rarely are these operators used one at a time. Often, multiple operators will be used in a single statement. When this happens, a lot of issues seem to arise. Consider the following:

```
Answer = 4 * 5 + 6 / 2 - 1;
```

What is the value of `Answer`? If you said 12, you are wrong. If you said 44 you are also wrong. The answer is 22.

**New Term** There is a set order in which different types of operators are executed. This set order is called *operator precedence*. The word *precedence* is used because some operators have a higher level of precedence than others. In the example, multiplication and division have a higher level of precedence than addition and subtraction. This means that 4 is multiplied by 5 and 6 is divided by 2, before any addition occurs.

Table 4.3 lists all the operators. The operators at each level of the table are at the same level of precedence. In almost all cases, there is no impact on the results. For example, 5 * 4 / 10 is the same whether 5 is multiplied by 4 first or 4 is divided by 10.

**Table 4.3** Operator Precedence

| *Level* | *Operator Types* | *Operators* |
|---|---|---|
| 1 | Primary operators | `()` `.` `[]` `x++` `x—` `new` `typeof` `sizeof` `checked` `unchecked` |
| 2 | Unary | `+` `-` `!` `~` `++x` `—x` |
| 3 | Multiplicative | `*` `/` `%` |
| 4 | Additive | `+` `-` |
| 5 | Shift | `<<` `>>` |
| 6 | Relational | `<` `>` `<=` `>=` `is` |
| 7 | Equality | `==` `!=` |
| 8 | Logical AND | `&` |
| 9 | Logical XOR | `^` |
| 10 | Logical OR | `\|` |
| 11 | Conditional AND | `&&` |
| 12 | Conditional OR | `\|\|` |
| 13 | Conditional | `?:` |
| 14 | Assignment | `=` `*=` `/=` `%=` `+=` `-=` `<<=` `>>=` `&=` `^=` `\|=` |

## Changing Precedence Order

You learned how to change the order of precedence by using parentheses punctuators earlier in today's lessons. Because parentheses have a higher level of precedence than the operators, what is enclosed in them is evaluated before operators outside of them. Using the earlier example, you can force the addition and subtraction to occur first by using parentheses:

```
Answer = 4 * ( 5 + 6 ) / ( 2 - 1 );
```

Now what will Answer be? Because the parentheses are evaluated first, the compiler first resolves the code to

```
Answer = 4 * 11 / 1;
```

The final result is 44. You can also have parentheses within parentheses. For example, the code could be written as

```
Answer = 4 * ( ( 5 + 6 ) / ( 2 - 1 ) );
```

The compiler would resolve this as

```
Answer = 4 * ( 11 / 1 );
```

Then it would resolve it as

```
Answer = 4 * 11;
```

and finally as the Answer of 44. In this case, the parentheses didn't cause a difference in the final answer; however, there are times when they do.



## Converting Data Types

When you move a value from one variable type to another, a conversion must occur. Additionally, if you want to perform an operation on two different data types, a conversion might also need to occur. There are two types of conversions that can occur: implicit and explicit.

**NEW TERM** *Implicit* conversions happen automatically without error. You've read about many of these within today's lesson. What happens when an implicit conversion is not available? For example, what if you want to put the value stored in a variable of type long into a variable of type int?

**NEW TERM** *Explicit* conversions are conversions of data that are forced. For the value data types that you learned about today, the easiest way to do an explicit conversion is with a cast. A *cast* is the forcing of a data value to another data type. The format of a cast is

```
ToVariable = (datatype) FromVariable;
```

where *datatype* is the data type you want the *FromVariable* converted to. Using the example of converting a long variable to an int, you enter the following statement:

```
int IntVariable = 0;
long LongVariable = 1234;
IntVariable = (int) LongVariable;
```

In doing casts, you take responsibility for making sure that the variable can hold the value being converted. If the receiving variable cannot store the received value, truncation or other changes can occur. There are a number of times when you are going to need to do explicit conversions. Table 4.4 contains a list of those times.

**Note** Explicit conversions as a group also encompass all the implicit conversions. It is possible to use a cast even if an implicit conversion is available.

Table 4.4. Required Explicit Conversions

| *From Type* | *To Type(s)* |
|---|---|
| `sbyte` | `byte, ushort, uint, ulong, or char` |
| `byte` | `sbyte or char` |
| `short` | `sbyte, byte, ushort, uint, ulong, or char` |
| `ushort` | `sbyte, byte, short, or char` |
| `int` | `sbyte, byte, short, ushort, uint, ulong, or char` |
| `uint` | `sbyte, byte, short, ushort, int, or char` |
| `long` | `sbyte, byte, short, ushort, int, uint, ulong, or char` |
| `ulong` | `sbyte, byte, short, ushort, int, uint, long, or char` |
| `char` | `sbyte, byte, short` |
| `float` | `sbyte, byte, short, ushort, int, uint, long, ulong, char, or decimal` |
| `double` | `sbyte, byte, short, ushort, int, uint, long, ulong, char, float, or decimal` |
| `decimal` | `sbyte, byte, short, ushort, int, uint, long, ulong, char, float, double` |

# Understanding Operator Promotion

**NEW TERM** Implicit conversions are also associated with *operator promotion,* which is the automatic conversion of an operator from one type to another. When you do basic arithmetic operations on two variables, they are converted to the same time before doing the math. For example, if you add a `byte` variable to an `int` variable, the `byte` variable is promoted to an integer before being added.

A numeric variable smaller than an `int` will be promoted to an `int`. The order of promotion after an `int` is

```
int
uint
long
ulong
float
double
    decimal
```

# For Those Brave Enough

For those brave enough, the following sections explain using the bitwise operators. This includes using the shift operators and the logical bitwise operators. Before understanding how these operators work, you need to understand how variables are truly stored.

**Tip**

It is valuable to understand the bitwise operators and how memory works; however, it is not critical to your understanding C#. This is considered an advanced topic by a lot of people.

4

## Storing Variables in Memory

To understand the bitwise operators, you must first understand bits. In yesterday's lesson on data types, you learned that the different data types take different numbers of bits to store. For example, a `char` data type takes 2 bytes. An integer takes 4 bytes. You also learned that there were maximum and minimum values that could be stored in these different data types.

Recall that a byte is 8 bits of memory. Two bytes is 16 bits of memory—two times eight. Four bytes is therefore 32 bits of memory. So the key to all of this is to understand what a bit is.

**NEW TERM** A bit is simply a single storage unit of memory that can be either turned on or turned off just like a light bulb. If storing information on a magnetic medium, a bit can be stored as either a positive charge or a negative charge. If working with something such as a CD-ROM, this can be stored as a bump or as an indent. In all these cases, one value is equated to `0` and the other is equated to `1`.

If a bit can store only a 0 or a 1, you are obviously very limited in what can be stored. To be able to store larger values, you use bits in groups. For example, if you use 2 bits, you can actually store four numbers, 00, 01, 10, and 11. If you use three bits, you can store 8 numbers, 000, 001, 010, 011, 100, 101, 110, and 111. If you use four bits, you can store 16 numbers. In fact x bits can store $2^x$ numbers, so a byte (8 bits), can store $2^8$ or 256 numbers. Two bytes can store $2^{16}$ or 65536 values.

Translating from these 1s and 0s is simply a matter of using the binary number system. Appendix D, "Understanding Different Number Systems" explains how you can work with the binary number system in detail. For now understand that the binary system is simply a number system.

You use the decimal number system to count. Where the decimal system uses 10 numbers (0 to 9) the binary system uses two numbers. When counting in the decimal system, you use 1s, 10s, 100s, 1000s, and so forth. For example, the number 13 is one 10 and three 1s. The number 25 is two 10s and five 1s.

The binary system works the same way except there are only two numbers, 0 and 1. Instead of 10s and 100s, you have 1s, 2s, 4s, 8s, and so on. In fact each group is based on taking 2 to the power of a number. The first group is 2 to the power of 0, the second is 2 to the power of 1, the third is 2 to the power of 3,and so on. Figure 4.2 illustrates this.

**FIGURE 4.2**

*Binary versus decimal.*

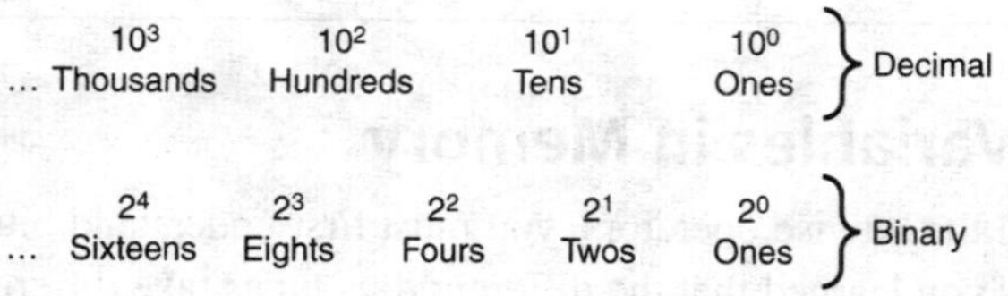


Presenting numbers in the binary system works the same way it does in the decimal system. The first position on the right is 1s, the second position from the right is 2s, the third is 4s, and so on. Consider the following number:

1101

To convert this binary number to decimal, you can take each value in the number times its positional value. For example, the value in the right column (1s) is 1. The 2s column contains a 0, the 4s column contains a 1, and the 8s column contains a 1. The result is

1 + (0 * 2) + (1 * 4) + (1 * 8)

The final decimal result is

1 + 0 + 4 + 8

which is 13. So 1101 in binary is equivalent to 13 in decimal. This same process can be applied to convert any binary number to decimal. As numbers get larger you need more bit positions. To keep things simpler, memory is actually separated into 8-bit units—bytes.

## Shift Operators

C# has two shift operators that can be used to manipulate bits. These operators do exactly what their names imply—they shift the bits. The shift operators can shift the bits to the right using the >> operator or to the left using the << operator. These operators shift the bits within a variable by a specified number of positions. The format is

```
New_value = Value [shift-operator] number-of-positions;
```

where `Value` is a literal or variable, `shift-operator` is either the right (>>) or left (<<) shift operator, and `number-of-positions` is how many positions you want to shift the bits. For example, if you have the number 13 stored in a byte, you know its binary representation is

00001101

If you use the shift operator on this, you change the value. Consider the following:

00001101 >> 2

This shifts the bits in this number to the right two positions. The result is

00000011

This binary value is equivalent to the value of 3. In summary, 13 >> 2 equals 3. Consider another example:

00001101 << 8

This example shifts the bit values to the left 8 positions. Because this is a single byte value, the resulting number is 0.

## Logical Operators

In addition to being able to shift bits, you can also combine the bits of two numbers. There are four bitwise logical operators, as shown in Table 4.5.

**TABLE 4.5** Logical Bitwise Operators

| *Operator* | *Description* |
|---|---|
| \| | Logical OR bitwise operator |
| & | Logical AND bitwise operator |
| ^ | Logical XOR bitwise operator |
| ~ | Logical NOT bitwise operator |

Each of these operators is used to combine the bits of two binary values together. Each has a different result.

### The Logical OR Bitwise Operator

When combining two values with the logical OR bitwise operator (|), you get the following results:

- If both bits are0, the result is 0.
- If either or both bits are 1, the result is 1.

Combining two byte values results in the following:

| | |
|---|---|
| Value 1: | 00001111 |
| Value 2: | 11001100 |
| Result: | 11001111 |

### The Logical AND Bitwise Operator

When combining two values with the logical AND bitwise operator (&), you get the following result:

- If both bits are 1, the result is 1.
- If either bit is 0, the result is 0.

Combining two byte values results in the following:

| | |
|---|---|
| Value 1: | 00001111 |
| Value 2: | 11001100 |
| Result: | 00001100 |

### The Logical NOT Operator

When combining two values with the logical NOT bitwise operator (^), you get the following result:

- If both bits are the same, the result is 0.
- If one bit is 0 and the other is 1, the result is 1.

Combining two byte values results in the following:

| | |
|---|---|
| Value 1: | 00001111 |
| Value 2: | 11001100 |
| Result: | 11000011 |

Listing 4.7 illustrates the three logical bitwise operators.

**LISTING 4.7** The Bitwise Operators

```
// bitwise.cs - Using the bitwise operators
//-----------------------------------------------

class bitwise
{
   static void Main()
   {
      int ValOne = 1;
      int ValZero = 0;
      int NewVal;

      // Bitwise NOT Operator

      NewVal = ValZero ^ ValZero;
      System.Console.WriteLine("\nThe NOT Operator: \n  0 ^ 0 = {0}",
➥NewVal);

      NewVal = ValZero ^ ValOne;
      System.Console.WriteLine("  0 ^ 1 = {0}", NewVal);

      NewVal = ValOne ^ ValZero;
      System.Console.WriteLine("  1 ^ 0 = {0}", NewVal);

      NewVal = ValOne ^ ValOne;
      System.Console.WriteLine("  1 ^ 1 = {0}", NewVal);

      // Bitwise AND Operator

      NewVal = ValZero & ValZero;
      System.Console.WriteLine("\nThe AND Operator: \n  0 & 0 = {0}",
➥NewVal);

      NewVal = ValZero & ValOne;
      System.Console.WriteLine("  0 & 1 = {0}", NewVal);

      NewVal = ValOne & ValZero;
      System.Console.WriteLine("  1 & 0 = {0}", NewVal);

      NewVal = ValOne & ValOne;
      System.Console.WriteLine("  1 & 1 = {0}", NewVal);

      // Bitwise OR Operator
```

**LISTING 4.7** continued

```
41:
42:             NewVal = ValZero | ValZero;
43:             System.Console.WriteLine("\nThe OR Operator: \n  0 | 0 = {0}",
➥NewVal);
44:
45:             NewVal = ValZero | ValOne;
46:             System.Console.WriteLine("  0 | 1 = {0}", NewVal);
47:
48:             NewVal = ValOne | ValZero;
49:             System.Console.WriteLine("  1 | 0 = {0}", NewVal);
50:
51:             NewVal = ValOne | ValOne;
52:             System.Console.WriteLine("  1 | 1 = {0}", NewVal);
53:         }
54:    }
```

**OUTPUT**

```
The NOT Operator:
  0 ^ 0 = 0
  0 ^ 1 = 1
  1 ^ 0 = 1
  1 ^ 1 = 0

The AND Operator:
  0 & 0 = 0
  0 & 1 = 0
  1 & 0 = 0
  1 & 1 = 1

The OR Operator:
  0 | 0 = 0
  0 | 1 = 1
  1 | 0 = 1
  1 | 1 = 1
```

**ANALYSIS** Listing 4.7 is a long listing; however, it summarizes the logical bitwise operators. Lines 8 and 9 define two variables and assign the values 1 and 0 to them. These two variables are then used repeatedly with the bitwise operators. A bitwise operation is done, and then the result is written to the console. You should review the output and see that the results are exactly as described in the earlier sections.

# Summary

Today's lesson presents a lot of information regarding operators and their use. You have learned about the types of operators, including arithmetic, multiplicative, relational, logical, and conditional. You also learned the order in which operators are evaluated (operator precedence). Finally, today's lesson ended with an explanation of bitwise operations and the bitwise operators.

# Q&A

**Q How important is it to understand operators and operator precedence?**

**A** You will use the operators in almost every application you create. Operator precedence is critical to understand. As you saw in today's lesson, if you don't understand operator precedence, you might end up with results different from what you expect.

**Q Today's lesson covered the binary number system briefly. Is it important to understand this number system? Also, what other number systems are i mportant?**

**A** Although it is not critical to understand binary, it *is* important. With computers today, information is stored in a binary format. Whether it is a positive versus negative charge, a bump versus an impression, or some other representation, all data is ultimately stored in binary. Knowing how the binary system works will make it easier for you to understand these actual storage values.

In addition to binary, many computer programmers also work with octal and hexadecimal. Octal is a base 8 number system and hexadecimal is a base 16 number system. Appendix D, "Understanding Number Systems," covers this in more detail.



# Workshop

The Workshop provides quiz questions to help you solidify your understanding of the material covered and exercises to provide you with experience in using what you've learned. Try to understand the quiz and exercise answers before continuing to the next day's lesson. Answers are provided in Appendix A, "Answers."

## Quiz

The following quiz questions will help verify your understanding of today's lessons.

1. What character is used for multiplication?
2. What is the result of 10 % 3?
3. What is the result of 10 + 3 * 2?
4. What are the conditional operators?
5. What C# keyword can be used to change the flow of a program?

6. What is the difference between a unary operator and a binary operator?
7. What is the difference between an explicit data type conversion versus an implicit conversion?
8. Is it possible to convert from a `long` to an integer?
9. What are the possible results of a conditional operation?
10. What do the shift operators do?

## Exercises

Please note that answers will not be provided for all exercises. The exercises will help you apply what you have learned in today's lessons.

1. What is the result of the following operation?

   2 + 6 * 3 + 5 – 2 *4

2. What is the result of the following operation?

   4 * (8 – 3 * 2) * (0 + 1) / 2

3. Write a program that checks to see whether a variable is greater than 65. If the value is greater than 65, print the statement `"The value is greater than 65!"`.
4. Write a program that checks to see whether a character contains the value of `'t'` or `'T'`.
5. Write the line of code to convert a long called `MyLong` to a short called `MyShort`.
6. **BUG BUSTER:** The following program has a problem. Enter it in your editor and compile it. Which lines generate error messages? What is the error?

```
class exercise
{
   static void Main()
   {
      int  value = 1;

      if ( value > 100 );
      {
         System.Console.WriteLine("Number is greater than 100");
      }
   }
}
```

7. Write the line of code to convert an integer, `IntVal`, to a short, `ShortVal`.
8. Write the line of code to convert a decimal, `DecVal`, to a long, `LongVal`.
9. Write the line of code to convert an integer, `ch`, to a character, `charVal`.

# WEEK 1

# DAY 5

# Control Statements

You've learned a lot in the previous four days. This includes knowing how to store information, knowing how to do operations, and even knowing how to avoid executing certain commands by using the `if` statement. You have learned a little about controlling the flow of a program using the `if` statement; however, there are often times where you need to be able to control the flow of a program even more. Today you

- See the other commands to use for program flow control
- Explore how to do even more with the `if` command
- Learn to switch between multiple options
- Investigate how to repeat a block of statements multiple times
- Discover how to abruptly stop the repeating of code

## Controlling Program Flow

By controlling the flow of a program, you are able to create functionality that results in something useful. As you continue to program, you will want to change the flow in a number of additional ways. You will want to repeat a piece of code a number of times, skip a piece of code altogether, or switch between a number of different pieces of code. Regardless of how you want to change the flow of a program, C# has an option for doing it. Most of the changes of flow can be categorized into two types:

- Selection statements
- Iterative statements

# Using Selection Statements

Selection statements enable you to execute specific blocks of code based on the results of a condition. The `if` statement that you learned about previously is a selection statement, as is the `switch` statement.

## Revisiting `if`

You've learned about the `if` statement; however, it is worth revisiting. Consider the following example:

```
if( gender == 'm' || gender == 'f' )
{
   System.Console.WriteLine("The gender is valid");
}
if( gender != 'm' && gender != 'f' )
{
   System.Console.WriteLine("The gender value, {0} is not valid", gender);
}
```

This example uses a character variable called `gender`. The first `if` statement checks to see whether `gender` is equal to an `'m'` or an `'f'`. This uses the OR operator you learned about in yesterday's lesson. A second `if` statement prints an error message in the case where the gender is not equal to `'m'` or `'f'`. This second `if` statement is an example of making sure that the variable has a valid value. If there is a value other than `'m'` and `'f'`, an error message is displayed.

If you look at these two statements and think that something is just not quite optimal, you are correct. C#, like many other languages, offers another keyword that can be used with the `if` statement: the `else` statement. The `else` statement is used specifically with the `if` statement. The format of the `if...else` statement is

```
if ( condition )
{
   // If condition is true, do these lines
}
else
{
```

```
    // If condition is false, do these lines
}
// code after if... statement
```

The `else` statement gives you the ability to have code that will be executed when the `if` statement's `condition` fails. You should also note that either the block of code after the `if` or the block of code after the `else` will execute—but not both. After either of these blocks of code is done executing, the program jumps to the first line after the `if...else` `condition`.

Listing 5.1 presents the gender code from earlier. This time, the code has been modified to use the `if...else` command. As you can see in the listing, this version is much more efficient and easier to follow than the one presented earlier.

**LISTING 5.1** ifelse.cs—Using the `if...else` Command

```
 1:  //  ifelse.cs - Using the if...else statement
 2:  //-----------------------------------------------------------
 3:
 4:  class ifelse
 5:  {
 6:     static void Main()
 7:     {
 8:        char gender = 'x';
 9:
10:        if( gender == 'm' || gender == 'f' )
11:        {
12:           System.Console.WriteLine("The gender is valid");
13:        }
14:        else
15:        {
16:           System.Console.WriteLine("The gender value, {0}, is not valid",
➥gender);
17:        }
18:        System.Console.WriteLine("The if statement is now over!");
18:     }
19:  }
```

**OUTPUT**

```
The gender value, x, is not valid
The if statement is now over!
```

**ANALYSIS** This listing declares a simple variable called `gender` of type `char` in line 8. This variable is set to a value of `'x'` when it is declared. The `if` statement starts in line 10. Line 10 checks to see whether `gender` is either `'m'` or `'f'`. If it is, a message is printed in line 12 saying that `gender` is valid. If `gender` is not `'m'` or `'f'`, the `if condition` fails and control is passed to the `else` statement in line 14. In this case, `gender` is equal to `'x'`, so the `else` command is executed. A message is printed stating that the `gender` value is invalid. Control is then passed to the first line after the `if...else` statement—line 18.

Modify line 8 to set the value of `gender` to either `'m'` or `'f'`. Recompile and rerun the program. This time the output will be

**OUTPUT**

```
The gender is valid
The if statement is now over!
```

**Caution**

What would you expect to happen if you set the value of gender to a capital `M` or `F`? Remember, C# is case sensitive. A capital letter is not the same thing as a lowercase letter.

## Nesting and Stacking `if` Statements

**NEW TERM** *Nesting* is simply the inclusion of one statement within another. Almost all C# flow commands can be nested within each other.

To nest an `if` statement, you place a second `if` statement within the first. You can nest within the `if` section or the `else` section. Using the `gender` example, you could do the following to make the statement a little more effective (the nested statement appears in bold):

```
if( gender == 'm' )
{
   // it is a male
}
else
{
   if ( gender == 'f' )
   {
      // it is a female
   }
   else
   {
      //neither a male or a female
   }
}
```

A complete `if...else` statement is nested within the `else` section of the original `if` statement. This code operates just as you expect. If `gender` is not equal to `'m'`, the flow goes to the first `else` statement. Within this `else` statement is another `if` statement that starts from its beginning. This second `if` statement checks to see whether the gender is equal to `'f'`. If not, the flow goes to the `else` statement of the nested `if`. At that point, you know that `gender` is neither `'m'` nor `'f'`, and you can add appropriate coding logic.

While nesting makes some functionality easier, you can also stack `if` statements. In the example of checking `gender`, stacking is actually a much better solution.

## Stacking `if` Statements

Stacking `if` statements combines the `else` with another `if`. The easiest way to understand stacking is to see the `gender` example one more time, stacked (see Listing 5.2).

**LISTING 5.2** stacking.cs—Stacking an `if` Statement

```
 1:  //  stacked.cs - Using the if...else statement
 2:  //--------------------------------------------------------------------
 3:
 4:  class stacked
 5:  {
 6:     static void Main()
 7:     {
 8:        char gender = 'x';
 9:
10:        if( gender == 'm' )
11:        {
12:           System.Console.WriteLine("The gender is male");
13:        }
14:        else if ( gender == 'f' )
15:        {
16:           System.Console.WriteLine("The gender is female");
17:        }
18:        else
19:        {
20:           System.Console.WriteLine("The gender value, {0}, is not valid",
➥gender);
21:        }
22:        System.Console.WriteLine("The if statement is now over!");
23:     }
24:  }
```

**OUTPUT**

```
The gender value, x, is not valid
The if statement is now over!
```

**ANALYSIS** The code presented in this example is very close to the code presented in the previous example. The primary difference is in line 14. The `else` statement is immediately followed by an `if`. There are no braces or a block. The format for stacking is

```
if ( condition 1 )
{
```

```
    // do something about condition 1
}
else if ( condition 2 )
{
    // do something about condition 2
}
else if ( condition 3 )
{
    // do something about condition 3
}
else if ( condition x )
{
    // do something about condition x
else
{
    // All previous conditions failed
}
```

This is relatively easy to follow. With the gender example, you had only two conditions. There are times when you might have more than two. For example, you could create a computer program that checks the roll of a die. You could then do something different depending on what the roll is. Each stacked condition could check for a different number (from 1 to 6) with the final else statement presenting an error because there can be only six numbers. The code for this would be

```
if (roll == 1)
    // roll is 1
else if (roll == 2)
            // roll is 2
else if (roll == 3)
            // roll is 3
else if (roll == 4)
            // roll is 4
else if (roll == 5)
            // roll is 5
else if (roll == 6)
            // roll is 6
else
    // it isn't a number from 1 to 6
```

This code is relatively easy to follow because it's easy to see that each of the 6 possible numbers is checked against the roll. If the roll is not one of the 6, the final else statement can take care of any error logic or reset logic.

**Note**

As you can see in the die code, there are no braces used around the if statements. If you are using only a single statement within the if or the else, you don't need the braces. You include them only when you have more than one statement.

## The `switch` Statement

C# provides a much easier way to modify program flow based on multiple values stored in a variable: the `switch` statement. The format of the `switch` statement is

```
switch ( value )
{
    case result_1 :
            // do stuff for result_1
            break;
    case result_2 :
            // do stuff for result_2
            break;
    ...
    case result_n :
            // do stuff for result_x
            break;
    default:
            // do stuff for default case
            break;
}
```

You can see by the format of the `switch` statement that there is no `condition`. Rather a *`value`* is used. This value can be the result of an expression, or it can be a variable. This value is then compared to each of the values in each of the `case` statements until a match is found. If a match is not found, the flow goes to the `default` case. If there is not a `default` case, the flow goes to the first statement following the `switch` statement.

When a match is found, the code within the matching `case` statement is executed. When the flow reaches another `case` statement, the `switch` statement is ended. Only one `case` statement will be executed at most. Flow then continues with the first command following the `switch` statement. Listing 5.3 shows the `switch` statement in action, using the earlier example of a roll of a six-sided die.



**LISTING 5.3** roll.cs—Using the `switch` Statement with the Roll of a Die

```
//  roll.cs- Using the switch statement.
//--------------------------------------------------------------------

class roll
{
    public static void Main()
    {
        int roll = 0;

        // The next two lines set the roll to a random number from 1 to 6
        System.Random rnd = new System.Random();
        roll = (int) rnd.Next(1,7);
```

**Listing 5.3** continued

```
13:
14:         System.Console.WriteLine("Starting the switch... ");
15:
16:         switch (roll)
17:         {
18:             case 1:
19:                         System.Console.WriteLine("Roll is 1");
20:                         break;
21:             case 2:
22:                         System.Console.WriteLine("Roll is 2");
23:                         break;
24:             case 3:
25:                         System.Console.WriteLine("Roll is 3");
26:                         break;
27:             case 4:
28:                         System.Console.WriteLine("Roll is 4");
29:                         break;
30:             case 5:
31:                         System.Console.WriteLine("Roll is 5");
32:                         break;
33:             case 6:
34:                         System.Console.WriteLine("Roll is 6");
35:                         break;
36:             default:
37:                         System.Console.WriteLine("Roll is not 1 through 6");
38:                         break;
39:         }
40:         System.Console.WriteLine("The switch statement is now over!");
41:     }
42: }
```

**Output**

```
Starting the switch...
Roll is 1
The switch statement is now over!
```

**Note**

Your answer for the roll in the output might be a number other than 1.

**Analysis** This listing is a little longer than a lot of the previous listings; however, it is also more functional. The first thing to focus on is lines 16 to 39. These lines contain the `switch` statement that is the center of this discussion. The `switch` statement uses the value stored in the roll. Depending on the value, one of the cases will be selected. If the number is something other than 1 though 6, the `default` statement starting in line 39 is executed. If any of the numbers are rolled (1 through 6), the appropriate `case` statement is executed.

You should note that at the end of each section of code for each `case` statement there is a `break` command, which is required at the end of each set of code. This signals the end of the statements within a `case`. If you don't include the `break` command, you will get a compiler error.

To make this listing a more interesting, lines 11 and 12 were added. Line 11 might look unfamiliar. This line creates a variable called `rnd`, which is an object that will hold a random number. In tomorrow's lesson, you revisit this line of code and learn the details of what it is doing. For now, simply know that it is setting up a variable for a random number.

Line 12 is also a line that will become more familiar over the next few days. The command, `(int) rnd.Next(1,7)` provides a random number from 1 to 6.

**Tip**

> You can use lines 11 and 12 to generate random numbers for any range by simply changing the values from 1 and 7 to the range you want numbers between. The first number is the lowest number that will be returned. The second number is one higher than the highest number that will be returned. For example, if you wanted a random number from 90 to 100, you could change line 12 to:
> `Roll = (int) rnd.Next(90, 101);`

## Multiple Cases for Single Solutions

Sometimes you might want to execute the same piece of code for multiple values. For example, if you want to switch based on the roll of a six-sided die, but you want to do something based only on odd or even numbers, you could group multiple `case` statements. The `switch` statement is

```
switch (roll)
{
    case 1:
    case 3:
    case 5:
            System.Console.WriteLine("Roll is odd");
            break;
    case 2:
    case 4:
    case 6:
            System.Console.WriteLine("Roll is even");
            break;
```

5

```
        default:
                  System.Console.WriteLine("Roll is not 1 through 6");
                  break;
}
```

The same code is executed if the roll is 1, 3, or 5. Additionally, the same code is executed if the roll is 2, 4, or 6.

**Caution**

If you are a C++ programmer, you learned that you could have code execute from multiple case statements by leaving out the break command. This causes the code to drop through to the next case statement. In C#, this is not valid. Code cannot drop through from one case to another. This means that if you are going to group case statements, you cannot place any code between them. You can place it only after the last case statement in each group.

## Executing More than One `case` Statement

There are times when you might want to execute more than one `case` statement within a `switch` statement. To do this in C#, you can use the `goto` command. The `goto` command can be used within the `switch` statement to go to either a `case` statement or to the default command. The following code snippet shows the `switch` statement from the previous section executed with `goto` statements instead of simply dropping through:

```
switch (roll)
{
     case 1:
                goto case 5;
                break;
     case 2:
                goto case 6;
                break;
     case 3:
                goto case 5;
                break;
     case 4:
                goto case 6;
                break;
     case 5:
                System.Console.WriteLine("Roll is odd");
                break;
     case 6:
                System.Console.WriteLine("Roll is even");
                break;
     default:
```

```
        System.Console.WriteLine("Roll is not 1 through 6");
        break;
}
```

Although this example illustrates using the goto, it is much easier to use the previous example of grouping multiple case statements. You will find there are times, however, when the goto provides the solution you need.

## Governing Types for switch Statements

A switch statement has only certain types that can be used. The data type—or the "governing type" for a switch statement—is the type that the switch statement's expression resolves to. If this governing type is sbyte, byte, short, ushort, int, uint, long, ulong, char, or a text string, this type is the governing type. There is another type called an enum that is also valid as a governing type. You will learn about enum types on Day 8, "Advanced Data Storage: Structures, Enumerators, and Arrays."

If the data type of the expression is something other than these types, the type must have a single implicit conversion that converts it to a type of sbyte, byte, short, ushort, int, uint, long, ulong, or a string. If there isn't a conversion available, or if there is more than one, you get an error when you compile your program.

**Note** If you don't remember what implicit conversions are, you should review Day 3, "Storing Information with Variables."

5

| Do | Don't |
|---|---|
| **DO** use a switch statement when you are checking for multiple different values in the same variable. | **DON'T** accidentally put a semicolon after the condition of a switch or if statement: `if ( condition );` |

# Using Iteration Statements

In addition to changing the flow through selection statements, there are times when you might want to repeat a piece of code multiple times. For times when you want to repeat code, C# provides a number of iteration statements. Iteration statements can execute a block of code zero or more times. Each execution of the code is a single iteration.

The iteration statements in C# are

- `while`
- `do`
- `for`
- `foreach`

## The `while` Statement

The `while` command is used to repeat a block of code as long as a condition is true. The format of the `while` statement is

```
while ( condition )
    Statement(s)
```

This format is also presented in Figure 5.1.

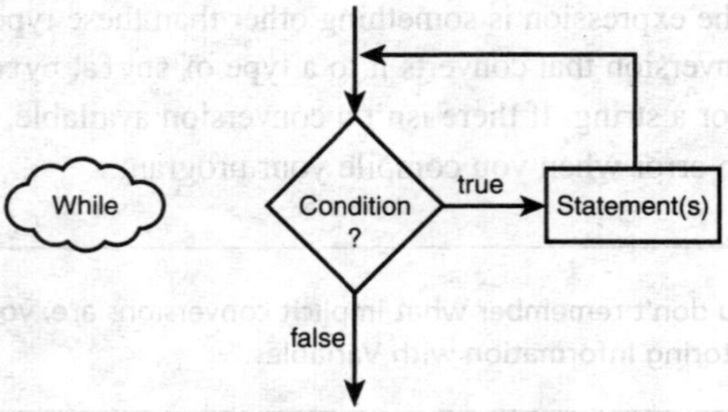


**FIGURE 5.1**
*The* `while` *command.*

As you can see from the figure, a `while` statement uses a conditional statement. If this conditional statement evaluates to true, the statement(s) are executed. If the condition evaluates to false, the statements are not executed and program flow goes to the next command following the `while` statement. Listing 5.4 presents a `while` statement that enables you to print the average of 10 random numbers from 1 to 10.

**LISTING 5.4** average.cs—Using the `while` Command

```
//  average.cs Using the while statement.
//  print the average of 10 random numbers that are from 1 to 10.
//-----------------------------------------------------------------

class average
{
   public static void Main()
   {
      int ttl = 0;  // variable to store the running total
```

**LISTING 5.4** continued

```
        int nbr = 0;  // variable for individual numbers
        int ctr = 0;  // counter

        System.Random rnd = new System.Random();  // random number

        while ( ctr < 10 )
        {
           //Get random number
           nbr = (int) rnd.Next(1,11);

           System.Console.WriteLine("Number {0} is {1}", (ctr + 1), nbr);

           ttl += nbr;          //add nbr to total
           ctr++;               //increment counter
        }

        System.Console.WriteLine("\nThe total of the {0} numbers is {1}"
➥ctr, ttl);
        System.Console.WriteLine("\nThe average of the numbers is {0}",
➥ttl/ctr );
     }
  }
```

**Note** The numbers in your output will differ from those shown here. Because random numbers are assigned, each time you run the program, the numbers will be different.

**OUTPUT**

```
Number 1 is 2
Number 2 is 5
Number 3 is 4
Number 4 is 1
Number 5 is 1
Number 6 is 5
Number 7 is 2
Number 8 is 5
Number 9 is 10
Number 10 is 2

The total of the 10 numbers is 37

The average of the numbers is 3
```

**ANALYSIS** This listing uses the code for random numbers that you saw earlier in today s lesson. Instead of a random number from 1 to 6, this code picks numbers from

1 to 10. You see this in line 18, where the value of 10 is multiplied against the next random number. Line 13 initialized the random variable before it was used in this manner.

The `while` statement starts in line 15. The condition for this `while` statement is a simple check to see whether a counter is less than 10. Because the counter was initialized to `0` in line 11, this condition evaluates to true, so the statements within the `while` will be executed. This `while` statement simply gets a random number from 1 to 10 in line 18 and adds it to the total counter, `ttl` in line 22. Line 23 then increments the counter variable, `ctr`. After this increment, the end of the `while` is reached in line 24. The flow of the program is automatically put back to the `while` condition in line 15. This condition is reevaluated to see whether it is still true. If true, the statements are executed again. This continues to happen until the `while` condition fails. For this program, the failure occurs when `ctr` becomes `10`. At that point, the flow goes to line 25 which immediately follows the `while` statement.

The code after the `while` statement prints the total and the average of the 10 random numbers that were found. The program then ends.

**Caution**

For a `while` statement to eventually end, you must make sure that you change something in the statement(s) that will impact the condition. If your condition can never be false, your `while` statement could end up in an infinite loop. There is one alternative to creating a false condition: the `break` statement. This is covered in the next section.

## Breaking Out Of or Continuing a `while` Statement

It is possible to end a `while` statement before the condition is set to false. It is also possible to end an iteration of a `while` statement before getting to the end of the statements.

To break out of a `while` and thus end it early, you use the `break` command. A `break` immediately takes control to the first command after the `while`.

You can also cause a `while` statement to jump immediately to the next iteration. This is done by using the `continue` statement. The `continue` statement causes the program's flow to go to the condition statement of the `while`. Listing 5.5 illustrates both the `continue` and `break` statements within a `while`.

**Listing 5.5** even.cs—Using `break` and `continue`

```
//  even.cs- Using the while with the break and continue commands.
//----------------------------------------------------------------

```

**LISTING 5.5** continued

```
 4:  class even
 5:  {
 6:     public static void Main()
 7:     {
 8:        int ctr = 0;
 9:
10:        while (true)
11:        {
12:           ctr++;
13:
14:           if (ctr > 10 )
15:           {
16:              break;
17:           }
18:           else if ( (ctr % 2) == 1 )
19:           {
20:              continue;
21:           }
22:           else
23:           {
24:              System.Console.WriteLine("...{0}...", ctr);
25:           }
26:        }
27:        System.Console.WriteLine("Done!");
28:     }
29:  }
```

**OUTPUT**

```
...2...
...4...
...6...
...8...
...10...
Done!
```



**ANALYSIS** This listing prints even numbers and skips odd numbers. When the value of the counter is greater than 10, the `while` statement is ended with a `break` statement.

This listing declares and sets a counter variable, `ctr`, to `0` in line 8. A `while` statement is then started in line 10. Because a `break` is used to end the loop, the condition in line 10 is simply set to `true`. This, in effect, creates an infinite loop. Because this is an infinite loop, a `break` statement is needed to end the `while` statement's iterations. The first thing done in the `while` statement is that `ctr` is incremented in line 12. Line 14 then checks to see whether the `ctr` is greater than 10. If `ctr` is greater than 10, line 16 executes a `break` statement, which ends the `while` and sends the program flow to line 27.

If ctr is less than 10, the else statement in line 18 is executed. This else statement is stacked with an if statement that checks to see whether the current number is odd. This is done using the modulus operator. If the counter is even, by using the modulus operator with 2, you get a result of 0. If it is odd, you get a result of 1. When an odd number is found, the continue statement is called in line 20. This sends control back to the top of the while statement where the condition is checked again. Because the condition is always true (literally), the while statement's statements are executed again. This starts with the increment of the counter in line 12 again, followed by the checks.

If the number is not odd, the else statement in line 22 will execute. This final else statement contains a single call to WriteLine, which prints the counter's value.

## The do Statement

If a while statement's condition is false on the initial check, the while statements will never execute. There are times, however, when you want statements to execute at least once. For these times, the do statement might be a better solution.

The format of the do statement is

```
do
Statement(s)
while ( condition );
```

This format is also presented in Figure 5.2.

**FIGURE 5.2**

*The do command.*

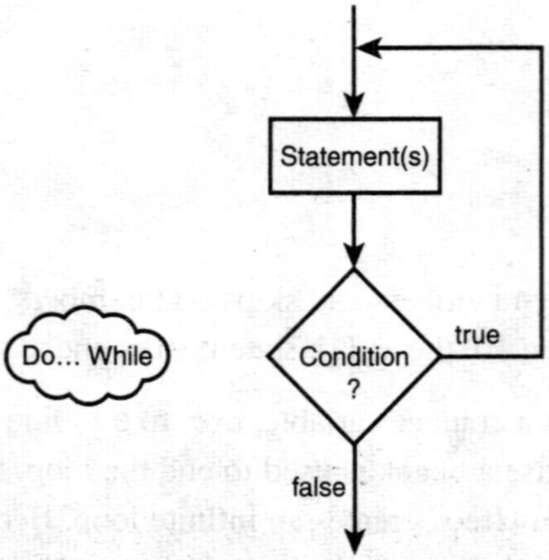


As you can see from the figure, a do statement first executes its statements. After executing the statements, a while statement is presented with a condition. This while statement and condition operate the same as the while you explored earlier in listing 5.4. If the condition evaluates to true, program flow returns to the statements. If the condition evaluates to false, the flow goes to the next line after the do...while. Listing 5.6 presents a do command in action.

> **Note**
> Because of the use of the while with the do statement, a do statement is often referred to as a do...while statement.

**Listing 5.6** do_it.cs—The do Command in Action

```
//  do_it.cs Using the do statement.
//  Get random numbers (from 1 to 10) until a 5 is reached.
//-----------------------------------------------------------------

class do_it
{
   public static void Main()
   {
      int ttl = 0;  // variable to store the running total
      int nbr = 0;  // variable for individual numbers
      int ctr = 0;  // counter

      System.Random rnd = new System.Random();  // random number

      do
      {
          //Get random number
          nbr = (int) rnd.Next(1,11);

          ctr++;              //number of numbers counted
          ttl += nbr;         //add nbr to total of numbers

          System.Console.WriteLine("Number {0} is {1}", ctr, nbr);

      } while ( nbr != 5 );

      System.Console.WriteLine("\n{0} numbers were read", ctr);
      System.Console.WriteLine("The total of the numbers is {0}", ttl);
      System.Console.WriteLine("The average of the numbers is {0}", ttl/ctr
➥);
   }
}
```

**Output**

```
Number 1 is 1
Number 2 is 6
Number 3 is 5

3 numbers were read
```

```
The total of the numbers is 12
The average of the numbers is 4
```

**ANALYSIS** As with the previous listings that used random numbers, your output will most likely be different from what is displayed. You will have a list of numbers, ending with 5.

For this program, you want to do something at least once—get a random number. You want to then keep doing this until you have a condition met—you get a 5. This is a great scenario for the do statement. This listing is very similar to an earlier listing. In lines 9 to 11, you set up a number of variables to keep track of totals and counts. In line 13, you again set up a variable to get random numbers.

Line 15 is the start of your do statement. The body of the do (lines 16 to 24) is executed. First, the next random number is obtained. Again, this is a number from 1 to 10 that is assigned to the variable nbr. Line 20 keeps track of how many numbers have been obtained by adding 1 to ctr each time a number is read. Line 21 then adds the value of the number read to the total. Remember, the following code:

```
ttl += nbr
```

is the same as

```
ttl = ttl + nbr
```

Line 23 prints the obtained number to the screen with the count of which number it is.

Line 25 is the conditional portion of the do statement. In this case, the condition is that nbr is not equal to 5. As long as the number obtained, nbr, is not equal to 5, the body of the do statement will continue to execute. When a 5 is received, the loop ends. If you look in the output of your program, you will find that there is always only one 5, and that it is always the last number.

Lines 27, 28, and 29 prints statistical information regarding the numbers you found.

## The for Statement

Although the do...while and the while statement give you all the functionality you really need to control iterations of code, they are not the only commands available. Before looking at the for statement, check out the code in the following snippet:

```
ctr = 1;
while ( ctr < 10 )
{
   //do some stuff
   ctr++;
}
```

In looking at this snippet of code, you can see that a counter is used to loop through a `while` statement. The flow if this code is this:

Step 1: Set a counter to the value of `1`.

Step 2: Check to see whether the counter is less than `10`.

If the counter is not less than `10` (the condition fails), go to the end.

Step 3: Do some stuff.

Step 4: Add `1` to the counter.

Step 5: Go to Step 2.

These steps are a very common use of iteration. Because this is a common use, you are provided with the `for` statement, which consolidates the steps into a much simpler format:

```
for ( initializer; condition; incrementor )
Statement(s);
```

You should review the format presented here for the `for` statement, which contains three parts within parentheses: the `initializer`, the `condition`, and the `incrementor`. Each of these three parts is separated by a semicolon. If one of these expressions is to be left out, you still need to include the semicolon separators.

The `initializer` is executed when the `for` statement begins. It is executed only once at the beginning and then never again.

After executing the `initializer`, the `condition` statement is evaluated. Just as the condition in the `while` statement, this must evaluate to either true or false. If this evaluates to true, the statement(s) are executed.

After the statement or statement block executes, program flow is returned to the `for` statement where the `incrementor` is evaluated. This `incrementor` can actually be any valid C# expression; however, it is generally used to increment a counter.

After the `incrementor` is executed, the `condition` is again evaluated. As long as the `condition` remains true, the statements will be executed, followed by the `incrementor`. This continues until the `condition` evaluates to false. Figure 5.3 illustrates the flow of the `for` statement.

Before jumping into a listing, let's revisit the `while` statement that was presented at the beginning of this section:

```
for ( ctr = 1; ctr < 10; ctr++ )
{
   //do some stuff
}
```

5

**FIGURE 5.3**

*The `for` statement.*

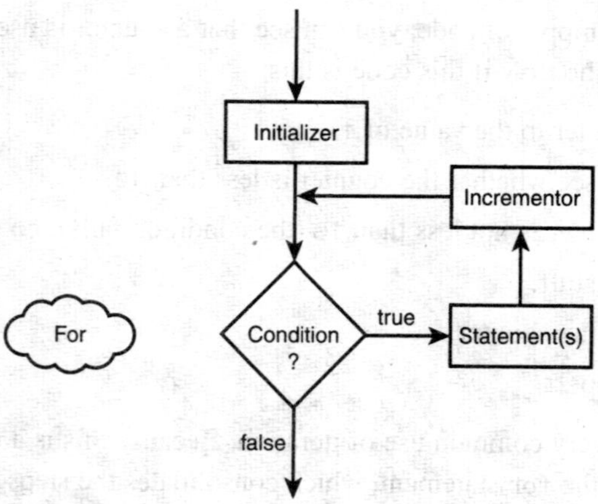


This `for` statement is much simpler than the code used earlier with the `while` statement. The steps that this `for` statement executes are

Step 1: Set a counter to the value of `1`.

Step 2: Check to see whether the counter is less than `10`.

If the counter is not less than `10` (condition fails), go to the end of the `for` statement.

Step 3: Do some stuff.

Step 4: Add `1` to the counter.

Step 5: Go to Step 2.

These are the same steps that were followed with the `while` statement snippet earlier. The difference is that the `for` statement is much more concise and easier to follow. Listing 5.7 presents a more robust use of the `for` statement. In fact, this is the same program you saw in sample code earlier, only now it is much more concise.

**LISTING 5.7** foravg.cs—Using the `for` Statement

```
//  foravg.cs Using the for statement.
//  print the average of 10 random numbers that are from 1 to 10.
//-----------------------------------------------------------------

class average
{
    public static void Main()
    {
        int ttl = 0;  // variable to store the running total
        int nbr = 0;  // variable for individual numbers
```

**LISTING 5.7** continued

```
11:         int ctr = 0;   // counter
12:
13:         System.Random rnd = new System.Random();   // random number
14:
15:         for ( ctr = 1; ctr <= 10; ctr++ )
16:         {
17:            //Get random number
18:            nbr = (int) rnd.Next(1,11);
19:
20:            System.Console.WriteLine("Number {0} is {1}", (ctr), nbr);
21:
22:            ttl += nbr;            //add nbr to total
23:         }
24:
25:         System.Console.WriteLine("\nThe total of the 10 numbers is {0}",
➥ttl);
26:         System.Console.WriteLine("\nThe average of the numbers is {0}",
➥ttl/10 );
27:      }
28:  }
```

**OUTPUT**

```
Number 1 is 10
Number 2 is 3
Number 3 is 6
Number 4 is 5
Number 5 is 7
Number 6 is 8
Number 7 is 7
Number 8 is 1
Number 9 is 4
Number 10 is 3

The total of the 10 numbers is 54

The average of the numbers is 5
```

**ANALYSIS** Much of this listing is identical to what you saw earlier in today's lessons. You should note, however, the difference. In line 15, you see the use of the `for` statement. The counter is initialized to `1`, which makes it easier to display the value in the `WriteLine` routine in line 20. The condition statement in the `for` statement is adjusted appropriately as well.

What happens when the program flow reaches the `for` statement? Simply put, the counter is set to `1`. It is then verified against the condition. In this case, the counter is less than or equal to 10, so the body of the `for` statement is executed. When the body in lines 16 to 23 is done executing, control goes back to the `incrementor` of the `for` statement in line 15. In this `for` statement's `incrementor`, the counter is incremented by `1`. The condition is then checked again and if true, the body of the `for` statement executes again. This continues until the condition fails. For this program, this happens when the counter is set to 11.

## The for Statement Expressions

You can do a lot with the initializer, condition, and incrementor. You can actually put any expressions within these areas. You can even put in more than one expression.

If you use more than one expression within one of the segments of the for statement, you need to separate them. The separator control is used to do this. The separator control is the comma. As an example, the following for statement initializes two variables and increments both:

```
for ( x = 1, y = 1; x + y < 100; x++, y++ )
   // Do something...
```

In addition to being able to do multiple expressions, you also are not restricted to using each of the parts of a for statement as described. The following example actually does all of the work in the for statement's control structure. The body of the for statement is an empty statement—a semicolon:

```
for ( x = 0; ++x <= 10; System.Console.WriteLine("{0}", x) )
   ;
```

This simple line of code actually does quite a lot. If you enter this into a program, it prints the numbers 1 to 10. You're asked to turn this into a complete listing in one of today's exercises at the end of the lesson.

**Caution**

> You should be careful about how much you do within the for statement's control structures. You want to make sure you don't make your code too complicated to follow.

## The foreach Statement

The foreach statement iterates in a way similar to the for statement. The foreach statement, however, has a special purpose. It can loop through collections such as arrays. The foreach statement, collections, and arrays are covered on Day 8.

## Revisiting break and continue

The use of break and continue were presented earlier with the while statement. Additionally, you saw the use of the break command with the switch statement. These two commands can also be used with the other program flow statements.

In the `do...while` statement, `break` and `continue` operate exactly like the `while` statement. The `continue` command loops to the conditional statement. The `break` command sends the program flow to the statement following the `do...while`.

With the `for` statement, the `continue` statement sends control to the `incrementor` statement. The condition is then checked, and if true, the `for` statement continues to loop. The `break` statement sends the program flow to the statement following the `for` statement.

The `break` command exits the current routine. The `continue` command starts the next iteration.

# Using `goto`

The `goto` statement is fraught with controversy, regardless of the programming language you use. Because the `goto` statement can unconditionally change program flow, it is very powerful. With power comes responsibility. Many developers avoid the `goto` statement because it is easy to create code that is hard to follow.

There are three ways the `goto` statement can be used. As you saw earlier, the `switch` statement is home to two of the uses of `goto`: `goto case` and `goto default`. You saw these in action earlier in the discussion on the `switch` statement.

The third `goto` statement takes the following format:

```
goto label;
```

With this form of the `goto` statement, you are sending the control of the program to a label statement.

## Labeled Statements

A label statement is simply a command that marks a location. The format of a label is

```
label_name:
```

Notice that this is followed by a colon, not a semicolon. Listing 5.8 presents the `goto` statement being used with labels.

**LISTING 5.8** Score.cs—Using the `goto` Statement with a Label

```
//  score.cs      Using the goto and label statements.
//  Disclaimer: This program shows the use of goto and label
//              This is not a good use; however, it illustrates
//              the functionality of these keywords.
```

**LISTING 5.8** continued

```
 5: //---------------------------------------------------------------------
 6:
 7: class score
 8: {
 9:     public static void Main()
10:     {
11:         int score = 0;
12:         int ctr = 0;
13:
14:         System.Random rnd = new System.Random();
15:
16:         Start:
17:
18:         ctr++;
19:
20:         if (ctr > 10)
21:             goto EndThis;
22:         else
23:             score = (int) rnd.Next(60, 101);
24:
25:         System.Console.WriteLine("{0} - You received a score of {1}",
26:                     ctr, score);
27:
28:         goto Start;
29:
30:       EndThis:
31:
32:         System.Console.WriteLine("Done with scores!");
33:     }
34: }
```

**OUTPUT**

```
1 - You received a score of 83
2 - You received a score of 99
3 - You received a score of 72
4 - You received a score of 67
5 - You received a score of 80
6 - You received a score of 98
7 - You received a score of 64
8 - You received a score of 91
9 - You received a score of 79
10 - You received a score of 76
Done with scores!
```

**ANALYSIS** The purpose of this listing is relatively simple; it prints 10 scores that are obtained by getting 10 random numbers from 60 to 100. This use of random numbers is similar to what you've seen before except for one small change. In line 23, instead of starting at `1` for the number to be obtained, you start at `60`. Additionally, because the numbers you want are from 60 to 100, the upper limit is set to 101. By using 101 as the second number, you get a number less than 101.

The focus of this listing is lines 16, 21, 28, and 30. In line 16 you see a label called `Start`. Because this is a label, the program flow skips past this line and goes to line 18 where a counter is incremented. In line 20, the condition within an `if` statement is checked. If the counter is greater than 10, a `goto` statement in line 21 is executed, which sends program flow to the `EndThis` label in line 30. Because the counter is not greater than 10, program flow goes to the `else` statement in line 22. The `else` statement gets the random score in line 23 that was already covered. Line 25 prints the score obtained. Program flow then hits line 28, which sends the flow unconditionally to the `Start` label. Because the `Start` label is in line 16, program flow goes back to line 16.

This listing does a similar iteration to what can be done with the `while`, `do`, or `for` statements. In many cases, you will find there are programming alternatives to using `goto`. If there is a different option, use it first.

> **Tip**
>
> Avoid using the `goto` whenever possible. It can lead to what is referred to as *spaghetti code*. Spaghetti code is code that winds all over the place and is therefore hard to follow from one end to the next.

## Nesting Flow

All of the program flow commands from today can be nested. When nesting program flow commands, make sure that the commands are ended appropriately. You can create a logic error and sometimes a syntax error if you don't nest properly.



| Do | Don't |
|---|---|
| **DO** comment your code to make it clearer what the program and program flow is doing. | **DON'T** use a `goto` statement unless it is absolutely necessary. |

## Summary

You learned a lot in today's lesson, and you'll use this knowledge in virtually every C# application you create.

In today's lesson, you once again covered some of the constructs that are part of the basic C# language. You first expanded on your knowledge of the `if` statement by learning about the else statement. You then learned about another selection statement, the switch. Selection statements were followed by a discussion of iterative program flow control statements. This included use of the while, do, and for statements. You learned that there is another command called the foreach that you will learn about on Day 8. In addition to learning how to use these commands, you also learned that they can be nested within each other. Finally, you learned about the goto statement and how it can be used with case, default, or labels.

# Q&A

**Q Are there other types of control statements?**

**A** Yes—throw, try, catch, and finally. You will learn about these in future lessons.

**Q Can you use a text string with a switch statement?**

**A** Yes. A string is a "governing type" for switch statements. This means that you can use a variable that holds a string in the switch and then use string values in the case statements. Remember, a string is simply text in quotation marks. In one of the exercises, you create a switch statement that works with strings.

**Q Why is the goto considered so bad?**

**A** The goto statement has gotten a bad rap. If used cautiously and in a structured, organized manner, the goto statement can help solve a number of programming problems. The use of goto case and goto default are prime examples of good uses of goto. goto has a bad rap because the goto statement is often not used cleanly; programmers use it to get from one piece of code to another quickly and in an unstructured manner. In an object-oriented programming language, the more structure you can keep in your programs, the better—and more maintainable—they will be.

# Workshop

The Workshop provides quiz questions to help you solidify your understanding of the material covered and exercises to provide you with experience in using what you've learned. Try to understand the quiz and exercise answers before continuing to the next day's lesson. Answers are provided in Appendix A, "Answers."

## Quiz

1. What commands are provided by C# for repeating lines of code multiple times?
2. What is the fewest times the statements in a while will execute?

3. What is the fewest times the statements in a do will execute?
4. Consider the following for statement:

   `for ( x = 1; x == 1; x++ )`

   What is the conditional statement?
5. In the for statement in question 4, what is the incrementor statement?
6. What statement is used to end a case expression in a select statement?
7. What punctuation character is used with a label?
8. What punctuation is used to separate multiple expressions in a for statement?
9. What is nesting?
10. What command is used to jump to the next iteration of a loop?

## Exercises

1. Write an if statement that checks to see whether a variable called file-type is 's', 'n', or 'j'. Print the following message based on the file-type:

```
s    The filer is single
m    The filer is married filing at the single rate
j    The filer is married filing at the joint rate
```

2. Is the following if statement valid? If so, what is the value of x after this code executes?

```
int x = 2;
int y = 3;
if (x==2) if (y>3) x=5; else x=9;
```

3. Write a while loop that counts from 99 to 1.
4. Rewrite the while loop in exercise 3 as a for loop.
5. **BUG BUSTER:** Is the following listing correct? If so, what does it do? If not, what is wrong with the listing (Ex5-5.cs)?

```
//  Ex5-5.cs. Exercise 5 for Day 5
//-----------------------------------------------------------------

class score
{
    public static void Main()
    {
        int score = 99;

        if ( score == 100 );
        {
            System.Console.WriteLine("You got a perfect score!");
```

5

```
        }
        else
            System.Console.WriteLine("Bummer, you were not perfect!");
    }
}
```

6. Create a `for` loop that prints the numbers `1` to `10` all within the initializer, condition, and incrementor sections of the `for`. The body of the `for` should be an empty statement.
7. Write the code for a `switch` statement that switches on the variable `name`. If the name is `"Robert"`, print a message that says `"Hi Bob"`. If the name is `"Richard"`, print a message that says `"Hi Rich"`. If the name is `"Barbara"`, print a message that says `"Hi Barb"`. If the name is `"Kalee"`, print a message that says `"You Go Girl!"`. On any other name, print a message that says `"Hi x"` where *x* is the person's name.
8. Write a program to roll a six-sided die 100 times. Print the number of times each of the sides of the die was rolled.

# WEEK 1

# DAY 6

# Classes

As you learned on Day 2, "Understanding C# Programs," classes are critical to an object-oriented language. Classes are also critical to C#. You have seen classes used in every example included in the book so far. Today you

- Revisit the concepts involved in object-oriented programming
- Learn how to declare a class
- Learn how to define a class
- Discover class members
- Create your own data members
- Implement properties in your classes
- Take your first serious look at namespaces

## Object-Oriented Programming Revisited

On Day 2, you learned that C# is considered an object-oriented language. You also learned that to take full advantage of C#, you should understand the concepts of object-oriented languages. In the next few sections, you briefly revisit the concepts you learned about in Day 2. You will then begin to see how these concepts are applied to actual C# programs.

Recall from Day 2 the key characteristics that make up an object-oriented language:

- Encapsulation
- Polymorphism
- Inheritance
- Reuse

## Encapsulation

Encapsulation is the concept of making classes (or "packages") that contain everything you need. In object-oriented programming, this means that you can create a class that stores all the variables that you need and all the routines to commonly manipulate this data. You can create a `Circle` class that stores information on a circle. This could include storing the location of the circle's center and its radius plus storing routines commonly used with a circle. These routines could include getting the circles area, getting its circumference, changing its center point, changing its radius, and much more.

By encapsulating a circle, you allow the user to be oblivious to how the circle works. You need to know only how to interact with the circle. This provides a shield to the inner workings of the circle, which means that the variables within the class could be changed and it would be invisible to the user. For example, instead of storing the radius of the circle, you could store the diameter. If you have encapsulated the functionality and the data, making this change impacts only your class. Any programs that use your class should not need to change. In today's and tomorrow's lessons, you see programs that work directly with a `Circle` class.

**Note** Encapsulation is often referred to as "black boxing." Black boxing refers to hiding the functionality or the inner workings of a process. For a circle, if you send in the radius, you can get the area. You don't care how it happens, as long as you know you are getting back the correct answer.

## Polymorphism

Polymorphism means to have the capability of assuming many forms, which means that the programs can work with what you send them. For example, you have used the `WriteLine()` routine in several of the previous days. You have seen that you can create a parameter field using `{0}`. What values does this field print? As you have seen, it can print a variable regardless of its type or it can print another string. The `WriteLine()` routine takes care of how it gets printed. The routine is polymorphic in that it adapts to most of the types you can send it.

Using a circle as an example, you might want to call a circle object to get its area. You can do this by using three points or by using a single point and the radius. Either way, you expect to get the same results. Additionally, you know that a circle is a shape. As such, a polymophic characteristic of a circle is to be capable of understanding and reacting as a shape.

## Inheritance

As you learned in Day 2, inheritance is the most complicated of the object-oriented concepts. Inheritance is when one class (object) is an expansion of another.

In many object-oriented programming books, an animal analogy is used to illustrate inheritance. The analogy starts with the concept of an animal as a living being.

Now consider reptiles, which are everything that an animal is, plus they are cold-blooded. A reptile contains all of the features of an animal, but it also adds its own unique features. Now consider a snake. A snake is a reptile that is long and skinny that has no legs. It has all the characteristics of a reptile, but it also has its own unique characteristics. A snake can be said to inherit the characteristics of a reptile. A reptile can be said to inherit the characteristics of an animal.

On Day 11, "Inheritance," you will see how this same concept is applied to classes and programming.

## Reuse

When you create a class, you can reuse it to create lots of objects. By using inheritance and some of the features described previously, you can create routines that can be used repeatedly in many programs and in many ways. By encapsulating functionality, you can create routines that have been tested and proven to work. You won't have to test the details of how the functionality works, only that you are using it correctly. This makes reusing these routines quick and easy.

## Objects and Classes

On Day 2, an illustration of a cookie cutter and cookies were used to illustrate classes and objects. Now you are done with cookies and snakes—it is time to jump into some code.

**Note** Over the next three days you are going to learn about classes, starting with extremely simple examples and building on them over the next several days.

# Defining a Class

To keep things simple, a keyword called `class` is used to define classes. The basic structure of a class is in the following format:

```
class identifier
{
    class-body ;
}
```

where *`identifier`* is the name given to the class and *`class-body`* is the code that makes up the class.

The name of a class is like any other variable name that can be declared. You want to give a class a meaningful name, something that describes what the class does.

The Microsoft .NET framework has a large number of built-in classes. You have actually been using one since the beginning of this book: the `Console` class. The `Console` class contains several data members and routines. You've already used many of these routines, including `Write` and `WriteLine`. The class name—the *identifier*—of this class is `Console`. The body of the `Console` class contains the code for the `Write` and `WriteLine` routines. By the end of tomorrow's lesson, you will be able to create and name your own classes that have routines similar to the `Console` class.

# Class Declarations

After a class is defined, you use it to create objects. A class is just a definition used to create objects. A class by itself does not have the capability of holding information or actually performing routines. Rather, a class is used to declare objects. The object can then be used to hold the data and perform the routines as defined by the class.

> **Note** The declaration of an object is commonly referred to as *instantiation*. Said differently, an object is an instance of a class.

The format of declaring an object from a class is as follows:

```
class_name object_identifier = new class_name();
```

where *`class_name`* is the name of the class and *`object_identifier`* is the name of the object being declared. For example, if you have a class called `point`, you could create an object called `startingPoint` with the following line of code:

```
point startingPoint = new point();
```

The name of the class is `point`, the name of the object declared is `startingPoint`. Because `startingPoint` is an object, it can contain data and routines if they were defined within the `point` class.

In looking at this declarative line of code, you might wonder what the other items are. Most importantly there is a keyword being used that you have not seen before; `new`.

As its name implies, the `new` keyword is used to create new items. In this case it creates a new point. Because `point` is a class, an object is created. The new keyword indicates that a new instance is to be created. In this case, the new instance is a `point` object.

When declaring an object with a class, you also have to provide parentheses to the class name on the right of the assignment. This enables the class to be constructed into a new object.

> **Caution** If you don't add the construction code, `new classname`, you will have declared a class, but the compiler won't have constructed its internal structure. You need to make sure you assign the `new classname` code to the declared object name to make sure everything is constructed. You will learn more about this initial construction in tomorrow's lesson.

Look at the statement again:

```
point startingPoint = new point();
```

The following breaks down what is happening:

```
point startingPoint
```

The `point` class is used to declare an object called `startingPoint`. This piece of the statement is like what you have seen with other data types, such as integers and decimals.

```
startingPoint =
```

As with variables, you assign the result of the right side of the assignment operator (the equal sign) to the variable on the left. In this case, the variable happens to be an object—which you now know is an object of type `point` called `startingPoint`.

```
new point()
```

This part of the statement does the actual construction of the `point` object. The class name with parentheses is a signal to construct—create—an object of the class type. The new keyword says to reserve some room in memory of this new object. Remember, a class is only a definition: it doesn't store anything. The object needs to store information, so it needs memory reserved. The new keyword reserves the memory.

Like all statements, this declaration is ended with a semicolon, which signals that the statement is done.

## The Members of a Class

Now that you know the overall structure of a class and how to create objects with a class, it is time to look at what can be held in a class. There are two primary types of items that can be contained within the body of a class: data members and function members.

Data members include variables and constants. These include variables of any of the types you learned about on Day 3, "Storing Information with Variables," and any of the more advanced types you will learn about later. These data members can even be other classes.

The other type of element that is part of a class's body is function members. Function members are routines that perform an action. These actions can be as simple as setting a value to something more complex, such as writing a line of text using a variable number of values—as you have seen with Write and WriteLine. Write and WriteLine are member functions of the Console class. In tomorrow's lesson, you will learn how to create and use member functions of your own. For now, it is time to visit data members.

# Data Members, aka Fields

**NEW TERM** Another name for a variable is a *field*. As stated previously, data members within a class are variables that are members of a class.

In the point class referenced earlier, you expect a data member to store the x and y coordinates of the point. These coordinates could be any of a number of data types; however, if these were integers, you define the point class as such:

```
class point
{
   int x;
   int y;
}
```

That's it. This is effectively the code for a very simple point class. There is one other item that you should include for now. This is an access modifier called public. Without adding the word public, you cannot access x or y outside the point class. A variable is accessible only within the block you declare it, unless you indicate otherwise. In this case, the block is the definition of the point class.

**Note** Remember, a block is a section of code between two braces {}. The body of a class is a block of code.

The change made to the `point` class is relatively simple. With the `public` accessor added, the class becomes

```
class point
{
   public int x;
   public int y;
}
```

Although the point class contains two integers, you can actually use any data type within this class. For example, you can create a `FullName` class that contains three strings that store the first, middle, and last names. You can create an `Address` class that contains a name class and additional strings to hold the different address pieces. You can create a customer class that contains a `long` value for a customer number, and an address class, a decimal account balance, a Boolean value for active or inactive, and more.

## Accessing Data Members

When you have data members declared, you want to get to their values. As you learned, the `public` accessor enables you to get to the data members from outside the class.

You cannot simply access data members from outside the class by their name. For example, if you have a program that declares a `startingPoint` from the `point` class, it would seem as if you should be able to get the point by using `x` and `y`—the names that are in the `point`. What happens if you declare both a `startingPoint` and an `endingPoint` in the same program? If you use `x`, which point is being accessed?

To access a data member, you use both the name of the object and the data member. The member operator, which is a period, separates these. To access the `startingPoint`'s coordinates, you therefore use

```
startingPoint.x
```

and

```
startingPoint.y
```

For the ending point, you use

```
endingPoint.x
```

and

```
endingPoint.y
```

At this time, you have the foundation to try out a program. Listing 6.1 presents the `point` class. This class is used to declare two objects, `starting` and `ending`.

**LISTING 6.1** point.cs—Declaring a Class with Data Members

```
1:  // point.cs- A class with two data members
2:  //--------------------------------------------------------------------
3:
4:  class point
5:  {
6:      public int x;
7:      public int y;
8:  }
9:
10: class pointApp
11: {
12:     public static void Main()
13:     {
14:        point starting = new point();
15:        point ending   = new point();
16:
17:        starting.x = 1;
18:        starting.y = 4;
19:        ending.x = 10;
20:        ending.y = 11;
21:
22:        System.Console.WriteLine("Point 1: ({0},{1})",
23:                                 starting.x, starting.y);
24:        System.Console.WriteLine("Point 2: ({0},{1})",
25:                                 ending.x, ending.y);
26:     }
27: }
```

**OUTPUT**

```
Point 1: (1,4)
Point 2: (10,11)
```

**ANALYSIS** A simple class called `point` is declared in lines 4 to 8.This class follows the structure that was presented earlier. In line 4, the `class` keyword is being used, followed by the name of the class, `point`. Lines 5 and 8 contain the braces that enclose the body of the class. Within the body of this class, two integers are declared, `x` and `y`. These are each declared as `public` so that you can use them outside of the class.

Line 10 contains the start of the main portion of your application. It is interesting to note that the main portion of your application is also a class! You will learn more about this later.

Line 12 contains the main routine that you should now be very familiar with. In lines 14 and 15, two objects are created using the `point` class, which follow the same format that was described earlier. In lines 17 to 20, values are set for each of the data members of the `point` objects. In line 17, the value `1` is assigned to the `x` data member of the starting class. The member operator, the period, separates the member name from the object name. Lines 18, 19, and 20 follow the same format.

Line 22 contains a `WriteLine` routine, which you have also seen before. This one is unique because you print the values stored within the `starting point` object. The values are stored in `starting.x` and `starting.y`, not just `x` and `y`. Line 24 prints the values for the `ending point`.

## Using Data Members

Listing 6.1 showed you how to assign a value to a data member as well as how to get its value. What if you want to do something more complex then a simple assignment or a simple display?

The data members of a class are like any other variable type. You can use them in operations, control statements, or anywhere that a regular variable can be accessed. Listing 6.2 expands on the use of the point class. In this example, the calculation is performed to determine the length of a line between two points. If you've forgotten your basic algebraic equation for this, Figure 6.1 illustrates the calculation to be performed.

**FIGURE 6.1**

*Calculating line length from two points.*

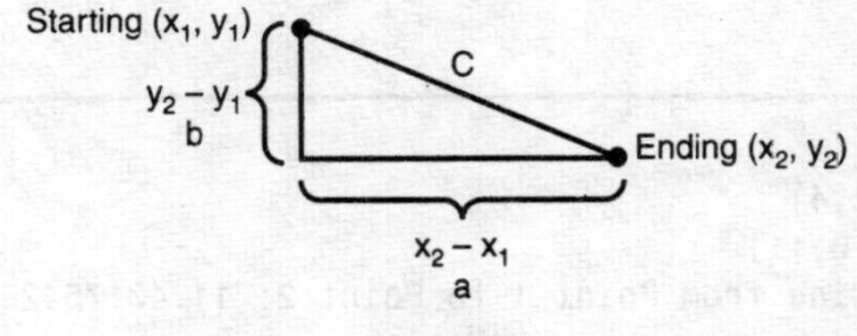


$$c^2 = a^2 + b^2$$

or

$$c = \sqrt{(x_2 - x_1)^2 + (y_2 - y_1)^2}$$

**LISTING 6.2** point2.cs—Working with Data Members

```
// line.cs- Calculate the length of a line.
//----------------------------------------------------------

class point
{
   public int x;
   public int y;
}

class lineApp
```

**LISTING 6.2** continued

```
11:  {
12:      public static void Main()
13:      {
14:          point starting = new point();
15:          point ending   = new point();
16:          double line;
17:
18:          starting.x = 1;
19:          starting.y = 4;
20:          ending.x = 10;
21:          ending.y = 11;
22:
23:          line = System.Math.Sqrt( (ending.x - starting.x)*(ending.x -
➥starting.x) +
24:                                   (ending.y - starting.y)*(ending.y -
➥starting.y) );
25:
26:          System.Console.WriteLine("Point 1: ({0},{1})",
27:                                    starting.x, starting.y);
28:          System.Console.WriteLine("Point 2: ({0},{1})",
29:                                    ending.x, ending.y);
30:          System.Console.WriteLine("Length of line from Point 1 to Point 2:
➥{0}",
31:                                    line);
32:      }
33:  }
```

**OUTPUT**

```
Point 1: (1,4)
Point 2: (10,11)
Length of line from Point 1 to Point 2: 11.4017542509914
```

**ANALYSIS** This listing is very similar to Listing 6.1. The biggest difference is the addition of a data member and some calculations that determine the length of a line. In line 16, you see that the new data member is declared of type `double` and called `line`. This variable will be used to hold the result of the length of the line between the two declared points.

Lines 23 and 24 are actually a single statement. This statement looks more complex than it is. Other than the `System.Math.Sqrt` part, you should be able to follow what the line is doing. `Sqrt` is a routine within the `System.Math` object that calculates the square root of a value. If you compare this formula to Figure 6.2, you will see that it is a match. The end result is the length of the line. The important thing to note is that the data members are being used within this calculation in the same manner that any other variable would be used. The only difference is the naming scheme.

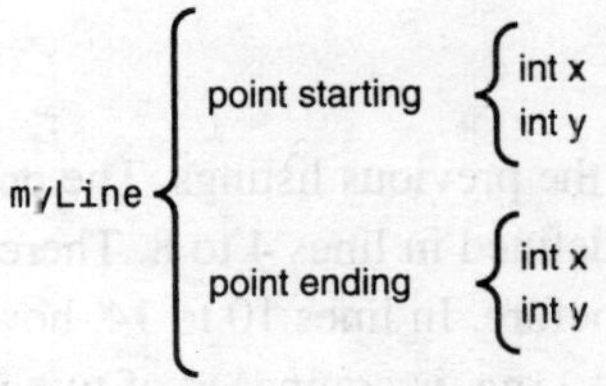


**FIGURE 6.2**
*The `myLine` class's data members.*

## Using Classes as Data Members

It was stated earlier that you can nest one class within another. A class is another type of data. As such, an object declared with a class type—which is just an advanced variable type—can be used in the same places as any other variable. Listing 6.3 presents an example of a line class. This class is composed of two points, `starting` and `ending`.

**LISTING 6.3** line2.cs—Nested Classes

```
// line2.cs- A class with two data members
//-----------------------------------------------

class point
{
    public int x;
    public int y;
}

class line
{
    public point starting = new point();
    public point ending = new point();
}

class lineApp
{
    public static void Main()
    {
        line myLine = new line();

        myLine.starting.x = 1;
        myLine.starting.y = 4;
        myLine.ending.x = 10;
        myLine.ending.y = 11;

        System.Console.WriteLine("Point 1: ({0},{1})",
                        myLine.starting.x, myLine.starting.y);
        System.Console.WriteLine("Point 2: ({0},{1})",
                        myLine.ending.x, myLine.ending.y);
    }
}
```

6

**OUTPUT**

```
Point 1: (1,4)
Point 2: (10,11)
```

**ANALYSIS** Listing 6.3 is very similar to the previous listings. The `point` class that you are coming to know and love is defined in lines 4 to 8. There is nothing different about this from what you have seen before. In lines 10 to 14, however, you see a second class being defined. This class, called `line`, is composed of two variables that are of type `point`, which is a class. These two variables are called `starting` and `ending`. When an object is declared using the `line` class, the `line` class will in turn create two `point` objects.

Continuing with the listing, you see in line 20 that a new line is called. This new line is given the name `myLine`. Line 20 follows the same format you saw earlier for creating an object from a class.

Lines 22 to 25 access the data members of the `line` class and assign them values. It is beginning to look a little more complex; however, looks can be deceiving. If you break this down, you will see that it is relatively straightforward. In line 22, you assign the constant value `1` to the variable `myLine.starting.x`. In other words, you are assigning the value `1` to the `x` member of the `starting` member of `myLine`. Going from the other direction, you can say that you are assigning the value `1` to the `myLine` object's `starting` member's `x` member. It is like a tree. Figure 6.2 illustrates the `myLine` class's members and their names.

## Nested types

On Day 3, you learned about the different standard data types that could be used. As you saw in Listing 6.3, an object created with a class can be used in the same places as any other variable created with a data type.

When used by themselves, classes really do nothing—they are only a description. For example, in Listing 6.3, the `point` class in lines 4 to 8, is only a description; nothing is declared and no memory is used. This description defines a type. In this case, the type is the class, or specifically a `point`.

It is possible to nest a type within another class. If `point` is going to be used only within the context of a line, it could be defined within the `line` class. This would enable `point` objects to be used in the `line` class.

The code for the nested `point` type is

```
class line
{
    public class point
    {
```

```
        public int x;
        public int y;
    }

    public point starting = new point();
    public point ending = new point();
}
```

One additional change was made. The `point` class had to be declared as `public` as well. If you don't declare the type as `public`, you get an error. The reason for the error should make sense if you think about it. How can the parts of the `point` or the `point` objects be `public` if the `point` itself isn't `public`?

# Static Variables

There are times when you will want a bunch of objects declared with the same class to share a value. For example, you might want to declare a number of line objects that all share the same originating point. If one `line` object changes the originating point, you want all lines to change it.

To share a single data value across all the objects declared by a single class, you add the `static` modifier. Listing 6.4 revisits the `line` class. This time, the same starting point is used for all objects declared with the `line` class.

**LISTING 6.4** statline.cs—Using the `static` Modifier with Data Members

```
//  statline.cs- A class with two data members
//-----------------------------------------------------------------

class point
{
   public int x;
   public int y;
}

class line
{
    static public point origin= new point();
    public point ending = new point();
}

class lineApp
{
   public static void Main()
   {
      line line1 = new line();
```

**Listing 6.4** continued

```
        line line2 = new line();

        // set line origin
        line.origin.x = 1;
        line.origin.y = 2;


        // set line1's ending values
        line1.ending.x = 3;
        line1.ending.y = 4;

        // set line2's ending values
        line2.ending.x = 7;
        line2.ending.y = 8;

        // print the values...
        System.Console.WriteLine("Line 1 start: ({0},{1})",
                                 line.origin.x, line.origin.y);
        System.Console.WriteLine("line 1 end:   ({0},{1})",
                                 line1.ending.x, line1.ending.y);
        System.Console.WriteLine("Line 2 start: ({0},{1})",
                                 line.origin.x, line.origin.y);
        System.Console.WriteLine("line 2 end:   ({0},{1})\n",
                                 line2.ending.x, line2.ending.y);

        // change value of line2's starting point
        line.origin.x = 939;
        line.origin.y = 747;

        // and the values again...

        System.Console.WriteLine("Line 1 start: ({0},{1})",
                                 line.origin.x, line.origin.y);
        System.Console.WriteLine("line 1 end:   ({0},{1})",
                                 line1.ending.x, line1.ending.y);
        System.Console.WriteLine("Line 2 start: ({0},{1})",
                                 line.origin.x, line.origin.y);
        System.Console.WriteLine("line 2 end:   ({0},{1})",
                                 line2.ending.x, line2.ending.y);
    }
}
```

**Output**

```
Line 1 start: (1,2)
line 1 end:   (3,4)
Line 2 start: (1,2)
line 2 end:   (7,8)
```

```
Line 1 start: (939,747)
line 1 end:   (3,4)
Line 2 start: (939,747)
line 2 end:   (7,8)
```

> **Caution** If you try to access a static data member with an object name, such as `line1`, you will get an error. You must use the class name to access a static data member.

**ANALYSIS** Listing 6.4 is not much different from what you have seen before. The biggest difference is in line 12, where the `origin` point is declared as `static` in addition to being `public`. The `static` keyword makes a big difference in this `line` class. Instead of each object that is created from the `line` class containing an origin point, there is only one origin point that is shared by all instances of `line`.

Line 18 is the beginning of your `Main` routine. Lines 20 and 21 declare two `line` objects called `line1` and `line2`. Lines 28 and 29 set the ending point of `line1`, and lines 33 and 34 set the ending point of `line2`. Going back to lines 24 and 25, you see something different from what you have seen before. Instead of setting the origin point of `line1` or `line2`, these lines set the point for the class name, `line`. This is important. If you try to set the origin on `line1` or `line2`, you will get a compiler error. In other words, the following line of code is an error:

```
line1.origin.x = 1;
```

Because the `origin` object is declared `static`, it is shared across all objects of type `line`. Because neither `line1` nor `line2` own this value, they cannot be used directly to set the value. Rather, you must use the class name. Remember, a variable declared `static` in a class is owned by the class, not the individual objects that are instantiated.

Lines 37 to 44 print the `origin point` and `ending point` for `line1` and `line2`. Again, notice that the class name is used to print the `origin` values, not the object name. Lines 47 and 48 change the `origin`, and the final part of the program prints the values again.

> **Note** A common use of a `static` data member is as a counter. Each time an object does something, it can increment the counter for all the objects.

# The Application Class

If you haven't already noticed, there is a class being used in all your applications that has not been discussed. If you look at line 16 of Listing 6.4, you see the following code:

```
class lineApp
```

You will notice a similar class line in every application you have entered in this book. C# is an object-oriented language. This means everything is an object—even your application. To create an object, you need a class to define it. Listing 6.4's application is `lineApp`. When you execute the program, the `lineApp` class is instantiated and creates a `lineApp` object, which just happens to be your program!

Like what you have learned above, your application class declares data members. In Listing 6.4, the `lineApp` class's data members are two classes: `line1` and `line2`. There is additional functionality in this class as well. In tomorrow's lesson, you will learn that this additional functionality can be included in your classes as well.

# Properties

Earlier it was stated that one of the benefits of an object-oriented program is the ability to control the internal representation or access to data. In the examples used so far in today's lesson, everything has been `public`, so access has been freely given to any code that wants to access the data members.

In an object-oriented program, you want to have more control over who can and can't get to data. In general, you won't want code to access data members directly. If you allow code to directly access these data members, you might lock yourself into being unable to change the data types of the values.

C# provides a concept called *properties* to enable you to create object-oriented fields within your classes. Properties use the keywords `get` and `set` to get the values from your variables and set the values in your variables. Listing 6.5 illustrates the use of `get` and `set` with the `point` class that you used earlier.

**LISTING 6.5** prop.cs—Using Properties

```
//  prop.cs- Using Properties
//-----------------------------------------------------------------

class point
{
    int my_X;  // my_X is private
    int my_Y;  // my_Y is private
```

**LISTING 6.5** continued

```

    public int x
    {
       get
       {
          return my_X;
       }
       set
       {
          my_X = value;
       }
    }
    public int y
    {
       get
       {
          return my_Y;
       }
       set
       {
          my_Y = value;
       }
    }
}

class MyApp
{
   public static void Main()
   {
      point starting = new point();
      point ending   = new point();

      starting.x = 1;
      starting.y = 4;
      ending.x = 10;
      ending.y = 11;

      System.Console.WriteLine("Point 1: ({0},{1})",
                          starting.x, starting.y);
      System.Console.WriteLine("Point 2: ({0},{1})",
                          ending.x, ending.y);
   }
}
```

**OUTPUT**

```
Point 1: (1,4)
Point 2: (10,11)
```

**ANALYSIS** Listing 6.5 creates properties for both the x and y coordinates of the point class. The point class is defined in lines 4 to 31. Everything on these lines is a part of the point class's definition. In lines 6 and 7, you see that two data members are created. These are called my_X and my_Y. Because these are not declared as public, they cannot be accessed outside the class. They are considered private variables. You will learn more about keeping things private on Day 8, " Advanced Data Storage: Structures, Enumerators, and Arrays."

Lines 9 to 19 and lines 20 to 30 operate exactly the same, except the first set of lines uses the my_X variable and the second set uses the my_Y variable. These sets of lines create the property abilities for the my_X and my_Y variables.

Line 9 looks like just another declaration of a data member. In fact, it is. In this line, you declare a public integer variable called x. Note that there is no semicolon at the end of this line; therefore, the declaration of the member variable is not complete. Rather, it also includes what is in the following code block in lines 10 to 19. Within this block of code you have two commands. Line 11 is a get statement, which is called whenever a program tries to get the value of the data member being declared—in this case, x. For example, if you assign the value of x to a different variable, you get the value of x and set it into the new variable. The set statement in line 15 is called whenever you are setting a value into the x variable. For example, setting x equal to 10 places the value of 10 into x.

When a program gets the value of x, the get property in line 11 is called. This executes the code within the get, which is line 13. Line 13 returns the value of my_X, which is the private variable in the point class.

When a program places a value into x, the set property in line 15 is called. This executes the code within the set, which is line 17. Line 17 sets something called value into the private variable, my_X, in the point class. value is the value being placed into x. (It is great when a name actually describes the contents.) For example, value is 10 in the following statement:

```
x = 10;
```

This statement places the value of 10 into x. The set property within x places this value into my_X.

Looking at the main application in lines 33 to 50, you should see that x is used as it had been used before. There is absolutely no difference to how you use the point class. The difference is that the point class could be changed to store my_X and my_Y differently and it would not impact the program.

Although the code in lines 9 to 30 is relatively simple, it doesn't have to be. You can do any coding and any manipulation you want within the get and set. You don't even have to write to another data member!

**Do**

**DO** make sure you understand data members and the class information presented in today's lesson before going to Day 7.

**DO** use property accessors to access your class's data members in programs you create.

## A First Look at Namespaces

As you begin to learn about classes, it is important to know that there is a large number of classes available that do a wide variety of functions. The .NET framework provides a substantial number of base classes that you can use. Additionally, you can obtain third-party classes that you can use.

**Note** Day 16, "Using the .NET Base Classes" focuses specifically on using a number of key .NET base classes.

As you continue through this book, you will be exposed to a number of key classes. You've actually used a couple of base classes already. As mentioned earlier, `Console` is a base class. You also learned that `Console` has a number of member routines called `Write` and `WriteLine`. For example, the following writes my name to the console:

```
System.Console.WriteLine("Bradley L. Jones");
```

You now know that `"Bradley L. Jones"` is a literal. You know that `WriteLine` is a routine that is a part of the `Console` class. You even know that `Console` is an object declared from a class. This leaves `System`.

Because of the number of classes, it is important that they be organized. Classes can be grouped together into namespaces. A namespace is a named grouping of classes. The `Console` class is a part of the `System` namespace.

`System.Console.WriteLine` is a fully qualified name. With a fully qualified name, you point directly to where the code is located. C# provides a shortcut method for using classes and methods that doesn't require you to always include the full namespace name. This is accomplished with the `using` keyword.

The `using` keyword enables you to include a namespace in your program. When the namespace is included, the program knows to search the namespace for routines and classes that might be used. The format for including a namespace is

```
using namespace_name
```

where *namespace_name* is the name of the namespace or the name of a nested namespace. For example, to include the `System` namespace, you include the following line of code near the top of your listing:

```
using System;
```

If you include this line of code, you do not need to include the `System` section when calling classes or routines within the namespace. Listing 6.6 calls the `using` statement to include the `System` namespace.

**LISTING 6.6** namesp.cs—Using using and Namespaces

```
// namesp.cs- Namespaces and the using keyword
//-----------------------------------------------------------------

using System;

class name
{
     public string first;
     public string last;
}

class NameApp
{
    public static void Main()
    {
       // Create a name object
       name you = new name();

       Console.Write("Enter your first name and press enter: ");
       you.first = Console.ReadLine();
       System.Console.Write("\n{0}, enter your last name and press enter: ",
                              you.first);
       you.last = System.Console.ReadLine();

       Console.WriteLine("\nData has been entered.....");
       System.Console.WriteLine("You claim to be {0} {1}",
                                   you.first, you.last);
    }
}
```

**OUTPUT**

```
Enter your first name and press enter: Bradley

Bradley, enter your last name and press enter: Jones

Data has been entered.....
You claim to be Bradley Jones
```

**Note** The bold text in the output is text that I entered. You can enter any text in its place. I suggest your own name rather than mine!

**ANALYSIS** Line 4 of Listing 6.6 is the focus point of this program. The `using` keyword includes the `System` namespace; when you use functions from the `Console` class, you don't have to fully qualify their names. You see this in lines 19, 20, and 25. By including the `using` keyword, you are not precluded from continuing to use fully qualified names, as lines 21, 23, and 26 show. There is, however, no need to fully qualify names, because the namespace was included.

This program uses a second routine from the `Console` class called `ReadLine`. As you can see by running this program, the `ReadLine` routine reads what is entered by users up to the time they press Enter. This routine returns what the user enters. In this case, the text entered by the user is assigned with the assignment operator to one of the data members in the name class.

## Nested Namespaces

Multiple namespaces can be stored together, and also are stored in a namespace. If a namespace contains other namespaces, you can add them to the qualified name, or you can include the sub-namespace qualified in a `using` statement. For example, the `System` namespace contains several other namespaces, including ones called `Drawing`, `Data`, and `Windows.Forms`. When using classes from these namespaces, you can either qualify these names or you can include them with `using` statements. To include a `using` statement for the `Data` namespace within the `System` namespace, you enter the following:

```
using System.Data;
```

# Summary

Today's and tomorrow's lessons are among two of the most important lessons in this book. Classes are the heart of object-oriented programming languages and therefore are the heart and key to C#. In today's lesson, you revisited the concepts of encapsulation, polymorphism, inheritance, and reuse. You then learned how to define the basic structure of a class and how to create data members within your class. You learned one of the first ways to encapsulate your program when you learned how to create properties using the `set` and `get` accessors. The last part of today's lesson introduced you to namespaces and the `using` statement.

6

# Q&A

**Q Would you ever use a class with just data members?**

**A** Generally you would not use a class with just data members. The value of a class and of object-oriented programming is the ability to encapsulate both functionality and data into a single package. You learned about only data today. In tomorrow's lesson, you learn how to add the functionality.

**Q Should all data members always be declared public so people can get to them?**

**A** Absolutely not! Although many of the data members were declared as public in today's lesson, there are times when you don't want people to get to your data for a number of reasons. One reason is to allow the ability to change the way the data is stored.

**Q It was mentioned that there are a bunch of existing classes. How can I find out about these?**

**A** Microsoft provided a bunch of classes called the .NET base classes. Microsoft also has provided documentation on what each of these classes can do. The classes are organized by namespace. At the time this book was written, the only way to get any information on them was through the use of online help. Microsoft included a complete references section for the base classes. You will learn more about the base classes on Day 19 of this book.

# Workshop

The Workshop provides quiz questions to help you solidify your understanding of the material covered and exercises to provide you with experience in using what you've learned. Try to understand the quiz and exercise answers before continuing to the next day's lesson. Answers are provided in Appendix A, "Answers."

## Quiz

1. What are the four characteristics of an object-oriented program?
2. What two key things can be stored in a class?
3. What is the difference between a data member declared as public and one that hasn't been declared as public?
4. What does adding the keyword `static` do to a data member?
5. What is the name of the application class in Listing 6.2?
6. What commands are used to implement properties?

7. When is `value` used?
8. Is `Console` a class, a data member, a namespace, a routine, or a type?
9. Is `System` a class, a data member, a namespace, a routine, or a type?
10. What keyword is used to include a namespace in a listing?

## Exercises

1. Create a class to hold the center of a circle and its radius.
2. Add properties to the `Circle` class created in exercise 1.
3. Create a class that stores an integer called `MyNumber`. Create properties for this number. When the number is stored, multiply it by 100. Whenever it is retrieved, divide it by 100.
4. **BUG BUSTER:** The following program has a problem. Enter it in your editor and compile it. Which lines generate error messages?

```
 1:// A bug buster program
 2:// Is something wrong? Or not?
 3://------------------------------------------
 4:  using System;
 5:  using System.Console;
 6:
 7:  class name
 8:  {
 9:      public string first;
10:  }
11:
12:  class NameApp
13:  {
14:     public static void Main()
15:     {
16:        // Create a name object
17:        name you = new name();
18:
19:        Write("Enter your first name and press enter: ");
20:        you.first = ReadLine();
21:        Write("\nHello {0}!", you.first);
22:     }
23:  }
```

5. Write a class called `die` that will hold the number of sides of a die, `sides`, and the current value of a roll, `value`.
6. Use the class in exercise 5 in a program that declares two dice objects. Set values into the side data members. Set random values into the stored roll values. Note, see Listing 5.3 for help with this program.

# WEEK 1

# DAY 7

# Class Methods and Member Functions

Yesterday you learned that there are several parts to a class. Most importantly, a class has the capability of defining objects used for storing data and routines. In yesterday's lesson you learned how the data is stored. Today you learn all about creating, storing, and using routines within your classes. These routines give your objects the power to do what you want. Although storing information can be important, the manipulation of the data brings life to your programs. Today you

- Build methods of your own
- Pass information to your routines with parameters
- Reevaluate the concepts of value and reference
- Understand the concepts of calling methods
- Discover the truth about constructors
- Learn to finalize or destruct your classes

# Getting Started with Methods

On previous days you learned how to store data and how to manipulate this data. You also learned how to manipulate program flow. Now you need to package some of this functionality into routines that you can reuse. Additionally, you need to associate these routines with the data members of a class.

Routines in C# are called either functions or methods. There is no real distinction between these two terms, so you can use them interchangeably.

**Note**

> Most C++ and C# developers refer to routines as methods. Most C programmers refer to them as functions. Regardless of what you call them, they all refer to the same thing.

**NEW TERM** A *method* is a named piece of independent code that is placed in a reusable format. A method can operate without interference from other parts of an application. If created correctly, it should perform a specific task that is indicated by its name.

As you will learn in today's lesson, methods can return a value. Additionally, many methods enable you to pass information to them.

# Using Methods

You have already used a number of methods in this book: `Write`, `WriteLine`, and `ReadLine`. Additionally, you used the `Main` method in every program you have created. Listing 7.1 presents the `Circle` class that you have seen before. This time, the routines for calculating the area and circumference have been added to the class as methods.

**LISTING 7.1** circle.cs—A Class with Member Methods

```
//  circle.cs - A simple circle class with methods
//-----------------------------------------------------

class Circle
{
    public int x;
    public int y;
    public double radius;

    public double area()
    {
```

**LISTING 7.1** continued

```
       double theArea;
       theArea = 3.14159 * radius * radius;
       return theArea;
    }

    public double circumference()
    {
       double theCirc;
       theCirc = 2 * 3.14159 * radius;
       return theCirc;
    }
}

class CircleApp
{
   public static void Main()
   {
      Circle first  = new Circle();
      Circle second = new Circle();

      double area;
      double circ;
      first.x = 10;
      first.y = 14;
      first.radius = 3;

      second.x = 10;
      second.y = 11;
      second.radius = 4;

      System.Console.WriteLine("Circle 1: Center = ({0},{1})",
                                first.x, first.y);
      System.Console.WriteLine("          Radius = {0}", first.radius);
      System.Console.WriteLine("          Area   = {0}", first.area());
      System.Console.WriteLine("          Circum = {0}", first.circumfer-
➥ence());

      area = second.area();
      circ = second.circumference();

      System.Console.WriteLine("\nCircle 2: Center = ({0},{1})",
                                second.x, second.y);
      System.Console.WriteLine("          Radius = {0}", second.radius);
      System.Console.WriteLine("          Area   = {0}", area);
      System.Console.WriteLine("          Circum = {0}", circ);
   }
}
```

7

**OUTPUT**

```
Circle 1: Center = (10,14)
          Radius = 3
          Area   = 28.27431
          Circum = 18.84954

Circle 2: Center = (10,11)
          Radius = 4
          Area   = 50.26544
          Circum = 25.13272
```

**ANALYSIS** Most of the code in Listing 7.1 should look familiar. The parts that might not seem familiar will be by the end of today's lesson.

Jumping into the listing, you see that line 4 starts the class definition for the circle. In lines 6 to 8, the same three data members that were declared in previous examples are declared. This includes an `x` and `y` value to store the center point of the circle and the variable `radius` to store the radius. The class continues after the declaration of the data members.

In lines 10 to 15, you see the first definition of a member method. The details of how this works are covered in the following sections. For now you can see that the name of this method is `area`. Lines 12 to 14 are the code within this method. This code calculates the area and returns it to the calling program. Lines 12 and 13 will be familiar. You'll learn more about line 14 later today. Lines 17 to 22 are a second method called `circumference`. This method calculates the value of the circumference and returns it to the calling program.

Line 25 is the beginning of the application class for this listing. Line 27 contains the `Main` method that starts every application. This routine creates two circles (lines 29 and 30) and then assigns values to the data members (lines 34 to 40). In lines 42 and 43, the data members are printed for the first circle. In lines 45 and 46, you see the `Console.WriteLine` method that you've seen before; the difference is the value you pass to be printed. In line 45, you pass `first.area`. This is a call to the first class's `area` member method, which was defined in lines 10 to 15. Line 48 calls the same method for the second class and assigns the result to the `area` variable.

**Tip**

> You know that `area` in the listing is a member method rather than a data member because the name is followed by parentheses when it is called. You'll learn more about this later.

If you haven't already, you should execute this listing and see what happens. The next few sections detail how to define your own methods and explain the way a method works. Additionally, you will learn how to send and receive values from a method.

# Program Flow with Methods

As you were told earlier, a method is an independent piece of code that is packaged and named so you can call it from your programs. When a method is called, program flow switches to the method. The method's code then executes before returning. Figure 7.1 presents the order of flow for Listing 7.1. When a method is called, program flow goes to the method, executes its code, and then returns to the calling routine. You can also see that a method can call another method with the same flow expectations.

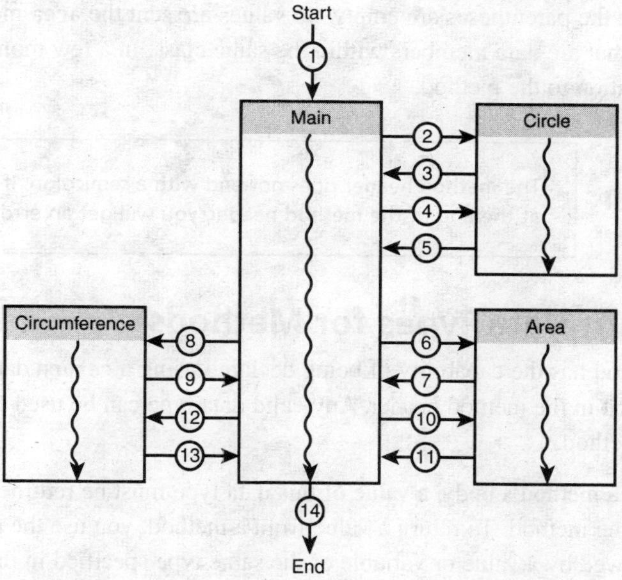


**FIGURE 7.1**
*The program flow of the circle application in Listing 7.1.*

# Format of a Method

It is important to understand the format of a method. Listing 7.1 has hinted at the format and the procedure for calling a method. The basic format of a method is

```
Method header
{
    Method body
}
```

## The Method Header

The method header defines several things about a method:

- The access that programs will have to the method
- The return data type of the method

7

- Any values that are being sent to the method
- The name of the method

If you look at line 10 of Listing 7.1, you see the header for the `area` method:

```
public double area()
```

This method is declared as `public`, which means it can be accessed by programs outside this class. Additionally, you see that the method has a return type of `double`. The method can return one `double` value to the calling program. The method's name is `area`. Finally, because the parentheses are empty, no values are sent the `area` method. Rather, it uses values that are data members within the same class. In a few moments, you will send information to the method.

**Caution** The method header does not end with a semicolon. If you place a semicolon at the end of the method header, you will get an error.

## Return Data Types for Methods

A method has the capability of being declared using a `return` data type. This data type is indicated in the method header. Any valid data type can be used as the `return` data type for a method.

Within a method's body, a value of this data type must be returned to the program that called the method. To return a value from a method, you use the return keyword, which is followed by a value or variable of the same type specified in the header. For example, the `area` method in Listing 7.1 was declared with a `return` type of double. In line 14, you can see that the return keyword is used to return a variable of type double. The area method returns the `double` value to the calling program

What if a method does not need to return a value? What data type is then used? If a method will not return a value, you use the void keyword with the method. void indicates that no value is to be returned.

## Naming Methods

It is important to name your methods appropriately. There are several theories on naming methods. You need to decide what is best for you or your organization. One rule of thumb is consistent: Always give your methods a meaningful name. If your method calculates and returns the area, the name `area` makes sense, as would names such as `GetArea`, `CalculateArea`, and `CalcArea`. Names such as `routine1` or `myRoutine` make less sense.

One popular guideline for naming methods is to always use a verb and noun combination. Because a method performs some action, you can always use a verb/noun combination. Using this guideline, `area` is considered a less useful name; however, the names `CalculateArea` or `CalcArea` are excellent choices.

## The Method Body

The method body contains the code that will be executed when the method is called. This code starts with an opening brace and ends with a closing brace. The code between can be any of the programming you've seen before. In general, however, the code modifies only the data members of the class it is a part of or data that has been passed into the method.

If the method header indicates that the method has a `return` type, the method needs to return a value of that type. You return a value by using the `return` keyword. The `return` keyword is followed by the value to be returned. Reviewing the `area()` method in Listing 7.1, you see that the method body is in lines 11 to 15. The area of the circle is calculated and placed into a double field called `theArea`. In line 14, this value is returned from the method using the `return` statement.

**Caution** The data type of the variable returned from a method must match the data type within the header of the method.

### Using Methods

To use a method, you call it. A method is called the same way a data member is called. You call the method by entering the object name followed by a period and then the method name. The difference between calling a method and calling data members is that you must also include parentheses and might include parameters when calling a method. In Listing 7.1, the `area` method is called for the first object with the following code:

```
first.area()
```

As with a variable, if the method has a `return` type, it is returned to the spot where the method is called. For example, the `area` method returns the area of a circle as a `double` value. In line 45 of Listing 7.1, this value is returned as the parameter to another method, `Console.WriteLine`. In line 48, the `return` value from the second object's `area` method is assigned to another variable called `area`.

## Using Data Members from a Method

The area method in Listing 7.1 uses the radius data member without identifying the class or object name. The code for the method is

```
public double area()
{
    double theArea;
    theArea = 3.14159 * radius * radius;
    return theArea;
}
```

Previously you had to include the name of the object when you used a data member. There is no object name included on this use of radius. How can the routine get away with omitting the object name? The answer is simple if you think it through.

When the area method is called, it is called using a specific object. If you call area with the circle1 object:

```
circle1.area()
```

you are calling the copy of the method within the circle1 object. The routine knows you called with circle1, so all the regular data members and other methods within circle1 are available. You don't need to use the object name because you are within the member method for that specific object.

You also see that additional variables can be declared within a class's member method. These variables are valid only for the time the method is operating. These variables are said to be local to the method. In the case of the area method, a double variable called theArea is created and used. When the method exits, the value stored in theArea—as well as theArea variable—goes away.

Listing 7.2 illustrates the use of a local variable and the program flow.

**LISTING 7.2** locals.cs—Using Local Versus Class Variables

```
//  locals.cs - Local variables
//-----------------------------------------------------

using System;

class loco
{
    public int x;

    public void count_x()
    {
        int x;
```

**LISTING 7.2** continued

```
13:
14:            Console.WriteLine("In count_x method. Printing X values...");
15:            for ( x = 0; x <= 10; x++)
16:            {
17:               Console.Write("{0} - ", x);
18:            }
19:            Console.WriteLine("\nAt the end of count_x method. x = {0}", x);
20:        }
21:    }
22:
23:  class CircleApp
24:  {
25:     public static void Main()
26:     {
27:        loco Locals = new loco();
28:
29:        int x = 999;
30:        Locals.x = 555;
31:
32:        Console.WriteLine("\nIn Main(), x = {0}", x);
33:        Console.WriteLine("Locals.x = {0}", Locals.x);
34:        Console.WriteLine("Calling Method");
35:        Locals.count_x();
36:        Console.WriteLine("\nBack From Method");
37:        Console.WriteLine("Locals.x = {0}", Locals.x);
38:        Console.WriteLine("In Main(), x = {0}", x);
39:     }
40:  }
```

**OUTPUT**

```
In Main(), x = 999
Locals.x = 555
Calling Method
In count_x method. Printing X values...
0 - 1 - 2 - 3 - 4 - 5 - 6 - 7 - 8 - 9 - 10 -
At the end of count_x method. x = 11

Back From Method
Locals.x = 555
In Main(), x = 999
```

**ANALYSIS** Listing 7.2 does not contain very good names; however, this listing illustrates a couple of key points. Several variables called `x` are declared in this listing. This includes a `public int x` declared in line 8 as a part of the `loco` class. There also is a local integer variable `x` declared in line 12 as part of the `count_x` method. Finally, there is a third integer variable called `x` declared in line 29 as part of the `Main` method. Although all three of these variables have the same name, they are three totally different variables.

The first of these variables, the one in the `loco` class, is easiest to recognize. It is part of a class. As you've seen before, to use this variable outside the class, you have to use an object name. This is done in line 30 of the listing, where an object declared with the name `Locals` is used to set a value in the `x` data member of `Locals`. This value is set to `555`. The `Main` routine's `x` value was set to the value of `999` in line 29. In lines 32 and 33, these two values contain their own values and are easy to differentiate from each other.

In line 35, the `Main` method calls the `count_x` method of the `loco` class that was declared in line 27. First, in lines 10 to 21, a variable called `x` is declared (line 12). This value overshadows any previous declarations of `x`, including the declaration of `x` in the class. In the rest of the method, this local variable `x` is used to loop and print numbers. When the loop is done, the value of `x` is printed one last time before the method ends.

With the end of the method, control is returned to the `Main` method, where the `x` variables are printed again. The `Locals` data member `x` was not touched. Additionally, the `x` variable that was a local within `Main` also retained its value of `999`. Each of these operated independently.

What happens if you want to work with the class data member `x` in the `count_x` method? You learned earlier that within a class's method, you can call a data member without using the object name. In fact, you can't use the object name because it can vary. How, then, can you use the data member `x` within a method if there is a local variable called `x`? Listing 7.3 is the `locals` listing with a slight change.

**LISTING 7.3** locals2.cs—Calling a Data Member Within a Method

```
 1:  //  locals.cs - Local variables
 2:  //-----------------------------------------------------
 3:
 4:  using System;
 5:
 6:  class loco
 7:  {
 8:      public int x;
 9:
10:      public void count_x()
11:      {
12:         int x;
13:
14:         Console.WriteLine("In count_x method. Printing X values...");
15:         for ( x = 0; x <= 10; x++)
16:         {
17:            Console.Write("{0} - ", x);
18:         }
19:
```

**LISTING 7.3** continued

```
20:        Console.WriteLine("\nDone looping.  x = {0}", x);
21:        Console.WriteLine("The data member x's value: {0}", this.x);
22:        Console.WriteLine("At the end of count_x method.");
23:     }
24: }
25:
26: class CircleApp
27: {
28:     public static void Main()
29:     {
30:        loco Locals = new loco();
31:
32:        int x = 999;
33:        Locals.x = 555;
34:
35:        Console.WriteLine("\nIn Main(), x = {0}", x);
36:        Console.WriteLine("Locals.x = {0}", Locals.x);
37:        Console.WriteLine("Calling Method");
38:        Locals.count_x();
39:        Console.WriteLine("\nBack From Method");
40:        Console.WriteLine("Locals.x = {0}", Locals.x);
41:        Console.WriteLine("In Main(), x = {0}", x);
42:     }
43: }
```

**OUTPUT**

```
In Main(), x = 999
Locals.x = 555
Calling Method
In count_x method. Printing X values...
0 - 1 - 2 - 3 - 4 - 5 - 6 - 7 - 8 - 9 - 10 -
Done looping.  x = 11
The data member x's value: 555
At the end of count_x method.

Back From Method
Locals.x = 555
In Main(), x = 999
```

**ANALYSIS** Line 21 is the unique part of this line— a value called `this.x` is printed. The keyword `this` always refers to the current object being used. In this case, `this` refers to the `Locals` object on which the method was called. Because it refers to the current object, the `x` value refers to the object's `x` data member—not the local data member. So, to access a data member from a method within the same class, you use the keyword `this`.

How can the class method access the value of `x` in the calling program—the local `x` åvariable declared in `Main` on line 32 of Listing 7.3? It can't unless it is passed in as a parameter.

# Passing Values to Methods

You now know how to access a method. You also know how to declare local variables within the method and how to use data members within the same class. What if you want to use a value, or multiple values, from another class or another method? For example, suppose you want a method that takes two numbers, multiplies them, and returns the result. You know how to return a single result, but how do you get the two numbers into the method?

A method header can receive values when called. To receive values, the header must have been defined with parameters. The format of a method header with parameters is

```
Modifiers ReturnType Name ( Parameters )
```

The parameters are passed within the parentheses of the method. Parameters are optional, so if no parameters are sent, the parentheses are empty—just as you've seen in the previous examples.

The basic format for passing parameters is

```
[Attribute] Type ArgumentName
```

where `Type` is the data type of the value being passed and `ArgumentName` is the name of the variable being passed. Optionally, you can have an attribute, which is covered later in this chapter. First, Listing 7.4 presents a simple program that takes two numbers, multiplies them, and returns the result.

**LISTING 7.4** Mult.cs—Passing Values

```
//  mult.cs - Passing values
//-----------------------------------------------

using System;

class Multiply
{
   static long multi( long nbr1, long nbr2 )
   {
      return (nbr1 * nbr2);
   }

   public static void Main()
   {
      long x = 1234;
      long y = 5678;
      long a = 6789;
      long b = 9876;
```

**Listing 7.4** continued

```
19:
20:         long result;
21:
22:         result = multi( x, y);
23:         Console.WriteLine("x * y : {0} * {1} = {2}", x, y, result);
24:
25:         result = multi(a, b);
26:         Console.WriteLine("a * b : {0} * {1} = {2}", a, b, result);
27:
28:         result = multi( 555L, 1000L );
29:         Console.WriteLine("With Long values passed, the result was {0}",
➥result);
30:     }
31: }
```

**Output**

```
x * y : 1234 * 5678 = 7006652
a * b : 6789 * 9876 = 67048164
With Long values passed, the result was 555000
```

**Analysis** Listing 7.4 illustrates the point of passing two values; however, it also illustrates a couple of other items. First, take a look at the method definition in lines 8 to 11. This method called `multi` takes two parameters as arguments. These are each `long` data types and have been given the names `nbr1` and `nbr2`. These two names are local variables used in the method. In line 10, you see how they are to be used. The two values are multiplied and the resulting value is returned to the caller. In the method header in line 8, the `multi` method is declared as a `long`, so it can return a single `long` value.

If you look at lines 22, 25, and 28 you see the `multi` method called three different times, each with different values. You see that you can pass data variables, as in lines 22 or 25. You can also pass literal values, as in line 28. When the `multi` method is called, the values passed are sent to the method and referenced with the variable names in the method header. So for line 22, `x` and `y` are passed to `nbr1` and `nbr2`; in line 25, `a` and `b` are passed to `nbr1` and `nbr2`. In line 28, the values `555` and `1000` are passed to `nbr1` and `nbr2`. These values are then used by the method.

It is important to note that the number of arguments sent to the method must match the number of parameters that were defined. In the case of the `multi` method, you must pass two values. If you don't, you get an error.

> **Note**
>
> For those of you who have programmed in languages such as C++, you should note that there are no default parameters in C#.

## Static Methods

You learned earlier that the `static` modifier caused a data member to be associated with a class instead of a specific object of a class. In Listing 7.4, a `static` method was used. Listing 7.4 contains only one class, which not only contains the `Main` method, but also the `multi` method.

The `multi` method could just as easily have been a part of another class. If so, you would have needed to declare an object for that class and then call the `multi` method with the object name. Because it is a part of the same class as the `Main` method and is declared as `static`, it is accessible to any part of the `Multiply` class. This enables it to be used within the `Main()` method.

## Different Parameter Access Attributes

In the previous example, you passed the values to the method. The method had copies of what was originally passed to it. These copies were used and then thrown out when the method finished its operations. Passing arguments to a method by value is only one means. There are three types of access attributes for parameters:

- Value
- Reference
- Out

### Using Value Access to Parameters

As already stated, value access to a parameter is when a copy is made of the data being sent to the method. The method then uses this copy and does not impact the original value.

### Using Reference Access to Parameters

There are times when you will want to modify the data stored in the original variable. In this case, you can pass a reference to the variable instead of the variable's value. A reference is a variable that has access to the original variable. If you change the reference, you change the original variable's value as well.

In more technical terms, a reference variable points to a location in memory where the data is stored. Consider Figure 7.2. The variable number is stored in memory. A reference could be created that points to where the number is stored. When the reference is changed, it changes the value in the memory, thus also changing the value of the number.

**FIGURE 7.2**

*Reference variables versus value variables.*

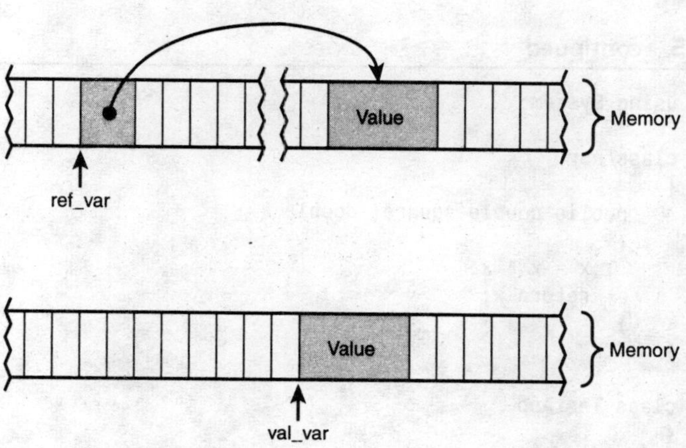


Because a reference variable can be pointed to different places, it is not tied to a specific location in memory the way a regular variable is. Each time a method is called with a parameter that has a reference attribute, the parameter is pointed to the new variable that is being sent to the routine. Because this points to the variable's location, any changes to the parameter variable also causes a change in the original variable.

When declaring a parameter, its attribute defaults to the attribute type of the data type. For the basic data types, this is by value. To cause a basic data type, such as an integer, to be passed by reference, you add the `ref` keyword to the method header before the data type. Listings 7.5 and 7.6 illustrate using the `ref` keyword and show the difference between using reference and value parameters. Listing 7.5 calls a method passing a `double`. This `double` is being passed by value. In Listing 7.6, a `double` is passed by reference. The difference between these two listings can be seen in their outputs.

> **Note**
>
> As you learned in Day 3, "Storing Information with Variables," the basic data types are attributed as value types by default. This means when you create a variable, it is given a specific location in memory to use where it can store its value. Data types such as classes are reference types by default. This means that the class name contains the address where the data within the class will be located rather than the data itself.

**LISTING 7.5** refnot.cs—Calling a Method by Value

```
//  refnot.cs - without reference variables (by value)
//-----------------------------------------------------

```

**LISTING 7.5** continued

```
using System;

class nbr
{
    public double square( double x )
    {
       x = x * x;
       return x;
    }
}

class TestApp
{
   public static void Main()
   {
      nbr doit = new nbr();

      double nbr1 = 3;
      double retVal = 0;

      Console.WriteLine("Before square -> nbr1 = {0}, retVal = {1}",
                         nbr1, retVal);

      retVal = doit.square( nbr1 );

      Console.WriteLine("After square -> nbr1 = {0}, retVal = {1}",
                         nbr1, retVal);
   }
}
```

**OUTPUT**

```
Before square -> nbr1 = 3, retVal = 0
After square -> nbr1 = 3, retVal = 9
```

**LISTING 7.6** refers.cs—Calling a Method by Reference

```
// refers.cs - Reference variables
//-----------------------------------------------------

using System;

class nbr
{
    public double square( ref double x )
    {
       x = x * x;
       return x;
    }
```

**LISTING 7.6** continued

```
13: }
14:
15: class TestApp
16: {
17:     public static void Main()
18:     {
19:         nbr doit = new nbr();
20:
21:         double nbr1 = 3;
22:         double retVal = 0;
23:
24:         Console.WriteLine("Before square -> nbr1 = {0}, retVal = {1}",
25:                           nbr1, retVal);
26:
27:         retVal = doit.square( ref nbr1 );
28:
29:         Console.WriteLine("After square -> nbr1 = {0}, retVal = {1}",
30:                           nbr1, retVal);
31:     }
32: }
```

**OUTPUT**

```
Before square -> nbr1 = 3, retVal = 0
After square -> nbr1 = 9, retVal = 9
```

**ANALYSIS** The output from these two listings tells the story of what is going on. In Listing 7.5, references are not used. As a result, the variable that is passed into the square method, `var1`, is not changed. It remains as the value of `3` both before and after the method is called. In Listing 7.6, a reference is passed. As you can see from the output of this listing, the variable passed to the square method is modified.

In the method header in Listing 7.6, the parameter is declared with the `ref` keyword added. A `double` is normally a `value` data type, so to pass it to the method as a reference you need to add the `ref` keyword before the variable being passed in. You see this in line 27.

## Using `out` Access to Parameters

The `return` type enables you to send back a single variable from a method; however, there are times when you will want more than one value to be returned. Although reference variables could be used to do this, C# has also added a special attribute type specifically for returning data out of a method.

You can add parameters to your method header specifically for returning values. These parameters are declared like any other parameter except that you also add the `out` keyword as an attribute. This keyword signifies that a value is being returned out of the method, but not coming in. When you call a method that has an `out` parameter, you must make sure to include a variable to hold the value being returned. Listing 7.7 illustrates the use of the out attribute.

**LISTING 7.7** Outter.cs—Using the out Attribute

```
//  outter.cs - Using output variables
//-----------------------------------------------

using System;

class nbr
{
    public void math_routines( double x,
                               out double half,
                               out double squared,
                               out double cubed )
    {
       half = x / 2;
       squared = x * x;
       cubed = x * x * x;
    }
}

class TestApp
{
   public static void Main()
   {
      nbr doit = new nbr();

      double nbr = 600;
      double Half_nbr = 0;
      double Squared_nbr = 0;
      double Cubed_nbr = 0;

      Console.WriteLine("Before method -> nbr = {0}", nbr);
      Console.WriteLine("                Half_nbr = {0}", Half_nbr);
      Console.WriteLine("             Squared_nbr = {0}", Squared_nbr);
      Console.WriteLine("               Cubed_nbr = {0}\n", Cubed_nbr);

      doit.math_routines( nbr, out Half_nbr, out Squared_nbr, out Cubed_nbr );

      Console.WriteLine("After method -> nbr = {0}", nbr);
      Console.WriteLine("               Half_nbr = {0}", Half_nbr);
      Console.WriteLine("            Squared_nbr = {0}", Squared_nbr);
      Console.WriteLine("              Cubed_nbr = {0}", Cubed_nbr);
   }
}
```

**OUTPUT**

```
Before method -> nbr = 600
            Half_nbr = 0
         Squared_nbr = 0
           Cubed_nbr = 0

After method -> nbr = 600
           Half_nbr = 300
        Squared_nbr = 360000
          Cubed_nbr = 216000000
```

**ANALYSIS** There are two key pieces of code to look at in Listing 7.7. First is the method header in lines 8 to 11. Remember, you can use whitespace to make your code easier to read. This method header has been formatted so each argument is on a different line. Notice that the first argument, `x`, is a regular `double` variable. The remaining three arguments have been declared with the `out` attribute. This means no value is being passed into the method. Rather, these three arguments are containers for values to be passed out of the method.

The second line of code to review is line 35, the call to the `math_routines` method. The variables being passed must also be attributed with the `out` keyword when calling the method. If you leave the `out` keyword off when calling the method, you get an error.

Overall, the code in this listing is relatively straightforward. The `math_routines` method within the `nbr` class does three math calculations on a number. In lines 30 to 33, the values of the variables that are to hold the results of the math calculations are printed. In line 37 to 40, the values are reprinted after having been filled within the `math_routines` method.

If you don't place a value in an output parameter, you get an error. It's important to know that you must assign a value to all output parameters within a method. For example, comment out line 14 in Listing 7.7:

```
14:         squared = x * x;
```

This removes the assignment to the square output variable. When you recompile this listing, you get the following error:

```
outter2.cs(8,17): error CS0177: The out parameter 'squared' must be assigned to
        before control leaves the current method
```

As you can see, if an output parameter is defined, it must be filled.

7

**Note**

A variable that is being used as an out variable does not have to be initialized before the method is called. For example, you can remove the initializations from lines 26 to 28 as follows:

```
26:          double Half_nbr;
27:          double Squared_nbr;
28:          double Cubed_nbr;
```

You will also need to remove lines 31 to 33. When you recompile, you will see that the method call in line 35 still works even though the three variables are not initialized.

| Do | Don't |
|---|---|
| **DO** use class and method names that are clear and descriptive. | **DON'T** confuse by value variables with reference variables. Remember, passing a variable by value creates a copy. Passing by reference enables you to manipulate the original variable's value. |

# Types of Class methods

You have learned the basics of using methods. There are a few special types of methods that you should be aware of:

- Property accessor methods
- Constructors
- Destructors/finalizers

## Property Accessor Methods

You actually worked with property accessor methods yesterday—`set` and `get`. These methods enable you to keep data members private.

## Constructors

When an object is first created, there are often times when you will want some setup to occur. There is a special type of method that is used specifically this initial setup—or construction—of objects. This method is called a constructor. There are actually two types of constructors: instance constructors, used when each instance or object is created; and `static` constructors, called before any objects are created for a class.

## Instance Constructors

An instance constructor is a method that is automatically called whenever an object is instantiated. This constructor can contain any type of code that a normal method could contain. A constructor is generally used to do initial setup for an object and can include functionality, such as initializing variables.

The format of a constructor is

```
modifiers classname()
{
   // Constructor body
}
```

This is a method that is defined using the class name that is to contain the constructor. Modifiers are the same modifiers you can add to other methods. Generally, you use only `public`. You don't include any `return` data type.

It is important to note that every class has a default constructor that is called, even if you don't create one. By creating a constructor, you gain the ability to control some of the setup.

The constructor class is automatically called whenever you create an object. Listing 7.8 illustrates using a constructor.

**LISTING 7.8** Constr.cs—Using a Constructor

```
//  constr.cs - constructors
//----------------------------------------------------------

using System;

public class myClass
{
    static public int sctr = 0;
    public int ctr = 0;

    public void routine()
    {
       Console.WriteLine("In the routine - ctr = {0} / sctr = {1}\n",
                            ctr, sctr );
    }

    public myClass()
    {
       ctr++;
       sctr++;
       Console.WriteLine("In Constructor- ctr = {0} / sctr = {1}\n",
```

**LISTING 7.8** continued

```
                           ctr, sctr );
    }
}

class TestApp
{
   public static void Main()
   {
      Console.WriteLine("Start of Main method...");

      Console.WriteLine("Creating first object...");
      myClass first = new myClass();
      Console.WriteLine("Creating second object...");
      myClass second = new myClass();

      Console.WriteLine("Calling first routine...");
      first.routine();

      Console.WriteLine("Creating third object...");
      myClass third = new myClass();
      Console.WriteLine("Calling third routine...");
      third.routine();

      Console.WriteLine("Calling second routine...");
      second.routine();

      Console.WriteLine("End of Main method");
   }
}
```

**OUTPUT**

```
Start of Main method...
Creating first object...
In Constructor- ctr = 1 / sctr = 1

Creating second object...
In Constructor- ctr = 1 / sctr = 2

Calling first routine...
In the routine - ctr = 1 / sctr = 2

Creating third object...
In Constructor- ctr = 1 / sctr = 3

Calling third routine...
In the routine - ctr = 1 / sctr = 3

Calling second routine...
In the routine - ctr = 1 / sctr = 3

End of Main method
```

**ANALYSIS** Listing 7.8 illustrates the use of a very simple constructor in lines 17 to 23. This listing also helps to reillustrate the use of a `static` class data member versus a regular data member. In lines 6 to 24, a class is defined called `myClass`. This class contains two data members that can be used as counters. The first data member is declared as `static` and is given the name `sctr`. The second data member is not `static` so its name is `ctr` (without the `s`).

> **Note** Remember, a class creates one copy of a `static` data member that is shared across all objects. For regular data members, each class has its own copy.

The test class contains two routines. The first is a method called `routine`, which prints a line of text with the current value of the two counters. The second routine has the same name as the class, `myClass`. Because of this, you automatically know that it is a constructor. This method is called each time an object is created. In this constructor, a couple of things are going on. First, each of the two counters is incremented by `1`. For the `ctr` variable, this is the first time it is incremented, because it is a new copy of the variable for this specific object. For `sctr`, the number might be something else. Because the `sctr` data member is `static`, it retains its value across all objects for the given class. The result is that for each copy of the class, `sctr` is incremented by `1`. Finally, in line 21, the constructor prints a message that displays the value stored in `ctr` and the value stored in `sctr`.

The application class for this program starts in line 26. This class prints messages and instantiates test objects. Nothing more. If you follow the messages that are printed in the output, you will see they match the listing. The one interesting thing to note is that when you call the `routine` method for the second object in line 46, the `sctr` is `3`, not `2`. Because `sctr` is shared across all objects, by the time you print this message, you have called the constructor three times.

One final item you should not call the constructor within your listing. Look at line 33:

```
33:        myClass first = new myClass();
```

This is the line that creates your object. Although the constructor is called automatically, notice the `myClass` call in this line!

> **Note** In tomorrow's lesson, you will learn how to pass parameters to a constructor!

7

## Static Constructors

As with data members and methods, you can also create `static` constructors. A constructor declared with the `static` modifier is called before the first object is created. It is called only once and then never used again. Listing 7.9 is a modified version of Listing 7.8. In this listing, a `static` constructor has been added to the `test` class.

Notice that this constructor has the same name as the other constructor. Because the `static` constructor includes the name `static`, the compiler can differentiate it from the regular constructor.

**LISTING 7.9** statcon.cs—Using a `static` Constructor

```
//  statcon.cs - static constructors
//-----------------------------------------------------

using System;

public class test
{
    static public int sctr;
    public int ctr;

    public void routine()
    {
       Console.WriteLine("In the routine - ctr = {0} / sctr = {1}\n",
                                           ctr, sctr );
    }

    static test()
    {
       sctr = 100;
       Console.WriteLine("In Static Constructor - sctr = {0}\n", sctr );
    }

    public test()
    {
       ctr++;
       sctr++;
       Console.WriteLine("In Constructor- ctr = {0} / sctr = {1}\n",
                                           ctr, sctr );
    }
}

class TestApp
{
   public static void Main()
   {
```

**LISTING 7.9** continued

```
        Console.WriteLine("Start of Main method...");

        Console.WriteLine("Creating first object...");
        test first = new test();
        Console.WriteLine("Creating second object...");
        test second = new test();

        Console.WriteLine("Calling first routine...");
        first.routine();

        Console.WriteLine("Creating third object... ");
        test third = new test();
        Console.WriteLine("Calling third routine...");
        third.routine();

        Console.WriteLine("Calling second routine...");
        second.routine();

        Console.WriteLine("End of Main method");
    }
}
```

**OUTPUT**

```
Start of Main method...
Creating first object...
In Static Constructor - sctr = 100

In Constructor- ctr = 1 / sctr = 101

Creating second object...
In Constructor- ctr = 1 / sctr = 102

Calling first routine...
In the routine - ctr = 1 / sctr = 102

Creating third object...
In Constructor- ctr = 1 / sctr = 103

Calling third routine...
In the routine - ctr = 1 / sctr = 103

Calling second routine...
In the routine - ctr = 1 / sctr = 103

End of Main method
```

**ANALYSIS** There is one key difference in the output of this listing from that of Listing 7.8. The third line printed in the output came from the `static` constructor. This printed the simple line `In Static Constructor....` This constructor (in lines 17 to 21) initializes the `static` data member, `sctr`, to `100` and then prints its message. The rest of the program operates exactly as it did for Listing 7.8. The output differs a little due to the fact that the `sctr` variable now starts at `100` rather than at `0`.

## Destructors/Finalizers

You can perform some operations when an object is destroyed. These are accomplished in the destructor.

A destructor is automatically executed at some point after the program is done using an object. Does "at some point after" sound vague? This is intentional. This destruction can happen from the point the object of a class is no longer used up to the point just before the program ends. In fact, it is possible that the program can end without calling the destructor, which means it would never be called. You don't have any real control over when the destructor will execute; therefore, the value of a destructor is limited.

**Caution**

In languages such as C++, a destructor can be called and the programmer can control when it will perform. This is not the case in C#.

**From the technical side of things . . .**

A destructor is generally called by the C# runtime after an object of a class is no longer in use. The C# runtime normally calls destructors just before checking to see whether there is any available memory that can be freed or released (a concept called "garbage collection"). If the C# runtime does not do any of this memory checking between the time the object is no longer used and the time the program ends, the destructor will never happen. It is possible to force garbage collection to happen; however, it makes more sense to just limit your use of destructors.

### Using a Destructor

A C# destructor is defined by using a tilde (~) followed by the class name and empty parentheses. For example, the destructor for an `xyz` class is

```
~xyz()
{
   // Destructor body
}
```

There are no modifiers or other keywords to be added to a destructor. Listing 7.10 presents a simpler version of Listing 7.8 with a destructor added.

**LISTING 7.10** destr.cs—Using a Destructor

```
//  destr.cs - constructors
//--------------------------------------------------------------------

using System;

public class test
{
   static public int sctr = 0;
   public int ctr = 0;

   public void routine()
   {
      Console.WriteLine("In the routine - ctr = {0} / sctr = {1}",
                          ctr, sctr);
   }

   public test()
   {
      ctr++;
      sctr++;
      Console.WriteLine("In Constructor");
   }

   ~test()
   {
      Console.WriteLine("In Destructor");
   }
}

class TestApp
{
  public static void Main()
  {
     Console.WriteLine("Start of Main method");

     test first = new test();
     test second = new test();

     first.routine();

     test third = new test();
     third.routine();

     second.routine();           // calling second routine last

     Console.WriteLine("End of Main method");
  }
}
```

**OUTPUT**

```
Start of Main method
In Constructor
In Constructor
In the routine - ctr = 1 / sctr = 2
In Constructor
In the routine - ctr = 1 / sctr = 3
In the routine - ctr = 1 / sctr = 3
End of Main method
In Destructor
In Destructor
In Destructor
```

**ANALYSIS** The destructor is called in the output after the final destruction of each of the objects. In this case, it happened after the `Main()` method ended; however, there is a chance that this destruction could have never happened.

> **Note**
>
> It is worth repeating—destructors are not guaranteed to happen. You may find that they don't execute when you run Listing 7.10.

### Destructors and Finalization

Destructors are often called "finalizers" because of something that happens internally. A destructor is related to a method called `Finalize`. The compiler converts your constructor into the correct code for this finalization.

## Summary

Today's lessons covered only a few topics; however, these topics were critical to your ability to program in C# and to program an object-oriented language. Yesterday you learned to add data members to your own classes. Today you learned how to add functionality in the form of methods to your classes. You learned that methods, functions, and routines are different terms that ultimately refer to the same thing.

After learning the basics of methods, you reviewed the difference between "by value" and "by reference." You learned how to pass information as arguments to the parameters specified in a method's header. You learned that by using keywords, such as `ref` and `out`, you can change the way the method treats the data passed.

Finally you learned about a few special types of methods, including constructors and destructors.

After the week in review, you will find tomorrow's lesson. In Day 8, "Advanced Data Storage: Structures, Enumerators, and Arrays," you will expand on what you've learned about methods today. You will explore overloading, delegates, and a number of other more advanced features of methods.

# Q&A

**Q What is the difference between a parameter and an argument?**

**A** A parameter is a definition of what is going to be sent into a method. A parameter occurs with the definition of a method in the method head. An argument is a value that is passed to a method. You will pass arguments to a method that match the parameters that were set in the method definition.

**Q Can you create a method outside a class?**

**A** Although in other languages you can create methods that are outside a class, in C# you cannot. C# is object-oriented, so all code must be within the framework of a class.

**Q Do methods and classes in C# operate the same way that they do for other languages, such as C++ and Java?**

**A** For the most part, methods and classes operate similarly. There are differences, however, between each language. It is beyond the scope of today's lesson to detail this here. As an example of a difference, C# does not allow defaulted parameters within a method. In languages such as C++, you can have a variable within a method default to a specified value if the calling method doesn't supply it This is not the case with C#. There are other differences as well.

**Q If I'm not suppose to count on destructors, how can I do cleanup code?**

**A** It is recommended that you create your own methods to do cleanup code and that you explicitly call these when you know you are done with an object. For example, if you have a class that creates a file object, you will want to close the file when you are done with it. Because a destructor might not be called, or it might not get called for a very long time, you should create your own closing method. You really wouldn't want to leave the file sitting open longer than you need to.

# Workshop

The Workshop provides quiz questions to help you solidify your understanding of the material covered and exercises to provide you with experience in using what you've learned. Try to understand the quiz and exercise answers before continuing to the next day's lesson. Answers are provided in Appendix A, "Answers."

## Quiz

1. What are the two key parts of a method?
2. What is the difference between a function and a method?
3. How many values can be returned from a method?
4. What keyword returns a value from a method?
5. What data types can be returned from a method?
6. What is the format of accessing a member method of a class? For example, if an object called `myObject` is instantiated from a class called `myClass`, which contains a method called `myMethod`, which of the following are correct for accessing the method?
   a. `myClass.myMethod`
   b. `myObject.myMethod`
   c. `myMethod`
   d. `myClass.myObject.myMethod`
7. What is the difference between passing a variable by reference versus passing a variable by value?
8. When is a constructor called?
9. What is the syntax for a destructor that has no parameters?
10. When is a destructor called?

## Exercises

1. Write the method header for a public method called `xyz`. This method will take no arguments and will return no values.
2. Write the method header for a method called `myMethod`. This method will take three arguments as its parameters. The first will be a `double` passed by value called `myVal`. The second will be an output variable called `myOutput`, and the third will be an integer passed by reference called `myReference`. The method will be publicly accessible and will return a byte value.
3. Using the circle class that you saw in Listing 7.1, add a constructor that defaults the center point to `(5, 5)` and the radius to `1`. Use this class in a program that prints with both the defaulted values and prints after you have set values. Instead of printing the circle information from the `Main()` method, create a method to print the circle information.

4. **BUG BUSTER:** The following code snippet has a problem. Which lines generate error messages?

```
public void myMethod()
{
    System.Console.WriteLine("I'm a little teapot short and stout");
    System.Console.WriteLine("Down came the rain and washed the spider
out");

    return 0;
}
```

5. Using the dice class you saw on previous days, create a new program. In this program, create a dice class that has three data members. These should be the number of sides of the dice, the value of the dice, and a `static` data member that contains the random number class (defined as `rnd` in previous examples). Declare a member method for this class called `roll()` that returns the next random value of the die.

# WEEK 1

# In Review

Congratulations! You have finished your first week of learning C#. During this week, you built the foundation for all the C# applications you will build. You learned how to store basic data, control the flow of the program, repeat pieces of code, and create classes that can store both data and methods—and you've learned a lot more.

Most of the listings and programs you have seen focus on only a single concept. The following code pulls together into a single listing the things you learned this past week. As you can see, when you pull it all together, the listing gets a bit longer.

When you execute this listing, you will be presented with a menu on the console from which you can make a selection. This selection is then used to create a class and execute some code.

> **Note**
>
> This listing doesn't use anything you haven't learned already. Over the next two weeks, you will learn ways to improve this listing. Such improvements will include better ways of performing some of the functionality, other ways to retrieve and convert data from the users, and much more.

## The WR01.cs Program

Enter, compile, and execute the WR01.cs listing. XML comments have been added to the listing. This means that you can produce XML documentation by including the /doc compiler switch that you learned about on Day 2.

**Note**

Although I believe the best way to learn is by typing a listing and making mistakes, the source code for the listings in this book are available on the publisher's Web site if you'd prefer to download them.

**LISTING WR1.1** WR01.cs—Week One in Review

```
        //  File:  wr01.cs
        //  Desc:  Week One In Review
        //         This program presents a menu and lets the user select a c
        //         a choice. Based on this choice, the program then executes
        //         a set of code that either manipulates a shape or exits the
CH. 2   //         program
        //-------------------------------------------------------------------

CH. 6   using System;

CH. 7   class WR01App
        {
           /// <summary>
CH. 2      /// Main() routine that starts the application
           /// </summary>
           public static void Main()
           {
CH. 3         int menuChoice = 99;

CH. 5         do
              {
CH. 7            menuChoice = GetMenuChoice();

                 switch( menuChoice )
                 {
                    case 0:  break;
                    case 1:  WorkWithLine();
                             break;
CH. 5               case 2:  WorkWithCircle();
                             break;
                    case 3:  WorkWithSquare();
                             break;
                    case 4:  WorkWithTriangle();
                             break;
                    default: Console.WriteLine("\n\nError... Invalid menu
➥option.");
                             break;
```

**LISTING WR1.1** continued

```
               }

CH. 4          if ( menuChoice !=0 )
               {
CH. 7             Console.Write("\nPress <ENTER> to continue...");
                  Console.ReadLine();
               }

CH. 5        } while ( menuChoice != 0 );
          }

          /// <summary>
          /// Displays a menu of choices.
CH. 2     /// </summary>
CH. 7     static void DisplayMenu()
          {
             Console.WriteLine("\n          Menu");
             Console.WriteLine("===========================\n");
             Console.WriteLine(" A - Working with Lines");
             Console.WriteLine(" B - Working with Circles");
             Console.WriteLine(" C - Working with Squares");
             Console.WriteLine(" D - Working with Triangles");
             Console.WriteLine(" Q - Quit\n");
             Console.WriteLine("===========================\n");
          }

CH. 2     /// <summary>
          /// Gets a choice from the user and verifies that it is valid.
          /// Returns a numeric value to indicate which selection was made.
          /// </summary>
CH. 7     static int GetMenuChoice()
          {
CH. 3        int  option = 0;
             bool cont = true;
             string buf;

CH. 5        while( cont == true )
             {
CH. 7           DisplayMenu();
                Console.Write(" Enter Choice: ");
                buf = Console.ReadLine();
CH. 2
                switch( buf )
                {
CH. 5              case "a":
                   case "A":   option = 1;
                               cont = false;
                               break;
```

**LISTING WR1.1** continued

```
             case "b":
             case "B":  option = 2;
                        cont = false;
                        break;
             case "c":
             case "C":  option = 3;
                        cont = false;
                        break;
             case "d":
             case "D":  option = 4;
                        cont = false;
                        break;
             case "q":
             case "Q":  option = 0;
                        cont = false;
                        break;

             default:   Console.WriteLine("\n\n--> {0} is not valid <--
➥\n\n", buf);
                        break;
          }
       }
Ch. 7  return option;
    }

Ch. 2  /// <summary>
    /// Method to perform code for Working with Line.
    /// </summary>
Ch. 7  static void WorkWithLine()
    {
Ch. 6  line myLine = new line();
Ch. 2
Ch. 6  myLine.start.x = 0;
       myLine.start.y = 0;
       myLine.end.x = 3;
       myLine.end.y = 3;

Ch. 7  myLine.DisplayInfo();
    }

Ch. 2  /// <summary>
    /// Method to perform code for Working with Circles.
    /// </summary>
Ch. 7  static void WorkWithCircle()
    {
Ch. 6  circle myCircle = new circle();

Ch. 2  myCircle.center.x = 1;
```

**LISTING WR1.1** continued

```
CH. 6         myCircle.center.y = 1;
CH. 2         myCircle.radius = 10;

CH. 7         myCircle.DisplayInfo();
          }

CH. 2     /// <summary>
          /// Method to perform code for Working with Squares.
          /// </summary>
CH. 7     static void WorkWithSquare()
          {
CH. 6         square mySquare = new square();

              mySquare.width.start.x = 1;
              mySquare.width.end.x = 10;
              mySquare.width.start.y = 0;
              mySquare.width.end.y = 0;
              mySquare.height.start.y = 2;
              mySquare.height.end.y = 8;
              mySquare.height.start.x = 0;
              mySquare.height.end.x = 0;
CH. 7
              mySquare.DisplayInfo();
          }

CH. 2     /// <summary>
          /// Method to perform code for Working with Triangles.
          /// </summary>
CH. 7     static void WorkWithTriangle()
          {
              Console.WriteLine("\n\nDo Triangle Stuff\n\n");
CH. 2         // This section left for you to do
          }
      }

      //---------------------------------------------------------------
      /// <summary>
      /// This is a point class. It is for storing and
      /// working with an (x,y) value.
      /// </summary>
CH. 6 class point
      {
          private int point_x;
          private int point_y;

          public int x {
              get { return point_x; }
              set { if ( value < 0 )
```

**LISTING WR1.1** continued

```
                 point_x = 0;
             else
                 point_x = value;  }
   }
   public int y {
       get { return point_y; }
       set { if ( value < 0 )
                 point_y = 0;
             else
                 point_y = value;  }
   }

   public point()
   {
CH. 3 x = 0;
      y = 0;
   }
}

CH. 2 //-----------------------------------------------------------
/// <summary>
/// This class encapsulates line functionality
/// <see>point</see>
/// </summary>
CH. 6 class line
{
   private point lineStart;
   private point lineEnd;

   public point start {
       get { return lineStart; }
       set { if ( value.x < 0 )
                 lineStart.x = 0;
CH. 5        else
                 lineStart.x = value.x;
             if ( value.y < 0 )
                 lineStart.y = 0;
CH. 5        else
CH. 6            lineStart.y = value.y;
           }
   }
   public point end {
       get { return lineEnd; }
       set { if ( value.x < 0 )
                 lineEnd.x = 0;
             else
                 lineEnd.x = value.x;
             if ( value.y < 0 )
```

**LISTING WR1.1** continued

```
                lineEnd.y = 0;
            else
                lineEnd.y = value.y;
        }
    }

    public double length()
    {
        int x_diff;
        int y_diff;
        double length;

        x_diff = end.x - start.x;
        y_diff = end.y - start.y;

        length = (double) Math.Sqrt((x_diff * x_diff) + (y_diff * y_diff));
        return (length);
    }

    public void DisplayInfo()
    {
        Console.WriteLine("\n\n---------------------------");
        Console.WriteLine("       Line stats:");
        Console.WriteLine("---------------------------");
        Console.WriteLine(" Length:        {0:f3}", length());
        Console.WriteLine(" Start Point: ({0},{1})", start.x, start.y);
        Console.WriteLine(" End Point:   ({0},{1})", end.x, end.y);
        Console.WriteLine("---------------------------\n");
    }

    public line()
    {
        lineStart = new point();
        lineEnd = new point();
    }
}

//----------------------------------------------------------------
/// <summary>
/// This class encapsulates square functionality
/// <see>line</see>
/// </summary>
class square
{
    private line squareHeight;
    private line squareWidth;

    public line height {
```

**LISTING WR1.1** continued

```
              get { return squareHeight; }
              set {  squareHeight.start.y = value.start.y;
                     squareHeight.end.y = value.end.y;
                  }
          }
          public line width {
              get { return squareWidth; }
              set {  squareWidth.start.x = value.start.x;
                     squareWidth.end.x = value.end.x;
                  }
          }

CH. 7     public double area()
          {
CH. 3         double total;

CH. 7         total = (width.length() * height.length());
              return (total);
          }

          public double border()
          {
CH. 3         double total;

              total = ((2 * width.length()) + (2 * (height.length())));
CH. 7         return (total);
          }

          public void DisplayInfo()
          {
               Console.WriteLine("\n\n--------------------------");
               Console.WriteLine("     Square stats:");
               Console.WriteLine("--------------------------");
               Console.WriteLine(" Area:         {0:f3}", area());
               Console.WriteLine(" Border:       {0:f3}", border());
               Console.WriteLine(" WIDTH Points: ({0},{1}) to ({2},{3})",
                                     width.start.x, width.start.y, width.end.x,
➥width.end.y);
               Console.WriteLine("       Length: {0:f3}", width.length());
               Console.WriteLine(" HEIGHT Points: ({0},{1}) to ({2},{3})",
                                     height.start.x, height.start.y,
➥height.end.x, height.end.y);
               Console.WriteLine("       Length: {0:f3}", height.length());

               Console.WriteLine("--------------------------\n");
          }

          public square()
```

**LISTING WR1.1** continued

```
            {
CH. 6           squareHeight = new line();
                squareWidth = new line();

                width.start.x = 0;
                width.start.x = 0;
                width.end.x = 0;
                width.end.y = 0;
                height.start.x = 0;
                height.start.y = 0;
                height.end.x = 0;
                height.end.y = 0;
            }
        }

CH. 2   //-------------------------------------------------------------
        /// <summary>
        /// This class encapsulates circle functionality
        /// <see>line</see>
        /// </summary>
CH. 6   class circle
        {
           private point circleCenter;
           private long circleRadius;

           public point center {
               get { return circleCenter; }
               set {  circleCenter.x = value.x;
                      circleCenter.y = value.y;
                   }
           }
           public long radius {
               get { return circleRadius; }
               set {  circleRadius = value; }
           }

CH. 7      public double area()
           {
               double total;

CH. 4          total = 3.14159 * radius * radius;
               return (total);
CH. 7      }

           public double circumference()
           {
CH. 3          double total;

```

**LISTING WR1.1** continued

```
CH. 4              total = 2 * 3.14159 * radius;
CH. 7              return (total);
              }

              public void DisplayInfo()
              {
                   Console.WriteLine("\n\n--------------------------");
                   Console.WriteLine("      Circle stats:");
                   Console.WriteLine("--------------------------");
                   Console.WriteLine(" Area:           {0:f3}", area());
                   Console.WriteLine(" Circumference: {0:f3}", circumference());
                   Console.WriteLine(" Center Points: ({0},{1})", center.x,
➥center.y);
                   Console.WriteLine(" Radius:         {0:f3}", radius);
                   Console.WriteLine("---------- ---------------\n");
              }

CH. 6         public circle()
CH. 6         {
                   circleCenter = new point();

                   center.x = 0;
                   center.y = 0;
                   radius = 0;
              }
         }
CH. 2    //---------------------- End of Listing ----------------------
```

When you execute this program, you are presented with the following:

**OUTPUT**

```
                 Menu
===========================

     A - Working with Lines
     B - Working with Circles
     C - Working with Squares
     D - Working with Triangles
     Q - Quit

===========================

     Enter Choice:
```

If you enter something other than the letters in the menu, then you get the following message:

OUTPUT

```
              Menu
==========================

  A - Working with Lines
  B - Working with Circles
  C - Working with Squares
  D - Working with Triangles
  Q - Quit
==========================

  Enter Choice: g


 --> g is not valid <--
```

The menu is then represented. Selecting one of the valid choices produces output like the following (this is the output for entering a choice of `c`):

OUTPUT

```
Enter Choice: c


 -------------------------
      Square stats:
 -------------------------
  Area:          54.000
  Border:        30.000
  WIDTH Points: (1,0) to (10,0)
        Length: 9.000
  HEIGHT Points: (0,2) to (0,8)
        Length: 6.000
 -------------------------


Press <ENTER> to continue...
```

## The XML Documentation

As stated earlier, you can produce XML documentation from this listing. The following is the content of the XML file that can be created by using the `/doc` compiler option:

```
<?xml version="1.0"?>
<doc>
    <assembly>
        <name>wr01</name>
    </assembly>
    <members>
        <member name="M:WR01App.Main">
            <summary>
            Main() routine that starts the application
            </summary>
```

```
        </member>
        <member name="M:WR01App.DisplayMenu">
            <summary>
            Displays a menu of choices.
            </summary>
        </member>
        <member name="M:WR01App.GetMenuChoice">
            <summary>
            Gets a choice from the user and verifies that it is valid.
            Returns a numeric value to indicate which selection was made.
            </summary>
        </member>
        <member name="M:WR01App.WorkWithLine">
            <summary>
            Method to perform code for Working with Line.
            </summary>
        </member>
        <member name="M:WR01App.WorkWithCircle">
            <summary>
            Method to perform code for Working with Circles.
            </summary>
        </member>
        <member name="M:WR01App.WorkWithSquare">
            <summary>
            Method to perform code for Working with Squares.
            </summary>
        </member>
        <member name="M:WR01App.WorkWithTriangle">
            <summary>
            Method to perform code for Working with Triangles.
            </summary>
        </member>
        <member name="T:point">
            <summary>
            This is a point class. It is for storing and
            working with an (x,y) value.
            </summary>
        </member>
        <member name="T:line">
            <summary>
            This class encapsulates line functionality
            <see>point</see>
            </summary>
        </member>
        <member name="T:square">
            <summary>
            This class encapsulates square functionality
            <see>line</see>
            </summary>
        </member>
```

```
            <member name="T:circle">
                <summary>
                This class encapsulates circle functionality
                <see>line</see>
                </summary>
            </member>
        </members>
    </doc>
```

## The Code at 50,000 Feet

**ANALYSIS** Now that you've seen some of the output and the XML documentation that can be created, it's time to look at some of the code.

At a 50,000-foot view, there are a few things to notice about this listing. First, line 9 includes the one namespace in this listing, `System`. As you learned on Day 6, "Classes," this means you don't have to type `System` when using items from the `System` namespace. This includes items such as the `Console` methods. You should also notice that there are five classes declared:

- `WR01App` class in lines 11 to 165
- `point` class in lines 172 to 197
- `line` class in lines 204 to 262
- `square` class in lines 270 to 335
- `circle` class in lines 342 to 394

The `line`, `square`, and `circle` classes are similar. The `point` class is used to help organize the other classes.

> **Note** You'll find in the next week that there is a better way to declare a point than by using a class—using the `struct` keyword.

## The `Main` Method

Looking closer at the listing, you see that the program flow will start in line 16 where the `Main` method is declared within the `WR01App` class. This method uses a `do...while` statement to continue processing a menu until the appropriate selection is made. The menu is displayed by calling another method, `GetMenuChoice`. Depending on the value returned from this function, one of a number of different routines will be executed. A `switch` statement in lines 24 to 37 is used to direct program flow to the correct statements.

In lines 39 to 43, an `if` statement is used to check the value of the menu choice. If `menuChoice` is `0`, the user chose to exit the program. If it was any other value, information was displayed on the screen. To pause the program before redisplaying the menu, lines 41 and 42 were added. Line 41 provides a message to the user saying to press the `<ENTER>` key to continue. Line 42 uses the `Console.ReadLine` method to wait for the `<ENTER>` key to be pressed. If the user entered any text before pressing the key, this listing ignores it. When the user continues, the `while` statement's condition is checked. If `menuChoice` is `0`, the `while` ends, as does the method and thus the program. If `menuChoice` is not `0`, the `do` statement loops, causing the menu to be redisplayed and the process to continue.

Looking in the `switch` statement, you see that each of the first four cases executes a method that is presented later in the `WR01App` class. If the `menuChoice` is not a value from 1 to 4, the `default` statement in the `switch` (line 35) is executed, thus printing an error.

## The `GetMenuChoice` Method

Stepping back, line 22 called `GetMenuChoice`. This method is in lines 67 to 107; it displays the menu and gets the choice from the user. In line 75, another method is called to do the actual display of the menu. After displaying the menu, line 77 uses the `Console.ReadLine` method to get the choice from the user and place it in the string variable, `buf`.

A `switch` statement then converts this choice to a numeric value that will be passed back to the calling method. This conversion is not absolutely necessary. This method has the purpose of getting the menu choice. You'll notice that there are two correct selections for each menu option. This `switch` statement takes each of these and converts it to a single correct option. There are a number of different ways you could have done this. Additionally, you could have chosen to return the character value rather then a numeric value. The lesson to learn here is that the functionality for obtaining a menu choice can be placed in its own method. By placing it in its own method, you can get the selection any way you want as long as you return a consistent set of final selection values. You could swap this method with another that returns a value from 0 to 4 and the rest of your code would work exactly the same.

## The Main Menu Options

Each of the four main menu options calls a method. Lines 112 to 122 contain the `WorkWithLine` method. This method declares an object, sets the initial values, and finally calls a method in the declared object that displays the information about the object. The `WorkWithSquare` and `WorkWithCircle` methods work the same way. The `WorkWithTriangle` was not filled coded. Rather, it was left for you to fill.

## The `point` Class

The `point` class is defined in lines 172 to 197. The `point` class contains two `private` data members, `START` and `END`. Because these data members are `private`, they cannot be accessed by any code outside of the `point` class. In lines 177 to 190, properties are declared with the `get` and `set` keywords. These provide access points for the user to get to the `point` data.

In line 192, the constructor for the `point` class is defined. This constructor sets the data values to `0`; this uses the properties to initialize the values.

If you want to change the way the `point` values are stored, you can change the properties. You won't need to change the methods!

## The `line` Class

The `line` class is similar to the `point` class. In lines 206 and 207, the data members are declared. In this case, the data members are `point` objects. The constructor in lines 258 to 263 instantiates the two `point` objects for this class. Note that default values are not set in this constructor. They don't need to be. When each of the `point` classes is instantiated, their constructors will set default values.

The `line` class also contains other methods that can be called. The coding in these methods is straightforward.

## The Other Classes

The rest of the classes in this program are similar to the `line` class. You can review their code on your own.

**Note**

> You should understand the code in this listing. If there is an area that you don't understand, you should go back and review the appropriate day's lesson. On future days, you will learn how to improve upon this listing

# WEEK 2

# At a Glance

You have completed your first week and only have two to go. In this, your second week, you are going to learn most of the remaining core topics to C#—not all of them, but most of them. By the end of this week, you will have the tools to build basic C# applications from scratch.

Day 8, "Advanced Data Storage, Structures, Enumerators, and Arrays" will teach you some alternative storage methods. This will include coverage of structures, which you will learn are similar to classes as well as enumerators and arrays.

On Day 9, "Advanced Method Access," you will expand on what you learned on Days 7 and 8. You will learn how to overload methods and how to use a variable number of parameters on a method. You will also learn about scope, which will allow you to limit access to your data and other type members. You'll discover the `static` keyword and you will learn how to create a class that cannot be used to create an object.

Creating programs that don't blow up on the user is important. On Day 10,"Handling Exceptions," you learn to add exception handling to your programs. Exception handling is a structured approach to catching and stopping problems before they cause your programs to go boom.

One of the key object-oriented features is inheritance. On Day 11, "Inheritance," you discover how to use inheritance with the classes you've created (or with someone else's classes). On this day you will learn several new keywords including `sealed`, `is`, and `as`.

Day 12, "Formatting and Retrieving Information," steps back from the super techie stuff and gives you a reprieve. On this day you will focus on presenting information and retrieving information to and from the console. You will learn how to format the data so that it is much more usable. This chapter will contain a number of tables that you will want to refer back to.

Day 13, "Interfaces," is another core topic for understanding the power of C#. This chapter expands on what you know about classes and structures as well as inheritance. On this day you will learn how to combine multiple features into a single new class using interfaces.

Finally the week ends with a single day focusing on three interesting topics. Day 14, "Indexers, Delegates, and Events," focus on exactly what its title states—indexers, delegates, and events. You will learn how to use index notation with a class' data. You also learn about delegates and events, which allow you to dynamically execute method as well as do event programming. Events will be key to your programming Windows-type applications.

By the end of this second week, you will have learned many of the core concepts for C# programming. You'll find that by the time you have completed this second week that you will understand most of the core concepts of most C# programs—not all, but most.

# WEEK 2

# DAY 8

# Advanced Data Storage: Structures, Enumerators, and Arrays

You've learned about the basic data types and you've learned about classes. C# also offers several other ways of storing information in your programs. In today's lesson, you learn about several of these alternative storage methods, including structures, enumerators, and arrays. More specifically, today you

- Learn how to store values in structures
- Discover how structures are similar, and different, from classes
- Understand what an enumerator is and how it can be used to make your programs easier to understand
- See how to declare and use arrays to hold lots of values of the same data type
- Work with the `foreach` keyword to manipulate arrays

# Structures

Structures are a data type provided by C# that are similar to classes. Like classes, structures can contain both data and method definitions. Also like a class, a structure can contain constructors, constants, fields, methods, properties, indexers, operators, and nested types.

## Structures Versus Classes

Although there are a lot of similarities between classes and structures, there is one primary difference and a few minor differences. The primary difference between a structure and a class is centered on how a structure is stored and accessed. A structure is a value data type, and a class is a reference data type.

Although the difference between value and reference data types has been covered before, it is worth covering several more times to ensure that you fully understand the difference. A value data type stores the actual values at the location identified by the data type's name. A reference data type actually stores a location that points to where the information is stored. Figure 8.1 is a repeat of the figure you saw on Day 7, "Class Methods and Member Functions." This figure illustrates the difference between value and reference data type storage.

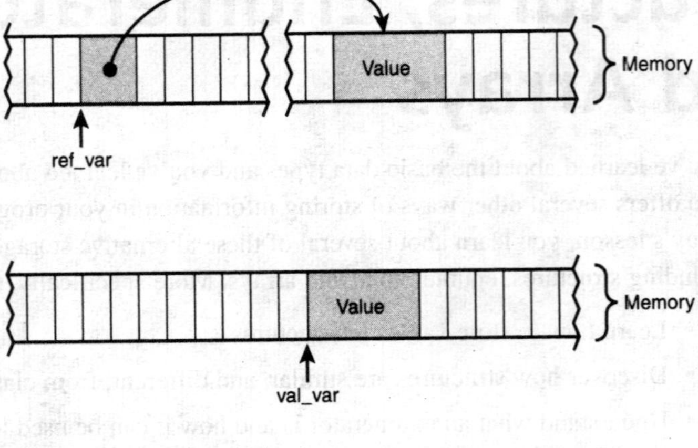


**FIGURE 8.1**
*Storage by reference versus by value.*

As you can see from Figure 8.1, a reference variable is actually more complicated to store than a value variable. The compiler, however, takes care of this complexity for you. Although there are benefits to storing information by reference, it results in extra overhead in memory. If you are storing small amounts of information, the extra overhead can actually outweigh the amount of information being stored.

A structure is stored by value. The overhead of reference is not included, so it is preferred when dealing with small amounts of data or small data values.

When dealing with large amounts of data, a reference type such as a class is a better storage method. This is especially true when passing the data to a method. A reference variable passes only the reference and not the entire data value. A value variable such as a structure is copied and passed to the method. Such copying can cause fat, slower programs if the structures are large.

A general rule of thumb is that if you need to decide between a class and a structure and the total size of the data members being stored is 16 bytes or less, use a structure. If it is greater than 16 bytes, consider how you are going to use the data.

## Structure Members

Declaring members in a structure is identical to declaring data members in a class. Following is a structure for storing a point:

```
struct point
{
   public int x;
   public int y;
}
```

This is similar to the class you've seen on previous days. The only real difference is that the `struct` keyword is used instead of the `class` keyword. You can also use this in a listing as you would use a class. Listing 8.1 uses this `point` structure.

**LISTING 8.1** point.cs—Using a Point Structure

```
//  point.cs- A structure with two data members
//-----------------------------------------------------------------

struct point
{
    public int x;
    public int y;
}

class pointApp
{
   public static void Main()
   {
      point starting = new point();
      point ending = new point();

      starting.x = 1;
```

**LISTING 8.1** continued

```
18:         starting.y = 4;
19:         ending.x = 10;
20:         ending.y = 11;
21:
22:         System.Console.WriteLine("Point 1: ({0},{1})",
23:                                  starting.x, starting.y);
24:         System.Console.WriteLine("Point 2: ({0},{1})",
25:                                  ending.x, ending.y);
26:     }
27: }
```

**OUTPUT**

```
Point 1: (1,4)
Point 2: (10,11)
```

**ANALYSIS** The primary difference between using the `point` structure and a class is the use of the `struct` keyword when defining the class (line 4). You could, in fact, replace the `struct` keyword with the `class` keyword and the listing would still work. As stated earlier, the biggest difference between using a structure and a class is how they are stored in memory. Figure 8.2 illustrates how a starting `point` object from a class could be placed in memory versus how an instance of the starting `point` structure could be stored.

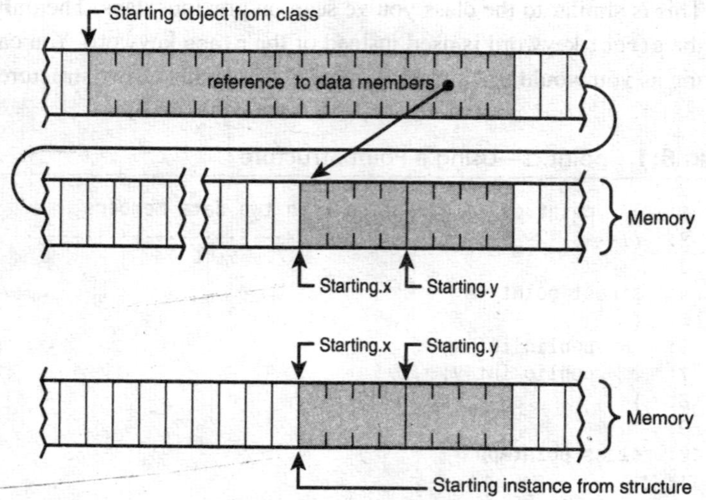


**FIGURE 8.2**
*Storing a starting point structure and class in memory.*

You can also see that members of a structure are accessed in the same manner that members of a class are accessed. This is by using the name of the structure instance, followed by the member operator (a period), followed by the name of the data member. For example, line 17 accesses the `x` data member of the `starting` instance of the `point` structure.

Declaring an instance from a structure can be simpler. Declaring instances from structures does not require that you use the new keyword, which means that lines 14 and 15 could be replaced with the following:

```
14:         point starting;
15:         point ending;
```

You should make this change and recompile Listing 8.1. You will see that the listing still compiles and works. If you replace the `struct` keyword with the `class` keyword in this modified version of the listing, the result is an error when you compile:

```
point.cs(17,7): error CS0165: Use of unassigned local variable 'starting'
point.cs(19,7): error CS0165: Use of unassigned local variable 'ending'
```

## Nesting Structures

Like classes, structures can contain any other data type, which includes other structures. Listing 8.2 illustrates a `line` structure that contains two `point` structures.

**LISTING 8.2** line.cs—A Line Structure

```
// line.cs- A line structure which contains point structures.
//--------------------------------------------------------------------

struct point
{
    public int x;
    public int y;
}

struct line
{
    public point starting;
    public point ending;
}

class lineApp
{
  public static void Main()
  {
     line myLine;

     myLine.starting.x = 1;
     myLine.starting.y = 4;
     myLine.ending.x = 10;
     myLine.ending.y = 11;

     System.Console.WriteLine("Point 1: ({0},{1})",
                              myLine.starting.x, myLine.starting.y);
```

**LISTING 8.2** continued

```
29:             System.Console.WriteLine("Point 2: ({0},{1})",
30:                                       myLine.ending.x, myLine.ending.y);
31:      }
32:  }
```

**OUTPUT**

```
Point 1: (1,4)
Point 2: (10,11)
```

**ANALYSIS** The `line` structure is set up similarly to the way the `line` class was set up on a previous day. The big difference is that when a line is instantiated, memory is allocated and directly stored.

In this listing, the `point` structure is declared in lines 4 to 8. In lines 10 to 14, a `line` structure is declared. Lines 12 and 13 contain `point` structures that are publicly accessible. Each of these has its own `x` and `y` point values.

Lines 22 to 25 set the individual values in the `line` structure. To access a value within a nested structure, you follow through the structure hierarchy. Member operators (periods) separate each step in the structure's hierarchy. In the case of line 22, you are accessing the `x` data member of the `starting` point structure in the `myLine` line structure. Figure 8.3 illustrates the line hierarchy.

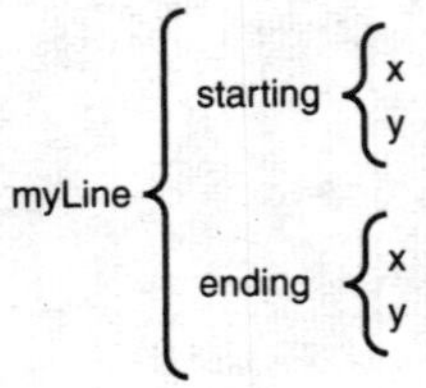


**FIGURE 8.3**
*The hierarchy of the line structure.*

## Structure Methods

Like classes, structures can also contain methods and properties. Methods and properties are declared exactly the same as classes. This includes using the modifiers and attributes you'd use with classes. You can overload these methods, pass values, and return values. Listing 8.3 presents the `line` class with a `length` method.

**LISTING 8.3** Line2.cs—Adding Methods to Structures

```
//  line2.cs - Adding methods to a structure.
//-----------------------------------------------------------------

struct point
```

**LISTING 8.3** continued

```
{
    public int x;
    public int y;
}

struct line
{
    public point starting;
    public point ending;

    public double length()
    {
        double len = 0;
        len = System.Math.Sqrt( (ending.x - starting.x)*(ending.x - start-
➥ing.x) +
                                (ending.y - starting.y)*(ending.y - start-
➥ing.y));
        return len;
    }
}

class lineApp
{
   public static void Main()
   {
      line myLine;

      myLine.starting.x = 1;
      myLine.starting.y = 4;
      myLine.ending.x = 10;
      myLine.ending.y = 11;

      System.Console.WriteLine("Point 1: ({0},{1})",
                          myLine.starting.x, myLine.starting.y);
      System.Console.WriteLine("Point 2: ({0},{1})",
                          myLine.ending.x, myLine.ending.y);
      System.Console.WriteLine("Length of line from Point 1 to Point 2:
➥{0}",
                          myLine.length());
   }
}
```

**OUTPUT**

```
Point 1: (1,4)
Point 2: (10,11)
Length of line from Point 1 to Point 2: 11.4017542509914
```

**ANALYSIS** Listing 8.3 adds the same `length` method you have seen in listings on prior days. This method is declared in lines 15 to 21 within the `line` structure. As was done previously, this structure uses the data members of the `line` class to calculate the length of the line. This value is placed in the `len` variable and returned from the method in line 20 as a `double` value.

The `length` method is used in the `lineApp` class. Its value is output using the `Console.WriteLine` method in lines 39 and 40.

Although the `line` class has only a single method, you could have created a number of methods and properties for the `line` structure. You could also have overloaded these methods.

## Structure Constructors

In addition to having regular methods, structures can also have constructors. Unlike classes, if you decide to declare a constructor, you must include declarations with parameters. You cannot declare a constructor for a structure that has no parameters. Listing 8.4 includes the `point` structure with a constructor added.

**LISTING 8.4** point2.cs—A Point Class with a Constructor

```
//  point2.cs- A structure with two data members
//-----------------------------------------------------------------

struct point
{
    public int x;
    public int y;

    public point(int x, int y)
    {
       this.x = x;
       this.y = y;
    }
//    public point()
//    {
//       this.x = 0;
//       this.y = 0;
//    }
}

class pointApp
{
   public static void Main()
   {
      point point1 = new point();
```

**LISTING 8.4** continued

```
26:         point point2 = new point(8, 8);
27:
28:         point1.x = 1;
29:         point1.y = 4;
30:
31:         System.Console.WriteLine("Point 1: ({0},{1})",
32:                                  point1.x, point1.y);
33:         System.Console.WriteLine("Point 2: ({0},{1})",
34:                                  point2.x, point2.y);
35:     }
36: }
```

**OUTPUT**

```
Point 1: (1,4)
Point 2: (8,8)
```

**ANALYSIS** A difference between structures and classes is that a structure cannot declare a constructor with no parameters. In Listing 8.4, you can see that such a constructor has been included in lines 14 to 18; however, it has been excluded with comments. If you remove the single-line comments on these lines and compile, you get the following error:

```
point2.cs(14,12): error CS0568: Structs cannot contain explicit parameterless
    constructors
```

Constructors with parameters can be declared. Lines 9 to 13 declare a constructor that can initialize the point values. The `x` and `y` values of the class are set with the `x` and `y` values passed into the constructor. To differ the passed-in `x` and `y` values from the structure instance `x` and `y` variables, the `this` keyword is used in lines 11 and 12.

Line 25 illustrates a normal instantiation using the `point` class. You could also have instantiated the `point1` structure instance by just entering

```
point point1;
```

without the new operator and empty constructor call. Line 26 illustrates using the constructor you created with parameters.

A constructor in a structure has an obligation. It must initialize all the data members of the structure. When the default (parameterless) constructor of a structure is called, it automatically initializes each data member with its default value. Generally the data members are initialized to zeros. If your constructor is called instead of this default constructor, you take on the obligation to initialize all the data members.

**Caution**

Although you can avoid the new operator when using the default constructor, you cannot avoid it when instantiating an instance of a structure with parameters. Replacing line 26 of Listing 8.4 with the following line will give you an error:

```
point point2(8,8);
```

## Structure Destructors

Classes can have destructors. Recall that destructors are not to be relied upon in classes even though they are available for you to use. With structures, you cannot declare a destructor. Structures cannot have destructors. If you try to add one, the compiler will give you an error.

# Enumerators

Another type that can be used in C# is enumerators. Enumerators enable you to create variables that contain a limited number of values. For example, there are only seven days in a week. Rather than referring to the days of a week as one, two, three, and so on, it would be much clearer to refer to them as `Day.Monday`, `Day.Tuesday`, `Day.Wednesday`, and so on. You could also have a toggle that could be either on or off. Rather than use values such as `0` and `1`, you could use values such as `Toggle.On` and `Toggle.Off`.

An enumerator enables you to create these values. Enumerators are declared with the `enum` keyword. The format of creating an enumerator is

```
modifiers enum enumName
{
    enumMember1,
    enumMember2,
    ...
    enumMemberN
}
```

where *`modifiers`* is either the new keyword or the access modifiers (`public` and `private`, which you are familiar with, or `protected` and `internal`, which you will learn about in later days). `enumName` is a name for the enumerator that is any valid identifier name. `enumMember1`, `enumMember2` to `enumMemberN` are the members of the enumeration that contain the descriptive values.

The following declares the toggle enumerator described previously with `public` access:

```
public enum toggle
{
```

```
    On,
    Off
}
```

The `enum` keyword is used, followed by the name of the enumerator, `toggle`. This enumeration has two values, `On` and `Off`, which are separated by a comma. To use the toggle `enum`, you declare a variable of type `toggle`. For example, the following declares a `myToggle` variable:

```
toggle myToggle;
```

This variable, `myToggle`, can contain two valid values—`On` or `Off`. To use these values, you use the name of the `enum` and the name of the value, separated by the member operator (a period). For example, `myToggle` can be set to `toggle.On` or `toggle.Off`. Using a `switch` statement, you can check for these different values. Listing 8.5 illustrates the creation of an enumerator to store a number of color values.

> **Note**
>
> By default, when an enumerator variable is initially declared, it is set to the value of `0`.

**LISTING 8.5** colors.cs—Using an Enumeration

```
//  color.cs- Using an enumeration
//           Note: Entering a nonnumeric number when running this
//                 program will cause an exception to be thrown.
//-----------------------------------------------------------------

using System;

class myApp
{
    enum Color
    {
        red,
        white,
        blue
    }

    public static void Main()
    {
        string buffer;
        Color myColor;

        Console.Write("Enter a value for a color: 0 = Red, 1 = White, 2 =
➥Blue): ");
```

**LISTING 8.5** continued

```
23:         buffer = Console.ReadLine();
24:
25:         myColor = (Color) Convert.ToInt32(buffer);
26:
27:         switch( myColor )
28:         {
29:            case Color.red:
30:               System.Console.WriteLine("\nSwitched to Red...");
31:               break;
32:            case Color.white:
33:               System.Console.WriteLine("\nSwitched to White...");
34:               break;
35:            case Color.blue:
36:               System.Console.WriteLine("\nSwitched to Blue...");
37:               break;
38:            default:
39:               System.Console.WriteLine("\nSwitched to default...");
40:               break;
41:         }
42:
43:         System.Console.WriteLine("\nColor is {0} ({1})", myColor, (int)
➥myColor);
44:      }
45:   }
```

**OUTPUT**

```
Enter a value for a color: 0 = Red, 1 = White, 2 = Blue): 1

Switched to White...

Color is white (1)
```

**OUTPUT**

```
Enter a value for a color: 0 = Red, 1 = White, 2 = Blue): 5

Switched to default...

Color is 5 (5)
```

**ANALYSIS** This listing was executed twice for this output. The first time, the value of `1` was entered and recognized as being equivalent to `white`. In the second execution, the value of `5` was entered, which does not equate to any colors.

Looking closer at the listing, you can see that the `Color` enumerator was declared in lines 10 to 15. This enumerator contains three members: `red`, `white`, and `blue`. When this enumerator is created, the value of `0` is assigned to the first member (`red`), `1` is assigned to the second (`white`), and `2` is assigned to the third (`blue`). All enumerators start with `0` as the first member and are then incremented by 1 for each additional member.

In line 20, the enumerator is used to create a variable called `myColor` that can store a value from the `Color` enumerator. This variable is assigned a value in line 25. The value that is assigned is worthy of some clarification. In line 22, a prompt is displayed to the screen. In line 23, the `ReadLine` of the `Console` class is used to get a value entered by the user. Because the user can enter any value, the program is open to errors. Line 25 assumes that the value entered by the user can be converted to a standard integer. A method called `ToInt32` in the `Convert` class is used to convert the buffer that contains the value entered by the user. This is cast to a `Color` type and placed in the `myColor` variable. If a value other than a number is entered, you get an exception error by the runtime and the program ends. On Day 10, "Handling Exceptions," you will learn one way to handle this type of error gracefully so that a runtime error isn't displayed and your program can continue to operate.

Line 27 contains a `switch` statement that switches based on the value in `myColor`. In lines 29 to 35, the `case` statements in the `switch` don't contain literal numbers; they contain the values of the enumerators. The value in the `myColor` enumerator will actually match against the enumerator word values. This `switch` really serves no purpose other than to show you how to switch based on different values of an enumerator.

Line 43 is worth looking at closely. Two values are printed in this line. The first is the value of `myColor`. You might have expected the numeric value that was assigned to the variable to be printed; however, it isn't. Rather, the actual enumerator member name is printed. For the value of `1` in `myColor`, the value `white` is printed—not `1`. If you want the numeric value, you have to explicitly force the number to print. This is done in line 43 using a cast.

## Changing the Default Value of Enumerators

The default value set to an enumerator variable is `0`. Even though this is the default value assigned to an enumerator variable, an enumerator does not have to have a member that is equal to `0`. Earlier, you were told that the values of the members in an enumerator definition start at `0` and are incremented by 1. You can actually change these default values. For example, you often want to start with `1` rather than `0`.

You have two options for creating an enumerator with values that start at `1`. First, you could put a filler value in the first position of the enumerator. This is an easy option if you want the values to start at `1`; however, if you want the values of the enumerator to be larger numbers, this can be a bad option.

The second option is to set the value of your enumerator members. You can set these values with literal values, the value of other enumerator members, or calculated values. Listing 8.6 doesn't do anything complex for setting the values of an enumerator. Rather it starts the first value at 1 rather than 0. The second value (February) is incremented from the first value. This means that it is 2 regardless of whether it is explicitly set, as in this listing.

**LISTING 8.6** bday.cs—Setting the Numeric Value of Enumerator Members

```
//  bday.cs- Using an enumeration, setting default values
//-----------------------------------------------------------

using System;

public class myApp
{
    enum Month
    {
        January = 1,
        February = 2,
        March = 3,
        April = 4,
        May = 5,
        June = 6,
        July = 7,
        August = 8,
        September = 9,
        October = 10,
        November = 11,
        December = 12
    }

    struct birthday
    {
        public Month bmonth;
        public int   bday;
        public int   byear;
    }

    public static void Main()
    {
        birthday MyBirthday;

        MyBirthday.bmonth = Month.August;
        MyBirthday.bday = 11;
        MyBirthday.byear = 1981;    // This is a lie...

        System.Console.WriteLine("My birthday is {0}, {1} {2}",
              MyBirthday.bmonth, MyBirthday.bday, MyBirthday.byear);
    }
}
```

8

**OUTPUT**

```
My birthday is August, 11 1981
```

**ANALYSIS** This listing creates an enumerator type called `Month`. This enumerator type contains the 12 months of the year. Rather than using the default values, which would be from `0` to `11`, this definition forces the values to be the more expected number of `1` to `12`. Because the values would be incremented based on the prior value, it is not necessary to explicitly set `February` to `2` or any of the additional values. It is done here for clarity. You could just as easily have set these values to other numbers. You could even have set them to formulas. For example, `June` could have been set to

```
May + 1
```

Because `May` is considered equal to `5`, this sets `June` to `6`.

The `Month` enumerator type is used in line 35 to declare a `public` data member within a structure. This data member called `bmonth` is declared as a `public Month` type. In line 33, the structure, called `birthday`, is used to declare a variable called `MyBirthday`. The data members of this structure instance are then assigned values in lines 26 to 28.The `bmonth` variable is assigned the value of `Month.August`. You could also have done the following to cast `August` to the `MyBirthday.bmonth` variable; however, the program would not have been as clear:

```
MyBirthday.bmonth = (Month) 8;
```

In line 39, you again see that the value stored in `MyBirthday.bmonth` is `August` rather than a number.

## Changing the Underlying Type of an Enumerator

In the examples so far, the underlying data type of the enumerators has been type `int`. Enumerators can actually contain values of type `byte`, `sbyte`, `int`, `uint`, `short`, `ushort`, `long`, and `ulong`. If you don't specify the type, the default is type `int`. If you know you need to have larger or smaller values stored in an `enum`, you can change the default underlying type to something else.

To change the default type, you use the following format:

```
modifiers enum enumName : typeName { member(s) }
```

This is the same definition as before, with the addition of a colon and the *`typeName`*, which is any of the types mentioned previously. If you change the type, you must make sure that if you assign numeric values, they are of the valid type.

Listing 8.7 illustrates a new listing using the color enumerator shown earlier. This time, because the values are small. the enumerator is set to use bytes to save a little memory.

**LISTING 8.7** color2—Displaying Random Byte Numbers

```
//  color2.cs- Using enumerations
//----------------------------------------------------------------

using System;

class myApp
{
   enum Color : byte
   {
      red,
      white,
      blue
   }

   public static void Main()
   {
      Color myColor;
      byte  roll;

      System.Random rnd = new System.Random();

      for ( int ctr = 0; ctr < 10; ctr++ )
      {
         roll = (byte) ((rnd.NextDouble() * 3 )); // random nbr form 0 to 2
         myColor = (Color) roll;

         System.Console.WriteLine("Color is {0} ({1} of type {2})",
                                  myColor, (byte) myColor,
➥myColor.GetTypeCode());
      }
   }
}
```

**OUTPUT**

```
Color is white (1 of type Byte)
Color is white (1 of type Byte)
Color is red (0 of type Byte)
Color is white (1 of type Byte)
Color is blue (2 of type Byte)
Color is red (0 of type Byte)
Color is red (0 of type Byte)
Color is red (0 of type Byte)
Color is blue (2 of type Byte)
Color is red (0 of type Byte)
```

**Note**

Your output will vary from this because of the random generator.

**ANALYSIS** This listing does more than just declare an enumerator using a byte. You'll see this in a minute. First, look at line 8. You can see that this time the `Color` enumerator type is created using bytes instead of type `int` values. You know this because of the inclusion of the colon and `byte` keyword. This means that `Color.red` will be a byte value of `0`, `Color.white` will be a byte value of `1`, and `Color.blue` will be a byte value of `2`.

In the `Main` method, this listing's functionality is different from the earlier listing. This listing uses the random logic that you have seen before. In line 24, you can see that a `random` number from `0` to `2` is created and explicitly cast as a `byte` value into the `roll` variable. The `roll` variable was declared as a `byte` in line 18. This `roll` variable is then explicitly cast to a `Color` type in line 25 and stored in the `myColor` variable.

Line 27 starts out similarly to what you have seen before. The `WriteLine` method is used to print the value of the `myColor` variable (which results in either `red`, `white`, or `blue`. This is followed by printing the numeric value using the explicit cast to `byte`. The third value being printed, however, is something new.

Enumerators are objects, as is everything else in C#. Because of this, there are some built-in methods that can be used on enumerators. The one you will find most useful is the `GetTypeCode` method, which returns the type of the variable stored. For `myColor`, the return type is `byte`, which is displayed in the output. If you add this parameter to one of the previous two listings, you will find that it prints `Int32`. Because the type is being determined at runtime, you get a .NET framework data type rather than the C# data type.

**Tip** To determine other methods of enumerators, check out the .NET framework documentation. Look up the `Enum` class.

| Do | Don't |
|---|---|
| **DO** use commas—not semicolons—to separate enumerator members. | **DON'T** place filler values as enumerator members. |

# Using Arrays to Store Data

In addition to storing different types of related information together as you can in classes and structure, you will also have times when you will want to store multiple pieces of information that are of the same data type. For example, a bank might keep track of monthly balances, or a teacher might want to keep track of the scores from a number of tests.

If you need to keep track of a number of items that are of the same data type, the best solution is to use an array. If you want to keep track of balances for each of the 12 months, without arrays you could create 12 variables to track these numbers:

```
decimal Jan_balance;
decimal Feb_balance;
decimal Mar_balance;
decimal Apr_balance;
decimal May_balance;
decimal Jun_balance;
decimal Jul_balance;
decimal Aug_balance;
decimal Sep_balance;
decimal Oct_balance;
decimal Nov_balance;
decimal Dec_balance;
```

To use these variables, you have to determine which month it is and then switch between the correct variable. This requires several lines of code that could include a large `switch` statement, such as the following:

```
...
switch (month)
{
   case 1:  // do January stuff
            Jan_balance += new_amount;
            break;
   case 2:  // do February stuff
            Feb_balance += new_amount;
            break;
...
```

This is obviously not the complete `switch` statement; however, it is enough to see that a lot of code needs to be written to determine and switch between the 12 monthly balances. Using an array of decimals, you can make it much more efficient to keep track of monthly balances.

## Creating Arrays

An array is a single data variable that can store multiple pieces of data, each of the same data type. Each of these data elements are stored sequentially in the computer's memory, thus making it easy to manipulate and navigate among them.

**Note** Because you declare one piece of data—or variable—after the other in a code listing does not mean that they will be stored together in memory. In fact, variables can be stored in totally different parts of memory even though they are declared together. An array is a single variable with multiple elements. Because of this, an array stores its values one after the other in memory.

To declare an array, you use the square brackets after the data type when you declare the variable. The basic format of an array declaration is

```
datatype[] name;
```

where *datatype* is the data type you will store. The square brackets indicate that you are declaring an array, and the *name* is the name of the array variable. The following definition sets up an array variable called `balances` that can hold decimal values:

```
decimal[] balances;
```

This declaration creates the variable and prepares it to be able to hold decimal values; however, it doesn't actually set aside the area to hold the variables. To do that, you need to do the same thing you do to create other objects, which is to initialize the variable using the `new` keyword. When you instantiate the array, you must indicate how many values will be stored. One way to indicate this number is to include the number of elements in square brackets when you do the initialization:

```
balances = new decimal[12];
```

You also can do this initialization at the same time that you define the variable. For the `balances` variable, this is the following:

```
decimal[] balances = new decimal[12];
```

As you can see, the format is

```
new datatype[nbr_of_elements]
```

where *datatype* is the same data type of the array and *nbr_of_elements* is a numeric value that indicates the number of items to be stored in the array. In the case of the `balances` variable, you can see that `12` decimal values can be stored.

**New Term** After you've declared and initialized an array, you can begin to use it. Each item in an array is called an *element*. Each element within the array can be accessed by using an index. An *index* is a number that identifies the offset—and thus the element—within the array.

The first element of an array is identified with an index of `0`, because the first element is at the beginning of the array and therefore there is no offset. The second element is indexed as `1` because it is offset by one element. The final index is at an offset that is one less than the size of the array. For example, the `balances` array declares `12` elements. The last element of the array will have an index of `11`.

To access a specific element within an array, you use the array name followed by the appropriate index within square brackets. To assign the value of `1297.50` to the first element of the `balances` array, you do the following:

```
balances[0] = 1297.50m;
```

To assign a decimal value the third element of the `balances` array, you do the following:

```
balances[2] = 1000m;
```

The index of `2` is used to get to the third element. Listing 8.8 illustrates using the balances array; Figure 8.4 illustrates the concept of elements and indexes. This figure uses a simpler array of `3` characters, which are declared as follows:

```
char[] initials = new char[3];
```

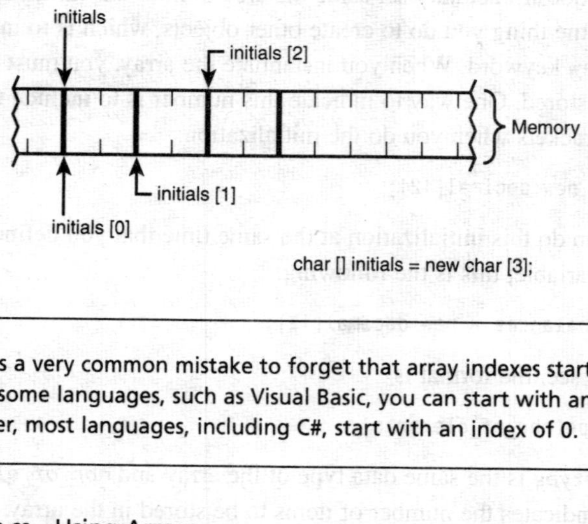


**FIGURE 8.4**
*An array in memory and its indexes.*

**Caution**

It is a very common mistake to forget that array indexes start at 0 and not 1. In some languages, such as Visual Basic, you can start with an index1; however, most languages, including C#, start with an index of 0.

**LISTING 8.8** balances.cs—Using Arrays

```
//  balances.cs - Using a basic array
//----------------------------------------------------

using System;

public class myApp
```

**LISTING 8.8** continued

```
{
   public static void Main()
   {
      decimal[] balances = new decimal[12];

      decimal ttl = 0m;
      System.Random rnd = new System.Random();

      // Put random values from 0 to 100000 into balances array

      for (int indx = 0; indx < 12; indx++ )
      {
         balances[indx] = (decimal) ((rnd.NextDouble() * 10000));
      }

      //values are initialized in balances

      for( int indx = 0; indx < 12; indx++ )
      {
         Console.WriteLine("Balance {0}: {1}", indx, balances[indx]);
         ttl += balances[indx];
      }

      Console.WriteLine("===============================");
      Console.WriteLine("Total of Balances = {0}", ttl);
      Console.WriteLine("Average Balance = {0}", (ttl/12));
   }
}
```

**OUTPUT**

```
Balance 0: 2276.50146106095
Balance 1: 4055.29556984794
Balance 2: 6192.0053633824
Balance 3: 2651.45477496621
Balance 4: 5885.39904257534
Balance 5: 2200.59107160223
Balance 6: 664.596651058922
Balance 7: 1079.63573237864
Balance 8: 2359.02580076783
Balance 9: 9690.85962031542
Balance 10: 934.673115114995
Balance 11: 7248.27192595614
===============================
Total of Balances = 45238.310129027017
Average Balance = 3771.54250645135085
```

**ANALYSIS** Listing 8.8 illustrates the use of a basic array called `balances`. In line 10, `balances` is declared as an array of decimal values. It is instantiated as a decimal array containing `12` elements. This listing creates a `Random` object called `rnd` (line 13), which is used to create random numbers to store in the array. This assignment of random numbers occurs in lines 17 to 20. Using an index counter, `indx`, this `for` loop goes from `0` to `11`. This counter is then used as the index of the array in line 19.

After the values are assigned, lines 24 to 28 loop through the array a second time. Technically, this loop is redundant; however, you generally wouldn't get your values elsewhere rather than assigning random numbers. In this second `for` loop, each of the `balances` items is written to the console (line 26). In line 27, each of the `balances` array elements is added to a total called `ttl`. Lines 31 and 32 provide some summary information regarding the random balances. Line 31 prints the total of the balances. Line 32 prints the average of each.

The `balances` array is much simpler than the code would have been if you had to use 12 different variables. When you use the indexes with the array name, such as `balance[2]`, it is like using a regular variable of the same data type.

## Initializing Array Elements with the Array

You can initialize the values of the individual array elements at the same time you declare and initialize the array. You can do this by declaring the values after the array declaration. The values are enclosed in a block and are separated by a comma. To initialize the values of the `balances` array, you do the following

```
decimal[] balances = new decimal[12] {1000.00m, 2000.00m, 3000.00m, 4000.00m,
                                      5000m, 6000m, 0m, 0m, 9m, 0m, 0m, 12000m};
```

This declaration creates the `balances` array and preassigns values into it. The first value of `1000.00` is placed into the first element, `balances[0]`. The second value, `2000.00`, is placed into the second element, `balances[1]`. The rest of the values are placed in the same manner.

It is interesting to note that if you initialize the values in this manner, you do not have to include the array size in the brackets. The following statement is equivalent to the previous statement:

```
decimal[] balances = new decimal[] {1000.00m, 2000.00m, 3000.00m, 4000.00m,
                                    5000m, 6000m, 0m, 0m, 9m, 0m, 0m, 12000m};
```

The compiler automatically defines this array as 12 elements because that is the number of items being initialized. Listing 8.9 creates and initializes a character array.

> **Note**
>
> You are not required to initialize all the values if you include the number of elements in your declaration. The following line of code is valid; the resulting array will have 12 elements with the first 2 elements being initialized to 111:
>
> ```
> decimal[] balances = new decimal[12] {111m, 111m};
> ```
>
> However, if you don't include the number of elements, you can't add more later. In the following declaration, the balances array can hold only 2 elements; it cannot hold more than 2.
>
> ```
> decimal[] balances = new decimal[] {111m, 111m};
> ```

**LISTING 8.9** fname.cs—Using Arrays

```
 1:  //  fname.cs - Initializing an array
 2:  //----------------------------------------------------
 3:
 4:  using System;
 5:
 6:  public class myApp
 7:  {
 8:     public static void Main()
 9:     {
10:           char[] name = new char[] {'B','r','a','d','l','e','y', (char) 0 };
11:
12:           Console.WriteLine("Display content of name array...");
13:
14:           int ctr = 0;
15:           while (name[ctr] != 0)
16:           {
17:              Console.Write("{0}", name[ctr]);
18:              ctr++;
19:           }
20:           Console.WriteLine("\n...Done.");
21:     }
22:  }
```

**OUTPUT**

```
Display content of name array...
Bradley
...Done.
```

**ANALYSIS** Listing 8.9 creates, initializes, and instantiates an array of characters called `name` in line 10. The `name` array is instantiated to hold `eight` elements. You know it can hold eight elements, even though this is not specifically stated, because eight items were placed into the array when it was declared.

This listing does something that you have not seen in previous listings. It puts a weird value (a character value of 0) in the last element of the array. This weird value is used to signal the end of the array. In lines 14 to 19, a counter called `ctr` is created to use as an index. The `ctr` is used to loop through the elements of the array until a character value of `0` is found. Then the `while` statement evaluates to `false` and the loop ends. This prevents you from going past the end of the array.

## Multidimensional Arrays

A multidimensional array is an array of arrays. You can even have a third level of arrays! This quickly starts getting complicated, so I recommend that you don't store more than three levels (or three dimensions) of arrays.

An array of arrays is often referred to as a two-dimensional array because it can be represented in two dimensions. To declare a two-dimensional array, you expand on what you do with a regular (or one-dimensional) array:

```
byte[,] scores = new byte[15,30];
```

A comma is added to the first part of the declaration, and two numbers separated by a command are used in the second part. This declaration creates a two-dimensional array that has 15 elements, each containing an array of 30 elements. In total, the `scores` array holds 450 values of data type `byte`.

To declare a simple multidimensional array that stores a few characters, you enter the following:

```
char[,] letters = new char[2,3];  // without initializing values
```

This declaration creates a two-dimensional array called `letters`, which contains `2` elements that are each arrays that have `3` character elements. You can initialize the elements within the `letters` array at the declaration time:

```
char[,] letters = new char[,] { {'a','b','c'},
                                {'X','Y','Z'} };
```

or you can initialize each element individually. To access the elements of a multidimensional array, you again use the indexes. The first element of the `letters` array is `letters[0,0]`. Remember, the indexes start at offset `0`, not `1`. `letters[0,1]` is the second element, which contains the letter `'b'`. The letter `'X'` is `letter[1,0]` because it is in the second array (offset `1`) and is the first element (offset `0`). To initialize the letters array outside the declaration, you could do the following:

```
letters[0,0] = 'a';
letters[0,1] = 'b';
letters[0,2] = 'c';
```

```
letters[1,0] = 'X';
letters[1,1] = 'Y';
letters[1,2] = 'Z';
```

## Creating an Array Containing Different-Sized Arrays

In the previous section, an assumption was made that in a two-dimensional array all the subarrays are the same size. This would make the arrays rectangular. What happens if you want to store arrays that are not the same size? Consider the following:

```
char[][] myname = new char[3][];
         myname[0] = new char[] { 'B', 'r', 'a', 'd', 'l', 'e', 'y'};
         myname[1] = new char[] { 'L', '.' };
         myname[2] = new char[] { 'J', 'o', 'n', 'e', 's' };
```

The `myname` array is an array of arrays. It contains three character arrays that are each a different length. Because they are different lengths, you work with their elements differently from the rectangular arrays you worked with before. Figure 8.5 illustrates the `myname` array.

**FIGURE 8.5**

*An array of different-sized arrays.*

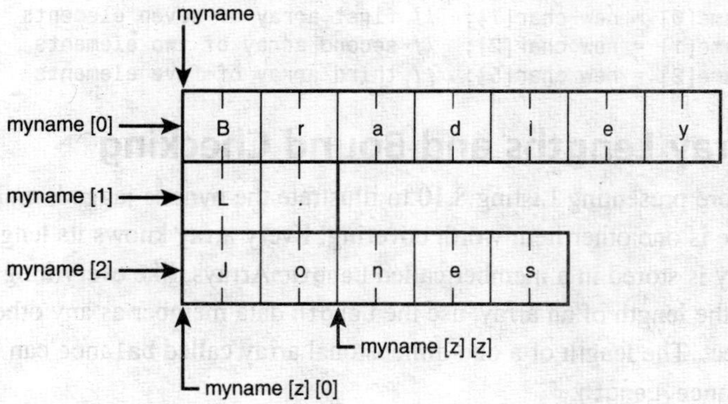


Instead of addressing each element by using index values separated by commas, you instead separate the elements into their own square brackets. For example, the following line of code uses the `WriteLine` method to print the array elements that would be my initials:

```
System.Console.WriteLine("{0}{1}{2}", myname[0][0], myname[1][0], myname[2][0]);
```

It would be wrong to address these as `myname[0,0]`, `myname[1,0]`, and `myname[2,0]`.

> **Note**
>
> A multidimensional array that contains subarrays of the same size is referred to as *rectangular*. A multidimensional array that has variable sized subarrays stored is referred to as *jagged*. In Figure 8.5, you can see the derivation of the name *jagged*.

What happens if you want to declare the `myname` array without initializing it, as was done previously? You know there are three parts to the name, so the first dimension is `3`; however, what should the second dimension be? Because of the variable sizes, you must make multiple instantiations to set up the full array. First, you declare the outside array that will hold the arrays:

```
char[][] myname = new char[3][];
```

This declares the `myname` variable as an array with three elements, each holding a character array. After you've done this declaration, you must initialize each of the individual arrays that will be stored in `myname[]`.Figure 8.5 illustrates this `myname` array:

```
myname[0] = new char[7];  // first array of seven elements
myname[1] = new char[2];  // second array of two elements
myname[2] = new char[5];  // third array of five elements
```

## Array Lengths and Bound Checking

Before presenting Listing 8.10 to illustrate the `myname` jagged, multidimensional array, there is one other item worth covering. Every array knows its length! The length of an array is stored in a member called `Length`. Arrays, like everything in C#, are objects. To get the length of an array, use the `Length` data member as any other data member and object. The length of a one-dimensional array called `balance` can be obtained from `balance.Length`.

In a multidimensional array, you still use `Length` or you can use a method of the array called `GetLength()` to get the length of a subarray. You pass the index number of the subarray to identify which length to return. Listing 8.10 illustrates the use of the `Length` member along with using a jagged array.

**LISTING 8.10** names.cs—Using a Jagged Two-Dimensional Array

```
//  names.cs - Using a two-dimensional array
//-----------------------------------------------------------

using System;

public class myApp
```

**LISTING 8.10** continued

```
{
    public static void Main()
    {
        char[][] name = new char[3][];

        name[0] = new char[7] {'B', 'r', 'a', 'd', 'l', 'e', 'y'};
        name[1] = new char[2] {'L', '.'};
        name[2] = new char[5] {'J', 'o', 'n', 'e', 's'};

        Console.WriteLine("Display the sizes of the arrays...\n");

        Console.WriteLine("Length of name array {0}", name.Length);

        for( int ctr = 0; ctr < name.Length; ctr++)
            Console.WriteLine("Length of name[{0}] is {1}", ctr, name[ctr].Length);

//---------------------------------------------------------------------

        Console.WriteLine("\n\nDisplaying the content of the name array...");

        for( int ctr = 0; ctr < name.Length; ctr++)
        {
            Console.Write("\n");  // new line
            for( int ctr2 = 0; ctr2 < name[ctr].Length; ctr2++ )
            {
                Console.Write("{0}", name[ctr][ctr2]);
            }
        }
        Console.WriteLine("\n...Done displaying");
    }
}
```

**OUTPUT**

```
Display the sizes of the arrays...

Length of name array 3
Length of name[0] is 7
Length of name[1] is 2
Length of name[2] is 5


Displaying the content of the name array...

Bradley
L.
Jones
...Done displaying
```

**ANALYSIS** Let's look at this listing in parts. The first part comprises lines 10 to 14. In line 10, a two-dimensional array called `name` is declared that contains three arrays of characters of possibly different lengths. In lines 12, 13, and 14, each of these arrays is instantiated. Although the size of the arrays is included in the square brackets, because the arrays are being initialized, you do not have to include the numbers. It is good practice to include the numbers, however, to be explicit in what you want.

The second part of this listing illustrates the `Length` member of the arrays. In line 18, the length of the `name` array is printed. You might have expected this to print `14`; however, it prints `3`. The `Length` member actually prints the number of elements. There are three elements in the `name` array and these three elements are each arrays.

In line 20, the `Length` member of the `name` array—which you now know is `3` in this example—is used as the upper limit for looping through each of the arrays. Using an index counter, the `length` method of each of the subarrays is printed. You can see that these values match what was declared.

The third part of this listing comprises lines 27 to 34. This portion of the listing displays the values stored in the individual names. This code has been set up to be dynamic by checking the `Length` member for each of the subarrays rather than hard-coding any values. If you change the code in lines 12 to 14, the rest of this listing still works.

## Using Arrays in Classes and Structures

An array is just another type that can be used to create variables. Arrays can be placed and created anywhere other data types can be used. This means that arrays can be used in structures or classes and other data types.

> **Note**
>
> Although basic data types are used in today's lesson, you can actually create arrays of any of the data elements. You can create arrays using classes, structures, or any other data type.

## Using the `foreach` Statement

It's time to address the keyword `foreach`, as promised on Day 5, "Control Statements." The `foreach` keyword can be used to make working with arrays much simpler, especially when you want to loop through an entire array. Additionally, rather than using the array name with a subscript, you can use a simple variable to work with the array. The downside of the `foreach` statement is that the simple variable you get to use is read-only—you can't do assignments to it. The format of the `foreach` command is

```
foreach( datatype varname in arrayName )
{
    statements;
}
```

where *datatype* is the data type for your array. *varname* is a variable name that can be used to identify the individual element of the array. *arrayName* is the name of the array the `foreach` is looping through. Listing 8.11 illustrates using `foreach` to loop through a name array.

**LISTING 8.11** foreach1.cs—Using `foreach` with an Array

```
 1:  // foreach1.cs - Initializing an array
 2:  //-----------------------------------------------------------------
 3:
 4:  using System;
 5:
 6:  public class myApp
 7:  {
 8:     public static void Main()
 9:     {
10:          char[] name = new char[] {'B','r','a','d','l','e','y'};
11:
12:          Console.WriteLine("Display content of name array...");
13:
14:          foreach( char x in name )
15:          {
16:               Console.Write("{0}", x);
17:          }
18:
19:          Console.WriteLine("\n...Done.");
20:     }
21:  }
```

**OUTPUT**

```
Display content of name array...
Bradley
...Done.
```

**ANALYSIS** This listing is shorter than the earlier listing. The big focus is in line 14. This line uses the `foreach` keyword to loop through the name array. It loops through each element of the name array and then ends. As it loops through, it refers to the individual elements as `x`. In the code in the statements of the `foreach`, you don't have to use `array[`*`index_ctr`*`]`; instead, you use `x`.

# Summary

Today's lesson covered three key advanced data types: the structure, the enumeration, and the array. You learned that structures operate similarly to classes, with the big difference being that structures are a value type and classes are a reference type. You learned that enumerations—declared with the `enum` keyword—are useful for making your code more readable. Enumerations enable you to create data types that take a range of values that you can control. Additionally, you can give these values more usable names.

The final topic of today's lesson was arrays. You learned how to create arrays. You also learned that arrays can have multiple dimensions. On arrays with more than one dimension, you can set the subarrays to have the same size array (a rectangular array), or you can assign arrays of different sizes (a jagged array).

Today's lesson concluded by covering the `foreach` keyword. You were shown how this keyword can make working with arrays much easier.

# Q&A

**Q Are there other differences between structures and classes that were not mentioned in today's lesson?**

**A** Yes, there are a few other differences that were not mentioned in today's lesson. You now know that structures are stored by value and classes are stored by references. You also learned that a structure cannot have a parameterless constructor. A structure is also not allowed to have a destructor. In addition to these differences, a structure is also different in that it is implicitly sealed. This concept will be explained when you learn about inheritance.

**Q I heard that enumerators can be used with bit fields. How is this done?**

**A** This is a more advanced topic that isn't covered in this book. You can use an enumerator to store the values of a bit. This can be done by using byte members and setting each of the members of the enumerator to one of the positions of the bits in the byte. The enumerator could be

```
enum Bits : byte
{
    first = 1,
    second = 2,
    third = 4,
    fourth = 8,
    fifth = 16,
    sixth = 32,
    seventh = 64,
    eighth = 128
}
```

You could then use bitwise operators to do bitwise math using these predefined values.

**Q Is an enumerator a value type or a reference type?**

**A** When a variable is declared as an enumerator, it is a value type. The value is actually stored in the enumerator variable.

**Q How many dimensions can you store in an array?**

**A** You can store more dimensions than you should. If you declare an array that is more than three dimensions, one of two things happens. Either you will waste a lot of memory because you are using rectangular arrays, or your code gets much more complicated. In almost all cases, you can find simpler ways to work with your information that don't require arrays of more than three dimensions.

# Workshop

The Workshop provides quiz questions to help you solidify your understanding of the material covered and exercises to provide you with experience in using what you've learned. Try to understand the quiz and exercise answers before continuing to the next day's lesson. Answers are provided in Appendix A, "Answers."

## Quiz

1. What is the difference between a value data type and a reference data type? Which is a structure?
2. What are the differences between a structure and a class?
3. How are structure constructors different from class constructors? (Or are they?)
4. What keyword is used to define an enumeration?
5. What data types can be stored in an enumerator?
6. What is the index value of the first element in an array?
7. What happens if you access an element of an array with an index larger than the number of elements in the array?
8. How many elements are in the array declared as `myArray[4,3,2]`? If this is a character array, how much memory will be used?
9. How can you tell the size of an array?
10. True or False (if False, what is wrong): The format of the `foreach` contains the same structure as the `for` statement?

## Exercises

1. Modify the point and line structures used in Listing 8.3 to include properties for the data members.
2. **ON YOUR OWN:** Modify the line structure to include a static data value that contains the longest line ever stored. This value should be checked and updated whenever the length method is called.
3. **BUG BUSTER:** The following code snippet has a problem. Can you fix it? (assume that myArray is an array of decimal values.)

```
foreach( decimal Element in myArray )
{
    System.Console.WriteLine("Element value is: {0}", Element);
    Element *= Element;
    System.Console.WriteLine("Element squared is: {0}", Element);
}
```

4. Write a program for a teacher. The program should have an array that can hold the test scores for 30 students. The program can randomly assign grades from 1 to 100. Determine the average score for the class.
5. Modify the listing you create in exercise 4 to keep track of scores for 15 tests used throughout a semester. It should keep track of these tests for the 30 students. Print the average score for each of the 15 tests and print each student's average score.
6. Modify the listing in exercise 5 to keep track of the same scores for 5 years. Do this with a three-dimensional array.

# WEEK 2

# DAY 9

# Advanced Method Access

You have learned quite a bit in the past eight days. Today you continue building on this foundation of knowledge by working further with class methods. In Days 6, "Classes," and 7, "Class Methods and Member Functions," you learned to encapsulate functionality and data into a class. In today's lesson, one of the key things you will learn is how to make your class more flexible. Today you

- Learn how to pass variable parameters to a method
- Discover how to overload methods
- Determine a method's Signatures
- Revisit scope
- Learn to create your own namespaces

## Overloading Methods

One of the key features of an object-oriented programming language is polymorphism. As you have previously learned, polymorphism is the capability of reaching a result even if different options are provided. One form of polymorphism is overloading. Previously, an example of a circle was provided.

In C#, the easiest place to see overloading in action is with methods. It is possible to create a class that can react to a number of different values and still reach the same conclusion. Consider Figure 9.1. In this figure, the black box illustrates your method for calculating the area of a circle.

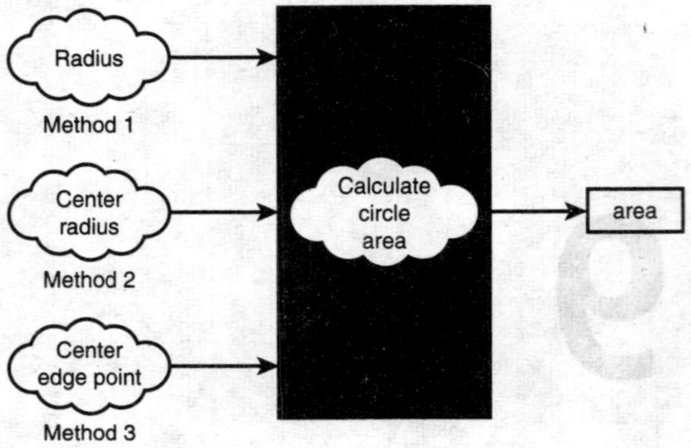


**FIGURE 9.1**

*A black box that calculates the area of a circle.*

Note that one of three possible solutions can be sent to this circle, and it still provides the appropriate answer. The first option sends just the radius of a circle. The second option sends the center point of the circle and the length of the radius. The third option sends the center point and a point on the circle. All three requests to the circle's `area` method return the area.

If you wrote a program to do the same functionality as this black box, you might be tempted to create three separate methods. You could call these `CalcArea`, `CalcAreaWithPoints`, `CalcAreaWithRadius`, or any of a million other unique names. If you were programming in a non–object-oriented language such as C, you would have to create multiple functions. In an object-oriented language with polymorphic abilities, there is an easier answer—method overloading.

## Overloading Functions

**NEW TERM** *Method overloading* is the process of creating multiple methods with the same name. Each of these methods is unique in some way so that the compiler will be able to tell the difference. Listing 9.1 presents a `Circle` class that has its `Area` method overloaded so that each of the calls illustrated in Figure 9.1 will work.

**LISTING 9.1** circle.cs—Polymorphism Illustrated with Method Overloading

```
//  circle1.cs - polymorphic area method
//-----------------------------------------------------------------

```

**LISTING 9.1** continued

```
using System;

public class Circle
{
    public int x;
    public int y;
    public double radius;
    private const float PI = 3.14159F;

    public double Area()  // Uses values from data members
    {
       return Area(radius);
    }

    public double Area( double rad )
    {
       double theArea;
       theArea = PI * rad * rad;
       Console.WriteLine("  The area for radius ({0}) is {1}", rad,
       ➥theArea);
       return theArea;
    }

    public double Area(int x1, int y1, double rad)
    {
        return Area(rad);
    }

    public double Area( int x1, int y1, int x2, int y2 )
    {
       int x_diff;
       int y_diff;
       double rad;

       x_diff = x2 - x1;
       y_diff = y2 - y1;

       rad = (double) Math.Sqrt((x_diff * x_diff) + (y_diff * y_diff));

       return Area(rad);
    }

    public Circle()
    {
       x = 0;
       y = 0;
       radius = 0.0;
    }
}
```

**LISTING 9.1** continued

```
53:  class CircleApp
54:  {
55:     public static void Main()
56:     {
57:        Circle myCircle = new Circle();
58:
59:        Console.WriteLine("Passing nothing...");
60:        myCircle.Area();
61:
62:        Console.WriteLine("\nPassing a radius of 3...");
63:        myCircle.Area( 3 );
64:
65:        Console.WriteLine("\nPassing a center of (2, 4) and a radius of
➥3...");
66:        myCircle.Area( 2, 4, 3 );
67:
68:        Console.WriteLine("\nPassing center of (2, 3) and a point of (5,
➥6)...");
69:        myCircle.Area( 2, 3, 4, 5 );
70:     }
71:  }
```

**OUTPUT**

```
Passing nothing...
  The area for radius (0) is 0

Passing a radius of 3...
  The area for radius (3) is 28.2743110656738

Passing a center of (2, 4) and a radius of 3...
  The area for radius (3) is 28.2743110656738

Passing center of (2, 3) and a point of (5, 6)...
  The area for radius (2.82842712474619) is 25.1327209472656
```

**ANALYSIS** The first things you should look at in this listing are lines 60, 63, 66, and 69. These lines all call the `Area` method of the `myCircle` object. Each of these calls, however, uses a different number of arguments. The program still compiles and works!

This is done using method overloading. If you look at the `Circle` class, you can see that four `Area` methods are defined. They differ based on the number of parameters being passed. In lines 13 to 16, an `Area` method is defined that doesn't receive any arguments but still returns a `double`. This method's body calls the `Area` method that contains one parameter. It passes the radius stored in the class `radius` data member.

In lines 18 to 24, the second `Area` method is defined. In this definition, a `double` value is passed into the method. This value is assumed to be the radius. In line 21, the area is calculated using the passed-in radius value. Line 22 prints the radius and the calculated area to the screen. The method ends by passing the area back to the calling routine.

**Tip**

Instead of using a constant value for PI throughout this listing, a constant variable was declared in line 11 instead. This enables you to change the value of PI in one location instead of potentially hard-coding it throughout your application. Maintenance will be much easier in the future.



In lines 26 to 29, you see the third defined `Area` method. This definition of the `Area` method is a little silly because only the radius is needed to calculate the area. Rather than repeat functionality in multiple places, this method passes its radius value, `rad`, to the `Area` method that requires only the radius. The area value is then passed back from each of the methods to the previous caller.

Lines 31 to 43 present the most complicated `Area` method. This method receives the center point of a circle and a point on the circle itself. The radius is the line that goes between these two points (Figure 9.2 illustrates this). Line 40 calculates the length of this line based on the two point values. After the length is obtained, it is passed to the `Area` method that requires only the radius where the rest of the work is done.

**FIGURE 9.2**

*The center point and a point on the circle.*

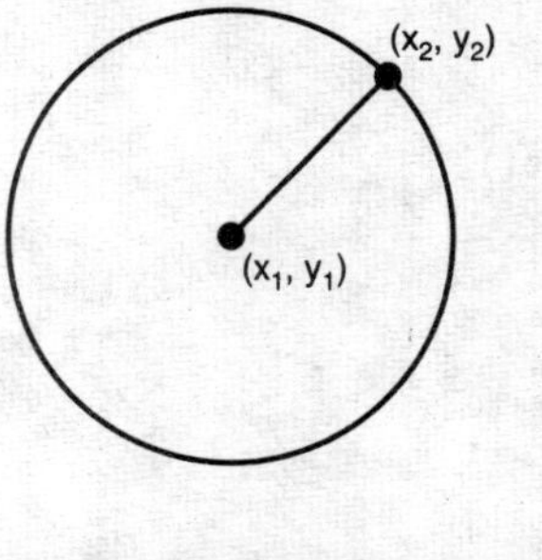


Although each of these methods calls another of the `Area` methods, this does not have to be the case. Each of these might do their coding completely independent of each other. How you code them is up to you. It is important that you can create multiple methods with the same name that can perform operations based on different sets of values.

**Caution**

Because you can code completely different functionality in methods with the same name, it doesn't mean that you should. Because the methods are named the same, the end results of each should be similar.

## Constructor Overloading

In addition to overloading regular methods, you can also overload constructors. An overloaded constructor enables you to pass values to an object at the same time it is created. Listing 9.2 illustrates a `Circle` class that has had the constructor overloaded. This `Circle` class is different from the one in Listing 9.1.

**LISTING 9.2** circle1.cs—Overloading the Constructor

```
//  circle1.cs - A simple circle class with overloaded constructors
//-----------------------------------------------------------------

using System;

public class Circle
{
    public int x;
    public int y;
    public int radius;
    private const float PI = 3.14159F;

    public double area()
    {
       double theArea;
       theArea = PI * radius * radius;
       return theArea;
    }

    public double circumference()
    {
       double Circ;
       Circ = 2 * PI * radius;
       return Circ;
    }

    public Circle()
    {
       x = 0;
       y = 0;
       radius = 0;
    }

    public Circle( int r )
    {
        x = 0;
        y = 0;
        radius = r;
    }
```

**LISTING 9.2** continued

```

    public Circle ( int new_x, int new_y )
    {
        x = new_x;
        y = new_y;
        radius = 0;
    }

    public Circle ( int new_x, int new_y, int r )
    {
        x = new_x;
        y = new_y;
        radius = r;
    }

    public void print_circle_info()
    {
      Console.WriteLine("Circle: Center = ({0},{1})", x, y);
      Console.WriteLine("         Radius = {0}", radius);
      Console.WriteLine("         Area   = {0}", area());
      Console.WriteLine("         Circum = {0}", circumference());
    }
}

class CircleApp
{
   public static void Main()
   {
      Circle first  = new Circle();
      Circle second = new Circle(4);
      Circle third  = new Circle(3,4);
      Circle fourth  = new Circle(1, 2, 5);

      Console.WriteLine("\nFirst Circle:");
      first.print_circle_info();

      Console.WriteLine("\nSecond Circle:");
      second.print_circle_info();

      Console.WriteLine("\nThird Circle:");
      third.print_circle_info();

      Console.WriteLine("\nFourth Circle:");
      fourth.print_circle_info();
   }
}
```

**OUTPUT**

```
First Circle:
Circle: Center = (0,0)
        Radius = 0
        Area   = 0
        Circum = 0

Second Circle:
Circle: Center = (0,0)
        Radius = 4
        Area   = 50.26544
        Circum = 25.13272

Third Circle:
Circle: Center = (3,4)
        Radius = 0
        Area   = 0
        Circum = 0

Fourth Circle:
Circle: Center = (1,2)
        Radius = 5
        Area   = 78.53975
        Circum = 31.41590001106262
```

**ANALYSIS** The constructors in the `Circle` class are the focus of this listing. There are a number of constructors, and each takes a different number of arguments. The first constructor is defined in lines 27 to 32. You have seen this constructor before—it takes no parameters. Declared as `public` and using the class name, this constructor follows the same format you learned about on Day 7.

In lines 34 to 39, you see the first of three additional `Circle` constructors. This constructor receives an integer that contains the radius. This value is applied to the class's radius field.

The code for the third `Circle` constructor is presented in lines 41 to 46. This constructor differs from the others in that it takes two integer values. These are the new values for the `x` and `y` coordinates of the center point. In lines 43 and 44, these values are set to the object's values.

The fourth and final constructor for the `Circle` class in this listing is in lines 48 to 53. This constructor takes three values. This includes the radius and the `x` and `y` coordinates for the center point.

All these methods are declared with the same name and in the same manner. The only difference is that each takes different parameters.

In lines 68 to 71 of the `CircleApp` class, you see these constructors in action. Line 68 creates a new `Circle` object called `first`. This is declared and created in the same way you've seen objects created before.

In line 69, the second object is different. When this object is created, instead of entering

```
new Circle()
```

an argument has been added—a `4`. The creation of the second object requires a constructor that can accept a single numeric value of 4. This matches the constructor that starts in line 34. The constructor in line 34 has the same format as the call in line 69.

9

Based on the description of the creation of the second object, it should be easy to see that the third and fourth objects call the constructors that are appropriate for them. The appropriate constructor is the one with parameters that match the call's arguments.

What happens if you created a `Circle` object as follows:

```
Circle myCircle = new Circle(1, 2, 3, 4);
```

This results in an error because it would pass four values. None of the constructors in the `Circle` class accept four values, so this declaration will not work.

## Understanding Method Signatures

Methods are overloaded because of the uniqueness of the individual methods. Each method has its own signature. As you learned in the previous section, the number of parameters in the method can determine the appropriate method. There are actually other ways that overloaded methods can differ from each other. Ultimately, these differences compose a method's signature.

A method's signature is composed of the number of parameters and their types. You saw with the `Circle` constructor that there were four signatures:

```
Circle()

Circle( int )

Circle( int, int )

Circle( int, int, int)
```

The `Area` method in Listing 9.1 has four signatures:

```
double Area()

double Area( double )

double Area(int, int, double )

double Area( int, int, int, int )
```

The following are valid to overload:

```
MyFunc( int )
MyFunc( float )
MyFunc( ref int )
MyFunc( val int)
```

There are a number of items that cannot be used as part of the signature. The `return` type cannot be used because the `return` type does not have to be used when calling a method.

Additionally, you cannot have a signature that differs because one method has a data type and another has an array. For example, if you overload with the following two signatures, you might get an error:

```
int myMethod( int )
int myMethod( int[] )
```

You also cannot use the `params` keyword to make signatures different. Using `params` will be covered later today. The following two methods together cause an error:

```
void myMethod( string, float )
void myMethod( string, params float[] )
```

You can overload a method as many times as you like, as long as each overloaded method has a unique signature.

# Using a Variable Number of Parameters

You've now learned how to create and use methods. You've learned how to pass information to methods. You learned that information could be passed in a number of ways. This includes passing information by value or by reference and passing variables that can be used to return output. You even learned to use the `return` keyword to pass a value back from a method. All these require a structured use of the methods.

What happens when you want to pass a variable number of items to a method? For example, suppose you want to add a set of numbers, but you don't know how many numbers there will be. You could call a routine multiple times, or you could set up a routine to take a variable number of parameters. Consider the `Console.WriteLine` and `Console.Write` methods. These methods both take a string and then a variable number of parameters of different values and different data types.

To accept an unknown number of parameters, you can use the `params` keyword. This keyword is used in the parameters list and declares the last value of the parameter list. The `params` keyword is used with an array data type.

Listing 9.3 presents the `params` keyword used with a method that takes a variable number of integers and adds them. It returns a `long` value with the total.

**LISTING 9.3** addem.cs—Using the `params` Keyword

```
// addem.cs - Using a variable number of arguments
//-----------------------------------------------------------------

using System;

public class AddEm
{
    public static long Add( params int[] args )
    {
       int ctr = 0;
       long Total = 0;

       for( ctr = 0; ctr < args.Length; ctr++)
       {
          Total += args[ctr];
       }
       return Total;
    }
}

class MyApp
{
   public static void Main()
   {
      long Total = 0;

      Total = AddEm.Add( 1 );
      Console.WriteLine("Total of (1) = {0}", Total);

      Total = AddEm.Add( 1, 2 );
      Console.WriteLine("Total of (1, 2) = {0}", Total);

      Total = AddEm.Add( 1, 2, 3 );
      Console.WriteLine("Total of (1, 2, 3) = {0}", Total);

      Total = AddEm.Add( 1, 2, 3, 4 );
      Console.WriteLine("Total of (1, 2, 3, 4) = {0}", Total);
   }
}
```

**OUTPUT**

```
Total of (1) = 1
Total of (1, 2) = 3
Total of (1, 2, 3) = 6
Total of (1, 2, 3, 4) = 10
```

**ANALYSIS** Your first reaction when looking at this listing should be to say, "Wait a minute—this could be done with a simple array of integers." If you caught this, you are absolutely right. This simple example could have been done without the `params` keyword and you could have made it work. But...

If you had declared this without the `params` keyword, you would not have gotten away with what is in lines 30, 33, and 36. Instead of being able to pass values to the method, you would have needed to place each of these values into a single `int` array and then pass that array. The `params` keyword enabled the compiler to take care of this for you.

If you take a closer look at this listing, you will see that it is not doing anything complex. In lines 6 to 19, a class called `AddEm` is created. This class has a single `static` function called `Add` that receives a variable number of integers stored in an array called `args`. Because the `params` keyword is used, you know that the integers can be passed individually rather than as a single, filled array.

The `AddEm` method is pretty straightforward. A `for` loop in lines 12 to 16 loops through the `args` array. Remember, this array was created from the integer values being passed into the `AddEm` method. Just like other arrays, you can check standard properties and methods. This includes using `args.Length` to get the length of the array. The `for` loop loops from `0` to the end of the `args` array and adds each of the numbers to a total called `Total`. This total is then returned in line 17 to the calling method.

The `MyApp` class in lines 21 to 39 uses the `AddEm` method to add numbers. You can see that the same method is called with various numbers of integers. You can continue to add integers to the method call and the method will still work.

**Note**

> No `AddEm` objects were created. Because the `Add` method is static, it is called using the class name, `AddEm`. This means the method can be used even though no objects were created.

## Using `params` with Multiple Data Types

The previous example used all integers within the variable parameter. Because all data types are based on the same class type, an `object`, you can actually use the `object` data type to get a variable number of different data types. Listing 9.4 presents a listing that is impractical for everyday use, but it does a great job of illustrating that you can pass anything.

**LISTING 9.4** garbage.cs—Passing Different Data Types

```
//  garbage.cs - Using a variable number of arguments
//               of different types
//-----------------------------------------------------------

using System;

public class Garbage
{
    public static void Print( params object[] args )
    {
        int ctr = 0;

        for( ctr = 0; ctr < args.Length; ctr++)
        {
            Console.WriteLine("Argument {0} is:  {1}", ctr, args[ctr]);
        }
    }
}

class MyApp
{
    public static void Main()
    {
        long ALong = 1234567890987654321L;
        decimal ADec = 1234.56M;
        byte Abyte = 42;
        string AString = "Cole McCrary";

        Console.WriteLine("First call...");
        Garbage.Print( 1 );    // pass a simple integer

        Console.WriteLine("\nSecond call...");
        Garbage.Print( );      // pass nothing

        Console.WriteLine("\nThird call...");
        Garbage.Print( ALong, ADec, Abyte, AString );  // Pass lots

        Console.WriteLine("\nFourth call...");
        Garbage.Print( AString, "is cool", '!' );     // more stuff
    }
}
```



**OUTPUT**

```
First call...
Argument 0 is:  1

Second call...

Third call...
Argument 0 is:  1234567890987654321
```

```
Argument 1 is:  1234.56
Argument 2 is:  42
Argument 3 is:  Cole McCrary

Fourth call...
Argument 0 is:  Cole McCrary
Argument 1 is:  is cool
Argument 2 is:  !
```

**ANALYSIS** This listing contains a method `Print` of the class `Garbage` in lines 9 to 17. The `Print` method is declared to take a variable number of objects. Any data type can be fitted into an object, so this enables the method to take any data type. The code within the method should be easy to follow. If you look at the output, you will see that in line 30 the first call to the `Garbage.Print` method prints a single value, `1`.

The second call in line 32 did not pass any arguments. The `Garbage.Print` method is still called; however, the logic in the method doesn't print anything. The `for` statement ends when it checks the `args.Length` value the first time.

The third and fourth calls to `Garbage` print various other values. By using a type of `object`, any data types can be passed in either as variables or as literals.

> **Note** Recall from the first week that a literal number that ends in an `L` is considered a long value. A literal number that ends in an `M` is considered a decimal. (See lines 24 and 25 of the listing).

## A More Detailed Look at `params`

It is worth reviewing what the `params` keyword is causing to happen in a little more detailed explanation. When values are passed to the method, first the compiler looks to see whether there is a matching method. If a match is found, that method is called. If a match is not found, the compiler checks to see whether there was a method with a `params` argument. If so, that method is used. The compiler then takes the values and places them into an array that is passed to the method. For example, using the last call to the `Add` method of `AddEm` in Listing 9.3:

```
AddEm.Add( 1, 2, 3, 4);
```

the compiler does the following behind the scenes:

```
int[] x = new int[4];
int[0] = 1;
int[1] = 2;
int[2] = 3;
int[3] = 4;
AddEm.Add(x);
```

In Listing 9.4, instead of declaring an array of type `int`, an array of type `object` is created and used.

**Caution**

Don't forget array members start at offset `0`, not `1`.

## The `Main` Method and Command-Line Arguments

You have already learned that the `Main` method is a special method because it is always called first. The `Main` method can also receive a variable number of parameters. You don't, however, need to use the `params` keyword with `Main`.

You don't need the `params` keyword because the command-line parameters are automatically packed into a string array. As you learned above, that is basically the same thing the `params` keyword would do for you. Because the values are already packed into an array, the `params` keyword becomes worthless.

When calling the `Main` method, it is standard practice to use the following format if parameters are expected:

```
public static [int | void] Main( string[] args )
```

Including either `void` or `int` is optional. If you return a different data type, generally your `Main` method will be void or return an integer. The focus here is in the parameter list: a string array called `args`. The name `args` can be changed to anything else; however, you will find that almost all C# programmers will use the variable `args`. Listing 9.5 Illustrates the use of command line parameters.

**Listing 9.5** command.cs—Using command line arguments

```
// command.cs - Checking for command-line arguments
//-----------------------------------------------------

using System;

class CommandLine
{
    public static void Main(string[] args)
    {
        int ctr=0;
        if (args.Length <= 0 )
        {
            Console.WriteLine("No Command Line arguments were provided.");
            return;
        }
```

**LISTING 9.5** continued

```
16:         else
17:         {
18:            for( ctr = 0; ctr < args.Length; ctr++)
19:            {
20:               Console.WriteLine("Argument {0} is {1}", ctr+1, args[ctr]);
21:            }
22:         }
23:      }
24: }
```

The first output illustrates executing this listing with no arguments.

**OUTPUT**

```
C:\code\Day09>command
No Command Line arguments were provided.
```

The second output illustrates calling the program with command-line arguments.

**OUTPUT**

```
C:\code\Day09>command xxx 123 456 789.012
Argument 1 is xxx
Argument 2 is 123
Argument 3 is 456
Argument 4 is 789.012
```

This listing is extremely short and to the point. The `Main` function, which starts in line 8, receives command-line arguments. It has been declared with the `string[] args` parameter, so it is set to capture any command-line arguments sent. In line 11, the `Length` data member of the `args` array is checked. If it is `0`, a message is printed saying that no command-line arguments were provided. If the value is something other than`0`, the lines 18 to 21 use a `for` loop to print each value. In line 20, instead of printing arguments starting with `0`, `1` is added to the counter. This is done so that the end user of the program doesn't have to wonder why the first argument is called `0`. After all, the end user might not be a C# programmer.

| Do | Don't |
|---|---|
| **DO** understand method overloading.<br>**DO** overload methods with the most common ways you believe a method could be used. | **DON'T** make things public if you don't need to. Use properties to give public access to private data members.<br>**DON'T** ignore command-line parameters in your programs. You can code your programs to accept command-line parameters and to return a value to the operating system. |

# Scope

**New Term** It is important to understand how long a variable exists before the runtime environment throws it out. This lifetime of a variable and its accessibility is referred to as *scope*. There are several levels of scope. The two most common are *local* and *global*.



A global scope is visible, and thus available to an entire listing. A variable that is available to a small area only is considered local to that area.

## Local Scope

The smallest level of scope is local to a block. A block can include a simple iterative statement. Consider the value of `x` in line 15 of Listing 9.6. What is the value of `x` in line 10?

**Listing 9.6** scope.cs—Local Variable out of Scope

```
 1: //  scope.cs - Local scope with an error
 2: //  *** You will get a compile error ***
 3: //----------------------------------------------------------------
 4:
 5: using System;
 6:
 7: class Scope
 8: {
 9:    public static void Main()
10:    {
11:        for( int x; x < 10; x++ )
12:        {
13:            Console.WriteLine("x is {0}", x);
14:        }
15:        Console.WriteLine("Out of For Loop. x is {0}", x);
16:    }
17: }
```

**Output**

```
scope.cs(15,55): error CS0103: The name 'x' does not exist in the class
or
        namespace 'Scope'
```

**Analysis** Although you might think that `x` should be `10`, it is actually in error. The variable is declared as part of the `for` statement in line 11. As soon as the `for` statement is complete, `x` goes out of scope. By being out of scope, it can no longer be used. This generates an error.

Now consider Listing 9.7. This listing contains a declaration in a `for` statement like the one in Listing 9.6; however, it declares `x` a second time in a second `for` statement. Will this lead to an error?

**LISTING 9.7** scope2.cs—Declaring More than One Local x

```
//  scope2.cs - Local scope.
//-----------------------------------------------------------------

using System;

class Scope
{
   public static void Main()
   {
       for( int x = 1; x < 5; x++ )
       {
           Console.WriteLine("x is {0}", x);
       }

       // Second for statement trying to redeclare x...
       for( int x = 1; x < 5; x++ )
       {
           Console.WriteLine("x is {0}", x);
       }
   }
}
```

**OUTPUT**

```
x is 1
x is 2
x is 3
x is 4
x is 1
x is 2
x is 3
x is 4
```

**ANALYSIS** This listing works! Each of the x variables is local to its own block (their `for` loops). Because of this, each x variable is totally independent of the other.

Now consider Listing 9.8 and its multiple use of x variables.

**LISTING 9.8** scope3.cs—Lots of x Variables

```
//  scope3.cs - Local scope.
//  *** Error if lines are uncommented ***
//-----------------------------------------------------------------

using System;

class Scope
{
   static int x = 987;

```

**LISTING 9.8** continued

```
11:     public static void Main()
12:     {
13:         Console.WriteLine("x is {0}", x);
14:
15: //       for( int x = 1; x < 5; x++ )
16: //       {
17: //           Console.WriteLine("x is {0}", x);
18: //       }
19:         Console.WriteLine("x is {0}", x);
20:     }
21: }
```

**OUTPUT**

```
x is 987
x is 987
```

**ANALYSIS** Notice that lines 15 to 18 are commented out in this listing. You should enter, compile, and run this listing with the commented lines intact as presented in the listing. When you do, you get the output shown. The x variable in lines 13 and 19 print the static x variable contained in the class, as you would expect.

Lines 15 to 18 contain a local variable x that is declared and used only within the for loop. Based on what you learned in the previous section, you might be tempted to believe that if you uncomment this code and compile, everything will work. The for loop uses its local x variable and the rest of the method uses the class x variable. Wrong! In line 17, how would the compiler know that you did not mean to use the class's x variable? It wouldn't. Uncomment lines 15 to 18 and recompile the listing. You get the following result:

**OUTPUT**

```
scope3.cs(15,17): error CS0136: A local variable named 'x' cannot be
➥declared in this scope because it would give a different meaning
➥to 'x', which is already used in a 'parent or current' scope to
denote something else
```

The compiler can't tell which x variable to use. The local variable conflicts with the class variable. There is a way around this problem.

## Differentiating Class Variables from Local Variables

One way to differentiate class variables from a local variable is to always refer to the class. You learned how to do this in an earlier lesson; however, it is worth reviewing here. The error provided in Listing 9.8 could be resolved in two ways: rename the local variable with a different name, or refer to the class variable in lines 14 and 19 more explicitly.

Depending on how you declared the variable, there are two ways to be more explicit on a class variable's name. If the class variable is a standard, non-`static` variable, you can use the `this` keyword. For accessing a class data member, `x`, you use `this.x`.

If the data member is `static`, like the one in Listing 9.8, you use the class name to reference the variable instead of the `this` keyword. For a review on the `this` keyword and accessing `static` data variables, go back to Day 7.

## Modifiers of Class Scope

Recall the two modifiers that can be used on methods and data members: `private` and `public`. You have learned about these throughout the last three days, and you will learn about others later in this book.

When the `public` modifier is used, a data member or member function can be accessed by methods that are outside a class. You've seen a number of examples of this. When the `private` modifier is used, the data member or method can be accessed only from within the defining class. Data members and methods are private by default.

> **Note**
>
> If you don't declare `private` or `public` on a variable within a class, it is created as `private`.
>
> Also, some languages have the ability to declare variables outside of any function or method. Such variables have global scope and are available to any portion of a program. C# cannot declare a variable outside of a class.

# Classes with No Objects

It is possible to create a class and prevent it from creating an object. You might wonder why you would ever want to do this, how a class can be used if you can't create an object to access it. In reality, you've used a number of classes already that you haven't created objects for. Consider the `Console` class. You have used its `WriteLine` and other methods without declaring a `Console` object. Additionally, classes such as the `Math` class enable you to use them without declaring objects.

How can you use a class without an object? A `static` method and data member is assigned to the class, not to the individual objects. If you declare a class with all `static` data and methods, declaring an object is of no value. Listing 9.9 presents `MyMath` class, which contains a number of methods for doing math.

**LISTING 9.9** MyMath.cs—Math Methods

```
 1:  //  MyMath.cs - Static members.
 2:  //-----------------------------------------------------------------
 3:
 4:  using System;
 5:
 6:  public class MyMath
 7:  {
 8:     public static long Add( params int[] args )
 9:     {
10:        int ctr = 0;
11:        long Answer = 0;
12:
13:        for( ctr = 0; ctr < args.Length; ctr++)
14:        {
15:           Answer += args[ctr];
16:        }
17:        return Answer;
18:     }
19:
20:     public static long Subtract( int arg1, int arg2 )
21:     {
22:        long Answer = 0;
23:        Answer = arg1 - arg2;
24:        return Answer;
25:     }
26:  }
27:
28:  class MyApp
29:  {
30:     public static void Main()
31:     {
32:        long Result = 0;
33:
34:        Result = MyMath.Add( 1, 2, 3 );
35:        Console.WriteLine("Add result is {0}", Result);
36:
37:        Result = MyMath.Subtract( 5, 2 );
38:        Console.WriteLine("Subtract result is {0}", Result);
39:     }
40:  }
```

**OUTPUT**

```
Add result is 6
Subtract result is 3
```

**ANALYSIS** The `MyMath` class in lines 6 to 26 declares two methods: `Subtract` and `Add`. Each of these subtracts or adds integers and returns the result. These could be more complex; however, that will be left for you to add.

There is no reason to create a `MyMath` object. There isn't anything, however, that prevents you from creating it, but it's possible to prevent an object from being created.

## Private Constructors

To prevent an object from being created, you create a `private` constructor. As you learned earlier, a method with the `private` keyword can be accessed only from within the class. This means that you can't call the constructor from outside the class. Because calling the constructor occurs when you create a class, you effectively prevent the class from being created by adding the `private` modifier to the constructor. Listing 9.10 is the `MyMath` class listing presented again with a private constructor.

**Listing 9.10** MyMath2.cs—`MyMath` Class with a Private Constructor

```
//  MyMath2.cs - Private constructor
//-----------------------------------------------------------------

using System;

public class MyMath
{
    public static long Add( params int[] args )
    {
       int ctr = 0;
       long Answer = 0;

       for( ctr = 0; ctr < args.Length; ctr++)
       {
          Answer += args[ctr];
       }
       return Answer;
    }

    public static long Subtract( int arg1, int arg2 )
    {
       long Answer = 0;
       Answer = arg1 - arg2;
       return Answer;
    }

    private MyMath()
    {
       // nothing to do here since this will never get called!
    }
}

class MyApp
```

**LISTING 9.10** continued

```
34:  {
35:     public static void Main()
36:     {
37:        long Result = 0;
38:
39:        // MyMath var = new MyMath();
40:
41:        Result = MyMath.Add( 1, 2, 3 );
42:        Console.WriteLine("Add result is {0}", Result);
43:
44:        Result = MyMath.Subtract( 5, 2 );
45:        Console.WriteLine("Subtract result is {0}", Result);
46:     }
47:  }
```



**OUTPUT**

```
Add result is 6
Subtract result is 3
```

**ANALYSIS** Lines 27 to 30 contain a constructor for this class. If you remove the comment from line 39 and recompile this listing, you get the following error:

```
MyMath3.cs(39,20): error CS0122: 'MyMath.MyMath()' is inaccessible due to its
    protection level
```

Creating an object is not possible. The `private` modifier stops you from creating an object. This is not an issue, however, because you can access the `public`, `static` class members anyway.

# Namespaces Revisited

Namespaces can be used to help organize your classes and other types. You've used a number of namespaces that are provided by the framework. This includes the `System` namespace that contains a number of system methods and classes, including the `Console` class that contains the reading and writing routines.

A namespace can contain other namespaces, classes, structures, enumerations, interfaces, and delegates. You are familiar with namespaces, classes, structures, and enumerations. You will learn about interfaces and delegates later in this book.

## Naming a Namespace

Namespaces can contain any name that is valid for any other type of identifier. This means that the name should be composed of the standard characters plus underscores. Additionally, namespaces can include periods in their names. As with other identifiers, you should use descriptive names for your namespaces.

## Declaring a Namespace

To create a namespace, you use the keyword `namespace` followed by the name that identifies it. You can then use braces to enclose the types that are contained within the namespace.

As stated earlier, a namespace can contain other namespaces. These namespaces are formatted in the same manner. Listing 9.11 contains a listing that declares namespaces.

**LISTING 9.11** namesp.cs—Declaring a Namespace

```
//  namesp.cs - Declaring namespaces
//-----------------------------------------------

using System;

namespace Consts
{
    public class PI
    {
        public static double value = 3.14159;
        private PI() {}  // private constructor
    }
    public class three
    {
        public static int value = 3;
        private three() {} // private constructor
    }
}

 namespace MyMath
 {
  public class Routine
  {
    public static long Add( params int[] args )
    {
        int ctr = 0;
        long Answer = 0;

        for( ctr = 0; ctr < args.Length; ctr++)
        {
            Answer += args[ctr];
        }
        return Answer;
    }

    public static long Subtract( int arg1, int arg2 )
    {
        long Answer = 0;
```

**Listing 9.11** continued

```
39:       Answer = arg1 - arg2;
40:       return Answer;
41:     }
42:   }
43: }
44:
45: class MyApp
46: {
47:   public static void Main()
48:   {
49:     long Result = 0;
50:
51:     Result = MyMath.Routine.Add( 1, 2, 3 );
52:     Console.WriteLine("Add result is {0}", Result);
53:
54:     Result = MyMath.Routine.Subtract( 5, 2 );
55:     Console.WriteLine("Subtract result is {0}", Result);
56:
57:     Console.WriteLine("\nThe value of PI is {0}", Consts.PI.value );
58:     Console.WriteLine("The value of three is {0}", Consts.three.value );
59:   }
60: }
```

**Output**

```
Add result is 6
Subtract result is 3

The value of PI is 3.14159
The value of three is 3
```

This listing is a modification of the `MyMath` listing you saw earlier. Additionally, some additional classes are declared, which are not practical. They do, however, help illustrate the namespace concepts.

In line 6, you see the first of two namespaces that are declared in this listing. The `Consts` namespace contains two classes—`PI` and `three`—which are used in lines 57 and 58. In these lines, the namespace has to be declared, along with the class and data member name. If you leave off `Consts` when accessing these classes from a different namespace (such as in lines 57 and 58), you get an error:

```
namespbad.cs(20,1): error CS1529: A using clause must precede all other
    namespace elements
```

You can, however, get around this error with the `using` keyword. Adding the following statement to the top of the listing will fix the error:

```
using Consts;
```

**Note**

> Every file provides a namespace even if you don't explicitly declare one. Each file contains a global namespace. Anything in this global namespace is available in any named namespace within the file.

## `using` and Namespaces

C# provides using, a keyword that makes using namespaces easier and which provides two functions. First, `using` can be used to alias a namespace to a different name. Second, `using` can be used to make it easier to access the types that are located in a namespace by shortcutting the need to fully qualify names.

### Shortcutting Fully Qualified Namespace Names

You've already seen how the `using` keyword can be used to shortcut the need to include a fully qualified name. By including the following line:

```
using System;
```

you no longer have to include the `System` namespace name when using the classes and types within the `System` namespace. This enabled you to use `Console.WriteLine` without the `System` namespace name being included. In Listing 9.11, you can add the following at line 5:

```
using Consts;
```

This enables you to use `PI.value` and `three.value` without fully qualifying the `Consts` namespace name.

**Caution**

> You must include `using` statements before other code elements. This means that they are best included at the top of a listing. If you try to include them later in a listing, you will get an error.

### Aliasing with `using`

You can also alias a namespace with the `using` keyword. This enables you to give a namespace—or even a class within a namespace—a different name. This alias can be an valid identifier name. The format of an alias is

```
using aliasname = namespaceOrClassName;
```

where *`aliasname`* is the name you want to use with the alias and *`namespaceOrClassName`* is the qualified namespace or class name. For example, consider the following line:

```
using doit = System.Console;
```

If you include this line in your listing, you can use `doit` in all the places that you would have used `System.Console`. To write a line to the console, you then type

```
doit.WriteLine("blah blah blah");
```

Listing 9.12 illustrates a `Hello World` program using aliasing of the `System.Console` class.

**Listing 9.12** useit.cs—Aliasing with using

```
 1:  // useit.cs
 2:  //-----------------------------------------------
 3:
 4:  using doit = System.Console;
 5:
 6:  class MyApp
 7:  {
 8:     public static void Main()
 9:     {
10:        doit.WriteLine("Hello World!");
11:     }
12:  }
```

**Output**

```
Hello World!
```

**Analysis** This is a very straightforward listing. Line 4 creates a `using` alias called `doit` in the `System.Console` class. The `doit` alias is then used in line 10 to print a message.

| Do | Don't |
| --- | --- |
| DO understand scope.<br>DO use the `using` keyword to make it easier to access members of namespaces.<br>DO use namespaces to organize your classes. | DON'T make data members `public` if they can be kept `private`.<br>DON'T forget that data members are `private` by default. |

# Summary

In today's lesson you expanded on some of what you have learned on previous days. You learned how to overload a method so it would be able to work with different numbers and types of parameters. You learned that this can be done by creating overloaded methods with unique signatures. In addition to overloading normal methods, you also learned how to overload a class's constructor.

You also learned more about the scope of class members. You learned that the `private` keyword isolates a member to the class itself. You learned that the `public` modifier enables the member to be accessed outside the class. You also learned that you can create local variables that exist only within the life of a block of code. You learned that the `this` keyword can be used to identify a data member that is part of a specific instance of a class.

You also learned about namespaces. This includes learning how to create your own namespaces. The `using` keyword was also addressed within the namespace discussion. The `using` keyword can be used to enable you to avoid the need to include the fully qualified name to a namespace's members, and also can be used to alias a namespace or class.

# Q&A

**Q Can you declare the `Main` method as `private`?**

**A** You can declare the `Main` method as `private`; however, you would be unable to access the class. To run a program, you need a `Main` method that is publicly accessible. If you can't access the `Main` method from outside the class, you can't run the program.

**Q Scope was briefly discussed in today's lesson. What are the default values of variables if they are not explicitly given a value?**

**A** A number of variable types are not initially assigned a value. This includes instance variables of an initially unassigned structure, output parameters, and local variables. A number of variable types are initially assigned. This includes static variables, instance variables of an object, instance variables of an structure variable that is initially assigned, array elements, value variables used as parameters in a method, and reference. Even though these are initially assigned, you should always set a value initially into all the variables you use.

**Q Why not keep things simple and declare everything public?**

**A** One of the benefits of an object-oriented language is to have the ability to encapsulate data and functions into a class that can be treated as a black box. By keeping members private, you make it possible to change the internals without impacting any programs that use the class.

# Workshop

The Workshop provides quiz questions to help you solidify your understanding of the material covered and exercises to provide you with experience in using what you've learned. Try to understand the quiz and exercise answers before continuing to the next day's lesson. Answers are provided in Appendix A, "Answers."



## Quiz

1. Is overloading functions an example of encapsulation, inheritance, polymorphism, or reuse?
2. How many times can a member function be overloaded?
3. Which of the following can be overloaded?
   a. Data members
   b. Member methods
   c. Constructors
   d. Destructors
4. What keyword is used to accept a variable number of parameters in a method?
5. What can you do to receive a variable number of parameters of different, and possibly unknown, data types?
6. To accept a variable number of parameters from the command line, what keyword do you include?
7. What is the default scope for a member of a class?
8. What is the difference between the `public` and `private` modifiers?
9. How can you prevent a class from being instantiated into an object?
10. What are two uses of the `using` keyword?

## Exercises

1. Write the line of code for a method header for a `public` function called `abc` that takes a variable number of short values. This method returns a byte.
2. Write the line of code needed to accept command-line parameters.
3. If you have a class called `aClass`, what code can you include to prevent the class from being instantiated into an object?

4. **BUG BUSTER:** Does the following program have a problem?. Enter it in your editor and compile it. If there is a problem, what is it?

```
using doit = System.Console.WriteLine;

class MyApp
{
    public static void Main()
    {
        doit("Hello World!");
    }
}
```

5. Create a namespace that contains a class and another namespace. This second namespace should also contain a class. Create an application class that uses both of these classes.

6. Create a program that has a number of overloaded methods. The overloaded method should have the following signatures. Are all these signatures legal? (overload.cs)

```
public myFunc()
public myFunc( int )
public myFunc( float )
public myFunc( ref int )
public myFunc ( ref float )
```

# WEEK 2

# DAY 10

# Handling Exceptions

If everyone wrote perfect code, if all users entered the correct information the first time, and if all computers disallowed errors, a large number of programmers today would be out of job. The reality is that computers, users, and programmers are not infallible. Because of this, you must write your programs to expect the unexpected. You must write your programs to handle the one thing that is different—the exception. Today you

- Learn about the concept of exception handling
- Discover the `try` and `catch` keywords
- Implement finality with the `finally` keyword
- Explore some common exceptions and their causes
- Understand how to pass an exception to a different routine
- Define your own exceptions
- Throw and rethrow exceptions

# The Concept of Handling Problems

When you create a program, you need to consider all possible problems that could arise. When creating programs that obtain information from a file, from a user, from a service, or even from another part of your program, you should always check to make sure that what you received or what you are using is what you expected. Consider the ListIt program that you entered in Day 2, "Understanding C# Programs." This program requires that you include a filename when you run the program. What happens when you don't include a filename? What happens if you include a filename for a file that doesn't exist? What happens if the filename given is for a machine code file? What if more than one filename is given?

You can choose not to worry about issues like these; however, you might find that people quit using your programs. Results of these types of errors can vary. When you write a program, you need to decide which issues are severe enough to worry about and which are not. A good programmer plans for the unusual or unwanted things that might happen.

## Preventing Errors via Logical Code

You will find that you can handle a lot of issues within your code with simple programming logic. If simple programming logic can prevent an error, you should add it. For example, you can check the length of a value, you can check for the presence of a command-line argument, or you can verify that a number is within a valid range. These types of checks can easily be performed using the programming constructs you learned in the first week.

Consider the following items. How would you handle these in your code?

- The user tries to open a file that doesn't exist.
- Too many items are assigned to an array.
- The code within a program assigns a string to an integer variable.
- A routine tries to use a reference variable that contains a null (empty) value.

You can write code to avoid these problems, but what happens when you miss one?

## What Causes Exceptions?

If you don't programmatically catch problems, an exception can occur. An exception is an uncaught programming error. This excludes logic errors, which are errors because of results that occur, not because of a coding issue. When an uncaught error occurs, the runtime can choke, and an exception is thrown. Listing 10.1 contains an error that throws an exception. Run this listing and see what happens when you access the nonexistent sixth element of a five-element array.

**Listing 10.1** Error.cs—Causing an Exception

```
 1:  // error.cs
 2:  // A program that throws an exception
 3:  //=============================================
 4:  using System;
 5:
 6:  class MyError
 7:  {
 8:     public static void Main()
 9:     {
10:        int [] myArray = new int[5];
11:
12:        for ( int ctr = 0; ctr < 10; ctr++ )
13:        {
14:           myArray[ctr] = ctr;
15:        }
16:     }
17:  }
```

**ANALYSIS** This listing compiles with no errors. It is not very practical because it doesn't create any real output or do anything of value. In line 10, an array of five integers is created called `myArray`. In lines 12 to 15, a `for` loop assigns the value of a counter to each value in the array. The value of `0` is assigned to `myArray[0]`, `1` is assigned to `myArray[1]`, and so on.

What happens when `ctr` becomes equal to `5`? The conditional statement in line 12 enables `ctr` to continue to be incremented as long as it is less than `10`. When `ctr` reaches `5`, however, there is a different problem. In line 14, `myArray[5]` is not valid—the array's highest element is `myArray[4]`. The runtime knows that the array cannot have an index value of`5`, so it throws out an error to indicate that something unusual, or exceptional, happened. When you run this program, you might receive a window that gives you an exception error such as the one shown in Figure 10.1. Additionally, you will see the following cryptic text displayed by the runtime:

```
Exception occurred: System.IndexOutOfRangeException: An exception of type System
.IndexOutOfRangeException was thrown.
  at MyError.Main()
```

The text was actually generated from an underlying object you are using in your program—the array.

The results of Listing 10.1 are not pretty, and are not what you want your users to see. For a program to be user friendly, you need to be able to handle these exception errors in a much friendlier manner. Additionally, this program abruptly stopped when the exception occurred. You will also want to be able to maintain control of your programs if these exceptions occur.

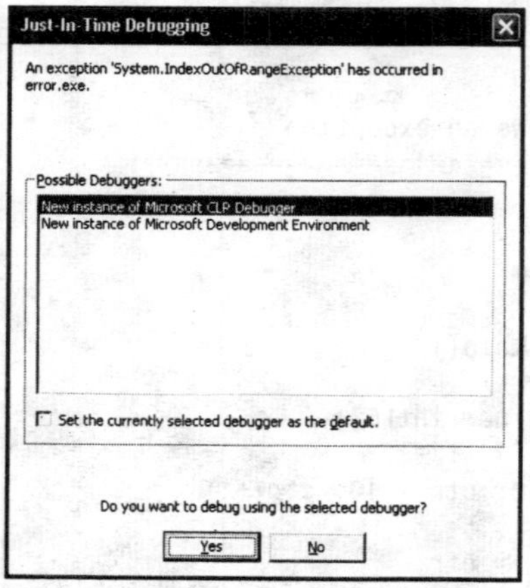


**FIGURE 10.1**
*An exception error being displayed by the runtime.*

**Tip**

Make a modification to Listing 10.1. Print the value of each array element after it is assigned. This can be done by adding the following after line 14:

```
Console.WriteLine("myArray[{0}] equals {1}", ctr, myArray[ctr]);
```

You will see that the listing stops before printing `myArray[5]`.

# Exception Handling

Exception handling refers to handling runtime errors such as the one created in Listing 10.1. You can add code to your programs that catch the problems and provide cleaner results than pop-up boxes, terminated programs, and cryptic messages. To do this, you use the `try` and `catch` keywords.

## Using `try` and `catch`

The `try` and `catch` keywords are the key to exception handling. The `try` command enables you to put a wrapper around a block of code that helps you route any exceptions that might occur.

The `catch` keyword enables you to catch the exceptions that the `try` command routes. By using a `catch`, you get the chance to execute code and control what happens, rather than letting the program terminate. Listing 10.2 illustrates a basic use of the `try` and `catch` commands.

**Listing 10.2** tryit.cs—Using try-catch

```
 1: // tryit.cs
 2: // A program that throws an exception
 3: //=============================================
 4: using System;
 5:
 6: class MyAppClass
 7: {
 8:    public static void Main()
 9:    {
10:       int [] myArray = new int[5];
11:
12:       try
13:       {
14:          for ( int ctr = 0; ctr < 10; ctr++ )  // Array only has 5
   ➥elements!
15:          {
16:             myArray[ctr] = ctr;
17:          }
18:       }
19:
20:       catch
21:       {
22:          Console.WriteLine("The exception was caught!");
23:       }
24:
25:    Console.WriteLine("At end of class");
25:    }
27: }
```

**OUTPUT**

```
The exception was caught!
At end of class
```

**ANALYSIS** This listing is similar to Listing 10.1, except it has basic exception handling added using `try` and `catch`. In this version of the listing, the main code is wrapped in a `try` statement. The `try` statement starts in line 12. It uses braces (lines 13 and 18) to enclose a block of code that is to be watched for exceptions. In this listing, the code that manipulates the array is enclosed in the `try` statement.

Following the `try` statement is a `catch` statement that starts in line 20 and includes the statements between its braces (lines 21 and 23). If an exception is found while executing the code within the `try` statement, control immediately goes to the `catch` statement. Instead of the results you saw in Listing 10.1, where a cryptic message was displayed and the program ended, in this listing the code within the `catch` statement's block executes. The program then continues to operate. In Listing 10.2, the `catch` statement prints a message and the program flow then continues. Line 25, which contains a call to the `WriteLine` method, is still executed.

## Catching Exception Information

In Listing 10.2, the `catch` statement catches any exception that might occur within the `try` statement's code. In addition to generically catching thrown exceptions, you can also determine which exception was thrown by including a parameter on your `catch`. The format of the `catch` is

```
catch( System.Exception e ) {}
```

The `catch` statement can receive the exception as a parameter. In this example, the exception is a variable named `e`. You could call this something more descriptive, but for this example, the name `e` works.

You can see that `e` is of type `System.Exception`, a fully qualified name meaning that the `Exception` type is defined in the `System` namespace. If you include the `System` statement with a `using` statement, you can shorten the `catch` call to

```
catch(Exception e) {}
```

The `Exception` type variable `e` contains descriptive information on the specific exception that was caused. Listing 10.3 is a modified version of Listing 10.2, containing a `catch` statement that receives any exceptions as a parameter. The changed lines are in boldface.

**Listing 10.3** tryit2.cs—Catching Exception Information

```
// tryit2.cs
// A program that throws an exception
//=============================================
using System;

class MyAppClass
{
    public static void Main()
    {
        int [] myArray = new int[5];

        try
        {
            for ( int ctr = 0; ctr < 10; ctr++ )  // Array only has 5 elements!
            {
                myArray[ctr] = ctr;
            }
        }

        catch( Exception e)
        {
            Console.WriteLine("The following exception was caught:\n{0}", e);
```

**LISTING 10.3** continued

```
23:         }
24:
25:         Console.WriteLine("At end of class");
26:     }
27: }
```

**OUTPUT**

```
The following exception was caught:
System.IndexOutOfRangeException: An exception of type
➥System.IndexOutOfRangeException was thrown.
    at MyAppClass.Main()
At end of class
```



**ANALYSIS** Listing 10.3 doesn't do much with the exception; however, you can gain a lot of information from what it does do. In line 22, `e` is printed using the `WriteLine` method. This displays information on the exception. Looking at the output, you see that the value of `e` indicates that the exception thrown was an `IndexOutOfRangeException` and it occurred in the `Main()` method of the `MyAppClass`—which is your program's class.

This listing catches all exceptions that occur within the `try` statement. The error printed is based on the type of exception executed. You can actually add code to your program to work with specific errors.

**Note**

> Once again, the exception was caught and the program continued to execute. Using a `catch` statement, you can prevent weird error messages from being automatically displayed. Additionally, the program doesn't terminate at the moment the exception occurs.

## Using Multiple Catches for a Single Try

The `catch` statement in Listing 10.2 is rather general. It can catch any exception that might have occurred in the code within the `try` statement code. You can include a `catch` statement that is more specific—in fact, you can write a `catch` statement for a specific exception. Listing 10.4 includes a `catch` statement that captures the exception you are already familiar with—`IndexOutOfRangeException`.

**Listing 10.4** catchIndex.cs—Catching a Specific Exception

```
// catchIndex.cs
// A program that throws an exception
//=============================================
using System;
```

**LISTING 10.4** continued

```
 5:
 6:  class MyAppClass
 7:  {
 8:     public static void Main()
 9:     {
10:        int [] myArray = new int[5];
11:
12:        try
13:        {
14:           for ( int ctr = 0; ctr < 10; ctr++ ) // Array only has 5
              ➥elements!
15:           {
16:              myArray[ctr] = ctr;
17:           }
18:        }
19:
20:        catch (IndexOutOfRangeException e)
21:        {
22:           Console.WriteLine("You were very goofy trying to use a bad array
              ➥index!!", e);
23:        }
24:
25:        catch (Exception e)
26:        {
27:           Console.WriteLine("Exception caught: {0}", e);
28:        }
29:
30:        Console.WriteLine("\nDone with the catch statements. Done with
           ➥program.");
31:     }
32:  }
```

**OUTPUT**

```
You were very goofy trying to use a bad array index!!

Done with the catch statements. Done with program.
```

**ANALYSIS** This listing uses the same array and same `try` command that you used in the previous listings, but lines 20 to 23 feature something new. Instead of having a parameter for a general exception, the `catch` statement in line 20 has a parameter for an `IndexOutOfRangeException` type. Like the general `Exception` type, this is in the `System` namespace. Just as its name implies, this exception type is specifically for indexes that go out of range. This `catch` statement captures only this type of exception though.

To be prepared for other exceptions that might occur, a second `catch` statement is included in lines 25 to 28. This `catch` includes the general `Exception` type parameter, so it will catch any other exceptions that might occur. Replace line 16 of Listing 10.4 with the following:

```
16:            myArray[ctr] = 100/ctr;    // division by zero....
```

When you recompile and run the program, you will get the following output:

```
Exception caught: System.DivideByZeroException: Attempted to divide by zero
   at MyAppClass.Main()

Done with the catch statements. Done with program.
```

The new line 16 causes a different error. The first time through the `for` loop in line 14, `ctr` is equal to `0`. Line 16 ends up dividing `100` by `0` (`ctr`). Division by `0` is not legal because it creates an infinite number, and thus an exception is thrown. This is not an index out of range, so the `catch` statement in line 20 is ignored because it doesn't match the `IndexOutOfRangeException` type. The `catch` in line 25 can work with any exception, and thus is executed. Line 27 prints the statement `"Exception Caught"`, followed by the exception description obtained with the variable `e`. As you can see by the output, the exception thrown is a `DivideByZeroException`.



## Understanding the Order of Handling Exceptions

In Listing 10.4, the order of the two `catch` statements is very important. You always include the more specific exceptions first and the most general exception last. Starting with the original Listing 10.4, if you change the order of the two `catch` statements:

```
catch (Exception e)
{
   Console.WriteLine("Exception caught: {0}", e);
}

catch (IndexOutOfRangeException e)
{
    Console.WriteLine("You were very goofy trying to use a bad array
    ➥index!!", e);
}
```

and then recompile, you will get an error. Because the general `catch(Exception e)` catches all the exceptions, no other `catch` statements will be executed.

# Adding Finality with `finally`

There are times when you will want to execute a block of code regardless of whether the code in a `try` statement succeeds or fails. C# provides the `finally` keyword to take care of this. The code in a `finally` block will always execute. Listing 10.5 shows the use of this keyword.

**Listing 10.5** final.cs—Using the `finally` Keyword

```
 1:  // final.cs
 2:  // A program that throws an exception
 3:  //=============================================
 4:  using System;
 5:
 6:  class MyAppClass
 7:  {
 8:     public static void Main()
 9:     {
10:        int [] myArray = new int[5];
11:
12:        try
13:        {
14:           for ( int ctr = 0; ctr < 10; ctr++ )  // Array only has 5
               ➥elements!
15:           {
16:              myArray[ctr] = ctr;
17:           }
18:        }
19:
20:  //      catch
21:  //      {
22:  //         Console.WriteLine("Exception caught");
23:  //      }
24:
25:        finally
26:        {
27:          Console.WriteLine("Done with exception handling");
28:        }
29:
30:        Console.WriteLine("End of Program");
31:     }
32:  }
```

**OUTPUT**

```
Exception occurred: System.IndexOutOfRangeException: An exception of type
➥System
.IndexOutOfRangeException was thrown.
   at MyAppClass.Main()
Done with exception handling
```

**ANALYSIS** This listing is the same listing you've seen before. The key change to this listing is in lines 25 to 28. A `finally` clause has been added. In this listing, the `finally` clause prints a message. It is important to note that even though the exception was not caught by a `catch` clause (lines 20 to 23 are commented out), the `finally` still executed before the program terminated. The `WriteLine` command in line 30, however, does not execute.

Remove the comments from lines 20 to 23 and rerun the program. This time you receive the following output:

**OUTPUT**

```
Exception caught.
Done with exception handling
End of Program
```

The use of a `catch` does not preclude the `finally` code from happening. If you change line 14 to the following:

```
14:            for ( int ctr = 0; ctr < 5; ctr++ )
```

and then recompile and run the program, you will get the following output:

**OUTPUT**

```
Done with exception handling
End of Program
```



Notice that this change to line 14 removed the problem that was causing the exception to occur. This means the listing ran without problems. As you can see from the output, the `finally` block was still executed. The `finally` block will be executed regardless of what else happens.

Now is a good time to show a more robust example that uses exception handling. Listing 10.6 illustrates a more practical program.

**Listing 10.6** ListFile.cs—Using Exception Handling

```
// ListFile.cs - program to print a listing to the console
//-----------------------------------------------------------

using System;
using System.IO;

class ListFile
{
  public static void Main(string[] args)
  {
    try
    {

       int ctr=0;
       if (args.Length <= 0 )
       {
          Console.WriteLine("Format: ListFile filename");
          return;
       }
       else
       {
          FileStream fstr = new FileStream(args[0], FileMode.Open);
          try
```

**LISTING 10.6** continued

```
            {
               StreamReader t = new StreamReader(fstr);
               string line;
               while ((line = t.ReadLine()) != null)
               {
                  ctr++;
                  Console.WriteLine("{0}:  {1}", ctr, line);
               }
            }
            catch( Exception e )
            {
               Console.WriteLine("Exception during read/write: {0}\n", e);
            }
            finally
            {
               fstr.Close();
            }
         }
      }

      catch (System.IO.FileNotFoundException)
      {
         Console.WriteLine ("ListFile could not find the file {0}", args[0]);
      }
      catch (Exception e)
      {
         Console.WriteLine("Exception: {0}\n\n", e);
      }
   }
}
```

**OUTPUT**

```
Format: ListFile filename
```

**ANALYSIS** If you run this program, you get the output displayed. You need to include a filename as a parameter to the program. If you run this program with ListFile.cs as the parameter, the output will be the listing with line numbers:

**OUTPUT**

```
 1:  // ListFile.cs - program to print a listing to the console
 2:  //-------------------------------------------------------------
 3:
 4:  using System;
 5:  using System.IO;
 6:
 7:  class ListFile
 8:  {
 9:    public static void Main(string[] args)
10:    {
11:      try
```

```
    {
        int ctr=0;
        if (args.Length <= 0 )
        {
           Console.WriteLine("Format: ListFile filename");
           return;
        }
        else
        {
           FileStream fstr = new FileStream(args[0], FileMode.Open);
           try
           {
              StreamReader t = new StreamReader(fstr);
              string line;
              while ((line = t.ReadLine()) != null)
              {
                 ctr++;
                 Console.WriteLine("{0}:  {1}", ctr, line);
              }
           }
           catch( Exception e )
           {
              Console.WriteLine("Exception during read/write: {0}\n",
➥e);
           }
           finally
           {
              fstr.Close();
           }
        }
    }

    catch (System.IO.FileNotFoundException)
    {
       Console.WriteLine ("ListFile could not find the file {0}",
➥args[0]);
    }
    catch (Exception e)
    {
       Console.WriteLine("Exception: {0}\n\n", e);
    }
  }
}
```



You can add different filenames and you will get the same results if the file exists. If you enter a file that doesn't exist, you get the following message (The filename xxx was used):

```
ListFile could not find the file xxx
```

Notice that the program isn't presenting the user with cryptic exception messages from the runtime; rather it is trying to provide useful information back to the user on what happened. This is done with a combination of programming logic and exception handling.

This listing incorporates everything you've been learning. In lines 4 and 5, you see that not only is the `System` namespace being used, but so is the `IO` namespace within `System`. The `IO` namespace contains routines for sending and receiving information (input/output).

In line 7, you see the start of the main application class, `ListFile`. This class has a `Main` routine, where program execution starts. In line 9, the `Main` method receives a string array named `args` as a parameter. The values within `args` are obtained from the command-line arguments you include when you run the program.

Line 11 starts the code that is the focus of today's lesson. In this line, a `try` block is declared. This `try` block encompasses the code from line 11 to line 42. You can see that this `try` block has lots of code in it, including another `try` command. If any of the code within this `try` block causes an exception to occur—and not be handled— the `try` statement fails and control goes to its `catch` blocks. It is important to note that only unhandled exceptions within this `try` block cause flow to go to this `try`'s `catch` statements.

There are two `catch` blocks defined for this overriding `try` statement. The first, in lines 44 to 47, catches a specific exception, `FileNotFoundException`. For clarity's sake, the exception name is fully qualified; however, you could have chosen to shorten this to just the exception type because `System.IO` was included in line 5. The `FileNotFoundException` occurs when you try to use a file that does not exist. In this case, if the file doesn't exist, a simple message is printed in line 46 that states the file couldn't be found.

Although the `FileNotFoundException` is expected with this program, lines 48 to 51 were added in case an unexpected exception happens. This allows a graceful exit rather than relying on the runtime.

Digging deeper into the code within the `try` statement, you get a better understanding of what this program is doing. In line 14, a simple counter variable, `ctr`, is created, which is used to place line numbers on a listing.

Line 15 contains programming logic that checks to make sure users include a filename when they run the program. If a filename is not included, you want to exit the program. In line 15, an `if` statement checks the value of the `Length` property of the `args` string. If the length is less than or equal to `0`, no command-line parameters were entered. The user should have entered at least one item as a command-line parameter. If no items were entered, a descriptive message is presented to the reader and the object is ended using the `return` statement.

If a command-line parameter is entered—`args.Length` is greater than `0`—the `else` statement in lines 20 to 41 are executed. In line 22, a new object called `fstr` is created. This object is of type `FileStream, which` has a constructor that takes two arguments. The first is a filename. The filename you are passing is the filename entered by the user and thus available in the first element of the `args` array. This is `args[0]`. The second parameter is an indicator as to what to do. In this case, you are passing a value called `FileMode.Open`, which indicates to the `FileStream` object that it should open a file so you can read its contents. The file that is opened is referenced using the `FileStream` object you are creating, `fstr`.



If line 22 fails and throws an exception, it goes to the `catch` in line 44. Line 44 contains the `catch` for the closest (without having gone past) `try` statement.

Line 23 starts a new `try` block. This `try` block has its own `catch` statement in line 33. Line 25 creates a variable called `t` of type `StreamReader`. This variable is associated to the file you opened in line 22 with the variable `fstr`. The file is treated as a stream of characters flowing into your program. The `t` variable is used to read this stream of characters.

Line 26 contains a string variable called `line`, which is used to hold a group of characters that are being streamed into your program. In line 27, you see how `line` is used.

Line 27 is doing a lot, so it is worth dissecting. First, a line of characters is streamed into your program using `t`. The `StreamReader` type has a method called `ReadLine` that provides a line of characters. A line of characters is all of the characters up until a newline character is found. Because `t` was associated to the `fstr` and `fstr` is associated to the file the reader entered, the `ReadLine` method returns the next line of characters from the user's file. This line of characters is then assigned to the `line` string variable. After reading this line of characters and placing it into the `line` variable, the value is compared to `null`. If the string returned was `null`, it was either the end of the file or a bad read. Either way, there is no reason to continue processing the file after the `null` value is encountered.

If the characters read and placed into `line` are not equal to `null`, the `while` statement processes its block commands. In this case, the line counter, `ctr`, is incremented and the `lineof` text is printed. The printing includes the line number, a colon, and the text from the file that is in the `line` variable. This processing continues until a `null` is found.

If anything goes wrong in reading a line of the file, an exception will most likely be thrown. Lines 33 to 36 catch any exceptions that might occur and add additional descriptive text to the exception message. This `catch` prevents the runtime from taking over. Additionally, it helps you and your users by giving additional information as to where the error occurred.

Lines 37 to 40 contain a `finally` that is also associated with the `try` in line 23. This `finally` does one thing—it closes the file that was opened in line 22. Because line 22 was successful—had it not been successful, it would have tossed an exception and program flow would have gone to line 44's `catch` statement—the file needs to be closed before the program ends. Whether an exception occurs in lines 24 to 32 or not, the file should still be closed before leaving the program. The `finally` clause makes sure that the `Close` method is called.

As you can see from this listing, `try-catch-finally` statements can be nested. Not only that, they also can be used to make your programs much more friendly for your users.

**Note** A program very similar to ListFile was used to add the line numbers to the listings in this book!

# Common Exceptions

There are a number of exceptions defined in the .NET Framework classes. You have seen a couple already. Table 10.1 lists many of the common exception classes within the `System` namespace.

**TABLE 10.1** Common Exceptions in the `System` Namespace

| *Exception Name* | *Description* |
|---|---|
| `MemberAccessException` | Access error. |
| | A type member, such as a method, cannot be accessed. |
| `ArgumentException` | Argument error. |
| | A method's argument is not valid. |
| `ArgumentNullException` | Null argument. |
| | A method was passed a null argument that cannot be accepted. |
| `ArithmeticException` | Math error. |
| | An exception caused because of a math operation. This is more general than `DivideByZeroException` and `OverflowException`. |

**TABLE 10.1** continued

| *Exception Name* | *Description* |
|---|---|
| `ArrayTypeMismatchException` | Array type mismatch.<br>Thrown when you try to store an incompatible type into an array. |
| `DivideByZeroException` | Divide by zero.<br>Caused by an attempt to divide by zero. |
| `FormatException` | Format is incorrect.<br>An argument has the wrong format. |
| `IndexOutOfRangeException` | Index out of range.<br>Caused when an index is used that is less than zero or higher than the top value of the array's index. |
| `InvalidCastException` | Invalid cast.<br>Caused when an explicit conversion fails. |
| `MulticastNotSupportedException` | Multicast not supported.<br>Caused when the combination of two non-null delegates fails. (Delegates are covered on Day 14, "Indexers, Delegates, and Events.") |
| `NotFiniteNumberException` | Not a finite number.<br>The number is not valid. |
| `NotSupportedException` | Method is not supported.<br>Indicates that a method is being called that is not implemented within the class. |
| `NullReferenceException` | Reference to null.<br>Caused when you refer to a reference object that is null. |
| `OutOfMemoryException` | Out of memory.<br>Caused when memory is not available for a new statement to allocate. |
| `OverflowException` | Overflow.<br>Caused by a math operation that assigns a value that is too large (or too small) when the checked keyword is used. |
| `StackOverflowException` | Stack overflow.<br>Caused when too many commands are on the stack. |
| `TypeInitializationException` | Bad type initialization.<br>Caused when a `static` constructor has a problem. |

**Note**

Table 10.1 provides the name with the assumption that you've included a `using` statement with the `System` namespace; otherwise, you need to fully qualify these names using `System.`*`ExceptionName`*, where *`ExceptionName`* is the name provided in the table.

# Defining Your Own Exception Classes

In addition to the exceptions that have been defined in the framework, you can also create your own. In C#, it is preferred that you throw an exception rather than pass back a lot of different error codes. Because of this, it is also important that your code always include exception handling in case an exception is thrown. Although this adds additional lines of code to your programs, it can make them much more friendly to your users.

After you create your own exception, you will want to cause it to occur. To cause an exception to occur, you *throw* the exception. To throw your own exception, you use the `throw` keyword!

You can throw a predefined exception or your own exception. Predefined exceptions are any that have been previously defined in any of the namespaces you are using. For example, you can actually throw any of the exceptions that were listed in Table 10.1. To do this, you use the `throw` keyword in the following format:

```
throw( exception );
```

If the exception doesn't already exist, you also will need to include the `new` keyword to create the exception. For example, Listing 10.7 throws a new `DivideByZeroException` exception. Granted, this listing is pretty pointless; however, it does illustrate the `throw` keyword in its most basic form.

**Note**

The use of parenthesis with the throw keyword is optional. The following two lines are the equivalent:

```
throw( exception );
```

```
throw exception;
```

**Listing 10.7** zero.cs—Throwing an Exception

```
// zero.cs
// Throwing a predefined exception.
// This listing gives a runtime exception error!
//===============================================
```

**Listing 10.7** continued

```
 5: using System;
 6:
 7: class SimpleApp
 8: {
 9:    public static void Main()
10:    {
11:       Console.WriteLine("Before Exception...");
12:       throw( new DivideByZeroException() );
13:       Console.WriteLine("After Exception...");
14:    }
15: }
```



**Output**

```
Before Exception...

Exception occurred: System.DivideByZeroException: Attempted to divide by
➥zero.
   at SimpleApp.Main()
```

**Analysis** This listing does nothing other than print messages and throw a `DivideByZeroException` exception in line 12. When this program executes, you get a runtime error that indicates the exception was thrown. Simple, but impractical.

When you compile this listing, you get a runtime error; line 13 will never be executed, because the `throw` command terminates the program. Remember, a `throw` command leaves the current routine immediately. You can remove line 13 from the listing—because it would never execute anyway—to avoid the compiler warning. It was added to this listing to emphasize what an exception does to program flow.

> **Note** You could replace the `DivideByZeroException` with any of the exceptions listed in Table 10.1. You would see that the output would display the appropriate information.

# Throwing Your Own Exceptions

Also possible—and more valuable—is being able to create and throw your own exceptions. To create your own exception, you must first declare it. Use the following format:

```
class ExceptionName : Exception {}
```

where *`ExceptionName`* is the name your exception will have. You can tell from this line of code that your exception is a class type. The rest of this line tells you that your exception is related to an existing class called `Exception`. You will learn more about this relationship in tomorrow's lessons on inheritance.

**Tip**

End your exception name with the word `Exception`. If you look at Table 10.1, you will see that this tip follows suit with the predefined exceptions.

One line of code is all that it takes to create your own exception that can then be caught. Listing 10.8 illustrates creating your own exception and throwing it.

**Listing 10.8** throwit.cs—Creating and Throwing Your Own Exception

```
// throwit.cs
// Throwing your own error.
//=================================================
using System;

class MyThreeException : Exception {}

class MyAppClass
{
    public static void Main()
    {
      int result;

      try
      {
          result = MyMath.AddEm( 1, 2 );
          Console.WriteLine( "Result of AddEm(1, 2) is {0}", result);

          result = MyMath.AddEm( 3, 4 );
          Console.WriteLine( "Result of AddEm(3, 4) is {0}", result);
      }

      catch (MyThreeException)
      {
          Console.WriteLine("Ack!  We don't like adding threes.");
      }

      catch (Exception e)
      {
         Console.WriteLine("Exception caught: {0}", e);
      }

      Console.WriteLine("\nAt end of program");
    }
}

class MyMath
{
    static public int AddEm(int x, int y)
```

**LISTING 10.8** continued

```
40:     {
41:        if(x == 3 || y == 3)
42:           throw( new MyThreeException() );
43:
44:        return( x + y );
45:     }
46: }
```

**OUTPUT**

```
Result of AddEm(1, 2) is 3
Ack!  We don't like adding threes.

At end of program
```

**ANALYSIS** This listing shows you how to create your own exception called `MyThreeException`. This exception is defined in line 6 using the format you learned earlier. This enables you to throw a basic exception.

Before jumping into the `MyAppClass`, first look at the second class in lines 37 to 46. This class called `MyMath` contains only a simple static method called `AddEm`. The `AddEm` method adds two numbers and returns the result. In line 41 an `if` condition checks to see whether either of the values passed to `AddEm` is equal to `3`; if so, an exception is thrown. This is the `MyThreeException` you declared in line 6.

In lines 8 to 34 you have the `Main` routine for the `MyAppClass`. This routine calls the `AddEm` method. These calls are done within a `try` statement, so if any exceptions are thrown, it is ready to react. In line 16, the first call to `AddEm` occurs using the value `1` and `2`. These values don't throw an exception, so program flow continues. Line 19 calls the `AddEm` method again. This time the first argument is a `3`, which results in the `AddEm` method throwing the `MyThreeException`. Line 23 contains a `catch` statement that is looking for a `MyThreeException` and thus catches and takes care of it.

If you don't catch the exception, the runtime throws an exception message for you. If you comment out lines 23 through 26 of Listing 10.8, you get the following output when you compile and rerun the program:

```
Result of AddEm(1, 2) is 3
Exception caught: MyThreeException: An exception of type MyThreeException was
➥thrown.
   at MyAppClass.Main()

At end of program
```

This is the same type of message that any other exception receives. You can also pass a parameter to the `catch` class that handles your exception. This parameter contains the information for the general system message. For example, if you change lines 23 to 26 to the following:

```
23:         catch (MyThreeException e )
24:         {
25:             Console.WriteLine("Ack!  We don't like adding threes. \n {0}" ,
            ➥e);
26:         }
```

you will see the following results (this assumes you uncommented the lines as well):

```
Result of AddEm(1, 2) is 3
Ack!  We don't like adding threes.
MyThreeException: An exception of type MyThreeException was thrown.
   at MyAppClass.Main()

At end of program
```

Your new exception is as fully functioning as any of the existing exceptions.

**Tip**

Listing 10.6 creates a basic exception. To be more complete, you should include three constructors for your new exception. The details of these overloads will become clearer after tomorrow's lesson on inheritance. For now, you should know that you are being more complete by including the following code, which contains three constructors:

```
class MyThreeException : Exception
{
  public MyThreeException()
  {
  }

  public MyThreeException( string e ) : base (e)
  {
  }

  public MyThreeException( string e, Exception inner ) :
          base ( e, inner )
  {
  }
}
```

You can replace the exception name of `MyThreeException` with your own exception.

## Rethrowing an Exception

It should come as no surprise that if you can throw your own exceptions, and if you can throw system expressions, it is also possible to rethrow an existing exception. Why might you want to do this? And *when* would you want to do this?

As you have seen, you can catch an exception and execute your own code in reaction. If you do this in a class that was called by another class, you might want to let the caller know there was a problem. Before letting the caller know, you might want to do some processing of your own.

Consider an example based on an earlier program. You could create a class that opens a file, counts the number of characters in the file, and returns this to a calling program. If you get an error when you open the file to begin your count, an exception will be thrown. You can catch this exception, set the count to `0` and return to the calling program. However, the calling program won't know that there was a problem opening the file. It will see only that the number of bytes returned was `0`.

A better action to take would be to set the number of characters to `0` and rethrow the error for the calling program to react to. This way the calling program knows exactly what happened.

To rethrow the error, you need to include a parameter of the error type in your `catch` statement. The following code illustrates how the generic `catch` statement could rethrow the catch to the calling routine:

```
catch (Exception e)
{
    // My personal exception logic here
    throw ( e );    // e is the argument received by this catch
}
```

**Note** As you begin to build more detailed applications, you might want to look deeper into exception handling. You have learned the most important features of exception handling today, but you can do a lot more with them. Such topics are beyond the scope of this book, however.

## checked Versus unchecked Statements

Two additional C# keywords determine whether placing a value that is too big or too small will cause an exception to be thrown: `checked` and `unchecked`.. If the code is `checked` and a value is placed in a variable that is too big or too small, an exception will occur. If the code is `unchecked`, the resulting value placed will be truncated to fit within the variable. Listing 10.9 illustrates these two keywords.

**Listing 10.9** checkit.cs—Using the *checked* Keyword

```
1:  // checkit.cs
2:  //===============================================
3:
4:  using System;
5:
6:  class MyAppClass
7:  {
8:     public static void Main()
9:     {
10:        int result;
11:        const int topval = 2147483647;
12:
13:        for( long ctr = topval - 5L;  ctr < (topval+10L); ctr++ )
14:        {
15:           checked
16:           {
17:              result = (int) ctr;
18:              Console.WriteLine("{0} assigned from {1}", result, ctr);
19:           }
20:        }
21:     }
22:  }
23:
```

**OUTPUT** You get the following error output; you also get an exception:

```
2147483642 assigned from 2147483642
2147483643 assigned from 2147483643
2147483644 assigned from 2147483644
2147483645 assigned from 2147483645
2147483646 assigned from 2147483646
2147483647 assigned from 2147483647

Exception occurred: System.OverflowException: An exception of type
➥System.Overfl
owException was thrown.
   at MyAppClass.Main()
```

**ANALYSIS** In line 11 of this listing, a variable called `topval` is created as a constant variable that contains the largest value that a regular integer variable can hold, `2147483647`. The `for` loop in line 13 loops to a value that is 10 higher than this top value. This is being placed in a `long` variable, which is okay. In line 17, however, the `ctr` value is being explicitly placed into `result`, which is an integer. When you execute this listing, you receive an error because the code in lines 16 to 19 is `checked`. This code tries to assign a value to `result` that is larger than the largest value it can hold.

**Note** If you remove the `+10` from line 13 of the listing and compile it, you will see that the listing works. This is because there is nothing wrong. It is when you try to go above the `topVal` that the overflow error occurs.

You should now change this listing to use the `unchecked` keyword. Change line 15 in the listing to the following:

```
13:     unchecked
```

Recompile and execute the listing. The listing will compile this time; however, the output might be unexpected results. The output this time is

OUTPUT

```
2147483642 assigned from 2147483642
2147483643 assigned from 2147483643
2147483644 assigned from 2147483644
2147483645 assigned from 2147483645
2147483646 assigned from 2147483646
2147483647 assigned from 2147483647
-2147483648 assigned from 2147483648
-2147483647 assigned from 2147483649
-2147483646 assigned from 2147483650
-2147483645 assigned from 2147483651
-2147483644 assigned from 2147483652
-2147483643 assigned from 2147483653
-2147483642 assigned from 2147483654
-2147483641 assigned from 2147483655
-2147483640 assigned from 2147483656
```

You should notice that this time an exception was not thrown because the code was `unchecked`. The results, however, are not what you would want.

## Formats for checked and unchecked

Within Listing 10.9, `checked` and `unchecked` were used as statements. The format of these was

```
[un]checked { //statements }
```

You can also use these as operators. The format of using these keywords as operators is

```
[un]checked ( expression )
```

where the expression being `checked`, or `unchecked`, is between the parentheses.

10

**Caution** You should not assume that `checked` or `unchecked` is the default. `checked` is generally defaulted; however, there are factors that can change this. You can force checking to occur by including `/checked` in your command-line compiler. If you are using an integrated development tool, you should be able to select a checked item on your compile options. You can force checking to be ignored by using `/checked-` in the command line.

# Summary

Today's lessons covered exception handling. You learned that the `try` command is used to check for exceptions occurring. If an exception is thrown, you learned that you can use the `catch` statement to handle the error in a more controlled fashion. You learned that you can have multiple `catch` statements so you can customize what you do for different exceptions, and that you can catch the type `Exception` which will catch any basic exception.

You also learned that you can create a block of code that will be executed after exception handling code (both `try` and `catch`) statements have executed. This block can be executed regardless of whether an exception was or was not thrown. This block is tagged with the `finally` keyword.

You ended the day's lessons by exploring two keywords that are related to handling overflow errors—`checked` and `unchecked`. An overflow error occurs when you place a value into a variable that is too big. You learned that you can force the checking of a section of code or an expression for overflow by using the `checked` keyword and can ignore overflow errors by using the `unchecked` keyword.

# Q&A

**Q Using `catch` by itself seems to be the most powerful. Why shouldn't I just use `catch` with no parameters and do all my logic there?**

**A** Although using `catch` by itself is the most powerful, it loses all the information about the exception that was thrown. Because of this, it is better to use `catch(Exception e)` instead. This enables you to get to the exception information that was thrown. If you chose not to use this information, you can then pass it on to any other classes that might call yours. This gives those classes the option to do something with the information.

**Q Are all exceptions treated equally?**

**A** No. There are actually two classes of exceptions, System exceptions and Application exceptions. Application exceptions will not terminate a program; System exceptions will. For the most part, today's lesson covered the more common exceptions, System level. For more details on exceptions and the differences between these two classes of exceptions, see the Framework or C# documentation.

**Q You said there was a lot more to learn about exception handling. Do I need to learn it?**

**A** Today's lesson about exception handling will get you through the coding you will do. By learning more about exception handling, you will be able to manipulate errors and messages better. Additionally, you can learn how to embed an exception within an exception—and more. It is not critical to know these advanced concepts; however, knowing them will make you a better, more expert, C# programmer.



# Workshop

The Workshop provides quiz questions to help you solidify your understanding of the material covered and exercises to provide you with experience in using what you've learned. Try to understand the quiz and exercise answers before continuing to the next day's lesson. Answers are provided in Appendix A, "Answers."

## Quiz

1. What keyword(s) are used with exceptions?
2. Which of the following should be handled by exception handling and which should be handled with regular code?
    a. A value entered by a user is not between a given range.
    b. A file cannot be read correctly.
    c. An argument passed to a method contains an invalid value.
    d. An argument passed to a method contains an invalid type.
3. What causes an exception?
4. When do exceptions occur?
    a. During coding
    b. During the compile
    c. During runtime
    d. When requested by the end user

5. What keyword is used to react to an exception?
6. When does the `finally` block execute?
7. How many `catch` statements are associated with a single `try` statement?
8. Does the order of `catch` statements matter? Why or Why not?
9. In what namespace are many of the common predefined exceptions defined?
10. What does the `throw` command do?

## Exercises

1. What code could be used to check the following line to see whether it causes an exception?

```
GradePercentage = MyValue/Total
```

2. **BUG BUSTER:** The following program has a problem. What is the cause of the error?

```
int zero = 0;
try
{
    int result = 1000 / zero;
}
catch (Exception e)
{
   Console.WriteLine("Exception caught: {0}", e);
}
catch (DivideByZeroException e)
{
    Console.WriteLine("This is my error message. ", e);
}
finally
{
    Console.WriteLine("Can't get here");
}
```

3. Write the code to create an exception class of your own that includes the three overloaded constructors suggested in the sidebar in today's lesson. Call the exception `NegativeValueException`.
4. Use the `NegativeValueException` you created in exercise 3 in a complete listing. Base this program on Listing 10.8. Create a class called `SubtractEm` that throws your `NegativeValueException` if the result of a subtraction operation is negative.

# WEEK 2

# DAY 11

# Inheritance

One of the key constructs of an object-oriented language is the ability to extend preexisting classes. This extending can be done through the concept of inheritance. Today you will

- Discover base classes
- Expand base classes with inheritance
- Learn to expand the functionality of a class using inheritance
- Protect, yet share, your data members with derived classes
- Discover how to be virtual and abstract with your class members
- Learn to seal a class
- Manipulate objects as different types using keywords `is` and `as`

## The Basics of Inheritance

Each of us inherits characteristics from our parents—for example, eye color, hair color and texture, and so forth. In addition to these characteristics, we also have our own characteristics that extend beyond our parents. Just as we derive and extend characteristics from our parents, classes can derive from other classes. Some of those characteristics are overridden with our own characteristics and some are not.

The concept of inheritance gives us the ability to create a new class based on an existing class. The new class can use all the features of the original class, it can override existing features, it can extend existing features, or it can add its own features.

A number of new classes can inherit from an original class; however, only one class can be inherited from. For example, you can have a base class called `control` that can be inherited by a number of different control types. Figure 11.1 helps illustrate this one-to-many relationship. Note from the figure that reading from left to right there can be a one-to-many relationship; however, reading from right to left, there is only one original class.

**FIGURE 11.1**
*Inheriting relationships.*

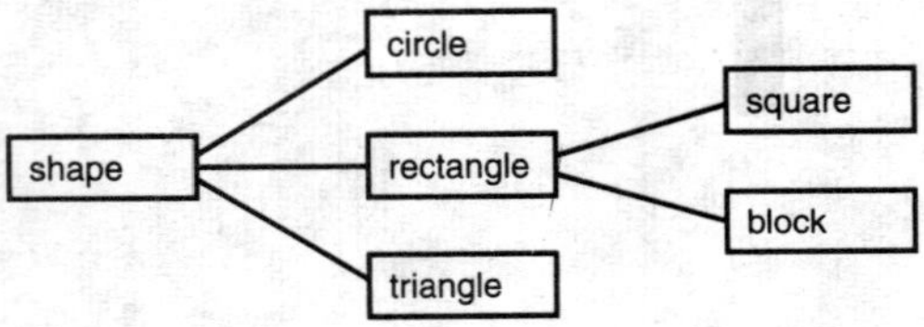


There are several basic terms that are commonly used when discussing inheritance:

| | |
|---|---|
| *Base class* | The original class. |
| *Parent class* | Another name for a base class. |
| *Derived class* | A new class, created by inheriting from a base class. |
| *Child class* | Another name for a derived class. |
| *Single inheritance* | A derived class created from one, and only one, base class. C# supports only single inheritance. The illustration in Figure 11.1 is for single inheritance. |
| *Multiple inheritance* | A derived class created from two or more base classes. C# does not support multiple inheritance. |

These are not the only important terms related to inheritance. Throughout today's lesson, you will learn a number of additional terms.

**Single Versus Multiple Inheritance**

Unlike C++, C# does not support multiple inheritance. Multiple inheritance occurs when a new, derived class is created by more than one base class. For example, you could use a

> name class and an address class and derive a business contact class from those two classes. The business class would include characteristics of both base classes. A number of issues, as well as additional complexities, accrue from multiple inheritance. Using interfaces, which are covered on Day 13, "Interfaces," you can obtain many of the same results.

## Simple Inheritance

The best way to understand inheritance is to see it in action. With inheritance, you need to start with a base class. Listing 11.1 illustrates a class that will be used to illustrate inheritance in today's lessons. A subset of this listing will also be used.



**Listing 11.1** A Base Class and a Class to Illustrate Its Use

```
// inherit01.cs
// A relatively simple class to use as a starting point
//=====================================================
using System;
using System.Text;

class Person
{
   private string firstName;
   private string middleName;
   private string lastName ;
   private int    age;

   // ToDo: Add properties to access the data members

   public Person()
   {
   }

   public Person(string fn, string ln)
   {
      firstName = fn;
      lastName = ln;
   }

   public Person(string fn, string mn, string ln)
   {
      firstName = fn;
      middleName = mn;
      lastName = ln;
   }

   public Person(string fn, string mn, string ln, int a)
```

**LISTING 11.1** continued

```
    {
        firstName = fn;
        middleName = mn;
        lastName = ln;
        age = a;
    }

    public void displayAge()
    {
        Console.WriteLine("Age {0}", age);
    }

    public void displayFullName()
    {
        StringBuilder FullName = new StringBuilder();

        FullName.Append(firstName);
        FullName.Append(" ");
        if( middleName[0] != "" )
        {
            FullName.Append(middleName[0]);
            FullName.Append(". ");
        }
        FullName.Append(lastName);

        Console.WriteLine(FullName);
    }
}

// NameApp class. Illustrates the use of the Person class
class NameApp
{
    public static void Main()
    {
        Person me = new Person("Bradley", "Lee", "Jones");
        Person myWife = new Person("Melissa", "Anne", "Jones", 21);

        me.displayFullName();
        me.displayAge();

        myWife.displayFullName();
        myWife.displayAge();
    }
}
```

**OUTPUT**

```
Bradley L. Jones
Age 0
Melissa A. Jones
Age 21
```

**ANALYSIS** The class that will be used for inheritance is the `Person` class defined in lines 7 to 61. Although this class is more complex than what is needed to illustrate inheritance, it also is more practical. In lines 9 to 12, you see four data members within the class. These store information about the person. The access modifier for each of these data members is `private`. Remember that `private` restricts access to the data members to within the class. To change these values outside the class, you should add properties to this listing.

> **Note** To cut down on the listing size, properties were left out of this listing. You should include properties in your own listings. You could also change the access modifiers to `public` to give access to the data members; however, it is recommended that you don't. It is best to encapsulate your data members and use properties.

In lines 16 to 39, there are four constructors created for this listing. This enables the user to create a `Person` object in a number of ways. Two member methods are also included in the class. In lines 41 to 44, a simple method, `displayAge`, displays the age of the person. Lines 46 to 60 present a more complex method, `displayFullName`.



The `displayFullName` method uses a new class type that you have not seen before. The `StringBuilder` class is available within the `System` namespace. More specifically, it is available within the `System.Text` namespace. In line 5, you will see that the `System.Text` namespace is being used in the listing. Line 5 was added for the `StringBuilder` class. The `StringBuilder` class creates a string that can be manipulated in ways that a normal string cannot. For example, the size of the string can be increased or decreased. It is easier to append to or change a `StringBuilder` object than a normal string.

In line 48, an object called `FullName` is being created that will be of type `StringBuilder`. This object will be used to hold the formatted full name of the person. In line 50, you append the first name, `firstName`, to the newly created `FullName` string. Because `FullName` will be blank, line 50 basically copies the first name into the `FullName`. Line 51 appends a space to the end of the first name. Lines 52 to 56 add the middle initial to the `FullName` rather then the full middle name. In line 52, an `if` statement is used to make sure that the middle name is not equal to "" (which is a blank string). If there is a middle name, line 54 appends the first character of the middle name (the initial). Line 55 then appends a period and a space. Finally, line 57 appends the last name.

The last line of the method displays the full name to the console. In your own listing, you might want to change the name of this method to `getFullName` and have it return the formatted name instead. This would enable calling programs to use the full name in other ways.

The rest of the listing contains the `NameApp` class. This class is provided so you can see the `Person` class being used. In lines 68 and 69, two objects of type `Person` are declared, `my` and `myWife`. In lines 71 to 75, the methods of the objects are called.

## Inheritance in Action

Although there is a lot of code in Listing 11.1, you should have been able to understand all of it. There is nothing new being presented here other than the `StringBuilder` class. In Listing 11.2, however, there are several new features. For example, to inherit from a base class, you use this format:

```
class derived_class : base_class
```

The colon (:) is used to indicate inheritance by separating the new, *`derived_class`*, from the original, *`base_class`*.

**Listing 11.2** inherit02.cs—Basic Inheritance

```
// inherit02.cs
// Basic inheritance.
//===============================================
using System;
using System.Text;

class Person
{
    protected string firstName;
    protected string middleName;
    protected string lastName;
    private int   age;

    //ToDo: Add properties to access data members

    public Person()
    {
    }

    public Person(string fn, string ln)
    {
        firstName = fn;
        lastName = ln;
    }

```

**LISTING 11.2** continued

```
   public Person(string fn, string mn, string ln)
   {
      firstName = fn;
      middleName = mn;
      lastName = ln;
   }

   public Person(string fn, string mn, string ln, int a)
   {
      firstName = fn;
      middleName = mn;
      lastName = ln;
      age = a;
   }

   public void displayAge()
   {
      Console.WriteLine("Age {0}", age);
   }

   public void displayFullName()
   {
      StringBuilder FullName = new StringBuilder();

      FullName.Append(firstName);
      FullName.Append(" ");
      if( middleName != "" )
      {
        FullName.Append(middleName[0]);
        FullName.Append(". ");
      }
      FullName.Append(lastName);

      Console.WriteLine(FullName);
   }
}

class Employee : Person
{
   private ushort hYear;

   public ushort hireYear
   {
     get { return(hYear); }
     set { hYear = value; }
   }

   public Employee() : base()
```

**LISTING 11.2** continued

```
    {
    }

    public Employee( string fn, string ln ) : base( fn, ln)
    {
    }

    public Employee(string fn, string mn, string ln, int a) :
            base(fn, mn, ln, a)
    {
    }

    public Employee(string fn, string ln, ushort hy) : base(fn, ln)
    {
       hireYear = hy;
    }

    public new void displayFullName()
    {
       Console.WriteLine("Employee: {0} {1} {2}",
                              firstName, middleName, lastName);
    }
}

class NameApp
{
    public static void Main()
    {
       Person myWife = new Person("Melissa", "Anne", "Jones", 21);
       Employee me = new Employee("Bradley", "L.", "Jones", 23);
       Employee you = new Employee("Kyle", "Rinni", 2000);

       myWife.displayFullName();
       myWife.displayAge();

       me.displayFullName();
       Console.WriteLine("Year hired: {0}", me.hireYear);
       me.displayAge();

       you.displayFullName();
       Console.WriteLine("Year hired of him: {0}", you.hireYear);
       you.displayAge();
    }
}
```

> **Tip**
> Okay, the listings are getting long. If you don't want to enter all this code, feel free to download the source code from the publisher's Web site at `www.samspublishing.com` or from my own Web site at `www.teachyourselfcsharp.com`.

**OUTPUT**

```
Melissa A. Jones
Age 21
Employee: Bradley L. Jones
Year hired: 0
Age 23
Employee: Kyle  Rinni
Year hired of him: 2000
Age 0
```

**ANALYSIS** This listing illustrates inheritance in its simplest form. As you will learn later in today's lessons, there are some issues that can arise as you begin to write more complex programs. For now, you should focus on understanding what is being done in this listing.

Lines 4 to 61 contain nearly the same `Person` class as Listing 11.1. There was a change made to this class. Did you notice it? In lines 9 to 11, the accessor type of the name variables was changed. Instead of `private`, these are now `protected`. Because a derived class is a new class outside the base class, it does not have access to the base class's `private` variables. `private` variables in the base class are accessible only within the base class. The `protected` modifier is still restrictive; however, it enables derived classes to also access the data members. This was the only change in the `Person` class. Later in today's lesson, you learn of a few changes that should be made to a class if you know it is going to be used as a base class.

In lines 63 to 96, you see the new, derived class, `Employee`. In line 63, the colon notation mentioned earlier is used. A new class called `Employee` is derived from a base class called `Person`. The `Employee` class contains all the functionality of the `Person` class. In line 65, the `Employee` class adds a data member called `hYear` that will contain the year the employee was hired. This is a `private` variable that is accessed through the use of the properties declared in lines 67 to 71.

Lines 73 to 89 contain constructors for the `Employee` class. These also contain a colon notation in what appears to be a different manner. Look at line 77. In this line, a constructor for `Employee` is being declared that takes two string parameters, `fn` and `ln`.

Following the colon, you see the use of the keyword base. The base keyword can be used in this manner to call the base class's constructor. In line 77, the base class constructor—Person—is called using the two variables passed to the Employee constructor, fn and ln. When the base class constructor is done executing, any code within the Employee constructor lines 78–79 will execute. In this case, there is no additional code. In the constructor in lines 86 to 95, the hireYear property is used to set the hYear value.

In lines 91 to 95, the Employee class has a method called displayFullName. The word new has been included in its declaration. Because this class has the same name as a base member and because the new keyword was used, this class overrides the base class's method. Any calls by an Employee object to the displayFullName method will execute the code in lines 91 to 95 rather than the code in lines 46 to 60.

In the last part of the listing, a NameApp class declares to illustrate the use of the derived class. In lines 102 to 103, three objects are declared. In the rest of the listing, calls to the objects are made. Listing 106 calls to the displayFullName method for the myWife object. Because myWife was declared as a person, you receive the Person class's method output, which abbreviates the middle name. In line 107, a call to the myWife object's displayAge method is made.

In line 109, the displayFullName method is called for the me object. This time, the Employee class's method is called because me was declared as an Employee in line 103. In line 111, a call to the displayAge method is made for the me object. Because the Employee class doesn't have a displayAge method, the program automatically checked to see whether the method was available in the base class. The base class's displayAge was then used.

Line 110 displayed hireYear, using the property created in the Employee class. What happens if you try to call the hireYear property using myWife? If you add the following line after 107, what would you expect to happen:

```
110:        Console.WriteLine("Year hired: {0}", myWife.hireYear);
```

This generates an error. A base class does not have any access to the routines in a derived class. Because Person does not have a hireYear, this line of code is not valid.

## Using Base Methods in Inherited Methods

The base keyword can also be used to directly call a base class's methods. For example, change lines 91 to 95 to the following:

```
public new void displayFullName()
{
   Console.Write("Employee: ");
   base.displayFullName();
}
```

This changes the new `displayFullName` method in the derived class. Now instead of doing all the work itself, it adds a little text and then calls the base class's version of `displayFullName`. This enables you to expand on the functionality of the base class without having to rewrite everything.

# Polymorphism and Inherited Classes

You've learned to this point a very simple use of inheritance. You have seen that you can extend a base class by adding additional data members and methods. You have also seen that you can call routines in the base class by using the `base` key word. Finally, you have learned that you override a previous version of a method by declaring a new method of the same name with the new keyword added.

Although all of this works, there are reasons to do things differently. One of the key concepts of an object-oriented language is that of polymorphism. If inheritance is done correctly, it can help you to gain polymorphic benefits within your classes. More specifically, you will be able to create a hierarchy of classes that can be treated in much the same way.



Consider the `Employee` and `Person` classes. An `Employee` is a `Person`. Granted an employee is more than a `Person`, but an `Employee` is everything a `Person` is and more. Listing 11.3 scales back the `Person` and `Employee` example to the bare minimum. Notice the declarations in the `MainApp` of this listing.

**Listing 11.3** inherit03.cs—Assigning a Person and Employee

```
// inherit03.cs
//===============================================
using System;

class Person
{
   protected string firstName;
   protected string lastName;

   public Person()
   {
   }

   public Person(string fn, string ln)
   {
      firstName = fn;
      lastName = ln;
   }

```

**LISTING 11.3** continued

```
    public void displayFullName()
    {
        Console.WriteLine("{0} {1}", firstName, lastName);
    }
}

class Employee : Person
{
    public ushort hireYear;

    public Employee() : base()
    {
    }

    public Employee( string fn, string ln ) : base( fn, ln)
    {
    }

    public Employee(string fn, string ln, ushort hy) : base(fn, ln)
    {
       hireYear = hy;
    }

    public new void displayFullName()
    {
       Console.WriteLine("Employee: {0} {1}", firstName, lastName);
    }
}

class NameApp
{
    public static void Main()
    {
        Employee me = new Employee("Bradley", "Jones", 1983);

        Person Brad = me;

        me.displayFullName();
        Console.WriteLine("Year hired: {0}", me.hireYear);

        Brad.displayFullName();
    }
}
```

**OUTPUT**

```
Employee: Bradley Jones
Year hired: 1983
Bradley Jones
```

**ANALYSIS** The key point of this listing is in lines 53 and 55. In line 53, an `Employee` object called `me` was created and assigned values. In line 55, a `Person` object called `Brad` was created and set equal to the `Employee` object, `me`. An `Employee` object was assigned to a `Person` object. How can this be done? Remember the statement earlier—an `Employee` *is* a `Person`. An `Employee` is a `Person` and more. All the functionality of a `Person` is contained within an `Employee`. Stated more generically, all aspects of a base class are a part of a derived class.

The `Brad` object can be used just as any other `Person` object can be used. In line 60, you see that the `displayFullName` method is called. Sure enough, the full name is displayed using the `Person` class's `displayFullName` method.

Because the `Person` object, `Brad`, had an `Employee` object assigned to it, can you call methods or use data members in the Employee class? For example, can you use `Brad.hireYear`? This is easily tested by adding the following after line 60:

```
Console.WriteLine("Year hired: ", Brad.hireYear);
```

You might think that `1983` will be displayed, but you are wrong! `Brad` is a `Person` object. The `Person` class does not have a `hireYear` member, so this will result in an error:

```
Inherit03.cs(61,45): error CS0117:  'Person' does not contain a definition for
➥'hireYear'
```

Although an `Employee` is everything a `Person` is, a `Person`—even if assigned an `Employee`—is not everything an `Employee` is. Said more generically, a derived class is everything a base class is, but a base class is *not* everything a derived class is.

How is this polymorphic? Simply put, you can make the same method call to multiple object types and the method call works. In this example, you called the `displayFullName` method on both a `Person` and an `Employee` object. Even though both were assigned the same values, the `displayFullName` method associated with the appropriate class type was called. You didn't have to worry about specifying which class's method to call.

11

## Virtual Methods

The use of the base class references to derived objects is common in object-oriented programming. Consider this question. In the previous example, `Brad` was declared as a `Person`, but was assigned an `Employee`. In the case of the call to the `displayFullName` method, which class's method was displayed? The base class was displayed, although the value assigned to method was of an `Employee`. In most cases, you will want the assigned class type's methods to be used.

**New Term** This is done using virtual methods in C#. A *virtual method* enables you to call the method associated with the actual assigned type rather than the base class type.

A method is declared as virtual within the base class. Using the `virtual` keyword in the method's definition does this. If such a method is overloaded, the actual class type of the data will be used at runtime rather than the data type of the declared variable. This means a base class can be used to point at multiple derived classes and the appropriate data will be displayed.

A deriving class must indicate when a virtual method is overridden. This is done using the `override` keyword in declaring the new method. Listing 11.4 is a modification of Listing 11.3. Notice the difference in the output!

**Note** A few of the constructors were removed from this listing to shorten the code. This has no impact on the example.

**Listing 11.4** inherit04.cs—Using Virtual Methods

```
// inherit04.cs - Virtual Methods
//===============================================
using System;

class Person
{
   protected string firstName;
   protected string lastName;

   public Person()
   {
   }

   public Person(string fn, string ln)
   {
      firstName = fn;
      lastName = ln;
   }

   public virtual void displayFullName()
   {
      Console.WriteLine("{0} {1}", firstName, lastName);
   }
}

class Employee : Person
{
   public ushort hireYear;
```

**LISTING 11.4** continued

```

    public Employee() : base()
    {
    }

    public Employee(string fn, string ln, ushort hy) : base(fn, ln)
    {
       hireYear = hy;
    }

    public override void displayFullName()
    {
       Console.WriteLine("Employee: {0} {1}", firstName, lastName);
    }
}

// A new class derived from Person...
class Contractor : Person
{
    public string company;

    public Contractor() : base()
    {
    }

    public Contractor(string fn, string ln, string c) : base(fn, ln)
    {
       company = c;
    }

    public override void displayFullName()
    {
       Console.WriteLine("Contractor: {0} {1}", firstName, lastName);
    }
}

class NameApp
{
    public static void Main()
    {

        Person Brad = new Person("Bradley", "Jones");
        Person me   = new Employee("Bradley", "Jones", 1983);
        Person Greg = new Contractor("Hill", "Batfield", "Data Diggers");

        Brad.displayFullName();
        me.displayFullName();
        Greg.displayFullName();
     }
}
```

**OUTPUT**

```
Bradley Jones
Employee: Bradley Jones
Contractor: Hill Batfield
```

**ANALYSIS** First, take a look at the changes that were made to this listing. A few constructors were removed to shorten the amount of code. More importantly, in line 20 you see the first key change. The `displayFullName` method of the `Person` class has been declared as `virtual`. This is an indicator that if the data assigned to a `Person` object is from a derived class, the derived class's method should be used instead.

In line 39, of the `Employee` class—which is derived from `Person`—you see the second key change. Here, the keyword `override` has been included instead of the keyword `new`. This indicates that for any data of the `Employee` type, this specific version of the `displayFullName` method should be used.

To make this listing a little more interesting and to help illustrate this example, a second class is derived from `Person` in lines 46 to 63. This class is for `Contractors`, and it has a data member of its own used to store the company from which the consultant has been hired. This class also contains an overridden version of the `displayFullName` method. When called, it indicates the fact that the person is a contractor.

The `Main` method within the `NameApp` has been changed to be straightforward. In lines 70 to 72, three objects of type `Person` are declared. However, each of these is assigned a different data object. In line 70, a `Person` object is assigned; in line 71, an `Employee` object is assigned; and in line 72, a `Contractor` object is assigned.

> **Caution**
>
> Although each of the variables in lines 70 to 72 (`Brad`, `me`, and `Greg`) are assigned objects of different types, only the data members and methods within its declared type, `Person`, are available.

In lines 74 to 76, you see the results of using virtual and overridden methods. Although all three of the variables calling `displayFullName` are `Person` types, each is calling the overridden method associated with the actual data that was assigned. They don't all call the `displayFullName` method of the `Person` class. This is almost always the result you will want.

## Working with Abstract Classes

In Listing 11.4, there was nothing requiring you to declare the `displayFullName` methods in the `Employee` and `Contractor` classes with override. If you change lines 39 and 59 to use `new` instead of `override`:

```
public new void displayFullName()
```

you will find that the results are different:

```
Bradley Jones
Bradley Jones
Hill Batfield
```

What has happened? Although the base class was declared as virtual, to be polymorphic and thus use the method based on the data type assigned to the variable, you have to use the `override` keyword in derived methods.

There is a way to force a class to override a method. Declaring the base class's method as abstract accomplishes this. An abstract method in the base class is declared with the keyword `abstract`. An abstract method is not given a body. Derived classes are expected to supply the body.

Whenever a method is declared as `abstract`, the class must also be declared as `abstract`. Listing 11.5 presents the use of the `abstract` class, once again using the `Person`, `Employee`, and `Contract` classes.



**Listing 11.5** inherit05.cs—Using Abstract Classes

```
// inherit05.cs - Abstract Methods
//===============================================
using System;

abstract class Person
{
   protected string firstName;
   protected string lastName;

   public Person()
   {
   }

   public Person(string fn, string ln)
   {
      firstName = fn;
      lastName = ln;
   }

   public abstract void displayFullName();
}

class Employee : Person
{
   public ushort hireYear;

```

**LISTING 11.5** continued

```
    public Employee() : base()
    {
    }

    public Employee(string fn, string ln, ushort hy) : base(fn, ln)
    {
       hireYear = hy;
    }

    public override void displayFullName()
    {
       Console.WriteLine("Employee: {0} {1}", firstName, lastName);
    }
}

// A new class derived from Person...
class Contractor : Person
{
    public string company;

    public Contractor() : base()
    {
    }

    public Contractor(string fn, string ln, string c) : base(fn, ln)
    {
       company = c;
    }

    public override void displayFullName()
    {
       Console.WriteLine("Contractor: {0} {1}", firstName, lastName);
    }
}

class NameApp
{
    public static void Main()
    {

//         Person Brad = new Person("Bradley", "Jones");
        Person me   = new Employee("Bradley", "Jones", 1983);
        Person Greg = new Contractor("Hill", "Batfield", "Data Diggers");

//         Brad.displayFullName();
        me.displayFullName();
        Greg.displayFullName();
    }
}
```

**OUTPUT**

```
Employee: Bradley Jones
Contractor: Hill Batfield
```

**ANALYSIS** Line 20 is the critical point to notice in this listing. The `displayFullName` method is declared as `abstract`. This indicates that the method will be implemented in a derived class. Because it will be implemented in a derived class, there is no body for the method.

> **Note** Line 20 ends with a semicolon.

Because the `Person` class now has an abstract method, the class itself must be declared as `abstract`. In line 5, the `abstract` keyword has been added.

In lines 36 and 56, you can see that the `Employee` and `Contractor` classes have both implemented overriding `displayFullName` methods. Finally, in the main application, you see in lines 68 and 69 that once again two variables of type `Person` are being explicitly assigned data of type `Employee` and `Contractor`. When lines 72 and 73 call the `displayFullName` methods, the method of the data type rather than the variable type is once again displayed.

Lines 67 and 71 were commented to prevent them from executing. If you uncomment line 67 and try to create data with the `Person` class, you will get an error:

```
Inherit05.cs(67, 22): error CS0144: Cannot create an instance of the abstract
➥class or interface 'Person'
```

An abstract class cannot be used to create an object!

You should also try to change the `override` keywords in lines 36 and 56 to `new` as you could do with Listing 11.4. When using abstract in your base class, this causes an error:

```
Inherit05.cs(23,7): error CS0534: 'Employee' does not implement inherited
➥ abstract member 'Person.displayFullName()'
Inherit05.cs(20,25): (Location of symbol related to previous error)
Inherit05.cs(43,7): error CS0534: 'Contractor' does not implement inherited
➥ abstract member 'Person.displayFullName()'
Inherit05.cs(20,25): (Location of symbol related to previous error)
```

The complier ensures that your base class abstract methods are overridden correctly.

11

## Sealing Classes

Abstract classes are created with the expectation that other classes will be derived from them. What if you want to prevent inheritance from a class? What if you want to seal off a class?

C# provides the `sealed` keyword to prevent derivation from a class. By including the `sealed` modifier when defining a class, you effectively prevent it from being inherited from. Listing 11.6 presents a very simple illustration of using a `sealed` class.

**Listing 11.6** inherit06.cs—Creatingkeyword to a `sealed` Class

```
// inherit06.cs - Sealed Classes
//===============================================
using System;

sealed public class number
{
   private float pi;

   public number()
   {
     pi = 3.14159F;
   }

   public float PI
   {
     get {
       return pi;
     }
   }
}

//public class numbers : number
//{
//    public float myVal = 123.456F;
//}

class myApp
{
   public static void Main()
   {
      number myNumbers = new number();
      Console.WriteLine("PI = {0}", myNumbers.PI);

//       numbers moreNumbers = new numbers();
//       Console.WriteLine("PI = {0}", moreNumbers.PI);
//       Console.WriteLine("myVal = {0}", moreNumbers.myVal);
   }
}keyword to
```

**OUTPUT** `PI = 3.14159`

**ANALYSIS** Most of this listing is straightforward. In line 5, the `number` class is declared with the `sealed` modifier. If you remove the comments from lines 22 to 25 and recompile, you get the following error:

```
inherit06b.cs(22,14): error CS0509: 'numbers' : cannot inherit from sealed class
      'number'
inherit06b.cs(5,21): (Location of symbol related to previous error)
```

This happens keyword to because you cannot inherit from a sealed class. Line 22 tries to inherit from `number` but can't.

> **Note** If you try to declare a data type as `protected` within a sealed class you will get a compiler warning. You should declare your data as private since the class won't be inherited.

# The Ultimate Base Class: `Object`



Everything within C# is a class. The ultimate base class in C# is the `Object` class, the root class in the .NET framework class hierarchy. This means it is the first base class.

Based on what you've learned today, everything is an `Object` in C#. This means that all data types and other classes are derived from the `Object` class. It also means that any methods available in the `Object` class are available in all .NET classes.

## The `Object` Class Methods

There are two methods of interest that instances of an `Object` can have and therefore all classes have. These are `GetType` and `ToString`. The `GetType` method returns the data type of an object. The `ToString` method returns a string that represents the current object. Listing 11.7 illustrates using these properties with one of the classes created earlier.

**Listing 11.7** obj.cs—Everything Is an Object

```
// obj.cs - Object Properties
//===============================================
using System;

sealed class PI
{
   public static float nbr;

```

**Listing 11.7** continued

```
 9:     static PI()
10:     {
11:         nbr = 3.14159F;
12:     }
13:
14:     static public float val()
15:     {
16:         return(nbr);
17:     }
18: }
19:
20: class myApp
21: {
22:     public static void Main()
23:     {
24:         Console.WriteLine("PI = {0}", PI.val());
25:
26:         Object x = new PI();
27:         Console.WriteLine("ToString: {0}", x.ToString());
28:         Console.WriteLine("Type: {0}", x.GetType());
29:
30:         Console.WriteLine("ToString: {0}", 123.ToString());
31:         Console.WriteLine("Type: {0}", 123.GetType());
32:     }
33: }
```

**Output**

```
PI = 3.14159
ToString: PI
Type: PI
ToString: 123
Type: System.Int32
```

**Analysis** To keep things simple, the first part of this listing is the `sealed PI` class you used in Listing 11.6. The difference comes in the `myApp` class. In line 24, the `PI` class `val` method is used again to display the value of the static data member in the `PI` class. As you see, this is still `3.14159`. Lines 26 to 31, however, are new.

In line 26, a new variable called `x` is declared. This variable is an `Object` data type; however, it points to a `PI` object. Because `Object` is a base class for all classes, including the `PI` class created in this listing, it is okay to use it to point to a new `PI` object. In lines 27 and 28, two of the `Object` class's methods are called, `GetType` and `ToString`. These methods tell you that `x` is of type `PI` and that `x` is holding a `PI` class.

In lines 30 and 31, you see something that might look strange. Remember, everything—including literals—is based on classes in C# and all classes derive from `Object`. This means a literal value such as the number `123` is in reality an object. Using the methods available to all `Objects` derived from the Object class, converting the number `123` to a string yields the value `123` (as a string). You also see that the data type for the number 123 is a `System.Int32` (which is the .NET framework equivalent of a standard `int` in C#.)

## Boxing and Unboxing

Now that you better understand the relationship between derived classes, there is another topic to explore—boxing and unboxing.

Earlier it was stated that everything is in C# is an object. That is not exactly true; however, everything can be *treated* as an object. On prior days you learned that value data types are stored differently than reference data types and that objects are reference types. In Listing 11.7, however, you treated a literal value as if it were an object. How was this possible?

In C# you have the ability to convert a value type to an object. This can happen automatically. In Listing 11.7, the value `123` was explicitly converted to an object. Remember, all objects are derived from the ultimate base object—`Object`. There are a number of things you can do with an object of type `Object` or any other object derived from this object. This includes determining the type of the data.



**New Term** *Boxing* is the conversion of a value type to a reference type (object). *Unboxing* is the explicit conversion of a reference type to a value type. A value unboxed must be put into a data type equivalent to the data stored.

Unboxing requires that that you explicitly convert the value from an object back to a value. This can be done using a cast. Listing 11.8 illustrates the simple boxing and unboxing of a value. Figure 11.2 and Figure 11.3 help to illustrate what is happening in the listing.

**Listing 11.8** boxIt.cs—Boxing and Unboxing

```
// boxIt.cs - boxing and unboxing
//===============================================
using System;

class myApp
{
   public static void Main()
   {

      float val = 3.14F;       // Assign a value type a value
      object boxed = val;      // boxing val into boxed
```

**LISTING 11.8** continued

```
12:
13:        float unboxed = (float) boxed;  // unboxing boxed into unboxed
14:
15:        Console.WriteLine("val: {0}", val);
16:        Console.WriteLine("boxed: {0}", boxed);
17:        Console.WriteLine("unboxed: {0}", unboxed);
18:
19:        Console.WriteLine("\nTypes...");
20:        Console.WriteLine("val: {0}", val.GetType());
21:        Console.WriteLine("boxed: {0}", boxed.GetType());
22:        Console.WriteLine("unboxed: {0}", unboxed.GetType());
23:    }
24: }
```

**OUTPUT**

```
val: 3.14
boxed: 3.14
unboxed: 3.14

Types...
val: System.Single
boxec: System.Single
unboxed: System.Single
```

**ANALYSIS** This listing focuses on boxing and unboxing. In line 10, a value data type is declared and assigned the value of `3.14`. In line 11, boxing occurs. The value type, `val`, is boxed into the variable, `boxed`. The `boxed` variable is an object. Figure 11.2 illustrates how these are different by showing how `val` and `boxed` are stored.

**FIGURE 11.2**
*Boxing a value.*

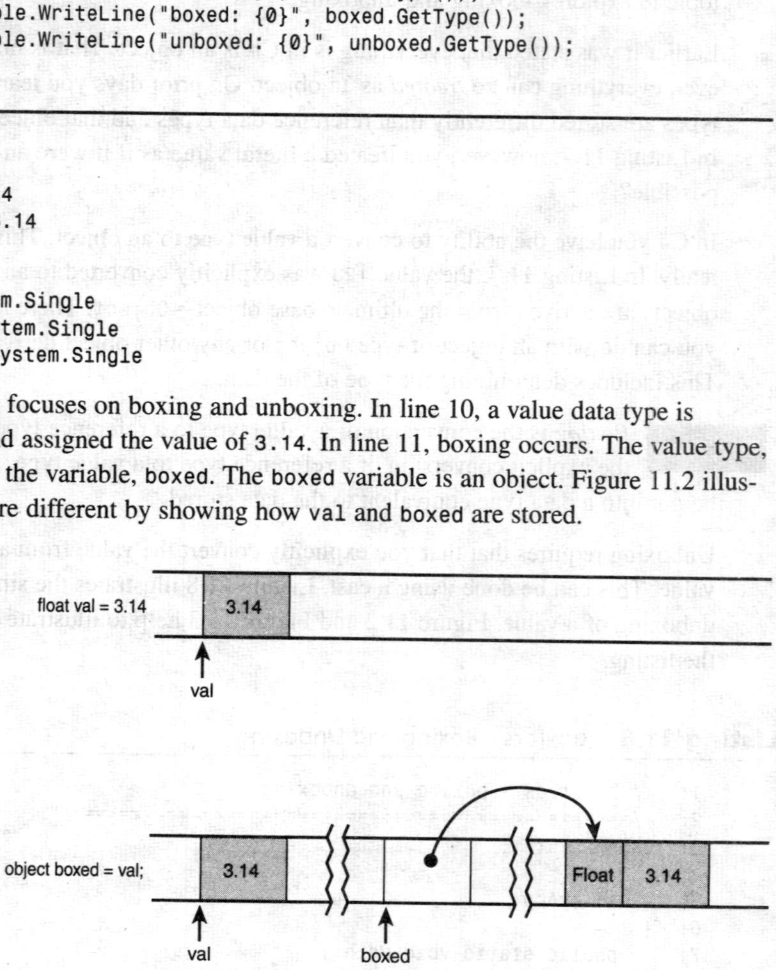


In line 13, the value in `boxed` is unboxed into a variable called `unboxed`. The `unboxed` variable is a value type that is given a copy of the value stored in `boxed`. In this listing, that value is `3.14`. Figure 11.3 helps illustrate how these are stored in memory.

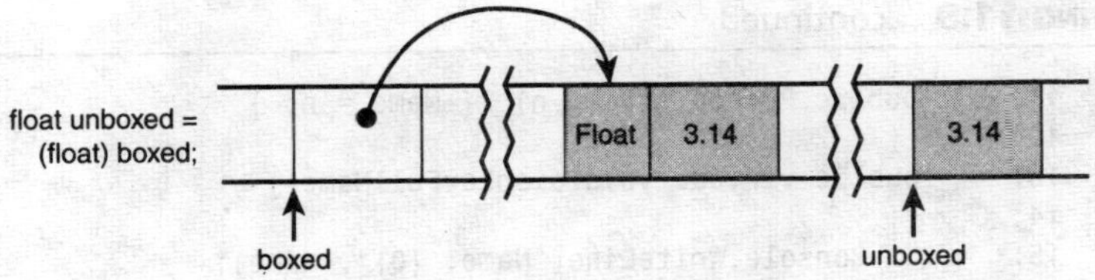


**FIGURE 11.3**
*Unboxing a value.*

Line 19 uses a method of the object type on each of the three variables. As you should know, `val` and `unboxed` are both value types. As such, you might wonder how the `GetType` method can work because the value types don't really store their type—they store only their value. In lines 20 and 22, the value types are automatically boxed, thus changing them to objects. This then enables methods such as `GetType` to be called.

# Using the `is` and `as` Keywords with Classes—Class Conversions

There are two keywords that can be used with classes: `is` and `as`.



## The `is` Keyword

The `is` keyword is used to determine whether a variable is of a specified type. The format of the `is` statement is

```
(expression is type)
```

where *`expression`* evaluates to a reference type and *`type`* is a valid *`type`*. Generally, *`type`* will be a class type.

If *`expression`* is compatible with *`type`*, this returns `true`. If *`expression`* is not compatible with *`type`*, `false` is returned. Listing 11.9 is not a practical listing; however, it illustrates the value of `is`.

**Listing 11.9** islist.cs—Using the `is` Keyword

```
// islist.cs - Using the is keyword
//================================================
using System;

class Person
{
    protected string Name;

    public Person()  { }

```

**LISTING 11.9** continued

```
    public Person(string n)  { Name = n; }

    public virtual void displayFullName()
    {
      Console.WriteLine("Name: {0}", Name);
    }
}

class Employee : Person
{
   public Employee() : base()    { }

   public Employee(string n) : base(n)  { }

   public override void displayFullName()
   {
      Console.WriteLine("Employee: {0}", Name);
   }
}

class IsApp
{
   public static void Main()
   {
      Person pers = new Person();
      Object emp = new Employee();
      string str = "String";

      if( pers is Person )
         Console.WriteLine("pers is a Person");
      else
         Console.WriteLine("pers is NOT a Person");

      if( pers is Object )
         Console.WriteLine("pers is an Object");
      else
         Console.WriteLine("pers is NOT an Object");

      if( pers is Employee )
         Console.WriteLine("pers is an Employee");
      else
         Console.WriteLine("pers is NOT an Employee");

      if( emp is Person )
         Console.WriteLine("emp is a Person");
      else
         Console.WriteLine("emp is NOT a Person");

```

**LISTING 11.9** continued

```
59:         if( str is Person )
60:             Console.WriteLine("str is a Person");
61:         else
62:             Console.WriteLine("str is NOT a Person");
63:     }
64: }
```

**OUTPUT**

```
pers is a Person
pers is an Object
pers is NOT an Employee
emp is a Person
str is NOT a Person
```

**ANALYSIS** This listing might give you warnings when you compile it. Some of the `is` comparisons are obvious to the compiler; thus it tells you that they are always going to be valid. The `is` keyword is a great tool for testing the type of a reference variable when a program is running.

This listing declares a couple of classes before getting to the `Main` method. These classes do very little. The first class is `Person`; the second class, `Employee`, is derived from `Person`. These classes are then used in the `Main` method.

In lines 35 to 37, three variables are declared. The first, `pers`, is a `Person` that is assigned a `Person`. The second, `emp`, is of data type of `Object` and is assigned an `Employee` type. As you learned earlier, you can assign a type to any of its base types. This means that an `Employee` can be assigned to an `Object` type, a `Person` type, or an `Employee` type. In line 37, a string is declared.

The rest of this listing does simple checks to see whether these three variables are of different types. You can review the output to see which passed and which did not.

> **Note** The `pers` variable is an `Object` and a `Person`. The `emp` variable is an `Employee`, a `Person`, and an `Object`. If this doesn't make sense, you should reread today's lesson.

## The as Keyword

The `as` operator works similarly to a cast. The `as` keyword cast an object to a different type. The type being cast to has to be compatible with the original type. The format of `as` is

```
expression as DataType
```

where *expression* results in a reference type and *DataType* is a reference type. A similar cast would take this form:

```
(DataType) expression
```

Although using the as keyword is similar to a cast, it is not the same. If you use a cast and there is a problem—such as trying to cast a string as a number—an exception will be thrown.

With as, if there is an error in setting the expression to the *DataType*, the expression will be set to the value of `null` and converted to the *DataType* anyway. However, no exception will be thrown.

# Arrays of Different Object Types

Before ending today's lesson, let's look at one additional topic. Using the keywords as and is, you can actually gain a lot of power. You can create an array of objects that are of different types by using a base type to define the variables. Listing 11.10 illustrates the use of the as keyword in addition to illustrating the storage of different object types in a single array. Different data types all have to be within the same inheritance hierarchy.

**Listing 11.10** objs.cs An Array of Objects

```
// objs.cs - Using an array containing different types
//===============================================
using System;

public class Person
{
   public string Name;

   public Person()
   {
   }

   public Person(string nm)
   {
      Name = nm;
   }

   public virtual void displayFullName()
   {
      Console.WriteLine("Person: {0}", Name);
   }
}

```

**LISTING 11.10** continued

```
class Employee : Person
{
//   public ushort hireYear;

   public Employee() : base()
   {
   }

   public Employee(string nm) : base(nm)
   {
   }

   public override void displayFullName()
   {
      Console.WriteLine("Employee: {0}", Name);
   }
}

// A new class derived from Person...
class Contractor : Person
{
//   public string company;

   public Contractor() : base()
   {
   }

   public Contractor(string nm) : base(nm)
   {
   }

   public override void displayFullName()
   {
      Console.WriteLine("Contractor: {0}", Name);
   }
}

class NameApp
{
   public static void Main()
   {
      Person [] myCompany = new Person[5];
      int ctr = 0;
      string buffer;

      do
      {
         do
         {
```

**LISTING 11.10** continued

```
            Console.Write("\nEnter \'c\' for Contractor, \'e\' for
➥Employee then press ENTER: ");
            buffer = Console.ReadLine();
         } while (buffer == "");

         if ( buffer[0] == 'c' || buffer[0] == 'C' )
         {
            Console.Write("\nEnter the contractor\'s name: ");
            buffer = Console.ReadLine();
            // do other Contractor stuff...
            Contractor contr = new Contractor(buffer);
            myCompany[ctr] = contr as Person;
         }
         else
         if ( buffer[0] == 'e' || buffer[0] == 'E' )
         {
            Console.Write("\nEnter the employee\'s name: ");
            buffer = Console.ReadLine();
            // Do other employee stuff...
            Employee emp = new Employee(buffer);
            myCompany[ctr] = emp as Person;
         }
         else
         {
            Person pers = new Person("Not an Employee or Contractor");
            myCompany[ctr] = pers;
         }

          ctr++;

        } while ( ctr < 5 );

        // Display the results of what was entered....

        Console.WriteLine( "\n\n\n===========================");

        for( ctr = 0; ctr < 5; ctr++ )
        {
           if( myCompany[ctr] is Employee )
           {
              Console.WriteLine("Employee: {0}", myCompany[ctr].Name);
           }
           else
           if( myCompany[ctr] is Contractor )
           {
              Console.WriteLine("Contractor: {0}", myCompany[ctr].Name);
           }
           else
           {
```

**LISTING 11.10** continued

```
                Console.WriteLine("Person: {0}", myCompany[ctr].Name);
            }
        }
        Console.WriteLine( "===========================");
    }
}
```

**OUTPUT**

```
Enter 'c' for Contractor, 'e' for Employee then press ENTER: C

Enter the contractor's name: Conner Bradshaw

Enter 'c' for Contractor, 'e' for Employee then press ENTER: E

Enter the employee's name: Tyler Truman

Enter 'c' for Contractor, 'e' for Employee then press ENTER: e

Enter the employee's name: Cody McCracker

Enter 'c' for Contractor, 'e' for Employee then press ENTER: c

Enter the contractor's name: Johnny Appleseed

Enter 'c' for Contractor, 'e' for Employee then press ENTER: Z


===========================
Contractor: Conner Bradshaw
Employee: Tyler Truman
Employee: Cody McCracker
Contractor: Johnny Appleseed
Person: Not an Employee or Contractor
===========================
```



**ANALYSIS** This is a long listing compared to what you have been seeing. This listing only partially implements everything it could do. One of today's exercises will have you expand on this listing.

The purpose of the listing is to enable you to enter people into the program. This is set up to take five people; however, you could have the user enter people until a set value is entered. The program prompts you to enter either an `'e'` or a `'c'` to indicate whether the person is an employee or a contractor. Based on what you enter, it gives you a custom prompt to enter the person's name. You could also ask for additional information; however, this hasn't been done here.

If the user enters a value other than an `'e'` or `'c'`, the program fills the person's name with an error message. You most likely would want different logic than this. You should also notice that although the program prompts for lowercase `'e'` or `'c'`, uppercase letters also work.

Most of the code should be familiar to you. The classes defined in this listing have been scaled back to a minimum amount of code. Lines 26 and 45 were left in the listing as comments. You will be asked to use these data members in one of today's exercises.

In line 63, you see the beginning of the `Main` method for this application. Lines 69 to 102 contain a `do...while` that loops for each person being entered. Lines 71 to 75 contain a nested `do...while`, which prompts the user to enter either an `'e'` or `'c'` to indicate the type of person being entered. Using a `ReadLine` in lines 74, the user's answer is obtained. Users who press Enter will be prompted again.

When a value is entered, `if...else` statements are used to determine what processing should occur. In line 77, only the first character of the text entered by the user is reviewed. The first character is stored in the zero position of the string—`buffer[0]`.

If the value entered starts with a `c`, lines 79 to 84 are executed. In line 79, the user is asked to enter a contractor's name. The `Write` method is used instead of `WriteLine` so that the reader can enter the name on the same line as the prompt. If you use `WriteLine`, a carriage return, line feed will occur and the user will have to enter the name on the next line.

In line 80, the name is retrieved using the `ReadLine` method. In line 82, a contractor object is created called `contr`. This object is initialized with the name obtained from the `ReadLine` method. In line 83, this new object is then assigned to the `myCompany` array. Because `myCompany` is an array of `Person`, the `contr` variable is assigned to the array as a `Person` type. Because `Person` is a base type for `Contractor`, you can do this—as you learned earlier today.

In lines 106 to 123, the program again loops through the `myCompany` array. This time, each element in the array is printed to the screen. In line 110, the element in the array is checked to see whether it is an `Employee`. If it is, a custom output for employees is displayed. If not, the `if` statement in line 115 is checked to see whether it is a `Contractor`. If so, a message is printed. If not, a message is printed indicating that it is just a `Person`.

Line 124 prints a dashed line to help format the output. The program then ends.

Using `is` and `as` enables you to store different data types in a single array, provided they work with the same base class. Because all objects inherit from `Object`, you will always have a base class that works in this manner. This listing illustrates key features of object-oriented programming.

## Summary

This has been one of your longest days. It is also one of the most important. In today's lesson, you learned about inheritance. You learned how to create base classes and how to derive from them. Additionally, you learned different keywords—such as `abstract`, `virtual`, and `protected`—that can impact what you can do with a base class and a derived class. You also learned how to seal a class to prevent inheritance.

Later in the day, you learned how to work with objects using types other than their own. You learned that an object can be assigned or accessed using a type in any of its base classes. Additionally, you learned that you could cast an object to a different type using the `as` keyword. The `as` keyword operates similarly to a cast operation, except that with an error, a null will be set instead of an exception being thrown. You also learned that you can use the `is` keyword to evaluate what type an object is.

## Q&A



**Q Can you inherit from a base class written in a language other than C#?**

**A** Yes. One of the features of .NET is that classes can inherit from classes written in other languages. This means that your C# classes can be derived from classes of other languages. Additionally, programmers of other languages can use your C# classes as base classes.

**Q Today's lesson presented an example of assigning a derived class to a base class in Listing 11.3. Can you assign a base class to a derived class?**

**A** Yes. If you are careful, you can. In Listing 11.3, a base class was assigned an object from a derived class. Although only the items available via the base class constructs can be used, the other portions of the derived class are not lost. It is possible to assign a derived class the value of a base class if you know the base class was assigned an object of the derived class's type. This assignment is done with a cast. In Listing 11.3, it would not be an error to do the following after line 55:

```
Employee you = (Employee) Brad;
```

This is valid because `Brad` was assigned with an `Employee` object. If `Brad` was not an `Employee` object, this line of code will throw an invalid cast exception, (`System.InvalidCastException`).

**Q What is data or method hiding?**

**A** Data or method hiding occurs when you create a method or data element in a derived class that replaces a base method or data element. This occurs when the `new` keyword is used to create the new class.

**Q What are upcasting and downcasting?**

**A** Downcasting is forcing an object to a type of a class derived from it. Upcasting is casting an object to a data type of a base class. Upcasting is considered safe to do and is an implicit operation in C#. Downcasting is considered unsafe. To Downcast, you must explicitly force the conversion.

# Workshop

The Workshop provides quiz questions to help you solidify your understanding of the material covered and exercises to provide you with experience in using what you've learned. Try to understand the quiz and exercise answers before continuing to tomorrow's lesson. Answers are provided in Appendix A, "Answers."

## Quiz

1. In C#, how many classes can be used to inherit from to create a single new class?
2. Which of the following is the same as a base class?

   a.Parent class

   b.Derived class

   c.Child class
3. What access modifier is used to protect data from being used outside of a single class? What access modifier will enable data to be used by only a base class and classes derived from the base class?
4. How is a base class's method hidden?
5. What keyword can be used in a base class to insure a derived class creates its own version of a method?
6. What keyword is used to prevent a class from being inherited?
7. Name two methods that all classes have.
8. What class is the ultimate base class from which all other classes are derived?
9. What does boxing do?
10. What is the as keyword used for?

## Exercises

1. Write a method header for declaring a constructor for the ABC class that receives two arguments, ARG1 and ARG2, that are both integers. This constructor should call a base constructor and pass it to the ARG2 integer. This should be done in the method header:

```
public ABC( int ARG1, int ARG2) : base( ARG2 )
{
}
```

2. Modify the following class to prevent it from being used as a base class:

```
class aLetter
{
     private static char A_ch;

     public char ch
     {
        get { return A_ch; }
        set { A_ch = value; }
     }

     static aLetter()
     {
         A_ch = 'X';
     }
}
```



3. **BUG BUSTER:** There is a problem with the following code. Which lines are in error?

```
// Bug Buster

//  Class definition for Person would need to be included here...

class NameApp
{
   public static void Main()
   {
       Person me = new Person();
       Object you = new Object();

       me = you;

       System.Console.WriteLine("Type: {0}", me.GetType());
   }
}
```

4. **ON YOUR OWN**: Modify Listing 11.9 to set the value of the hireyear or company. Print these values when appropriate with the output that is displayed.

# WEEK 2

# DAY 12

# Better Input and Output

The last few days you covered a lot of hard-core C# development topics that will be critical to your development of professional-level applications. Before trudging into additional hard-core topics, today's lesson offers some diversion. In today's lesson, you

- Review the difference between input and output
- Discover more of the formatting options available when displaying information in the console
- Get a detailed explanation of reading information from the console
- Learn how to parse information read from the console
- Format and work with strings
- Examine the concept of streams
- Manipulate basic file information

**Note**

Today's lesson contains much more reference information than most of the other days in this book.

# Understanding Console Input and Output

You've seen the terms *input* and *output* before. In today's lesson, you step back and focus on providing output in a much better presentation format. Additionally, you learn a little more about getting information from your users via input from the console.

You also learn a lot more about strings in today's lessons. The `Write` and `WriteLine` methods actually do string formatting behind the scenes. In today's lesson, you learn how to format these strings using other methods.

# Formatting Information

When displaying information, it is often easiest if you convert the information to a string first. As you have already seen, the `Write` and `WriteLine` methods for the `Console` class use strings for displaying output. Additionally, the .NET framework provides a number of methods and specifiers that can be used with strings. A *specifier* indicates that information is to be formatted.

Format specifiers can be used with any string. The following sections cover a number of format specifiers. This includes specifiers for working with each of the following:

- Standard numeric formats
- Formatting currency
- Formatting exponential numbers
- Formatting exponentials
- Creating custom numeric formats
- Formatting dates and times
- Formatting enumerators

There are several ways to use these format specifiers. The most obvious way is to use the specifiers with the `Write` and `WriteLine` methods to provide additional formatting.

In some cases you can use the format specifiers when calling the `ToString` method. As you learned in yesterday's lesson, the `Object` class contains a `ToString` method. Because all classes are derived from `Object`, all objects have access to a `ToString` method. In classes such as the Int32 class, this method can be passed a formatting specifier to format the data. For example, if `var` is an integer variable containing the value `123`, by using the currency formatter (`"C"`), the following line:

```
var.ToString("C");
```

returns this value:

```
$123.00
```

A third way to use the specifiers is with the `string` data type. The `string` class has a static method called `Format`. Because `Format` is a static method, it can be used directly with the class as `string.Format`. The format for using this method follows the same format as the parameters of the `Console` display methods:

```
string newString = string.Format("format_string", value(s) );
```

where *`newString`* is the new string that will be formatted. The *`format_string`* is a string that contains formatting specifiers. These specifiers are the same as those that can be used in `Write` and `WriteLine`. *`value(s)`* contains the values that will be formatted into the string.

**Note** You will learn more about formatting values as you learn about some of the specifiers.

The character `C` is the format specifier for currency. As stated previously, you can indicate this format to the `ToString` method by passing it between quotes as an argument. When formatting information within a string, such as with `WriteLine`, you include this format specifier with the variable placeholder. The following is the basic format:

```
{hldr:X#}
```



where *`hldr`* is the placeholder number for the variable. *`X`* is the specifier used to format the number. This would be `C` for currency format. The `#` is an optional value, which is the number of digits you want. This number can do different types of padding depending on the specifier. With the currency specifier, this number indicates the number of decimal places. Listing 12.1 presents the three ways of using specifiers that were mentioned earlier. It presents a small example of using the currency and other specifiers. More details will be provided later today on these and other specifiers.

**LISTING 12.1** formatit.cs—Basic Formatting Methods

```
// formatit.cs - Different places for specifiers
//               to be used.
//-----------------------------------------------

using System;

class myApp
```

**LISTING 12.1** continued

```
{
  public static void Main()
  {
    int var = 12345;

    // Format using WriteLine

    Console.Write("You can format text using Write");
    Console.WriteLine(" and WriteLine. You can insert");
    Console.Write("variables (such as {0}) into a string", var );
    Console.WriteLine(" as well as do other formatting!");
    Console.WriteLine("\n{0:C}\n{0:C4}", var);
    Console.WriteLine("\n{0:f}\n{0:f3}", var);


    // Format using ToString

    string str1 = var.ToString("C");
    string str2 = var.ToString("C3");
    string str3 = var.ToString("E8");

    Console.WriteLine("\nYou can also format using ToString");
    Console.WriteLine(str1);
    Console.WriteLine(str2);
    Console.WriteLine(str3);

    // Formatting with string.Format

    string str4 = string.Format("\nOr, you can use string.Format: ");
    string str5 = string.Format("Nbr {0:F3} \n{0:C} \n{0:C0}", var);

    Console.WriteLine(str4);
    Console.WriteLine(str5);
  }
}
```

**OUTPUT**

```
You can format text using Write and WriteLine. You can insert
variables (such as 12345) into a string as well as do other formatting!

$12,345.00
$12,345.0000

12345.00
12345.000

You can also format using ToString
$12,345.00
$12,345.000
1.23450000E+004
```

```
Or, you can use string.Format:
Nbr 12345.000
$12,345.00
$12,345
```

**ANALYSIS** A full analysis of this listing isn't going to be provided here. Rather, this listing is presented to touch on some of the formatting you can do. You can see that formatting is done in this listing. The `var` number is formatted as currency, a decimal number, and as an exponential. More important to notice here is that the numbers included after the specifier helped determine the number of decimals or zero positions included.

## Formatting Numbers

There are a number of format specifiers you can use to format numeric values. Table 12.1 lists these specifiers.

**TABLE 12.1** Characters Used for Numeric Formatting

| *Specifier* | *Description* | *Default Format* | *Example Output* |
|---|---|---|---|
| C or c | Currency | $xx,xxx.xx | $12,345.67 |
| | | ($xx,xxx.xx) | ($12,345.67) |
| D or d | Decimal | xxxxxxx | 1234567 |
| | | -xxxxxxx | -1234567 |
| E or e | Exponential | x.xxxxxxE+xxx | 1.234567E+123 |
| | | x.xxxxxxe+xxx | 1.234567e+123 |
| | | -x.xxxxxxxE+xxx | -1.234567E+123 |
| | | -x.xxxxxxxe+xxx | -1.234567e+123 |
| | | x.xxxxxxE-xxx | 1.234567E-123 |
| | | x.xxxxxxe-xxx | 1.234567e-123 |
| | | -x.xxxxxxxE-xxx | -1.234567E-123 |
| | | -x.xxxxxxxe-xxx | -1.234567e-123 |
| F or f | Fixed point | xxxxxx.xx | 1234567.89 |
| | | -xxxxx.xx | -1234567.89 |
| N or n | Numeric | xx,xxx.xx | 12,345.67 |
| | | -xx,xxx.xx | -12,345.67 |
| X or x | Hexadecimal | | 12d687<br>12D687 |

12

**Table 12.1** continued

| *Specifier* | *Description* | *Default Format* | *Example Output* |
|---|---|---|---|
| `G` or `g` | General | varies (will use the most compact format) | |
| `R` or `r` | Roundtrip | Maintains precession when numbers are converted to and then back from a string | |

You can use these and the other format specifiers in today's lesson in the ways described earlier. When using the specifiers with the `ToString` method, you enclose the appropriate character between quotes and pass it as a parameter. You saw the earlier example of `123` being formatted as currency:

```
string newString = var.ToString("C");
```

This results in `newString` containing the value `$123.00`. The following sections discuss each of these formats briefly.

**Caution** The formatting specifiers might differ depending on your system's locale settings.

## Standard Formats (Fixed, Decimal, Numeric)

The standard format specifiers work with their related number types. `F` works for floating-point numbers. `D` works with standard whole numbers, such as integers and longs. If you try to use `D` with a floating-point number, you get an exception.

The number specifier (`N`) presents numbers in a nicer format. The number specifier adds two decimal places and commas to the number's format.

## Formatting Currency

By now you should know that the currency specifier is `C`. You can use `C` by itself to have currency displayed with two decimal positions. If you want to avoid decimals, use `C0`. The `0` indicates that no decimals positions should be included.

## Formatting Exponential Numbers

Exponential numbers are often presented in scientific notation due to their overly large, or overly small, size. The `E` and `e` specifiers can be used to format these numbers. You should note that the case of the `E` in the format specifier is the same case that will be used in the output.

## General Formatting of Numbers

The general formatting specifier (`G` or `g`) is used to format a number into the smallest string representation possible. Based on the number, this formatter determines whether an exponential representation or a standard format results in the smallest string. Whichever is smaller is returned. Listing 12.2 illustrates the different formats this specifier can return.

**Listing 12.2** general.cs—Using the General Specifier

```
 1:  // general.cs - Using the General format specifier
 2:  //-----------------------------------------------
 3:  using System;
 4:
 5:  class myApp
 6:  {
 7:     public static void Main()
 8:     {
 9:         float f1 = .000000789F;
10:         float f2 = 1.2F;
11:
12:         Console.WriteLine("f1   ({0:f}). Format (G): {0:G}", f1);
13:         Console.WriteLine("f2   ({0:f}). Format (G): {0:G}", f2);
14:     }
15:  }
```

**Output**

```
f1   (0.00). Format (G): 7.89E-7
f2   (1.20). Format (G): 1.2
```

**Analysis** This listing initializes and prints two variables. In lines 9 and 10, two float variables are created. One is a very small decimal value, the other is a simple number.

In lines 12 and 13, these values are written to the console. The first placeholder in each of these lines displays the floating-point value as a fixed-point number using the `F` specifier. The second placeholder prints the same variable in the general format using the `G` format. In the output, `f1` is much more concise as an exponential number, and `f2` is more concise as a regular number.



## Formatting Hexadecimal Numbers

Hexadecimal numbers are numbers based on the Base16 number system. This number system is often used with computers. Appendix D, "Working with Number Systems" covers using hexadecimal. The letter x—either upper- or lower-case—is used to specify a hexadecimal number. The hexadecimal specifier automatically converts and prints a value as a hexadecimal value.

## Maintaining Precession (Roundtripping)

When you convert a number from one format to another, you run the risk of losing precision. A specifier has been provided to help maintain precision in case you might want to convert a string back to a number: the `R` (or `r`) specifier. By using this specifier, the runtime tries to maintain the precision of the original number.

## Creating Custom Formats Using Picture Definitions

There are times when you will want to have more control over a number's format. For example, you might want to format a driver's license number or social security number with dashes. You might want to add parentheses and dashes to a phone number. Table 12.2 presents some of the formatting characters that can be used with the specifiers to create custom formats for output. Listing 12.3 provides examples of these specifiers.

**TABLE 12.2** Formatting Characters for Picture Definitions

| *Specifier* | *Description* |
|---|---|
| `0` | Zero placeholder. Filled with digit if available. |
| `#` | Blank placeholder. Filled with digit if available. |
| `.` | Displays a period. Used for decimal points. |
| `,` | Uses a comma for separating groups of numbers. It can also be used as a multiplier (see Listing 12.3). |
| `%` | Displays the number as a percentage value (for example, 1.00 is 100%). |
| `\` | Used to indicate that a special character should be printed. This can be one of the escape characters, such as the newline character (`\n`). |
| `'xyz'` | Displays text within the apostrophes. |
| `"xyz"` | Displays text within the quotes. |

**LISTING 12.3** picts.cs—Using the Picture Specifiers

```
// picts.cs - Using picture specifiers
//-----------------------------------------------

using System;
```

**LISTING 12.3** continued

```

class myApp
{
   public static void Main()
   {
      int var1 = 1234;
      float var2 = 12.34F;

      // Zero formatter
      Console.WriteLine("\nZero...");
      Console.WriteLine("{0} -->{0:0000000}", var1);
      Console.WriteLine("{0} -->{0:0000000}", var2);

      // Space formatter
      Console.WriteLine("\nSpace...");
      Console.WriteLine("{0} -->{0:0####}<--", var1);
      Console.WriteLine("{0} -->{0:0####}<--", var2);

      // Group separator and mulitplier (,)
      Console.WriteLine("\nGroup Multiplier...");
      Console.WriteLine("{0} -->{0:0,,}<--", 1000000);
      Console.WriteLine("Group Separator...");
      Console.WriteLine("{0} -->{0:##,###,##0}<--", 2000000);
      Console.WriteLine("{0} -->{0:##,###,##0}<--", 3);

      // Percentage formatter
      Console.WriteLine("\nPercentage...");
      Console.WriteLine("{0} -->{0:0%}<--", var1);
      Console.WriteLine("{0} -->{0:0%}<--", var2);

     // Literal formatting
      Console.WriteLine("\nLiteral Formatting...");
      Console.WriteLine("{0} -->{0:'My Number: '0}<--", var1);
      Console.WriteLine("{0} -->{0:'My Number: '0}<--", var2);
      Console.WriteLine("\n{0} -->{0:Mine: 0}<--", var1);
      Console.WriteLine("{0} -->{0:Mine: 0}<--", var2);
   }
}
```

**OUTPUT**

```
Zero...
1234 -->0001234
12.34 -->0000012

Space...
1234 -->01234<--
12.34 -->00012<--
```

```
Group Multiplier...
1000000 -->1<--
Group Separator...
2000000 -->2,000,000<--
3 -->3<--

Percentage...
1234 -->123400%<--
12.34 -->1234%<--

Literal Formatting...
1234 -->My Number: 1234<--
12.34 -->My Number: 12<--

1234 -->Mine: 1234<--
12.34 -->Mine: 12<--
```

**ANALYSIS** This listing uses the format specifiers in Table 12.2 and applies them to two variables. Looking at the comments and the output, you can see how a number of the specifiers work.

## Formatting Negative Numbers

There are also times when you want a negative number treated differently than a positive number. The specifiers you have learned about will work with both positive and negative numbers.

The placeholder for specifying the format can actually be separated into either two or three sections. If the placeholder is separated into two sections, the first is for positive numbers and zero and the second is for negative numbers. If it is broken into three sections, the first is for positive values, the middle is for negative values, and the third is for zero.

The placeholder is broken into these sections using a semicolon. The placeholder number is then included in each. For example, to format a number to print with three levels of precision when positive, five levels when negative, and no levels when zero, you do the following:

```
{0:D3;D5;'0'}
```

Listing 12.4 presents this example in action and one or two examples.

**LISTING 12.4** threeway.cs.

```
// threeway.cs - Controlling the formatting of numbers
//-----------------------------------------------------
```

**LISTING 12.4** continued

```
using System;

class myApp
{
  public static void Main()
  {
    Console.WriteLine("\nExample 1...");
    for ( int x = -100; x <= 100; x += 100 )
    {
      Console.WriteLine("{0:000;-00000;'0'}", x);
    }

    Console.WriteLine("\nExample 2...");
    for ( int x = -100; x <= 100; x += 100 )
    {
      Console.WriteLine("{0:Pos: 0;Neg: -0;Zero}", x);
    }

    Console.WriteLine("\nExample 3...");
    for ( int x = -100; x <= 100; x += 100 )
    {
      Console.WriteLine("{0:You Win!;You Lose!;You Broke Even!}", x);
    }
  }
}
```

**OUTPUT**

```
Example 1...
-00100
0
100

Example 2...
Neg: -100
Zero
Pos: 100

Example 3...
You Lose!
You Broke Even!
You Win!
```



**ANALYSIS** This listing helps illustrate how to break the custom formatting into three pieces. A `for` loop is used to create a negative number, increment the number to zero, and finally increment it to a positive number. The result is that the same `WriteLine` can be used to display all three values. This is done three separate times for three different examples.

In line 13, you see that the positive value will be printed to at least three digits because there are three zeros in the first formatting position. The negative number will include a negative sign followed by at least 5 numbers. You know this because the dash is included in the format for the negative sign, and there are five zeros. If the value is equal to zero, a zero will be printed.

In the second example, text is included with the formatting of the numbers. This is also done in the third example. The difference is that in the second example, zero placeholders are also included so the actual numbers will print. This is not the case with the third example where only text is displayed.

As you can see by all three of these examples, it is easy to cause different formats to be used based on the sign (positive or negative) of a variable.

## Formatting Date and Time Values

Date and time values can also be formatted. There are a number of specifiers that can help you format everything from the day of the week to the full data and time string. Before presenting these format characters, you should first understand how to obtain the date and time.

### Getting the Date and Time

C# and the .NET framework provide a class for storing dates and times—the `DateTime` class located in the `System` namespace. The `DateTime` class stores both a full date and the full time.

The `DateTime` class has a number of properties and methods that you will find useful. Additionally, there are a couple of static members. The two static properties that you will be likely to use are `Now` and `Today`. `Now` contains the date and time for the moment the call is made. `Today` returns just the current date. Because these are static properties, their values can be obtained using the class name rather than an instant name:

```
DateTime.Now
```

```
DateTime.Today
```

You can review the online documents for information on all the methods and properties. A few of the ones you might find useful are

| | |
|---|---|
| `Date` | Returns the date portion of a `DateTime` object |
| `Month` | Returns the month portion of a `DateTime` object |
| `Day` | Returns the day of the month of a `DateTime` object |
| `Year` | Returns the year portion of the `DateTime` object |

| | |
|---|---|
| `DayOfWeek` | Returns the day of the week of a `DateTime` object |
| `DayOfYear` | Returns the day of the year of a `DateTime` object |
| `TimeOfDay` | Returns the time portion of a `DateTime` object |
| `Hour` | Returns the hour portion of a `DateTime` object |
| `Minute` | Returns the minutes portion of a `DateTime` object |
| `Second` | Returns the seconds portion of a `DateTime` object |
| `Millisecond` | Returns the milliseconds component of a `DateTime` object |
| `Ticks` | Returns a value equal to the number of 100-nanoseconds ticks for the given `DateTime` object |

**Note** The `DateTime.Today` property gives you only a valid date. It does not give you the current time.

## Formatting the Date and Time

There are a number of specifiers that can be used with dates, times, or both. These include the capability of displaying information in short and long format. Table 12.3 contains the date and time specifiers.

**TABLE 12.3** Date And Time Formatting Characters

| *Specifier* | *Description* | *Default Format* | *Example Output* |
|---|---|---|---|
| `d` | Short date | `mm/dd/yyyy` | `5/6/2001` |
| `D` | Long date | `day, month dd, yyyy` | `Sunday, May 06, 2001` |
| `f` | Full date/short time | `day, month dd, yyyy hh:mm AM/PM` | `Sunday, May 06, 2001 12:30 PM` |
| `F` | Full date/ full time | `day, month dd, yyyy HH:mm:ss AM/PM` | `Sunday, May 06, 2001 12:30:54 PM` |
| `g` | Short date/ short time | `mm/dd/yyyy HH:mm` | `6/5/2001 12:30 PM` |
| `G` | Short date/ long time | `mm/dd/yyyy hh:mm:ss` | `6/5/2001 12:30:54 PM` |
| `M` or `m` | Month day | `month dd` | `May 06` |
| `R` or `r` | RFC1123 | `ddd, dd Month yyyy hh:mm:ss GMT` | `Sun, 06 May 2001 12:30:54 GMT` |
| `s` | Sortable | `yyyy-mm-dd hh:mm:ss` | `2001-05-06T12:30:54` |

**TABLE 12.3** continued

| *Specifier* | *Description* | *Default Format* | *Example Output* |
|---|---|---|---|
| t | Short time | hh:mm AM/PM | 12:30 PM |
| T | Long time | hh:mm:ss AM/PM | 12:30:54 PM |
| u | Sortable (universal) | yyyy-mm-dd hh:mm:ss | 2001-05-06 12:30:54Z |
| U | Sortable (universal) | day, month dd, yyyy hh:mm:ss AM/PM | Sunday, May 06, 2001 12:30:54 PM |
| Y or y | Year/month | month, yyyy | May, 2001 |

> **Caution**
>
> s is used as a specifier for printing a sortable date. Note that this is a lower case *s*. An uppercase *S* is not a valid format specifier and will generate an exception if used.

The date and time specifiers are easy to use. Listing 12.5 defines a simple date variable and then prints it in all the formats presented in Table 12.3.

**LISTING 12.5** dtformat.cs—The Date Formats

```
// dtformat.cs - date/time formats
//-----------------------------------------------

using System;

class myApp
{
  public static void Main()
  {
     DateTime CurrTime = DateTime.Now;

     Console.WriteLine("d: {0:d}", CurrTime );
     Console.WriteLine("D: {0:D}", CurrTime );
     Console.WriteLine("f: {0:f}", CurrTime );
     Console.WriteLine("F: {0:F}", CurrTime );
     Console.WriteLine("g: {0:g}", CurrTime );
     Console.WriteLine("G: {0:G}", CurrTime );
     Console.WriteLine("m: {0:m}", CurrTime );
     Console.WriteLine("M: {0:M}", CurrTime );
     Console.WriteLine("r: {0:r}", CurrTime );
     Console.WriteLine("R: {0:R}", CurrTime );
     Console.WriteLine("s: {0:s}", CurrTime );
//     Console.WriteLine("S: {0:S}", CurrTime );  // error!!!
```

**Listing 12.5** continued

```
24:         Console.WriteLine("t: {0:t}", CurrTime );
25:         Console.WriteLine("T: {0:T}", CurrTime );
26:         Console.WriteLine("u: {0:u}", CurrTime );
27:         Console.WriteLine("U: {0:U}", CurrTime );
28:         Console.WriteLine("y: {0:y}", CurrTime );
29:         Console.WriteLine("Y: {0:Y}", CurrTime );
30:     }
31: }
```

**Output**

```
d: 5/6/2001
D: Sunday, May 06, 2001
f: Sunday, May 06, 2001 1:06 PM
F: Sunday, May 06, 2001 1:06:51 PM
g: 5/6/2001 1:06 PM
G: 5/6/2001 1:06:51 PM
m: May 06
M: May 06
r: Sun, 06 May 2001 13:06:51 GMT
R: Sun, 06 May 2001 13:06:51 GMT
s: 2001-05-06T13:06:51
t: 1:06 PM
T: 1:06:51 PM
u: 2001-05-06 13:06:51Z
U: Sunday, May 06, 2001 6:06:51 PM
y: May, 2001
Y: May, 2001
```



**Analysis** In line 10, this listing declares an object to hold the date and time. This is done using the `DateTime` class. This object is called `CurrTime`. It is assigned the static value from the `DateTime` class, `Now`, which provides the current date and time. Looking at the output, you can see that it was midday in May when I ran this listing. Lines 12 to 29 present this same date and time in all the date/time formats.

Line 23 is commented. This line uses the `S` specifier, which is not legal. If you uncomment this line, you will see that the listing throws an exception.

## Displaying Values from Enumerations

When you worked with enumerators on Day 8, "Advanced Data Storage: Structures, Enumerators, and Arrays," you saw that the output when using `Write` and `WriteLine` displayed the descriptive value of the enumerator rather than the numeric value. With string formatting, you can control the numeric value or the text value. You can also force a hexadecimal representation to be displayed. Table 12.4 presents the formatting characters for enumerators. Listing 12.6 presents a listing using these key values in this table.

**Table 12.4** Formatting Characters for Enumerators

| *Specifier* | *Description* |
|---|---|
| D or d | Displays the numeric value from the enumerator element |
| G or g | Displays the string value from the enumerator element |
| X or x | Displays the hexadecimal equivalent of the numeric value from the enumerator element |

**Listing 12.6** enums.cs—Formatting Enumeration Values

```
// enums.cs - enumerator formats
//-----------------------------------------------

using System;

class myApp
{
   enum Pet
   {
      Cat,
      Dog,
      Fish,
      Snake,
      Rat,
      Hamster,
      Bird
   }

   public static void Main()
   {
      Pet myPet = Pet.Fish;
      Pet yourPet = Pet.Hamster;

      Console.WriteLine("Using myPet: ");
      Console.WriteLine("d: {0:d}", myPet );
      Console.WriteLine("D: {0:D}", myPet );
      Console.WriteLine("g: {0:g}", myPet );
      Console.WriteLine("G: {0:G}", myPet );
      Console.WriteLine("x: {0:x}", myPet );
      Console.WriteLine("X: {0:X}", myPet );

      Console.WriteLine("\nUsing yourPet: ");
      Console.WriteLine("d: {0:d}", yourPet );
      Console.WriteLine("D: {0:D}", yourPet );
      Console.WriteLine("g: {0:g}", yourPet );
      Console.WriteLine("G: {0:G}", yourPet );
      Console.WriteLine("x: {0:x}", yourPet );
```

**LISTING 12.6** continued

```
38:         Console.WriteLine("X: {0:X}", yourPet );
39:     }
40: }
```

**OUTPUT**

```
Using myPet:
d: 2
D: 2
g: Fish
G: Fish
x: 00000002
X: 00000002

Using yourPet:
d: 5
D: 5
g: Hamster
G: Hamster
x: 00000005
X: 00000005
```

**ANALYSIS** This listing creates an `enum` that holds pets. In lines 21 and 22, two objects are created, `myPet` and `yourPet`, that are used to illustrate the format specifiers. Lines 24 to 30 use the specifiers with the `myPet` object. Lines 32 to 38 use `yourPet`. As you can see by the output, the case of the specifiers doesn't matter.

## Working Closer with Strings



Now that you know all about formatting strings, it is worth stepping back and learning a few more details about string specifics. Recall that strings are a special data type that can hold textual information.

As you should know, `string` is a C# keyword. The `string` keyword is simply a different name for the `String` class in the `System` namespace. As such, `string` has all the methods and properties of the `String` class.

A value stored in a string cannot be modified. When string methods are called or when you make changes to a string, a new string is actually created. If you tried to change a character in a string, you would find that you get an error. Listing 12.7 is a simple listing you can enter to prove this point.

**Listing 12.7** str_err.cs—Strings Cannot Be Changed

```
 1: // str_err.cs - Bad listing. Generates error
 2: //-----------------------------------------------
 3: using System;
 4:
 5: class myApp
 6: {
 7:   public static void Main()
 8:   {
 9:      string str1 = "abcdefghijklmnop";
10:
11:      str1[5] = 'X';       //  ERROR!!!
12:
13:      Console.WriteLine( str1 );
14:   }
15: }
```

**Output**

This listing generates the following error:

```
str_err.cs(11,6): error CS0200: Property or indexer 'string.this[int]'
➥cannot be
         assigned to — it is read only
```

**Analysis**

This listing helps illustrate that you can't change a string. Remember, a string is an array of characters. Line 11 attempts to change the sixth character to a capital X. This generates an error because you can't modify a string's value.

If strings can't be modified, you might believe their usefulness is greatly limited. Additionally, you might wonder how methods and properties can work with strings. You will find that methods that make modifications to a string actually create a new string. Additionally, if you really need to modify a string, C# provides another class that can be used. This class, called `StringBuilder`, is covered later today.

> **Note**
>
> Strings are said to be immutable. Immutable means "can't be changed."

## String Methods

There are also a number of extremely useful methods that can be used with string comparisons. Table 12.5 presents some of the key string methods along with descriptions of their use.

**TABLE 12.5** Common String Methods

| *Method* | *Description* |
|---|---|
| | **Static Methods of `String/string`** |
| `Compare` | Compares the values of two strings. |
| `CompareOrdinal` | Compares the values of two strings without compensating for language or other internationalization issues. |
| `Concat` | Concatenates (joins) two or more strings into one string. |
| `Copy` | Creates a new string from an existing string. |
| `Equals` | Compares two strings to determine whether they contain the same value. Returns true if the two values are equal; otherwise, returns false. |
| `Format` | Replaces format specifiers with their corresponding string values. Specifiers were covered earlier today. |
| `Join` | Concatenates two or more strings. A specified "separator string" is placed between each of the original strings. |
| | **Methods and Properties of Each Instance** |
| `Char` | Returns the character at a given location. |
| `Clone` | Returns a copy of the stored string. |
| `CompareTo` | Compares the value of this string with another string. Returns a negative number if this string is less than the compared string, a zero if equal, and a positive number if the value of this string is greater. |
| `CopyTo` | Copies a portion or all of a string to a new string or character array. |
| `EndsWith` | Determines whether the end of the value stored in the string is equal to a string value. If they are equal, `true` is returned; otherwise, `false` is returned. |
| `Equals` | Compares two strings to determine whether they contain the same value. Returns `true` if the two values are equal; otherwise, returns `false`. |
| `IndexOf` | Returns the index (location) of the first match for a character or string. Returns `-1` if the value is not found. |
| `Insert` | Inserts a value into a string. This is done by returning a new string. |
| `LastIndexOf` | Returns the index (location) of the last match for a character or string. Returns `-1` if the value is not found. |

12

**TABLE 12.5** continued

| *Method* | *Description* |
|---|---|
| `Length` | Returns the length of the value stored in the string. The length is equal to the number of characters contained. |
| `PadLeft` | Right-justifies the value of a string and then pads any remaining spaces with a specified character (or space). |
| `PadRight` | Left-justifies the value of a string and then pads any remaining spaces with a specified character (or space). |
| `Remove` | Deletes a specified number of characters from a specified location within a string. |
| `Split` | The opposite of `Join`. Breaks a string into substrings based on a specified value. The specified value is used as a breaking point. |
| `StartsWith` | Determines whether the value stored in a string starts with a specified character or set of characters. Returns `true` if there is a match and false if not. If specified character is `null`, `true` is also returned. |
| `Substring` | Returns a substring from the original string starting at a specified location. The number of characters for the substring might also be specified, but is not required. |
| `ToCharArray` | Copies the characters in the current string value to a `char` array. |
| `ToLower` | Returns a copy of the current value in all lowercase letters. |
| `ToUpper` | Returns a copy of the current value in all uppercase characters. |
| `Trim` | Removes copies of a specified string from the beginning and end of the current string. |
| `TrimEnd` | Removes copies of a specified string from the end of the current string. |
| `TrimStart` | Removes copies of a specified string from the beginning of the current string. |

Many of these methods and properties are used throughout the rest of this book.

## The Special String Formatter—@

You have seen a number of special characters used in many of the listings. For example, to use a quote in a string, you use an escape character. The following prints `"Hello World"` including quotes:

```
System.Console.WriteLine("\"Hello World\"");
```

To use a backslash, you also have to use an escape character:

```
System.Console.WriteLine("My Code: C:\\Books\\TYCSharp\\Originals\\");
```

C# provides a special formatting character that you can use to shortcut using the escape characters: @. When this precedes a string, the string's value will be taken literally. In fact, this string is referred to as a *verbatim string literal*. The following is equivalent to the previous directory strings:

```
System.Console.WriteLine(@"My Code: C:\Books\TYCSharp\Originals\");
```

When using the @ string formatter, you will find that the only tricky issue is using a double-quote. If you want to use a double-quote in a string formatted with @, you need to use two double-quotes. The following is the equivalent code for the "Hello World" example:

```
System.Console.WriteLine(@"""Hello World!""");
```

**Note** You might be thinking, "Wait a minute, he said use two double-quotes, but he used three!" One of the quotes is for enclosing the string. In this example, the first quote starts the string. The second quote would normally end the string; however, because it is followed by another quote, the system knows to display a quote. The fourth quote would then normally end the string, but because it also is followed by a quote, it is converted to display a quote. The sixth quote checks to see whether it can end the string. Because it is not followed by another quote, the string value is ended.

12

## Building Strings

The StringBuilder class is provided in the System.Text namespace to create an object that can hold a changeable string value. An object created with the StringBuilder class operates similarly to a string. The difference is that methods of a StringBuilder can directly manipulate the value stored. The methods and properties for a StringBuilder object are listed in Table 12.6.

**TABLE 12.6** The StringBuilder Methods and Properties

| *Method* | *Method or Property* |
|---|---|
| Append | Appends an object to the end of the current StringBuilder. |
| AppendFormat | Inserts objects into a string base on formatting specifiers. |
| Capacity | Sets or gets the number of characters that can be held. Capacity can be increased up to the value of MaxCapacity. |

**TABLE 12.6** continued

| *Method* | *Method or Property* |
|---|---|
| `Chars` | Sets or gets the character at a given index position using indexer notation. |
| `EnsureCapacity` | Ensures that the capacity of `StringBuilder` is at least as big as a provided value. If the value is passed to `EnsureCapacity`, the value of the Capacity property is set to this new value. If `MaxCapacity` is less than the value passed, an exception is thrown. |
| `Equals` | Determines whether the current `StringBuilder` is equal to the value passed. |
| `Insert` | Places an object into `StringBuilder` at a given location. |
| `Length` | Sets or gets the length of the current value stored in `StringBuilder`. Length cannot be larger than the Capacity of `StringBuilder`. If the current value is shorter than Length, the value is truncated. |
| `MaxCapacity` | Gets the maximum capacity for `StringBuilder`. |
| `Remove` | Removes a specified number of characters starting at a specified location within the current `StringBuilder` object. |
| `Replace` | Changes all copies of a given character with a new character. |
| `ToString` | Converts `StringBuilder` to String. |

The `StringBuilder` class can be used like other classes. Listing 12.8 uses the `StringBuilder` object and several of the methods and properties presented in Table 12.6. This listing has a user enter first, last, and middle names. The values are combined into a `StringBuilder` object.

**LISTING 12.8** strbuilder.cs—Using the `StringBuilder` Class.

```
// strbuilder.cs - String Builder
//-----------------------------------------------
using System;
using System.Text;     //For StringBuilder

class buildName
{
  public static void Main()
  {
     StringBuilder name = new StringBuilder();
     string buffer;
     int marker = 0;

```

**Listing 12.8** continued

```
        Console.Write("\nEnter your first name: ");
        buffer = Console.ReadLine();

        if ( buffer != null )
        {
          name.Append(buffer);
          marker = name.Length;
        }

        Console.Write("\nEnter your last name: ");
        buffer = Console.ReadLine();

        if ( buffer != null )
        {
          name.Append(" ");
          name.Append(buffer);
        }

        Console.Write("\nEnter your middle name: ");
        buffer = Console.ReadLine();

        if ( buffer != null )
        {
          name.Insert(marker+1, buffer);
          name.Insert(marker+buffer.Length+1, " ");
        }

        Console.WriteLine("\n\nFull name: {0}", name);

        // Some stats....
        Console.WriteLine("\n\nInfo about StringBuilder string:");
        Console.WriteLine("value: {0}", name);
        Console.WriteLine("Capacity: {0}", name.Capacity);
        Console.WriteLine("Maximum Capacity: {0}", name.MaxCapacity);
        Console.WriteLine("Length: {0}", name.Length);
    }
}
```

**Output**

```
Enter your first name: Bradley

Enter your last name: Jones

Enter your middle name: Lee

Full name: Bradley Lee Jones
```

```
Info about StringBuilder string:
value: Bradley Lee Jones
Capacity: 32
Maximum Capacity: 2147483647
Length: 17
```

**ANALYSIS** The first thing to note about this listing is that line 4 includes a `using` statement for the `System.Text` namespace. Without this, you would need to fully qualify the `StringBuilder` class as `System.Text.StringBuilder`.

In line 10, a new `StringBuilder` object called `name` is created. This is used to hold the string that the listing will be building. In line 11, a string is created called `buffer` that will be used to get information from the user. This information is obtained in lines 15, 24, and 33, using the `ReadLine` method in `Console`. The first value obtained is the first name. This is appended into the name `StringBuilder` object. Because `name` was empty, this is placed at the beginning. The length of the first name is placed in a variable called `marker`. This variable will be used to determine where to place the middle name.

The last name is obtained second. This is appended to the `name` object (line 29) right after a space is appended (line 28). Finally, the middle name is obtained and inserted into the middle of `name` using the `Insert` method. The marker saved earlier is used to determine where to insert the middle name.

The resulting full name is displayed in line 41. Lines 44 to 48 display some general information. In line 45, the value of the `StringBuilder` `name` object is printed. In line 46, you see the current capacity that the `name` object can hold. In line 47, you see the maximum value that this can be extended to. In line 48, the current length of the value is stored in `name`.

# Getting Information from the Console

So far, today's lesson has focused on formatting and displaying information. In addition to producing output, you also need to have more flexibility in obtaining input—information entered into your program.

You have seen the `Read` and `ReadLine` methods of the `Console` class used in this book. The following sections provide more information on obtaining input and converting it to a more usable format.

## Using the `Read` Method

There are two methods in the `Console` class in the `System` namespace that can be used to get information from your users: `ReadLine` and `Read`.

The Read method reads a single character at a time from the input stream. The method returns the character as an integer (int). If the end of the stream is read, -1 is returned. Listing 12.9 reads characters from the console using Read.

**Tip**

To end the stream of characters coming from the console, you can press Ctrl+z.

**LISTING 12.9** The Read Method

```
// readit.cs - Read information from Console
//-----------------------------------------------
using System;
using System.Text;

class myApp
{
  public static void Main()
  {
     StringBuilder Input = new StringBuilder();

     int ival;
     char ch = ' ';

     Console.WriteLine("Enter text. When done, press CTRL+Z:");

     while ( true )
     {
        ival = Console.Read();
        if ( ival == -1 )
           break;
        ch = ( char ) ival;

        Input.Append(ch);
     }
     Console.WriteLine("\n\n==========>\n");
     Console.Write( Input );
     Console.Write("\n\n");
  }
}
```

**OUTPUT**

```
Enter text. When done, press CTRL+Z:
Mary Had a little lamb,
Its fleece was white as snow.
Everywhere that Mary went,
that lamb was sure to go!
==========>
```

```
Mary Had a little lamb,
Its fleece was white as snow.
Everywhere that Mary went,
that lamb was sure to go!
```

**ANALYSIS** The output shows that four lines of text were entered. After entering the text, Ctrl+Z was pressed to end the input.

In lines 17 to 25, a `while` loop is used to read characters. Line 19 does the actual read. The value read is placed in the `ival` variable. If `ival` is equal to `-1`, the end of the input has been reached and a `break` command is used to get out of the `while` loop. If the `ival` character is valid, this numeric value is cast to a character value in line 22. The character value is then appended to the string `Input`.

After the entry of characters is completed, line 27 prints the full value of the `Input` string. All the characters were stored, as well as the carriage returns and line feeds.

> **Note**
>
> For Windows and Web applications, you obtain information differently. On Days 15 through 17, you will learn more about obtaining data on these platforms.

## Using the `ReadLine` method

The `ReadLine` method has been used a number of times in this book. You should already be aware of what it does. In review, the `ReadLine` method reads a line of text up to a carriage return, a line feed, or both. The `ReadLine` method then returns all characters read except the carriage return and line feed. If the end of the stream is reached, the value `null` is returned.

The following is similar to Listing 12.9. To end this listing you can use Ctrl+Z.

**LISTING 12.9** readln.csUsing `ReadLine` to Read Characters

```
// readln.cs - Read information from Console
//-----------------------------------------------
using System;
using System.Text;

class myApp
{
   public static void Main()
   {
      StringBuilder Input = new StringBuilder();
      string buff;
```

**LISTING 12.9** continued

```
12:
13:         Console.WriteLine("Enter text. When done, press Ctrl+Z:");
14:
15:         while ( (buff = Console.ReadLine()) != null )
16:         {
17:             Input.Append(buff);
18:             Input.Append("\n");
19:         }
20:         Console.WriteLine("\n\n==========>\n");
21:         Console.Write( Input );
22:         Console.Write("\n\n");
23:     }
24: }
```

**OUTPUT**

```
Enter text. When done, press Ctrl+Z:
Twinkle, twinkle little star
How I wonder where you are
up above the sky so high
like a diamond in the sky

==========>

Twinkle, twinkle little star
How I wonder where you are
up above the sky so high
like a diamond in the sky
```

**ANALYSIS** This listing provides the same functionality as the previous listing. Instead of reading a character at a time, a line is read (line 15). If the line read is equal to `null`, the input is ended. If information was read, it is appended to the `Input` string (line 17). Because line feed information is removed from the string, line 18 adds a line feed back to the string being created so that the final output displayed in line 21 will match what the user entered.

How could you prevent Ctrl+Z from being used? Suppose you wanted to end this listing by entering a blank line. Exercise 3 at the end of today's lessons asks you how to change this listing so a blank line ends the input. The answer is provided in Appendix A, "Answers."

## The `Convert` Class

The key to using information read in by the `Read` and `ReadLine` methods is not in just getting the data, but in converting it to the format you want to use. This can be meshing the text in a string to a different string value or converting it to a different data type.

The `System` namespace contains a class that can be used to convert data to a different data type: the `Convert` class.

The `Convert` class is a sealed class containing a large number of static methods. These methods convert to different data types. Because they are static, the format for using them is

```
Convert.method( orig_val );
```

This assumes you have included a `using` statement with the `System` namespace. *`method`* is the name of the conversion method you want to use. *`orig_val`* is the original value that you are converting to the new type. It is very important to know that this is a class in the base class library. This means that the class also can be used with other programming languages. Instead of converting to C# data types, the `Convert` class converts to a base data type. Not to fret—as you learned on Day 3, "Storing Information with Variables," there are equivalent base types for each of the C# data types.

Table 12.7 contains several of the methods in the `Convert` class. You should consult the framework documentation for a complete list of methods. Listing 12.10 presents a brief example of using a `Convert` method. This listing converts a `string` value entered by `ReadLine` into an integer.

**Note** The `Convert` class is being used to convert from strings to numbers in this lesson; however, it can be used to convert from other data types as well.

**TABLE 12.7** The Conversion Methods

| *Method* | *Converts To* |
|---|---|
| `ToBoolean` | Boolean |
| `ToByte` | 8-bit unsigned integer |
| `ToChar` | Unicode character |
| `ToDateTime` | `DateTime` |
| `ToDecimal` | Decimal number |
| `ToDouble` | Double number |
| `ToInt16` | 16-bit signed integer |
| `ToInt32` | 32-bit signed integer |
| `ToInt64` | 64-bit signed integer |
| `ToSByte` | 8-bit signed integer |
| `ToSingle` | Single precision floating-point number |
| `ToString` | String |

**TABLE 12.7** continued

| *Method* | *Converts To* |
|---|---|
| `ToUInt16` | 16-bit unsigned integer |
| `ToUInt32` | 32-bit unsigned integer |
| `ToUInt64` | 64-bit unsigned integer |

**LISTING 12.10** conv.cs—Using a `Convert` Method

```
// conv.cs - Converting to a data type
//-----------------------------------------------
using System;
using System.Text;

class myApp
{
  public static void Main()
  {
     string buff;
     int age;

     Console.Write("Enter your age: ");

     buff = Console.ReadLine();

     try
     {
        age = Convert.ToInt32(buff);

        if( age < 21 )
           Console.WriteLine("You are under 21.");
        else
           Console.Write("You are 21 or older.");
     }
     catch( ArgumentException )
     {
        Console.WriteLine("No value was entered... (equal to null)");
     }
     catch( OverflowException )
     {
        Console.WriteLine("You entered a number that is too big or too
➥small.");
     }
     catch( FormatException )
     {
        Console.WriteLine("You didn't enter a valid number.");
     }
     catch( Exception e )
     {
```

**LISTING 12.10** continued

```
40:             Console.WriteLine("Something went wrong with the conversion.");
41:             throw;
42:         }
43:     }
44: }
```

**OUTPUT** The following is output from running the listing several times from the command line:

```
C:\Day12>conv
Enter your age: 12
You are under 21.

C:\Day12>conv
Enter your age: 21
You are 21 or older.

C: \Day12>conv
Enter your age: 65
You are 21 or older.

C:\Day12>conv
Enter your age: 9999999999999999
You entered a number that is too big or too small.

C:\\Day12>conv
Enter your age: abc
You didn't enter a valid number.

C:\Day12>conv
Enter your age: abc123
You didn't enter a valid number.

C:\Day12>conv
Enter your age: 123abc
You didn't enter a valid number.

C:\Day12>conv
Enter your age: 123 123
You didn't enter a valid number.
```

**ANALYSIS** The first thing you will notice about this listing is that exception handling was used. You should use exception handling whenever there is a possibility of an exception being thrown. The conversion method being used in line 19, `ToInt32`, has the possibility of throwing three exceptions if bad information is entered. Lines 26, 30, and 34 catch these three different types of exceptions. Line 38 catches any other unexpected exceptions. If an exception is not thrown, a message is displayed based on whether the age is less than 21 or not.

This sets up the foundation for you to be able to get information from the end user, convert it to a more usable format, and verify the information to make sure it is valid.

# Summary

You explored a lot of information in today's lesson. Mark the pages that contain the tables of methods; having them handy will help as you continue your programming.

In today's lesson, you learned how to format information to make it more presentable. In addition to learning how to format regular data types, you also learned how to get and format dates and times.

The second half of today's lesson focused more on working with strings and the methods available to use with them. Because strings are immutable—they can't be changed—you also learned about the `StringBuilder` class. Using this class, you learned how to manipulate string information.

Today ended by focusing on obtaining information from the console. You revisited the `Read` and `ReadLine` methods. To these you combined what you had learned with formatting strings and with a new conversion class. You now know how to retrieve information from the console and format it into a usable format, which can include different data types.

# Q&A

**Q I'm confused. You said strings can't be changed; yet there are a number of string methods that seem to change strings. What gives?**

**A** The methods that work directly with a string type do not change the original string. Rather, they create a new string with the changes and then replace the original. With the `StringBuilder` class, the original string information can be manipulated.

**Q You said the `Convert` class works with the base data types. I didn't follow what you meant. Please explain.**

**A** You should review Day 3. When you compile your programs, the C# data types are all converted to data types in the runtime. For instance, a C# type `int` is converted to a `System.Int32`. You can actually use `int` or `System.Int32` interchangeably in your programs.

# Workshop

The Workshop provides quiz questions to help you solidify your understanding of the material covered and exercises to provide you with experience in using what you've

12

learned. Try to understand the quiz and exercise answers before continuing to the next day's lesson. Answers are provided in Appendix A, "Answers."

## Quiz

1. What method can be used to convert and format an integer data type to a string?
2. What method within the `string` class can be used to format information into a new string?
3. What specifier can be used to indicate that a number should be formatted as currency?
4. What specifier can be used to indicate that a number should be formatted as a decimal number with commas and containing one decimal place (for example, 123,890.5)?
5. What will the following display be if `x` is equal to `123456789.876`?

   ```
   Console.WriteLine("X is {0:'a value of '#,.#'.'}", x);
   ```

6. What would be the specifier used to format a number as a decimal with a minimum of five characters displayed if positive, a decimal with a minimum of eight characters displayed if negative, and the text `<empty>` if a value of zero?
7. How would you get today's date?
8. What is the key difference between a string and a `StringBuilder` object?
9. What special character is used for the string formatter, and what does this do to the string?
10. How can you get a numeric value out of a string?

## Exercises

1. Write the line of code to format a number so that it has at least three digits and two decimal places.
2. Write the code to display a date value written as day of week, month, day, full year (for example, Monday, January 1, 2002).
3. Modify Listing 12.9 so that the input ends when a blank line is entered.
4. Modify Listing 12.10. If the user enters information with a space, crop the information and use the first part of the string. For example, if the user enters `123 456`, crop to 123 and then convert.
5. **ON YOUR OWN:** Write a program that has a person enter full name, age, and phone number. Display this information with formatting. Also display the person's initials.

# DAY 13

# Interfaces

Today, you expand on your understanding of the object-oriented programming. This includes expanding on your use of inheritance and polymorphism with the use of interfaces. Today, you learn how to inherit traits from multiple sources and how to perform methods on a number of different data types. More specifically, today you

- Learn about interfaces
- Discover what the basic structure of an interface is
- Define and use interfaces
- Understand about implementing multiple interfaces
- Derive new interfaces from existing ones
- See how to hide interface members from a class

On Day 6, "Classes," you began learning about classes. On Day 11, "Inheritance," you learned how to inherit from one class to another. Today, you learn how to inherit characteristics from multiple sources into a single new class.

## Interfaces—A First Look

Consider the following. What do you notice about this class?

```
public abstract class cShape
{
     public abstract long Area();
     public abstract long Circumference();
     public abstract int sides();
}
```

You should notice that this is an `abstract` class and that all its methods are abstract. You learned about abstract classes on Day 11.

To review, `abstract` classes are classes that generally contain at least one abstract method. Abstract methods are methods that must be overridden when inherited.

Interfaces are another reference type similar to classes, and very similar to the `cShape` class shown. An interface has the purpose of defining what will be contained within a class that will be declared; however, an interface does not define the actual functionality. An interface is like an abstract method and is very similar to the class shown.

In fact, the `cShape` class can be changed to an interface by dropping the modifiers on the methods and class and by changing the word `class` to `interface`:

```
public interface IShape
{
     long Area();
     long Circumference();
     int sides();
}
```

### Classes Versus Interfaces

An interface is like a pure abstract class. An interface differs from a class in a number of ways.

First and primarily, an interface does not provide any implementation code. This will be done by the classes that implement the interface. An interface is said to provide a specification or guideline for what will be happening, but not the details.

An interface differs from a class; all of its members are assumed to be `public`. If you try to declare a different scope modifier for a member of an interface, you will get an error.

Interfaces contain only methods, properties, events, and indexers. They do not contain data members, constructors, or destructors. They also cannot contain any `static` members.

An abstract class has similar traits to those described, but differs in what you can do with an interface. You'll understand this by the end of today's lesson.

## Using Interfaces

An interface might not seem as all-powerful as a class, but interfaces can be used where a class can't. A class can inherit from only one other class. A class can implement multiple interfaces. Additionally, structures cannot inherit from other structures or classes. They can, however, implement interfaces. You'll learn more about implementing multiple interfaces later today.

**Note**

> C# does not support multiple inheritance of classes as C++ and other object-oriented languages do. The capability of multiple inheritance was intentionally left out because of the trouble caused by its complex implementation. C# provides the functionality and benefit of multiple inheritance by enabling multiple interfaces to be implemented.

## Why Use Interfaces?

There are benefits to using interfaces. You can figure out a couple from the previous sections.

First, you can use interfaces as a means of providing some inheritance features with structures. Additionally, you can implement multiple interfaces with a class, thus gaining functionality you can't obtain with an abstract class.

One of the biggest values to using an interface is that you can add characteristics to a class that it would not otherwise have. If you add these same characteristics to other classes, you can begin to make assumptions about your class's functionality. Actually, by using interfaces, you can *avoid* making assumptions.

Another benefit is that by using an interface rather than a class, you force the new class to implement all the defined characteristics of the interface. If you inherit from a base class with virtual members, you can get away without implementing code for them. This opens your new class, and the programs that use it, to errors.

13

# Defining Interfaces

As you saw earlier, an interface is declared as a guide to what will need to be implemented by classes. The basic structure is

```
interface IName
{
   members;
}
```

where *IName* is the name of the interface. This can be any name that you want to give it. I recommend that you use an I at the beginning of the name to indicate that this is an interface. This is in line with what is generally done by most programmers.

*members* designates the members of the interface. These are any of the types mentioned before: properties, events, methods (virtual methods that is), and indexers.

You'll learn about events and indexers tomorrow. Methods are specified without the need for a scope modifier. As stated earlier, the methods will be assumed public. Additionally, you won't implement the bodies for the methods. In most cases, you state the return type and the method name, followed by a parenthesis and a semicolon:

```
interface IFormatForPrint
{
   void FormatForPrint(PrintClass PrinterType);
   int  NotifyPrintComplete();
}
```

This interface defines two methods that need to be defined by any classes implementing it. These are FormatForPrint, which takes a PrintClass object and returns nothing, and NotifyPrintComplete, which returns an integer.

## Defining an Interface with Method Members

Enough theory—it's time to take a look at some code. Listing 13.1 contains code to define an interface called IShape. The IShape interface is then implemented by two classes, Circle and Square.

The definition for the IShape interface is

```
public interface IShape
{
  double Area();
  double Circumference();
  int    Sides();
}
```

By using this interface, you guarantee a couple of things. First, you guarantee that Circle and Square will both fully implement the methods in the interface. In this case, you guarantee that both classes will contain implementations for Area, Sides, and Circumference. Just as important, you guarantee that both contain the characteristic of IShape. You've seen the value of this before on Day 12, "Better Input and Output."

You'll see the value of this again in Listing 13.1.

**LISTING 13.1** shape.cs—Using the `IShape` Interface

```
//  shape.cs -
//-----------------------------------------------------------------------------

using System;

public interface IShape
{
   double Area();
   double Circumference();
   int    Sides();
}

public class Circle : IShape
{
   public int x;
   public int y;
   public double radius;
   private const float PI = 3.14159F;

   public double Area()
   {
      double theArea;
      theArea = PI * radius * radius;
      return theArea;
   }

   public double Circumference()
   {
      return ((double) (2 * PI * radius));
   }

   public int Sides()
   {
      return 1;
   }

   public Circle()
   {
      x = 0;
      y = 0;
      radius = 0.0;
   }
}

public class Square : IShape
{
```

**LISTING 13.1** continued

```
   public int side;

   public double Area()
   {
      return ((double) (side * side));
   }

   public double Circumference()
   {
      return ((double) (4 * side));
   }

   public int Sides()
   {
      return 4;
   }

   public Square()
   {
      side = 0;
   }
}

public class myApp
{
   public static void Main()
   {
      Circle myCircle = new Circle();
      myCircle.radius = 5;

      Square mySquare = new Square();
      mySquare.side = 4;

      Console.WriteLine("Displaying Circle information:");
      displayInfo(myCircle);

      Console.WriteLine("\nDisplaying Square information:");
      displayInfo(mySquare);
   }

   static void displayInfo( IShape myShape )
   {
      Console.WriteLine("Area: {0}", myShape.Area());
      Console.WriteLine("Sides: {0}", myShape.Sides());
      Console.WriteLine("Circumference: {0}", myShape.Circumference());
   }
}
```

**OUTPUT**

```
Displaying Circle information:
Area: 78.5397529602051
Sides: 1
Circumference: 31.415901184082

Displaying Square information:
Area: 16
Sides: 4
Circumference: 16
```

**ANALYSIS** This listing defines the `IShape` interface in lines 6 to 11. As you can see, this is the same interface as presented earlier. In line 13, you see how an interface is implemented:

```
public class Circle : IShape;
```

An interface is implemented in the same manner that a class is inherited—you include it after your new class's name, using a colon as a separator.

Within the `Circle` class, you can see that there are a number of data members. Additionally, you can see that the methods from the `IShape` interface have been provided code. All three of the methods in the `IShape` interface have been defined in the `Circle` class. Each of these methods include the same parameter types and return types as the method names in the interface.

In line 45, you see that the same is true of the `Square` class. It also implements the `IShape` interface. Because it also implements this interface, it also includes definitions for the three `IShape` methods.

In line 70, the application class starts. The `Main` method for this class creates a `Circle` object and a `Square` object. Each of these is assigned a value. In line 81, the `displayInfo` method is called. This method is passed the `myCircle Circle` object. In line 84, the `displayInfo` method of the application class is called again. This time it is called with the `mySquare Square` object.

Is this method overloaded to take both `Circle` and `Square` objects? No! As you learned on Day 11 with classes, you see here with interfaces. The `displayInfo` method takes an `IShape` value. Technically, there is no such thing as an `IShape` object. There are, however, objects that have `IShape` characteristics. This method is polymorphic; it can work with any object that has implemented the `IShape` interface. It can then use the methods that were defined within the `IShape` interface.

**Note** You can also use the `is` and `as` keywords within the `displayInfo` method to determine whether different class methods can be used. See Day 11 on how to use these keywords.

13

## Specifying Properties in Interfaces

A property specification can also be included in an interface. As with other members of an interface, no specific implementation code is included. The format for declaring a property within an interface is

```
modifier(s) datatype name
{
   get;
   set;
}
```

Listing 13.2 is a scaled-down listing that shows how to define a property within an interface and then how to use that property from a class. This listing is of no real value other than to illustrate this concept.

**LISTING 13.2** props.cs—Defining Properties in an Interface

```
//  props.cs - Using properties in an interface
//-----------------------------------------------------------------

using System;

public interface IShape
{
   int Sides
   {
      get;
      set;
   }

   double Area();
}

public class Square : IShape
{
   private int sides;
   public  int SideLength;

   public double Area()
   {
      return ((double) (SideLength * SideLength));
   }

   public int Sides
   {
      get { return sides; }
      set { sides = value; }
   }
```

**Listing 13.2** continued

```
32:
33:     public Square()
34:     {
35:        Sides = 4;
36:     }
37:  }
38:
39:  public class myApp
40:  {
41:     public static void Main()
42:     {
43:        Square mySquare = new Square();
44:        mySquare.SideLength = 5;
45:
46:        Console.WriteLine("\nDisplaying Square information:");
47:        Console.WriteLine("Area: {0}", mySquare.Area());
48:        Console.WriteLine("Sides: {0}", mySquare.Sides);
49:     }
50:  }
```

**Output**

```
Displaying Square information:
Area: 25
Sides: 4
```

> **Caution**
>
> Remember, C# is case sensitive. It may seem confusing, but it is perfectly legal to use variables of the same name with different character cases. An example is the use of `side` and `Side` in this listing. It is a common practice to use property names that have the same name as their data names, but with a different case.

**Analysis** This listing focuses on the use of a property rather than all the other code in the previous listing. You can see that the number of sides for the shape is now accessed via a property instead of a method. In lines 8 to 12, the `IShape` interface has a declaration for a property called `Sides` that will be used with an integer. This will have both the `get` and `set` methods. You should note that you are not required to specify both here. It would be perfectly acceptable to specify just a `get` or just a `set`. If both are specified in the interface, all classes that implement the interface must implement both.

**Note**

In the `IShape` interface used here, it would make sense to specify only the `get` property for `Sides`. Many shapes have a `set` number of sides that could be set in the constructor and then never changed. The `get` method could still be used. If `set` were not included in the interface, a class could still implement `set`.

The `IShape` interface is implemented in a `Square` class starting in line 17. In lines 27 to 31, the actual definitions for the `get` and `set` properties are defined. The code for the `Square` class's implementation is straightforward. The `Sides` property sets the `sides` data member.

The use of a property that has been implemented via an interface is no different than any other property. You can see the use of the `Sides` property in the previous listing in a number of lines. This includes getting the value in line 48. The value is set in line 35 of the constructor.

**Note**

Many people will say that a class inherits from an interface. In a way this is true; however, it is more correct to say that a class *implements* an interface.

# Using Multiple Interfaces

One of the benefits of implementing interfaces instead of inheriting from a class is that you can implement more than one interface at a time. This gives you the power to do multiple inheritance without some of the downside.

To implement multiple interfaces, you separate them with a comma. To include both an `IShape` and a `IShapeDisplay` interface in a `Square` class, you use the following:

```
class Square : IShape, IShapeDisplay
{
   ...
}
```

You then need to implement all the constructs within both interfaces. Listing 13.3 illustrates the use of multiple interfaces.

**LISTING 13.3** multi.cs—Implementing Multiple Interfaces in a Single Class

```
//  multi.cs -
//-----------------------------------------------------------------

```

**LISTING 13.3** continued

```
using System;

public interface IShape
{
   // Cut out other methods to simplify example.
   double Area();
   int Sides { get; }
}

public interface IShapeDisplay
{
   void Display();
}

public class Square : IShape, IShapeDisplay
{
   private int sides;
   public  int SideLength;

   public int Sides
   {
      get { return sides; }
   }

   public double Area()
   {
      return ((double) (SideLength * SideLength));
   }

   public double Circumference()
   {
      return ((double) (Sides * SideLength));
   }

   public Square()
   {
      sides = 4;
   }

   public void Display()
   {
      Console.WriteLine("\nDisplaying Square information:");
      Console.WriteLine("Side length: {0}", this.SideLength);
      Console.WriteLine("Sides: {0}", this.Sides);
      Console.WriteLine("Area: {0}", this.Area());
   }
}

```

**LISTING 13.3** continued

```
52: public class myApp
53: {
54:     public static void Main()
55:     {
56:         Square mySquare = new Square();
57:         mySquare.SideLength = 7;
58:
59:         mySquare.Display();
60:     }
61: }
```

**OUTPUT**

```
Displaying Square information:
Side length: 7
Sides: 4
Area: 49
```

**ANALYSIS** You can see that two interfaces are declared and used in this listing. In line 18, you can see that the `Square` class is going to implement the two interfaces. Because both are included, all members of both interfaces must be implemented by the `Square` class. In looking at the code in lines 23 to 49, you see that all the members are implemented.

# Explicit Interface Members

So far, everything has gone smoothly with implementing interfaces. What happens, however, when you implement an interface that has a member name that clashes with another name already in use? For example, what would happen if the two interfaces in Listing 13.3 both had a `Display` method?

If a class includes two or more interfaces with the same member name, that member needs to be implemented only once. This single implementation of the method will satisfy both interfaces.

There might be times where you want to implement the method independently for both interfaces. In this case, you need to use explicit interface implementations. An explicit implementation is done by including the interface name with the member name when you define the member. You must also use casting to call the method. This casting will be shown in Listing 13.4.

**LISTING 13.4** explicit.cs

```
//  explicit.cs
//-----------------------------------------------------------------

using System;

public interface IShape
{
   double Area();
   int Sides { get; }
   void Display();
}

public interface IShapeDisplay
{
   void Display();
}

public class Square : IShape, IShapeDisplay
{
   private int sides;
   public  int SideLength;

   public int Sides
   {
      get { return sides; }
   }

   public double Area()
   {
      return ((double) (SideLength * SideLength));
   }

   public double Circumference()
   {
      return ((double) (Sides * SideLength));
   }

   public Square()
   {
      sides = 4;
   }

   void IShape.Display()
   {
      Console.WriteLine("\nDisplaying Square Shape\'s information:")
      Console.WriteLine("Side length: {0}", this.SideLength);
      Console.WriteLine("Sides: {0}", this.Sides);
      Console.WriteLine("Area: {0}", this.Area());
```

**LISTING 13.4** continued

```
49:     }
50:     void IShapeDisplay.Display()
51:     {
52:        Console.WriteLine("\nThis method could draw the shape...");
53:     }
54:
55:  }
56:
57:  public class myApp
58:  {
59:     public static void Main()
60:     {
61:        Square mySquare = new Square();
62:        mySquare.SideLength = 7;
63:
64:        IShape ish = (IShape) mySquare;
65:        IShapeDisplay ishd = (IShapeDisplay) mySquare;
66:
67:        ish.Display();
68:        ishd.Display();
69:     }
70:  }
```

**OUTPUT**

```
Displaying Square Shape's information:
Side length: 7
Sides: 4
Area: 49

This method could draw the shape...
```

**ANALYSIS** This listing is a bit more complicated, but the result is that you can explicitly declare and then use methods from different interfaces with the same name within a single class.

This listing has two methods called `Display`. Each of these is explicitly defined within the `Square` class. You can see in lines 43 and 50 that the explicit definitions use the explicit name of the method. The explicit name is the interface name and member name separated by a period.

To use these explicit interfaces requires more work than calling the method. After all, if you call the method using the standard class name, which `Display` method would be used? To use one of the methods, you must cast the class to the interface type. In this case, it is a matter of casting the class to either `IShape` or `IShapeDisplay`. In line 64, a variable, `ish`, is declared that is of type `IShape`. This is assigned to the `mySquare` class. A cast makes sure that the `mySquare` class is treated as an `IShape` type.

In line 65, the `myShape` class is cast to a variable, `ishd`, that is of type `IShapeDisplay`. You can see in lines 67 and 68 that these variables of interface types can then be used to call the appropriate `Display` method.

The end result of this listing is that you can have multiple interfaces with similarly named methods. Using explicit definitions and a little casting, you can make sure the correct method is called. Why might you do this? For the previous listing, the `IShapeDisplay` interface might be used with shapes to ensure that all the classes have the capability of doing a graphical display method. The `Display` method in the `IShape` might have the purpose of providing detailed textual information. By implementing both, you have the ability to get both types of display.

# Deriving New Interfaces from Existing Ones

As with classes, an interface can be derived from another interface. This inheritance of interfaces is done in a similar manner to inheriting classes. The following snippet shows how the `IShape` interface created earlier could be extended:

```
public interface IShape
{
     long Area();
     long Circumference();
     int Sides{ get; set; };
}
interface I3DShape : IShape

{
   int Depth { get; set; }
}
```

The `I3DShape` contains all the members of the `IShape` class and any new members it adds. In this case, a `Depth` property member is added. You can then use the `I3DShape` interface as you would any other interface. Its members would be `Area`, `Circumference`, `Sides`, and `Depth`.



# Hiding Interface Members

It is possible to implement an interface member, and yet hide its access from the base class. This can be done to meet the requirement of implementing the interface and avoid cluttering up your class with additional members.

To hide an interface, you explicitly define it in the class. Listing 13.5 provides an example of hiding an interface member.

**LISTING 13.5** hide.cs—Hiding an Interface Member from a Class

```
//  hide.cs
//-----------------------------------------------------------------

using System;

public interface IShape
{
   // members left out to simplify example...
   int ShapeShifter( int val );
   int Sides { get; set; }
}

public class Shape : IShape
{
   private int sides;

   public int Sides
   {
      get { return sides; }
      set { sides = value; }
   }

   int IShape.ShapeShifter( int val )
   {
      Console.WriteLine("Shifting Shape....");
      val += 1;
      return val;
   }

   public Shape()
   {
      Sides = 5;
   }
}

public class myApp
{
   public static void Main()
   {
      Shape myShape = new Shape();

      Console.WriteLine("My shape has been created.");
      Console.WriteLine("Using get accessor. Sides = {0}", myShape.Sides);

//    myShape.Sides = myShape.ShapeShifter(myShape.Sides);   // error

      IShape tmp = (IShape) myShape;
      myShape.Sides = tmp.ShapeShifter( myShape.Sides);
```

**LISTING 13.5** continued

```
49:
50:         Console.WriteLine("ShapeShifter called. Sides = {0}", myShape.Sides);
51:     }
52: }
```

**OUTPUT**

```
My shape has been created.
Using get accessor. Sides = 5
Shifting Shape....
ShapeShifter called. Sides = 6
```

**ANALYSIS** This listing uses a scaled-down version of the `IShape` interface you've seen used throughout today's lessons. The focus of this listing is to illustrate the point of hiding an interface's member from a class. In this case, the `ShapeShifter` method is hidden from the `Shape` class. Line 45 is commented out, and there is an attempt to use the `ShapeShifter` method as a member of the `Shape` class. If you remove the comments from the beginning of this line and try to compile and run this program, you get the following error:

```
hide2.cs(45,21): error CS0117: 'Shape' does not contain a definition for
    'ShapeShifter'
```

As you can see, `Shape` objects can't directly access the `ShapeShifter` method—it is hidden from them.

How is this done? When defining the interface member, you need to do it explicitly. In line 23, you see that the definition of the `ShapeShifter` method includes such an explicit definition. The name of the interface is explicitly included in this line.

When calling the explicitly defined member, you need to do what was done in lines 47 and 48. You need to declare a variable of the interface type and then use a cast of the interface type using the object you want to access. In line 47, you see that a variable called `tmp` is created that is of the interface type `IShape`. The `myShape` object is then cast to this variable using the same interface type. In line 48, you see that this variable of the interface type (`IShape`) can be used to get to the `ShapeShifter` method. The output from line 50 proves that the method was appropriately called.

The `tmp` variable can access the method because it is of the same type as the explicit declaration in line 23.

## Summary

Today's lesson was shorter than most that you've seen so far, but it contained a lot of important information. You learned about interfaces, a construct that enables you to define what must be implemented. They can be used to ensure that different classes have similar implementations within them. You learned a number of things about interfaces, including how to use them, how to extend them, and how to implement—yet hide—some of their members from the base classes.

## Q&A

**Q Is it important to understand interfaces?**

**A** Yes. You will find interfaces are used through C# programming. Many of the preconstructed methods provided within the class libraries include the use of interfaces.

**Q You said the `as` and `is` keywords can be used with interfaces; yet you did not show an example. How does the use of these keywords differ from what was shown with classes?**

**A** The use of `as` and `is` with interfaces is nearly identical to their use with classes. Because the use is so similar, the coding examples with interfaces would also be virtually the same as what was shown on Day 11.

## Workshop

The Workshop provides quiz questions to help you solidify your understanding of the material covered and exercises to provide you with experience in using what you've learned. Try to understand the quiz and exercise answers before continuing to tomorrow's lesson. Answers are provided in Appendix A, "Answers."

### Quiz

1. Are interfaces a reference type or a value type?
2. What is the purpose of an interface?
3. Are members of an interface declared as `public`, `private`, or `protected`?
4. What is the primary difference between an interface and a class?
5. What inheritance is available with structures?
6. What types can be included in an interface?

7. How would you declare a public class called `AClass` that inherits from a class called `baseClass` and implements an interface called `IMyInterface`?
8. How many classes can be inherited at one time?
9. How many interfaces can be inherited (implemented) at one time?
10. How is an explicit interface implementation done?

## Exercises

1. Write the code for an interface called `Iid` that has a property called `ID` as its only member.
2. Write the code that would declare an interface called `IPosition`. This interface should contain a method that takes a `Point` value and returns a Boolean.
3. **BUG BUSTER:** The following code snippet might have a problem. If so, what is it?

```
public interface IDimensions
{
   long   Width;
   long   Height;
   double Area();
   double Circumference();
   int    Sides();
}
```

4. Implement the `IShape` interface declared in Listing 13.1 into a class called `Rectangle`.

# WEEK 2

# DAY 14

# Indexers, Delegates, and Events

You've learned many of the foundational topics related to C# programming. In today's lesson, you learn about several additional topics that are foundational for your full understanding of C#. Today you

- Learn about indexers
- Build your own indexers
- Explore delegates
- Discover event programming
- Create your own events and event handlers
- Learn to multicast

## Using an Indexer

**NEW TERM** On Day 8, "Advanced Data Storage," you learned about arrays. Today, you learn about indexers. An *indexer* enables you to use an index on an object to obtain values stored within the object. In essence this enables you to treat an object like an array.

An indexer is also similar to a property. As with properties, you use `get` and `set` when defining an indexer. Unlike properties, you are not obtaining a specific data member; rather, you are obtaining a value from the object itself. When you define a property, you define a property name. With indexers, instead of creating a name as you do with properties, you use the `this` keyword, which refers to the object instance and thus the object name is used. The format for defining an indexer is

```
public dataType this[int index]
{
    get
    {
        // Do whatever you want...
        return aValue;
    }
    set
    {
        // Do whatever you want
        // Generally you should set a value within the class
        // based on the index and the value they assign.
    }
}
```

Creating an indexer enables you to use bracket notation ([]) with an object to set and get a value from an object. As you can see in the format shown earlier, you state the *dataType* that will be set and returned by the indexer. In the `get` section, you return a value that is of *dataType*. In the `set` block, you will be able to do something with a value of *dataType*. As with properties and member functions, you can use the `value` keyword. This is the value passed as the argument to the `set` routine. Listing 14.1 presents a simple example of using an indexer.

**LISTING 14.1** indexer.cs—Using an Indexer

```
//  indx2.cs - Using an indexer
//--------------------------------------------------------------------

using System;

public class SpellingList
{
    protected string[] words = new string[size];
    static public int size = 10;

    public SpellingList()
    {
        for (int x = 0; x < size; x++ )
            words[x] = String.Format("Word{0}", x);
    }
```

**LISTING 14.1** continued

```

    public string this[int index]
    {
       get
       {
          string tmp;

             if( index >= 0 && index <= size-1 )
                tmp = words[index];
             else
                tmp = "";

             return ( tmp );
       }
       set
       {
             if( index >= 0 && index <= size-1 )
                words[index] = value;
       }
    }
 }

 public class TestApp
 {
    public static void Main()
    {
       SpellingList myList = new SpellingList();

       myList[3] = "=====";
       myList[4] = "Brad";
       myList[5] = "was";
       myList[6] = "Here!";
       myList[7] = "=====";

       for ( int x = 0; x < SpellingList.size; x++ )
           Console.WriteLine(myList[x]);
    }
 }
```

**OUTPUT**

```
Word0
Word1
Word2
=====
Brad
was
Here!
=====
Word8
Word9
```

**ANALYSIS** This listing creates an indexer to be used with the `SpellingList` class. The `SpellingList` class contains an array of strings called `words` that can be used to store a list of words. This list is set to the size of the variable declared in line 9.

Lines 11 to 15 contain a constructor for `SpellingList` that sets initial values into each element of the array. You could just as easily have requested the words from the reader or read them from a file. This constructor assigns the string value `Word##` to each of the elements in the array, where `##` is the element number of the array.

Jumping down to the `TestApp` class in lines 38 to 53, you see how the `SpellingList` class is going to be used. In line 42, the `SpellingList` class is used to instantiate the `myList` object that will hold the words. Line 42 also causes the constructor to be executed. This initializes the `Word##` values. Lines 44 to 48 then change some of these values.

If you think back to how you worked with arrays, you should be saying, "wait a minute" as you look at lines 44 to 48. To access the value of one of the words, you would normally have to access the data member within the object. When using arrays as a data member, you learned that you would assign a value to the fourth element as

```
MyList.words[3] = "=====";
```

Line 44, however, is accessing the fourth element within the object, which has been set to be the fourth element in the `words` array.

An indexer has been created for the `SpellingList` class in lines 17 to 35. This indexer enables you to access the elements within the `words` array using just the object name.

Line 17 is the defining line for the indexer. You know this is an indexer rather than a property because the `this` keyword is used instead of a name. Additionally, this is given an index (called `index`). The indexer will return a string value.

Lines 19 to 29 contain the `get` portion of the indexer. The `get` block returns a value based on the `index`. In this class, this value is an element from the `words` array. You can return any value you want. The value should, however, make sense. In line 23, a check is done to make sure the `index` value is valid. If you don't check the value of the `index`, you risk having an exception thrown. In this listing, if the `index` is out of the range, a null value is returned (line 26). If the `index` is valid, the value stored in the `words` array at the `index` location will be returned.

The `set` portion of the indexer is in lines 30 to 34. This block can be used to set information within the object. As with properties, the `value` keyword contains the value being assigned. In this code, the `index` value is again checked to make sure it is valid. If it is, a word in the `words` array will be updated at the `index` location with the value assigned.

Looking again at the test class, you see that the `set` indexer block is used to assign values in lines 44 to 48. For line 44, the `set` indexer block will be called with `value` equal to ===== and will be passed with an `index` value of `3`. In line 45, `value` will be `Brad` and the `index` is `4`. In line 51, the `get` indexer block is called with an `index` value of `x`. The value returned will be the string value returned by the `get` indexer block.

**Note**

There are times to use indexers and there are times to not use them. You should use indexers when it makes your code more readable and easier to understand. For example, you can create a stack that can have items placed on it and taken off of it. Using an indexer, you could access items within the stack without needing to remove items.

# Exploring Delegates

**NEW TERM** You are now going to learn about a more advanced topic—delegates. A *delegate* is a reference type, which defines the signature for a method call. The delegate can then accept and execute methods that are of the format of this signature. Delegates are often compared to interfaces. You learned in yesterday's lesson that an interface is a reference type that defines the layout for a class, but does not itself define any of the functionality. A delegate defines the layout for a method, but does not actually define a method. Rather, it can accept and work with methods that match its layout (signature).

An example will help make delegates clearer. The example presented here creates a program that sorts two numbers, either ascending or descending. In the example, the sort is in the code presented; however, you could ask the reader to enter the direction of the sort. Based on the direction—ascending or descending—a different method will be used. Although a different method will be used, only one call, to a delegate, will be made. The delegate will be given the appropriate method to execute.

The format for declaring a delegate is

```
public delegate returnType DelegateName(parameters);
```

where `public` can be replaced with appropriate access modifiers, and `delegate` is the keyword used to indicate this is a delegate. The rest of the definition is for the signature of the method the delegate will work with. As you should know from previous lessons, the signature includes the data type to be returned by the method (*`returnType`*) as well as the name of the parameters that will be received by the method (*`parameters`*). The name of the delegate goes where the method name would normally go. Because the delegate will be used to execute multiple methods that fit the *`returnType`* and parameters, you don't know the specific method names.

The example used here creates a delegate called `Sort` that can take multiple sorting methods. These methods will not return a value, thus making their return type `void`. The methods that will be used for sorting will pass in two integer variables that will be reference types. This enables the sorting functions to switch the values if necessary. The delegate definition for the example will be

```
public delegate void Sort(ref int a, ref int b);
```

Notice the semicolon at the end. Although this looks similar to a method definition, it is not a method definition. There is no body, because a delegate is just a template for methods that can be executed. Methods are actually delegated to this delegate to be executed.

A delegate is a template for multiple methods. For example, the `Sort` delegate can be used with methods that don't return a value and take two reference integers as parameters. The following is an example of a method that can be used with the `Sort` delegate:

```
public static void Ascending( ref int first, ref int second )
{
   if (first > second )
   {
      int tmp = first;
      first = second;
      second = tmp;
   }
}
```

This method, `Ascending`, is of type `void`. Additionally, it receives two values that are both `ref int`. This matches the signature of the `Sort` delegate so it can be used. This method takes the two values and checks to see whether the first is greater than the second. If it is, the two values are swapped using a simple `sort` routine. Because these values are `ref` types, the calling routine will have the values swapped as well.

A second method called `Descending` can also be created:

```
public static void Descending( ref int first, ref int second )
{
   if (first < second )
   {
      int tmp = first;
      first = second;
      second = tmp;
   }
}
```

This method is similar to `Ascending` except that the larger value is kept in the first position. You could declare additional sort routines to use with this delegate as long as the signature of your methods matched. Additionally, different programs could use the `Sort` delegate and have their own logic within their methods.

Now that a delegate has been declared and there are multiple functions that can be used with it, what is next?

You need to associate your methods with the delegate. Instantiating delegate objects can do this. A delegate object is declared like other objects, with the parameter for the initializer being the method name you are assigning (delegating) to the delegate. For example, to declare a delegate that can be used with the `Ascending` method, you code the following:

```
Sort up = new Sort(Ascending);
```

This creates a delegate object called `up` that can then be used. `up` is associated with the `Ascending` method that was declared. The following creates a `Sort` delegate associated with the `Descending` method. This delegate is called `down`.

```
Sort down = new Sort(Descending);
```

Now you've declared your delegate, created methods that can be used with it, and associated these methods to delegate objects. How do you get the delegated methods to execute? You create a method that receives a delegate object as a parameter. This generic method can then execute the method from the delegate:

```
public void DoSort(Sort ar)
{
    ar(ref val1, ref val2);
}
```

As you can see, the `DoSort` method receives a delegate called `ar` as its parameter. This method then executes `ar`. You should notice that `ar` has the same signature as your delegate. If your delegate has a return type, `ar` will have a return type. The method of the `ar` call also matches your delegate. In essence, the `DoSort` method executes whichever method is passed as a `Sort` delegate object. For our example, if `up` is passed, `ar(...)` is equivalent to calling the `Ascending` method. If `down` is passed, `ar(...)` is equivalent to calling the `Decending` method.

You have now seen all the key pieces to working with a delegate. Listing 14.2 pulls the entire sample together into a workable application.

**Listing 14.2** deleg1.cs—Using a Simple Delegate

```
//  deleg1.cs - Using a delegates
//-----------------------------------------------------------

using System;

```

**LISTING 14.2** continued

```
public class SortClass
{
    static public int val1;
    static public int val2;

    public delegate void Sort(ref int a, ref int b);

    public void DoSort(Sort ar)
    {
        ar(ref val1, ref val2);
    }
}

public class SortProgram
{
   public static void Ascending( ref int first, ref int second )
   {
      if (first > second )
      {
         int tmp = first;
         first = second;
         second = tmp;
      }
   }

   public static void Descending( ref int first, ref int second )   {
      if (first < second )
      {
         int tmp = first;
         first = second;
         second = tmp;
      }
   }

   public static void Main()
   {
      SortClass.Sort up = new SortClass.Sort(Ascending);
      SortClass.Sort down = new SortClass.Sort(Descending);

      SortClass doIT = new SortClass();

      SortClass.val1 = 310;
      SortClass.val2 = 220;

      Console.WriteLine("Before Sort: val1 = {0}, val2 = {1}",
                        SortClass.val1, SortClass.val2);
      doIT.DoSort(up);
      Console.WriteLine("After Sort: val1 = {0}, val2 = {1}",
                        SortClass.val1, SortClass.val2);
```

**LISTING 14.2** continued

```
56:
57:         Console.WriteLine("Before Sort: val1 = {0}, val2 = {1}",
58:                           SortClass.val1, SortClass.val2);
59:         doIT.DoSort(down);
60:         Console.WriteLine("After Sort: val1 = {0}, val2 = {1}",
61:                           SortClass.val1, SortClass.val2);
62:     }
63: }
```

**OUTPUT**

```
Before Sort: val1 = 310, val2 = 220
After Sort: val1 = 220, val2 = 310
Before Sort: val1 = 220, val2 = 310
After Sort: val1 = 310, val2 = 220
```

**ANALYSIS** This listing starts by declaring a sorting class that will contain the `Sort` delegate. This class holds two `static public` variables in lines 8 and 9 that will be used to hold the two values to be sorted. These were declared as `static` to make the coding easier in the rest of the listing. Line 11 contains the delegate definition followed by the method that will execute the delegated methods, `DoSort`, in lines 13 to 16. As you can see, the `DoSort` method receives a delegate object as its parameter. The delegate object is used in line 15 as a method call using the same signature that was used with the delegate definition in line 11.

The `SortProgram` class uses the `Sort` delegate. This class defines the methods that will be delegated—`Ascending` and `Descending`. The class also contains a `Main` method that will perform the key logic. In lines 43 and 44, two delegate objects are created. These are the `up` and `down` objects you saw earlier.

In line 46, an object is created of type `SortClass`. This is necessary to use the `DoSort` method. In lines 48 and 49, two values are set into the sorting variables. Line 51 prints these values to the console. Line 53 then calls the `DoSort` method passing a delegate object. In this case, the `up` object is passed. This causes the `Ascending` method to be used. As the output from line 57 shows, the sort was accomplished. Line 59 then calls the `DoSort` method again. This time it is with the `down` object. This causes the `Descending` method to be used, as can be seen by the final output.

You could actually get around declaring a `doIT` object in line 46 by declaring the `DoSort` method as `static`. The `DoSort` method could then be accessed using the class name instead of an object:

```
SortClass.DoSort(...);
```

This example uses delegates with hard-coded values and with specific calls. The value of delegates becomes more apparent when you begin to create more dynamic programs. For example, Listing 14.2 could be modified to use data from a file or information entered by the user. This would give the sorting more value. Additionally, you could have your user enter whether they wanted to sort ascending, descending, or some other way. Based on what they enter, you could then make a single call to `DoSort` with the appropriate delegate object being passed.

**Note**

In today's exercises, you will be asked to create a delegate that can accept a method for sorting an array of integers. An answer for this will be provided. You could actually take the answer one step further, make the array work with objects, and then create a delegate for sorting data of any type.

# Working with Events

You will find that you will use delegates primarily when you are working with events. An event is a notification from a class that something has occurred. Other classes can then do something based on this notification.

The most common example of event processing is Microsoft Windows. Within Windows, a dialog or window is displayed. Users can then do a number of different things. They can click a button, select a menu, enter text, and so forth. Whenever the user does one of these actions, an event occurs. Event handlers within Windows then react based on the event that occurred. For example, if a user selects a button, a `ButtonClick` event notification might occur. A `ButtonClick` event handler would then handle any actions that need to occur.

# Creating Events

There are several steps to creating and using an event. This includes setting up the delegate for the event, creating a class to pass arguments for the event handlers, declaring the code for the event, creating code that should occur when the event happens (the handler), and finally causing the event to occur.

## An Event's Delegate

The first step to working with events is to create a delegate for the event. The delegates you create for an event follow a specific format:

```
delegate void EventHandlerName(object source, xxxEventArgs e);
```

The *EventHandlerName* is the name of the delegate for the event handler. A delegate for an event always takes two parameters. The first parameter, `object` *source*, will contain the source that raised the event. The second parameter, *xxxEventArgs* `e`, is a class containing data that can be used by a handler for the event. This class is derived from the `EventArgs` class, which is part of the `System` namespace.

The following line of code creates a delegate for an event. This event checks assigned characters. If a certain character is assigned, an event is executed. The delegate could be defined as

```
delegate void CnarEventHandler(object source, CharEventArgs e);
```

This declares the delegate named `CharEventHandler`. From this declaration, you can see that a class called `CharEventArgs` needs to be created by deriving it from `EventArgs`.

## The EventArgs Class

The `EventArgs` class is used to pass data to an event handler. This class can be inherited into a new class that contains data members for any necessary values. The format of a derived class should be

```
public class xxxEventArgs : EventArgs
{
    // Data members

    public xxxEventArgs( type name )
    {
        //Set up values
    }
}
```

As you can see, `xxxEventArgs` inherits from `EventsArgs`. You can rename `xxxEventArgs` to any name you want. Using a name that ends with `EventArgs` makes the use of this class more obvious.

**Tip**

> Although you can name the xxxEventArgs class anything you want, you should end your class name with EventsArgs. This indicates what the purpose of the class is and is more consistent with how others are programming.



You can then add data members to this derived class and add logic to initialize these values within the class's constructor. This class will be passed to the event handler. Any data that your event handler will need should be included in this class.

In the example from the previous section, you saw that a delegate was created called `CharEventHandler`. This delegate passed an object of class `CharEventArgs`. The `CharEventArgs` code follows:

```
public class CharEventArgs : EventArgs
{
    public char CurrChar;
    public CharEventArgs(char CurrChar)
    {
       this.CurrChar = CurrChar;
    }
}
```

As you can see, `CharEventArgs` is a new class derived from `EventArgs`. Regardless of the event you are doing, you will need to create a class that is derived in the same fashion from `EventArgs`. This class contains a single char value, `CurrChar`, which will be usable by the code that will be written to handle this event. This class also contains a constructor that receives a character when the class is created. The character passed to the constructor is assigned the data member within the class.

## The Event Class Code

A class can be created that serves the purpose of kicking off the event. This class contains a declaration for the event. This declaration takes the following format:

```
public event xxxEventHandler EventName;
```

where *`xxxEventHandler`* is the delegate definition that was created for this event. *`EventName`* is the name of the event being declared. In summary, this line of code uses the `event` keyword to create an event instance called *`EventName`* that is a delegate of type *`xxxEventHandler`*. *`EventName`* will be used to assign methods to the delegate as well as to do the execution of the methods.

Here is an example of creating an event class:

```
class CharChecker
{
    char curr_char;
    public event CharEventHandler TestChar;
    public char Curr_Char
    {
        get { return curr_char; }
        set
        {
            if (TestChar != null)
            {
                CharEventArgs args = new CharEventArgs(value);
                TestChar(this, args);
```

```
14:                 curr_char = args.CurrChar;
15:             }
16:         }
17:     }
18: }
```

This class contains the code that will kick off the event if the appropriate condition is met. Your code can vary from this example; however, there are a couple of things that will be similar. In the fourth line, an event object is created using the delegate `CharEventHandler`, which was created earlier. This event object will be used to execute any assigned event handlers. The next section of this class is a properties definition for `Curr_Char` (lines 5 to 17). As you can see, a `get` property returns the value of the `curr_char` data member from this class (line7).

The `set` property in lines 8 to 16 is unique. The first thing done is to verify that the `TestChar` object is not equal to `null` (line 10). Remember, the `TestChar` object was just declared as an event. This event object will be `null` only if there are no event handlers created. You'll learn more about this in the next section. If there is an event handler, line 12 creates a `CharEventArgs` object. As you learned in the previous section, this object will hold any values needed for the event handling routines. The value entered into the `set` routine is passed to the `CharEventArgs` constructor. As you saw in the previous section, this contains a character that will be available to the event handlers.

Line 13 is the call to the event delegate. Using the event object created in line 4, a call to the delegate is being made. Because this is an event, it checks for all the methods that have been associated to this event object. As you can see, two values are passed to this event object. The first is `this`, which is the object that is making the call to the event. The second value is `args`, which is the `CharEventArgs` object you declared in the previous line.

Line 14 is specific to this particular event. This line assigns the character that is in the `CharEventArgs` object back to the `curr_char` data member. If any event handlers called in line 13 change the data, this makes sure that the event class has an updated value and is thus set—which is the purpose of the `set` property!

## Creating Event Handlers

You have now created a delegate, created a structure to pass information to your event handlers, and created code to execute the event. Now you need event handlers. An event handler is a piece of code that gets notified when an event occurs. An event handler is a method created using the same format as your delegate. The format of the method is the following:

```
void handlername(object source, xxxEventArgs argName)
{
   // Event Handler code
}
```

`handlername` is the name of the method that will be called when an event occurs. The two parameters being passed should look very familiar by this time. The first is the object that executed the event. The second is the class derived from `EventArgs` that contains the values for the event handler to use. The *`Event Handler code`* can be any code you want. If the event was a button click, this code would be the code executed when the button is clicked. If it was a `Cancel` button, this code would do the logic for canceling. If it was an `Okay` button, this code would do the logic for things being okay.

Going back to our `Character` event example, an event can be declared to replace the letter `'A'` whenever it is entered with an 'X'. This is a goofy example, but it is easy to follow:

```
static void Drop_A(object source, CharEventArgs e)
{
   if(e.CurrChar == 'a' || e.CurrChar == 'A' )
   {
      Console.WriteLine("Don't like 'a'!");
      e.CurrChar = 'X';
   }
}
```

As you can see, this event handler receives the `CharEventArgs` parameter. The `CurrChar` value is retrieved from this object and checked for its value. If the user enters an `'A'` or an `'a'`, the event handler displays a message and changes the current character to an `'X'` instead. If it is any other character, nothing happens.

## Associating Events and Event Handlers

Now you have almost all the pieces. It's time to associate your event handler to the event—in case it happens. This occurs in your primary program.

To associate a handler with an event, you must first declare an object containing an event. For the `Character` example, this is done by declaring a `CharChecker` object:

```
CharChecker tester = new CharChecker();
```

As you can see, this object is instantiated like any other object. When this object is created, your event is available. Whenever the `set` logic of a `CharChecker` object is called, the logic within it will be followed, including the creation of the event and the execution of the event object in its `set` statements.

Right now, however, you still have not associated your event handler to this object. To associate an event handler to the object, you need to use the += operator. This is used in the following format:

```
ObjectWithEventName.EventObj += new EventDelegateName(EventName);
```

where *ObjectWithEventName* is the object you just declared using the event class. For the example, this is `tester`. *EventObj* is the event object you declared in the event class. For the example, this would be `TestChar`. The += operator follows as an indicator that the following will be an event to be added to the event handler. The `new` keyword indicates that the following handler should be created. Finally, the name of the event handler, *EventName*, is passed to the delegate, *EventDelegateName*. The final statement for the example is

```
tester.TestChar += new CharEventHandler(Drop_A);
```

## Pulling It All Together

Whew! That is a lot to do; however, when this is completed, a line as simple as the following can be used to execute the event:

```
tester.Curr_Char = 'B';
```

Listing 14.3 wraps it all up.

**Listing 14.3** Using an Event and Event Handlers

```
// events.cs - Using events
//-----------------------------------------------------------------

using System;

delegate void CharEventHandler(object source, CharEventArgs e);

public class CharEventArgs : EventArgs
{
     public char CurrChar;
     public CharEventArgs(char CurrChar)
     {
        this.CurrChar = CurrChar;
     }
}

class CharChecker
{
    char curr_char;
    public event CharEventHandler TestChar;
    public char Curr_Char
```

**LISTING 14.3** continued

```
   {
      get { return curr_char; }
      set
      {
         if (TestChar != null )
         {
             CharEventArgs args = new CharEventArgs(value);
             TestChar(this, args);
             curr_char = args.CurrChar;
         }
      }
   }
}

class myApp
{
   static void Main()
   {
      CharChecker tester = new CharChecker();

      tester.TestChar += new CharEventHandler(Drop_A);

      tester.Curr_Char = 'B';
      Console.WriteLine("{0}", tester.Curr_Char);

      tester.Curr_Char = 'r';
      Console.WriteLine("{0}", tester.Curr_Char);

      tester.Curr_Char = 'a';
      Console.WriteLine("{0}", tester.Curr_Char);

      tester.Curr_Char = 'd';
      Console.WriteLine("{0}", tester.Curr_Char);

   }

   static void Drop_A(object source, CharEventArgs e)
   {
      if(e.CurrChar == 'a' || e.CurrChar == 'A' )
      {
         Console.WriteLine("Don't like 'a'!");
         e.CurrChar = 'X';
      }
   }
}
```

**OUTPUT**

```
B
r
Don't like 'a'!
X
d
```

**ANALYSIS** If you look at this listing, it contains all the sections of code discussed in the previous sections. The only real new code is in the `Main` routine in lines 44 to 54. This code assigns characters to the `Curr_Char` value in the tester class. If an `'a'` or an `'A'` is found, a message is printed and it is changed to an `'X'`. The change is shown by displaying the `Curr_Char` value using a `Console.WriteLine` call.

The event class can be any class that you want to create. For example, I could have changed the `CharChecker` class in this example to a class that stores a full name or other textual information. In other words, this example doesn't do much: Your code can.

## Multiple Event Handlers (Multicasting)

You can declare multiple event handlers for a single event with multicasting. Additional event handlers should follow the same format of receiving an object and a derived object of type `EventArgs` as well as returning `void`. To add the additional events, you use the `+=` operator in the same way you saw earlier. Listing 14.4 is a new version of Listing 14.3, with a second event handler added.

**LISTING 14.4** Events2.cs—Multiple Event Handlers

```
//  events2.cs - Using multiple event handlers
//-----------------------------------------------------------------

using System;

delegate void CharEventHandler(object source, CharEventArgs e);

public class CharEventArgs : EventArgs
{
     public char CurrChar;
     public CharEventArgs(char CurrChar)
     {
        this.CurrChar = CurrChar;
     }
}

class CharChecker
{
    char curr_char;
    public event CharEventHandler TestChar;
    public char Curr_Char
```

**Listing 14.4** continued

```
    {
        get { return curr_char; }
        set
        {
            if (TestChar != null )
            {
                CharEventArgs args = new CharEventArgs(value);
                TestChar(this, args);
                curr_char = args.CurrChar;
            }
        }
    }
}

class MyApp
{
    static void Main()
    {
        CharChecker tester = new CharChecker();

        tester.TestChar += new CharEventHandler(Drop_A);
        tester.TestChar += new CharEventHandler(Change_D);

        tester.Curr_Char = 'B';
        Console.WriteLine("{0}", tester.Curr_Char);

        tester.Curr_Char = 'r';
        Console.WriteLine("{0}", tester.Curr_Char);

        tester.Curr_Char = 'a';
        Console.WriteLine("{0}", tester.Curr_Char);

        tester.Curr_Char = 'd';
        Console.WriteLine("{0}", tester.Curr_Char);
    }

    static void Drop_A(object source, CharEventArgs e)
    {
        if(e.CurrChar == 'a' || e.CurrChar == 'A' )
        {
            Console.WriteLine("Don't like 'a'!");
            e.CurrChar = 'X';
        }
    }

// new event handler....
    static void Change_D(object source, CharEventArgs e)
    {
        if(e.CurrChar == 'd' || e.CurrChar == 'D' )
```

**LISTING 14.4** continued

```
71:         {
72:             Console.WriteLine("D's are good!");
73:             e.CurrChar = 'Z';
74:         }
75:     }
76: }
```

**OUTPUT**

```
B
r
Don't like 'a'!
X
D's are good!
Z
```

**ANALYSIS** Lines 68 to 75 add a new event handler called `Change_D`. As you can see, it follows the format required—it returns `void` and receives the appropriate two parameters. This event checks for the letter `'D'` or `'d'`. If found, it converts it to a `'Z'` after displaying a message. Not exciting, but effective.

This event handler is added to the event object in line 43. As you can see, it is added in the same manner as the original event, `Drop_A`. Now when a letter is assigned, both events will be executed.

## Removing an Event Handler

Event handlers can be added, and they can also be removed. To remove an event, use the -= operator instead of the += operator. Listing 14.5 contains a new `Main` routine for the `CharChecker` program.

> **Caution**
>
> Listing 14.5 is not a complete listing. It is only the `Main` routine. You can substitute this code for the main routine in Listing 14.4. Alternatively, you can obtain the listing, `events3.cs`, from the source code available online at `www.TeachYourselfCSharp.com`.

**LISTING 14.5** events3.cs—Removing an Event

```
static void Main()
{
    CharChecker tester = new CharChecker();

    tester.TestChar += new CharEventHandler(Drop_A);
    tester.TestChar += new CharEventHandler(Change_D);
```

**LISTING 14.4** continued

```
 7:
 8:        tester.Curr_Char = 'B';
 9:        Console.WriteLine("{0}", tester.Curr_Char);
10:
11:        tester.Curr_Char = 'r';
12:        Console.WriteLine("{0}", tester.Curr_Char);
13:
14:        tester.Curr_Char = 'a';
15:        Console.WriteLine("{0}", tester.Curr_Char);
16:
17:        tester.Curr_Char = 'd';
18:        Console.WriteLine("{0}", tester.Curr_Char);
19:
20:        // Remove event handler...
21:        Console.WriteLine("\nRemoving event handler....");
22:        tester.TestChar -= new CharEventHandler(Change_D);
23:
24:        // Try D-a-d...
25:
26:        tester.Curr_Char = 'D';
27:        Console.WriteLine("{0}", tester.Curr_Char);
28:
29:        tester.Curr_Char = 'a';
30:        Console.WriteLine("{0}", tester.Curr_Char);
31:
32:        tester.Curr_Char = 'd';
33:        Console.WriteLine("{0}", tester.Curr_Char);
34:     }
```

**OUTPUT**

```
B
r
Don't like 'a'!
X
D's are good!
Z

Removing event handler....
D
Don't like 'a'!
X
d
```

**ANALYSIS** As you can see by the output, when line 22 is executed, the `Change_D` event is no longer active. The `Change_A` event handler, however, continues to work.

**Caution**

> If multiple event handlers are assigned to an event, there is no guarantee as to which will be executed first. In Listing 14.5, there is no guarantee that `Change_A` will execute before `Change_D`.
>
> Additionally, event handlers and events can throw exceptions and do all the things other code can do. If an exception is thrown, there is no guarantee that other event handlers will be executed.

## Summary

In today's lesson, you learned about some of the more complicated topics within C#. You first learned about indexers. Indexers can be used with a class so that you can access the class using index notation. This makes your classes "array-like."

You then learned about delegates. You learned that delegates are like interfaces: They state a definition for accessing, but don't actually provide the implementation. Delegates set up a format for using methods. You learned that you can use a delegate to dynamically call different methods with a single method call.

The last part of today's lesson focused on events. You learned that you can create code to cause an event to happen. More importantly, you learned that you can create code—event handlers— to react when an event happens.

## Q&A

**Q Today's concepts were hard. How important is it to understand them?**

**A** There is a lot you can do with C# without understanding the concepts presented today; however, there is a lot more you won't be able to do. If you plan to program applications for Windows or other graphical environments, you will find that events are critical. And, as you learned today, delegates are critical for working with events.

Many of the C# editors, such as Visual Studio .NET, will help by automatically creating a lot of the code for you. For example, Visual Studio .NET adds code for many of the standard events.

**Q In today's lesson, events were declared in properties. Do they have to be declared in a property?**

**A** No. You can declare an event call within a property or a method.

**Q Multiple event handlers were assigned to an event. Can multiple methods be assigned to a single delegate?**

**A** Yes. It is possible to assign more than one method to a single delegate so that multiple methods execute with a single call. This is also called multicasting.

**Q What is a function pointer?**

**A** In languages such as C and C++, there is a construct called a function pointer. A function pointer is used to accomplish the same task as a delegate. A delegate, however, is type-safe and secure. In addition to being used to reference methods, delegates are also used by events.

# Workshop

The Workshop provides quiz questions to help you solidify your understanding of the material covered and exercises to provide you with experience in using what you've learned. Try to understand the quiz and exercise answers before continuing to tomorrow's lesson. Answers are provided in Appendix A, "Answers."

## Quiz

1. You are in your living room and the phone rings. You get up and answer the phone. The ringing of the phone is best associated with which of the following concepts?
   a. Indexer
   b. Delegate
   c. Event
   d. Event handler
   e. Exception handler
2. Your answering the phone is best associated with which of the following concepts:
   a. Indexer
   b. Delegate
   c. Event
   d. Event handler
   e. Exception handler

3. What is the point of an indexer?
4. When declaring an indexer, what keyword is used?
5. An indexer definition is similar to which of the following:
    a. A class definition
    b. An object definition
    c. A property definition
    d. A delegate definition
    e. An event definition
6. What are the different steps to creating and using an event?
7. What operator is used to add an event handler?
8. What is it called when multiple event handlers are added to an event?
9. Which is true (note—none or both are possible answers):

    An event is an instantiation based on a delegate.

    A delegate is an instantiation based on an event.
10. Where within a class can an event be instantiated?

## Exercises

1. Add an indexer to the following class. Use the class in a simple program.

```
public class SimpleClass
{
    int[] numbers;

    public SimpleClass(int size)
    {
       numbers = new int[size];           // declare size elements
       for ( int x = 0; x < size; x++ )   // initialize values to 0.
           numbers[x] = 0;
    }
}
```

2. Rewrite Listing 14.1 without using indexers.
3. Modify Listing 14.2 so that you don't have to declare a `doIT` object.
4. Write a program using a delegate that sorts an array of integers. You can use Listing 14.2 as a starting point.
5. Add an event handler to the code in Listing 14.5. This event handler should change any lowercase vowels to uppercase.

# Week 2

# In Review

You've succeeded in making it through the second week of learning C#! At this point you have learned many of the key foundational topics in C#.

The following listing pulls together many of these concepts into a program that is a little more functional than the examples in the lessons. This program is longer, but as you will see, it is a little more fun.

This listing presents a limited blackjack, or "21," card game. This program displays the cards in your hand and the first card in the computer dealer's hand. The idea of blackjack is to accumulate cards totaling as close to 21 as you can without going over. Face cards (jacks, queens, and kings) are worth 10 points, and the other cards are worth their basic value. An ace can be worth 1 point or 11 points—you decide.

The computer dealer must have a total of at least 17. If the computer's hand is less than 17, the dealer must draw another card. If the dealer goes over 21, it busts. If you go over 21, you bust and the computer automatically wins.

**Listing WR2.1** The Game of Blackjack

Ch. 8

```
//  cards.cs -
//     Blackjack
//------------------------------------------------------------------------

using System;

public enum CardSuit
{
      Zero_Error,
      clubs,
      diamonds,
      hearts,
      spades
}

public enum CardValue
{
      Zero_Error,
      Ace,
      two,
      three,
      four,
      five,
      six,
      seven,
      eight,
      nine,
      ten,
      Jack,
      Queen,
      King
}

// Structure: card
//==============================================
struct card
{
    public CardSuit suit;  // 1 - 4
    public CardValue val;  // 1 - 13

    public int CardValue
    {
       get
       {
          int retval;

          if( (int) this.val >= 10)
             retval = 10;
          else
          if( (int) this.val == 1 )
```

**LISTING WR2.1** continued

```
               retval = 11;
            else
               retval = (int) this.val;

            return retval;
         }
      }
```

CH. 11

```
      public override string ToString()
      {
         return (string.Format("{0} of {1}", this.val.ToString("G"),
                                     this.suit.ToString("G")));
      }
   }

   // Class: deck
   //==============================================
   class deck
   {
```

CH. 8

```
      public card [] cards = new card[53] ;
      int next;

      // deck()
      //   Constructor for setting up a regular deck
      //==============================================
      public deck()
      {
         next = 1;   // initialize pointer to point to first card.

         // Initialize the cards in the deck
         cards[0].val = 0;  // card 0 is set to 0.
         cards[0].suit = 0;

         int currcard = 0;
```

CH. 9

```
         for( int suitctr = 1; suitctr < 5; suitctr++ )
         {
            for( int valctr = 1; valctr < 14; valctr++ )
            {
               currcard = (valctr) + ((suitctr - 1) * 13);
               cards[currcard].val = (CardValue) valctr;
               cards[currcard].suit  = (CardSuit) suitctr;
            }
         }
      }

      // shuffle()
      //   Randomizes a deck's cards
      //==============================================
      public void shuffle()
      {
```

**LISTING WR2.1** continued

```
      Random rnd = new Random();
      int sort1;
      int sort2;
      card tmpcard = new card();

      for( int ctr = 0; ctr < 100; ctr++)
      {
         sort1 = (int) ((rnd.NextDouble() * 52) + 1);
         sort2 = (int) ((rnd.NextDouble() * 52) + 1);

         tmpcard = this.cards[sort1];
         this.cards[sort1] = this.cards[sort2];
         this.cards[sort2] = tmpcard;
      }

      this.next = 1;  // reset pointer to first card
   }

   // dealCard()
   //   Returns next card in deck
   //==========================================
   public card dealCard()
   {
      if( next > 52 )
      {
         // At end of deck
         return (this.cards[0]);
      }
      else
      {
         // Returns current card and increments next
         return this.cards[next++];
      }
   }
}

// Class: CardGame
//==========================================

class CardGame
{
   static deck mydeck = new deck();
   static card [] pHand = new card[10];
   static card [] cHand = new card[10];

   public static void Main()
   {
      int pCardCtr = 0;
```

**Listing WR2.1** continued

```
        int pTotal = 0;
        int cTotal = 0;

        bool playing = true;

        while ( playing == true )
        {
           //CLEAR HANDS
           pTotal = 0;
           cTotal = 0;
           pCardCtr = 0;

Ch. 9      for ( int ctr = 0; ctr < 10; ctr++)
           {
Ch. 8         pHand[ctr].val = 0;
              pHand[ctr].suit = 0;
           }

           Console.WriteLine("\nShuffling cards...");
           mydeck.shuffle();

           Console.WriteLine("Dealing cards...");

           pHand[0] = mydeck.dealCard();
Ch. 8      cHand[0] = mydeck.dealCard();
           pHand[1] = mydeck.dealCard();
           cHand[1] = mydeck.dealCard();

Ch. 8      // Set computer total equal to its first card...
           cTotal = cHand[0].CardValue;

Ch. 9      bool playersTurn = true;

           do
           {
              Console.WriteLine("\nPlayer\'s Hand:");
              pCardCtr = 0;
              pTotal = 0;

              do
              {
                 Console.WriteLine("  Card {0}:  {1}",
                                   pCardCtr + 1,
                                   pHand[pCardCtr].ToString());

                 // Add card value to player total
```

**Listing WR2.1** continued

```
                  pTotal += pHand[pCardCtr].CardValue;

                  pCardCtr++;

               } while ((int) pHand[pCardCtr].val != 0);

               Console.WriteLine("Dealer\'s Hand:");

               Console.WriteLine("  Card 1:  {0}",
                           cHand[0].ToString());


               Console.WriteLine("----------------------------");
               Console.WriteLine("Player Total = {0} \nDealer Total = {1}",
                                  pTotal, cTotal);


               if( pTotal <= 21 )
               {
                  playersTurn = GetPlayerOption(pCardCtr);
               }
               else
               {
                  playersTurn = false;
               }

            } while(playersTurn == true);

            // Player's turn is done

            if ( pTotal > 21 )
            {
               Console.WriteLine("\n\n**** BUSTED ****\n");
            }
            else // Determine computer's score
            {
               // Tally Computer's current total...
Ch. 8          cTotal += cHand[1].CardValue;

               int cCardCtr = 2;
Ch. 9
               Console.WriteLine("\n\nPlayer\'s Total:  {0}", pTotal);
               Console.WriteLine("\nComputer: ");
               Console.WriteLine("  {0}", cHand[0].ToString());
               Console.WriteLine("  {0} TOTAL: {1}",
Ch. 8                             cHand[1].ToString(),
                                  cTotal);
```

**LISTING WR2.1** continued

```
         
         while ( cTotal < 17 )  // Less than 17, must draw
         {
            cHand[cCardCtr] = mydeck.dealCard();
CH. 8       cTotal += cHand[cCardCtr].CardValue;
            Console.WriteLine("  {0} TOTAL: {1}",
                              cHand[cCardCtr].ToString(),
                              cTotal);
            cCardCtr++;
         }

         if (cTotal > 21 )
         {
            Console.WriteLine("\n\nComputer Busted!");
            Console.WriteLine("YOU WON!!!");
         }
         else
         {
            if( pTotal > cTotal)
            {
               Console.WriteLine("\n\nYOU WON!!!");
            }
            else
            if( pTotal == cTotal )
            {
               Console.WriteLine("\n\nIt\'s a push");
            }
            else
            {
               Console.WriteLine("\n\nSorry, The Computer won");
            }
         }
      }

      Console.Write("\n\nDo you want to play again?  ");
CH. 9 string answer = Console.ReadLine();

CH. 10 try
      {
CH. 8    if( answer[0] != 'y' && answer[0] != 'Y' )
         {
            //Quitting
            playing = false;
         }
      }
CH. 10 catch( System.IndexOutOfRangeException )
      {
         // Didn't enter a value so quit
```

**LISTING WR2.1** continued

```
                playing = false;
            }
        }
    }

    // GetPlayerOption()
    //   Returns true to hit, false to stay
    //===========================================

    static bool GetPlayerOption( int cardctr )
    {
        string buffer;
        bool cont = true;
        bool retval = true;

        while(cont == true)
        {
            Console.Write("\n\nH = Hit, S = Stay ");
            buffer = Console.ReadLine();

CH. 10      try
            {
CH. 8           if ( buffer[0] == 'h' || buffer[0] == 'H')
                {
                    pHand[cardctr] = mydeck.dealCard();
                    cont = false;
                }
CH. 8           else if( buffer[0] == 's' || buffer[0] == 'S' )
                {
                    // Turn is over, return false...
                    retval = false;
                    cont = false;
                }
                else
                {
                    Console.WriteLine("\n*** Please enter an H or S and press ENTER...");
                }
            }
CH. 10      catch( System.IndexOutOfRangeException )
            {
                // Didn't enter a value, so ask again
                cont = true;
            }
        }
        return retval;
    }
}
//------------- END OF LISTING -------------//
```

Output

```
Shuffling cards...
Dealing cards...

Player's Hand:
  Card 1:  four of clubs
  Card 2:  six of hearts
Dealer's Hand:
  Card 1:  Jack of hearts
----------------------------
Player Total = 10
Dealer Total = 10


H = Hit, S = Stay h

Player's Hand:
  Card 1:  four of clubs
  Card 2:  six of hearts
  Card 3:  King of diamonds
Dealer's Hand:
  Card 1:  Jack of hearts
----------------------------
Player Total = 20
Dealer Total = 10


H = Hit, S = Stay s


Player's Total:  20

Computer:
  Jack of hearts
  seven of diamonds TOTAL: 17

YOU WON!!!


Do you want to play again?

Shuffling cards...
Dealing cards...

Player's Hand:
  Card 1:  three of clubs
  Card 2:  Jack of spades
Dealer's Hand:
  Card 1:  seven of clubs
```

```
-----------------------------
Player Total = 13
Dealer Total = 7


H = Hit, S = Stay h

Player's Hand:
  Card 1:  three of clubs
  Card 2:  Jack of spades
  Card 3:  five of hearts
Dealer's Hand:
  Card 1:  seven of clubs
-----------------------------
Player Total = 18
Dealer Total = 7


H = Hit, S = Stay s


Player's Total:  18

Computer:
  seven of clubs
  two of diamonds TOTAL: 9
  three of diamonds TOTAL: 12
  five of clubs TOTAL: 17


YOU WON!!!


Do you want to play again?
```

**ANALYSIS** This output chooses cards from a standard 52-card deck that has been randomly shuffled, so your output will be different. This program is not a perfect blackjack game. For example, this game does not indicate whether you actually get a blackjack (21 with two cards). This game also does not keep track of history—how many wins you have had versus the computer. These are enhancements you can feel free to add!

This listing uses a number of the concepts you have learned throughout the previous 14 days. The following sections analyze some of the parts of this listing.

## Enumerations for the Cards

On Day 8, "Advanced Data Storage: Structures, Enumerators, and Arrays," you learned about enumerations. This program uses enumerations to make it easier to work with individual cards. Two enumerations are used. First, an enumeration is used in lines 7 to 14 to hold the different values for suits. To make it easier, numerically, to work with the cards, the first position is set as an error. Each of the suits, starting with clubs, will be assigned a value from 1 to 4. You could have left out line 9 and made these same numerical assignments by changing line 10 to the following:

```
clubs = 1,
```

I chose to include the zero position to use as an error value, if needed, in card games I can create with this structure.

The second enumeration is for card values. The `CardValue` enumeration is defined in lines 16 to 32. This enables each card to be represented. Notice that again I skipped zero and provided a placeholder. This was so that an ace would be equal to 1, a two equal to 2, and so on. Again, I could have obtained this numbering by assigning 1 to the ace, as the following shows, and by removing line 18:

```
Ace = 1,
```

## A card Type

The `card` type is defined in lines 36 to 64, as a structure instead of a class. You could just as easily declare a card as a class; however, because of its small size, it is more efficient to use a structure.

The `card` structure has just a few members. In lines 38 and 39, a member variable is created to store a `CardSuit` and a `CardValue`. These are variables based on the enumerators you had just created. Additionally, the `card` type contains a property that enables you to get the value of a card. This is based on each face card being valued at 10 (lines 47 to 48), an ace at 11 (lines 50 to 51), and any other card at its standard value (lines 52 to 53).

The final member of the `card` structure is the `ToString` method. As you learned in the previous week, all classes derive from the base class `Object`. The `Object` class includes a number of existing methods that your classes can use. One of those methods is `ToString`. You also learned on Day 11, "Inheritance," that you can override an existing method with your own functionality by using the `override` keyword. Lines 59 to 63 override the `ToString` method.

The overriding prints the value of an individual card in a more readable manner, using a formatting string of `"G"`. This string prints the textual value of an enumeration. You learned about using formatting strings with enumerations and other data types on Day 12, "Better Input and Output."

## A deck Class

Having a card is great, but to play a game, you need a deck of cards. A class is used to define a deck of cards. If you were asked what type should be used to hold a deck of cards, you might be tempted to answer an array. Although you could create an array of cards—and the `deck` class actually does—a deck needs to do more than just hold card information.

A class is more appropriate for a deck of cards, because in addition to holding the cards, you will also want to create a couple of methods to work with the cards in the deck. The `deck` class in this listing includes methods to shuffle the deck as well as to deal a card. The class also keeps track of the current card position and more.

The `deck` class includes an array of cards in line 70. The individual card structures in this array are initialized in the constructor of the deck (lines 76 to 94). This initialization is done by looping through the suits and through the card values. In lines 90 and 91, the actual assignments take place. The numeric values are cast to the `CardValue` or `CardSuit` types and placed into the card structure within the deck's card array.

The location in the array where `CardValue` and `CardSuit` are being placed is tracked using `currcard`. The calculation in line 89 might seem strange; however, this is used to create a number from 1 to 52. If you follow this line's logic, you will see that with each increment of the loops, the value calculated into `currcard` increments one higher.

The `deck` class also contains a method for shuffling the cards in lines 99 to 118. This method determines two random numbers from 1 to 52 in lines 108 and 109. These cards in the card array, in these two locations, are then switched in lines 111 to 113. The number of times this is done is determined by the `for` loop started in line 106. In this case, there will be 100 switches, which is more than enough to randomize the deck.

## The Card Game

The main application portion of this program is called `CardGame`. As stated earlier, this is a simplified version of 21. You could create a number of other card games that use the `deck` class and its methods. You could even create a program that uses multiple decks.

This listing has a number of comments and display commands to help you understand the code. I'm going to highlight only a few points within the game itself. In lines 143 and 144, a player and a computer hand are both created. The hands are declared to hold as many as 10 cards; it is rare to have a hand with 5 cards. The chance of needing 10 cards is so low that this should be sufficient.

Most of the code in the card game is straightforward. In lines 279 to 291, exception handling has been added. In line 279, a `try` statement encloses a check to see whether an answer array's first character is a `'y'` or `'Y'`. If it is one of these values, the player wants to play again. If it isn't, it is assumed that the player doesn't want to continue. What happens, however, if the user presses enter without entering any value? If this happens, the answers array will not have a value in the first position, and an exception will be thrown when you try to access the first character. This exception is an `IndexOutOfRangeException`, which is caught with the `catch` in line 287. Similar logic is used to determine whether the player wants to hit or stay in lines 310 to 332.

# Looking at the Entire Deck

You can take a quick look at all the cards in the deck by cycling through it. The listing currently does not do this; however, you can with just a few lines of code:

```
deck aDeck = new deck();
card aHand;

for( int ctr = 1; ctr < 53; ctr++)
{
   aHand = aDeck.dealCard();
   Console.WriteLine(aHand.ToString());
}
```

This declares a new deck called `aDeck`. A temporary card called `aCard` is also declared. This holds a card that is dealt from the deck, `aDeck`. A `for` loop then loops through the deck dealing a card to the temporary card and the card is displayed on the screen. This code prints the cards in the deck whether they have been shuffled or not.

# Summary

This listing uses only some of the complex topics learned in the last few days. There is a lot you can do with the basic constructs of the C# language. You'll also find that parts of this code can be reused. This includes the `card` and `deck` classes. You can use these to create other card games. Additionally, when you combine this listing with what you'll learn next week, you'll be able to create a graphical interface that makes playing the card game much more fun and easier to follow.

Although this listing is not perfect, it does accomplish quite a bit in a few lines of code. You'll find that in your coding you will want to include lots of comments, including XML documentation comments. You will also want to include more exception handling than this listing has.

# WEEK 3

# At a Glance

You have now completed two weeks and have only one remaining. You learned a lot of details about C# in Week 2. Week 3 teaches you about some of the preexisting code that is available for you to use. This is followed by quickly hitting on a number of advanced topics.

More specifically, on the first day of your third week, you are going to jump into the Base Class Libraries (BCL). These are a set of preexisting classes and types that you can use within your program. On Day 15, "Using the .NET Base Classes," you will work with your computer's directories, with math routines, and even with files. You will do all of this with the help of the BCL.

On Days 16, "Creating Windows Forms," and 17, "Creating Windows Applications," you will have fun learning about forms-based programming. You will learn how to create and customize a basic form and how to add some of the basic controls and functionality to your form. This includes adding menus and dialog boxes. These two days are not intended to be all-inclusive; covering just windows-based form programming could take a book larger than this one! These two days will give you the foundation to apply your C# knowledge to windows-based form programming.

Day 18, "Web Programming," follows up the windows-based form programming with an overview of what you can do with C# regarding Web-based programming. This day assumes you have some Web experience. If you don't, you might find this day's lesson tough to digest. Not to fret, though. There will be entire books written on the topics presented on this day.

Day 19, "The Two D's, Directives and Debugging," returns from using base classes to the world of C# programming. On Day 19, you learn a little bit about debugging your C# applications. Additionally, you learn how to use the directives to determine what code gets compiled—or not compiled—in your listings. You'll learn what directives are available and how to use them to do this psuedo-preprocessing.

Day 20, "Overloading Operators," presents a topic that many people believe to be complex, but is relatively easy to implement in C#: operator overloading. You've already learned how to overload methods. On Day 20, you'll learn how to overload operators!

The book ends with Day 21, "Odds and Ends." By the time you reach this day, you will have a basic understanding of most of the key topics within C#. This day's lesson presents a few advanced-level C# topics for your basic understanding, including attributes and versioning. By the time you finish reviewing Day 21, you will find that you are well equipped to build C# applications.

# WEEK 3

# DAY 15

# Using the .NET base classes

On the previous 14 days, you learned how to create your own types, including classes, interfaces, enumerators, and more. During this time, you used a number of classes and types that were a part of the C# class libraries. This week starts by focusing on these existing base classes. Today, you

- Learn about the existing base class libraries
- Review namespaces and their organization
- Discover many of the standardized types by working with
  - Timers
  - Directory information
  - The system environment
  - Math routines
  - Files and data
  - Much more

Today and the next two days, you will dig into a number of classes and other types that have been written by Microsoft and provided within a set of libraries.

Today's lesson presents a variety of preexisting classes and other types that you will find interesting. Tomorrow and the next day, the focus tightens to cover Windows programming. Day 18, "Web Development," follows with classes that focus specifically on doing Web-centric development. This includes coverage of creating Web forms and Web services.

# Classes in the .NET Framework

The .NET framework contains a number of classes, enumerators, structures, interfaces, and other data types. In fact, there are thousands of them. These classes are available for you to use in your C# programs.

You'll learn about several of these types in today's lesson. Most of today's lesson is organized with small example listings that show how to use a number of different classes. You'll be able to easily expand on these examples within your own programs.

## The Common Language Specification

The classes within the framework have been written with the Common Language Specification (CLS) in mind. The CLS was mentioned at the beginning of this book when discussing the C# runtime.

The CLS is a set of rules that all languages that run on the .NET platform must follow. This set of rules also includes the common type system that you learned about when you were working with the basic data types on Day 3, "Storing Information with Variables." By adhering to this set of rules, the common runtime will be able to execute a program regardless of the language syntax used.

The advantage of following the CLS is that code written in one language can be called using another language. Because the routines within the framework follow the CLS, they can be used not only by C#, but also by any other CLS-compliant language, such as Visual Basic.NET and JScript.NET.

**Note**

Over 20 languages will be able to use the code within the framework. The way each language calls a piece of code in the framework may be slightly different; however, the code will perform the same functionality.

## Namespace Organization of Types

The code within the framework is organized within namespaces. There are hundreds of namespaces within the framework that are used to organize the thousands of classes and other types.

Some of the namespaces are stored within other namespaces. For example, you have used the `DateTime` type, which is located in the `System` namespace. You have also used the `Random` type, also located in the `System` namespace. Many of the input and output types are stored in a namespace within the `System` namespace called `System.IO`. Many of the routines for working with XML data are within the `System.XML` namespace. You can check the online documents for a complete list of all the namespaces within the framework.

## ECMA Standards

Not all of the types within namespaces are necessarily compatible with all other languages. Additionally, development tools created by other companies for doing C# might not include equivalent code routines.

When C# was originated, Microsoft submitted a large number of types to the same standards board that was given C# to standardize. By submitting these types to the standards board, the door is open for other developers to create tools and compilers for C# that use the same namespaces and types. This enables the code created within Microsoft's tools to be compatible with any other company's tools.

**Note** When this book was written, Microsoft had the only C# compiler and the only runtime environment. By submitting the C# language and the base class library to the standards boards, other people and companies have the ability to create tools for C#—including compilers and runtimes.

The classes that were standardized are located within the `System` namespace. There are other namespaces that include classes that have not been standardized. If a class is not part of the standard, it might not be supported on all operating systems and runtimes that are written to support C#. For example, Microsoft includes several namespaces with its SDK. This includes `Microsoft.VisualBasic`, `Microsoft.CSharp`, `Microsoft.JScript`, and `Microsoft.Win32`. These namespaces were not a part of the ECMA standard submission, so they might not be available in all development environments.

**Note** Information on ECMA and the C# standard can be found at `Msdn.Microsoft. com/net/ecma`.

## Checking Out the Framework Classes

There are thousands of classes and other types within the base class libraries. It would fill several books this size to effectively cover all of them. Before you start writing your own programs, take the time to review the online documentation to verify that similar functionality doesn't already exist. All the classes and other types covered in today's lessons are a part of the standards that were submitted to ECMA.

**Note** Not only can you directly use the types within the class libraries, you can also extend many of them.

# Working with a Timer

Listing 15.1 presents a neat little program that is not well designed. It is simple, and there is nothing new presented in it.

**LISTING 15.1** timer.cs—Displaying the Time

```
// Timer01.cs - Displaying Date and Time
//      Not a great way to do the time.
//      Press Ctrl+C to end program.
//-----------------------------------------
using System;

class myApp
{
   public static void Main()
   {
      while (true)
      {
         Console.Write("\r{0}", DateTime.Now);
      }
   }
}
```

**OUTPUT**

```
5/26/2001 9:34:19 PM
```

**ANALYSIS** As you can see, this listing was executed at 9:34 on May 26. This listing presents a clock on the command line, which seems to update the time every second. Actually, it updates much more often than that; however, you notice the changes every second only when the value being displayed actually changes. This program runs until you break out of it by using Ctrl+C.

The focus of today's lesson is on using classes and types from the base class libraries. In line 13, a call to `DateTime` is made. `DateTime` is a structure available from the `System` namespace within the base class libraries. This structure has a static property called `Now` that returns the current time. There are many additional data members and methods within the `DateTime` structure. You can check out the .NET Framework class library documentation for information on these.

**NEW TERM** A better way to present a date on the screen is with a timer. A *timer* enables a process—in the form of a delegate—to be called at a specific time or after a specific period of time has passed. The framework includes a class for timers within the `System.Timers` namespace. This class is appropriately called `Timer`. Listing 15.2 is a rewrite of Listing 15.1 using a `Timer`.

**LISTING 15.2** Timer02.cs—Using a Timer with the DateTime

```
1:  // Timer02.cs - Displaying Date and Time
2:  //     Using the Timer class.
3:  //     Press Ctrl+C or 'q' followed by Enter to end program.
4:  //------------------------------------------------------------
5:  using System;
6:  using System.Timers;
7:
8:  class myApp
9:  {
10:    public static void Main()
11:    {
12:       Timer myTimer = new Timer();
13:       myTimer.Elapsed += new ElapsedEventHandler( DisplayTimeEvent );
14:       myTimer.Interval = 1000;
15:       myTimer.Start();
16:
17:
18:       while ( Console.Read() != 'q' )
19:       {
20:          ;   // do nothing...
21:       }
22:    }
23:
24:    public static void DisplayTimeEvent( object source, ElapsedEventArgs e )
25:    {
26:       Console.Write("\r{0}", DateTime.Now);
27:    }
28: }
```

**OUTPUT**

```
5/26/2001 10:04:13 PM
```

**ANALYSIS** As you can see, this listing's output is like that of the previous listing. This listing, however, operates much better. Instead of constantly updating the date and time being displayed, this listing updates it only every `1000` ticks, which is equal to 1 second.

Looking closer at this listing, you can see how a timer works. In line 12, a new `Timer` object is created. In line 14, the interval that is to be used is set. In line 13, the method that is to be executed after the interval is associated to the timer. In this case, the `DisplayTimeEvent` will be executed. This method is defined in lines 24 to 27.

In line 15, the `Start` method is called, which will start the interval. Another member for the `Timer` class is the `AutoReset` member. If you change the default value from `true` to `false`, the `Timer` event will happen only once. If the `AutoReset` is left at its default value of `true`, or set to `true`, the `Timer` will fire an event and thus execute the method every time the given interval passes.

Lines 18 to 21 contain a loop that continues to operate until the reader enters the letter `'q'` and presses Enter. Then the end of the routine is reached and the program ends; otherwise, the program continues to spin in this loop. Nothing is done in this loop in this program. You can do other processing in this loop if you want. There is no need to call the `DisplayTimeEvent` in this loop because it will be automatically called at the appropriate interval.

This timer is used to display the time on the screen. Timers and timer events also can be used for numerous other programs. You could create a timer that fires off a program at a given time. You could create a backup routine that copies important data at a given interval. You could also create a routine to automatically log off a user or end a program after a given time period with no activity. There are numerous ways to use timers.

> **Note**
>
> Listing 15.2 uses events with slightly different names than what you saw on Day 14, "Indexers, Delegates, and Events." These slightly different names are customized versions of the routines you learned about on Day 14.

# Getting Directory and System Environment Information

A plethora of information is available to your programs about the computer running a program. How you choose to use this information is up to you. Listing 15.3 presents a listing that shows information about a computer and its environment. This is done using the `Environment` class, which has a number of static data members you will find interesting.

**LISTING 15.3** env01.cs—Using the `Environment` Class

```
//  env01.cs - Displaying information with the
//                     Environment class
//-----------------------------------------------
using System;

class myApp
{
   public static void Main()
   {
     // Some Properties...
       Console.WriteLine("=================================");
       Console.WriteLine(" Command: {0}", Environment.CommandLine);
       Console.WriteLine("Curr Dir: {0}", Environment.CurrentDirectory);
       Console.WriteLine(" Sys Dir: {0}", Environment.SystemDirectory);
       Console.WriteLine(" Version: {0}", Environment.Version);
       Console.WriteLine(" OS Vers: {0}", Environment.OSVersion);
       Console.WriteLine(" Machine: {0}", Environment.MachineName);
       Console.WriteLine("  Memory: {0}", Environment.WorkingSet);

     // Some methods...
       Console.WriteLine("=================================");
       string [] args = Environment.GetCommandLineArgs();
       for ( int x = 0; x < args.Length; x++ )
       {
           Console.WriteLine("Arg {0}: {1}", x, args[x]);
       }

       Console.WriteLine("=================================");
       string [] drives = Environment.GetLogicalDrives();
       for ( int x = 0; x < drives.Length; x++ )
       {
           Console.WriteLine("Drive {0}: {1}", x, drives[x]);
       }

       Console.WriteLine("=================================");
       Console.WriteLine("Path: {0}",
                      Environment.GetEnvironmentVariable("Path"));
       Console.WriteLine("=================================");

   }
}
```

**OUTPUT** From my notebook computer:

```
=================================
 Command: C:\MYDOCU~1\BOOKS\98-CODE\DAY15\ENV01.EXE
Curr Dir: C:\My Documents\Books\98-code\Day15
 Sys Dir: C:\WINDOWS\SYSTEM
 Version: 1.0.2914.16
 OS Vers: Microsoft Windows 98 4.90.73010104.0
 Machine: HP-PIII
  Memory: 0
=================================
Arg 0: C:\MYDOCU~1\BOOKS\98-CODE\DAY15\ENV01.EXE
=================================
Drive 0: A:\
Drive 1: C:\
Drive 2: D:\
=================================
Path:
C:\WINDOWS;C:\WINDOWS\COMMAND;C:\WINDOWS\MICROS~1.NET\FRAMEW~1\V10~1.291
;
=================================
```

From my desktop computer:

```
=================================
 Command: ENV01
Curr Dir: C:\WORKAREA\DAY15
 Sys Dir: C:\WINDOWS\System32
 Version: 1.0.2914.16
 OS Vers: Microsoft Windows NT 5.1.2462.0
 Machine: HPBETA30
  Memory: 3629056
=================================
Arg 0: ENV01
Arg 1: aaa
Arg 2: bbbbb
Arg 3: ccccc
=================================
Drive 0: A:\
Drive 1: C:\
Drive 2: D:\
Drive 3: E:\
=================================
Path: C:\WINDOWS\system32;C:\WINDOWS;C:\WINDOWS\System32\Wbem;C:\PRO-
GRA~1\MICROS
~2\80\Tools\BINN
=================================
```

**ANALYSIS** The operation of the `Environment` class is pretty straightforward. There are lots of static members that provide information about the user's system. This application was run on two different machines. The first output was done on my notebook computer, which is running Windows ME (although the output said Windows 98). I have three drives in this machine: A, C, and D. You can also see the current directory and the system directory. The drives on my machine and additional directory information also are presented in the output.

I ran the second set of output on Windows XP (NT 5). You can also see lots of other information about my machine. One thing you can tell that is different about this output is that three command-line parameters were used: `aaa`, `bbbbb`, and `ccccc`.

Most of the information can be obtained by calling a `static` member from the `Environment` class. A number of `static` members are called in lines 12 to 18. A couple of the methods within this class return string arrays. This includes the command-line arguments method `GetCommandLineArgs` and the `GetLogicalDrives` method. Simple loops are used in Listing 15.3 to print the values from these string arrays. Lines 22 to 26 print the command-line arguments, and lines 29 to 33 display the valid drives.

The `Environment` class includes a couple of other methods you might be interested in. `GetEnvironmentVariable` gets the environment variables and their values from the current system. `GetEnvironmentVariable` can be used to get the value stored in one of the current system's environment variables.

# Working with Math Routines

Basic math operators—such as plus, minus, and modulus—can get you only so far. It will only be a matter of time before you find you need more robust math routines. C# has access to a set of math routines within the base classes. These are available from within the `System.Math` namespace. Table 15.1 presents a number of the math methods available.

The `Math` class is `sealed`. Recall that a `sealed` class cannot be inherited from. Additionally all the classes and data members are `static`, so you won't be able to create an object of type `Math`. Rather, you will use the members and methods with the class name.

**TABLE 15.1** Math Routines in the `Math` Class

| *Method* | *Description* |
|---|---|
| `Abs` | Returns the absolute value of a number. |
| `Ceiling` | Returns a value that is the smallest whole number greater than or equal to a given number. |
| `Exp` | Returns `E` raised to a given power. This is the inverse of `Log`. |
| `Floor` | Returns a value that is the largest whole number that is less than or equal to the given number. |

**TABLE 15.1** continued

| *Method* | *Description* |
|---|---|
| `IEEERemainder` | Returns the result of a division of two specified numbers. This division operation conforms to the remainder operation stated within Section 5.1 of ANSI/IEEE Std 754-1985; IEEE Standard for Binary Floating-Point Arithmetic; Institute of Electrical and Electronics Engineers, Inc; 1985. |
| `Log` | Returns a value that is the logarithmic value of the given number. |
| `Log10` | Returns a value that is the base 10 logarithm of a given value. |
| `Max` | Returns the larger of two values. |
| `Min` | Returns the smaller of two values. |
| `Pow` | Returns the value of a given value raised to a given power. |
| `Round` | Returns a rounded value for a number. You can specify the precision of the rounded number. The number `.5` would be rounded down. |
| `Sign` | Returns a value indicating the sign of a value. `-1` is returned for a negative number, `0` for zero, and `1` for a positive number. |
| `Sqrt` | Returns the square root for a given value. |
| `Acos` | Returns the value of an angle whose cosine is equal to a given number. |
| `Asin` | Returns the value of an angle whose sine is equal to a given number. |
| `Atan` | Returns the value of an angle whose tangent is equal to a given number. |
| `Atan2` | Returns the value of an angle whose tangent is equal to the quotient of two given numbers. |
| `Cos` | Returns a value that is the cosine of a given angle. |
| `Cosh` | Returns a value that is the hyperbolic cosine for a given angle. |
| `Sin` | Returns the sine for a given angle. |
| `Sinh` | Returns the hyperbolic sine for a given angle. |
| `Tan` | Returns the tangent of a specified angle. |
| `Tanh` | Returns the hyperbolic tangent of a given angle. |

The `Math` class also includes two constants: `PI` and `E`. `PI` returns the value of $\prod$ as `3.14159265358979323846`. The `E` data member returns the value of the logarithmic base, `2.7182818284590452354`.

Most of the math methods in Table 15.1 are easy to understand. Listing 15.4 presents a couple of the routines in use.

**LISTING 15.4** Math.cs—Using Some of the Math Routines

```
//  math.cs - Using a Math routine
//-----------------------------------------------
using System;

class myMathApp
{
   public static void Main()
   {
      int val2;
      char disp;

      for (double ctr = 0.0; ctr <= 10; ctr += .2)
      {
         val2 = (int) Math.Round( ( 10 * Math.Sin(ctr))) ;
         for( int ctr2 = -10; ctr2 <= 10; ctr2++ )
         {
            if (ctr2 == val2)
               disp = 'X';
            else
               disp = ' ';

            Console.Write("{0}", disp);
         }
         Console.WriteLine(" ");
      }
   }
}
```

**OUTPUT**

```
          X
            X
              X
                X
                 X
                  X
                   X
                    X
                    X
                    X
                   X
                  X
                 X
               X
             X
           X
```

```
         X
       X
      X
    X
  X
 X
X
X
X
X
 X
  X
    X
     X
       X
         X
           X
             X
               X
                 X
                  X
                   X
                    X
                    X
                    X
                   X
                   X
                 X
                001X
              X
            X
          X
        X
      X
     X
```

**ANALYSIS** This listing maps out the `Sin` method. A `for` statement in lines 12 to 25 loops through double values, incrementing them by `.2` each iteration. The sine of this value is obtained using the `Math.Sin` method in line 14. The sine will be a value from `-1.0` to `1.0`. To make the display easier, this value is converted to a value from `-10` to `10`. This conversion is done by multiplying the returned sine value by 10 and then rounding the value with the `Math.Round` method.

The result of doing the multiplication and rounding is that `val2` is a value from `-10` to `10`. A `for` loop in line 15 displays a single line of characters. This line of characters will be spaces, with the exception of the character in the position equal to `val2`. Line 24 prints another space to start a new line. The result of this work is a rough display of a sine curve.

15

# Working with Files

The ability to write information to a file or to read information from a file can make your programs much more usable. Additionally, there are lots of times when you will want to be able to work with existing files. The following sections touch on a few basic features of working with files. This will be followed by an explanation of a key file concept called streams.

## Copying a File

A file class exists within the base class called `File`, located within the `System.IO` namespace. The `File` class contains a number of static methods that can be used to work with files. In fact, all the methods within the `File` class are `static`. Table 15.2 lists many of the key methods.

**TABLE 15.2** File Methods

| *Method* | *Description* |
|---|---|
| `AppendText` | Appends text to a file. |
| `Copy` | Creates a new file from an existing file. |
| `Create` | Creates a new file at a specified location. |
| `CreateText` | Creates a new file that can hold text. |
| `Delete` | Deletes a file at a specified location. File must exist or an exception is thrown. |
| `Exists` | Determines whether a file actually exists at a specified location. |
| `GetAttributes` | Returns information on the given file's attributes. This includes information on whether the file is compressed, whether it is a directory name, whether it is hidden or read-only, whether it is a system file, whether it is temporary, and much more. |
| `GetCreationTime` | Returns the date and time the file was created. |
| `GetLastAccessTime` | Returns the date and time the file was last accessed. |
| `GetLastWriteTime` | Returns the date and time of the last write to the file. |
| `Move` | Enables a file to be moved to a new location and enables the file to be renamed. |
| `Open` | Opens a file at a given location. By opening a file you are then able to write information to it or read information from it. |
| `OpenRead` | Creates a file that can only be read from. |
| `OpenText` | Opens a file that can then be read as text. |
| `OpenWrite` | Opens a specified file for writing to. |

**TABLE 15.2** continued

| *Method* | *Description* |
|---|---|
| `SetAttributes` | Sets file attributes for a specified file. |
| `SetCreationTime` | Sets the date and time of a file's creation. |
| `SetLastAccessTime` | Sets the date and time the file was last accessed. |
| `SetLastWriteTime` | Sets the date and time that the file was last updated. |

Listing 15.5 presents a small listing that uses the `File` class to create a copy of a file.

**LISTING 15.5** Filecopy.cs—Copying a File

```
//  filecopy.cs - Copies a file
//-----------------------------------------------
using System;
using System.IO;

class myApp
{
   public static void Main()
   {
      string[] CLA = Environment.GetCommandLineArgs();

      if ( CLA.Length < 3 )
      {
          Console.WriteLine("Format: {0} orig-file new-file", CLA[0]);
      }
      else
      {
        string origfile = CLA[1];
        string newfile  = CLA[2];

        Console.Write("Copy....");

        try
        {
           File.Copy(origfile, newfile);
        }

        catch (System.IO.FileNotFoundException)
        {
          Console.WriteLine("\n{0} does not exist!", origfile);
          return;
        }

        catch (System.IO.IOException)
        {
```

**LISTING 15.5** continued

```
            Console.WriteLine("\n{0} already exists!", newfile);
            return;
         }

         catch (Exception e)
         {
            Console.WriteLine("\nAn exception was thrown trying to copy
➥file.");
            Console.WriteLine;
            return;
         }

         Console.WriteLine("...Done");
      }
   }
}
```

**OUTPUT**

```
Copy.......Done
```

**ANALYSIS** This output is a result of running this program with the following command line:

```
filecopy filecopy.cs filecopy.bak
```

filecopy.cs existed and filecopy.bak did not exist before this command was executed. After the program executes, filecopy.bak will be created and therefore exist. If you execute this same command a second time—with filecopy.bak already existing—you get the following output:

```
Copy....
filecopy.bak already exists!
```

If you execute this program without any parameters, or with only one parameter, you get the following output:

```
Format: C:\MYDOCU~1\BOOKS\98-CODE\DAY15\FILECOPY.EXE orig-file new-file
```

Finally, it is worth looking at the output you get if the file you are trying to copy does not exist:

```
Copy....
BadFileName does not exist!
```

As you can see by all this output, Listing 15.5 does a great job of trying to react to all the possible situations that could be thrown at it. You'll see that this is done with both programming logic and exception handling.

Looking at the listing, you see that line 4 includes the `System.IO` namespace. This enables the program to use the `File` class without fully qualifying it. In line 10, you see the first key line of the `Main` method. In this line, the command-line arguments are obtained using the `Environment` class method you saw earlier today.

Line 12 checks to verify that there are at least `3` values in the command-line arguments variable, `CLA`. If there are less than three, the user didn't provide enough information. Remember, using the `GetCommandLineArgs` method, you are given the name of the program as the first value. The rest of the values on the command line follow. This means you need three values to have the program name, original file, and new file. If there are not three values, a "usage" method is presented to the user (line 14). This usage method includes passing the actual name of the program read in by the `GetCommandLineArgs`.

**Tip**

> The value of using `GetCommandLineArgs` is that it gives you the actual program name the user executed. You can then use this actual name to present your "usage" message rather than a hard-coded value. The benefit of this is that the `filecopy` program can be renamed, and yet the usage information will still be correct—it will present the actual name of the executed program.

If the necessary number of parameters are there, the processing of the files occurs. Lines 18 and 19 assign the information from the command line to file variables with easier-to-follow names. Technically, you do not need to do this; however, it makes the rest of the program easier to read.

In line 21, a simple message is presented to the reader stating that the copy has started. Line 25 does the actual copy with the `Copy` method of the `File` class. As you can see, this copy is very straightforward.

Although the use of `Copy` is straightforward, it is important to notice what this listing has done. It has wrapped the copy in exception handling logic. This includes the `try` in line 23 and the three instances of `catch` that follow. Because there are so many things that can go wrong with a file operation, it is critical that you make sure your programs are prepared to react appropriately. The best way to prepare your program is with exception handling.

Most of the `File` methods have exceptions already defined for a number of key errors that can occur. When you look at the online documentation for a class, you will find that any exceptions that are defined for a given method call are also included. It is a good programming practice to include exception handling whenever an exception is possible.

In line 28, you see the first exception handler for the call to the `Copy` method. This exception is thrown when the file you are trying to copy is not found. It is named, appropriately, `FileNotFoundException`.

> **Note**
>
> In this listing, the exception name is fully qualified. Because the `System.IO` namespace was included, you could have left `System.IO` off.

Line 34 catches an `IOException`. This exception is thrown as a result of a number of other exceptions. This includes a directory not being found (`DirectoryNotFoundException`), an end of a file being found (`EndOfStreamException`), a problem loading a file (`FileLoadException`), or a file-not-found exception, which would have been caught by the earlier exception. This exception was thrown when the new filename already existed.

Finally, line 40 catches the unexpected error by using the standard, generic exception. Because it is unknown what would cause this exception, it presents a general message followed by a display of the exception itself.

If an exception was not thrown, the file was successfully copied. Line 47 displays a messaging stating this success.

| Do | Don't |
|---|---|
| **DO** use exception handling when using file routines. | **DON'T** assume the user provided you with everything you need when using command-line arguments. |

## Getting File Information

In addition to the `File` class, the `FileInfo` class is also available for working with files. Listing 15.6 presents the `FileInfo` class in use. This program takes a single filename and displays the size and key dates regarding it. For the output, the filesize.cs file was used.

**Listing 15.6** Filesize.cs—Using the `FileInfo` Class

```
//  fileinfo.cs
//-----------------------------------------------
using System;
using System.IO;
```

**LISTING 15.6** continued

```

class myApp
{
   public static void Main()
   {
      string[] CLA = Environment.GetCommandLineArgs();

      FileInfo fiExe = new FileInfo(CLA[0]);

      if ( CLA.Length < 2 )
      {
         Console.WriteLine("Format: {0} filename", fiExe.Name);
      }
      else
      {
        try
        {
          FileInfo fiFile = new FileInfo(CLA[1]);

          if(fiFile.Exists)
          {
            Console.WriteLine("===================================");
            Console.WriteLine("{0} - {1}", fiFile.Name, fiFile.Length );
            Console.WriteLine("===================================");
            Console.WriteLine("Last Access: {0}", fiFile.LastAccessTime);
            Console.WriteLine("Last Write:  {0}", fiFile.LastWriteTime);
            Console.WriteLine("Creation:    {0}", fiFile.CreationTime);
            Console.WriteLine("===================================");
          }
          else
          {
            Console.WriteLine("{0} doesn't exist!", fiFile.Name);
          }
        }

        catch (System.IO.FileNotFoundException)
        {
          Console.WriteLine("\n{0} does not exist!", CLA[1]);
          return;
        }
        catch (Exception e)
        {
          Console.WriteLine("\nAn exception was thrown trying to copy
➥file.");
          Console.WriteLine;
          return;
        }
```

**LISTING 15.6** continued

```
51:         }
52:     }
53: }
```

**OUTPUT**

```
==================================
filesize.cs - 1547
==================================
Last Access: 5/27/2001 12:00:00 AM
Last Write:  5/27/2001 2:57:34 PM
Creation:    5/27/2001 2:57:32 PM
==================================
```

**ANALYSIS** This listing is similar to the `filecopy` listing presented earlier. The `FileInfo` class creates an object that is associated to a specific file. In line 12, a `FileInfo` object was created called `fiExe` that is associated to the program being executed (fileinfo.exe). If the user doesn't enter an argument on the command line, the value of `fiExe` is printed with program usage information (line 14).

In line 22, a second `FileInfo` object is created using the argument passed to the program. In lines 26 to 32, information is displayed about this file.

# Working with Data Files

Getting information about files and copying files is great, but it's more valuable to read and write information to and from files.

## Understanding Streams

The term *file* is generally associated with information stored on a disk drive or in memory. When working with files, you generally employ the use of a stream. Many people are confused about the difference between files and streams. A stream is a flow of information. It does not have to be associated with a file, nor does it have to be text.

A stream can be used to send or receive information from memory, the network, the Web, a string, and more. A stream is also used to go to and from a data file.

## The Order for Reading Files

When reading or writing to a file, you need to follow a process. You must first open the file. If you are creating a new file, you generally open the file at the same time you create it. When it's open, you need to use a stream to place information into the file or to pull information out of the file. When you create the stream, you need to indicate the direction information will be flowing. After you have the stream associated to the file, you can then begin the actual reading or writing of data. If you are reading information from a file, you might need to check for the end of the file. When you are done reading or writing, you need to close the file.

> **Basic Steps to Working with a File**
>
> Step 1: Open/create the file.
>
> Step 2: Set up a stream to/from the file.
>
> Step 3: Place information into or read information from the file.
>
> Step 4: Close the stream/file.

## Methods for Creating and Opening Files

There are different types of streams. You will use different streams and different methods depending on the type of data within your file. In this section, you focus on reading and writing text information. In the next section, you will learn how to read and write binary information. Binary information includes the capability of storing numeric values and any of the other data types.

To open a disk file for reading or writing text, you can use either the `File` or `FileInfo` classes. Several methods can be used from either of these classes, including the following:

| | |
|---|---|
| `AppendText` | Opens a file that can be used to have text appended to it (creates a `StreamWriter` to be used to append the text) |
| `Create` | Creates a new file |
| `CreateText` | Creates and opens a file to use with text (actually creates a `StreamWriter Stream`) |
| `Open` | Opens a file for reading and/or writing (actually opens a `FileStream`) |
| `OpenRead` | Opens a file for reading |
| `OpenText` | Opens an existing file to be used to read from (creates a `StreamReader` to be used) |
| `OpenWrite` | Opens a file for reading and writing |

How do you know when to use the `File` class rather than the `FileInfo` class if they both contain similar methods? These two classes are different. The `File` class contains all static methods. Additionally, the `File` class automatically checks permissions on a file. The

`FileInfo` class is used to create instances of a `FileInfo`. If you are opening a file once, using the `File` class is okay. If you are planning on using a file multiple times within a program, you are better off using the `FileInfo` class. If in doubt, you can use the `FileInfo` class.

## Writing to a Text File

The best way to understand working with files is to jump right into the code. Listing 15.7 presents a listing that creates a text file and then writes information to it.

**LISTING 15.7** Writing.cs—Writing to a Text File

```
//  writing.cs - Writing to a text file.
//  Exception handling left out to keep listing short.
//-----------------------------------------------------
using System;
using System.IO;

public class WritingApp
{
   public static void Main(String[] args)
   {
      if( args.Length < 1 )
      {
         Console.WriteLine("Must include file name.");
      }
      else
      {
        StreamWriter myFile = File.CreateText(args[0]);

        myFile.WriteLine("Mary Had a Little Lamb,");
        myFile.WriteLine("Whose Fleece Was White as Snow.");

        for ( int ctr = 0; ctr < 10; ctr++ )
            myFile.WriteLine ("{0}", ctr);

        myFile.WriteLine("Everywhere that Mary Went,");
        myFile.WriteLine("That Lamb was sure to go.");

        myFile.Close();
      }
   }
}
```

**OUTPUT** Running this listing does not produce any viewable output unless you don't include a filename. You need to include a filename as a parameter. This file will then be created and will contain the following:

```
Mary Had a Little Lamb,
Whose Fleece Was White as Snow.
0
1
2
3
4
5
6
7
8
9
Everywhere that Mary Went,
That Lamb was sure to go.
```

**ANALYSIS** This listing does not contain exception handling. This means that it is possible for this listing to throw unhandled exceptions. The exception handling was left out to enable you to focus on the file methods. This also cuts down the size of the listing for the example.

Looking at the listing, you can see that lines 11 to 14 check to see whether a filename was included as a command-line parameter. If not, an error message is displayed. If a filename was included, processing continues in line 17.

In line 17, you see that the `CreateText` method of the `File` class is called to create a new `StreamWriter` object called `myFile`. The argument passed is the name of the file being created. The end result of this line is that a file is created that can hold text. This text will be sent to the file through the `StreamWriter` called `myFile`. Figure 15.1 illustrates the result of this statement.

**Caution** If a file already exists with the same name as the filename you pass into this listing, that original file will be overwritten.

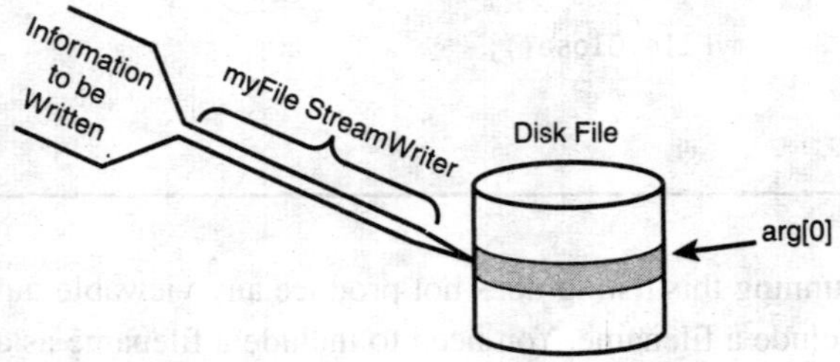


**FIGURE 15.1**
*Using a stream to write a file.*

When the stream is set up and pointing to the file, you can write to the stream and thus write to the file. Line 19 indicates that you can write to the stream in the same way you write to the `Console`. Instead of using `Console`, though, you use the stream name—in this case, `myFile`. Lines 19 and 20 call the `WriteLine` method to write sentences to the stream. Lines 22 to 23 write numbers to the stream; these numbers are written as text. Finally, lines 25 and 26 write two more lines to the file.

When you are done writing to the file, you need to close the stream. Line 28 closes the stream by calling the `Close` method.

The steps to working with a file are all followed in this example.

## Reading Text from a File

Reading information from a text file is very similar to writing information. Listing 15.8 presents a listing that can be used to read the file you created with Listing 15.7. This program reads text data.

**LISTING 15.8** reading.cs—Reading a Text File

```
//  reading.cs - Read text from a file.
//  Exception handling left out to keep listing short.
//----------------------------------------------------
using System;
using System.IO;

public class ReadingApp
{
    public static void Main(String[] args)
    {
        if( args.Length < 1 )
        {
           Console.WriteLine("Must include file name.");
        }
        else
        {
          string buffer;

          StreamReader myFile = File.OpenText(args[0]);

          while ( (buffer = myFile.ReadLine()) != null )
          {
             Console.WriteLine(buffer);
          }

          myFile.Close();
        }
    }
}
```

**OUTPUT**

```
Mary Had a Little Lamb,
Whose Fleece Was White as Snow.
0
1
2
3
4
5
6
7
8
9
Everywhere that Mary Went,
That Lamb was sure to go.
```

**ANALYSIS** Jumping right into this listing, you can see that a string is declared in line 17. This string, `buffer`, is going to be used to hold the information being read from the file. Line 19 presents a line similar to the one in the Writing.cs listing. Instead of using the `CreateText` method, you use the `OpenText` method of the `File` class. This opens the file passed into the program (`arg[0]`). Again, a stream is associated to this file. In line 21, a while loop is used to loop through the file. The ReadLine method is used to read lines of text from the `myFile` stream until a line is read that is equal to `null`. The `null` indicates that the end of the file has been reached.

As each line is read, it is printed to the `Console` (line 23). After all the lines have been read, the file is closed in line 26.

## Writing Binary Information to a File

If you use a text file, you must convert all your numbers to and from text. There are a lot of times when you would be better off if you could write values directly to a file and read them back in. For example, if you write a bunch of integer numbers to a file as integers, you can pull them out of the file as integers. If you write them as text, you have to read the text from the file and then convert each value from a string to an integer. Rather than going through the extra steps of converting text, you can associate a binary stream type (`BinaryStream`) to a file and then read and write binary information through this stream.

Listing 15.9 presents a listing that writes binary data to a file. Although this file writes 100 simple integers to a file, it could just as easily write any other data type.

**Note** Binary information is information that retains its data type's storage format rather than being converted to text.

**LISTING 15.9** binwrite.cs—Writing to a Binary File

```
 1: //  binWrite.cs -
 2: //  Exception handling left out to keep listing short.
 3: //----------------------------------------------------
 4: using System;
 5: using System.IO;
 6:
 7: class MyStream
 8: {
 9:    public static void Main(String[] args)
10:    {
11:       if( args.Length < 1 )
12:       {
13:          Console.WriteLine("Must include file name.");
14:       }
15:       else
16:       {
17:          FileStream myFile = new FileStream(args[0], FileMode.CreateNew);
18:          BinaryWriter bwFile = new BinaryWriter(myFile);
19:
20:          // Write data to Test.data.
21:          for (int i = 0; i < 100 ; i++)
22:          {
23:             bwFile.Write(i );
24:          }
25:
26:          bwFile.Close();
27:          myFile.Close();
28:       }
29:    }
30: }
```

**ANALYSIS** A filename should be included as a command-line parameter. If it is included, no output will be written to the console. Rather, information will be written to a file. If you look at the file, you will see extended characters displayed. You won't see readable numbers.

This listing also lacks exception handling. If you try to write this information to an existing file, an exception will be thrown because of line 17. In this listing, you open a file differently than the way you opened it for text. In line 17, you create a `FileStream` object called `myFile`. This file stream is associated to a file using the constructor for `FileStream`. The first argument of the constructor is the name of the file you are creating (`arg[0]`). The second parameter is the mode you are opening the file in. This second parameter is a value from the `FileMode` enumerator. In this listing, the value being used is `CreateNew`. This means that a new file will be created. Table 15.3 lists other mode values that can be used from the `FileMode` enumeration.

**Table 15.3** FileMode Enumeration Values

| *Value* | *Definition* |
|---|---|
| `Append` | Opens an existing file or creates a new file. |
| `Create` | Creates a new file. If the filename already exists, it is deleted and a new file is created with the same name. |
| `CreateNew` | Creates a new file. If the filename already exists, an exception is thrown. |
| `Open` | Opens an existing file. |
| `OpenOrCreate` | Opens a file or creates a new file if the file doesn't already exist. |
| `Truncate` | Opens an existing file and deletes its contents. |

After you create the `FileStream`, you need to set it up to work with binary data. Line 18 accomplishes this by connecting a type that can be used to write binary data to a stream: the `BinaryWriter` type. In line 18, a `BinaryWriter` called `bwFile` is created. `myFile` is passed to the `BinaryWriter` constructor, thus associating `bwFile` with `myFile`.

Line 23 indicates that information can be written directly to the `BinaryWriter`, `bwFile`, using a `Write` method. The data being written can be of a specific data type. In this listing, an integer is being written. When you are done writing to the file, you need to close the streams that you have opened.

## Reading Binary Information from a File

Now that you have written binary data to a file, you will most likely want to read it. Listing 15.10 presents a program that reads binary information from a file.

**Listing 15.10** binread.cs—Reading Binary Information

```
//  binRead.cs
//  Exception handling left out to keep listing short.
//-----------------------------------------------
using System;
using System.IO;

class MyStream
{
   public static void Main(String[] args)
   {
      if( args.Length < 1 )
      {
         Console.WriteLine("Must include file name.");
      }
      else
```

**Listing 15.10** continued

```
16:       {
17:           FileStream myFile = new FileStream(args[0], FileMode.Open);
18:           BinaryReader brFile = new BinaryReader(myFile);
19:
20:           // Read data
21:           Console.WriteLine("Reading file....");
22:           while( brFile.PeekChar() != -1 )
23:           {
24:               Console.Write("<{0}> ", brFile.ReadInt32());
25:           }
26:
27:           Console.WriteLine("....Done Reading.");
28:
29:           brFile.Close();
30:           myFile.Close();
31:
32:       }
33:   }
```

**Output**

```
Reading file....
<0> <1> <2> <3> <4> <5> <6> <7> <8> <9> <10> <11> <12> <13> <14> <15>
➥<16> <17>
<18> <19> <20> <21> <22> <23> <24> <25> <26> <27> <28> <29> <30> <31>
➥<32> <33>
<34> <35> <36> <37> <38> <39> <40> <41> <42> <43> <44> <45> <46> <47>
➥<48> <49>
<50> <51> <52> <53> <54> <55> <56> <57> <58> <59> <60> <61> <62> <63>
➥<64> <65>
<66> <67> <68> <69> <70> <71> <72> <73> <74> <75> <76> <77> <78> <79>
➥<80> <81>
<82> <83> <84> <85> <86> <87> <88> <89> <90> <91> <92> <93> <94> <95>
➥<96> <97>
<98> <99> ....Done Reading.
```

**Analysis** With this application, you can read the data you wrote with the previous listing. In line 17, you create your `FileStream`. This time, the file mode being used is `Open`. You then associate this to a `BinaryReader` stream in line 18, which helps you read binary information.

In line 22, you see something a little different. The `PeekChar` method of the `BinaryReader` class is used. This method takes a look at the next character in the stream. If the next character is the end of the file, `-1` is returned; otherwise, the next character is returned. It does this without changing the location within the stream. It lets you peek at the next character!

As long as the next character is not the end of the file, line 24 is used to read an integer from the `BinaryStream` object, `brFile`. The method being used to read the integer, `ReadInt32`, uses a type name from the framework rather than the C# name. Remember, these are all classes from the framework being called by C#—they are not a part of the C# languages. These classes are usable by languages other than C# as well.

The `BinaryReader` class has methods similar to the `ReadInt32` for each of the other base data types. Each of these read methods are used in the same manner that `ReadInt32` is being used in this listing.

## Working with Other File Types

The previous sections showed you how to read and write basic text and binary data. There are also classes for reading other types of data including XML. Additionally, a lot of functionality can be gleamed from the classes and other types presented in today's lessons.

Namespaces that contain classes and other types support more advanced file access. Although these classes offer greater functionality with less coding, you need to know the trade-off for using them. Such classes might not follow the .NET standards and thus might not be portable.

# Summary

Today, you took a look at some of the base classes available through the .NET Framework. At the time this book was written, the classes presented in today's lesson had been submitted for standardization. This means they should be as portable as your C# programs.

You started the day by looking at timers, which can be used to kick off an event after a given amount of time. You then learned how to obtain information about the current directories and files as well as about the system itself. Math routines are often needed, and today you learned about a bunch of methods available through the `Math` class.

Finally, you focused on accessing files. You learned how to read and write to both text and binary files.

# Q&A

**Q I tried to use one of the classes in the help documents; however, when I compiled I was told that I was missing an assembly. What do I need to do?**

**A** If you find that you have done all the appropriate coding, but you are still getting an error saying you are missing a file or assembly, you might need to include a reference to an assembly from the framework in the compile command. This is done by using the `/r:` switch along with the name of the disk file containing the namespace you want included. The help documents will tell you what file is needed for each class. For example, the `System.TextReader` type is stored in the Mscorlib.dll assembly. To compile the xxx.cs program with this assembly, use this command line:

```
csc /r:Mscorlib.dll xxx.cs
```

**Q Today I learned that I could get the command-line arguments using the `GetCommandLineArgs` method of the Environment class. I learned earlier in the book that I could get the command-line values by using a string parameter within the `Main` method. Which is better?**

**A** Either method works. The difference is that using the `GetCommandLineArgs` you can also get the name of the program that was executed. The `Main` arguments' first value is the first parameter—not the name of the program being executed.

**Q Are XML and ADO both a part of the standard classes?**

**A** No. There are a number of classes that are being standardized for XML; however, ADO is a Microsoft technology that is not part of the standards.

# Workshop

The Workshop provides quiz questions to help you solidify your understanding of the material covered and exercises to provide you with experience in using what you've learned. Try to understand the quiz and exercise answers before continuing to the next day's lesson. Answers are provided in Appendix A, "Answers."

## Quiz

1. How many ticks are needed to make a second?
2. Which of the following does a timer use?
   a. A delegate
   b. An event

c. An orphomite

d. An exception

3. Which standards organization is standardizing C# and the Base Class Libraries?
4. What is the difference between using `Environment.GetCommandLineArgs` and `Main( String args[] )`?
5. When would you create an instance of the `Math` class (when would you create a `Math` object)?
6. What class or method can be used to determine whether a file actually exists?
7. What is the difference between a file and a stream?
8. Which `FileMode` value can be used to create a new file?
9. What are some of the classes for working with XML?

## Exercises

1. Create a program that uses the binary file methods to write to a file. Create a structure to hold a person's name, age, and membership status. Write this information to the file. (*Note:* Age can be an integer. Membership can be a boolean).
2. Rewrite Listing 15.4 to use the `Cosine` method of the `Math` class.
3. Create a program that reads text from the console and writes it to the file. The user should enter a blank line to end input.
4. **BUG BUSTER:** Does the following program have a problem?

```
using System;
using System.IO;

class MyStream
{
   public static void Main(String[] args)
   {
         FileStream myFile = new FileStream(args[0], FileMode.Open);
         BinaryReader brFile = new BinaryReader(myFile);
         while( brFile.PeekChar() != -1 )
         {
            Console.Write("<{0}> ", brFile.ReadInt32());
      }
   }
}
```

# WEEK 2

# DAY 16

# Creating Windows Forms

The base class libraries from Microsoft provide a number of classes for creating and working with forms-based windows applications, including the creation of Windows forms and controls. Today, you

- Learn how to create a Windows form
- Customize the look and feel of a form
- Ad controls to a Windows form
- Work with text boxes, labels, and more
- Customize the look of a control by setting its properties
- Associate events with a control

## Working with Windows and Forms

Most operating systems today use event-driven programming and forms to interact with users. If you have done development for Microsoft Windows, you most likely used a set of routines within the Win32 libraries that helped you to create windows and forms. Yesterday you learned about the Base Class Libraries (BCL). Within the BCL is a set of classes for doing similar windows and forms development. The benefit of the classes in the base classes is that they can be used by any of the programming languages within the framework. Additionally, they have been created to make developing forms-based applications simple.

# Creating Windows Forms

To create a windows form application, you create a class that inherits from the `Form` class. The `Form` class is located within the `System.Windows.Forms` namespace. Listing 16.1 presents firstfrm.cs, which is the code required to create what is probably the most minimal windows form application.

**LISTING 16.1** firstfrm.csA Simple Windows Form Application

```
// firstfrm.cs - A super simplistic windows form application
//-----------------------------------------------------------------

using System.Windows.Forms;

public class frmHelloApp : Form
{
    public static void Main( string[] args )
    {
        frmHelloApp frmHello = new frmHelloApp();
        Application.Run(frmHello);
    }
}
```

As you can see, this listing is extremely short when you consider what it can do. To see what it can do though, you need to compile it. In the next section, you'll see what you need to do in order to compile this listing.

## Compiling Options

Compiling Listing 16.1 needs to be done differently than you have done before. You might need to include a reference in the `compile` command to the base classes you are using, which was briefly covered yesterday.

The `Form` classes are contained within an assembly called System.Windows.Forms.dll. You might need to include a reference to this assembly when you compile the program. Just including the `using` statement at the top of a listing does not actually include any files in your program; it provides only a reference to a point within the namespace stored in the file. As you have learned and seen, this enables you to use a shortened version of the name rather than a fully qualified name. Most of the common windows form controls and forms functionality is within this assembly.

To ensure that this assembly is used when you compile your program, you use the reference command-line parameter when you compile. This is `/reference:filename`, where filename is the name of the assembly. Using the `Forms` assembly to compile the firstfrm.cs program in Listing 16.1, you type the following command line:

```
csc /reference:System.Windows.Forms.dll firstfrm.cs
```

Alternatively, you can shorten `/reference:` to just `/r:`. When you execute the `compile` command, your program will execute.

If you execute the firstfrm application from the command prompt, you will see the window in Figure 16.1 displayed.

**FIGURE 16.1**
*The firstfrm application's form.*

This is exactly what you want. But wait. If you run this program from directly within an operating system such as Microsoft Windows, you will notice a slightly different result. The result will be a command-line box as well as the windows form (See Figure 16.2). The command-line dialog is not something you want created.

To stop this from displaying, you need to tell the compiler that you want the program created to be targeted to a Microsoft Windows operating system. This is done using the `/target:` flag with the `winexe` option. You can use `/t:` as an abbreviation. Recompiling the firstfrm.cs program in Listing 16.1 with the following command results in the solution wanted:

```
csc /r:System.Windows.Forms.dll /t:winexe firstfrm.cs
```

When you execute the program, it does not first create a command window.

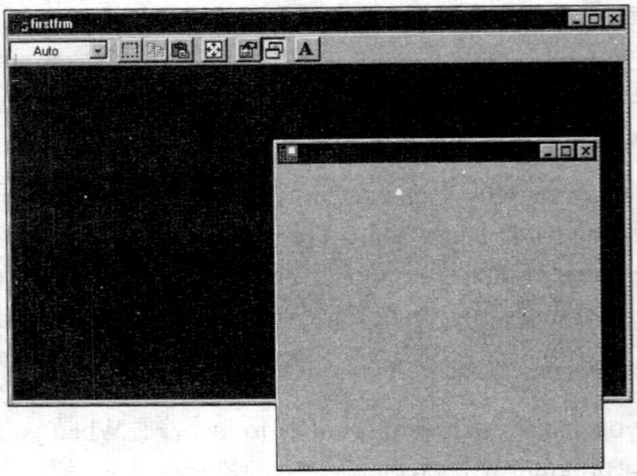


**FIGURE 16.2**
*The actual display from the firstfrm application.*

**Note** You should be aware that some of the assemblies might be automatically included when you compile. For example, development tools such as Microsoft Visual C# include a few assemblies by default. If an assembly is not included, you get an error when you compile, stating that an assembly might be missing.

## Analyzing Your First Windows Form Application

Now that you can compile and execute a windows form application, you should begin understanding the code. Look back at the code in Listing 16.1.

In line 4, the listing uses the `System.Windows.Forms` namespace, which enables the `Form` and `Application` class names to be shortened. In line 6, this application is in a class called `frmHelloApp`. The new class you are creating inherits from the `Form` class, which provides all the basic functionality of a Windows form.

**Note** As you will learn in today's lesson, the `System.Windows.Forms` namespace also includes controls, events, properties, and other code that will make your windows forms more usable.

With the single line of code (line 4), you have actually created the Forms application class. In line 10, you instantiate an object from this class. In line 11, you call the `Run` method of the `Application` class. This is covered in more detail in a moment. For now, know that it causes the application to display the form and keep running until you close the form. You could call the Show method of the Form class instead by replacing line 11 with the following:

```
frmHello.Show();
```

Although this seems more straightforward, you will find the application ends with a flaw. The program shows the form and then moves on to the next line, which is the end of the program. Because the end of the program is reached, the processing ends and the form closes. This is not the result you want. The Application class gets around this problem.



**Note** Later today, you will learn about a form method that will display a form and wait.

## The Application.Run Method

A windows application is an event-driven program that will generally display a form containing controls. The program then spins in a loop until the user does something on the form or within the windowed environment. Messages are created whenever something occurs. These messages cause an event to occur. If there is an event handler for a given message, it will be executed. If there is not, the loop will continue. Figure 16.3 illustrates this looping.

**FIGURE 16.3**
*Flow of a standard windows program.*

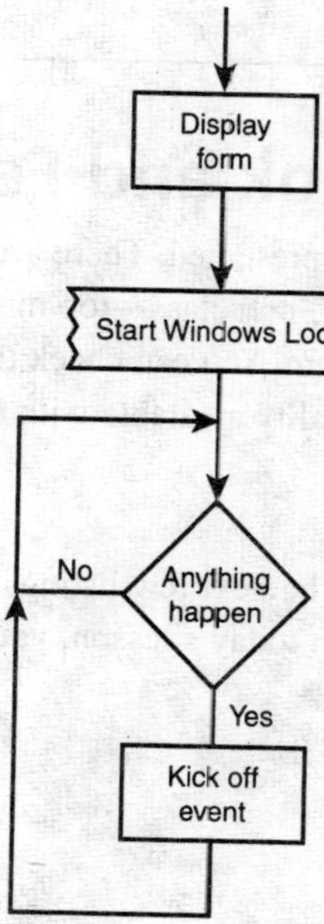

As you can see, the loop never seems to end. Actually, an event can end the program. The basic form that you inherit from (`Form`) includes the close button as well as a close item in the Command menu. These controls can kick off an event that closes the form and ends the loop.

By now you should be guessing what the `Application` class does for you—or more specifically what the `Application` class's `Run` method does for you. The `Run` method takes care of creating the loop and keeping the program running until an event that ends the program loop is executed. In the case of Listing 16.1, selecting the close button on the form or selecting the Close option on the command menu causes an event to be fired that will end the loop and thus close the form.

The `Application.Run` method also displays a form for you. Line 11 of Listing 16.1 receives a form object—`frmHello`. This is an object derived from the `Form` class. The `Application.Run` method displays this form and then loops.

**Note**

The loop created by the `Application` class's `Run` method actually processes messages that are created. These messages can be created by the operating system, your application, or other applications that are running. The loop will process these methods. For example, when you click a button, there will be a number of messages created. This will include messages for a mouse down, mouse up, button click, and more. If a message matches with an event handler, the event handler will be executed. If no event handler is defined, the message is ignored.

# Customizing a Form's Look and Feel

In the previous listing, you saw a basic form presented. There are a number of properties, methods, and events associated with the `Form` class—too many to cover in this book. However, it is worth touching on a few of them. You can check the online documentation for a complete accounting of all the functionality available with this class.

## Caption Bar on a Form

Listing 16.1 presented a basic, blank form. The next few listings continue to work with this blank form; however, with each listing in today's lesson, you will learn to take a little more control of the form.

The form from Listing 16.1 comes with a number of items already available, including the control menu and the minimize, maximize, and close buttons. You can control whether these features are on or off with your forms by setting properties:

| | |
|---|---|
| `ControlBox` | Determines whether the control box is displayed. |
| `HelpButton` | Indicates whether a help button is displayed on the caption of the form. This will be displayed only if both the `MaximizeBox` and `MinimizeBox` values are false. |
| `MaximizeBox` | Indicates whether the maximum button is included. |
| `MinimizeBox` | Indicates whether the minimize button is included. |
| `Text` | The `Caption` for the form. |

Some of these values impact others. For example, the `HelpButton` will display only if both the `MaximizeBox` and `MinimizeBox` properties are false (turned off). Listing 16.2 gives you a short listing that enables you to play with these values; Figure 16.4 shows the output. Enter this listing, compile it, and run it. Remember to include the `/t:winexe` flag when compiling.

**LISTING 16.2** form2.cs—Sizing a Form

```
// form2.cs - Caption Bar properties
//-----------------------------------------------------------

using System.Windows.Forms;

public class frmHelloApp : Form
{
    public static void Main( string[] args )
    {
       frmHelloApp frmHello = new frmHelloApp();

       // Caption bar properties
       frmHello.MinimizeBox = true;
       frmHello.MaximizeBox = false;
       frmHello.HelpButton = true;
       frmHello.ControlBox = true;
       frmHello.Text = @"My Form's Caption";

       Application.Run(frmHello);
    }
}
```

**OUTPUT**

**FIGURE 16.4**
*Output for Listing 16.2.*

**ANALYSIS** This listing is easy to follow. In line 6, a new class is created called `frmHelloApp` that inherits from the `Form` class. In line 10, a new form object is instantiated from the `Application` class. This form has a number of caption bar values set in lines 13 to 17. In line 19, the `Run` method of the `Application` class is called to display the form. You should look at the output in Figure 16.4. Both the Maximize and Minimize buttons are displayed; however, the Maximize button is to be active. This is because you set it to `false` in line 14. If you set both values to `false`, neither button will show.

You should also notice that the Help button is turned to true in line 15. The Help button displays only if both the Minimize and Maximize buttons are turned off (false). This means that line 15 is ignored. Change the property in line 13 so that the resulting properties in lines 14 to 16 are the following:

```
13:          frmHello.MinimizeBox = false;
14:          frmHello.MaximizeBox = false;
15:          frmHello.HelpButton = true;
16:          frmHello.ControlBox = true;
```

Recompile and run this program. The new output will be Figure 16.5.

**FIGURE 16.5**
*Output with a help button.*

As you can see, the output reflects the values that have been set.

One additional combination is worth noting. When you set `ControlBox` to `false`, the Close button and the Control Box are both hidden. Additionally, if `ControlBox`, `MinimizeBox`, and `MaximizeBox` are all set to false and if there is no text for the caption, the caption bar will be completely gone. Remove line 17 from Listing 16.2 and set the values for the properties in lines 13 to 16 to false. Recompile and run the program. The output you will receive is displayed in Figure 16.6.



You might wonder why you would want to remove the caption bar. One possible reason is to display a splash screen. You'll learn more about creating a splash screen later.

**FIGURE 16.6**
*Output without the caption bar.*

> **Note**
> In Microsoft Windows, Alt+F4 closes the current window. If you disable the Control Box, you end up removing the close button as well. You'll need Alt+F4 to close the window!

## The Size of a Form

The next thing to take control of is the form's size. There are a number of methods and properties that can be used to manipulate the form's shape and size. Table 16.1 presents the ones used here.

**TABLE 16.1** Sizing Functionality in the `Form` Class

| | |
|---|---|
| `AutoScale` | The form automatically adjusts itself, based on the font and/or controls used on it. |
| `AutoScaleBaseSize` | The base size used for autoscaling the form. |
| `AutoScroll` | The form will have the automatic capability of scrolling. |
| `AutoScrollMargin` | The size of the margin for the auto-scroll. |
| `AutoScrollMinSize` | The minimum size of the auto-scroll. |

**TABLE 16.1** continued

| | |
|---|---|
| `AutoScrollPosition` | The location of the auto-scroll position. |
| `ClientSize` | The size of the client area of the form. |
| `DefaultSize` | The protected property that sets the default size of the form. |
| `DesktopBounds` | The size and location of the form. |
| `DesktopLocation` | The location of the form. |
| `Height` | The height of the form |
| `MaximizeSize` | The maximum size for the form. |
| `MinimizeSize` | The minimum size for the form. |
| `Size` | The size of the form. `set` or `get` a `Size` object that contains an `x`, `y` value. |
| `SizeGripStyle` | The style of the size grip used on the form. A value from the `SizeGripStyle` enumerator. Values are `Auto` (automatically displayed when needed), `Hide` (hidden), `Show` (always shown). |
| `StartPosition` | The starting position of the form. This is a value from the `FormStartPosition` enumerator. Possible `FormStartPosition` enumeration values are `CenterParent` (centered within the parent form), `CenterScreen` (centered in the current display screen), `Manual` (location and size determined by starting position), `WindowsDefaultBounds` (Positioned at the default location), and `WindowsDefaultLocation` (positioned at the default location, with dimensions based on specified values for the size). |
| `Width` | The width of the form |

The items listed in Table 16.1 are only a few of the methods and properties available that work with a form's size. Listing 16.3 presents some of these in another simple application; Figure 16.7 shows the output.

**LISTING 16.3** form3.cs—Sizing a Form

```
// form3.cs - Form Size
//-----------------------------------------------------------------------------

using System.Windows.Forms;
```

**LISTING 16.3** continued

```
 5: using System.Drawing;
 6:
 7: public class frmHelloApp : Form
 8: {
 9:     public static void Main( string[] args )
10:     {
11:        frmHelloApp myForm = new frmHelloApp();
12:        myForm.Text = "Form Sizing";
13:
14:        myForm.Width = 400;
15:        myForm.Height = 100;
16:
17:        Point FormLoc = new Point(200,350);
18:        myForm.StartPosition = FormStartPosition.Manual;
19:        myForm.DesktopLocation = FormLoc;
20:
21:
22:        Application.Run(myForm);
23:     }
24: }
```

**OUTPUT**

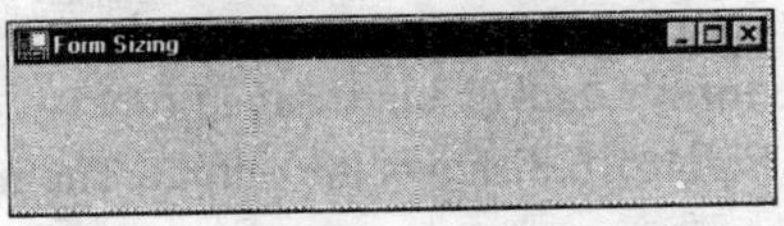


**FIGURE 16.7**

*Positioning and sizing the form.*

**ANALYSIS** Setting the size of a form is simple. Lines 14 and 15 set the size of the form in Listing 16.3. As you can see, the `Width` and `Height` properties can be set. You can also set both of these at the same time by using a `Size` object.

Positioning the form takes a little more effort. In line 17, a `Point` object is created that contains the location on the screen that you want the form positioned. This is then used in line 19 by applying it to the `DesktopLocation` property. To use the `Point` object without fully qualifying its name, you need to include the `System.Drawing` namespace, as in line 5.

In line 18, you see that an additional property has been set. If you leave line 18 out, you will not get the results you want. You must set the starting position for the form by setting the `StartPosition` property to a value in the `FormStartPosition` enumerator. Table 16.1 contained the possible values for this enumerator. You should note the other values for `FormStartPosition`. If you want to center a form on the screen, you can replace lines 17 to 19 with one line:

```
myForm.StartPosition = FormStartPosition.CenterScreen;
```

This single line of code takes care of centering the form on the screen regardless of the screen's resolution.

## Colors and Background of a Form

Working with the background color of a form requires setting the `BackColor` property to a color value. The color values can be taken from the `Color` structure located in the `System.Drawing` namespace. Table 16.2 lists some of the common colors.

To set a color is as simple as assigning a value from Table 16.2:

```
myForm.BackColor = Color.HotPink;
```

Of equal value to setting the form's color is to place a background image on the form. An image can be set into the form's `BackgroundImage` property. Listing 16.4 sets an image onto the background; Figure 16.8 shows the output. The image placed is passed as a parameter to the program.

**Caution** Be careful with this listing. For brevity, it does not contain exception handling. If you pass a filename that doesn't exist, the program will throw an exception.

**TABLE 16.2** Colors

| | | | | | |
|---|---|---|---|---|---|
| AliceBlue | AntiqueWhite | Aqua | Aquamarine | Azure | Beige |
| Bisque | Black | BlanchedAlmond | Blue | BlueViolet | Brown |
| BurlyWood | CadetBlue | Chartreuse | Chocolate | Coral | CornflowerBlue |
| Cornsilk | Crimson | Cyan | DarkBlue | DarkCyan | DarkGoldenrod |
| DarkGray | DarkGreen | DarkKhaki | DarkMagenta | DarkOliveGreen | DarkOrange |
| DarkOrchid | DarkRed | DarkSalmon | DarkSeaGreen | DarkSlateBlue | DarkSlateGray |
| DarkTurquoise | DarkViolet | DeepPink | DeepSkyBlue | DimGray | DodgerBlue |
| Firebrick | FloralWhite | ForestGreen | Fuchsia | Gainsboro | GhostWhite |
| Gold | Goldenrod | Gray | Green | GreenYellow | Honeydew |
| HotPink | IndianRed | Indigo | Ivory | Khaki | Lavender |
| LavenderBlush | LawnGreen | LemonChiffon | LightBlue | LightCoral | LightCyan |
| LightGoldenrodYellow | LightGray | LightGreen | LightPink | LightSalmon | LightSeaGreen |
| LightSkyBlue | LightSlateGray | LightSteelBlue | LightYellow | Lime | LimeGreen |
| Linen | Magenta | Maroon | MediumAquamarine | MediumBlue | MediumOrchid |
| MediumPurple | MediumSeaGreen | MediumSlateBlue | MediumSpringGreen | MediumTurquoise | MediumVioletRed |
| MidnightBlue | MintCream | MistyRose | Moccasin | NavajoWhite | Navy |
| OldLace | Olive | OliveDrab | Orange | OrangeRed | Orchid |
| PaleGoldenrod | PaleGreen | PaleTurquoise | PaleVioletRed | PapayaWhip | PeachPuff |
| Peru | Pink | Plum | PowderBlue | Purple | Red |
| RosyBrown | RoyalBlue | SaddleBrown | Salmon | SandyBrown | SeaGreen |
| SeaShell | Sienna | Silver | SkyBlue | SlateBlue | SlateGray |
| Snow | SpringGreen | SteelBlue | Tan | Teal | Thistle |
| Tomato | Transparent | Turquoise | Violet | Wheat | White |
| WhiteSmokeYellow | YellowGreen | | | | |

**LISTING 16.4** form4.cs—Using Background Images

```
// form4.cs - Form Backgrounds
//-----------------------------------------------------------------

using System.Windows.Forms;
using System.Drawing;

public class frmApp : Form
{
    public static void Main( string[] args )
    {
       frmApp myForm = new frmApp();
       myForm.BackColor = Color.HotPink;
       myForm.Text = "Form4 - Backgrounds";

       if (args.Length >= 1)
       {
          myForm.BackgroundImage = Image.FromFile(args[0]);

          Size tmpSize = new Size();
          tmpSize.Width = myForm.BackgroundImage.Width;
          tmpSize.Height = myForm.BackgroundImage.Height;
          myForm.ClientSize = tmpSize;

          myForm.Text = "Form4 - " + args[0];
       }

       Application.Run(myForm);
    }
}
```

**OUTPUT**

**FIGURE 16.8**
*Using a background image.*

**ANALYSIS** This program presents an image on the form background. This image is provided on the command line. If no image is entered on the command line, the background color is set to Hot Pink. I ran the listing using a picture of my nephews. The command line I entered was:

```
form4 pict1.jpg
```

The pict1.jpg was in the same directory as the form4 executable. If it was in a different directory, I would have needed to enter the full path. You can pass a different image as long as the path is valid. If you enter an invalid filename, you get an exception.

Looking at the listing, you can see that to create an application to display images is extremely easy. The framework classes take care of all the difficult work for you. In line 12, the background color was set to be Hot Pink. This is done by setting the form's `BackColor` property with a color value from the `Color` structure.

In line 15, a check is done to see whether a value was included on the command line. If a value was not included, lines 17 to 24 are skipped and the form is displayed with a hot pink background. If a value was entered, this programming makes the assumption (which your programs should not do) that the parameter passed was a valid graphics file. This file is then set into the `BackgroundImage` property of the form. The filename needs to be converted to an actual image for the background by using the `Image` class. More specifically, the `Image` class includes a `static` method, `FromFile`, that will take a filename as an argument and return an `Image`. This is exactly what is needed for this listing.

**Note**

> If you want a specific image for your background, you could get rid of the if statement and replace line 17's arg[0] value with the hard-coded name of the file you want as the background.

The `BackgroundImage` property holds an `Image` value. Because of this, properties and methods from the `Image` class can be used on this property. The `Image` class includes `Width` and `Height` properties that are equal to the width and height of the image contained. Lines 20 and 21 use these values to a temporary Size variable that will in turn be assigned to the form's client size in line 22. The size of the form's client area is set to the same size as the image. The end result is that the form displayed will always display the full image. If you don't do this, you will see either only part of the image or tiled copies of the image.

## Borders

Controlling the border will not only impact the look of the form, but will also determine whether the form can be resized. To modify the border, you set the `Form` class's `BorderStyle` property with a value from the `FormBorderStyle` enumeration. Possible values for the `BorderStyle` property are listed in Table 16.3. Listing 16.5 presents a form with the border modified; Figure 16.9 shows the output.

**TABLE 16.3** FormBorderStyle Enumerator Values

| *Value* | *Description* |
|---|---|
| `Fixed3D` | Fixed, 3D border |
| `FixedDialog` | Fixed, thick border |
| `FixedSingle` | Fixed, single-line border |
| `FixedToolWindow` | Non-resizable, tool window border |
| `None` | No border |
| `Sizeable` | Resizable |
| `SizeableToolWindow` | Resizable tool window border |

**LISTING 16.5** border.cs—Modifying a Form's Border

```
// border.cs - Form Borders
//-----------------------------------------------------------

using System.Windows.Forms;
using System.Drawing;

public class frmApp : Form
{
    public static void Main( string[] args )
    {
       frmApp myForm = new frmApp();
       myForm.BackColor = Color.SteelBlue;
       myForm.Text = "Borders";

       myForm.FormBorderStyle = FormBorderStyle.Fixed3D;

       Application.Run(myForm);
    }
}
```

**OUTPUT**

**FIGURE 16.9**
*Modifying a form's border.*

**ANALYSIS** As you can see, the border is fixed in size. If you try to resize the form at runtime you will not be able to.

If you do make the form resizable, you have another option you can set as well: `SizeGripStyle`. `SizeGripStyle` determines whether the form will be marked with a resize indicator. Figure 16.10 has the resize indicator circled. You can set your form to automatically show this indicator or to always hide or always show it. This is done using one of three values in the `SizeGripStyle` enumerator: `Auto`, `Hide`, or `Show`. The indicator in Figure 16.10 was shown by including the line

```
myForm.SizeGripStyle = SizeGripStyle.Show;
```

**FIGURE 16.10**
*The size grip.*

**Caution** Don't get confused by using conflicting properties. For example, if you use a fixed-sized border and you set the size grip to display, your results will not match these settings. The fixed border means that the form cannot be resized; therefore, the size grip will not display regardless of how you set it.

# Adding Controls to a Form

Up to this point, you have been working with the look and feel of a form; however, without controls a form is virtually worthless. Controls make a windows application usable.

A control can be a button, a list box, a text box, an image, or even simple plain text being displayed. The easiest way to add such controls is to use a graphical development tool such as Microsoft's Visual C#. A graphical tool enables you to drag and drop controls onto a form. It also adds all the basic code needed to display the control.

A graphical development tool, however, is not needed. Even if you use a graphical tool, it is still valuable to understand what the tool is doing for you. Some of the standard controls provided in the framework are listed in Table 16.4. Additional controls can be created and used as well.

**TABLE 16.4** Some Standard Controls in the Base Class Libraries

| | | | |
|---|---|---|---|
| `Button` | `CheckBox` | `CheckedListBox` | `ComboBox` |
| `ContainerControl` | `DataGrid` | `DateTimePicker` | `DomainUpDown` |
| `Form` | `GroupBox` | `HScrollBar` | `ImageList` |
| `Label` | `LinkLabel` | `ListBox` | `ListView` |
| `MonthCalendar` | `NumericUpDown` | `Panel` | `PictureBox` |
| `PrintReviewControl` | `ProgressBar` | `PropertyGrid` | `RadioButton` |
| `RichTextBox` | `ScrollableControl` | `Splitter` | `StatusBar` |
| `StatusBarPanel` | `TabControl` | `TabPage` | `TabStrip` |
| `TextBox` | `Timer` | `ToolBar` | `ToolBarButton` |
| `ToolTip` | `TrackBar` | `TreeView` | `VScrollBar` |
| `UserControl` | | | |

**FIGURE 16.11**
*The control architecture in the .NET classes.*

The controls in Table 16.4 are defined in the `System.Windows.Forms` namespace. The following sections cover some of these controls. Be aware, however, that the coverage here is very minimal. There are hundreds of properties, methods, and events associated with the controls listed in Table 16.4. It would take a book bigger than this one to cover all the details of each control. Here, you will learn how to use some of the key controls. The process of using the other controls will be very similar to those presented here. Additionally, you will see only a few of the properties. All the properties can be found in the help documentation available with the C# compiler or with your development tool.

## Working with Labels and Text Display



You use the `Label` control to display simple text on the screen. The `Label` control is in the `System.Windows.Forms` namespace with the other built-in controls.

To add a control to a form, you first create the control. Then you can customize the control via its properties and methods. When you have made the changes you want, you can then add it to your form.

**New Term** A *label* is a control that displays information to the user, but does not allow the user to directly change its values. You create a label like any other object:

```
Label myLabel = new Label();
```

After it's created, you have an empty label that can be added to your form. Listing 16.6 illustrates a few of the label's properties, including setting the textual value with the `Text` property; Figure 16.11 shows the output. To add the control to your form, you use the `Add` method with the `Controls` property of your form. Simply shown, to add the `myLabel` control to the `myForm` you've used before, you use

```
myForm.Controls.Add(myLabel);
```

To add other controls, you replace `myLabel` with the control's name.

**Listing 16.6** Control1.cs—Using a `Label` Control

```
// control1.cs - Working with controls
//-----------------------------------------------------------------

using System;
using System.Windows.Forms;
using System.Drawing;

public class frmApp : Form
{
    public static void Main( string[] args )
    {
        frmApp myForm = new frmApp();

        myForm.Text = Environment.CommandLine;
        myForm.StartPosition = FormStartPosition.CenterScreen;

```

**LISTING 16.6** continued

```
17:         // Create the controls...
18:         Label myDateLabel = new Label();
19:         Label myLabel = new Label();
20:
21:         myLabel.Text = "This program was executed at:";
22:         myLabel.AutoSize = true;
23:         myLabel.Left = 50;
24:         myLabel.Top = 20;
25:
26:         DateTime currDate = DateTime.Now;;
27:         myDateLabel.Text = currDate.ToString();
28:
29:         myDateLabel.AutoSize = true;
30:         myDateLabel.Left = 50 + myLabel.PreferredWidth + 10;
31:         myDateLabel.Top = 20;
32:
33:         myForm.Width = myLabel.PreferredWidth + myDateLabel.PreferredWidth +
➥110;
34:         myForm.Height = myLabel.PreferredHeight+ 100;
35:
36:         // Add the control to the form...
37:         myForm.Controls.Add(myDateLabel);
38:         myForm.Controls.Add(myLabel);
39:
40:         Application.Run(myForm);
41:     }
42: }
```

**OUTPUT**

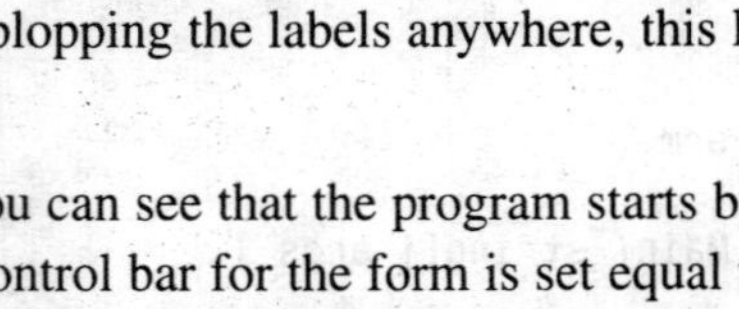


**FIGURE 16.11**

*Using a* `Label` *control.*

**ANALYSIS** This program creates two label controls and displays them in your form. Rather than just plopping the labels anywhere, this listing positions them somewhat centered in the form.

Stepping back, you can see that the program starts by creating a new form in line 12. The title on the control bar for the form is set equal to the command-line value from the `Environment` class. If you remember this from yesterday, you will know that this is the program name along with the complete path. In line 15, the `StartPosition` property for the form is set to center the form on the screen. At this point, no size for the form has been indicated. That will be done in a minute.

In lines 18 and 19, two label controls are created. The first label, `myDateLabel`, will be used to hold the current date and time. The second label control will be used to hold descriptive text. Recall that a label is a control that displays information to the user, but does not allow the user to directly change its values—so these two uses of a label are appropriate.

In lines 21 to 24, properties for the `myLabel` label are set. In line 21, the text to be displayed is assigned to the `Text` property of the label. In line 22, the `AutoSize` property is set to `true`. You can control the size of the label or you can let it determine the best size for itself. Setting the `AutoSize` property to `true` gives the label the ability to resize itself. In lines 23 and 24, the `Left` and `Top` properties are set to values. These values are for the location on the form that the control should be placed. In this case, the `myLabel` control will be placed 50 pixels from the left side of the form and 20 pixels down into the client area of the form.



The next two lines of the listing (26 and 27) are a roundabout way to assign the current date and time to the `Text` property of your other label control, `myDateLabel`. As you can see, a `DateTime` object is created and assigned the value of `Now`. This value is then converted to a string and assigned to the `myDateLabel`.

In line 29, the `AutoSize` property for the `myDateLabel` is also set to `true` so that the label will be displayed in an appropriately sized manner. In lines 30 and 31, the position of the `myDateLabel` are set. The `Top` position is easy to understand—it will be at the same vertical location as the other label—but the `Left` position is a little more complex. The `myDateLabel` label is to be placed to the right of the other label. To place it to the right of the other label, you need to move it over a distance equal to the size of the other label plus any offset from the edge of the window to the other label. This would be 50 plus the width of the `myLabel` label. Because you have said to auto size your labels, the width will be equal to the preferred width. A label's preferred width can be obtained from the `PreferredWidth` property of the control. The end result is that to place the `myDateLabel` to the right of `myLabel`, you add the preferred width of `myLabel` plus the offset added to `myLabel`. To add a little buffer between the two labels, an additional 10 pixels are added. Figure 16.12 helps illustrate what is happening in line 30.

**FIGURE 16.12**

*Positioning of the* `Label`.

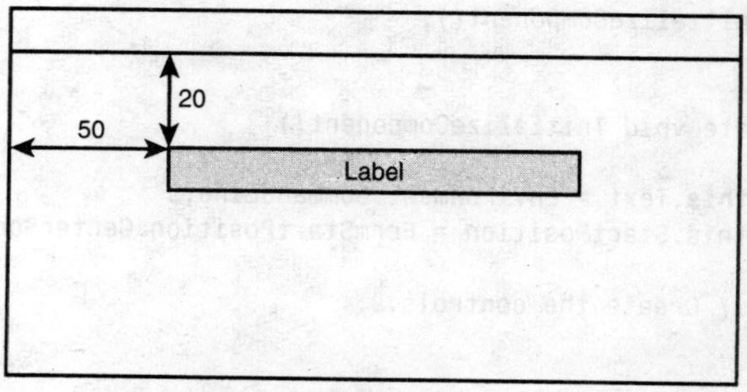

Lines 33 and 34 set the width and height of the form. As you can see, the Width is set to center the labels on the form. This is done by balancing the offsets and using the widths of the two labels. The height is set to make sure there is a lot of space around the text.

In lines 37 and 38, you see that adding these controls to the form is a simple call. The `Add` method of the `Controls` property is called for each of the controls. The `Run` method of the `Application` is then executed in line 40 so that the form is displayed. The end result is that you now have text displayed on your form!

For the most part, this same process is used for all other types of control. This involves creating the control, setting its properties, and then adding it to the form.

## A Suggested Approach for Using Controls

The process presented in the previous section is appropriate for using controls. The most common development tool for creating windowed applications is expected to be Microsoft Visual Studio .NET, and thus Microsoft Visual C# for C# applications. This development tool provides a unique structure to programming controls. Although not necessary, this structure does organize the code so that the graphical design tools can better follow the code. Because the amount of effort to follow this approach is minimal, it is worth considering. Listing 16.7 represents Listing 16.6 in this slightly altered structure. This structure is similar to what is generated by Microsoft Visual C#.

**LISTING 16.7** ctrl1b.cs—Structuring Your Code for Integrated Development Environments

```
// cntrl1b.cs - Working with controls
//-----------------------------------------------

using System;
using System.Windows.Forms;
using System.Drawing;

public class frmApp : Form
{
   public frmApp()
   {
      InitializeComponent();
   }

   private void InitializeComponent()
   {
       this.Text = Environment.CommandLine;
       this.StartPosition = FormStartPosition.CenterScreen;

       // Create the controls...
```

**LISTING 16.7** continued

```
21:        Label myDateLabel = new Label();
22:        Label myLabel = new Label();
23:
24:        myLabel.Text = "This program was executed at:";
25:        myLabel.AutoSize = true;
26:        myLabel.Left = 50;
27:        myLabel.Top = 20;
28:
29:        DateTime currDate = new DateTime();
30:        currDate = DateTime.Now;
31:        myDateLabel.Text = currDate.ToString();
32:
33:        myDateLabel.AutoSize = true;
34:        myDateLabel.Left = 50 + myLabel.PreferredWidth + 10;
35:        myDateLabel.Top = 20;
36:
37:        this.Width = myLabel.PreferredWidth + myDateLabel.PreferredWidth +
➥110;
38:        this.Height = myLabel.PreferredHeight+ 100;
39:
40:        // Add the control to the form...
41:        this.Controls.Add(myDateLabel);
42:        this.Controls.Add(myLabel);
43:    }
44:
45:    public static void Main( string[] args )
46:    {
47:       Application.Run( new frmApp() );
48:    }
49: }
```

**ANALYSIS** The output for this listing is identical to that shown in Figure 16.12 for the previous listing. This listing illustrates a different structure for coding. Again, I include this listing and analysis so you won't be surprised if you use a tool such as Visual C# and see that it followed a different structure than what I had previously presented.

Looking at this listing, you can see that the code is broken into a couple of methods instead of being placed into the `Main` method. Additionally, you can see that rather than declaring a specific instance of a form, an instance is created at the same time the `Application.Run` method is called.

When this application is executed, the `Main` method in lines 45 to 48 is executed first. This method has one line of code that creates a new `frmApp` instance and passes it to the `Application.Run` method. This one line of code kicks off a series of other activities. The first thing to happen is that the `frmApp` constructor is called to create the new `frmApp`. A constructor has been included in lines 10 to 13 of the listing. The constructor again has one simple call, `InitializeComponent`. This call causes the code in lines 17 to 43 to execute. This is the same code that you saw earlier, with one minor exception. Instead of using the name of the form, you use the `this` keyword. Because you are working within an instance of a form, `this` refers to the current form. Everywhere you referred to the `myForm` instance in the previous listing, you now refer to `this`. When the initialization of the form items is completed, control goes back to the constructor, which is also complete. Control is therefore passed back to `Main`, which then passes the newly initialized `frmApp` object to the `Application.Run` method. This displays the form and takes care of the windows looping until the program ends.

The nice thing about this structure is that it moves all your component and form initialization into one method that is separate from a lot of your other programming logic. In larger programs, you will find this more beneficial.

## Working Buttons

One of the most common controls used in windows applications are buttons. Buttons can be created using the—you guessed it—`Button` class! Buttons differ from labels, so you will most likely want an action to occur when the user clicks on a button.

Before jumping into creating button actions, it is worth taking a minute to cover creating and drawing buttons. As with labels, the first step to using a button is to instantiate a button object with the class:

```
Button myButton = new Button();
```

After you've created the button object, you can then set properties to customize it to the look and feel you want. As with the `Label` control, there are too many properties, data members, and methods to list here. You can get the complete list from the help documents. Table 16.5 lists a few of the properties.

**TABLE 16.5** A Few Button Properties

| *Property* | *Description* |
|---|---|
| `BackColor` | Returns or sets the background color of the button. |
| `BackgroundImage` | Returns or sets an image that will display on the button's background. |
| `Bottom` | Returns the distance between the bottom of the button and the top of the container the button resides in. |
| `Enabled` | Returns or sets a value indicating whether the control is enabled. |
| `Height` | Returns or sets a value indicating the height of the button. |

**TABLE 16.5** continued

| *Property* | *Description* |
|---|---|
| `Image` | Returns or sets an image on the button. |
| `Left` | Returns or sets the position of the left side of the button. |
| `Right` | Returns or sets the position of the right side of the button. |
| `Text` | Returns or sets the text on the button. |
| `TextAlign` | Returns or sets the button's text alignment. |
| `Top` | Returns or sets a value indicating the location of the top of the button. |
| `Visible` | Returns or sets a value indicating whether the button is visible. |
| `Width` | Returns or sets the width of the button. |

**Note**

Take a close look at the properties in Table 16.5. These should look like some of the same properties you used with `Label`. There is a good reason for this similarity. All the controls inherit from a more general `Control` class. This class enables all the controls to use the same methods or the same names to do similar tasks. For example, `Top` is the property for the top of a control regardless of whether it is a button, text, or something else.

## Button Events

Recall that buttons differ from labels; you generally use a button to cause an action to occur. When the user clicks on a button, you want something to happen. To cause the action to occur, you use events.

After you create a button, you can associate one or more events to it. This is done in the same manner that you learned on Day 14, "Indexers, Delegates, and Events." First, you create a method to handle the event, which will be called when the event occurs. As you learned on Day 14, this method must take two parameters, the object that caused the event and a `System.EventArgs` variable. This method must also be protected and of type `void`. The format is

```
protected void methodName( object sender, System.EventArgs args )
```

When working with windows, you generally name the method based on what control caused the event followed by what event occurred. For example, if button ABC was clicked, the method name for the handler could be `ABC_Click`.

To activate the event, you need to associate it to the appropriate delegate. A delegate object called `System.EventHandler` takes care of all the windows events. By associating your event handlers to this delegate object, they will be called when appropriate. The format is

```
ControlName.Event += new System.EventHandler(this.methodName);
```

where *`ControlName.Event`* is the name of the control and the name of the event for the control. `this` is the current form, and *`methodName`* is the method that will handle the event (as mentioned previously).

Listing 16.8 presents a modified version of Listing 16.7; Figure 16.13 shows the output. You will see that the date and time are still displayed in the form. You will also see, however, that a button has been added. When the button is clicked, an event fires that will update the date and time. Additionally, four other event handlers have been added to this listing for fun. These events are kicked off whenever the mouse moves over or leaves either of the two controls.

**LISTING 16.8** button1.cs—Using Buttons and Events

```
// button1.cs - Working with buttons and events
//-----------------------------------------------------------

using System;
using System.Windows.Forms;
using System.Drawing;

public class frmApp : Form
{
   private Label myDateLabel;
   private Button btnUpdate;

   public frmApp()
   {
      InitializeComponent();
   }

   private void InitializeComponent()
   {
      this.Text = Environment.CommandLine;
      this.StartPosition = FormStartPosition.CenterScreen;
      this.FormBorderStyle = FormBorderStyle.Fixed3D;

      myDateLabel = new Label();        // Create label

      DateTime currDate = new DateTime();
      currDate = DateTime.Now;
      myDateLabel.Text = currDate.ToString();

```

**LISTING 16.8** continued

```
            myDateLabel.AutoSize = true;
            myDateLabel.Location = new Point( 50, 20);
            myDateLabel.BackColor = this.BackColor;

            this.Controls.Add(myDateLabel);  // Add label to form

            // Set width of form based on Label's width
            this.Width = (myDateLabel.PreferredWidth + 100);

            btnUpdate = new Button();  // Create a button

            btnUpdate.Text = "Update";
            btnUpdate.BackColor = Color.LightGray;
            btnUpdate.Location = new Point(((this.Width/2) - (btnUpdate.Width /
2)),
                                           (this.Height - 75));

            this.Controls.Add(btnUpdate);  // Add button to form

            // Add a click event handler using the default event handler
            btnUpdate.Click += new System.EventHandler(this.btnUpdate_Click);
            btnUpdate.MouseEnter += new
➥System.EventHandler(this.btnUpdate_MouseEnter);
            btnUpdate.MouseLeave += new
➥System.EventHandler(this.btnUpdate_MouseLeave);

            myDateLabel.MouseEnter += new
➥System.EventHandler(this.myDataLabel_MouseEnter);
            myDateLabel.MouseLeave += new
➥System.EventHandler(this.myDataLabel_MouseLeave);
        }

        protected void btnUpdate_Click( object sender, System.EventArgs e)
        {
            DateTime currDate =DateTime.Now ;
            this.myDateLabel.Text = currDate.ToString();
        }


        protected void btnUpdate_MouseEnter( object sender, System.EventArgs e)
        {
            this.BackColor = Color.HotPink;
        }

        protected void btnUpdate_MouseLeave( object sender, System.EventArgs e)
        {
            this.BackColor = Color.Blue;
        }

```

**LISTING 16.8** continued

```
74:     protected void myDataLabel_MouseEnter( object sender, System.EventArgs
➥e)
75:     {
76:        this.BackColor = Color.Yellow;
77:     }
78:
79:     protected void myDataLabel_MouseLeave( object sender, System.EventArgs
➥e)
80:     {
81:        this.BackColor = Color.Green;
82:     }
83:
84:
85:     public static void Main( string[] args )
86:     {
87:        Application.Run( new frmApp() );
88:     }
89: }
```

**OUTPUT**

**FIGURE 16.13**
*Using a button and events.*

**ANALYSIS** This listing uses the windows designer format even though a designer was not used. This is a good way to format your code, so I follow the format here.

You will notice that I made a change to the previous listing. In lines 10 and 11, the label and button are declared as members of the form rather than members of a method. This enables all the methods within the form's class to use these two variables. They are `private`, so only this class can use them.

The `Main` method and the constructor are no different from the previous listing. The `InitializeComponent` method has changed substantially; however, most of the changes are easy to understand. Line 31 offers the first new item. Instead of using the `Top` and `Left` properties to set the location of the `myDateLabel` control, a `Point` object was used. This `Point` object was created with the value `(50, 20)` and immediately assigned to the `Location` property of the label.

**Tip** You might find that creating an object and immediately assigning it can be easier to follow than doing multiple assignments. Either method works. Use whichever you are most comfortable with or whichever is easiest to understand.

In line 39, a button called `btnUpdate` is created. It is then customized by assigning values to several properties. Don't be confused by the calculations in lines 43 and 44. This is just like line 31, except that instead of using literals, calculations are used. Also keep in mind that `this` is the form, so `this.Width` is the width of the form.

Line 46 adds the button to the form. As you can see, this is done exactly the same way that any other control would be added to the form.

In lines 49 to 54, you see the fun part of this listing. These lines are assigning handlers to various events. On the left side of these assignments, you see the controls and one of their events. This event is assigned to the method name that is being passed to the `System.EventHandler`. For example, in line 49, the `btnUpdate_Click` method is being assigned to the `Click` event of the `btnUpdate` button. In lines 50 and 51, events are being assigned to the `MouseEnter` and `MouseLeave` events of `btnUpdate`. Lines 53 and 54 assign events to the `MouseEnter` and `MouseLeave` events of `myDataLabel`. Yes, a label control can have events too! Virtually all controls have events.

**Note** There are too many events associated with each control type to list in this book. To know which events are available, check the help documentation.

For the event to work, you must actually create the methods you associated to them. In lines 57 to 82, you see a number of very simple methods. These are the same methods that were associated in lines 49 to 54.

## Creating an OK Button

A common button that can be found on many forms is an OK button. This button is clicked when users complete what they are doing. The result of this button is that the form is usually closed.

If you created the form and are using the `Application` class's `Run` method, you can create an event handler for a button click that ends the `Run` method. This method can be as simple as

```
protected void btnOK_Click( object sender, System.EventArgs e)
{
   // Final code logic before closing form
   Application.Exit();    // Ends the Application.Run message loop.
}
```

If you don't' want to exit the entire application or application loop, then you can use the `Close` method on the form instead. The `Close` method will close the form.

There is an alternative method for implementing the logic of OK. This involves taking a slightly different approach. First, instead of using the `Application` class's `Run` method, you can use a `Form` object's `ShowDialog` method. The `ShowDialog` method displays a dialog and waits for the dialog to complete. A dialog is simply a form. All other logic for creating the form is the same.

In general, if a user presses the Enter key on a form, the form will activate the OK button. You can associate the Enter key with a button using the `AcceptButton` property of the form. You set this property equal to the button that will be activated when the Enter key is pressed.

## Working with Text Boxes

Another popular control is the text box. The text box control is used to obtain text input from the users. Using a text box control and events, you can obtain information from your users that you can then use. Listing 16.9 illustrates the use of text box controls; Figure 16.14 shows the output.

**LISTING 16.9** text1.csUsing Textbox Controls

```
// text1.cs - Working with text controls
//-----------------------------------------------------------

using System;
using System.Windows.Forms;
using System.Drawing;

public class frmGetName : Form
{
   private Button btnOK;

   private Label  lblFirst;
   private Label  lblMiddle;
   private Label  lblLast;
   private Label  lblFullName;
   private Label  lblInstructions;

   private TextBox txtFirst;
   private TextBox txtMiddle;
```

**LISTING 16.9** continued

```
   private TextBox txtLast;

   public frmGetName()
   {
      InitializeComponent();
   }

   private void InitializeComponent()
   {
      this.FormBorderStyle = FormBorderStyle.Fixed3D;
      this.Text = "Get User Name";
      this.StartPosition = FormStartPosition.CenterScreen;

      // Instantiate the controls...
      lblInstructions = new Label();
      lblFirst    = new Label();
      lblMiddle   = new Label();
      lblLast     = new Label();
      lblFullName = new Label();

      txtFirst    = new TextBox();
      txtMiddle   = new TextBox();
      txtLast     = new TextBox();

      btnOK = new Button();

      // Set properties

      lblFirst.AutoSize = true;
      lblFirst.Text     = "First Name:";
      lblFirst.Location = new Point( 20, 20);

      lblMiddle.AutoSize = true;
      lblMiddle.Text     = "Middle Name:";
      lblMiddle.Location = new Point( 20, 50);

      lblLast.AutoSize = true;
      lblLast.Text     = "Last Name:";
      lblLast.Location = new Point( 20, 80);

      lblFullName.AutoSize = true;
      lblFullName.Location = new Point( 20, 110 );

      txtFirst.Width = 100;
      txtFirst.Location = new Point(140, 20);

      txtMiddle.Width = 100;
      txtMiddle.Location = new Point(140, 50);
```

**Listing 16.9** continued

```

            txtLast.Width = 100;
            txtLast.Location = new Point(140, 80);

            lblInstructions.Width = 250;
            lblInstructions.Height = 60;
            lblInstructions.Text = "Enter your first, middle, and last name." +
                                   "\nYou will see your name appear as you
➥type." +
                                   "\nFor fun, edit your name after entering
➥it.";
            lblInstructions.TextAlign = ContentAlignment.MiddleCenter;
            lblInstructions.Location =
                new Point(((this.Width/2) - (lblInstructions.Width / 2 )), 140);

            this.Controls.Add(lblFirst);  // Add label to form
            this.Controls.Add(lblMiddle);
            this.Controls.Add(lblLast);
            this.Controls.Add(lblFullName);
            this.Controls.Add(txtFirst);
            this.Controls.Add(txtMiddle);
            this.Controls.Add(txtLast);
            this.Controls.Add(lblInstructions);

            btnOK.Text = "Done";
            btnOK.BackColor = Color.LightGray;
            btnOK.Location = new Point(((this.Width/2) - (btnOK.Width / 2)),
                                       (this.Height - 75));

            this.Controls.Add(btnOK);  // Add button to form

            // Event handlers
            btnOK.Click += new System.EventHandler(this.btnOK_Click);
            txtFirst.TextChanged += new
➥System.EventHandler(this.txtChanged_Event);
            txtMiddle.TextChanged += new
➥System.EventHandler(this.txtChanged_Event);
            txtLast.TextChanged += new
➥System.EventHandler(this.txtChanged_Event);
        }

        protected void btnOK_Click( object sender, System.EventArgs e)
        {
           Application.Exit();
        }

        protected void txtChanged_Event( object sender, System.EventArgs e)
        {
```

**LISTING 16.9** continued

```
111:        lblFullName.Text = txtFirst.Text + " " + txtMiddle.Text + " " +
➥txtLast.Text;
112:     }
113:
114:     public static void Main( string[] args )
115:     {
116:        Application.Run( new frmGetName() );
117:     }
118:  }
```



**OUTPUT**

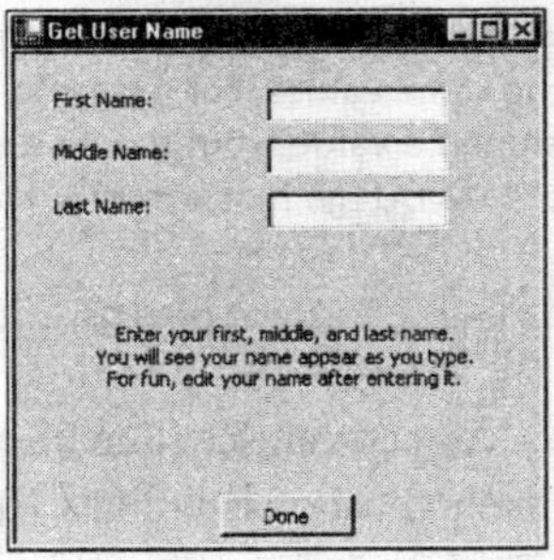


**FIGURE 16.14**
*Using the text box control.*

**ANALYSIS** As you can see by looking at the output of this listing, the applications you are creating are starting to look useful. The text box controls in this listing enable your users to enter their name. This name is concatenated and displayed to the screen.

Although Listing 16.9 is long, much of the code is repetitive because of the three similar controls for first, middle, and last names. In lines 10 to 20, a number of controls are declared within the `frmGetName` class. These controls are instantiated (lines 34 to 44) and assigned values within the `InitializeComponent` method. In lines 48 to 58, the three labels for first, middle, and last names are assigned values. They first have their `AutoSize` property set to `true` so the control will be large enough to hold the information. The text value is then assigned. Finally, each are positioned on the form. As you can see, they are each placed 20 pixels from the edge. They also are spaced vertically at different positions.

In lines 60 to 61, the full name label is declared. Its `Text` property is not assigned a value at this point. It will obtain its `Text` assignment when an event is called.

Lines 63 to 70 assign locations and widths to the text box controls that are being used in this program. As you can see, these assignments are done in the same manner as for the controls you've already learned about.

In lines 72 to 79, instructions are added via another label control. Don't be confused by all the code being used here. In line 74, three lines of text are being added to the control;

however, this is really just one very long string of text that has been broken to make it easier to read. The plus sign concatenates the three pieces and assigns them all as a single string to the `lblInstructions.Text` property. Line 77 uses another property you have not seen before. This is the `TextAlign` property that aligns the text within the label control. This property is assigned a value from the `ContentAlignment` enumeration. In this listing, `MiddleCenter` was used. Other valid values from the `ContentAlignment` enumerator include `BottomCenter`, `BottomLeft`, `BottomRight`, `MiddleLeft`, `MiddleRight`, `TopCenter`, `TopLeft`, and `TopRight`.

**Caution**

Although different controls have properties with the same name, such properties might not accept the same values. For example, the label control's `TextAlign` property is assigned a value from the `ContentAlignment` enumeration. The text box control's `TextAlign` is assigned a `HorizontalAlignment` enumeration value.

Lines 98 to 101 add exception handlers. As you can see, line 98 adds a handler for the `Click` event of the `btnOK` button. The method called is in lines 104 to 107. This method exits the application loop, thus helping end the program.

Lines 99 to 101 add event handlers for the `TextChanged` event of the text box buttons. Whenever the text within one of the three text boxes is changed, the `txtChanged_Event` will be called. As you can see, the same method can be used with multiple handlers. This method concatenates the three name fields and assigns the result to the `lblFullNameText` control.

## Working with Other Controls

Listing 16.9 provides the basis of what you need to build basic applications. There are a number of other controls that you can use. For the most part, basic use of the controls is similar to the use you've seen in the listings in today's lessons. You create the control, you modify the properties to be what you need, you create event handlers to handle any actions you want to react to, and finally you place the control on the form. Some controls, such as list boxes, are a little more complex for assigning initial data, but overall the process of using such controls is the same.

As mentioned earlier, covering all the controls and their functionality would be a very, very thick book on its own. The online documentation is a great starting point for working the details of these. Although it is beyond the scope of this book to go into too much depth, the popularity of windows-based programming warrants covering a few additional windows topics in tomorrow's lesson before moving on to Web forms and services.

# Summary

Today's lesson was a lot of fun. As you have learned, using the classes, methods, properties, and events defined in the `System.Windows.Forms` namespace can help you create windows-based applications with very little code. Today, you learned how to create and customize a form. You also learned how to add basic controls to the form and how to work with events to give your forms functionality. Although only a few of the controls were introduced, you will find that using the other controls is similar in a lot of ways to working with the ones presented today.

Tomorrow, you continue to expand on what you learned today. On Day 18, "Web Development," you'll learn how windows forms differ from Web forms.

# Q&A

**Q Where can I learn more about Windows forms?**

**A** You can learn more about Windows forms from the documentation that comes with the .NET SDK. This includes a Windows Forms Quick Start.

**Q I noticed that `Form` is listed in the table of controls. Why?**

**A** A form is a control. Most of the functionality of a control is also available to a form.

**Q Why didn't you cover all the properties, events, and methods for the controls presented today?**

**A** There are over 40 controls within the framework classes. Additionally, many of these controls have well over a hundred methods, events, and properties. To cover over 4,000 items with just a line each would take roughly 80 pages.

# Workshop

The Workshop provides quiz questions to help you solidify your understanding of the material covered and exercises to provide you with experience in using what you've learned. Try to understand the quiz and exercise answers before continuing to the next day's lesson. Answers are provided in Appendix A, "Answers."

## Quiz

1. What is the name of the namespace where most of the windows controls are located?
2. What method can be used to display a form?

3. What are the three steps involved in getting a control on a form?
4. What do you enter on the command line to compile the program xyz.cs as a windows program?
5. If you want to include the assembly myAssmb.dll when you compile the program xyz.cs, what do you enter on the command line?
6. What does the `Show()` method of the `Form` class do? What is the problem with using this method?
7. Which of the following causes the `Application.Run` method to end?
   a. A method
   b. An event
   c. The last line of code in the program is reached
   d. It never ends
   e. None of the above
8. What are the possible colors you can use for a form? What namespace needs to be included to use such colors?
9. What property can be used to assign a text value to a label?
10. What is the difference between a text box and a label?

## Exercises

1. Write the shortest Windows application you can.
2. Create a program that centers a 200-x-200–pixel form on the screen.
3. Create a form that contains a text field that can be used to enter a number. When the user presses a button, display a message in a label that states whether the number is from 0 to 1000.
4. **BUG BUSTER**: The following program has a problem. Enter it in your editor and compile it. Which lines generate error messages?

```
1:  using System.Windows.Forms;
2:
3:  public class frmHello : Form
4:  {
6:      public static void Main( string[] args )
7:      {
8:          frmHello frmHelloApp = new frmHello();
9:          frmHelloApp.Show();
10:     }
11: }
```

# WEEK 3

# DAY 17

# Creating Windows Applications

Yesterday, you learned how to create a windows form and to add controls to it Today, you will see a couple of additional controls and also learn to enhance your forms in several ways. Today, you

- Use radio buttons within groups
- Take a look at containers
- Add items to a list box control
- Enhance your applications by adding menus
- Discover the `MessageBox` class
- See how to use a few existing dialog boxes

**Note**

Today's lesson continues yesterday's introduction to windows forms functionality; however, this is merely a foundation that you can expand upon. To effectively cover the controls and the

> functionality of windows forms would take another 1,000-page book. You will find, however, that much of the functionality is very similar to what you learn in these two days.

# Working with Radio Buttons

In yesterday's lesson, you learned how to create a couple of basic controls. You were told that most controls are created and implemented in the same manner:

1. Instantiate a control object.
2. Set property values.
3. Add it to the form.

Radio buttons can be created the same way. Radio buttons are controls that are generally used in groups. When one button is selected, any others grouped with it are generally unselected. As such, they are helpful when the user has a limited number of choices to make. They are also handy when you want all the choices to be displayed—for example, when selecting gender, male or female, or selecting marital status, single or married. To create a radio button, you use the `RadioButton` class.

## Grouping Radio Buttons

Radio buttons differ from other controls in how they are generally used. Often you will want to group a set of radio buttons. If one button in the group is selected, you want the others to be unselected. Listing 17.1 presents a form that includes two groups of radio buttons. The main form for this listing is presented in Figure 17.1.

**LISTING 17.1** radio1.cs—Using and Grouping Radio Buttons

```
// radio1.cs - Using Radio Buttons
//            - Not quite right...
//-----------------------------------------------------------------

using System.Drawing;
using System.Windows.Forms;

public class Form1 : Form
{
   private RadioButton rdMale;
```

**LISTING 17.1** continued

```
   private RadioButton rdFemale;
   private RadioButton rdYouth;
   private RadioButton rdAdult;
   private Button btnOK;
   private Label lblText1;
   private Label lblText2;

   public Form1()
   {
      InitializeComponent();
   }

   private void InitializeComponent()
   {
      this.rdMale   = new System.Windows.Forms.RadioButton();
      this.rdFemale = new System.Wincows.Forms.RadioButton();
      this.lblText1 = new System.Wincows.Forms.Label();
      this.rdYouth  = new System.Windows.Forms.RadioButton();
      this.rdAdult  = new System.Windows.Forms.RadioButton();
      this.lblText2 = new System.Windows.Forms.Label();
      this.btnOK = new System.Windows.Forms.Button();

      // Form1
      this.ClientSize = new System.Drawing.Size(350, 225);
      this.Text       = "Radio Buttons 1";

      // rdMale
      this.rdMale.Location = new System.Drawing.Point(50, 65);
      this.rdMale.Size     = new Size(90, 15);
      this.rdMale.TabIndex = 0;
      this.rdMale.Text     = "Male";

      // rdFemale
      this.rdFemale.Location = new System.Drawing.Point(50, 90);
      this.rdFemale.Size     = new System.Drawing.Size(90, 15);
      this.rdFemale.TabIndex = 1;
      this.rdFemale.Text     = "Female";

      // lblText1
      this.lblText1.Location = new System.Drawing.Point(50, 40);
      this.lblText1.Size     = new System.Drawing.Size(90, 15);
      this.lblText1.TabIndex = 2;
      this.lblText1.Text     = "Sex";

      // rdYouth
```

**LISTING 17.1** continued

```
        this.rdYouth.Location = new System.Drawing.Point(220, 65);
        this.rdYouth.Size     = new System.Drawing.Size(90, 15);
        this.rdYouth.TabIndex = 3;
        this.rdYouth.Text     = "Over 21";


        // rdAdult
        this.rdAdult.Location = new System.Drawing.Point(220, 90);
        this.rdAdult.Size     = new System.Drawing.Size(90, 15);
        this.rdAdult.TabIndex = 4;
        this.rdAdult.Text     = "Under 21";

        // lblText2
        this.lblText2.Location = new System.Drawing.Point(220, 40);
        this.lblText2.Size     = new System.Drawing.Size(90, 15);
        this.lblText2.TabIndex = 5;
        this.lblText2.Text     = "Age Group";

        // btnOK
        this.btnOK.Location = new System.Drawing.Point(130, 160);
        this.btnOK.Size     = new System.Drawing.Size(70, 30);
        this.btnOK.TabIndex = 6;
        this.btnOK.Text     = "OK";
        this.btnOK.Click   += new System.EventHandler(this.btnOK_Click);

        this.Controls.Add(rdMale);
        this.Controls.Add(rdFemale);
        this.Controls.Add(lblText1);
        this.Controls.Add(rdYouth);
        this.Controls.Add(rdAdult);
        this.Controls.Add(lblText2);
        this.Controls.Add(btnOK);
    }

    private void btnOK_Click(object sender, System.EventArgs e)
    {
        Application.Exit();
    }

    static void Main()
    {
        Application.Run(new Form1());
    }
}

```

**OUTPUT**

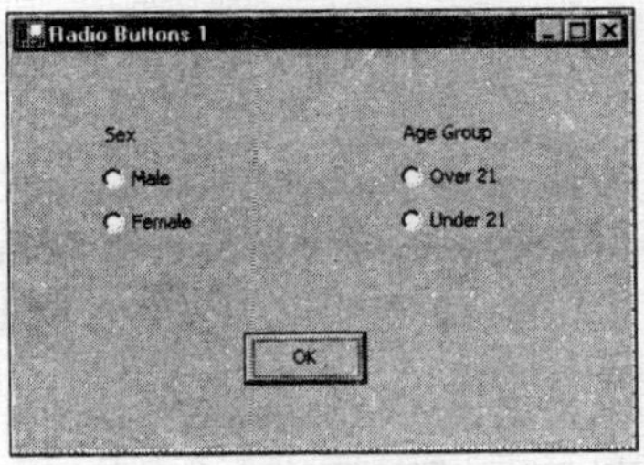


**FIGURE 17.1**
*Radio buttons in use.*

**ANALYSIS** This listing creates a form with four radio buttons and a command button. There are also two label controls used to provide descriptive information back to the person using the program. When you run this program, you will see that the radio buttons operate as you would expect them to—almost. When you select one radio button, all the others are unselected—that is the standard way radio buttons operate. The problem is that when you select one of the two buttons in the sex category, the choice in the age group category is unselected. It would be better if these two categories were separated. Before showing you how to resolve this issue, it is worth a few minutes to review this listing.



In lines 5 and 6, the `using` statements include the `Drawing` and the `Windows.Forms` namespaces within the `System` namespace. The `Drawing` namespace is used to shorten the names of the `Point` class. The `Windows.Forms` namespace is included to shorten the names of the classes used for forms and controls.

Line 8 presents the beginning statement for the class. In this line, the new form, `Form1`, is defined. It inherits from the `Form` class.

In lines 10 to 16, a number of `private` members are declared for the `Form1` class. This includes the four radio buttons that will be used (lines 10 to 14), the OK button (line 14), and the two text labels (lines 15 and 16). These are instantiated and defined values later in the listing.

Lines 18 to 21 contain the standard constructor for the form. This should look familiar because it is the same format used in yesterday's later listings. The method `InitializeComponent` is called, which will do all the work of setting up the base form for the application.

The `InitializeComponent` method starts by instantiating each of the controls (lines 25 to 31). Notice that I included the explicit names for the constructors. Because of the earlier `using` statement, these could have been condensed to just the name of the constructor. For example, line 25 could have been

```
this.rdMail = new RadioButton();
```

I included the full names so you could see which namespaces were being used. I did this throughout this listing.

Starting with line 34, the first values are set for the form. In line 34, the size of the application's form is set. The `ClientSize` property of the current form (`this`) is set by assigning a `Size` value. In line 35, the `Text` for the form is set. Remember, the `Text` property sets the title that will be used on the form.

In line 25, the first of the radio buttons is instantiated. It is then set up, starting in line 38. First, the location is set by assigning a `Point` value to the radio button's `Location` property. The point will be an (x,y) location on the form. In this case, the button will be positioned 50 pixels over and 65 pixels down. The size of the control is set in line 39. This will be the amount of space given to the little button as well as the text. In line 40, the `TabIndex` property is set. Finally, in line 41 the text included on the radio button is set. In this case, the button is set to equal `Male`. In the following lines of the listing, the `rdFemale`, `rdYouth`, and `rdAdult` radio buttons are set up in the same manner.

**Note** The `TabIndex` property is on most controls. This is the order that the controls will be selected when the Tab button is pressed. The first control will be index 0, the second index 1, the third index 2, and so on. Setting the tab index enables you to control the order that the user can navigate through a form's controls.

The two labels on the form are set up in lines 49 to 53 and lines 69 to 72. In lines 75 to 79, the OK button is set up with an event handler that will exit the program when the button is selected.

The final set of initializing the form is adding all the controls to the actual form. This is done using `Controls.Add` in lines 81 to 87. When this is completed, the form is initialized and ready to display with all the controls.

There was no logic needed to actually manipulate the radio buttons. They already contain the code necessary to select and unselect. As mentioned earlier though, this listing is not operating exactly as preferred. A change needs to be made to enable the two sets of radio buttons to operate independently.

## Working with Containers

The answer to the issue in Listing 17.1 is obtained by using containers. A container enables you to group a set of controls. You have already been using a container—your main form. You can also create your own containers, which you can place in the form's container or any other container. By placing your two sets of radio buttons in Listing 17.1 into their own containers, you separate them.

You also can separate the controls by using another control, a group box. The group box operates in the same fashion as a container, and it gives you added functionality, including the ability to display a text label as part of the group box.

Listing 17.2 drops the label controls from Listing 17.2 and replaces them with group boxes. This listing also drops the use of explicit names. The explicit names were included in Listing 17.1 to help you know where different classes and types were stored. Figure 17.2 shows the radio buttons positioned within the group boxes.



**LISTING 17.2** radio2.cs—Grouping Radio Buttons

```
// radio2.cs - Using Radio Buttons
//           - Using Groups
//-----------------------------------------------------------------

using System.Drawing;
using System.Windows.Forms;

public class Form1 : Form
{
   private GroupBox gboxAge;
   private GroupBox gboxSex;

   private RadioButton rdMale;
   private RadioButton rdFemale;
   private RadioButton rdYouth;
   private RadioButton rdAdult;
   private Button btnOK;

   public Form1()
   {
      InitializeComponent();
   }

   private void InitializeComponent()
   {
      this.gboxAge = new GroupBox();
      this.gboxSex = new GroupBox();
      this.rdMale   = new RadioButton();
      this.rdFemale = new RadioButton();
      this.rdYouth  = new RadioButton();
      this.rdAdult  = new RadioButton();
      this.btnOK    = new Button();

```

**LISTING 17.2** continued

```
        // Form1
        this.ClientSize = new Size(350, 200);
        this.Text       = "Grouping Radio Buttons";

        // gboxSex
        this.gboxSex.Location = new Point(15, 30);
        this.gboxSex.Size     = new Size(125, 100);
        this.gboxSex.TabStop  = false;
        this.gboxSex.Text     = "Sex";

        // rdMale
        this.rdMale.Location = new Point(35, 35);
        this.rdMale.Size     = new Size(70, 15);
        this.rdMale.TabIndex = 0;
        this.rdMale.Text     = "Male";

        // rdFemale
        this.rdFemale.Location = new Point(35, 60);
        this.rdFemale.Size     = new Size(70, 15);
        this.rdFemale.TabIndex = 1;
        this.rdFemale.Text     = "Female";

        // gboxAge
        this.gboxAge.Location = new Point(200, 30);
        this.gboxAge.Size     = new Size(125, 100);
        this.gboxAge.TabStop  = false;
        this.gboxAge.Text     = "Age Group";

        // rdYouth
        this.rdYouth.Location = new Point(35, 35);
        this.rdYouth.Size     = new Size(70, 15);
        this.rdYouth.TabIndex = 3;
        this.rdYouth.Text     = "Over 21";

        // rdAdult
        this.rdAdult.Location = new Point(35, 60);
        this.rdAdult.Size     = new Size(70, 15);
        this.rdAdult.TabIndex = 4;
        this.rdAdult.Text     = "Under 21";

        // btnOK
        this.btnOK.Location = new Point(130, 160);
        this.btnOK.Size     = new Size(70, 30);
        this.btnOK.TabIndex = 6;
        this.btnOK.Text     = "OK";
        this.btnOK.Click   += new System.EventHandler(this.btnOK_Click);

        this.Controls.Add(gboxSex);
```

**LISTING 17.2** continued

```
82:         this.Controls.Add(gboxAge);
83:
84:         this.gboxSex.Controls.Add(rdMale);
85:         this.gboxSex.Controls.Add(rdFemale);
86:         this.gboxAge.Controls.Add(rdYouth);
87:         this.gboxAge.Controls.Add(rdAdult);
88:
89:         this.Controls.Add(btnOK);
90:      }
91:
92:      private void btnOK_Click(object sender, System.EventArgs e)
93:      {
94:         Application.Exit();
95:      }
96:
97:      static void Main()
98:      {
99:         Application.Run(new Form1());
100:     }
101:  }
102:
```



**OUTPUT**

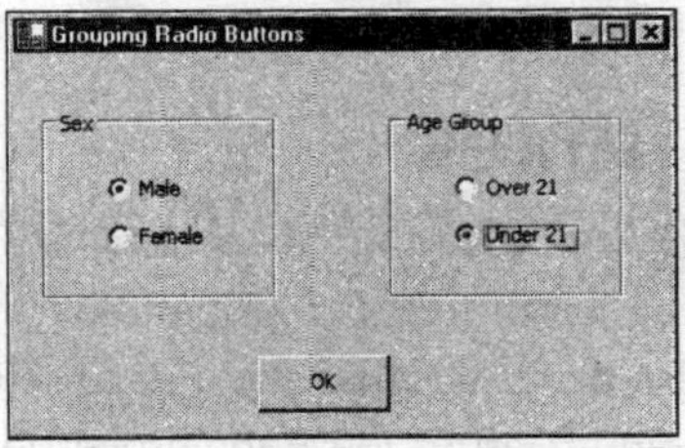


**FIGURE 17.2**
*Grouped radio buttons.*

**ANALYSIS** The focus of this listing is on the use of the group boxes. If you used containers instead of group boxes, the coding would be similar to this listing, except that you would not set `Text` and other properties on the container. Instead you would need to use other controls (such as labels) to create custom look-and-feel attributes on the container.

Lines 10 and 11 declare the two group box members that will be used in the form. The label controls were removed, because a text description can be included on a group box. In lines 26 and 27, the two group boxes are instantiated by calling the `GroupBox` constructor.

Lines 39 to 42 set the characteristics of the first group box control, `gboxSex`. Like other controls, the `Location`, `Size`, `TabStop`, and `Text` properties can be set. You can set other properties as well. Lines 57 to 60 set the properties for the `gboxAge` group box.

**Tip**

Consult the online documentation for a complete list of all the properties and members of the group box. Like all the controls, there are lots—too many to cover here!

The big difference to notice in this listing is in lines 81 to 87. In line 81 and 82, the two groups, `gboxSex` and `gboxAge`, are added to the form. The radio buttons are not added to the form. In lines 84 to 87, the radio buttons are added to the group boxes instead. The group box is a part of the form (`this`), so the radio buttons will appear on the form within the group box.

By adding the radio buttons within the group buttons, they are within separate containers. When you run this listing, you will see that selecting a `Sex` option has no impact on the `Age` category.

**Note**

You could have a selection of one of the Sex options impact an Age selection. To do this, you would include an event that included code to manipulate the properties of the other control.

# Working with List Boxes

Another common control that you want to use on your forms is a list box. A list box is a control that allows you to list a number of items in a small box. The list box can be set to scroll through the items. It can also be set to allow the user to select one or more items. Because a list box requires a little more effort to set the properties with values, it is worth taking a brief look at its base functionality.

A list box is set up like all the other controls you've seen so far. First you define the list box control as part of your form:

```
private ListBox myListBox;
```

You then need to instantiate it:

```
myListBox = new ListBox();
```

Of course you can do both of these statements on a single line:

```
private ListBox myListBox = new ListBox();
```

After it's created, you can add it to your form—again, the same way you added the other controls:

```
this.Controls.Add(myListBox);
```

A list box is different because you want it to contain a list of items.

## Adding Items to the List

Adding items to a list box is done in a couple of steps. The first step is to let the list box know you are going to update it. This is done by calling the `BeginUpdate` method on the list box. For a list box called `myListBox`, this would be done as follows:

```
myListBox.BeginUpdate();
```



After you've called this method, you can then begin adding items to the list box by calling the `Add` method of the `Items` member of the list box. This is easier than it sounds. To add `"My First Item"` as an item to `myListBox`, you enter the following:

```
myListBox.Items.Add("My First Item");
```

Other items can be added in the same manner:

```
myListBox.Items.Add("My Second Item");
myListBox.Items.Add("My Third Item");
```

When you are finished adding your items, you need to indicate to the list box that you are done. This is done calling the `EndUpdate` method:

```
myListbox.EndUpdate();
```

That's it! That is all it takes to add items to the list box. Listing 17.3 uses two list boxes. You can see in the output presented in Figure 17.3 that they are presented differently.

**LISTING 17.3** list1.cs—Using List Boxes

```
// list1.cs - Working with list box controls
//-----------------------------------------------------------------

using System.Windows.Forms;
using System.Drawing;

public class frmGetName : Form
{
    private Button  btnOK;
    private Label   lblFullName;
    private TextBox txtFullName;
    private ListBox lboxSex;
    private Label   lblSex;
```

**LISTING 17.3** continued

```
    private ListBox lboxAge;

    public frmGetName()
    {
       InitializeComponent();
    }

    private void InitializeComponent()
    {
        this.FormBorderStyle = FormBorderStyle.Fixed3D;
        this.Text = "Get User Info";
        this.StartPosition = FormStartPosition.CenterScreen;

        // Instantiate the controls...
        lblFullName  = new Label();
        txtFullName  = new TextBox();
        btnOK        = new Button();
        lblSex       = new Label();
        lboxSex      = new ListBox();
        lboxAge      = new ListBox();

        // Set properties
        lblFullName.Location = new Point(20, 40);
        lblFullName.AutoSize = true;
        lblFullName.Text = "Name:";

        txtFullName.Width = 170;
        txtFullName.Location = new Point(80, 40);


        btnOK.Text = "Done";
        btnOK.Location = new Point(((this.Width/2) - (btnOK.Width / 2)),
                                   (this.Height - 75));

        lblSex.Location = new Point(20, 70);
        lblSex.AutoSize = true;
        lblSex.Text = "Sex:";

        // Set up ListBox
        lboxSex.Location = new Point(80, 70);
        lboxSex.Size = new Size(100, 20);
        lboxSex.SelectionMode = SelectionMode.One;

        lboxSex.BeginUpdate();
          lboxSex.Items.Add("          ");
          lboxSex.Items.Add(" Boy      ");
          lboxSex.Items.Add(" Girl     ");
          lboxSex.Items.Add(" Man      ");
```

**LISTING 17.3** continued

```
            lboxSex.Items.Add(" Lady   ");
        lboxSex.EndUpdate();

        // Set up ListBox
        lboxAge.Location = new Point(80, 100);
        lboxAge.Size      = new Size(100, 60);
        lboxAge.SelectionMode = SelectionMode.One;
        lboxAge.BeginUpdate();
          lboxAge.Items.Add("          ");
          lboxAge.Items.Add(" Under 21 ");
          lboxAge.Items.Add("    21    ");
          lboxAge.Items.Add(" Over 21  ");
        lboxAge.EndUpdate();
        lboxAge.SelectedIndex = 0;

        this.Controls.Add(btnOK);          // Add button to form
        this.Controls.Add(lblFullName);
        this.Controls.Add(txtFullName);
        this.Controls.Add(lboxSex);
        this.Controls.Add(lblSex);
        this.Controls.Add(lboxAge);

        // Event handlers
        btnOK.Click += new System.EventHandler(this.btnOK_Click);
    }

    protected void btnOK_Click( object sender, System.EventArgs e)
    {
      Application.Exit();
    }

    public static void Main( string[] args )
    {
      Application.Run( new frmGetName() );
    }
}
```



**OUTPUT**

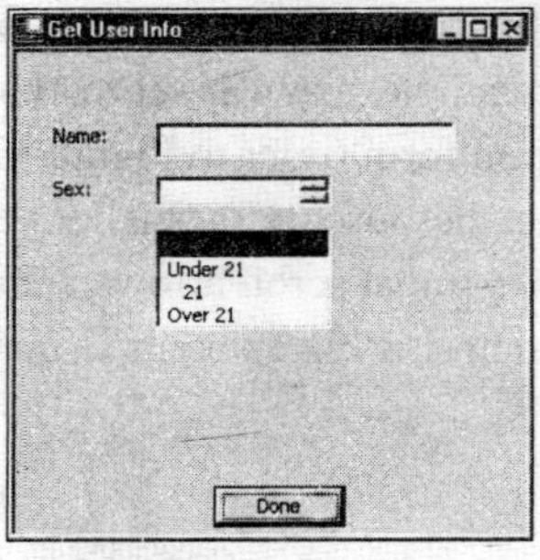


**FIGURE 17.3**
*Using list boxes.*

**ANALYSIS** Listing 17.3 uses list boxes to display the selections for `Age` and `Sex`. Additionally, the listing contains a text box for users to enter their name. In Figure 17.3, the default selections for the two list boxes are blanks. A blank value was entered as the first item for each list box.

In lines 9 to 14, the controls for the form in this application are defined. In lines 12 and 14, the list boxes are declared. In lines 28 to 33, all the controls are instantiated. The two list box controls are instantiated in lines 32 and 33.

The details of the list boxes are set later in the listing. The first list box, `lboxSex`, is defined in lines 53 to 63. First, the location and size are set up in lines 53 and 54. In line 55, the selection mode is set. The possible selection modes for a list box are listed in Table 17.1. In line 55, the mode for the `lboxSex` is `SelectionMode.One`. Only one item can be selected at a time.

**TABLE 17.1** `ListBox` Selection Modes

| *Mode* | *Description* |
|---|---|
| `SelectionMode.One` | Only one item can be selected at a time. |
| `SelectionMode.MultiExtended` | Multiple items can be selected. Shift, Ctrl, and the arrow keys can be used to make multiple selections. |
| `SelectionMode.MultiSimple` | Multiple items can be selected. |
| `SelectionMode.None` | No items can be selected. |

In lines 57 to 63, the different selection items are added to the `lboxSex` list box. This is done as shown earlier. First, the `BeginUpdate` method is called. Each item is then added by using the `Items.Add` method. Finally, the additions are ended by calling the `EndUpdate` method.

In lines 66 to 75, the `lboxAge` is set up in a similar manner. There are two distinct differences you should notice. The first is that the `SelectedIndex` is set in line 75 for the `lboxAge` control. This determines which item is to be initially selected in the list box. The second difference is in the size of the control. For the `lboxSex` control, the size was set to `100` by `20` (line 54). For the `lboxAge`, the size was set to `100` by `60` (line 67). You can see the results of this on the displayed form (refer to Figure 17.3). The `lboxSex` control can display only one option at a time because of its smaller vertical size. Because the items don't fit in the size of the control, vertical scroll arrows are automatically added to the control. For the `lboxAge` box, the control is big enough, so no vertical scroll bar was needed.

Everything else about a list box is similar to the other controls. You can create events to determine when a selection has changed or when the user has left the control. You can add logic to your form to make sure that a selection was made. Or, you can do a lot more.

# Adding Menus to Your Forms

Controls are one way to make your forms functional. Another way is to add menus. Most windowed applications include a menu of some sort. At a minimum, there is generally a File or a Help menu item. When selected, these usually list a set of submenu items for selection. You also can add menus to your forms.

## Creating a Basic Menu

Listing 17.4 is the form you saw yesterday that displays the current date and time (see Figure 17.4). Instead of using a button to update the current date and time, this form uses a menu option. Although this is not a great use of a menu item, it illustrates a number of key points. First, you add a menu to your form. Second, you explore how the menu items are associated to an event item. Finally, you see how to code a menu item's event.

**LISTING 17.4** menu1.cs—Basic Menu

```
// menu1.cs - menus
//-----------------------------------------------------------

using System;
using System.Windows.Forms;
using System.Drawing;

public class frmApp : Form
{
   private Label myDateLabel;
   private MainMenu myMainMenu;

   public frmApp()
   {
      InitializeComponent();
   }

   private void InitializeComponent()
   {
      this.Text = "STY Menus";
      this.StartPosition = FormStartPosition.CenterScreen;
      this.FormBorderStyle = FormBorderStyle.Fixed3D;

```

**LISTING 17.4** continued

```
        myDateLabel = new Label();      // Create label

        DateTime currDate = new DateTime();
        currDate = DateTime.Now;
        myDateLabel.Text = currDate.ToString();

        myDateLabel.AutoSize = true;
        myDateLabel.Location = new Point( 50, 70);
        myDateLabel.BackColor = this.BackColor;

        this.Controls.Add(myDateLabel);  // Add label to form

        // Set width of form based on Label's width
        this.Width = (myDateLabel.PreferredWidth + 100);

        myMainMenu = new MainMenu();

        MenuItem menuitemFile = myMainMenu.MenuItems.Add("File");
        menuitemFile.MenuItems.Add(new MenuItem("Update Date",
                                       new
➥EventHandler(this.MenuUpdate_Selection)));
        menuitemFile.MenuItems.Add(new MenuItem("Exit",
                                       new
➥EventHandler(this.FileExit_Selection)));
        this.Menu = myMainMenu;
    }

    protected void MenuUpdate_Selection( object sender, System.EventArgs e )
    {
        DateTime currDate = new DateTime();
        currDate = DateTime.Now;
        this.myDateLabel.Text = currDate.ToString();
    }
    protected void FileExit_Selection( object sender, System.EventArgs e )
    {
       this.Close();
    }

    public static void Main( string[] args )
    {
       Application.Run( new frmApp() );
    }
}
```

**OUTPUT**

**FIGURE 17.4**
*The basic menu selected on the form.*

**ANALYSIS** In Figure 17.4, the listing creates a simple File menu that contains two items, Update Date and Exit. Selecting Update Date updates the date and time on the screen. Selecting Exit ends the program by calling closing the current form using `this.Close()`.



The primary menu on a form is called the main menu, which contains File as well as any other options that appear across the top of the application. In line 11 of Listing 17.4, a `MainMenu` type called `myMainMenu` is declared for the `frmApp` form.

In line 39, the `myMainMenu` data member is instantiated. In lines 41 to 44, it is set up, and in line 46, it is added to the form.

Looking closer, you can see that a lot of work is done in lines 41 to 46. In fact, a lot of work is done in line 41 alone. In line 41, a new data member is declared called `menuitemFile`. Additionally, the following statement:

```
MyMainMenu.MenuItems.Add("File");
```

adds a new item—the first item—to the `myMainMenu` menu. This item is called File, and it is then assigned to the `menuitemFile` data member.

In general terms, to add a menu item, you can call the `MenuItems.Add` method on either a menu data member or another menu item data member. If you call this on the main menu, you get the primary items in the main menu. If you call `MenuItems.Add` on a menu item, you get a submenu, menu item.

In line 42, the menu item containing `File`, `menuitemFile`, has its `MenuItems.Add` method called. This means that a submenu item is being added to `File`. In the case of line 42, this is the item `"Update Date"`. In line 44, the submenu item `"Exit"` is added.

Wait a minute. If you look closely, you will see that the call in line 41 to the `MenuItems.Add` method is different from the ones in Lines 42 and 44. It should be obvious to you that this method had been overloaded. If only one parameter string is passed, it is assumed to be the text item that will be displayed. In the calls in lines 42 and 44, two parameters are passed. The first is a new `MenuItem` that is assigned directly to the menu rather than an intermediary variable.

The second is a new event handler. This is the event handler that will be called if and when the menu item is selected. Event handler methods have been created (starting in lines 49 and 54) for the two event handlers passed in lines 43 and 45.

Line 49 contains the event handler for the Update Date menu option. This method call has the same name passed to the `MenuItems.Add` method in line 42. Don't forget that when you set up the actual event handler methods, you will have two parameters, the sender and the `EventArgs`. When the Update Date menu option is selected, the event handler in lines 49 to 54 will be called. This method updates the date and time on the form. This could just as easily have done something else.

The event handler in lines 55 to 58 is called when Exit is selected. This handler exits the application by closing the form.

## Creating Multiple Menus

In this section, you add a second menu item to the main menu and control key access to your menu items. Listing 17.5 presents a program that contains both a File and a Help menu option on the main menu (see Figure 17.5). Each of these options contains its own submenu selections.

**LISTING 17.5** menu2.cs—Multiple Items on the Main Menu

```
// menu2.cs - menus
//-----------------------------------------------------------------

using System;
using System.Windows.Forms;
using System.Drawing;

public class frmApp : Form
{
   private Label myDateLabel;
   private MainMenu myMainMenu;

   public frmApp()
   {
      InitializeComponent();
```

**LISTING 17.5** continued

```
    }

    private void InitializeComponent()
    {
        this.Text = "STY Menus";
        this.StartPosition = FormStartPosition.CenterScreen;
        this.FormBorderStyle = FormBorderStyle.Fixed3D;

        myDateLabel = new Label();      // Create label

        DateTime currDate = new DateTime();
        currDate = DateTime.Now;
        myDateLabel.Text = currDate.ToString();

        myDateLabel.AutoSize = true;
        myDateLabel.Location = new Point( 50, 70);
        myDateLabel.BackColor = this.BackColor;

        this.Controls.Add(myDateLabel);  // Add label to form

        // Set width of form based on Label's width
        this.Width = (myDateLabel.PreferredWidth + 100);

        CreateMyMenu();
    }

    protected void MenuUpdate_Selection( object sender, System.EventArgs e)
    {
        DateTime currDate = new DateTime();
        currDate = DateTime.Now;
        this.myDateLabel.Text = currDate.ToString();
    }

    protected void FileExit_Selection( object sender, System.EventArgs e)
    {
       this.Close();
    }

    protected void FileAbout_Selection( object sender, System.EventArgs e)
    {
       // display an about form
    }

    public void CreateMyMenu()
    {
       myMainMenu = new MainMenu();

       MenuItem menuitemFile = myMainMenu.MenuItems.Add("&File");
       menuitemFile.MenuItems.Add(new MenuItem("Update &Date",
```

**LISTING 17.5** continued

```
65:                                  new
➥EventHandler(this.MenuUpdate_Selection),
66:                                  Shortcut.CtrlD));
67:       menuitemFile.MenuItems.Add(new MenuItem("E&xit",
68:                                  new EventHandler(this.FileExit_Selection),
69:                                  Shortcut.CtrlX));
70:
71:       MenuItem menuitemHelp = myMainMenu.MenuItems.Add("&Help");
72:       menuitemHelp.MenuItems.Add(new MenuItem("&About",
73:                                  new
➥EventHandler(this.FileAbout_Selection)));
74:
75:       this.Menu = myMainMenu;
76:    }
77:
78:    public static void Main( string[] args )
79:    {
80:       Application.Run( new frmApp() );
81:    }
82: }
```

**OUTPUT**

**FIGURE 17.5**
*Multiple items on the main menu.*

**ANALYSIS** This listing is similar to Listing 17.4. One major difference is that the menu creation has been pulled into its own method to help organize the code better. This method, `CreateMyMenu`, is in lines 59 to 76. The `InitializeComponent` method calls `CreateMyMenu` in line 39 as a part of its initial form setup.

Lines 42 to 57 contain the events that might be activated by different menu selections. The first two, `MenuUpdate_Selection` and `FileExit_Selection`, are like the ones in Listing 17.4. The third, `FileAbout_Selection`, will be associated to the About menu item on the Help menu. Line 56 does not contain any code; however, any code could be placed here. In the case of an About menu selection, that would most likely be the display of an informative dialog box. Later today, you'll see an example of such a dialog box.

The focus of this listing related to menus is in lines 59 to 76, and it takes the same approach as in the prior listing. In line 61, the main menu is instantiated. In line 63, the File item is added to `myMainMenu`. There is one difference in this call. An ampersand (`&`)has been added to File. This indicates that a letter—the letter following the ampersand—should be underlined on the display. For a `MainMenu` item, it also indicates that the given item should be selectable by using the Alt key with the letter following the ampersand. In this case, pressing Alt+F automatically selects the File menu option.

In lines 64 and 67, you see the addition of menu items to the File menu similar to the ones in the prior listing; however, yet another version of the `MenuItems.Add` method is called. This time a third parameter is included, which specifies that the menu item should indicate that a keyboard shortcut can be used to select the given menu item. If you look at the two submenu items on the File menu, you will see that they have additional text indicating that a shortcut key is available (see Figure 17.6).



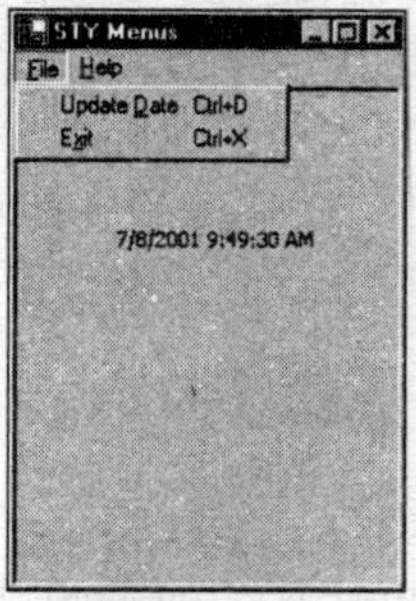


**FIGURE 17.6**
*Shortcut key indicators on a menu item.*

**Note**

Fortunately, there are shortcut keys already defined in the `Shortcut` data type. In general, you can use `Shortcut.Ctrl*`, where `*` is any letter.

Adding the second menu item to the main menu is done the same way the first item was added. The About menu item was added in line 71. Because this menu item will have submenu items, you need to assign it to a `MenuItem` variable. In this case, it is `menuitemHelp`. `menuitemHelp` then has its items added using its `MenuItems.Add` method.

## Using Checked Menus

One other common feature of using menus is the ability to check or uncheck a menu item. When checked it is active; when unchecked it is not active. Listing 17.6 illustrates how to add checking to a menu item and also provides an alternate way of declaring and defining menus (see Figure 17.7). This method requires more code; however, some people consider it easier to read and follow.

**Listing 17.6** menu3.cs—Checking Menus

```
// menu3.cs - menus
//-----------------------------------------------

using System;
using System.Windows.Forms;
using System.Drawing;

public class frmApp : Form
{
   private Label myDateLabel;
   private MainMenu myMainMenu;

   private MenuItem menuitemFile;
   private MenuItem menuitemUD;
      private MenuItem menuitemActive;
   private MenuItem menuitemExit;
   private MenuItem menuitemHelp;
   private MenuItem menuitemAbout;

   public frmApp()
   {
      InitializeComponent();
   }

   private void InitializeComponent()
   {
      this.Text = "STY Menus";
      this.StartPosition = FormStartPosition.CenterScreen;
      this.FormBorderStyle = FormBorderStyle.Sizable;

      myDateLabel = new Label();      // Create label

      DateTime currDate = new DateTime();
      currDate = DateTime.Now;
      myDateLabel.Text = currDate.ToString();

      myDateLabel.AutoSize = true;
      myDateLabel.Location = new Point( 50, 70);
      myDateLabel.BackColor = this.BackColor;

      this.Controls.Add(myDateLabel);  // Add label to form

      // Set width of form based on Label's width
      this.Width = (myDateLabel.PreferredWidth + 100);

      CreateMyMenu();
   }

```

**LISTING 17.6** continued

```
    protected void MenuUpdate_Selection( object sender, System.EventArgs e)
    {
      if( menuitemActive.Checked == true)
      {
        DateTime currDate = new DateTime();
        currDate = DateTime.Now;
        this.myDateLabel.Text = currDate.ToString();
      }
      else
      {
        this.myDateLabel.Text = "** " + this.myDateLabel.Text + " **";
      }
    }

    protected void FileExit_Selection( object sender, System.EventArgs e)
    {
      Application.Exit();
    }

    protected void FileAbout_Selection( object sender, System.EventArgs e)
    {
      // display an about form
    }

    protected void ActiveMenu_Selection( object sender, System.EventArgs e)
    {
      MenuItem tmp;
      tmp = (MenuItem) sender;

      if ( tmp.Checked == true )
        tmp.Checked = false;
      else
        tmp.Checked = true;
    }

    public void CreateMyMenu()
    {
      myMainMenu = new MainMenu();

      // FILE MENU
      menuitemFile = myMainMenu.MenuItems.Add("&File");

      menuitemUD = new MenuItem();
      menuitemUD.Text = "Update &Date";
      menuitemUD.Shortcut = Shortcut.CtrlD;
      menuitemUD.Click += new EventHandler(this.MenuUpdate_Selection);
      menuitemFile.MenuItems.Add( menuitemUD );

```

**LISTING 17.6** continued

```
      menuitemExit = new MenuItem();
      menuitemExit.Text = "E&xit";
      menuitemExit.Shortcut = Shortcut.CtrlX;
      menuitemExit.ShowShortcut = false;
      menuitemExit.Click += new EventHandler(this.FileExit_Selection);
      menuitemFile.MenuItems.Add( menuitemExit );

      // HELP MENU
      menuitemHelp = myMainMenu.MenuItems.Add("&Help");

      menuitemActive = new MenuItem();
      menuitemActive.Text = "Active";
      menuitemActive.Click += new EventHandler(this.ActiveMenu_Selection);
      menuitemActive.Checked = true;
      menuitemHelp.MenuItems.Add( menuitemActive );

      menuitemAbout = new MenuItem();
      menuitemAbout.Text = "&About";
      menuitemAbout.Shortcut = Shortcut.CtrlA;
      menuitemAbout.ShowShortcut = false;
      menuitemAbout.Click += new EventHandler(this.FileAbout_Selection);
      menuitemHelp.MenuItems.Add( menuitemAbout );

      this.Menu = myMainMenu;
   }

   public static void Main( string[] args )
   {
      Application.Run( new frmApp() );
   }
}
```

**OUTPUT**

**FIGURE 17.7**
*Checked menus.*

**ANALYSIS** This listing is a little longer than the previous two, partly because of the alternate way of creating the menu.

Instead of declaring a `MainMenu` data item and only the top-level menu items, this listing declares a `MainMenu` item in line 11 and then `MenuItem` variables for each menu item that will exist. Lines 13 to 18 declare a `MenuItem` variable to hold each of the individual menu items.

As in the previous listing, the functionality to create the menu is placed in its own method, starting in line 84. In line 86, the `MainMenu` item, `myMainMenu`, is declared.

In line 89, the first menu item, File, is declared in the same way as you've seen before. The declaration of the submenu items is different this time. The Update Date menu item is created in lines 91 to 95. First, a menu item variable, `menuitemUD`, is instantiated as a menu item. This is followed by setting individual property values on this menu item (lines 92 and 93). In line 94, an event handler is associated to the `Click` event of this menu item. This event handler will be called whenever the menu item is selected. Finally, in line 95, the menu item is attached to its parent menu item. In this case, the `menuitemUD` is added to the File menu, `menuitemFile`.



All the other menu items are added in the same manner. In some cases, different properties are set.

This listing also uses a new feature you've not used before. The Active menu item on the Help menu can be checked on and off. If checked on, the date and time is updated when the Date Update menu item is selected. If checked off, the date and time is enclosed in asterisks when displayed. This is done by setting the checked property on the menu item, as in line 110, and by adding a little code to the menu item's event handler, `ActiveMenu_Selection`.

The `ActiveMenu_Selection` event handler is in lines 73 to 83. There is nothing new in this routine, but a few lines are worth reviewing. As with other event handlers, this method receives an object as its first argument. Because this event was caused by a menu selection, you know this object actually contains a `MenuItem`. In lines 75 and 76, a temporary `MenuItem` variable is created and the argument is cast to this temporary variable. This temporary variable, `tmp`, can then be used to access all `MenuItem` properties and methods.

You also know that this event was activated by the Active menu selection. In line 78, you check to see whether the Checked property of the Active menu item is true and thus checked. If it is, you uncheck it in line 79 by setting the Checked property to false. If it wasn't checked, you set the Checked property to true. The result of this method is that it toggles the Active menu's check on and off.

The `MenuUpdate` event handler has also been modified in this listing. This event handler displays the current date if the active menu item is checked. If it isn't checked, the current date and time value is enclosed in asterisks and redisplayed. The main point of this event handler is not what is being displayed. Rather, it is that the checked menu item can be used to determine what should occur.

## Creating a Pop-Up Menu

In addition to the standard menus you have seen up to this point, you can also create pop-up menus. Listing 17.7 presents a pop-up menu that is displayed by pressing the right mouse button (see Figure 17.8).

**LISTING 17.7** popup.cs—Using a Pop-Up Menu

```
// popup.cs - popup menus
//-----------------------------------------------------------------

using System;
using System.Windows.Forms;
using System.Drawing;

public class frmApp : Form
{
   private ContextMenu myPopUp;

   public frmApp()
   {
      InitializeComponent();
   }

   private void InitializeComponent()
   {
      this.Text = "STY Pop-up Menu";
      this.StartPosition = FormStartPosition.CenterScreen;

      CreatePopUp();
   }

   protected void PopUp_Selection( object sender, System.EventArgs e)
   {
      // Determine menu item and do logic...
      this.Text = ((MenuItem) sender).Text;
   }

   private void CreatePopUp()
   {
      myPopUp = new ContextMenu();

      myPopUp.MenuItems.Add("First Item",
                      new EventHandler(this.PopUp_Selection));
```

**LISTING 17.7** continued

```
37:
38:          myPopUp.MenuItems.Add("Second Item",
39:                               new EventHandler(this.PopUp_Selection));
40:
41:          myPopUp.MenuItems.Add("-");
42:
43:          myPopUp.MenuItems.Add("Third Item",
44:                               new EventHandler(this.PopUp_Selection));
45:
46:          this.ContextMenu = myPopUp;
47:
48:       }
49:
50:       public static void Main( string[] args )
51:       {
52:          Application.Run( new frmApp() );
53:       }
54:    }
```

**OUTPUT**

**FIGURE 17.8**
*A custom pop-up menu.*

**ANALYSIS** Rather than creating a `MainMenu` object, to create a popup menu, you create a `ContextMenu` item. This is done in Listing 17.7 in line 33, where `myPopUp` is instantiated as a `ContextMenu`. `myPopUp` was declared as a variable in line 10.

You can add items to a `ContextMenu` the same way you add them to a `MainMenu`—by using the `MenuItems.Add` method. In this listing, four items are added to this menu. The first, second, and fourth items are added the way you've seen before. The third item in line 41 is the unique one. In line 41, it appears that a single dash is being added to the menu. However, adding a single dash actually creates a line across the menu. You can see this in the output in Figure 17.8. When the items are all added to the `ContextMenu` item, `myPopUp`, the menu is added as a `ContextMenu` to the current form.

You should also notice that all three of the actual menu items use the same event handler, `PopUp_Selection`. This event handler is defined in lines 25 to 29, with the actual functionality contained on line 28. Line 28 assigns a new value to the `Text` property of the current form. Remember, the `Text` property is the title on the form. The value assigned is the `Text` of the object that called the event handler. This will be the text of the menu item that was selected. The code in line 28 casts the sender object to a `MenuItem` and then uses the text value of this `MenuItem`. This is a shortcut way of doing the same thing that was done in lines 75 to 76 of the previous listing.

# Displaying Pop-Up Dialogs and Forms

You now know how to display controls and menus on your forms. You have also learned to create event handlers to react to events that occur on your forms. The one procedure that has been missing from the examples shown so far is the displaying of another dialog box or form.

The following sections cover three topics related to displaying a new form or dialog. First, you use the basic functionality of the `MessageBox` class. Then you explore a few dialogs that exist in Microsoft Windows. Finally, you learn about creating your own dialog form, which is not nearly the same as using the custom dialogs.

## The `MessageBox` Class

A class that is often used when doing windows programming is a message box class. A message box class is defined in the Base Class Libraries (BCL) as well. This class enables you to display a message in a pop-up box. Listing 17.8 uses the `MessageBox` class to pop up messages. You can see this by the output in Figures 17.9–17.12.

**LISTING 17.8** msgbox.cs—Using the `MessageBox` Class

```
// msgbox.cs - Using the MessageBox class
//-----------------------------------------------------------------------

using System;
using System.Windows.Forms;
using System.Drawing;

public class frmApp : Form
{
   private ContextMenu myPopUp;

   public frmApp()
   {
      MessageBox.Show( "You have started the application.", "Status");
      InitializeComponent();
      CreatePopUp();
```

**LISTING 17.8** continued

```
        MessageBox.Show( "Form has been initialized.", "Status");
     }

     private void InitializeComponent()
     {
        this.Text = "STY C# Pop-up Menu";
        this.StartPosition = FormStartPosition.CenterScreen;
     }

     protected void PopUp_Selection( object sender, System.EventArgs e)
     {
       // Determine menu item and do logic...
       MessageBox.Show( ((MenuItem) sender).Text, this.Text + " Msg Box");
     }

     private void CreatePopUp()
     {
       myPopUp = new ContextMenu();

       myPopUp.MenuItems.Add("First Item",
                           new EventHandler(this.PopUp_Selection));
       myPopUp.MenuItems.Add("Second Item",
                           new EventHandler(this.PopUp_Selection));
       myPopUp.MenuItems.Add("-");
       myPopUp.MenuItems.Add("Third Item",
                           new EventHandler(this.PopUp_Selection));

       this.ContextMenu = myPopUp;
     }

     public static void Main( string[] args )
     {
       Application.Run( new frmApp() );
       MessageBox.Show( "You are done with the application", "Status");

     }
  }
```



**OUTPUT**

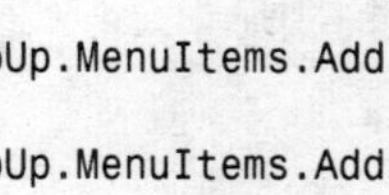


**FIGURE 17.9**
*A message box displayed at the start of this program.*

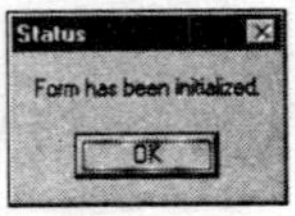


**FIGURE 17.10**

*A message box displayed when the form has completed its initialization.*

**FIGURE 17.11**

*A message box displayed by selecting an item from the context menu.*

**FIGURE 17.12**

*A message box displayed at the end of the program.*

**ANALYSIS** This listing uses a `MessageBox` object to display a message at a number of different times throughout the program's execution.

The basic usage of the `MessageBox` class enables you to display a text string within a dialog box containing an OK button. You can also specify the title that will appear in the dialog. Listing 17.8 uses a number of message boxes. The first is called in the constructor at line 14. Two parameters are used with this basic call to the `Show` method of `MessageBox`. The first is the message that will be displayed in the dialog. The second argument is the title of the dialog box. You can see that this is true by comparing the code in line 14 to the dialog presented in Figure 17.9. The dialog box in line 14 is displayed immediately.

Lines 15 and 16 initialize the application's main form and set up a pop-up menu. This is followed by another message box, which indicates that the initialization has been completed. This message box is the second that displayed.

When the OK button is pressed in the second message box, the constructor code (`frmApp()`) concludes and the application's main form is displayed. This form is an empty form that contains a menu that pops up with a right click of the mouse. When you select an item from this menu, the `PopUp_Selection` event handler in lines 26 to 30 is called. This event handler calls the message box class regardless of which item was selected.

Figure 17.12 shows the final message box that is displayed when you exit this program. This dialog results from the `MessageBox.Show` call in line 50, and it doesn't display until after the main form has exited.

## Preexisting Dialogs You Can Use in Microsoft Windows

In addition to the `MessageBox` class, there are a number of more complex dialog boxes that have been defined. The following are useful dialogs:

- Color selection dialog (`ColorDialog`)
- Print preview dialog (`PrintPreviewDialog`)
- Fonts dialog(`FontDialog`)
- File open dialog(`OpenFileDialog`)
- File save dialog(`SaveFileDialog`)

These dialogs are within the BCL. Listing 17.9 shows how easy it is to incorporate the basic features of these dialogs into your list, as shown in Figures 17.13–17.15.

**LISTING 17.9** canned.cs—Using Some of the Canned Dialogs

```
// canned.cs - using existing dialogs
//-----------------------------------------------------------------

using System;
using System.Windows.Forms;
using System.Drawing;

public class frmApp : Form
{
   private MainMenu myMainMenu;

   public frmApp()
   {
      InitializeComponent();
   }

   private void InitializeComponent()
   {
      this.Text = "Canned Dialogs";
      this.StartPosition = FormStartPosition.CenterScreen;
      this.FormBorderStyle = FormBorderStyle.Sizable;
      this.Width = 400;
```

**LISTING 17.9** continued

```

      myMainMenu = new MainMenu();

      MenuItem menuitemFile = myMainMenu.MenuItems.Add("&File");
      menuitemFile.MenuItems.Add(new MenuItem("Colors Dialog",
                                 new EventHandler(this.Menu_Selection)));
      menuitemFile.MenuItems.Add(new MenuItem("Fonts Dialog",
                                 new EventHandler(this.Menu_Selection)));
      menuitemFile.MenuItems.Add(new MenuItem("Print Preview Dialog",
                                 new EventHandler(this.Menu_Selection)));
      menuitemFile.MenuItems.Add("-");
      menuitemFile.MenuItems.Add(new MenuItem("Exit",
                                 new EventHandler(this.Menu_Selection)));
      this.Menu = myMainMenu;
   }

   protected void Menu_Selection( object sender, System.EventArgs e )
   {
      switch (((MenuItem) sender).Text )
      {
        case "Exit":
             Application.Exit();
             break;

        case "Colors Dialog":
             ColorDialog myColorDialog = new ColorDialog();
             myColorDialog.ShowDialog();
             break;

        case "Fonts Dialog":
             FontDialog myFontDialog = new FontDialog();
             myFontDialog.ShowDialog();
             break;

        case "Print Preview Dialog":
             PrintPreviewDialog myPrintDialog =
                                   new PrintPreviewDialog();
             myPrintDialog.ShowDialog();
             break;

        default:
             MessageBox.Show("DEFAULT", "PopUp");
             break;
      }
   }

   public static void Main( string[] args )
   {
      Application.Run( new frmApp() );
   }
}
```

**OUTPUT**

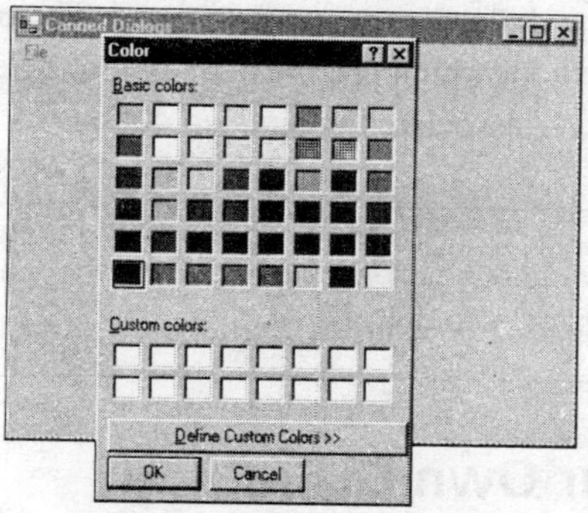


**FIGURE 17.13**

*Displaying the basic color dialog.*

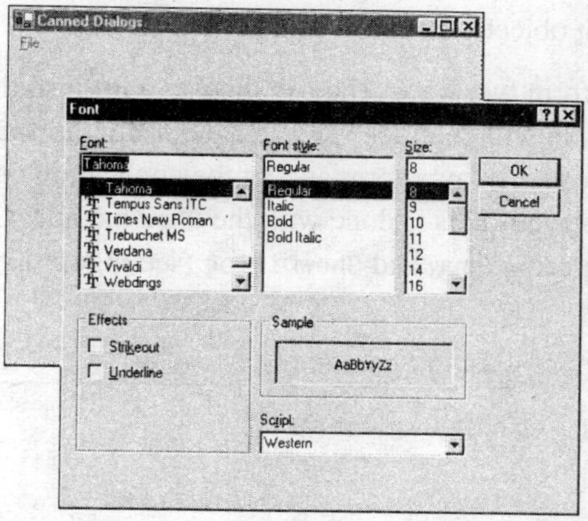


**FIGURE 17.14**

*Displaying the basic font dialog.*



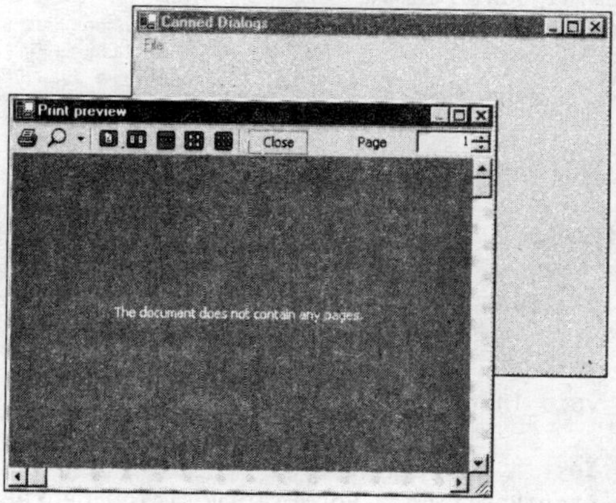


**FIGURE 17.15**

*Displaying the print preview dialog.*

**ANALYSIS** This listing uses functionality that has been presented in earlier listings to display the dialogs. A File menu has been added to the form. This menu contains items for displaying three dialogs. Each of these dialogs is displayed in the same manner. A new object of the dialog's type is instantiated. The object is then displayed by calling the `ShowDialog` method, which presents the dialog. Selecting each of the menu options provides you with the associated precreated dialog.

**Note** To learn more about customizing and using the features of these dialogs, check the online help documents.

## Popping Up Your Own Dialog

You also can create your own dialogs. You do this in the same way you create your base form: define a form object, add controls, and then display it.

You can display a form two ways. You can display a form so that it must be responded to before the application will continue. This is done using the `ShowDialog` method. Alternatively, you can display a form and let the application continue or let other forms continue to be displayed. This is done with the `Show` method. Listing 17.10 illustrates the difference between using `Show` and `ShowDialog` (see Figure 17.16).

**LISTING 17.10** myform.cs—Using `Show` Versus `ShowDialog`

```
// myform.cs - displaying subforms
//-----------------------------------------------------------------

using System;
using System.Windows.Forms;
using System.Drawing;

public class frmApp : Form
{
   private MainMenu myMainMenu;

   public frmApp()
   {
      InitializeComponent();
   }

   private void InitializeComponent()
   {
      this.Text = "Canned Dialogs";
      this.StartPosition = FormStartPosition.CenterScreen;
      this.FormBorderStyle = FormBorderStyle.Sizable;
      this.Width = 400;

      myMainMenu = new MainMenu();
```

**LISTING 17.10** continued

```

      MenuItem menuitemFile = myMainMenu.MenuItems.Add("&File");
      menuitemFile.MenuItems.Add(new MenuItem("My Form",
                                 new EventHandler(this.Menu_Selection)));
      menuitemFile.MenuItems.Add(new MenuItem("My Other Form",
                                 new EventHandler(this.Menu_Selection)));
      menuitemFile.MenuItems.Add("-");
      menuitemFile.MenuItems.Add(new MenuItem("Exit",
                                 new EventHandler(this.Menu_Selection)));
      this.Menu = myMainMenu;
   }

   protected void Menu_Selection( object sender, System.EventArgs e )
   {
      switch (((MenuItem) sender).Text )
      {
        case "Exit":
             Application.Exit();
             break;

        case "My Form":
             subForm aForm = new subForm();
             aForm.Text = "A Show form";
             aForm.Show();
             break;

        case "My Other Form":
             subForm bForm = new subForm();
             bForm.Text = "A ShowDialog form";
             bForm.ShowDialog();
             break;

        default:
             MessageBox.Show("DEFAULT", "PopUp");
             break;
      }
   }

   public static void Main( string[] args )
   {
      Application.Run( new frmApp() );
   }
}


public class subForm : Form
{
   private MainMenu mySubMainMenu;
```

**LISTING 17.10** continued

```
      
   public subForm()
   {
      InitializeComponent();
   }

   private void InitializeComponent()
   {
      this.Text = "My sub-form";
      this.StartPosition = FormStartPosition.CenterScreen;
      this.FormBorderStyle = FormBorderStyle.FixedDialog;
      this.Width = 300;
      this.Height = 250;

      mySubMainMenu = new MainMenu();

      MenuItem menuitemFile = mySubMainMenu.MenuItems.Add("&File");
      menuitemFile.MenuItems.Add(new MenuItem("Close",
                              new EventHandler(this.CloseMenu_Selection)));
      this.Menu = mySubMainMenu;
   }

   protected void CloseMenu_Selection( object sender, System.EventArgs e )
   {
      this.Close();
   }
}
```

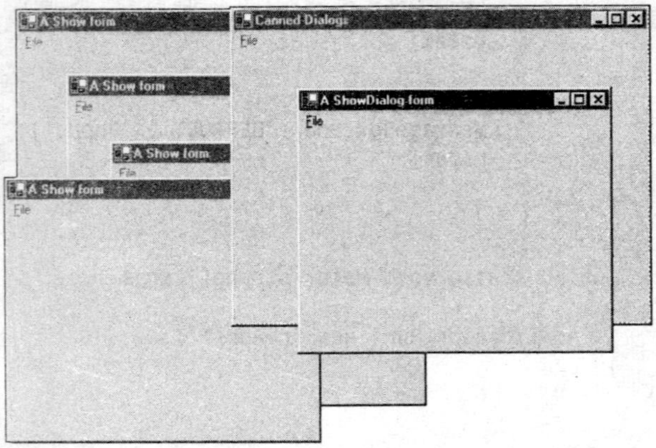


**FIGURE 17.16**
*Only one* ShowDialog *form can be displayed at a time, but multiple* Show *forms can be displayed.*

**ANALYSIS** When you run this program, you will find that you can create multiple ShowDialog forms. You can even change focus between them and the main application form. When you create a `ShowDialog` form, you cannot do anything else in this program until you close it.

**Note** A form that must be responded to before giving up focus is called *modal*.

# Summary

Today's lesson ended up being among the longest in the book; however, you saw a lot of code. Today you expanded on what you learned yesterday regarding the creation of windows based development. While the information covered today is not a part of the ECMA standard C# language, it is applicable to programming on Microsoft's Windows. Other platforms supporting .NET will most likely have similar—if not the same—functionality.

Today's lesson started with coverage of two more controls, radio buttons and list boxes. You learned how to group controls with the group box. Additionally, you learned how to add both main menus and context (popup) menus to your applications. Creating an application with multiple forms and dialogs was also displayed. Not only did you learn to use the message box dialog, you also learned how to create your own dialogs or to use pre-existing dialogs.

The two days of windows coverage were not intended to be complete coverage. You do, however, have a foundation for beginning to develop windows-based applications.

# Q&A

**Q How important was the information learned today and yesterday if I use a tool such as Visual Studio or Microsoft Visual C#?**

**A** The graphical IDEs will do a lot of the coding for you. For example, using Visual Studio, you can drag and drop controls onto a form and set properties by using a dialog within the tool. This makes it very easy to create dialogs. Yesterday's and today's lessons help you understand the code these tools are creating for you. By understanding generated code, you can better understand your programs and how they operate.

**Q Isn't there a lot more to learn about windows programming?**

**A** Yesterday and today barely scratched the surface of windows-based programming, but they do give you a solid foundation from which to start such programming.

**Q Is what I learned yesterday and today portable to other platforms?**

**A** Because all of the routines presented are a part of the base class libraries, it is hoped that they will be ported to new platforms. In reality, these classes were not all part of the ECMA standard created for C#, so there is no guarantee that these window classes or control classes will be converted to other platforms. I believe there is a good chance they will be ported.

# Workshop

The Workshop provides quiz questions to help you solidify your understanding of the material covered and exercises to provide you with experience in using what you've learned. Try to understand the quiz and exercise answers before continuing to the next day's lesson. Answers are provided in Appendix A, "Answers."

## Quiz

1. What class can be used to create a radio button control?
2. What namespace contains controls such as radio buttons and list boxes?
3. How do you set the tab order for a form's controls?
4. What are the steps involved in adding items to a list box?
5. What is the difference between a `MainMenu` and a `ContextMenu` item?
6. What is an easy way to display a dialog with a simple message in a simple dialog?
7. What are some of the preexisting dialogs you can use from the base class library?
8. If you want to display a form and not allow any other forms to be displayed or activated in the same application, what method should you use?
9. How many forms can be displayed with the `Show` method at the same time?

## Exercises

1. Write the code to add two radio buttons called `butn1` and `butn2` to a group box called `grpbox`.
2. What code would you use to add a line to the `MYMENU` menu?
3. Create an application that uses the `ColorDialog` form. Set the background of your main form to the color returned from the `ColorDialog` form you display. The color returned is stored in the `Color` property. *Hint:* Create a variable of type `ColorDialog`. When you return from calling the dialog, the selected color should be in the `Color` property.

4. **BUG BUSTER:** Does the following code have a problem? If so, what is it?

```
using System;
using System.Windows.Forms;
using System.Drawing;

public class frmApp : Form
{
    private Label myDateLabel;
    private MainMenu myMainMenu;

    public frmApp()
    {
        this.Text = "STY Menus";
        this.FormBorderStyle = FormBorderStyle.Fixed3D;

        myDateLabel = new Label();       // Create label

        DateTime currDate = new DateTime();
        currDate = DateTime.Now;
        myDateLabel.Text = currDate.ToString();
        myDateLabel.AutoSize = true;
        myDateLabel.Location = new Point( 50, 70);
        myDateLabel.BackColor = this.BackColor;
        this.Controls.Add(myDateLabel);  // Add label to form
        this.Width = (myDateLabel.PreferredWidth + 100);

        CreateMyMenu();
    }

    protected void MenuUpdate_Selection( object sender,
➥System.EventArgs e)
    {
        DateTime currDate;
        currDate = DateTime.Now;
        this.myDateLabel.Text = currDate.ToString();
    }

    protected void FileExit_Selection( object sender, System.EventArgs
e)
    {
       this.Close();
    }

    public void CreateMyMenu()
    {
       myMainMenu = new MainMenu();

       MenuItem menuitemFile = myMainMenu.MenuItems.Add("&File");
       menuitemFile.MenuItems.Add(new MenuItem("Update &Date",
```

```
                                      new
➥EventHandler(this.MenuUpdate_Selection),
                                      Shortcut.CtrlH));
         menuitemFile.MenuItems.Add(new MenuItem("E&xit",
                                      new
➥EventHandler(this.FileExit_Selection),
                                      Shortcut.CtrlX));
         this.Menu = myMainMenu;
      }

      public static void Main( string[] args )
      {
         Application.Run( new frmApp() );
      }
   }
```

5. **ON YOUR OWN:** Create an application that contains a menu. The menu should display a dialog that contains a number of controls including an OK button.
6. Modify Listing 17.6 to include an `About` dialog.

# WEEK 3

# DAY 18

# Web Development

Over the last couple of days you have learned about creating applications that use windows forms. If you are building applications for the Internet, or more specifically, the Web, you might not be able to use windows-based forms that use the `System.Windows.Forms` namespace. Rather, you might want to take advantage of the Web's capability of working with numerous different systems by using general standards, such as HTML and XML. Today, you

- Learn the basics about Web services
- Create a simple Web service using C#
- Understand how to generate a proxy file for using a Web service
- Use your Web service from a client program
- Obtain an overview of what Web forms are
- Evaluate some of the basic controls used in Web forms
- Discover the differences between server and client controls
- Create a basic Web form application

**Caution**

The topic of today's lesson—Web Development—could fill an entire book on its own. To avoid adding a large number of pages to today's lesson, I am going to make some assumptions. If you don't fit all these assumptions, don't fret—you will still find lots of value in the concepts and code presented in today's lessons.

My assumptions are

- In the Web Services section, it is assumed you have access to a Web server or a Web service provider that can host Web services written to the .NET runtime.
- You are familiar with basic Web development concepts, including the use of HTML and basic client-side scripting.
- You are using a computer that has a Web server running that supports Active Server Pages and ASP.NET (such as Microsoft Internet Information Server—IIS).
- Your Web server is set up with the standard Inetpub/wwwroot directory. Today's lesson references this directory as the base directory or root directory of your Web server. If you know how to set up virtual directories, you can use those as well.

# Creating Web Applications

There are two types of Web applications that are going to be covered in today's lesson: Web services and Web forms. Each of these types has its own use and its own applications. Let's start with Web services.

# The Concept of a Component

**NEW TERM** Before tackling the concept of a Web service, it is worth looking at the concept of components. A *component* is a piece of software that has a well-defined interface, hidden internals, and the capability of being discovered. By "discovered," I mean that you can determine what the component does without needing to see the code within it. In a lot of ways, a component is similar to a method. It can be called with arguments that fit a set of parameters, and it has the capability of returning results.

# Web Services

**NEW TERM** The use of methods as components has been moved to the Web. A Web component can be referred to as a Web service. A *Web service* is a component that performs a function or service. A Web service may also return information to the caller. This service resides somewhere on the Web and can be accessed from other locations on the Web. For this service to be called, there are a number of elements that must be in place. First, the caller must know how to call the service. Second, the call must be made across the Web. Finally, the Web service must know how to respond. Figure 18.1 illustrates the Web service process.

**FIGURE 18.1**
*Web services.*

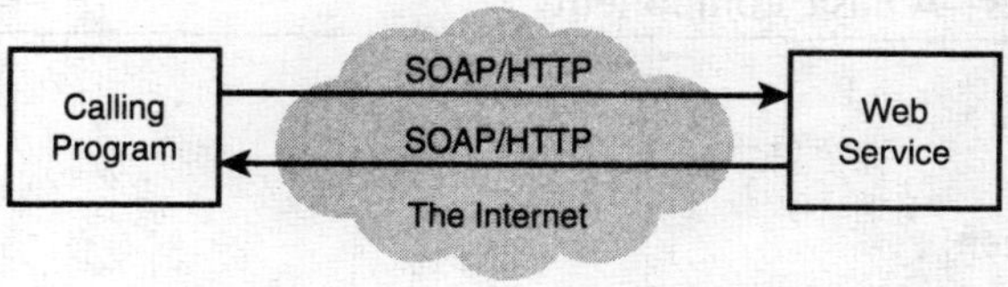


In the figure, the Simple Object Access Protocol (SOAP) has been created to communicate between a program and a Web service. SOAP is a standardized way of formatting information about method calls and data. This formatting is based on the XML standard. Using SOAP, a program can communicate to a Web service and the Web service can communicate back.

The calling program can be a C# program or a program written in any other programming language. Additionally, the calling program can be a browser or even another Web service, and the Web service can be written in C# or any other language. Because a standardized protocol—SOAP—is being used, the calling program is able to interact with the Web service and vice versa.



**Note** Although understanding SOAP is valuable, it is not critical for creating Web services.

There are three basic steps to setting up a Web service and using it:

1. Create the actual Web service.
2. Create a program to use the service.
3. Create a file that can help your program call the service. This helper program is called a *Web proxy*.

**NEW TERM**

You'll learn about creating each of these three parts in the following sections.

## Creating a Simple Component

Before creating a Web service, you create a simple class. This class will then be used as the basis of your first Web service. This class will be compiled as a routine within a library. Listing 18.1 contains the simple routine that will be used.

**LISTING 18.1** Calc.cs—A Basic Component

```
1:  // Calc.cs
2:  //-----------------------------------
3:
4:  using System;
5:
6:  public class Calc
7:  {
8:     public static int Add( int x, int y )
9:     {
10:       return x + y;
11:    }
12:    public static int Subtract( int x, int y )
13:    {
14:       return x - y;
15:    }
16: }
```

**ANALYSIS** To make this an external class that you can call, you need to compile the listing as a library. You create a library by targeting the output as a library. This is done by using `library` with the command-line target flag:

```
csc /t:library Calc.cs
```

The result is a file called Calc.dll instead of Calc.exe.

Looking at the listing, you see that the component will contain two methods in a class called `Calc`. `Add` in lines 8 to 11 will add two numbers. `Subtract` in lines 12 to 15 will return the difference of two numbers. Listing 18.2 presents a routine that can use these methods.

**LISTING 18.2** main.cs—Using `Add` and `Subtract`

```
// main.cs
// Calling a component
//------------------------------

using System;

```

**LISTING 18.2** continued

```
public class myApp
{
    public static void Main()
    {
        Console.WriteLine("Using Calc component");
        Console.WriteLine("Calc.Add( 11, 33); = {0}",
                                Calc.Add(33, 11));
        Console.WriteLine("Calc.Subtract(33, 11); = {0}",
                                Calc.Subtract(33,11));

    }
}
```

**OUTPUT**

```
Using Calc component
Calc.Add( 11, 33); = 44
Calc.Subtract(33, 11); = 22
```

**ANALYSIS** If you compile this routine the normal way:

```
csc main.cs
```

you get an error saying a type or namespace could not be found. As you learned earlier in this book, you need to include a reference to the component you will be using—in this case `Calc`. Compile the main listing by including a reference to the file with the component you created in Listing 18.1. This is done by using the reference compile flag:



```
csc /r:Calc.dll main.cs
```

The `/r:` is the reference flag. It tells the compiler to include the identified file, Calc.dll. The result is that main.cs will be able to use the classes and methods in Calc.dll.

Looking at the code in Listing 18.2, you can see that there is nothing different from what you have done before. The `Main` routine makes calls to the classes that are available. Because you included the Calc.dll in your compile command, the `Calc` class and its `Add` and `Subtract` methods are available.

## Creating a Web Service

The `Calc` class and its methods are nice, but the example in Listings 18.1 and 18.2 are for a class located on a local machine. A Web service uses a component across the Web. You want to have the `Calc` methods operate as Web services so that they will be accessible across the Web by any Web-based application. This obviously adds complexity to the use of the class.

To create a Web service based on the `Calc` class, you need to make some changes. Listing 18.3 presents the `Calc` routine as a Web service.

**LISTING 18.3** WebCalc.asmx—Using `Calc`

```
1:  <%@WebService Language="C#" Class="Calc"%>
2:
3:  //----------------------------------
4:  // WebCalc.asmx
5:  //----------------------------------
6:
7:  using System;
8:  using System.Web.Services;
9:
10: public class Calc : WebService
11: {
12:    [WebMethod]
13:    public int Add( int x, int y )
14:    {
15:       return x + y;
16:    }
17:
18:    [WebMethod]
19:    public int Subtract( int x, int y )
20:    {
21:       return x - y;
22:    }
23: }
```

**ANALYSIS** Several changes were made to this listing to make it a Web service. As you can see by glancing at the listing, none of these changes were major.

The first change is in the name of the file. Instead of ending with a .cs extension, a Web service always ends with an .asmx extension. This extension is a signal to the runtime and to a browser that this is a Web service.

The first coding change is in line 1—a line with lots of weird stuff:

```
<%@WebService Language="C#" Class="Calc"%>
```

The `<%@` and `%>` are indicators to the Web server. The Web server will see that this is a Web service written in the language `C#`. It will also know that the primary routine is called `Calc`. Because the language is specified as C#, the server will know to read the rest of the file as C# and not as some other language.

When this service is first called, it will be compiled. You will not need to do the actual compile yourself. The Web server will call based on the language specified in the `Language=` command.

The next change you will see is the inclusion of the `System.Web.Service` namespace in line 8. This is included so that the use of `WebMethod` and `WebService` can be done without explicitly including the namespace name throughout the rest of the listing.

In line 10, the `Calc` class is derived from `WebService`. This gives your class the Web service traits as defined within the .NET framework.

The only remaining change is to identify each of the methods that you want to have available to anyone accessing your service. These are identified by including `[WebMethod]` before the method, as has been done in lines 12 and 18.

That's it. This is a Web service that is ready to go!

**Note**

If you are using Visual Studio .NET, you have the option to create a Web service project. This project provides you with the basic infrastructure for a Web service. Like many other Visual Studio .NET projects, it includes a lot of additional code.

**Caution**

Because a Web service is accessed across the Web, and because a Web service could be called from any platform, you should avoid using a graphical user interface (GUI) within a Web service.

18

In the following sections, you learn how to create a proxy and how to call your Web service. You probably can't wait to see your Web service in action—and you don't have to.

If you are running a Web server such as Microsoft's IIS, you will have a directory on your machine called Inetpub. This directory will have a subdirectory called wwwroot. You can copy your Web service (WebCalc.asmx) to this directory.

When your new Web service is in that directory, you can call it by using your browser. You use the following address to call the WebCalc.asmx service:

```
http://localhost/WebCalc.asmx
```

When you use this address, you get a page similar to the page in Figure 18.2. If you have an error in your Web service, you might get a different page, indicating the error.

Looking at this page, you can see that a lot of information is displayed regarding your Web service. Most important is that this page lists the two operations that can be performed, `Add` and `Subtract`. These are the two methods from your Web services class.

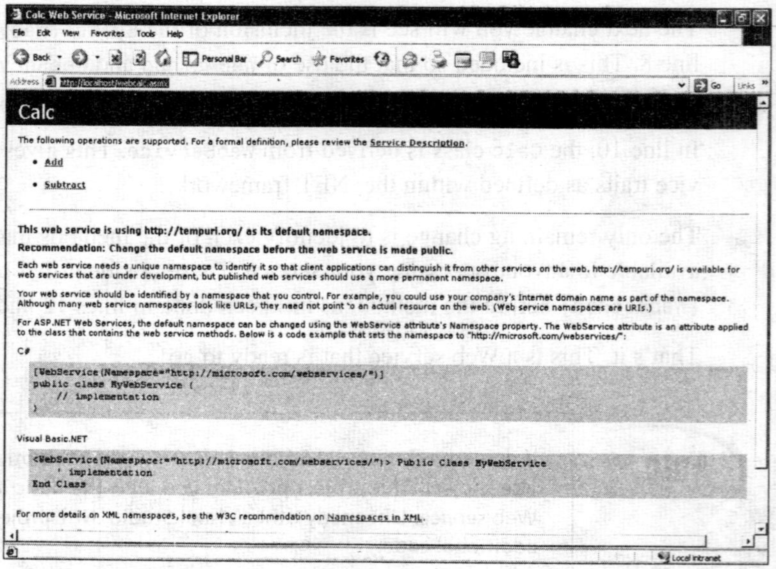


**FIGURE 18.2**
*The WebCalc.asmx Web service displayed in Internet Explorer.*

If you click on either of these methods, you are taken to a second screen (see Figure 18.3), which enables you to enter the parameters that your method expects.

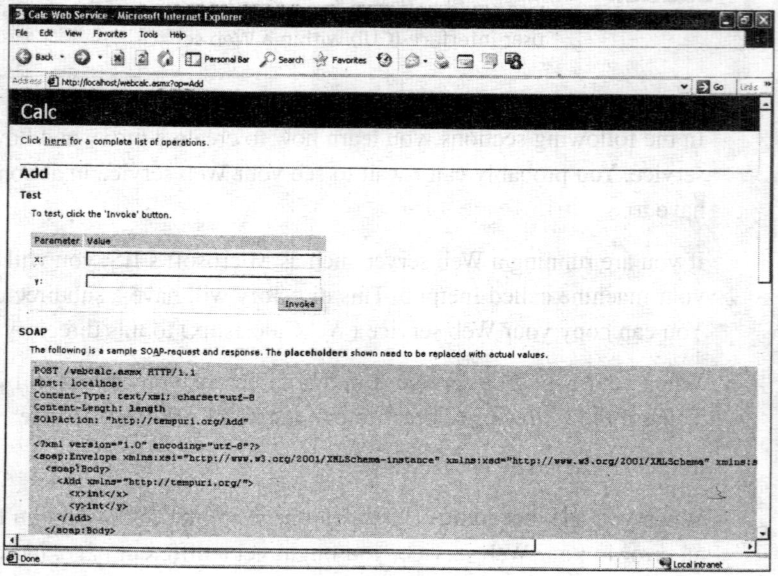


**FIGURE 18.3**
*The* `Add` *method within the Web service.*

In the case of the `Add` method, two parameters are expected: `x` and `y`. This matches your code in Listing 18.3. If you enter the values of `5` and `10`, as you did in Listing 18.2, you will see the result:

```
<?xml version="1.0" encoding="utf-8" ?>
<int xmlns="http://tempuri.org/">15</int>
```

The result of 15 is in there, but so is a bunch of other stuff! The other stuff is the SOAP information needed to send the information back to the calling routine.

## Creating a Proxy

The previous section showed you how to see your Web service in action by using your browser on your local machine; however, it is more likely that you will want to use the service from another program. To do this, you need to set up a Web proxy.

As mentioned earlier, this proxy will help your local program know where on the Web to find the Web service. It will also contain the details for communicating to the Web service (the SOAP stuff).

Writing a proxy can be a lot of work; however, there are utilities to help make this easier. One such utility is wsdl.exe, provided by Microsoft in its framework. This command-line tool can be run using the following parameters:

```
wsdl webservice_file?wsdl /out:proxyfile
```

where `wsdl` is the name of the utility you are executing and *`webservice_file`* is the name and location of your Web service file. The Web service name is followed by `?wsdl`, which indicates that this is to generate a file using the `wsdl` standard. For the `Calc` programming example, this is currently on your `localhost` server; this could easily be on a different server, in which case this would be the URL to the service.



The `/out:` flag is optional and is used to give your proxy a name. If you don't use the `/out:` flag, your proxy will be named the same as your service. I suggest adding `proxy` to the name of your proxy. The following line creates the proxy file for the `webcalc.asmx` service and places it in the `inetpub\wwwroot\` directory with the name of `calcproxy.cs`:

```
wsdl http://localhost/WebCalc.asmx?wsdl /out:c:\inetpub\wwwroot\calcproxy.cs
```

The proxy file has a .cs extension, which means it is C# code that can be compiled. Listing 18.4 contains the code that was generated by `wsdl` using the WebCalc.asmx file you created earlier (no line numbers are provided).

**LISTING 18.4** calcproxy.cs—Generated Code from `wsdl`

```
//------------------------------------------------------------------------------
// <autogenerated>
//     This code was generated by a tool.
```

**LISTING 18.4** continued

```
//     Runtime Version: 1.0.2914.16
//
//     Changes to this file may cause incorrect behavior and will be lost if
//     the code is regenerated.
// </autogenerated>
//------------------------------------------------------------------------------

//
// This source code was auto-generated by wsdl, Version=1.0.2914.16.
//
using System.Diagnostics;
using System.Xml.Serialization;
using System;
using System.Web.Services.Protocols;
using System.Web.Services;


[System.Web.Services.WebServiceBindingAttribute(Name="CalcSoap",
            Namespace="http://tempuri.org/")]
public class Calc : System.Web.Services.Protocols.SoapHttpClientProtocol {

    [System.Diagnostics.DebuggerStepThroughAttribute()]
    public Calc() {
        this.Url = "http://localhost/WebCalc.asmx";
    }

    [System.Diagnostics.DebuggerStepThroughAttribute()]
    [System.Web.Services.Protocols.SoapDocumentMethodAttribute(
        "http://tempuri.org/Add",
        Use=System.Web.Services.Description.SoapBindingUse.Literal,
        ParameterStyle=
           System.Web.Services.Protocols.SoapParameterStyle.Wrapped)]
    public int Add(int x, int y) {
        object[] results = this.Invoke("Add", new object[] {
                    x,
                    y});
        return ((int)(results[0]));
    }

    [System.Diagnostics.DebuggerStepThroughAttribute()]
    public System.IAsyncResult BeginAdd(int x, int y, System.AsyncCallback
                callback, object asyncState) {
        return this.BeginInvoke("Add", new object[] {
                    x,
                    y}, callback, asyncState);

    }

    [System.Diagnostics.DebuggerStepThroughAttribute()]
```

**LISTING 18.4** continued

```
    public int EndAdd(System.IAsyncResult asyncResult) {
        object[] results = this.EndInvoke(asyncResult);
        return ((int)(results[0]));
    }

    [System.Diagnostics.DebuggerStepThroughAttribute()]
    [System.Web.Services.Protocols.SoapDocumentMethodAttribute(
        "http://tempuri.org/Subtract",
        Use=System.Web.Services.Description.SoapBindingUse.Literal,
        ParameterStyle=
            System.Web.Services.Protocols.SoapParameterStyle.Wrapped)]
    public int Subtract(int x, int y) {
        object[] results = this.Invoke("Subtract", new object[] {
                    x,
                    y});
        return ((int)(results[0]));
    }

    [System.Diagnostics.DebuggerStepThroughAttribute()]
    public System.IAsyncResult BeginSubtract(int x, int y,
            System.AsyncCallback callback, object asyncState) {
        return this.BeginInvoke("Subtract", new object[] {
                    x,
                    y}, callback, asyncState);
    }

    [System.Diagnostics.DebuggerStepThroughAttribute()]
    public int EndSubtract(System.IAsyncResult asyncResult) {
        object[] results = this.EndInvoke(asyncResult);
        return ((int)(results[0]));
    }
}
```

It is beyond the scope of this book to explain the code in this listing. The important thing to note is that it takes care of the SOAP stuff for you. Before you can use it, however, you need to compile it. As you've done before, you need to compile this listing as a library. Remember, this is done using the target flag (`/t:library`):

```
csc /t:library calcproxy.cs
```

The result is a file called calcproxy.dll that you will use with the programs that call your Web service.

## Calling a Web Service

The final step for using a Web service is to create the program that will call the service. Listing 18.5 presents a simple program that can use the `WebCalc` service.

**LISTING 18.5** WebClient.csClient to Use `WebCalc`.

```
 1:  // WebClient.cs
 2:  // Calling a Web service
 3:  //-----------------------------
 4:
 5:  using System;
 6:
 7:  public class myApp
 8:  {
 9:     public static void Main()
10:     {
11:        Calc cSrv = new Calc();
12:
13:        Console.WriteLine("cSrv.Add( 11, 33); = {0}",
14:                                cSrv.Add(33, 11));
15:        Console.WriteLine("cSrv.Subtract(33, 11); = {0}",
16:                                cSrv.Subtract(33,11));
17:     }
18:  }
```

**OUTPUT**

```
cSrv.Add( 11, 33); = 44
cSrv.Subtract(33, 11); = 22
```

**ANALYSIS** When you compile this listing, you need to include a reference to the proxy file you previously compiled. You do this the same way you include any library, with the `/r:` flag:

```
csc /r:calcproxy.dll WebClient.cs
```

After it's compiled, you have a program that can use the Web proxy (via the calcproxy program you generated) to access the Web service you created (WebCalc.cs). You can see in Listing 18.5 that using the Web service is very easy. In line 11, you create a `Calc` object called `cSrv`. This is then used to call the methods within the service. In reality, this is the same as if you were using a local library. The difference is that you created and used the Web proxy file that took care of connecting to the `Calc` routines on the Web server.

**Note** You could move the WebCalc.asmx file to a different Web server. You would then need to create a new proxy file and recompile your local program.

# Creating Regular Web Applications

The second type of Web application that was promised to be covered today is Web forms. Web forms are different from Web services. As a technology, Web forms are closer to window forms and the standard applications that you are used to. A Web form is a building block to build dynamic Web sites.

A Web form application is not created as a file with a .cs extension. Rather, it is created as a part of ASP.NET. ASP.NET stands for Active Server Pages *dot* Net, or Active Server Pages for *dot* Net. As such, Web form applications end with an .aspx extension.

ASP.NET applications, and thus Web forms, are applications that an end user sees from within a browser. These applications can use any general markup language, such as HTML. Additionally, they can be viewed in any standard browser. Most importantly, they can use programming code that can be executed on a Web server.

You should already be familiar with HTML and how a Web page is displayed. You should also be aware of how a basic browser works. You should know that a browser (the client) sends a request for a Web page. This request is routed and received by the appropriate Web server (the server). The Web server then processes the request and sends the HTML for the Web page across the Internet back to the browser machine (the client) that made the request. The delivered HTML can then be processed and displayed by the browser (see Figure 18.4).

18

**FIGURE 18.4**
*Request for a Web page.*

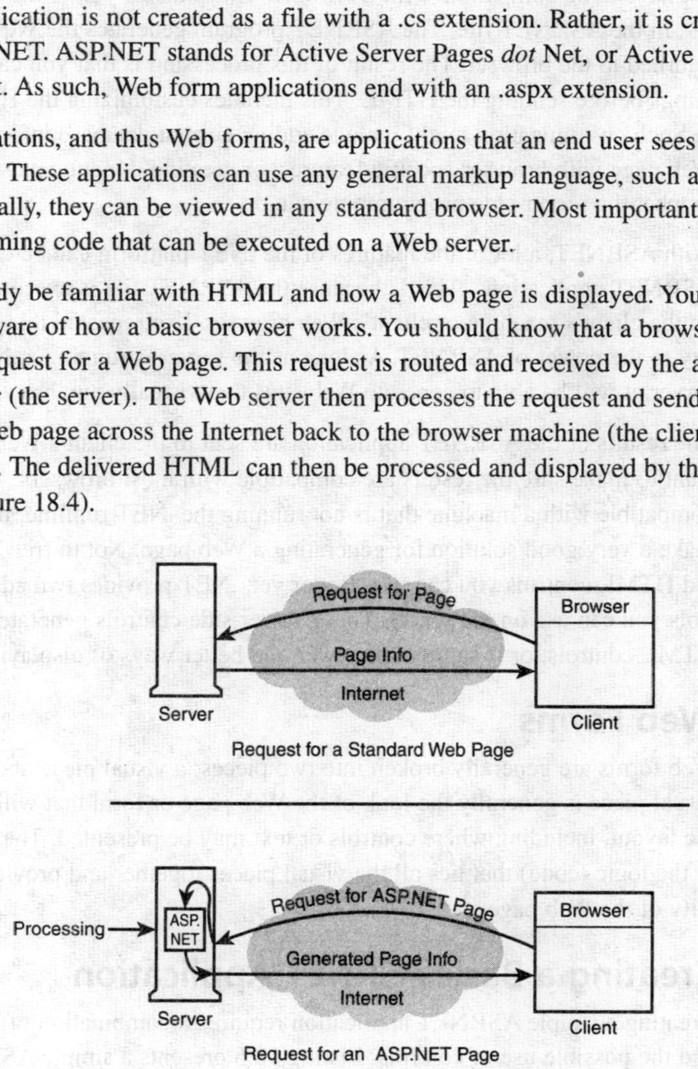

In a basic Web page, the request received by the server causes the server to send HTML back to the browser. Microsoft provided Active Server Pages to intervene in this process. ASP enables greater control over what is being sent to a browser.

When the request is made for an ASP.NET page, the server executes the ASP.NET page. This page runs on the server, not on the browser. This means that an ASP.NET page does not have to be compatible with a browser. This enables you to include real code, such as C#, in the ASP.NET file. The ASP.NET program generates the Web page that will be returned to the browser. The result of this processing is that you can do lots of cool things before sending the HTML. This includes customizing the HTML before sending it. Such customization might include adding current database information, modeling the Web page with browser-specific features, or creating dynamic pages. There are no limits to what the server-side programming can do.

With ASP.NET, a lot of the features of the .NET platform can be carried into these ASP.NET applications. This is because the ASP.NET file is executed on the server, not on the client's machine or client's Web browser. I've repeated this several times—it is the key to the power of ASP.NET. As long as the server is running a .NET runtime and Web server, it will be able to generate Web sites that virtually any browser can view.

The results of the ASP.NET application are sent to the client's Web browser, so you will want to make sure the results are compatible with most browsers. Windows forms are not compatible with a machine that is not running the .NET runtime; therefore, they don't make a very good solution for generating a Web page. Not to fret. There are the standard, old HTML controls you can use. Better yet, .NET provides two additional types of controls you can use on the server. These server-side controls generate appropriate standard HTML controls, or if supported, newer and better ways of displaying information.

## Web Forms

Web forms are generally broken into two pieces; a visual piece and a code piece. The visual piece is generally the look of the Web page or form that will be created. This is the layout, including where controls or text may be presented. The code piece is generally the logic (code) that ties all the visual pieces together and provides the actual functionality of the Web page.

## Creating a Basic ASP.NET Application

Creating a simple ASP.NET application requires a combination of HTML, ASP scripting, and the possible use of controls. Listing 18.6 presents a simple ASP.NET application.

**LISTING 18.6** firstasp.aspx—Simple ASP.NET Application

```
<%@ Page Language="C#" %>

<HTML>
<HEAD>
     <SCRIPT runat="server">
     protected void btnMyButton_Click(object Source, EventArgs e)
     {
          lblMyLabel.Text="The button was <b>clicked</b>!";
     }
     </SCRIPT>
</HEAD>

<BODY>
     <H3>Simple Web Form Example</H3>

     <FORM runat=server>
          <asp:Button id=btnMyButton
                      runat="server"
                      Text="My Button"
                      onclick="btnMyButton_Click" />
          <br>
          <br>
          <asp:Label id=lblMyLabel
                     runat=server />
     </FORM>
</BODY>
</HTML>
```



**OUTPUT**

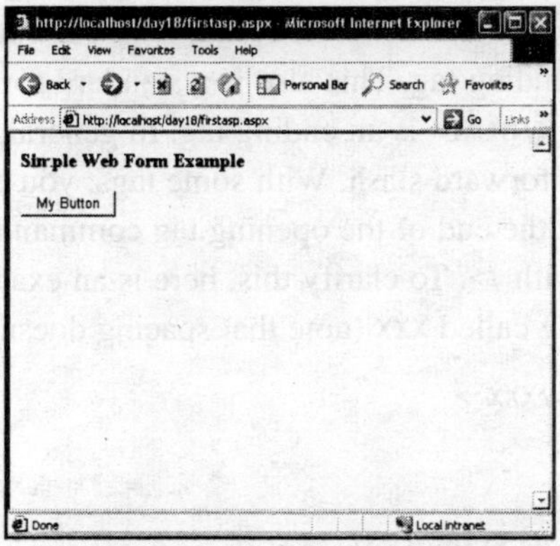


**FIGURE 18.5**
*The result of the firstasp.aspx application.*

**ANALYSIS** Enter this listing and save it as `firstasp.aspx`. You don't need to compile this listing. Rather, as with the Web service program, you copy this program to the Web server. If you place this application in the inetpub\wwwroot\ directory, you can call it using `localhost`. After you copy the program, use the following URL in the browser to execute the ASP.NET application:

```
http://localhost/firstasp.aspx
```

The initial result is shown in Figure 18.5. As you can see, the page displays standard HTML. The file extension of .aspx identifies this as an ASP.NET page and thus a Web form. The Web server will know that any files with an .aspx extension are to be treated as ASP.NET applications.

An ASP.NET application can use a number of different languages. The first line of Listing 18.6 includes a standard ASP directive that indicates that this page will use the language `C#`. By including this line at the top of your page, you will be able to use C# with your ASP.NET page. If for some strange reason you wanted to use a different language, you would change C# to the language you are going to use. For example, to use Visual Basic, you would change the `C#` to `VB`.

This directive will be intercepted by the Web server. The Web server will know to process this as an ASP.NET page because of the `<%`. The Web server will treat everything between the `<%` and `%>` tags as ASP.NET directives.

The rest of this listing should look similar to a standard Web page that contains a scripting element. The unique items can be seen in lines 5, 17, 18, 20, 23, and 24. There are two things to notice. First, there are the `runat=server` statements and the use of `asp:` in front of the control names. These items are addressed in the following sections.

The other unique item you should notice is the slight change in style of the HTML. Instead of regular HTML, an XHTML or XML format is used. You'll see that all the control tags must include an ending tag. This also is a standard for XML. For example, `<html>` is an opening tag and `</html>` is an ending tag. In general, ending tags use the same tag name preceded by a forward slash. With some tags, you can abbreviate this by including the forward slash at the end of the opening tag commands. The controls in Listing 18.6 do this, ending with `/>`. To clarify this, here is an example of the two ways to open and close a generic tag called `XXX` (note that spacing doesn't matter):

```
< XXX  attributes > text < /XXX >

< XXX  attributes  />
```

The *`attributes`* are optional, as is the *`text`*.

Before continuing, you should click the button on the Web page. You will see that doing so causes the `btnMyButton_Click` event to be executed. In line 8, this event assigns a value to the `Text` property of the label control, `lblMyLabel`. Figure 18.6 shows the results of clicking the button.

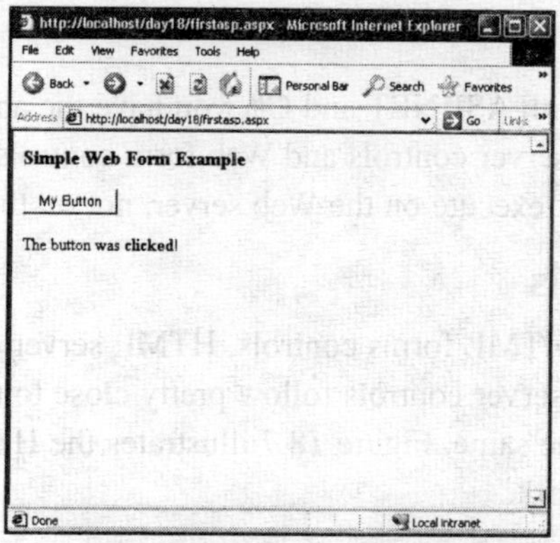


**FIGURE 18.6**

*The browser code after clicking the button.*

You should do one more thing before continuing: Within your browser, open the source file using the View Source option. Do you see the firstasp.aspx code shown earlier? No! You should see the following (after you've clicked the button):

```
<HTML>
<HEAD>

</HEAD>

<BODY>
    <H3>Simple Web Form Example</H3>

    <form name="ctrl0" method="post" action="firstasp.aspx" id="ctrl0">
<input type="hidden" name="__VIEWSTATE"
value="dDw1ODM3NzA0MzM7dDw7bDxpPDI+Oz47bDx0PDtsPGk8Mz47PjtsPHQ8cDxwPGw8VGV4dDs+O
2w8VGhlIGJ1dHRvbiB3YXMgXDxiXD5jbGlja2VkXDwvYlw+ITs+Pjs+Ozs+Oz4+Oz4+Oz4=" />

        <input type="submit" name="btnMyButton" value="My Button"
id="btnMyButton" />
        <br>
        <br>
        <span id="lblMyLabel">The button was <b>clicked</b>!</span>
    </form>
</BODY>
</HTML>
```

Remember, your browser is not getting the ASP.NET file; it is getting the *results generated* by the file. This includes the HTML code and browser-friendly controls. You might notice that the `lblMyLabel` control was converted to an HTML `span` tag rather than a control. This is the result that the Web server determined appropriate and thus generated.

## ASP.NET Controls

When creating Web pages with ASP.NET and C#, you have the ability to use two different sets of controls: HTML server controls and Web form controls. Like ASP.NET in general, both sets of controls execute on the Web server, not on the client's machine.

### HTML Server Controls

If you are familiar with the HTML forms controls, HTML server controls will look very familiar. In fact, the HTML server controls follow pretty close to the standard HTML controls—but they are not the same. Figure 18.7 illustrates the HTML server controls that are in the .NET framework.

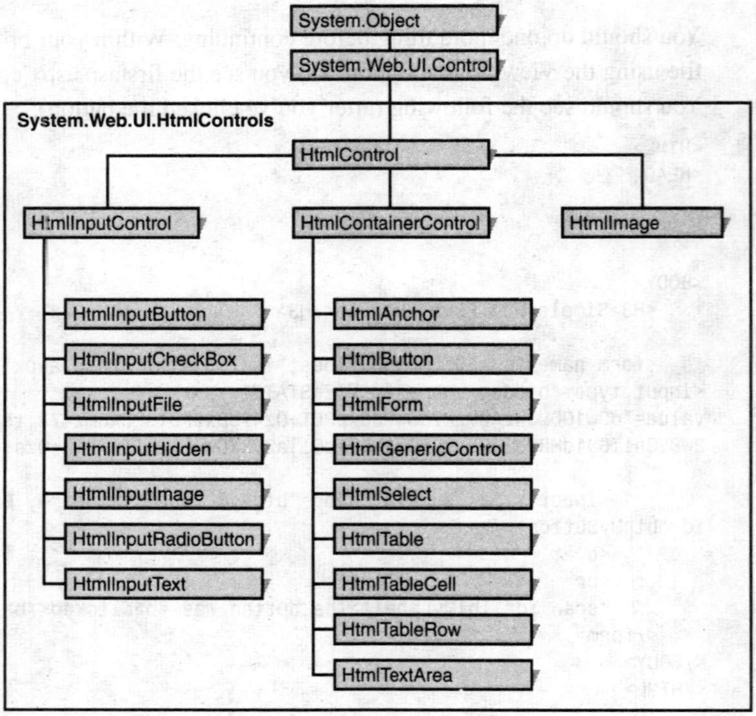


**FIGURE 18.7**
*The HTML server controls.*

Even though the primary purpose of these controls is to provide a migration path for previous versions of ASP, you can still use them. Listing 18.6 presents a Web page application that uses HTML server controls.

Table 18.1 shows you which HTML server control maps to which standard HTML control.

**Table 18.1** HTML Server Controls

| *Control* | *Standard HTML Control* |
|---|---|
| `HtmlAnchor` | `<a>` |
| `HtmlButton` | `<button>` |
| `HtmlForm` | `<form>` |
| `HtmlGenericControl` | `<span>`, `<div>`, `<body>`, `<font>`, or other tags not specified an existing HTML server control |
| `HtmlImage` | `<img>` |
| `HtmlInputButton` | `<input type=button>`, `<input type=submit>`, and `<input type=reset>` |
| `HtmlInputCheckBox` | `<input type=checkbox>` |
| `HtmlInputFile` | `<input type=file>` |
| `HtmlInputHidden` | `<input type=hidden>` |
| `HtmlInputImage` | `<input type=image>` |
| `HtmlInputRadioButton` | `<input type=radio>` |
| `HtmlInputText` | `<input type=text>` and `<input type=password>` |
| `HtmlSelect` | `<select>` |
| `HtmlTable` | `<table>` |
| `HtmlTableCell` | `<td>` and `<th>` |
| `HtmlTableRow` | `<tr>` |
| `HtmlTextArea` | `<textarea>` |



Although Figure 18.7 lists a bunch of controls with names that are different from the HTML controls, you will see a pattern. The difference is that each of the standard HTML server controls have been named after the standard HTML control, with `Html` added to the beginning.

When the ASPX file is originally parsed, all the standard HTML controls in the page are left alone. Yes, left alone. They are assumed to be standard HTML controls that should be passed to the calling Web page. However, if you add `runat=server` to the control's list of attributes, the parser converts the control to the related HTML server control in Table 18.1. By converting to the HTML server equivalent, you are then able to manipulate the controls on the server. If you don't include `runat=server`, you won't be able to manipulate the controls on the server; they will be sent to the browser instead.

Listing 18.7 is a rather long listing that uses HTML server controls. This listing displays a form, which enables you to enter a username and a password. In the code, the username is `Brad` and the correct password is `Swordfish`. The form contains two input boxes and two buttons. They all have `runat=server` included, so all the controls will be executed on the server as HTML server controls.

**Listing 18.7** htmlcontrols.cs—Using HTML Server Controls

```
<html>
   <script Language="C#"  runat="server">

      protected void SubmitBtn_Click(object source, EventArgs e)
      {
         if ((Name.Value == "Brad") &&
                     (Password.Value == "Swordfish"))
         {
            Message.InnerHtml = "You Pass!";
         }
         else
         {
            Message.InnerHtml = "Incorrect user name or password.";
         }
      }

      protected void ResetBtn_Click(object source, EventArgs e)
      {
         Name.Value = "";
         Password.Value = "";
      }
   </script>
   <body>
         <form method=post runat="server">
            Enter Name:        
                    <input id="Name"
                           type=text
                           size=50
                           runat="server">
<br/><br/>
            Enter Password: <input id="Password"
                                type=password
                                size=50
                                runat="server">
<br/><br/>     

            <input type=submit value="Enter"
                           size=30
                           OnServerClick="SubmitBtn_Click"
                           runat="server">
     

            <input type=reset OnServerClick="ResetBtn_Click"
```

**LISTING 18.7** continued

```
44:                                    size=30
45:                                    runat="server">
46:                  <h1>
47:                  <span id="Message" runat="server"> </span>
48:                  </h1>
49:              </form>
50:        </body>
51:  </html>
```

**OUTPUT**

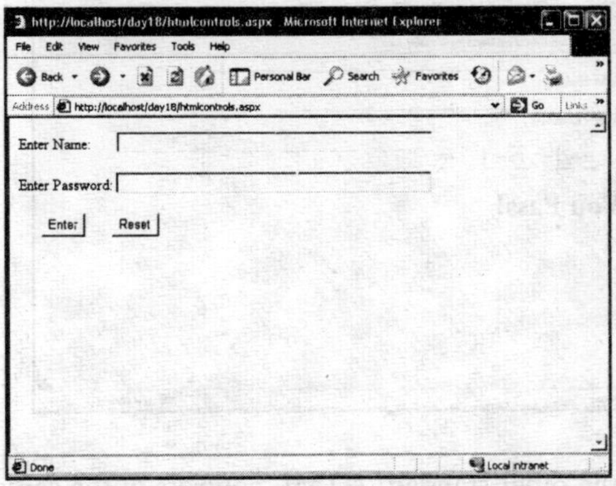


**FIGURE 18.8**

*The result of using HTML server controls.*



**ANALYSIS** The structure of this listing is slightly different from the preceding one. Instead of using the ASP.NET `Page` directive at the top of the listing, this one jumps right into HTML. In line 2, a set of script code is included. This is a standard script tag—or is it? Actually, it includes the `runat=server` directive, so it is actually ASP code that will run on the server! This means the script functionality will be available when this form executes on the server. If the `runat=server` was not included, this would be a standard script tag that would be sent off to the browser!

The next several lines are C# code used in the script. Because this script is executed on the server, C# is fine to use. The code checks to see whether the password and name are valid. They set a message field based on the results.

The form starts in line 24. The controls on the form all look standard. The only thing that is unique is that they include `runat="server"` attributes. This changes the controls and the form to HTML server controls. If you know standard HTML, you should be able to follow the rest of this listing.

**Caution**

> If you don't know standard HTML, you should learn it before tackling Web forms and ASP.NET.

You should run this ASP.NET page. Figure 18.9 shows the output when the correct name and password are entered.

**FIGURE 18.9**

*The HTML server controls program with correct login.*

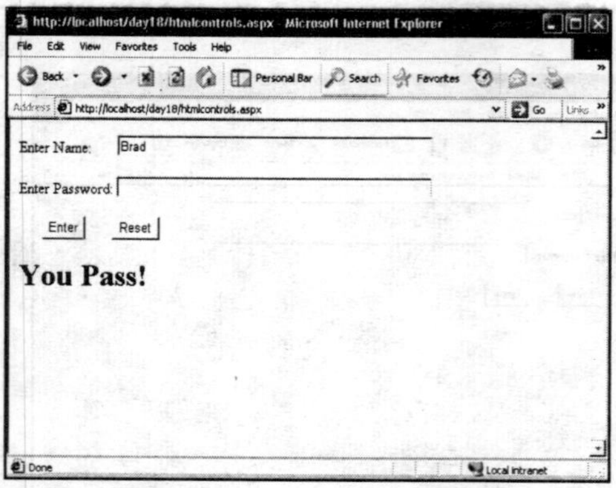


You can use any of the other standard HTML controls in the same manner as the input button. For specific properties you can manipulate with each control, check the online documentation for each of the controls listed in Table 18.1.

**Tip**

> You should notice that label controls were not used in the form. You are generating HTML. Standard text will be treated as part of the HTML file that is sent to the browser. This means you don't need to use a label control to display information; rather you can use standard HTML. You should use a label only when you need to change displayed information.

## Web Server Controls

In addition to the HTML server controls, there are also Web server controls that can be used with your ASP.NET applications. These controls are very similar to the window form controls that you learned to use on Days 16, "Creating Windows Forms," and 17, "Creating Windows Applications." The common Web server controls are presented in Figure 18.10.

**FIGURE 18.10**
*The Web server controls.*

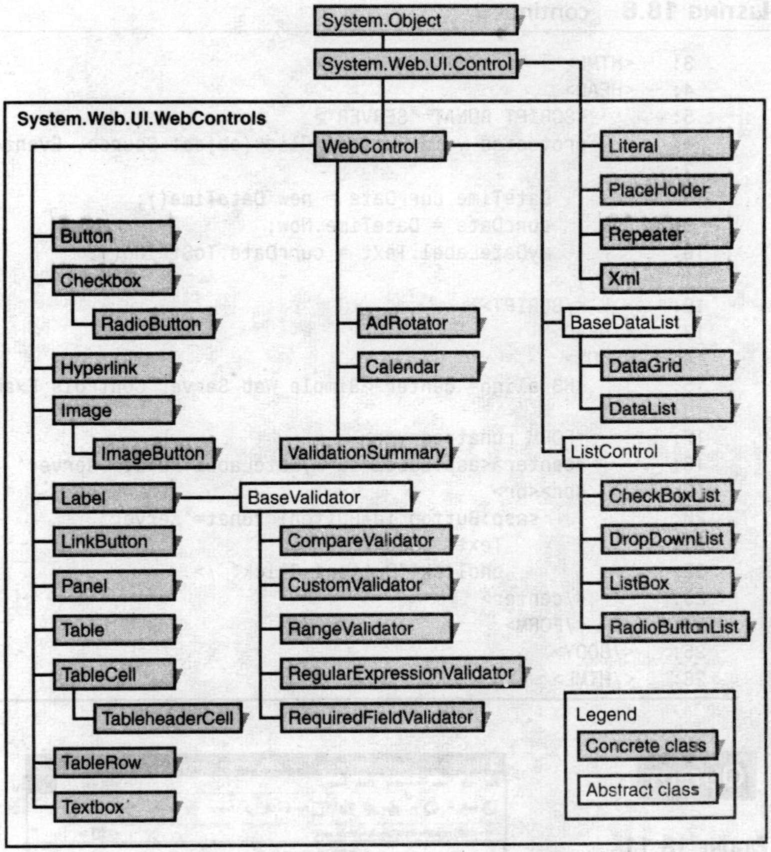


You generally use the Web server controls to create Web forms. You will be able to identify the Web server controls in a listing, because in addition to the `runat=server` directive, Web server controls are preceded by `asp:`. You'll see this in Listing 18.8, which shows another simple Web form application—this time, using the Web server controls.

> **Caution**
> Don't confuse the extensions between Web form applications and Web service applications. Web service programs end in .asmx. Web form applications end in .aspx.

**LISTING 18.8** webform.aspx—Using Web Server Controls

```
<%@ Page Language="C#" %>

```

**LISTING 18.8** continued

```
3:   <HTML>
4:   <HEAD>
5:       <SCRIPT RUNAT="SERVER">
6:       protected void Button1_Click(object Source, EventArgs e)
7:       {
8:          DateTime currDate = new DateTime();
9:          currDate = DateTime.Now;
10:         myDateLabel.Text = currDate.ToString();
11:      }
12:      </SCRIPT>
13:  </HEAD>
14:  <BODY>
15:      <H3 align="center">Simple Web Server Controls Example</H3>
16:
17:      <FORM runat=server>
18:      <center><asp:Label id=myDateLabel runat="server" />
19:      <br><br>
20:          <asp:Button id=Button1 runat="server"
21:             Text="Update"
22:             onclick="Button1_Click" />
23:      </center>
24:      </FORM>
25:  </BODY>
26:  </HTML>
```

**OUTPUT**

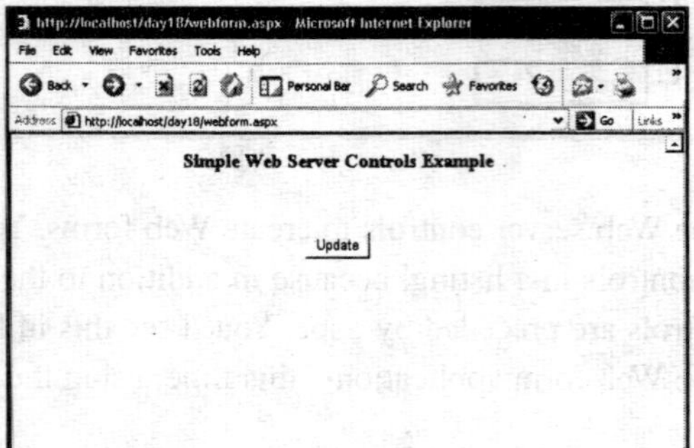


**FIGURE 18.11**
*The results of webform.aspx displayed in the browser.*

**ANALYSIS** You'll see that this listing looks very similar to Listing 18.6. The page starts with the Page directive, which indicates the language that will be used. This listing displays the date and time when you press an Update button. This is the same type of application you created with windows forms, and the code in lines 8 through 10 is the same. This code calculates the date value and assigns it to a label control. In line 18, this label control is a Web server control. You know this because it is preceded by the asp: and ends with a runat=server. Obviously, a timer would make this listing work better; however, that wouldn't allow me to illustrate the use of a Web server button with a label control.

This listing displays the date and time when the Update button is pressed (see Figure 18.12). Is this the time on the server or the time on the browser? The correct answer is that it is the server's time because the code is executed on the server!

**FIGURE 18.12**

*The webform.aspx output after the Update button is clicked.*

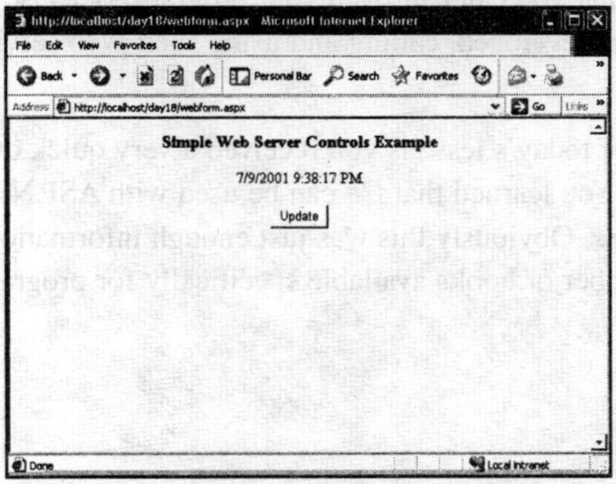




You should again take a look at the HTML sent to the browser. It has been stated a number of times that the Web HTML and server controls execute on the server. Take a look at the source code associated with Listing 18.8's browser output. You can do this by selecting the option to view source from the browser. You will see something like the following:

```
<HTML>
<HEAD>

</HEAD>
<BODY>
    <H3 align="center">Simple Web Server Controls Example</H3>

    <form name="ctrl0" method="post" action="webform.aspx" id="ctrl0">
<input type="hidden" name="__VIEWSTATE"
value="dDwtMTA2MDQwMDUyMDt0PDtsPGk8Mj47PjtsPHQ8O2w8aTwxPjs+O2w8dDxwPHA8bDxUZXh0O
z47bDw3LzkvMjAwMSA5OjQwOjAxIFBNOz4+Oz47Oz47Pj47Pj47Pg==" />

    <center><span id="myDateLabel">7/9/2001 9:40:01 PM</span>
    <br><br>
        <input type="submit" name="Button1" value="Update" id="Button1" />
    </center>
    </form>
```

```
</BODY>
</HTML>
```

This code is definitely different than the codes included in the original listing.

# Summary

Today's lesson was broken into two parts. You spent the first part on setting up and using a simple Web service. You learned that a Web service is a piece of code residing somewhere on the Web that you can call from your program. Because of communication standards that have been developed, calling and using such Web services has become relatively easy.

In the second half of today's lessons you received a very quick overview on Web-based forms applications. You learned that C# can be used with ASP.NET to create Web-centric dynamic applications. Obviously this was just enough information to whet your appetite. There will be a number of books available specifically for programming ASP.NET and Web forms.

# Q&A

**Q Today's lesson covered a lot of material, but barely went into any depth. Why didn't you provide more coverage and more depth?**

**A** As mentioned at the beginning of today's lesson, Web services and Web forms could each fill a book on their own. Additionally, these topics are an application of C# rather than a part of the C# languages. As such, many C# books don't even cover the topics. I believe the topics are important and of interest to most people, and worth giving you a taste of the Web technologies associated with Web development.

**Q The code in the Web service and in the client using the Web service is not very different from normal code. Shouldn't this be more complex?**

**A** The code presented in today's Web service and client was very simple. A lot of work has gone into creating standards for communicating across the Web. The complexity of Web services is in the communication. The `wsdl` tool created the complex code for you. By creating standards for communicating interaction, much of the complexity has been removed from the applications. Your applications can focus on what they need to do, rather than communicating.

**Q Do I have to use wsdl.exe to generate the proxy code file?**

A No. You can write this code by hand, or you can use a development tool such as Visual Studio that can help generate some of the code needed.

**Q I'm confused. You stated there are server controls and HTML controls, but the HTML controls are not the same as standard HTML controls used in a browser. Which controls are HTML controls?**

A Microsoft has created a set of controls called HTML controls that run on the Web server. These controls match up to the original HTML controls that run on a browser. In fact, the HTML server controls generally generate HTML browser controls. The important thing to know is that the HTML controls that run on the server will be able to adapt to what any calling browser can handle.

# Workshop

The Workshop provides quiz questions to help you solidify your understanding of the material covered and exercises to provide you with experience in using what you've learned. Try to understand the quiz and exercise answers before continuing to the next day's lesson. Answers are provided in Appendix A, "Answers."



## Quiz

1. What is a Web service?
2. What is the file called that helps a client application communicate with a Web service?
3. What program can be used to create the code to communicate with a Web server?
4. How can you tell a Web service from an ASP.NET page?
5. How do you execute an ASP.NET page?
6. What are the two types of controls used for Web forms?
7. Does Listing 18.6 use HTML controls, HTML server controls, or Web server controls?
8. What is the difference between a standard HTML control and an HTML server control?
9. What is the server equivalent of the standard HTML table tag?
10. How can you tell a server-side HTML control from a standard HTML control?

## Exercises

1. What is the first line of a C# program that will be used as a Web service? Assume the Web service class name is `DBInfo` and the first method is called `GetData`.
2. What changes need to be made to a method to use it in a Web service?
3. Add a `Multiply` and `Subtract` method to the `Calc` Web service.
4. Create a new client that uses the `Multiply` and `Divide` classes created in Exercise 3.
5. **ON YOUR OWN:** Create a Web page that uses HTML server controls. Rewrite the application to use ASP server controls.
6. **ON YOUR OWN:** Review the online documentation that might have come with your compiler. Look up HTML server controls and Web server controls. Review the different properties, methods, and events that are associated with these controls.

# WEEK 3

# DAY 19

# Two *D*'s in C#—Directives and Debugging

Today, you jump into an area that most programmers want to avoid. You are going to learn a little bit about the concept of debugging. Additionally, you are going to learn about using directives. Specifically, today you

- Learn what debugging is
- Review the primary types of errors your programs can have
- Discover how to tell the compiler to ignore parts of your listings
- Generate your own warnings and errors when compiling
- Change the line numbers reported by the compiler
- Understand how to define symbols in both your code and when compiling
- Define regions in your listing that can be used by IDEs

## What Is Debugging?

When something goes wrong with the compiling or execution of a program, it is up to you to determine what the problem is. In small programs such as those used as examples in this book, it is usually relatively easy to look through the listing to figure out what the problem is. In larger programs, finding the error can be much harder.

**New Term** The process of looking for and removing an error is called *debugging*. An error is often referred to as a bug in a program. One of the first computer problems was caused by a bug—specifically a moth. This bug was found in the computer and removed. Although this error was caused by an actual bug, it has become common to refer to all computer errors as bugs.

> **Tip** Knowing that this bug was a moth was a million-dollar question on *Who Wants to Be a Millionaire*. It is good to know that such trivial facts can sometimes become very valuable to know.

## Types of Errors

**New Term** As you learned on one of the first days of this book, there are a number of different types of errors. Most errors must be caught before you are able to run your program. The compiler will catch these problems and let you know about them in the form of errors and warnings. Other errors are harder to find. For example, you can write a program that compiles with no errors, but doesn't perform as you expect. These errors are called *logic errors*. You can also cleanly compile a listing but run into errors when the end user enters bad information, when data is received that your program does not expect, when data is missing, or when any of a nearly infinite number of things is not quite right.

## Finding Errors

Syntax errors are generally identified when you compile your listing. At compile time, the compiler will identify these problems with errors and warnings. The compiler will provide the location of these errors with a description.

Runtime errors are caused by several issues. You've learned to prevent some of these from crashing your programs by adding exception handling to your programs. For example, if a program tries to open a file that doesn't exist, an exception will be thrown. By adding exception handling you are able to catch and handle runtime exception errors.

Other runtime errors can be caused by a user entering bad information. For example, if you use an integer to capture a person's age, the user could theoretically enter 30,000 or some other invalid number. This won't throw an exception or cause any other type of error. It is, however, still a problem for your program, because it is bad data. This type of issue is easily resolved with a little extra programming logic to check the value entered by the user of the program.

A number of runtime errors are harder to find. These are logic errors that are syntactically correct and don't cause the program to crash. Rather, they provide you with erroneous results. These runtime errors along with some of the more complex exceptions might require you to employ more effort to find them than simply reading through your listing's code. These errors require serious debugging.

**NEW TERM** Some of the ways you can find these more complex errors are to walk through your code line by line. You can do this by hand or you can use an automated tool. Such automated tools are called *debuggers*. You can also use a few of the features provided within C# to find the errors. This includes using directives or using a couple of built-in classes.

## Code Walkthroughs: Tracing Code

A code walkthrough involves reading your code one line at a time. You start at the first line of code that would execute and read each line as it would be executed. You can also read through each class definition to verify that the logic is contained correctly within the class. This is a tedious, long process that when done by hand can take a lot of time and is prone to errors. The positive side of doing these manual code walkthroughs is that you should understand fully the code within your program.

19

**Note** Many companies have code walkthroughs as a standard part of the development process. Generally, these involve sitting down with one or more other people on a project and reading through the code with them. It is your job in these walkthroughs to explain the code to these other participants. You might think there is little value to this; however, often you will find better ways to complete the same task. Additionally, you will find that you understand your code better.

## Preprocessor Directives

C# provides a number of directives that can be used within your code. These directives can determine how the compiler treats your code. If you have programmed in C or C++, you might be familiar with directives such as these. In C#, however, there are fewer directives. Table 19.1 presents the directives available in C#. The following sections cover the more important of these.

**Note**

In C and C++, these directives are called *preprocessor* directives because before compiling the code, the compiler preprocesses the listing and evaluates any preprocessor directives. The name preprocessor is still associated with these directives; however, preprocessing isn't necessary for the compiler to evaluate them.

**TABLE 19.1** C# Directives

| *Directive* | *Description* |
|---|---|
| `#define` | Defines a symbol. |
| `#else` | Starts an `else` block. |
| `#elif` | Combination of an `else` and `if` statement. |
| `#endregion` | Identifies the end of a region. |
| `#endif` | Ends an `#if` statement. |
| `#if` | Tests a value. |
| `#error` | Sends a specified error message when compiled. |
| `#line` | Specifies a line source code line number. It can also include a filename that will appear in the output. |
| `#region` | Identifies the start of a region. A region is a section of code that can be expanded or collapsed in an IDE. |
| `#undef` | Undefines a symbol. |
| `#warning` | Sends a specified warning message when compiled. |

## Preprocessing Declarations

Directives are easy to identify. They start with a pound sign and are the first item on a coding line. Directives don't, however, end with a semicolon.

The first directives to be aware of are `#define` and `#undef`. These directives enable you to define or undefine a symbol that can be used to determine what code is included in your listings. By being able to exclude or include code in your listing, you can allow the same code to be used in multiple ways.

One of the most common ways to use these directives is for debugging. When you are creating a program, you often would like to have it generate extra information that you won't want displayed when in production. Rather than adding and removing this code all the time, you can use defining directives and then define or undefine a value.

The basic format of `#define` and `#undef` is

`#define xxxx`

and

`#undef xxxx`

where *xxxx* is the name of the symbol being defined or undefined. Listing 19.1 uses a listing from earlier in the book. This listing displays the contents of a file provided on the command line.

**Caution**

> This listing does not include exception handling code so you can create errors. For example, if you try to open a file that doesn't exist, an exception will be thrown.



**LISTING 19.1** reading.cs—Using the `#define` Directive

```
//  reading.cs - Read text from a file.
//  Exception handling left out to keep listing short.
//-----------------------------------------------------

#define DEBUG

using System;
using System.IO;

public class ReadingApp
{
   public static void Main(String[] args)
   {
      if( args.Length < 1 )
      {
         Console.WriteLine("Must include file name.");
      }
      else
      {

#if DEBUG

   Console.WriteLine("==============DEBUG INFO===============");
```

**LISTING 19.1** continued

```
        for ( int x = 0; x < args.Length ; x++ )
        {
           Console.WriteLine("Arg[{0}] = {1}", x, args[x]);
        }
        Console.WriteLine("=======================================");

     #endif

              string buffer;

              StreamReader myFile = File.OpenText(args[0]);

              while ( (buffer = myFile.ReadLine()) != null )
              {
     #if DEBUG
        Console.Write( "{0:D3} - ", buffer.Length);
     #endif
                   Console.WriteLine(buffer);
              }

              myFile.Close();
          }
        }
     }
```

**OUTPUT**

```
==============DEBUG INFO===============
Arg[0] = reading.cs
=======================================
041 - //  reading.cs - Read text from a file.
054 - //  Exception handling left out to keep listing short.
054 - //-----------------------------------------------------
000 -
013 - #define DEBUG
000 -
013 - using System;
016 - using System.IO;
000 -
023 - public class ReadingApp
001 - {
041 -    public static void Main(String[] args)
004 -    {
027 -       if( args.Length < 1 )
007 -       {
055 -           Console.WriteLine("Must include file name.");
007 -       }
010 -       else
007 -       {
000 -
```

```
009 - #if DEBUG
000 -
064 -     Console.WriteLine("==============DEBUG INFO===============");
043 -     for ( int x = 0; x < args.Length ; x++ )
004 -     {
054 -         Console.WriteLine("Arg[{0}] = {1}", x, args[x]);
004 -     }
065 -     Console.WriteLine("========================================");
000 -
006 - #endif
000 -
023 -             string buffer;
000 -
054 -             StreamReader myFile = File.OpenText(args[0]);
000 -
055 -             while ( (buffer = myFile.ReadLine()) != null )
010 -             {
010 - #if DEBUG
046 -     Console.Write( "{0:D3} - ", buffer.Length);
006 - #endif
039 -                 Console.WriteLine(buffer);
010 -             }
000 -
024 -             myFile.Close();
007 -         }
004 -     }
001 - }
```



**Analysis** This listing includes a number of directive commands within it. When `DEBUG` is defined, this listing provides additional output. `DEBUG` is defined in line 5, so every time this is compiled it will produce the extra output. If you comment out line 5 (or remove it) and recompile, the extra information does not get displayed.

What is the extra information? In line 21, you see another directive being used, the `#if` directive. If the value after the `#if` is defined, this evaluates to `true`. If it isn't defined, it evaluates to `false`. Because `DEBUG` was defined in line 5, the `if` code is included. Had it not been, control would have jumped to the `#endif` statement in line 30.

Lines 22 to 29 print out the command-line parameters so you can see what was entered. Again, when released to production, the `DEBUG` statement will be left out and this information won't be displayed because it will be dropped out of the listing when compiled.

Line 38 contains a second `#if` check, again for `DEBUG`. This time a value is printed at the beginning of each line. This value is the length of the line being printed. This length information can be used for debugging purposes. Again, when the listing is released, by undefining `DEBUG` this information won't be included.

As you can see, defining a value is relatively easy. One of the values of using directives was to prevent the need to change code; yet to change whether `DEBUG` is defined, you have to change line 5 in Listing 19.1. An alternative to this is to define a value when compiling.

## Defining Values on the Command Line

Remove line 5 from Listing 19.1 and recompile. You will see that the extra debugging information is left out. To define `DEBUG` without adding line 5 back into the listing, you can use the `/define` flag on the compile option. The format of this compile option is

```
csc /define:DEBUG reading.cs
```

where `DEBUG` is any value you want defined in the listing and where `reading.cs` is your listing name. If you compile Listing 19.1 using the `/define` switch, `DEBUG` is once again defined without the need to change your code. Leaving the `/define` off of the command line stops the debugging information from being displayed. The end result is that you can turn the debugging information on and off without the need to change your code!

**Tip**

You can use `/d` as a shortcut for `/define`.

**Note**

If you are using an IDE, check its documentation regarding the defining of directives. There should be a dialog box that enables you to enter symbols to define.

## Position of `#define` and `#undef`

Although it has not been shown, you can also undefine values using `#undef`. From the point where the `#undef` is encountered to the end of the program, the symbol in the `#undef` command will no longer be defined.

The `#undef` and the `#define` directives must occur before any real code in the listing. They can appear after comments and other directives, but not after a declaration or other code occurs.

**Caution**

Neither `#define` nor `#undef` can appear in the middle of a listing.

## Conditional Processing (#if, #elif, #else, #endif)

As you have already seen, you can use `if` logic with defined values. C# provides full `if` logic by including `#if`, `#elif`, `#else`, and `#endif`. This gives you `if`, `if...else`, and `if...else if` logic structures. Regardless of which format you use, you always end with an `#endif` directive. You've seen `#if` used in Listing 19.1. A common use of the `if` logic is to determine whether the listing being compiled is a development version or a release version:

```
#if DEBUG
// do some debug stuff
#elif PRODUCTION
// do final release stuff
#else
// display an error regarding the compile
#endif
```

The listing can produce different results based on the defined values.

### Preprocessing Expressions (!, ==, !=, &&, ||)

The `if` logic with directives can include several operators: `!`, `==`, `!=`, `&&`, and `||`. These operate exactly as they do with a standard `if` statement. The `!` checks for the `not` value. The `==` operator checks for equality. The `!=` checks for inequality. Using `&&` checks to see whether multiple conditions are all true. Using `||` checks to see whether either condition is true.

A common check that can be added to your listings is the following:

```
#if DEBUG && PRODUCTION
//Produce an error and stop compiling
```

If both `DEBUG` and `PRODUCTION` are defined, there is a problem. The next section shows you how to indicate that there was a problem.



## Reporting Errors and Warning in Your Code (#error, #warning)

Because the directives are a part of your compiling, it makes sense that you would want them to be able to indicate warnings and errors. In the previous section you saw that if both `DEBUG` and `PRODUCTION` are defined, there is a serious problem and thus an error should occur. You can cause such an error using the `#error` directive. If you want the listing to still compile and create an executable—if everything else was okay—you can produce a warning instead by using the `#warning` directive. Listing 19.2 uses these directives in a modified version of the reading listing.

**LISTING 19.2** reading2.cs—Using #warning and #error

```
//  reading.cs - Read text from a file.
//  Exception handling left out to keep listing short.
//  Using the #error & #warning directives
//-----------------------------------------------

#define DEBUG
#define BOOKCHECK

#if DEBUG
  #warning Compiled listing in Debug Mode
#endif
#if BOOKCHECK
  #warning Compiled listing with Book Check on
#endif
#if DEBUG && PRODUCTION
  #error Compiled with both DEBUG and PRODUCTION!
#endif

using System;
using System.IO;

public class ReadingApp
{
   public static void Main(String[] args)
   {
      if( args.Length < 1 )
      {
         Console.WriteLine("Must include file name.");
      }
      else
      {

#if DEBUG

   Console.WriteLine("==============DEBUG INFO===============");
   for ( int x = 0; x < args.Length ; x++ )
   {
      Console.WriteLine("Arg[{0}] = {1}", x, args[x]);
   }
   Console.WriteLine("======================================");

#endif

         string buffer;

         StreamReader myFile = File.OpenText(args[0]);

         while ( (buffer = myFile.ReadLine()) != null )
```

**LISTING 19.2** continued

```
49:             {
50:
51:  #if BOOKCHECK
52:
53:        if (buffer.Length > 72)
54:        {
55:           Console.WriteLine("*** Following line too wide to present in book
➥***");
56:        }
57:        Console.Write( "{0:D3} - ", buffer.Length);
58:
59:  #endif
60:                  Console.WriteLine(buffer);
61:             }
62:
63:             myFile.Close();
64:          }
65:       }
66:  }
```

**OUTPUT** When you compile this listing, you receive two warnings:

```
reading2.cs(10,12): warning CS1030: #warning: 'Compiled listing in Debug
➥Mode'
reading2.cs(13,12): warning CS1030: #warning: 'Compiled listing with
➥Book Check
          on'
```

If you define `PRODUCTION` on the command line, you get the following warnings plus an error:

```
reading2.cs(10,12): warning CS1030: #warning: 'Compiled listing in Debug Mode'
reading2.cs(13,12): warning CS1030: #warning: 'Compiled listing with Book Check
     on'
reading2.cs(16,10): error CS1029: #error: 'Compiled with both DEBUG and
     PRODUCTION!'
```

**Note**

`PRODUCTION` is defined on the command line using `/d:PRODUCTION` when compiling.

**ANALYSIS** This listing uses the `#warning` and `#error` directives in the first few lines of the listing. Warnings are provided to enable the person compiling the listing to know the modes that are being used. In this case, there is a `DEBUG` mode and a `BOOKCHECK` mode. In line 15, a check is done to verify that the listing is not being compiled with both `DEBUG` and `PRODUCTION` defined.

Most of this listing is straightforward. The addition of the BOOKCHECK is for me as the author of this book. There is a limitation to the width of a line that can be displayed on a page. This directive is used to include code in lines 52 to 58 that check to see whether the length of the code lines is okay. If a line is longer than 72 characters, a message is written to the screen followed by the line of code with its width included. If the line is not too long, the line prints normally. By undefining BOOKCHECK, I can have this logic removed.

## Changing Line Numbers

Another directive that is provided is the `#line` directive. This directive enables you to change the number of the lines in your code. The impact of this can be seen when you print error messages. Listing 19.3 presents a listing using the `#line` directive.

**LISTING 19.3** lines.cs—Using the `#line` Directive

```
//  lines.cs -
//-----------------------------------------------

using System;

public class linesApp
{
   #line 100
   public static void Main(String[] args)
   {
      #warning In Main...
      Console.WriteLine("In Main....");
      myMethod1();
      myMethod2();
      #warning Done with main
      Console.WriteLine("Done with Main");
   }

   #line 200
   static void myMethod1()
   {
      Console.WriteLine("In Method 1");
      #warning In Method 1...
      int x;   // not used. Will give warning.
   }

   #line 300
   static void myMethod2()
   {
      Console.WriteLine("in Method 2");
      #warning In Method 2...
```

**Listing 19.3** continued

```
    int y; // not used. Will give warning.
  }
}
```

**Output** You will receive the following warnings when you compile this listing:

```
lines.cs(102,16): warning CS1030: #warning: 'In Main...'
lines.cs(106,16): warning CS1030: #warning: 'Done with main'
lines.cs(203,16): warning CS1030: #warning: 'In Method 1...'
lines.cs(303,16): warning CS1030: #warning: 'In Method 2...'
lines.cs(204,11): warning CS0168: The variable 'x' is declared but never
➥used
lines.cs(304,11): warning CS0168: The variable 'y' is declared but never
➥used
```

The following is the output of the listing:

```
In Main....
In Method 1
in Method 2
Done with Main
```

**Analysis** This listing has no practical use; however, it illustrates the `#line` directive. Each method is started with a different line number. The main listing starts at line 100 and goes from there. `myMethod1` starts at line 200 and is numbered from there. `myMethod2` starts with line number 300. This enables you tell which location in the listing has a problem based on the line number.

You can see in the compiler output that the warnings are numbered based on the `#line` values and not on the actual line numbers. Obviously, there are not 100 lines in this listing! These directive line numbers are used in the `#warning` directives as well as warnings and errors produced by the compiler.

You also can return line numbers within a section of the listing back to their default values:

```
#line default
```

This returns the line numbers to their default values from that point in the listing forward.

**Tip**

> If you do ASP.NET development with C#, you will find line numbers useful; otherwise, it is generally better to stick with the actual line numbers.

## A Brief Look at Regions

The other directives that you saw in Table 19.1 were `#region` and `#endregion`. These directives are used to block in regions of a code listing. These regions are used by graphical development environments, such as Visual Studio.NET, to open and collapse code. `#region` indicates the beginning of a block. `#endregion` indicates the end of a block.

**Tip**

A great way to use directives to help debugging is to include messages that are written to the console. These messages can contain information about variable contents, where you are in the listing, or anything that will help you. These messages can be contained within `#if` blocks that can be excluded by undefining—or by never defining—a symbol, such as `DEBUG`.

**Note**

The base class libraries include some classes that do tracing and debugging. These classes use `DEBUG` and `TRACE` symbols to help display information on what is happening in a listing. It is beyond the scope of this book to cover these classes; however, you can check the class library reference for information on the `Systems.Diagnostics` namespace, which includes classes called `Trace` and `Debug`.

# Using Debuggers

One of the primary purposes of a debugger is to automate the process of walking through a program line by line. A debugger enables you to do exactly this—run a program one line at a time. You will be able to view the value of variables and other data members after each line of a program lists. You can jump to different parts of the listing. You can even skip lines of code to prevent them from happening.

**Note**

It is beyond the scope of this book to cover the use of debuggers. Visual Studio and many other of the C# IDEs have built-in debuggers. Additionally, the Microsoft .NET Framework ships with a command-line debugger called CORDBG.

# Summary

Today, you learned about using directives to indicate to the compiler what should and should not happen while your listing is compiled. This included learning how to include or exclude code by defining or undefining symbols. It also included learning about the `#if`, `#ifel`, `#else`, and `#endif` statements, which can be used to make decisions. You learned how to change the line numbers that are used by the compiler to indicate errors. Speaking of errors and warnings, you also learned how to generate your own errors or warnings when compiling, by using the `#error` and `#warning` directives.

# Q&A

**Q Which is better, to define values in a listing or to define them on the compile line?**

**A** If you define a value in a listing, you must remove it or undefine it in the listing. By defining on the command line, you don't have to mess with the code when switching between defining and undefining values.

**Q What happens if I undefine a symbol that was never defined?**

**A** Nothing. You also can undefine a symbol more than once without an error.

# Workshop

The Workshop provides quiz questions to help you solidify your understanding of the material covered and exercises to provide you with experience in using what you've learned. Try to understand the quiz and exercise answers before continuing to the next day's lesson. Answers are provided in Appendix A, "Answers."

## Quiz

19

1. What is debugging?
2. Do preprocessing directives end with a semicolon?
3. What bug is credited with forever associating the term *debugging* with computers?
4. Which type of error will the compiler find?
5. When doing a code walkthrough, which parts of a listing should you review?
6. Which language has the fewest directives: C, C++, or C#?
7. What are the directives for defining and undefining a symbol in your code listing?
8. What flag is used to define a symbol on the command line?
9. What directive enables you to change the line numbers used by the compiler? What value can be used to change the line numbers back to the real line numbers?
10. What classes are provided in the base class libraries to help do debugging and other diagnostics?

## Exercises

1. What code would you use to define a symbol to be used for preprocessing? Call the symbol SYMBOL.
2. Write the code that you would need to add to your listing to have the line numbers start with 1000.
3. Does the following compile? If so, what does this listing do?

```
//  fun.cs - Using Directives in a goofy way
//-----------------------------------------------------

#define AAA
#define BBB
#define CCC
#define DDD
#undef  CCC
using System;
#warning This listing is not practical...
#if DDD
public class
#endif
#if CCC
destroy();
#endif
#if BBB || EEE
myApp { public static void
#endif
#region
#if GGG
Main(){Console.WriteLine("Lions");
#elif AAA
Main(){Console.WriteLine(
#elif GGG
Console.ReadLine(
#else
Console.DumpLine(
#endif
 "Hello"
#if AAA
+ " Goofy "
#else
+ " Strange "
#endif
#if CCC && DDD
+ "Mom"
#else
+ "World"
#endif
);}
```

```
#endregion
}

```

4. **BUG BUSTER:** Does the following program have a problem? If so, which line(s) generate error messages? You should define the symbol `MYLINES` when you compile this listing.

```
1:  //  bugbust.cs -
2:  //-----------------------------------------------
3:
4:  using System;
5:
6:  public class ReadingApp
7:  {
8:     #if MYLINES
9:     #line 100
10:    #endif
11:    public static void Main(String[] args)
12:    {
13:       Console.WriteLine("In Main....");
14:       myMethod1();
15:       myMethod2();
16:       Console.WriteLine("Done with Main");
17:    }
18:
19:    #if MYLINES
20:    #line 200
21:    #endif
22:    static void myMethod1()
23:    {
24:       Console.WriteLine("In Method 1");
25:    }
26:
27:    #if MYLINES
28:    #line 300
29:    #endif
30:    static void myMethod2()
31:    {
32:       Console.WriteLine("in Method 2");
33:    }
34:    #undef MYLINES
35: }
```

5. **ON YOUR OWN**. Add directives to one of the listings you've created on a previous day. Use the directives to print messages as to where in the listing you are. These messages should be displayed only if a symbol called `REPORT` is defined.

6. **ON YOUR OWN**. Add directives to one of the listings you created. The directives should cause the comments to be printed if a symbol called `COMMENTS` is defined. The rest of the listing (the actual code) should be ignored.

# WEEK 3

# DAY 20

# Operator Overloading

In today's lesson, you delve deeper into some of the functionality available when working with classes. This includes exploring overloading in much greater detail. You've seen method overloading; today, you

- Revisit method and constructor overloading
- Learn about operator overloading
- Discover how to overload unary, binary, relational, and logical operators.
- Understand the difference in overloading the logical operators
- Review the individual operators that can and can't be overloaded

## Overloading Functions Revisited

On Day 9, "Advanced Method Access," you learned that you can overload a method multiple times. The key issue with overloading a method is that you must ensure that each time you overload the method it has a different signature. A signature is determined by the return type and parameters of a method. For example, all of the following are different signatures:

```
int mymethod( int x, int y )

int mymethod( int x )

int mymethod( long x )

int mymethod( char x, long y, long z )

int mymethod( char x, long y, int z )
```

On Day 9, you learned that you could overload constructors as well as regular methods. Today, you go beyond overloading methods. Today, you learn how to overload a class's operators.

## Operator Overloading

In addition to overloading constructors and accessors, many object-oriented languages give you the ability to overload operators as well. C# is no exception. C# enables you to overload many of the mathematical operators—such as addition (+) and subtraction (-)—as well as many of the relational and logical operators.

Why would you want to overload these operators? There is no reason you *have* to overload them, but there are times when it can make your program's code easier to follow and your classes easier to use.

The `String` class is a great example of a class that has had an operator overloaded. Normally, the addition operator would not work on a class type, but in C#, you can actually add two strings together with the addition operator. This addition does what you would expect—it concatenates two strings. For example:

```
"animal" + " " + "crackers"
```

results in this string:

```
"animal crackers"
```

To accomplish this, the `String` class and the `string` data type overload the addition operator. You will find that overloading operators can help make some of your programs work better as well. Take a look at Listing 20.1. This listing gives you an error when you compile. The error is shown in the listing's output.

**Note** This listing is not a great example of using operator overloading; however, it is simple so you can focus on the concepts rather than try to understand the code in a complex listing. A few of the other listings in today's lesson will be much more practical.

**LISTING 20.1** over1a.cs—A Program with a Problem

```
//  over1a.cs - A listing with a problem
//----------------------------------------------

using System;

public class AChar
{
   private char CH;

   public AChar() { this.ch = ' '; }
   public AChar(char val) { this.ch = val; }

   public char ch
   {
      get{ return this.CH; }
      set{ this.CH = value; }
   }
}

public class myAppClass
{

   public static void Main(String[] args)
   {
      AChar aaa = new AChar('a');
      AChar bbb = new AChar('b');

      Console.WriteLine("Original value: {0}, {1}", aaa.ch, bbb.ch);

      aaa = aaa + 3;
      bbb = bbb - 1;

      Console.WriteLine("Final values: {0}, {1}", aaa.ch, bbb.ch);
   }
}
```



**OUTPUT** The following errors are generated when you try to compile this listing:

```
over1.cs(30,13): error CS0019: Operator '+' cannot be applied to
operands of
        type 'AChar' and 'int'
over1.cs(31,13): error CS0019: Operator '-' cannot be applied to
operands of
        type 'AChar' and 'int'
```

**ANALYSIS** This listing is easy to follow. A class is created called `AChar`. This class is not practical, but its simplicity makes it easy to use as an illustration for overloading. A second class will be used in later listings today.

The `AChar` class stores a single character. The class has two constructors in lines 10 and 11. The first is called when no arguments are provided. It sets the character value stored in an instantiated object to a space. The second constructor takes a single character that is placed into the instantiated object's private character variable. The class uses an accessor in lines 13 to 17 to do the actual setting of the character value.

The `AChar` class is used in the `myAppClass` class. In lines 25 and 26, two `AChar` objects are created. `aaa` will contain `'a'`, and `bbb` will contain `'b'`. In line 33, these values are printed. In line 30, the value of `3` is added to `aaa`. What would you expect to happen when you add `3` to an `AChar` object? Note that this is not a type `char` object, or even a numeric object. It is an `AChar` object.

This listing is trying to add `3` to the actual object, not to a member of the object. The result—as you can see by the compiler output—is an error.

In line 31, the value of `1` is subtracted from an `AChar` object. An error is produced because you can't add or subtract from an object like this. If lines 30 and 31 had worked, line 33 would have printed their values.

You can make the addition work by manipulating an object's members instead of the class itself. Changing lines 30 and 31 to the following allows the listing to compile:

```
aaa.ch = (char) (aaa.ch + 3);
bbb.ch = (char) (bbb.ch - 1);
```

Although this works, it is not the ultimate solution. There is too much casting and the code is not as simple as it can be. Another solution to make this clear is to add methods to the class that allow an end user to do addition and subtraction—or other types of operations—with a class's objects. Listing 20.2 presents this approach.

**LISTING 20.2** over1b.cs—Operators for Mathematical Functions

```
//  over1b.cs - Using methods for mathematic operations
//-----------------------------------------------------------

using System;

public class AChar
{
   private char CH;

   public AChar() { this.CH = ' '; }
```

**LISTING 20.2** continued

```
11:     public AChar(char val) { this.CH = val; }
12:
13:     public char ch
14:     {
15:        get{ return this.CH; }
16:        set{ this.CH = value; }
17:     }
18:
19:     static public AChar Add ( AChar orig, int val )
20:     {
21:        AChar result = new AChar();
22:        result.ch = (char)(orig.ch + val);
23:        return result;
24:     }
25:     static public AChar Subtract ( AChar orig, int val )
26:     {
27:        AChar result = new AChar();
28:        result.ch = (char)(orig.ch - val);
29:        return result;
30:     }
31:  }
32:
33:  public class myAppClass
34:  {
35:     public static void Main(String[] args)
36:     {
37:        AChar aaa = new AChar('a');
38:        AChar bbb = new AChar('b');
39:
40:        Console.WriteLine("Original value: {0}, {1}", aaa.ch, bbb.ch);
41:
42:        aaa = AChar.Add( aaa, 3 );
43:        bbb = AChar.Subtract( bbb, 1 );
44:
45:        Console.WriteLine("Final values: {0}, {1}", aaa.ch, bbb.ch);
46:     }
47:  }
```



**OUTPUT**

```
Original value: a, b
Final values: d, a
```

**ANALYSIS** This listing is better than the last listing—it compiles! It also provides routines for doing mathematical operations on the class. This is accomplished with the `static` methods `Add` and `Subtract` declared in lines 19 to 24 and 25 to 30, respectively.

The `Add` method increments the original `AChar` character value (`ch`) by the number specified. In the `myAppClass` class, the `AChar.Add` method is called to increment `aaa` by `3`, which results in an `'a'` becoming a `'d'`. The `Add` method returns a new `AChar` class that can overwrite the original. In this way, a number can be added to the class and returned to overwrite the original value. The `Subtract` method works in the same manner, except that the `ch` value is decremented by the given number.

This listing is relatively simple. If there were other data members as a part of the class, the `Add` and `Subtract` operations would become more complex and be more valuable. Consider a few examples:

- A `Deposit` class that contains members for the person making the deposit, an account number, and the value being deposited. In this case, the `Add` method would manipulate only the value being deposited.
- A `currency` class that contains an enumeration value that indicates the type of currency and multiple numeric values to store different money types, such as dollars and cents.
- A `salary` class that contains an employee name, employee ID number, the date of hire, and the actual salary for the employee.

## Overloading Operators

Using methods such as those presented in Listing 20.2 is a perfectly acceptable way to increment and decrement values of a class. There are times, however, when overloading an operator would make the class easier to use. The three examples given are such cases, as is the `String` concatenation example from earlier.

The `AChar` class is probably not a good class to overload the operators with. Why? Simply put, if you overload an operator it should be obvious to everyone using the class what the overloaded operator is doing. Consider the following lines of code. What would you expect the results to be? What would everyone else expect the results to be?

```
Salary = Salary + 1000;

MyChar = MyChar + 3;

MyChar = MyChar + 'a';

Deposit = Deposit - 300;
```

The `Salary` and the `Deposit` lines should be obvious. The `MyChar + 3` line might seem obvious, but is it? The `MyChar + 'a'` is even more cryptic. The + operator could be overloaded for all these cases to make these examples work. The `MyChar` example would probably be better with a more descriptive named method.

There are a number of operators that can be overloaded. This includes the basic binary mathematics operators, most of the unary operators, the relational operators, and the logical operators.

## Overloading the Basic Binary Mathematical Operators

The binary operators are operators that use two values. These operators include addition (+), subtraction (-), multiplication (*), division (/), and modulus (%). All of these can be overloaded within your classes. The total list of binary operators that can be overloaded is

```
+
-
*
/
%
&
|
^
<<
>>
```

The format for overloading a binary operator is similar to the format for creating other methods. The general format for overloading an operator is

```
public static return_type operator op ( type x, type y )
{
   ...
   return return_type;
}
```

where *return_type* is the data type that is being returned by the overloaded operator. For the `AChar` class in the earlier example, *return_type* was *AChar*. This type is preceded by the `public` and `static` modifiers. An overloaded operator must always be `public` so that it can be accessed. It must always be `static` so that it can be accessed at the class level rather than at an individual object level.

The term `operator` is then used to indicate that this is an operator overloading method. The operator being overloaded (*op*) will then be presented. If you were overloading the addition operator, for example, this would be a plus sign. Finally, the parameters for the operation are presented.

In this example, a binary operator is being overloaded, so there are two parameters. One of the parameters must be of the type of the class whose operator is being overloaded. The other parameter's type can be of any type. When setting up operator overloading, you will often set these two types to be the same. It is perfectly acceptable to make the second type a different type as well. In fact, if you are overloading an operator, you should make sure to set up overloaded methods for any possible data types that might be added to the original class.

Looking back at the `AChar` class, the following is the method header for overloading the addition operator so that you can add an integer value to an `AChar` value:

```
public static AChar operator+ (AChar x, int y)
```

Although `x` and `y` are used as the parameter names, you can use any variable names you'd like. An integer value is the second parameter because that is what was added to the `AChar` objects in the earlier listings. Listing 20.3 presents the `AChar` class one more time. This time, however, the addition and subtraction operators are overloaded.

> **Note**
>
> You might have noticed that the format description earlier had a space between the word `operator` and the *op* sign. In the example just presented for the `AChar` class, there is no space; the operator is connected to the word operator. Either format works.

**LISTING 20.3** over1c—Overloading the Binary Operators

```
//  over1c.cs - Overloading an operator
//-----------------------------------------------

using System;

public class AChar
{
   private char CH;

   public AChar() { this.CH = ' '; }
   public AChar(char val) { this.CH = val; }

   public char ch
   {
      get{ return this.CH; }
      set{ this.CH = value; }
   }

   static public AChar operator+ ( AChar orig, int val )
```

**LISTING 20.3** continued

```
20:     {
21:        AChar result = new AChar();
22:        result.ch = (char)(orig.ch + val);
23:        return result;
24:     }
25:     static public AChar operator- ( AChar orig, int val )
26:     {
27:        AChar result = new AChar();
28:        result.ch = (char)(orig.ch - val);
29:        return result;
30:     }
31:  }
32:
33:  public class myAppClass
34:  {
35:     public static void Main(String[] args)
36:     {
37:        AChar aaa = new AChar('a');
38:        AChar bbb = new AChar('b');
39:
40:        Console.WriteLine("Original value: {0}, {1}", aaa.ch, bbb.ch);
41:
42:        aaa = aaa + 25;
43:        bbb = bbb - 1;
44:
45:        Console.WriteLine("Final values: {0}, {1}", aaa.ch, bbb.ch);
46:     }
47:  }
```

**OUTPUT**

```
Original value: a, b
Final values: z, a
```

**ANALYSIS** Lines 19 to 30 contain the overloading of the addition and subtraction operators of the AChar class. In line 19, the overloading follows the format presented earlier and an AChar type is returned. The first type being added is also an AChar.

In this example, an integer value is being added to an AChar type. You could have used another AChar object, or any other type that would make sense instead of the integer. In fact, you can overload the addition operator multipie times, with each adding a different data type to the AChar type, as long as the resulting overloads have unique signatures.

The overloaded addition operator's functionality is presented in lines 21 to 23. A new AChar object is instantiated in line 21. The ch value within this new AChar object is assigned a value based upon the values received with the addition operator. When this value is updated, the new AChar object, `result`, is returned. The code in this method could be changed to anything you would like; however, it should be related to the values received by the addition operator.

The subtraction operator is set up in the same manner as the addition operator. In an exercise at the end of today's lesson, you create a second overloaded method for the subtraction operator. The second method will take two `AChar` values and return the number of positions between them.

This listing overloaded only the addition and subtraction operators. Overloading the multiplication, division, modulus, and other binary operators is done in the same way.

## Overloading the Basic Unary Mathematical Operators

The unary operators work with only one element. The unary operators that can be overloaded are

```
+
-
++
--
!
~
true
false
```

The unary operators are overloaded similarly to the binary operators. The difference is that only one value is declared as a parameter. This single value will be of the same data type as the class containing the overload. A single parameter is all that is passed, because a unary operator operates on a single value. Two examples are presented in Listings 20.4 and 20.5. Listing 20.4 presents the positive (+) and negative (-) unary operators. These are used with the `AChar` class you've already seen. A positive `AChar` capitalizes the character. A negative `AChar` converts the character to lowercase.

Listing 20.5 uses the increment and decrement (--) operators. This listing increments the character to the next character value or decrements the character to the preceding value. Note that this is moving through the character values, so incrementing `'Z'` or decrementing `'A'` will take you to a non-letter character. You could add logic, however, to prevent the incrementing or decrementing past the end or beginning of the alphabet.

**LISTING 20.4** over2.cs—Overloading the + and - Unary Operators

```
//  over2b.cs - Overloading
//-----------------------------------------------

using System;
using System.Text;

public class AChar
{
   private char CH;

   public AChar() { this.CH = ' '; }
   public AChar(char val) { this.CH = val; }

   public char ch
   {
      get{ return this.CH; }
      set{ this.CH = value; }
   }

   static public AChar operator+ ( AChar orig )
   {
      AChar result = new AChar();
      if( orig.ch >= 'a' && orig.ch <='z' )
         result.ch = (char) (orig.ch - 32 );
      else
         result.ch = orig.ch;

      return result;
   }
   static public AChar operator- ( AChar orig )
   {
      AChar result = new AChar();
      if( orig.ch >= 'A' && orig.ch <='Z' )
         result.ch = (char) (orig.ch + 32 );
      else
         result.ch = orig.ch;

      return result;
   }

}

public class myAppClass
{
   public static void Main(String[] args)
   {
      AChar aaa = new AChar('g');
      AChar bbb = new AChar('g');
```

20

**LISTING 20.4** continued

```
49:         AChar ccc = new AChar('G');
50:         AChar ddd = new AChar('G');
51:
52:         Console.WriteLine("ORIGINAL:");
53:         Console.WriteLine("aaa value: {0}", aaa.ch);
54:         Console.WriteLine("bbb value: {0}", bbb.ch);
55:         Console.WriteLine("ccc value: {0}", ccc.ch);
56:         Console.WriteLine("ddd value: {0}", ddd.ch);
57:
58:         aaa = +aaa;
59:         bbb = -bbb;
60:         ccc = +ccc;
61:         ddd = -ddd;
62:
63:         Console.WriteLine("\n\nFINAL:");
64:         Console.WriteLine("aaa value: {0}", aaa.ch);
65:         Console.WriteLine("bbb value: {0}", bbb.ch);
66:         Console.WriteLine("ccc value: {0}", ccc.ch);
67:         Console.WriteLine("ddd value: {0}", ddd.ch);
68:     }
69: }
```

**OUTPUT**

```
ORIGINAL:
aaa value: g
bbb value: g
ccc value: G
ddd value: G


FINAL:
aaa value: G
bbb value: g
ccc value: G
ddd value: g
```

**ANALYSIS** As you can see by the output of Listing 20.4, using the + operator changes a lowercase letter to uppercase. It has no affect on a letter that is already uppercase. Using the - operator does the opposite. It changes an uppercase letter to lowercase. It has no effect on a character that is lowercase.

Lines 20 to 39 contain the overloaded operator methods. These are unary overloaded operator methods because they each have only one parameter (see lines 20 and 30). The code within these overloaded operators is relatively straightforward. The code checks to see whether the original character is an alphabetic character that is either uppercase (line 33) or lowercase (line24). If the character is one of these, it is changed to the other case by either adding 32 or subtracting 32.

**Note**

Remember, characters are stored as numeric values. The letter 'A' is stored as 65. The letter 'a' is stored as 97. Each letter of the same case is stored sequentially after.

Listing 20.4 overloaded the unary positive and negative operators; Listing 20.5 overloads the increment and decrement operators.

**LISTING 20.5** over2b.cs—Overloading the Increment and Decrement Operators

```
//  over2b.cs - Overloading
//-----------------------------------------------------------------

using System;

public class AChar
{
    private char CH;

    public AChar() { this.CH = ' '; }
    public AChar(char val) { this.CH = val; }

    public char ch
    {
       get{ return this.CH; }
       set{ this.CH = value; }
    }

    static public AChar operator++ ( AChar orig )
    {
       AChar result = new AChar();
       result.ch = (char)(orig.ch + 1);
       return result;
    }
    static public AChar operator-- ( AChar orig )
    {
       AChar result = new AChar();
       result.ch = (char)(orig.ch - 1);
       return result;
    }

}

public class myAppClass
{
    public static void Main(String[] args)
    {
```

**LISTING 20.5** continued

```
38:         AChar aaa = new AChar('g');
39:         AChar bbb = new AChar('g');
40:
41:         Console.WriteLine("Original value: {0}, {1}", aaa.ch, bbb.ch);
42:
43:         aaa = ++aaa;
44:         bbb = --bbb;
45:
46:         Console.WriteLine("Current values: {0}, {1}", aaa.ch, bbb.ch);
47:
48:         aaa = ++aaa;
49:         bbb = --bbb;
50:
51:         Console.WriteLine("Final values: {0}, {1}", aaa.ch, bbb.ch);
52:
53:     }
54: }
```

**OUTPUT**

```
Original value: g, g
Current values: h, f
Final values: i, e
```

**ANALYSIS** This listing is similar to the previous listing. Instead of overloading the `-` and `+` operators, the `--` and `++` operators are overloaded. When overloaded, these operators can be used with objects of the given class. You see this in lines 43, 44, 48, and 49. The other unary operators can be overloaded in the same way.

## Overloading the Relational and Logical Operators

The relational operators can also be overloaded. This includes the following operators:

```
<
<=
>
>=
```

as well as the logical operators:

```
==
!=
```

These differ from the previous operators in how they are declared. Rather than returning a value of the class type, these return a Boolean value. This should make sense. The idea of these operators is to compare two values and determine a truth about them.

Listing 20.6 uses a more realistic class to illustrate a couple of the relational operators being overloaded. This class defines a `Salary` value. You will notice that the == and the != are not illustrated in this listing. They require a slightly different approach, which is covered in the next section.

**LISTING 20.6** over3.cs—Overloading the Relational Operators

```
//  over3a.cs - Overloading Relational Operators
//----------------------------------------------------

using System;
using System.Text;

public class Salary
{
   private int AMT;

   public Salary() { this.amount = 0; }
   public Salary(int val) { this.amount = val; }

   public int amount
   {
      get{ return this.AMT; }
      set{ this.AMT = value; }
   }

   static public bool operator < ( Salary first, Salary second )
   {
      bool retval;

      if ( first.amount < second.amount )
         retval = true;
      else
         retval = false;

      return retval;
   }

   static public bool operator <= ( Salary first, Salary second )
   {
      bool retval;

      if ( first.amount <= second.amount )
         retval = true;
      else
         retval = false;

      return retval;
   }
```

**LISTING 20.6** continued

```
   static public bool operator > ( Salary first, Salary second )
   {
      bool retval;

      if ( first.amount > second.amount )
         retval = true;
      else
         retval = false;

      return retval;
   }

   static public bool operator >= ( Salary first, Salary second )
   {
      bool retval;

      if ( first.amount >= second.amount )
         retval = true;
      else
         retval = false;

      return retval;
   }

   public override string ToString()
   {
      return( this.amount.ToString() );
   }
}

public class myAppClass
{
   public static void Main(String[] args)
   {
      Salary mySalary   = new Salary(24000);
      Salary yourSalary = new Salary(24000);
      Salary PresSalary = new Salary(200000);

      Console.WriteLine("Original values: ");
      Console.WriteLine("      my salary: {0}", mySalary);
      Console.WriteLine("    your salary: {0}", yourSalary);
      Console.WriteLine(" a Pres' salary: {0}", PresSalary);
      Console.WriteLine("\n--------------------------\n");

      if ( mySalary < yourSalary )
         Console.WriteLine("My salary less than your salary");
      else if ( mySalary > yourSalary )
```

**LISTING 20.6** continued

```
91:          Console.WriteLine("My salary is greater than your salary");
92:       else
93:          Console.WriteLine("Our Salaries are the same");
94:
95:       if ( mySalary >= PresSalary )
96:          Console.WriteLine("\nI make as much or more than a president.");
97:       else
98:          Console.WriteLine("\nI don't make as much as a president.");
99:    }
100: }
```

**OUTPUT**

```
Original values:
      my salary: 24000
    your salary: 24000
  a Pres' salary: 200000

--------------------------

Our Salaries are the same

I don't make as much as a president.
```

**ANALYSIS** This listing creates a `Salary` class. The `Salary` class contains a person's salary. Although this example doesn't include it, you could also include information such as the last time the person received a raise, the amount of the raise, and more. Regardless of what you include, the basic information you'd expect from this class is a person's salary.

For this example, several of the relational operators are overloaded. Each is overloaded in the same manner, so only one needs to be reviewed here. Line 20 overloads the less than operator (<).

The return type is a `bool`. The result of the method is to return `true` or `false`. The method also receives two `Salary` objects as parameters: the value before and the value after the less than sign when it is used in code:

```
first < second
```

Using these two values, you can make the determinations that fit for the class. In this case, a check is done in line 24 to see whether the first `Salary` object's `amount` is less than the second `Salary` object's `amount`. If so, `true` is set for a return value. If not, `false` is set for the return value. Line 29 then returns the value.

In the `myAppClass` class, using the overloaded relational operators is no different than using relational operators with the basic data types. You can easily compare one salary to another, as done in lines 88, 90, and 95.

Another part of this listing that needs to be covered is not related to operator overloading. In lines 68 to 71, the `ToString()` method is overridden by using the `override` keyword. The `ToString` method was inherited automatically from the base class, `Object`. Remember from the days on inheritance that all classes derive from `Object` automatically. As such, all classes contain the functionality of methods that were contained in `Object`. This includes the `ToString` method.

The `ToString` method can be overridden in any class. It should always return a string representation of a class. In the case of a `Salary` class that could contain lots of members, you could return a number of possible items. Returning a string representation of the actual amount value makes the most sense, however. This is exactly what line 70 does.

More importantly, by overloading the `ToString` method (lines 83 to 85), you gain the ability to "print" the class. When you display the class as shown in these lines, the `ToString` method is automatically called.

## Overloading the Logical Operators

Overloading the equality and inequality logical operators takes more effort than overloading the other relational operators. First, you can not overload just one of these. If you want to overload one, you must overload both. Additionally, if you want to overload these operators, you must also overload two methods, `Equals()` and `GetHashCode()`. Like the `ToString` method, these methods are a part of the base object (`Object`) and are automatically inherited when you create a class. These methods must be overloaded because the logical operators use them behind the scenes.

When comparing two objects of the same class, you should define an `Equals` method that overrides the base class's `Equals` method. This method takes the following format:

```
public override bool Equals(object val)
{
   // determine if classes are equal or not
   // return (either true or false)
}
```

This method can be used to see whether one object is equal to another. You can do whatever logic within this method you want. This might include checking a single value or checking multiple values. For example, are two salaries equal if the amount is equal? If the `Salary` class includes hire dates, would two salaries that are of the same annual amount be equal if the hire dates were different? These are the type of decisions you must make to code the logic within the `Equals` method.

The `GetHashCode` must also be overridden if you want to override the `==` and `!=` operators. The `GetHashCode` method returns an integer value used to identify a specific instance of a class. In general, you are not going to want to make any changes to this method. You can override this method and return the hash code of the current instance by including the following `override` method:

```
public override int GetHashCode()
{
   return this.ToString().GetHashCode();
}
```

After you have overridden the `Equals` and `GetHashCode` methods, you need to define the overload methods for `==` and `!=`. This is done with the same initial method structure as used with the relational operators. One difference is that you should use the `Equals` method rather than repeating any comparison code. In Listing 20.7, the `!=` operatcr basically calls the `Equals` method and returns the not (`!`) value of it.

> **Note**
>
> The `Equals` method actually uses the return values from the `GetHashCode` method to determine whether two objects are equal.

**Listing 20.7** over4.cs—Overloading Equals and Not Equals

```
//  over4.cs - Overloading
//-----------------------------------------------

using System;
using System.Text;

public class Salary
{
   private int AMT;

   public Salary() { this.amount = 0; }
   public Salary(int val) { this.amount = val; }

   public int amount
   {
      get{ return this.AMT; }
      set{ this.AMT = value; }
   }

   public override bool Equals(object val)
```

**Listing 20.7** continued

```
   {
      bool retval;

      if( ((Salary)val).amount == this.amount )
         retval = true;
      else
         retval = false;

      return retval;
   }

   public override int GetHashCode()
   {
      return this.ToString().GetHashCode();
   }

   static public bool operator == ( Salary first, Salary second )
   {
      bool retval;

      retval = first.Equals(second);

      return retval;
   }
   static public bool operator != ( Salary first, Salary second )
   {
      bool retval;

      retval = !(first.Equals(second));

      return retval;
   }

   public override string ToString()
   {
      return( this.amount.ToString() );
   }

}

public class myAppClass
{
   public static void Main(String[] args)
   {
      string tmpstring;

      Salary mySalary   = new Salary(24000);
      Salary yourSalary = new Salary(24000);
```

**LISTING 20.7** continued

```
69:         Salary PresSalary = new Salary(200000);
70:
71:         Console.WriteLine("Original values: {0}, {1}, {2}",
72:             mySalary, yourSalary, PresSalary);
73:
74:         if (mySalary == yourSalary)
75:            tmpstring = "equals";
76:         else
77:            tmpstring = "does not equal";
78:
79:         Console.WriteLine("\nMy salary {0} your salary", tmpstring);
80:
81:         if (mySalary == PresSalary)
82:            tmpstring = "equals";
83:         else
84:            tmpstring = "does not equal";
85:
86:         Console.WriteLine("\nMy salary {0} a president\'s salary",
87:                                                        tmpstring);
88:     }
89: }
```

**OUTPUT**

```
Original values: 24000, 24000, 200000

My salary equals your salary

My salary does not equal a president's salary
```

**ANALYSIS** Most of the code in this listing was analyzed before the listing. You'll find the overloaded `Equals` method in lines 20 to 30. The overloaded `GetHashCode` method is in lines 32 to 35. For fun, you can remove one of these two methods and try to compile the listing. You will see that your listing will generate errors without them.

Line 27 starts the method for overloading the == operator. Earlier, I stated that you should use the `Equals` method for comparing classes. This is exactly what the overloaded == method is doing. It calls the `Equals` method and returns the value from it. The `!=` method does the same thing in lines 45 to 52, except that the value is changed by using the `!` operator.

In the `Main` method of the `myAppClass` class, using the `==` and `!=` operators is as easy as using the other overloaded operators. You can compare two classes and you'll receive a response of `true` or `false`.

**Caution**

> When overloading the logical operators, `==` and `!=`, you must always overload both. You can't overload just one or the other.

## Summarizing the Operators to Overload

A number of operators can be overloaded. To repeat an earlier point, you should overload operators only when the resulting functionality will be clear to a person using the class. If in doubt, you should use regular methods instead. The operators that are available to overload are presented in Table 20.1. The operators that cannot be overloaded are presented in Table 20.2.

**TABLE 20.1** Operators That Can Be Overloaded

```
+   -   ++   --   !   ~   true   false
+   -   *   /   %   &   |   ^   <<   >>
<   <=   >   >=   ==   !=
```

**TABLE 20.2** Operators That Cannot Be Overloaded

```
=   .   ?:   &&   ||   new   is
sizeof   typeof   checked   unchecked
```

You also cannot overload parentheses `()` or any of the compound operators (`+=`, `-=`, and so forth). The compound operators will use the binary overloaded operators.

The only operators that are left are the brackets `[]`. As you learned earlier in the book, these are overloaded by using indexers.

# Summary

Today's lessons covered the final OOP topic that is covered in this book. Today you learned how to overload operators. While many people believe that operator overloading is complex, it is really quite simple. You learned to overload the unary, binary, relational, and logical operators. The final section of today's lessons presented two tables containing the operators that could and couldn't be overloaded.

With today's lessons you have learned nearly all the basics of C#. This includes having learned nearly all the basic constructs of the language as well as their use. Tomorrow's lessons present a number of different advanced topics in brief detail. Although you have all the building blocks needed to create complex C# applications, there are a few advanced topics worth being exposed to. These will be overviewed tomorrow.

# Q&A

**Q Which is better, to use methods such as `Add()` or to overload operators?**

**A** Either will work. Many people expect operators to be overloaded when working with advanced languages such as C++ and C#. As long as it is clear what should be expected when two classes are added or manipulated with an operator, you should consider overloading the operator. In the end, it can actually make your code easier to follow and understand.

**Q Why couldn't compound operators such as += be overloaded?**

**A** This was actually answered in today's lesson. The compound operators are always broken out into being

```
xxx = xxx op yyy
```

So,

```
x += 3
```

is broken out to

```
x = x + 3
```

This means the overloaded binary operator can be used. If you overload the addition operator (+),you essentially also overload the compound addition operator (+=).

**Q I want a different method for postfix and prefix versions of the decrement and increment operators. What do I do?**

**A** Sorry, but C# doesn't support this. You get to define only a single overloaded method for the increment and decrement operators.



# Workshop

The Workshop provides quiz questions to help you solidify your understanding of the material covered and exercises to provide you with experience in using what you've learned. Try to understand the quiz and exercise answers before continuing to tomorrow's lesson. Answers are provided in Appendix A, "Answers."

## Quiz

1. How many times can a single operator be overloaded in a single class?
2. What determines how many times an operator can be overloaded?

3. What method or methods must be overloaded to overload the equality operator (==)?
4. Which of the following are good examples of using overloaded operators?
   a. Overloading the plus operator (+) to concatenate two string objects.
   b. Overloading the minus operator (-) to determine the distance between two `MapLocation` objects.
   c. Overloading the plus operator (+) to increment an amount once, and incrementing the ++ operator to increment the amount twice.
5. How do you overload the `/=` operator?
6. How do you overload the `[]` operator?
7. What relational operators can be overloaded?
8. What unary operators can be overloaded?
9. What binary operators can be overloaded?
10. What operators cannot be overloaded?
11. What modifiers are always used with overloaded operators?

## Exercises

1. What would the method header be for the overloaded addition operator used to add two type `XYZ` objects together?
2. Modify Listing 20.3. Add an additional subtraction overloaded method that takes two `AChar` values. The result should be the numerical difference between the character values stored in the two `AChar` objects.
3. **BUG BUSTER:** Does the following code snippet have a problem? If so, what is the problem? If not, what does this snippet do?

```
static public int operator >= ( Salary first, Salary second )
{
   int retval;

   if ( first.amount <= second.amount )
      retval = 1;
   else
      retval = 0;

   return retval;
}
```

4. Modify Listing 20.7 to include a method that will compare a salary to an integer value. Also add a method to compare a salary to a `long` value.

# WEEK 3

# DAY 21

# A Day for Reflection and Attributes

At this point you have worked through 21 of learning C#. You have learned about data types, classes, object-oriented programming, and much more. You have learned all the basics of C# programming. You have the ability to create C# programs, including programs that use the Base Class Libraries (BCL) class and more. These can be Windows-based, Web-based, or within the console. In today's lesson, you touch on two advanced-level topics within C# that you might come across and complete your learning of the C# foundations. Today, you

- Discover the concept of reflection
- Use reflection to determine the contents of a program
- Learn how to use predefined attributes
- Explore the creation of custom attributes
- See how to associate custom attributes with your code
- Write the code to evaluate attributes at runtime

# Reflection

Sometimes it is good to sit back and reflect on life. More specifically, you can sit back and reflect on yourself. Often you will discover information you didn't realize about yourself.

Just as *you* can reflect, it is also possible to have a C# program reflect upon *itself*. Such reflection can be used to learn about an application. For example, you can have a class reflect upon itself and tell you the methods or properties it contains. You'll find that being able to reflect on a program, class, or other item will give you the ability to take more advantage of it.

The key to getting information on a type is to use a reflection method. For example, the `GetMembers` method can be used to get a type's members. You get the list of members by passing `GetMembers` a `Type` type. Yes, `Type` is a type that holds types. Read that sentence slowly and it should make sense. When you have a `Type`, you can use it to get the members within it using the `GetMembers` method.

Stepping back, you can see that the first step for reflection is to get the type of a type. You get the type of a class (or other type) using the `static` method `Type.GetType`. The return value of this method is a type that can be assigned to a `Type` object. The `GetType` method uses virtually any data type as a parameter. For example, to get the type of a class called `testclass` and assign it to a `Type` object called `MyTestObject`, you do the following:

```
Type MyTypeObject = Type.GetType(testclass);
```

`MyTypeObject` then contains the type for `testclass`. You can use the `MyTypeObject` to get the members of a `testclass`. As stated, this is done using the `GetMembers` method. The `GetMembers` method returns an array of `MemberItems`. To call the `GetMember` method on the `MyTypeObject` (which contains the type of a `testclass` in this example), you do the following:

```
MemberInfo[] Mymemberarray = MyTypeObject.GetMembers();
```

An array of `MemberInfo` objects called `Mymemberarray` is created, which is assigned the return value of the call to `GetMembers` for the type stored in `MyTypeObject`.

After you've done this assignment, the `Mymemberarray` contains the members of your type. You can loop through this array and evaluate each member. Listing 21.1 pulls all this together into a single listing. For fun, this listing reflects on the `System.Reflection.PropertyInfo` class.

The `MemberInfo` type is a part of the `Reflection` namespace. You need to include `System.Reflection` to use the shortened version of the name.

**LISTING 21.1** reflect.cs—Using Reflection

```
using System;
using System.Reflection;

class Mymemberinfo
{
   public static int Main()
   {
      //Get the Type and MemberInfo.
      string testclass = "System.Reflection.PropertyInfo";

      Console.WriteLine ("\nFollowing is the member info for class: {0}",
                                                testclass);

      Type MyType = Type.GetType(testclass);

      MemberInfo[] Mymemberinfoarray = MyType.GetMembers();

      //Get the MemberType method and display the elements

      Console.WriteLine("\nThere are {0} members in {1}",
              Mymemberinfoarray.GetLength(0),
              MyType.FullName);

      for ( int counter = 0;
            counter < Mymemberinfoarray.GetLength(0):
            counter++ )
      {
         Console.WriteLine( "{0}. {1} Member type - {2}",
                 counter,
                 Mymemberinfoarray[counter].Name,
                 Mymemberinfoarray[counter].MemberType.ToString());
      }
      return 0;
   }
}
```

**OUTPUT**

```
Following is the member info for class: System.Reflection.PropertyInfo

There are 36 members in System.Reflection.PropertyInfo
0. get_CanWrite Member type - Method
1. get_CanRead Member type - Method
2. get_Attributes Member type - Method
3. GetIndexParameters Member type - Method
4. GetSetMethod Member type - Method
```

21

```
5. GetGetMethod Member type - Method
6. GetAccessors Member type - Method
7. SetValue Member type - Method
8. SetValue Member type - Method
9. GetValue Member type - Method
10. GetValue Member type - Method
11. get_PropertyType Member type - Method
12. IsDefined Member type - Method
13. GetCustomAttributes Member type - Method
14. GetCustomAttributes Member type - Method
15. get_ReflectedType Member type - Method
16. get_DeclaringType Member type - Method
17. get_Name Member type - Method
18. get_MemberType Member type - Method
19. GetHashCode Member type - Method
20. Equals Member type - Method
21. ToString Member type - Method
22. GetAccessors Member type - Method
23. GetGetMethod Member type - Method
24. GetSetMethod Member type - Method
25. get_IsSpecialName Member type - Method
26. GetType Member type - Method
27. MemberType Member type - Property
28. PropertyType Member type - Property
29. Attributes Member type - Property
30. IsSpecialName Member type - Property
31. CanRead Member type - Property
32. CanWrite Member type - Property
33. Name Member type - Property
34. DeclaringType Member type - Property
35. ReflectedType Member type - Property
```

Before digging into the code, take a look at the output. You can see that there are 36 members in the `System.Reflection.PropertyInfo` class. In the line numbered 0 of the output, the first member is the `get_CanWrite` member, which is a method. Other members are `get_CanRead`, `get_Attributes`, `GetIndexParameters`, and so forth. Look at the lines numbered 13 and 14 of the output. They appear to be the same—both contain `GetCustomAttributes`. Is this an error? No! Each overloaded method is a separate member, as it should be.

**ANALYSIS** The first thing to note about the code is that the `System.Reflection` namespace is included in line 2. This is necessary for the reflection members that will be used in the listing.

In line 9, I assigned a specific class name to a variable. This makes it easy for you to reflect on different classes—just change the name stored in this string.

A great enhancement to this listing would be to capture a command-line parameter that indicates which class to reflect upon. I'll leave that to you to add! By making it a command-line value, you don't need to recompile each time you want to change the class. It would also illustrate a key point to you—reflection can happen at runtime.

In line 14, the name of a class is passed to the `Type.GetType` method. The returned type is assigned to the variable `MyType`. The `MyType` object is then used to get the members of the type it contains. These are assigned to a `MemberInfo` array called `Mymemberinfoarray` in line 16. Lines 24 to 32 then loop through this array and print the `Name` and the `MemberType` values for each element. As you can see, the `Name` element contains the name of the member. The `MemberType` when displayed as a string tells you the type of the individual member.

Getting basic information is relatively easy. If you want to get more specific information, a little more work is involved. Before getting to that, look at a second listing illustrating the `MemberInfo` objects. Listing 21.2 presents another look at the process of reflection.

**LISTING 21.2** reflect2.cs—A Second Look at Reflection

```
// reflect2.cs
//-----------------------------------
using System;
using System.Reflection;

namespace Reflect
{

 class Mymemberinfo
 {
    int MYVALUE;

    public void THIS_IS_A_METHOD()
    {
      //
    }

    public int myValue       // property
    {
        set { MYVALUE = value; }
    }

    public static int Main()
    {
```

**Listing 21.2** continued

```
        //The following is the class being checked
        string testclass = "Reflect.Mymemberinfo";

        Console.WriteLine ("\nFollowing is the member info for class: {0}",
                                      testclass );

        Type MyType = Type.GetType(testclass);

        MemberInfo[] Mymemberinfoarray = MyType.GetMembers();

        //Get the MemberType method and display the elements

        Console.WriteLine("\nThere are {0} members in {1}",
                Mymemberinfoarray.GetLength(0),
                MyType.FullName);

        for ( int counter = 0;
              counter < Mymemberinfoarray.GetLength(0);
              counter++ )
        {
           Console.WriteLine( "{0}. {1} Member type - {2}",
                   counter,
                   Mymemberinfoarray[counter].Name,
                   Mymemberinfoarray[counter].MemberType.ToString());
        }
        return 0;
     }
  }
}
```

**Output**

```
Following is the member info for class: Reflect.Mymemberinfo

There are 9 members in Reflect.Mymemberinfo
0. GetHashCode Member type - Method
1. Equals Member type - Method
2. ToString Member type - Method
3. THIS_IS_A_METHOD Member type - Method
4. set_myValue Member type - Method
5. Main Member type - Method
6. GetType Member type - Method
7. .ctor Member type - Constructor+
8. myValue Member type - Property
```

**Analysis** This listing uses the same reflection that you saw in Listing 21.1. The base of the listing is the same, but in this one, the listing reflects on itself. More importantly, a few different member types were added to this listing to help illustrate what can be reflected on using the `MemberInfo` type. This includes a property called `myValue`.

The `MemberInfo` type enables you to get general information. You can also use a number of other types to restrict the information you retrieve. For example, you could declare a `FieldInfo` array and discover information on fields within the type. By using a more focused method—such as `FieldInfo`—you also gain the ability to obtain more specific information on each item. For example, the `FieldInfo` type enables you to discover information, such as what the access modifiers are on a field, and provides implementation details. It also enables you to get and set values. Table 21.1 contains some classes that you might find useful for reflection.

**TABLE 21.1** Types for Discovering Specific Information

| *Reflection Types* | *Description* |
|---|---|
| `Assembly` | Work with assemblies. |
| `ConstructorInfo` | Work with constructors. Determine information such as name, parameters, access modifiers, and implementation details of constructors. |
| `EventInfo` | Work with events. Determine information such as name, event-handling information, custom attributes, and more. |
| `FieldInfo` | Work with fields. Determine information such as name, access modifiers, and implementation of fields. |
| `MethodInfo` | Work with methods. Determine information such as name, return type, parameters, access modifiers, and the implementation details of methods. |
| `Module` | Work with modules. Determine information such as classes. |
| `ParameterInfo` | Work with parameters. Determine information such as a parameter's name, data type, type (for example, input or output), and position of the parameter in a method's signature. |
| `PropertyInfo` | Work with properties. Determine information such as name, data type, declaring type, and more. |

# Attributes

As time passes, things change—just as you are changing topics now. Over the years, programming languages such as basic and C have also needed to change. These changes are usually to add new functionality that wasn't initially known or considered. If a language can't easily adapt—without breaking existing programs—the language tends to get left behind. Languages such as C and COBOL were not designed for paradigms such as object-oriented programming.

In addition to things changing, it is not unexpected that you want your programs to interact with other programs. Most programming languages are not set up to be able to interact with other systems or languages.

## What Are Attributes?

The designers of C# have included a way for the language to extend itself. This extensibility is gained through the use, of attributes.

One of the key reasons for using attributes is to associate additional information with the code in your C# programs. This information can then be obtained later at runtime.

You've actually already used an attribute in this book without realizing it. On Day 18, "Web Development," you included the code `[WebMethod]` before each method you wanted exposed in your Web services. You actually associated an attribute to your methods. Later, when the program was executed, these attributes could be queried using reflection to know which methods could be used as `WebMethods`.

A number of attributes are available throughout the .NET framework and are defined in the BCL. These include classes for documentation, multithreading, Web services, and much more. In addition to being able to use or extend these, you can also create your own custom attributes. Some examples of existing attributes in the framework include

- `CLSCompliant`indicates that the target is compliant with the CLS.
- `Conditional` indicates whether a method can be called. It is based on a defined value in the calling code.
- `Obsolete` indicates that a type is no longer current.
- `WebMethod` indicates that a method should be available within a Web service.

There are three steps that are usually associated with using attributes. The first step is to define the attribute. You have to create an attribute to use it—although there are some preexisting attributes in the .NET framework. The second is to associate the attribute with code elements. The third step is to query the attributes at runtime. If you don't use the attributes by querying them, there really is no point in having them!

## Using Attributes

As you might have guessed from the `WebMethod` attribute, attributes are included in your code listings before the element you are associating them with. You might have also speculated that attributes are indicated by the use of square brackets to enclose them. On Day 18, you associated the `WebMethod` attribute to the method within your class as follows:

```
[WebMethod]
public static int Add( int x, int y )
{
   return x + y;
}
```

In general, an attribute is associated with the code element that follows it. Some of the code elements that an attribute can be associated with are listed in Table 21.2.

**TABLE 21.2** Elements Associated with Attributes

| *Element* | *Explicit Specifier* |
|---|---|
| Assembly | `assembly` |
| Event method | `event` |
| Field | `field` |
| Method | `method` |
| Program module | `module` |
| Parameter | `param` |
| Property | `property` |
| Return value | `return` |
| Class or structure | `type` |

From Table 21.2, you can see that there are a number of different elements that an attribute can be associated with. Consider the following example:

```
[MyAttribute]
class MyClass {}
```

The `MyAttribute` attribute appears before a class. The attribute would therefore be associated to the `MyClass` class.

Now consider a second example:

```
[MyAttribute]
public int MyMethod() {}
```

This looks very similar to the `WebMethod` attribute. What is this attribute associated with? Table 21.2 lists a number of elements. Is `MyAttribute` associated to the method? Couldn't it be associated to the return type as well? Yes, it could.

C# gives you a way to make it explicit where you want the attribute associated. This is done using one of the explicit terms in Table 21.2. The ambiguity can be resolved by including the explicit term at the beginning of the attribute with a colon for separation. To associate the `MyAttribute` attribute with the return value, you use the following:

```
[return:MyAttribute]
public int MyMethod() {}
```

To associate it with the method, you use the following:

```
[method:MyAttribute]
public int MyMethod() {}
```

**Tip** Because there is no harm in using an explicit specifier on an attribute, you should use them liberally.

## Using Multiple Attributes

You can associate more than one attribute with a single code element. This can be accomplished by listing each attribute separately:

```
[FirstAttr]
[SecondAttr]
class myClass {}
```

Although this example shows the attributes on separate lines, you could include them on the same line. Additionally, you can combine attributes into a single declaration. In this case, you separate each attribute with a comma:

```
[FirstAttr, SecondAttr]
class myClass {}
```

## Using Attributes That Have Parameters

Attributes can have parameters. The purpose of including parameters with an attribute is to provide additional information.

There are two types of parameters used with attributes: positional parameters and named parameters. Positional parameters are also called *unnamed parameters*.

**NEW TERM** *Positional parameters* gain their name from the fact that their position is important. Because they must be placed in a set position, their name becomes less important. The order that *named parameters* are presented in is not important. Named parameters get their name from the fact that their name is included with the specification of the parameter. By including the name, you automatically know what the parameter is.

You can define both positional and named parameters in a single attribute. As you should be able to guess, if you are including positional parameters, they must be declared first because their position is important. Consider the following example:

```
[CodeStatus("Tested", Coder="Brad")]
class MyClass {}
```

The `CodeStatus` attribute has two parameters. These parameters are included in a similar manner to what you use with a method call. All the parameters are enclosed in a single set of parentheses, just as a method's parameters are. Additionally, each parameter is separated by a comma.

In looking at the example, you should be able to tell that the first parameter is a positional parameter. It includes just the data being supplied. In this case, the data is `"Tested"`. The second parameter includes a name that is set equal to a data value. This is a named parameter called `Coder` that is associated with the data `"Brad"`.

**Note** To clarify, positional parameters are just data. Named parameters are the name of the field set equal to the data value.

## Defining Your Own Attribute

It is important to understand that while attributes appear somewhat different from the other C# code in your programs, they are not different. Attributes are simply classes put to a special use. Because they are just classes, you can define your own to use.

Attributes are derived from an existing class in the framework, `System.Attribute`. You derive an attribute just as you would any other class:

```
public myAttribute : System.Attribute
{
   ...
}
```

When you derive a new class, you need to define a `public` constructor. Any parameters within the constructor will be considered positional parameters. You then will need to define any additional data members to be used with the attribute. Named parameters will be associated to `public` data members within the class. Specifically, the named parameters are `public` properties or fields. Finally, you need to include information to define the usage of the class.

### Restricting an Attribute

An attribute can be restricted. You can create an attribute that can be associated with only specific types of code or specific targets. For example, you can create an attribute that can be associated with only constructors. You can also create an attribute that can be associated with only methods or properties. This restriction is done with another attribute, `AttributeUsage`.

21

`AttributeUsage` is associated to the attribute class you create. The `AttributeUsage` class takes a parameter that indicates what your attribute can be associated with—it indicates your attribute's usage! Table 21.3 lists the different targets that an attribute can be restricted to.

**Caution**

Don't be confused by Tables 21.2 and 21.3. The values in Table 21.2 are used when you place your attributes in your program. The values in Table 21.3 are used when you create the attribute. Obviously, there should be some correlation between the two within your programs. If you create an attribute to work only with properties, you shouldn't place it anywhere other than with properties.

**TABLE 21.3** `AttributeUsage` Targets

| *Flag* | *Usage* |
|---|---|
| `All` | Can be used anywhere |
| `Assembly` | Can be used with an assembly |
| `Class` | Can be used with a class |
| `Constructor` | Can be used with constructors |
| `Delegate` | Can be used with delegates |
| `Enum` | Can be used with enumerators |
| `Event` | Can be used with events |
| `Field` | Can be used with fields |
| `Interface` | Can be used with interfaces |
| `Method` | Can be used with methods |
| `Module` | Can be used with modules |
| `Parameter` | Can be used with a method parameter |
| `Property` | Can be used with properties |
| `ReturnValue` | Can be used with a method's return value |
| `Struct` | Can be used with structures |

You can actually associate more than one target with an attribute you create. The restriction is accomplished by using the attribute with a parameter indicating the specific target. The parameter is composed of values from the `AttributeTargets` enumeration. These values in this enumeration are the flags listed in Table 21.3. To include more than one attribute restriction from the table, you use the | operator. The following shows how to use the `AttributeUsage` attribute to restrict a new attribute to structures and classes:

```
[AttributeUsage(AttributeTargets.Class | AttributeTargets.Struct)]
```

## Defining the Attribute Class

You define an attribute similarly to defining a regular class. After all, an attribute is really just another class—an attribute class. You've already seen the class header for declaring an attribute. In addition to the header, you need to set up any parameters and the elements within the body.

There are restrictions on the parameters for an attribute class. You can use only simple types, such as `bool`, `byte`, `char`, `short`, `int`, `long`, `float`, and `double`. Additionally, you can use `string`, `System.Type`, and `enum`. A parameter can also be defined as a one-dimensional array as long as the array type is one of the standard types already mentioned. Finally, a parameter can be of type `object`. If it is declared of type `object`, when a value is passed to an instantiated object of the attribute class, it must also be of the types already mentioned.

Listing 21.3 presents a code snippet, which is a custom attribute that can be used to track the status of a code listing, who the coder is, and who the tester is.

**LISTING 21.3** attr1.cs—A Custom Attribute Class

```
using System;

[AttributeUsage(AttributeTargets.All)]
public class CodeStatusAttribute : System.Attribute
{
   private string STATUS;
   private string TESTER;
   private string CODER;

   public CodeStatusAttribute( string Status )
   {
      this.STATUS = Status;
   }

   public string Tester
   {
      set
      {
         TESTER = value;
      }
      get
      {
```

**LISTING 21.3** continued

```
23:            return TESTER;
24:        }
25:    }
26:
26:    public string Coder
27:    {
28:        set
29:        {
30:            CODER = value;
31:        }
32:        get
33:        {
34:            return CODER;
35:        }
36:    }
37:
38:    public override string ToString()
39:    {
40:        return STATUS;
41:    }
42: }
```

**Note** C# enables you to use an attribute called *xxx*Attribute by simply typing [*xxx*()].

**ANALYSIS** Listing 21.3 creates a custom attribute class called CodeStatusAttribute. You can see in line 3 that this class is restricted to All, which really means it isn't restricted—it can be used at all the locations specified in Listing 21.3. You can see that AttributeUsage is an attribute that is passed one positional parameter. You know it is an attribute because it is enclosed in square brackets.

The attribute class actually starts in line 4. As you can see, the CodeStatusAttribute class inherits from System.Attribute and thus is an attribute class. The rest of the class contains standard code that you should be able to follow. There are three private variables that are all accessed using properties.

There are a few things you should note. Parameters that are defined as part of the constructor are positional. The first parameter used in the CodeStatusAttribute attribute will be the Status parameter. Two named parameters are also available: the other two public members, Coder and Tester.

## Using a Custom Attribute

Now that you've defined an attribute, you'll want to use it. Using the `CodeStatusAttribute` attribute in a listing is done just as the attributes used earlier were used. You need to include the positional parameter, and you have the option of including the named parameters. Listing 21.4 presents a code fragment with several classes. These classes use the `CodeStatusAttribute` attribute to indicate the status of the coding efforts.

**LISTING 21.4** attrUsed.cs—`CodeStatusAttribute` in Use with a Class

```
// attrUsed.cs - using the CodeStatus attribute
//-----------------------------------------------

[CodeStatus("Beta", Coder="Brad")]
public class Circle
{
    public Circle()
    {
        // Set up and build a circle class
    }
}

[CodeStatus("Final", Coder="Fred", Tester="John")]
public class Square
{
    public Square()
    {
        // Set up and build a square class
    }
}

[CodeStatus("Alpha")]
public class Triangle
{
    public Triangle()
    {
        // Set up and build a triangle class
    }
}

[CodeStatus("Final", Coder="Bill")]
public class Rectangle
{
    public Rectangle()
    {
        // Set up and build a rectangle class
    }
}
```

**Caution**

> This is not a complete listing, so it won't compile correctly.

**Analysis** This class uses the `CodeStatusAttribute` attribute. You might wonder whether there is an error in lines 4, 13, 22, and 31. These lines use `CodeStatus` rather than `CodeStatusAttribute`. This is not an error. You can change all of these to `CodeStatusAttribute` and the program will work; however, you don't have to. The .NET framework enables you to define attributes with the word `Attribute` at the end of the name. When you do use the attribute, you can drop the word `Attribute`. This helps make your listings a little more readable, and it makes your attribute definitions easy to identify.

In line 4, the `CodeStatus` attribute called with the positional attribute parameter filled with `"Beta"` and one named parameter is used, `Coder`. It is assigned the value `"Brad"`. In line 13, you can see that a `Tester` named parameter is also included. Line 21 contains the minimum parameters—it contains only a positional value.

## Accessing the Associated Attribute Information

If you couldn't access the attribute information at runtime, there would be little point of using attributes. You can access the attribute information via reflection. Listing 21.5 presents the code that can be used to see what attributes are associated with a class.

**Listing 21.5** reflAttr.cs—Reflection on the `CodeStatus` Attributes

```
// retrAttr.cs -
//-----------------------------------------------
class myApp
{
   public static void Main()
   {
      PrintAttributes(typeof(Rectangle));
   }

   public static void PrintAttributes( Type psdType )
   {
      Console.WriteLine("\nAttributes for: {0}", psdType.ToString());

      Attribute[] attribs = Attribute.GetCustomAttributes(psdType);
      foreach (Attribute attr in attribs)
      {
         CodeStatus item = (CodeStatus) attr;
         Console.WriteLine(
```

**LISTING 21.5** continued

```
19:                     "Status is {0}. Coder is {1}. Tester is {2}.",
20:                     item.ToString(), item.Coder, item.Tester);
21:          }
22:       }
23: }
```

**ANALYSIS** This code snippet enables you to evaluate what attributes are associated with a class. The bulk of the listing is in the `PrintAttributes` method in lines 10 to 22. This method takes a type and then prints out the types associated to that type. The `Main` method of this code snippet shows how the `PrintAttributes` method can be called with the `Rectangle` class. You should remember from Day 7, "Class Methods and Member Functions," that a class is itself a type. This means a `Rectangle` object is a `Rectangle` type. Because you can't pass the name, a method from the .NET framework is used to convert the class name to a `Type`. This is the `typeof` operator.

First, in the `PrintAttributes` method, the name of the type passed into the method, `psdType`, is printed. For the `Rectangle` class, this is `Rectangle`.

In line 14, an array of type `Attribute` is created. This array is called `attribs`. It is assigned the value of the attributes from the type that was passed into the method. This is done using a method within the `Attribute` class called `GetCustomAttributes`, returns the individual attributes associated with the argument. In the case of `psdType`, which contains the `Rectangle` type, there was one attribute (in line 31 of Listing 21.4. If there were additional attributes, they would be assigned to this array as well.

In lines 15 to 21, a `foreach` statement is used to loop through the `attribs` array of `Attribute` values. A variable called `attr` is defined as a single `Attribute` in line 15 as a part of the `foreach` statement. This is assigned the current value from the `attribs` array. For each `Attribute` in the array (`attr`), the three possible parameter values are printed. This is done by first changing the current `attr` value to be a `CodeStatus` value using casting (line 17). If line 15 is confusing, you will want to review the inheritance lessons on Days 11, "Inheritance," and 13, "Interfaces." When you have cast the `attr` to a `CodeStatus`, you can then use the methods, properties, and fields as if it were a normal `CodeStatus` type (which it is).

## Pulling It All Together



Up to this point you have seen all the parts of creating an attribute, associating it with your classes, and getting the information at runtime. Listing 21.6 pulls this all together into a listing that can be compiled and executed. You'll see that this listing is composed of the previous three listings and nothing more.

**LISTING 21.6** complete.cs—Using a Custom Attribute

```
// complete.cs -
//------------------------------------------------------------------
using System;

[AttributeUsage(AttributeTargets.All)]
public class CodeStatusAttribute : System.Attribute
{
   private string STATUS;
   private string TESTER;
   private string CODER;

   public CodeStatusAttribute( string Status )
   {
      this.STATUS = Status;
   }

   public string Tester
   {
      set
      {
         TESTER = value;
      }
      get
      {
          return TESTER;
      }
   }

   public string Coder
   {
      set
      {
         CODER = value;
      }
      get
      {
         return CODER;
      }
   }

   public override string ToString()
   {
      return STATUS;
   }
}

// attrUsed.cs - using the CodeStatus attribute
//----------------------------------------------
```

**LISTING 21.6** continued

```
[CodeStatus("Beta", Coder="Brad")]
public class Circle
{
    public Circle()
    {
        // Set up and build a circle class
    }
}

[CodeStatus("Final", Coder="Fred", Tester="John")]
public class Square
{
    public Square()
    {
        // Set up and build a square class
    }
}

[CodeStatus("Alpha")]
public class Triangle
{
    public Triangle()
    {
        // Set up and build a triangle class
    }
}

[CodeStatus("Final", Coder="Bill")]
public class Rectangle
{
    public Rectangle()
    {
        // Set up and build a rectangle class
    }
}

class myApp
{
   public static void Main()
   {
      PrintAttributes(typeof(Circle));
      PrintAttributes(typeof(Triangle));
      PrintAttributes(typeof(Square));
      PrintAttributes(typeof(Rectangle));
   }

   public static void PrintAttributes( Type psdType )
```

**LISTING 21.6** continued

```
 97:     {
 98:        Console.WriteLine("\nAttributes for: {0}", psdType.ToString());
 99:
100:        Attribute[] attribs = Attribute.GetCustomAttributes(psdType);
101:        foreach (Attribute attr in attribs)
102:        {
103:            CodeStatusAttribute item = (CodeStatusAttribute) attr;
104:            Console.WriteLine(
105:                "Status is {0}. Coder is {1}. Tester is {2}.",
106:                item.ToString(), item.Coder, item.Tester);
107:        }
108:     }
109:  }
```

**OUTPUT**

```
Attributes for: Circle
Status is Beta. Coder is Brad. Tester is.

Attributes for: Triangle
Status is Alpha. Coder is . Tester is.

Attributes for: Square
Status is Final. Coder is Fred. Tester is John.

Attributes for: Rectangle
Status is Final. Coder is Bill. Tester is.
```

**ANALYSIS** The first part of the listing defines the custom attribute `CodeStatusAttribute`. This attribute is then used with its shortened name, `CodeStatus`, with the classes throughout the middle part of the listing. Finally, the `myApp` class checks the attributes on each of the classes.

Lines 90 and 91 are additions. In the prior listing, only the `Rectangle` class was included. In this listing, each of the different class types are used with the `PrintAttributes` method. The output shows that the appropriate attributes are printed for each.

> **Note**
>
> Although this is all included in a single listing, you could have included the custom attribute in a separate file and/or namespace. You could have included it using a `using` statement.

## Single-Use Versus Multi-Use Attributes

One other point regarding attributes deserves some attention. If you tried to associate the `CodeStatus` to the same class more than once, you will get an error. For example, consider the following:

```
[CodeStatus("Beta", Coder="Brad")]
[CodeStatus("Testing", Tester="Bill")]
class Rectangle()
...
```

This generates an error. What if, however, you changed the attribute to be information on the coder of the class? The attribute could contain the coder's name as a positional parameter. Additional named parameters could include information such as the last date modified or the status. It would make sense that you could then have multiple coders on a single class.

To be able to use multiple attributes of the same type on an item is simple. All you need to do is specify that multiple associates are allowed when you initially declare the attribute. When you declared an attribute earlier, you included the following information as an attribute on your attribute declaration:

```
[AttributeUsage(AttributeTargets)]
```

where `AttributeTargets` is a positional parameter that specifies the valid targets for your attribute. You can also include the `AllowMultiple` named parameter. Setting this parameter to `true` enables you to use the same attribute multiple times on the same target. Although the default is false, you can state this value by assigning false to `AllowMultiple`.

To allow multiple `CodeStatus` attributes to be used, you change a single line in the complete.cs listing. Changing line 5 to the following is all that is required:

```
5:  [AttributeUsage(AttributeTargets.All, AllowMultiple=true)]
```

When you've done this, you can add multiple `CodeStatus` attributes to your listing.

# Summary

In today's final lesson, you covered two advanced topics within C# programming. Both enable you to get technical programming information at runtime. First you discovered reflection. You learned that through reflection you can learn what methods, properties, events, and other members are available within a program.

After discovering reflection you learned about attributes. Attributes enable the C# language to be extended in a structured manner. Additionally, attributes enable you to associate additional information to portions of your programs. You learned how to create custom attributes. You learned how to associate them to your own classes. Finally, you learned how to query the information about attributes on a program at runtime.

# Congratulations!

Congratulations, you've made it through 21 days of C#. You've learned a lot in just twenty-one lessons. There is more to learn, like today's topics, most of what you could continue to learn is an extension of what you already know. Attributes are just another application of classes within your listings. Reflection uses classes and information in the base class library. If you understood most of what was in this book, you are ready to tackle almost any basic C# project. The best way to become an expert or guru is to apply what you've learned. Write programs. The more programs you write, the quicker you will most likely go from simply knowing C# to being a full-fledged expert.

# Q&A

**Q If an attribute is supposed to appear before the element it is associated with, where do you put an attribute associated to an assembly?**

**A** Attributes for assemblies and modules are placed in your code listings after your `using` clauses for namespaces and before your code. This is the only location they can go for an assembly.

**Q Can reflection be used with attributes?**

**A** Reflection is used to determine attribute values.

# Workshop

The Workshop provides quiz questions to help you solidify your understanding of the material covered and exercises to provide you with experience in using what you've learned. Answers are provided in Appendix A, "Answers."

## Quiz

1. What can be used to get the type of an object, class, or other item?
2. What type can be used to hold a type value? What namespace is this type in?
3. What concept provides information about a class at runtime?
4. What type would you use to get detailed information on a method's parameter(s)?
5. What has been included in C# to help the language be expanded in the future or to help the language handle concepts not currently discovered?
6. Was the `WebMethod` tag you used in creating Web Services on Day 16 an example of reflection or an example of attributes?
7. Name three predefined attributes.

8. What are five things within a program that an attribute can be associated with?
9. What are the two types of parameters used with Attributes? What is the difference between the two?
10. How can you limit what items an attribute can be assigned to?
11. **BONUS:** What data types can an attribute parameter be?

## Exercises

1. Modify the Reflect.cs listing (Listing 21.1) to reflect on the `Object` class (`System.Object`).
2. What methods are available in the `Object` class? Which methods in the `Object` type are also in the types you displayed in today's exercises?
3. Modify Listing 22.2 to use the `FieldInfo` type instead of the `MemberInfo`. Use this type to evaluate a listing for its field values.
4. Modify the complete.cs listing to allow multiple attributes to be assigned to a single target. Assign two `CodeStatus` attributes to a single class.

# WEEK 3

# In Review

Congratulations! You have come to the end of this book. You have learned the fundamentals of programming with C#. In addition to learning the fundamentals of C#, you also learned to use some of the classes and other types within the standard class libraries, including the Base Class Libraries (BCL).

You learned that by using preexisting classes you have the ability to create applications that are windows-based, Web-based, or services-based. You learned that there are a number of existing classes that you can use to instantly gain large amounts of functionality.

## Apply What You Know

The best way to ensure that you have learned C# is to apply what you have learned. You should create as many C# programs as you can. You will find that the more you use C#, the easier it becomes.

## Show What You Know

As you continue to use C#, you will most likely create a number of programs or classes that you are proud of or that you believe will be useful to others. If so, send a copy of your listing along with a couple of paragraphs of text that detail what your listing does and what is special about it. As time permits, I will post these listings along with your description on the `www.TeachYourselfCSharp.com` Web site. At the same time, you will be able to review the listings that have been submitted. For specific submission guidelines, see the Web site.

# APPENDIX A

# Answers

## Day 1 Answers

### Quiz

1. Give three reasons why C# is a great choice of programming language.
    - C# is simple.
    - C# is modern.
    - C# is object-oriented.
    - C# is powerful and flexible.
    - C# is a language of few words.
    - C# is modular.
    - C# will be popular.
2. What do IL and CLR stand for?

   IL stands for Intermediate Language. CLR stands for Common Language Runtime.

3. What are the steps in the Program Development Cycle?
   a. Create the source file.
   b. Compile the program.
   c. Execute the program.
4. What command do you enter to compile a program called my_prog.cs with your compiler?

   ```
   csc my_prog.cs
   ```
5. What extension should you use for your C# source files?

   .cs
6. Is filename.txt a valid name for a C# source file?

   Yes; however, it is not recommended.
7. If you execute a program that you have compiled and it doesn't work as you expected, what should you do?

   You should review the code to verify that you didn't create a logic error.
8. What is machine language?

   It is the language that a computer can understand.
9. On what line did the following error most likely occur?

   ```
   my_prog.cs(35,6): error CS1010: Newline in constant
   ```
   It most likely occurred on line 35. If not on line 35, line 34 would be the next likely line.
10. Near what column did the following error most likely occur?

    ```
    my_prog.cs(35,6): error CS1010: Newline in constant
    ```
    Column 6

## Exercises

1. The listing should look like mumbled and jumbled text. It could include weird characters and more.
2. This program prints the area and circumference of a circle with a radius of size 4.

   ```
   Radius = 4, PI = 3.1459
   The area is 50.3344
   The circumference is 25.1672
   ```
3. The program prints out a block of X's:

   ```
   XXXXXXXXXX
   XXXXXXXXXX
   XXXXXXXXXX
   ```

```
XXXXXXXXXX
XXXXXXXXXX
XXXXXXXXXX
XXXXXXXXXX
XXXXXXXXXX
XXXXXXXXXX
XXXXXXXXXX
```

4. The program was missing quotation marks on lines 5 and 6:

```
1:  class Hello
2:  {
3:     static void Main()
4:     {
5:        System.Console.WriteLine("Keep Looking!");
6:        System.Console.WriteLine("You'll find it!");
7:     }
8:  }
```

The program prints out a block of smiley faces instead of X's.

# Day 2 Answers

## Quiz

1. What are the three types of comments you can use in a C# program?

   Single line, multiline, and document comments

2. How are each of the three types of comments entered into a C# program?

   Single line comments start anywhere on a line with two forward slashes (//).

   Multiline comments start with a forward slash followed by an asterisk (/*), and end with an asterisk followed by a forward slash (*/).

   Document comments start with three forward slashes (///).

3. What impact does whitespace have on a C# program?

   Whitespace makes a C# program easier to read. When compiled, whitespace is almost always removed, so it has no impact on the execution of the program. Whitespace is not removed in quoted text.

4. `as`, `object`, `throw`, and `catch` are keywords. The others are not.

5. What is a literal?

   A literal is a hard-coded value that cannot be changed. For example, the number 10 is simply 10. Text in quotation marks is also a literal.

6. Statements are made up of expressions.

7. What is an empty statement?

   The semicolon (;) by itself is an empty statement.

8. What are the key concepts of object-oriented programming?

   Encapsulation, polymorphism, inheritance, and reuse

9. What is the difference between `WriteLine()` and `Write()`?

   `WriteLine()` prints on a new line. `Write()` writes on the same line.

10. What do you use as a placeholder when printing a value with `WriteLine()` or `Write()`?

    You use a number between braces {}, starting with 0.

## Exercises

1. There is no answer to this exercise. This listing should compile with no errors.
2. If you run the program on its own, you get the following output:

   ```
   Format: ListIT filename
   ```

   If you run the program with a filename following it, you get the file displayed to the screen with line numbers added. Running listit.cs results in the following:

   ```
    1:  // ListIT.cs - program to print a listing with line numbers
    2:  //-----------------------------------------------------------
    3:
    4:  using System;
    5:  using System.IO;
    6:
    7:  class ListIT
    8:  {
    9:     public static void Main(string[] args)
   10:     {
   11:       try
   12:       {
   13:
   14:          int ctr=0;
   15:          if (args.Length <= 0 )
   16:          {
   17:             Console.WriteLine("Format: ListIT filename");
   18:             return;
   19:          }
   20:          else
   21:          {
   22:             FileStream f = new FileStream(args[0], FileMode.Open);
   23:             try
   24:             {
   ```

```
                StreamReader t = new StreamReader(f);
                string line;
                while ((line = t.ReadLine()) != null)
                {
                   ctr++;
                   Console.WriteLine("{0}:  {1}", ctr, line);
                }
                f.Close();
             }
             finally
             {
                f.Close();
             }
          }
       }
       catch (System.IO.FileNotFoundException)
       {
          Console.WriteLine ("ListIT could not find the file
➥{0}", args[0]);
       }

       catch (Exception e)
       {
          Console.WriteLine("Exception: {0}\n\n", e);
       }
    }
}
```

3. The program prints the numbers 1 to 10 with 0s padding each number. Following is the output:

```
001 002 003 004 005 006 007 008 009 010
```

4. **BUG BUSTER:** The bugbust.cs listing does not generate an error when you compile it. When you run the program, you will get an error. An exception is thrown. The problem is in line 8. When printing a value, the first value should be `{0}` not `{1}`.

```
8:          System.Console.WriteLine("\nA fun number is {0}", 123 );
```

5. Write the line of code that prints your name on the screen. The following are two possible answers. Of course, you can replace `"your name"` with your name!

```
System.Console.WriteLine("your name");
```

Or

```
System.Console.Write("your name");
```

# Day 3 Answers

## Quiz

1. What are the by value data types available in C#?

   `int, uint, long, ulong, bool, char, short, ushort, float, double, decimal, sbyte, and ubyte`

2. What is the difference between a signed and unsigned variable?

   An unsigned variable holds only positive values. A signed variable can hold negative values.

3. What is the smallest data type you can use to store the number 55?

   A `byte`

4. What is the biggest number that a type `short` variable can hold?

   32767 if it is signed, 65535 if it is unsigned

5. What numeric value is the character *B*?

   `66`

6. How many bits in a byte?

   There are 8 bits in a byte.

7. What literal values can be assigned to a Boolean variable?

   `true` or `false`

8. Name three of the reference data types.

   Classes, strings, interfaces, arrays, and delegates

9. Which floating-point data type has the best precision?

   `decimal`

10. What .NET data type is equivalent to the C# `int` data type?

    `System.Int32`

## Exercises

1. Change the range of values in Listing 3.6 to print the lowercase letters.

```
// Ex03_01.cs
//--------------------------------------------------------------


using System;

class chars
```

```
{
    public static void Main()
    {
        int ctr;
        char ch;

        Console.WriteLine("\nNumber    Value\n");

        for( ctr = 97; ctr <= 122; ctr = ctr + 1)
        {
            ch = (char) ctr;
            Console.WriteLine( "{0} is {1}", ctr, ch);
        }
    }
}
```

2. Write the line of code that would declare a variable named `xyz` of type `float` and assign the value of `123.456` to it.

   `float xyz = 123.456;`

3. Which of the following variable names are valid?

   a) `X` Valid

   b) `PI` Valid

   c) `12months` Invalid, can't start with a number

   d) `sizeof` Invalid, can't use a C# keyword

   e) `nine` Valid

4. **BUG BUSTER:** The following program has a problem. Enter it in your editor and compile it. Which lines generate error messages?

   ```
   BugBuster3_4.cs(13,22): error CS0029: Cannot implicitly convert type
   ➥'double' to 'decimal'
   ```

   By default, the `3.14` declared in lines 12 and 13 are of type `double`. Line 13 assigns a `double` to a `decimal` value. This won't work. You need to change `3.14` to `3.14m`

5. Exercise 6 was on your own. *HINT:* Don't forget to add suffixes.

# Day 4 Answers

## Quiz

1. What character is used for multiplication?

   The asterisk (*)

2. What is the result of 10 % 3?

   1

3. What is the result of 10 + 3 * 2?

   The answer is 16, not 26.

4. What are the conditional operators?

   The conditional operators are && (AND) and || (OR). There are also three bitwise conditional operators; & (AND), | (OR), and ^ (NOT).

5. What C# keyword can be used to change the flow of a program?

   The `if` statement can be used to change program flow.

6. What is the difference between a unary operator and a binary operator?

   A unary operator works on one variable. A binary operator works with two.

7. What is the difference between an explicit data type conversion and an implicit conversion?

   An explicit conversion requires you to add code to make the conversion happen. An implicit conversion happens automatically (you do nothing).

8. Is it possible to convert from a long to an integer?

   Yes; however, you need to make sure that the value from the long will fit into the integer or you will get an erroneous result. Additionally, this will require an explicit conversion.

9. What are the possible results of a conditional operation?

   The possible results are either true or false.

10. What do the shift operators do?

    The shift operators move the bits in a value either to the left or to the right.

## Exercises

1. The result is 17.
2. The result is 4.
3. The following is one option:

```
class exercise
{
    static void Main()
    {
        int  value = 1;

        if ( value > 65 )
        {
```

```
            System.Console.WriteLine("The value is greater than 65!");
        }
    }
}
```

4. A complete listing is not provided. The following is the critical line of code (`var` is a `char` data type):

```
if ( var == 't' || var == 'T' )
{
   // do something
}
```

5. The code is

```
MyShort = (short) MyLong;
```

6. **BUG BUSTER:** There should not be a semicolon at the end of line 7.

7. The code is

```
ShortVal = (short) IntVal;
```

8. The code is

```
LongVal = (long) DecVal;
```

9. The code is

```
charVal= (char) ch;
```

# Day 5 Answers

## Quiz

1. What commands are provided by C# for repeating lines of code multiple times?

   The `while`, `do`, `for`, and `foreach` can all be used to cause code to repeat multiple times. The `goto` can also be used with labels to do this as well; however, the `goto` is not recommended.

2. What is the fewest times the statements in a `while` will execute?

   If the condition in a `while` evaluates to `false`, the statements will never execute.

3. What is the fewest times the statements in a `do` will execute?

   The statements in a `do` will always execute at least once.

4. What is the conditional statement?

```
x == 1
```

5. What is the incrementor statement?

```
x++
```

6. What statement is used to end a case expression in a `select` statement?

   `break;`

7. What punctuation character is used with a label?

   A colon.

8. What punctuation is used to separate multiple expressions in a `for` statement?

   A semicolon is used to separate the initializer, condition, and incrementor. A comma is used to separate multiple expressions in each of these.

9. What is nesting?

   Nesting occurs when one command is placed fully within another.

10. What command is used to jump to the next iteration of a loop?

    `continue`

## Exercises

1. The following is one possible answer. This is a complete listing rather than just the `if` statement:

```
//  Ex5-1. Exercise 1 for Day 5
//------------------------------------------------------------------

class taxstatus
{
   public static void Main()
   {
      char file_type = 'm';

      if ( file_type == 's' )
      {
         System.Console.WriteLine("The filer is single");
      }
      else if ( file_type == 'm' )
      {
         System.Console.WriteLine("The filer is married filing at the sin-
gle rate");
      }
      else if ( file_type == 'j' )
      {
         System.Console.WriteLine("The filer is married filing at the
joint rate");
      }
      else
      {
         System.Console.WriteLine("The file type is not valid");
      }
   }
}
```

2. The `if` statement is valid. `x` equals `9` because `x` is equal to `2`; however, `y` is not greater than `3`.
3. The following listing is a `while` loop that counts from `99` to `1`.

**Note** The `Write` routine that is used in the following listing works just like the `WriteLine` routine. The difference is that `WriteLine` always starts on a new line whereas the `Write` routine does not.

```
//  Ex5-3.cs. Exercise 3 for Day 5
//  Count from 1 to 99
//-----------------------------------------------------------------

class while99
{
   public static void Main()
   {
      int ctr = 1;

      while ( ctr <= 99 )
      {
         System.Console.Write("{0} ", ctr);
         ctr++;
      }
   }
}
```

4. The following is a `for` loop that counts from `99` to `1`.

```
//  Ex5-4.cs. Exercise 4 for Day 5
//  Count from 1 to 99
//-----------------------------------------------------------------

class for99
{
   public static void Main()
   {
      int ctr;

      for ( ctr = 1; ctr <= 99; ctr++)
         System.Console.Write("{0} ", ctr);
   }
}
```

5. **BUG BUSTER:** The `if` statement has a semicolon after its condition. This can cause the body (statements) of the `if` to always be executed. The semicolon

needs to be removed. Following are the errors you will get when you try to compile the listing:

```
Ex5-5.cs(10,26): warning CS0642: Possible mistaken null statement
Ex5-5.cs(14,7): error CS1525: Invalid expression term 'else'
Ex5-5.cs(15,11): error CS1002: ; expected
```

Following is the corrected listing (Ex5-5fix.cs):

```
//  Ex5-5fix.cs. Exercise 5 for Day 5 (corrected BUG BUSTER)
//--------------------------------------------------------------------

class score
{
   public static void Main()
   {
      int score = 99;

      if ( score == 100 )
      {
          System.Console.WriteLine("You got a perfect score!");
      }
      else
          System.Console.WriteLine("Bummer, you were not perfect!");
   }
}
```

6. The following is one possible answer:

```
//  Ex5-6.cs. Exercise 6 for Day 5
//--------------------------------------------------------------------

class allinone
{
   public static void Main()
   {
      int ctr;

      // One solution:

      for (ctr = 1; ctr <= 10; System.Console.WriteLine("{0}", ctr++))
           ;  // empty statement.

      // Another solution:

      for (ctr = 0; ++ctr <= 10; System.Console.WriteLine("{0}", ctr))
           ;  // empty statement.
   }
}
```

A

7. The following is one possible answer:

```
//  Ex5-7.cs. Exercise 7 for Day 5
//-----------------------------------------------------------------------

class names
{
   public static void Main()
   {
      string name = "Kalee";

      System.Console.WriteLine("Starting the switch... {0}", name);

      switch (name)
      {
          case "Robert":
                    System.Console.WriteLine("Hi Bob!");
                    break;
          case "Richard":
                    System.Console.WriteLine("Hi Rich!");
                    break;
          case "Barbara":
                    System.Console.WriteLine("Hi Barb!");
                    break;
          case "Kalee":
                    System.Console.WriteLine("You Go Girl!");
                    break;
          default:
                    System.Console.WriteLine("Hi {0}", name);
                    break;
      }
      System.Console.WriteLine("The switch statement is now over!");
   }
}
```

8. The following is one possible answer (ex_roll.cs):

```
//  ex_roll.cs- Exercise 5.8. Using the switch statement.
//-----------------------------------------------------------------------

class ex_roll
{
   public static void Main()
   {
      int roll = 0;
      int ctr = 0;
      int range = 6;

      int nbr_1 = 0;    //variables used to hold totals
      int nbr_2 = 0;
      int nbr_3 = 0;
      int nbr_4 = 0;
```

```
        int nbr_5 = 0;
        int nbr_6 = 0;

        // Create random number variable
        System.Random rnd = new System.Random();

        for (ctr = 0; ctr < 100; ctr++ )
        {
          // The next line set the roll to a random number from 1 to the
          // value set in range
          roll = (int) rnd.Next(1, range + 1);

          System.Console.WriteLine("Roll {0} is {1}", ctr+1, roll);

          switch (roll)
          {
            case 1:
                      nbr_1++;
                      break;
            case 2:
                      nbr_2++;
                      break;
            case 3:
                      nbr_3++;
                      break;
            case 4:
                      nbr_4++;
                      break;
            case 5:
                      nbr_5++;
                      break;
            case 6:
                      nbr_6++;
                      break;
            default:
                      System.Console.WriteLine("Roll is not 1 through 6");
                      break;
          }
        }
       System.Console.WriteLine("\n\nThe results are:");
       System.Console.WriteLine("ones:     {0}", nbr_1);
       System.Console.WriteLine("twos:     {0}", nbr_2);
       System.Console.WriteLine("threes:   {0}", nbr_3);
       System.Console.WriteLine("fours:    {0}", nbr_4);
       System.Console.WriteLine("fives:    {0}", nbr_5);
       System.Console.WriteLine("sixes:    {0}", nbr_6);
    }
}
```

# Day 6 Answers

## Quiz

1. What are the four characteristics of an object-oriented program?

   Polymorphism, encapsulation, inheritance, and reuse

2. What two key things can be stored in a class?

   Data and routines can be stored in classes. You can also store types in a class.

3. What is the difference between a data member declared as public and one that hasn't been declared as public?

   A data member declared as public can be accessed by applications. A data member that hasn't been declared as public is private to the class—only code within the class can access it.

4. What does adding the keyword `static` do to a data member?

   Adding `static` to a data member causes only one copy of the data member to exist for all the objects created from a class.

5. What is the name of the application class in Listing 6.2?

   The application class is called lineApp.

6. What commands are used to implement properties?

   `set` and `get`

7. When is `value` used?

   `value` is used in the `set` property code. It contains the value being passed to the `set` property.

8. Is `Console` a class, a data member, a namespace, a routine, or a type?

   `Console` is a class within the `System` namespace.

9. Is `System` a class, a data member, a namespace, a routine, or a type?

   `System` is a namespace.

10. What keyword is used to include a namespace in a listing?

    `using`

## Exercises

1. Create a class to hold the center of a circle and its radius

```
class circle
{
    public int x;
    public int y;
```

```
    public double radius;
}
```

2. Add properties to the `Circle` class created in exercise 1. The following adds the properties and then uses the class in a short program:

```
//  ex0602.cs
//-----------------------------------------------

using System;

class circle
{
    int center_x;
    int center_y;
    double Radius;

    public int x
    {
       get { return center_x; }
       set { center_x = value; }
    }
    public int y
    {
       get { return center_y; }
       set { center_y = value; }
    }
    public double radius
    {
       get { return Radius; }
       set { Radius = value; }
    }
}

class MyApp
{
   public static void Main()
   {
      circle myCircle = new circle();

      myCircle.x = 10;
      myCircle.y = 10;
      myCircle.radius = 8;

      Console.WriteLine("Center: ({0},{1})", myCircle.x, myCircle.y);
      Console.WriteLine("Radius: {0}", myCircle.radius);
      Console.WriteLine("Circumference: {0}", (double) (2 * 3.14159 *
➥myCircle.radius));
   }
}
```

OUTPUT

```
Center: (10,10)
Radius: 8
Circumference: 50.26544
```

3. Create a class called `MyNumber` that stores an integer. Create properties for this number. When the number is stored, multiply it by 100. Whenever it is retrieved, divide it by 100.

```
class MyNumber
{
    int Nbr;

    public int value
    {
      get
      {
          return (Nbr / 100);
      }
      set
      {
          Nbr = value * 100;
      }
    }
}
```

4. **BUG BUSTER:** The program does indeed have a problem. Line 5 tries to include a class name. You can only use the `using` statement to include namespaces. `Console` is a class, so this causes an error. You also get an error on lines 19, 20, and 21 where the routines within the `Console` class are being used without the `Console` class name.

```
 1:  // A bug buster program
 2:  // fixed
 3:  //-------------------------------------------
 4:  using System;
 5:
 6:
 7:  class name
 8:  {
 9:     public string first;
10:  }
11:
12:  class NameApp
13:  {
14:    public static void Main()
15:    {
16:       // Create a name object
17:       name you = new name();
18:
19:       Console.Write("Enter your first name and press enter: ");
```

```
            you.first = Console.ReadLine();
            Console.Write("\nHello {0}!", you.first);
        }
    }
```

5. Write a class called `die` that will hold the number of sides of a die, `sides`, and the current value of a roll, `value`.

```
class die
{
    public int sides;
    public int value;
}
```

6. Use the class in exercise 5 in a program that declares two dice objects. Set values into the side data members. Set random values into the stored roll values. Note, see Listing 5.3 for help with this program.

```
//  dice1.cs - A class with two data members
//-----------------------------------------------------------------------

using System;

class die
{
    public int sides;
    public int value;
}

class diceApp
{
    public static void Main()
    {
        die dice1 = new die();
        die dice2 = new die();

        dice1.sides = 6;
        dice2.sides = 12;

        // The next two lines set the roll to a random number
        // based on the number of sides.
        Random rnd = new Random();
        dice1.value = (int) ((rnd.NextDouble() * dice1.sides) + 1);
        dice2.value = (int) ((rnd.NextDouble() * dice2.sides) + 1);

        Console.WriteLine("dice 1; sides = {0}, value = {1}",
                                    dice1.sides, dice1.value);
        Console.WriteLine("dice 2; sides = {0}, value = {1}",
                                    dice2.sides, dice2.value);
    }
}
```

# Day 7 Answers

## Quiz

1. What are the two key parts of a method?

   The method header and the method body

2. What is the difference between a function and a method?

   There is no difference between a function and a method. These two terms can be used interchangeably in C#.

3. How many values can be returned from a method?

   This is a tricky question. Only one value can be *returned* from a method; however, you can use `ref` variables or `out` variables to *change* more than one variable in a calling program.

4. What keyword returns a value from a method?

   The `return` keyword

5. What data types can be returned from a method?

   Any data type can be returned from a method. Additionally, any data type can be passed to a method. This includes objects. A data type does not have to be returned.

6. What is the format of accessing a member method of a class? For example, if an object called `myObject` is instantiated from a class called `myClass`, which contains a method called `myMethod`, which of the following are correct for accessing the method?

   a. `myClass.myMethod()` is correct if the `myMethod` method is declared as `static`. If `myMethod` is not declared as `static`, this is in error.

   b. `myObject.myMethod()` is the standard way of calling a method within a class for an instance of an object. If the method had been declared as `static`, this would be wrong (and (a) would be correct).

   c. `myMethod` is correct only if `myMethod` is a part of the same class that is calling `myMethod`. If `myMethod` is declared in a different class, this would be an error.

   d. `myClass.myObject.myMethod` is not correct.

7. What is the difference between passing a variable by reference versus passing a variable by value?

   Passing by value sends a copy of a variable, which means the original variable in the calling method is not modified. Passing by reference sends information to the method that points back to the location of the original variable, which means the method can change the variable's value in the calling method.

8. When is a constructor called?

   The constructor for a class is called each time an object is instantiated (created) with the class. If the constructor is declared as `static`, it is instantiated some time before the first object is instantiated.

9. What is the syntax for a destructor that has no parameters?

   The syntax is a tilde (~) followed by the class name and empty parentheses. This is followed by the body. For the `xyz` class, the destructor is

```
~xyz()
{
   // body
}
```

10. When is a destructor called?

    A destructor is called some time after the last object of a class is no longer in use and before the program totally ends.

## Exercises

1. Write the method header for a public method called `xyz`. This method will take no arguments and will return no values.

```
public void xyz()
```

2. Write the method header for a method called `myMethod`. This method will take three arguments as its parameters. The first will be a double passed by value called `myVal`. The second will be an output variable of type string called `myOutput`, and the third will be an integer passed by reference called `myReference`. The method will be publicly accessible and will return a byte value.

```
public byte MyMethod(double myVal, out string myOutput, ref int
➥myReference)
```

3. The following is one possible solution:

```
//  ex_circ.cs - A simple circle class
//------------------------------------------------------------------

public class Circle
{
    public int x;
    public int y;
    public int radius;

    public double area()
```

```
        {
           double theArea;
           theArea = 3.14159 * radius * radius;
           return theArea;
        }

        public double circumference()
        {
           double theCirc;
           theCirc = 2 * 3.14159 * radius;
           return theCirc;
        }

        public Circle()
        {
           x = 5;
           y = 5;
           radius = 1;
        }

        public void print_circle_info()
        {
          System.Console.WriteLine("\nCircle: Center = ({0},{1})", x, y);
          System.Console.WriteLine("           Radius = {0}", radius);
          System.Console.WriteLine("           Area   = {0}", area());
          System.Console.WriteLine("           Circum = {0}", circumfer-
➥ence());
        }
    }

    class CircleApp
    {
       public static void Main()
       {
          Circle first  = new Circle();
          Circle second = new Circle();

          first.x = 10;
          first.y = 14;
          first.radius = 3;

          first.print_circle_info();
          second.print_circle_info();
       }
    }
```

The following is the output for this listing:

**OUTPUT**

```
Circle: Center = (10,14)
        Radius = 3
        Area   = 28.27431
        Circum = 18.84954
```

```
Circle: Center = (5,5)
        Radius = 1
        Area   = 3.14159
        Circum = 6.28318
```

4. **BUG BUSTER:** The following code snippet has a problem. Which lines generate error messages?

   This method is declared with a `void` return type; therefore it cannot return a value. The `return` statement generates an error.

```
public void myMethod()
{
    System.Console.WriteLine("I'm a little teapot short and stout");
    System.Console.WriteLine("Down came the rain and washed the spider
out");
}
```

5. The following is one possible answer for this exercise:

```
//  ex_dice.cs- A class with two data members and member methods
//-----------------------------------------------------------------

class die
{
    public int sides;
    public int value;

    // The following declares a data member called rnd that is an
    // object of type System.Random.
    static System.Random rnd = new System.Random();

    public int roll()
    {
        value = (int) ((rnd.NextDouble() * sides) + 1);
        return value;
    }

    // A constructor to default values in the data members.
    public die()
    {
        sides = 6;
        value = 0;
    }
}

class diceclass
{
    public static void Main()
    {
        die dice1 = new die();
        die dice2 = new die();
```

A

```
        dice1.sides = 6;
        dice2.sides = 12;

        // The next two lines set the value data member to randon number
        // based on the number of sides. This is done with the roll()
        // method.
        dice1.roll();
        dice2.roll();

        System.Console.WriteLine("dice 1; sides = {0}, value = {1}",
                                 dice1.sides, dice1.value);
        System.Console.WriteLine("dice 2; sides = {0}, value = {1}",
                                 dice2.sides, dice2.value);
    }
}
```

The following is the output for this listing:

OUTPUT

```
dice 1; sides = 6, value = 4
dice 2; sides = 12, value = 9
```

# Day 8 Answers

## Quiz

1. What is the difference between a value data type and a reference data type? Which is a structure?

   A structure is a value data type. A value data type stores the actual value(s) being assigned. A reference data type actually stores information as to where the values are located.

2. What are the differences between a structure and a class?

   The primary difference is that a structure is a value data type and a class is a reference data type. Other differences include the fact that structures don't have default constructors with no parameters and don't have destructors.

3. How are structure constructors different from class constructors? (Or are they?)

   A structure cannot have a default constructor that takes no parameters.

4. What keyword is used to define an enumeration?

   The `enum` keyword is used.

5. What data types can be stored in an enumerator?

   `byte`, `sbyte`, `int`, `uint`, `short`, `ushort`, `long`, and `ulong`

6. What is the index value of the first element in an array?

   Zero.

7. What happens if you access an element of an array with an index larger than the number of elements in the array?

   You will get a runtime error.

8. How many elements are in the array declared as `myArray[4,3,2]`? If this is a character array, how much memory will be used?

   This array will have 24 elements. If each element is a character, this array will require 48 bytes of memory.

9. How can you tell the size of an array?

   You can use the `Length` member of the array. This returns the number of elements in the array.

10. True or False (if False, what is wrong): The format of the `foreach` contains the same structure as the `for` statement?

    A `foreach` statement has a different format than the `for` statement. The `foreach` statement has a single data element declared, which is used in the array. The format is

    ```
    foreach(datatype varname in arrayName)
    ```

## Exercises

1. The following is one possible answer.

```
// ex_line.cs- A line structure which contains point structures. (ex
➥8.1)
//-----------------------------------------------------------------------------
➥---

struct point
{
        private int point_x;
        private int point_y;

        public int x
        {
            get { return point_x; }
            set { point_x = value; }
        }
        public int y
        {
            get { return point_y; }
            set { point_y = value; }
        }
```

```
}

struct line
{
   private point line_starting;
   private point line_ending;

   public point starting
   {
      get { return line_starting; }
      set { line_starting = value; }
   }
   public point ending
   {
      get { return line_ending; }
      set { line_ending = value; }
   }
}

class lineApp
{
   public static void Main()
   {
      line myLine = new line();

      point tmp_point = new point();

      tmp_point.x = 1;
      tmp_point.y = 4;
      myLine.starting = tmp_point;

      tmp_point.x = 10;
      tmp_point.y = 11;
      myLine.ending = tmp_point;

      System.Console.WriteLine("Point 1: ({0},{1})",
                              myLine.starting.x, myLine.starting.y);
      System.Console.WriteLine("Point 2: ({0},{1})",
                              myLine.ending.x, myLine.ending.y);
   }
}
```

2. Exercise 2 is on your own.
3. **BUG BUSTER:** The problem with the code snippet is the following line:

```
Element *= Element;
```

The shortcut variable that you create with a `foreach` is read-only. You cannot assign a value to it.

4. The following is one possible answer (score.cs):

```
//  score.cs- Using an array to find the score for a class (Ex 8.4)
//-------------------------------------------------------------------

using System;

public class ClassScore
{
   public static void Main()
   {
      // Set up array to hold 30 scores...
      int [] scores = new int[30];
      // Create a total variable for calculations....
      int ttl = 0;

      // Set up random variable...
      System.Random rnd = new System.Random();

      Console.Write("Initializing scores.");

      // set random scores into array...
      for( int ctr = 0; ctr < 30; ctr++ )
      {
         scores[ctr] = (int) ((rnd.NextDouble() * 100) + 1);
         Console.Write(".");
      }
      Console.WriteLine("...done.\n");

      // Display scores to console...
      for( int ctr = 0; ctr < 30; ctr++ )
      {
         Console.WriteLine("Student {0} score: {1}", ctr+1,
➥scores[ctr]);
         ttl += scores[ctr];
      }
      Console.WriteLine("========================");
      Console.WriteLine("Average Score = {0}", (ttl/30));
   }
}
```

**OUTPUT**

```
Initializing scores...............................done.

Student 1 score: 30
Student 2 score: 79
Student 3 score: 41
. . .
Student 28 score: 98
Student 29 score: 74
Student 30 score: 7
========================
Average Score = 54
```

5. The following is just one possible solution (score2.cs).

```
//  score2.cs- Using a array to find the score for a class (Ex 8.5)
//---------------------------------------------------------------

using System;

public class ClassScore
{
   public static void Main()
   {
      // Set up array to hold 30 scores...
      int [,] scores = new int[15,30];
      // Create a total variable for calculations....
      int ttl = 0;
      int testTotal = 0;

      // Set up random variable...
      System.Random rnd = new System.Random();

      Console.Write("Initializing scores.");

      // set random scores into array...
      for ( int test = 0; test < 15; test++ )
      {
        // Loop through students for each test...
        for( int student = 0; student < 30; student++ )
        {
            scores[test,student] = (int) ((rnd.NextDouble() * 100) +
➥1);
            Console.Write(".");
        }
      }
      Console.WriteLine("...done.\n");

      //Loop through each test...
      for( int test = 0; test < 15; test++ )
      {
        testTotal = 0;    // set total accumulator to zero for a new
➥test.
        for( int student = 0; student < 30; student++ )
        {
//                Console.WriteLine("Student {0} score: {1}", student+1,
➥scores[test,student]);
            testTotal += scores[test,student];
        }
        // print out average test score...
        Console.WriteLine("Average score for test {0} is {1}",
➥test+1, testTotal/30);
        ttl += testTotal;  // Add test total to overall total
      }
```

```
        Console.WriteLine("=====================================");
        Console.WriteLine("Average score for all tests = {0}",
➥(ttl/(15*30)));
    }
}
```

**OUTPUT**

```
Initializing
scores.................................................................
...........................................................................
➥........
...........................................................................
➥........
...........................................................................
➥........
...........................................................................
➥........
...........................................................................
➥.done.

Average score for test 1 is 52
Average score for test 2 is 48
Average score for test 3 is 52
Average score for test 4 is 55
Average score for test 5 is 49
Average score for test 6 is 42
Average score for test 7 is 46
Average score for test 8 is 46
Average score for test 9 is 31
Average score for test 10 is 48
Average score for test 11 is 47
Average score for test 12 is 56
Average score for test 13 is 56
Average score for test 14 is 46
Average score for test 15 is 59
=====================================
Average score for all tests = 49
```

6. The following is just one possible solution (score3.cs).

```
//  score3.cs- Using an array to find the score for a class (Ex 8.6)
//-----------------------------------------------------------------------

using System;

public class ClassScore
{
   public static void Main()
   {
      // Set up array to hold 30 scores...
      int [,,] scores = new int[5,15,30];
      // Create a total variable for calculations....
```

```
        int ttl = 0;
        int yearTotal = 0;
        int testTotal = 0;

        // Set up random variable...
        System.Random rnd = new System.Random();

        Console.Write("Initializing scores.");

        // set random scores into array...
        for( int year = 0; year < 5; year++ )
        {
          // loop through tests for a given year...
          for ( int test = 0; test < 15; test++ )
          {
            // Loop through students for each test...
            for( int student = 0; student < 30; student++ )
            {
              scores[year,test,student] = (int) ((rnd.NextDouble() *
➥100) + 1);
              Console.Write(".");
            }
          }
        }
        Console.WriteLine("...done.\n");

        for( int year = 0; year < 5; year++ )
        {
          yearTotal = 0;
          //Loop through each test...
          for( int test = 0; test < 15; test++ )
          {
            testTotal = 0;   // set total accumulator to zero for a new
➥test.
            for( int student = 0; student < 30; student++ )
            {
//              Console.WriteLine("Student {0} score: {1}",
//                          student+1, scores[year,test,student]);
              testTotal += scores[year,test,student];
            }
            // print out average test score...
            Console.WriteLine("Average score for test {0} is {1}",
                                               test+1, testTotal/30);
            yearTotal += testTotal;  // Add test total to overall total
          }
          Console.WriteLine("====> YEAR {0} Average: {1} <====",
                                              year+1,
➥yearTotal/(15*30));
          ttl += yearTotal;
        }
        Console.WriteLine("=====================================");
```

A

```
61:         Console.WriteLine("Average score for all tests = {0}",
62:
➥(ttl/(5*15*30)));
63:     }
64: }
```

# Day 9 Answers

## Quiz

1. Is overloading functions an example of encapsulation, inheritance, polymorphism, or reuse?

   Overloading is best described as an example of polymorphism.

2. How many times can a member function be overloaded?

   There is no limit to the number of times a member function can be overloaded as long as each overload definition has a unique signature.

3. Which of the following can be overloaded?

   a. Data members

   b. Member methods

   c. Constructors

   d. Destructors

   Member functions and constructors can be overloaded. The destructor cannot be overloaded, nor can a data member be overloaded.

4. What keyword is used to accept a variable number of parameters in a method?

   The `params` keyword is used to identify that a variable number of parameters can be used.

5. What can you do to receive a variable number of parameters of different, and possibly unknown, data types?

   You can declare the parameter to be of type `object`. This will enable you to accept any data type.

6. To accept a variable number of parameters from the command line, what keyword do you include?

   The `Main` method does not require you to use the `params` keyword. You need to declare an array only to accept the command-line values. Generally this is an array of strings.

7. What is the default scope for a member of a class?

   The default scope is `private`.

8. What is the difference between the `public` and `private` modifiers?

   The `private` modifier restricts access to the class. The `public` modifier enables access outside the class.

9. How can you prevent a class from being instantiated into an object?

   You can prevent objects from being created by declaring a `private` constructor.

10. What are two uses of the `using` keyword?

    The `using` keyword can be used to shortcut fully qualified namespace names or it can be used to create aliases for a namespace or class.

## Exercises

1. Write the line of code for a method header for a public function called `abc` that takes a variable number of short values. This method returns a byte.

   ```
   public byte abc( params short [] args )
   ```

2. Write the line of code needed to accept command-line parameters.

   ```
   public static void Main( string [] args )
   ```

3. If you have a class called `aClass`, what code can you include to prevent the class from being instantiated into an object?

   You can add a `private` constructor:

   ```
   private aClass() {}
   ```

4. **BUG BUSTER:** The code does contain an error. An alias can be created for a namespace or type. You cannot create an alias to a method.

5. Create a namespace that contains a class and another namespace. This second namespace should also contain a class. Create an application class that uses both of these classes. The following is one possible answer:

   ```
   // ex0605.cs - Exercise 5 of Day 6
   //-----------------------------------------------

   using System;

   namespace Numbers
   {
      public class one
      {
         public static int value = 1;
         private one() {}
      }
      public class two
      {
         public static int value = 2;
   ```

```
        private two() {}
    }

    namespace Special
    {
        public class PI
        {
            public static double value = 3.1459;
            private PI() {}
        }
    }
}

class MyApp
{
    public static void Main()
    {
        Console.WriteLine("One is {0}", Numbers.one.value);
        Console.WriteLine("Two is {0}", Numbers.two.value);
        Console.WriteLine("PI is {0}", Numbers.Special.PI.value);
    }
}
```

**OUTPUT**

```
One is 1
Two is 2
PI is 3.1459
```

6. The following is just one possible answer:

```
//  overload.cs - Overloading functions
//---------------------------------------------------------------

using System;

public class myFunc
{

    public myFunc()
    {
        Console.WriteLine("Signature: myFunc()");
    }

    public myFunc( int x )
    {
        Console.WriteLine("Signature: myFunc( int )");
    }

    public myFunc( float x )
    {
        Console.WriteLine("Signature: myFunc( float )");
    }
```

A

```
        public myFunc( ref int x )
        {
            Console.WriteLine("Signature: myFunc( ref int )");
        }

        public myFunc ( ref float x)
        {
            Console.WriteLine("Signature: myFunc( ref float )");
        }
    }

    class myApp
    {
        public static void Main()
        {
            int i = 99;
            float f = 100.00F;

            myFunc first   = new myFunc();
            myFunc second  = new myFunc( 1 );
            myFunc third   = new myFunc( 2.2F);
            myFunc fourth  = new myFunc( ref i );
            myFunc fifth   = new myFunc( ref f );
            myFunc sixth   = new myFunc( 123L );
            myFunc seventh = new myFunc( (byte) 12 );
        }
    }
```

**OUTPUT**

```
Signature: myFunc()
Signature: myFunc( int )
Signature: myFunc( float )
Signature: myFunc( ref int )
Signature: myFunc( ref float )
Signature: myFunc( float )
Signature: myFunc( int )
```

# Day 10 Answers

## Quiz

1. What keyword(s) are used with exceptions?

   `try`, `catch`, `finally`, and `throw`

2. Which of the following should be handled by exception handling and which should be handled with regular code?

   a. A value entered by a user is not between a given range.

      This would be best handled with regular code.

b. A file cannot be read correctly.

   This would be best with exception handling.

c. An argument passed to a method contains an invalid value.

   This would be best handled with program logic.

d. An argument passed to a method contains an invalid type.

   This would be best with exception handling.

3. What causes an exception?

   If your program doesn't catch a severe programming error, it causes an exception. Additionally, the `throw` statement can cause an exception.

   Exceptions occur during runtime; however, if the compiler knows that the code will cause an exception—such as an overflow— a compile error could occur. Exceptions don't occur during coding or when requested.

5. What keyword is used to react to an exception?

   The `catch` keyword is used to react to an exception. The `try` keyword is used to route an exception to a `catch`.

6. When does the `finally` block execute?

   A `finally` block executes after a `try-catch` set has completed. The `finally` block is executed whether the `try-catch` caught an error or not.

7. How many `catch` statements are associated with a single `try` statement?

   A `try` statement can have zero or more `catch` statements. There is no limit to the number of `catch` statements; however, you should make sure they go from most specific to least specific.

8. Does the order of `catch` statements matter? Why or Why not?

   Yes, the order of `catch` statements matters. The catch statements should be in the order of the most specific to the least specific. If you put a general (least specific) `catch` first, it will `catch` an exception before a more specific catch statement gets a chance. Normally, only one `catch` clause will be executed.

9. In what namespace are many of the common predefined exceptions defined?

   Many of the predefined namespaces are defined within the System namespace.

10. What does the `throw` command do?

    The `throw` command enables you to throw, or rethrow, an exception.

## Exercises

1. The answer follows:

```
try
{
   GradePercentage = MyValue/Total
}
```

2. **BUG BUSTER:** The listing contains a specific `catch` statement after the more generic `catch` statement. The second `catch` statement for an `IndexOutOfRangeException` will never be executed and will thus result in a compiler error.
3. See the Answer for exercise 4.
4. The following is one possible answer:

```
// throwit2.cs
// Throwing your own error.
//===============================================
using System;

class NegativeNumberException : Exception
{
  public NegativeNumberException()
  {
  }

  public NegativeNumberException( string e ) : base
  {
  }

  public NegativeNumberException( string e, Exception inner ) :
          base ( e, inner )
  {
  }
}

class MyAppClass
{
   public static void Main()
   {
      int result;

      try
      {
         result = MyMath.SubtractEm( 10, 2 );
         Console.WriteLine( "Result of SubtractEm(10, 2) is {0}",
➥result);

         result = MyMath.SubtractEm( 2, 10 );
```

```
            Console.WriteLine( "Result of SubtractEm(2, 10) is {0}",
➥result);
        }

        catch (NegativeNumberException msg)
        {
            Console.WriteLine("Sorry, you can't subtract to a result
➥less than zero!");
            Console.WriteLine("\nPassed Error Message: \n{0}", msg);
        }

        catch (Exception e)
        {
           Console.WriteLine("Exception caught: {0}", e);
        }

        Console.WriteLine("At end of program");
    }
}

class MyMath
{
    static public int SubtractEm(int x, int y)
    {
        if( y > x )
           throw( new NegativeNumberException() );

        return( x - y );
    }
}
```

# Day 11 Answers

## Quiz

1. In C#, how many classes can be used to inherit from to create a single new class?

   You can inherit from only one class.

2. Which of the following is the same as a base class?

   a. Parent class

   b. Derived class

   c. Child class

   A parent class is the same as a base class. Parent and derived classes are not the same.

3. What access modifier is used to protect data from being used outside of a single class? What access modifier will enable data to be used by only a base class and classes derived from the base class?

   `private` is used to protect data within a class. `protected` is used to limit a data member to be used by a base class and classes derived from the base class.

4. How is a base class's method hidden?

   You hide a base class's method in a derived class by declaring a method with the same name using the `new` keyword.

5. What keyword can be used in a base class to insure a derived class creates its own version of a method?

   The `abstract` keyword is used in a base class to force a derived class to create its own version of a method.

6. What keyword is used to prevent a class from being inherited?

   The `sealed` keyword.

7. Name two methods that all classes have.

   All classes have a `ToString` method and a `GetType` method, which they get from the `Object` base class.

8. What class is the ultimate base class from which all other classes are derived?

   The `Object` class.

9. What does boxing do?

   Boxing is the conversion of a value type to a reference type (object).

10. What is the as keyword used for?

    The `as` keyword is used to cast a value to a data type. The benefit of the `as` keyword over a regular cast is that the `as` keyword sets a value to null instead of throwing an exception, if the value being cast is invalid for the conversion.

## Exercise

1. Write a method header for declaring a constructor for the `ABC` class that receives two arguments, `ARG1` and `ARG2`, that are both integers. This constructor should call a base constructor and pass it the `ARG2` integer. This should be done in the method header;

```
public ABC( int ARG1, int ARG2) : base( ARG2 )
{
}
```

2. Modify the following class to prevent it from being used as a base class:

```
sealed class aLetter
{
     private static char A_ch;

     public char ch
     {
        get { return A_ch; }
        set { A_ch = value; }
     }

     static aLetter()
     {
         A_ch = 'X';
     }
}
```

3. **BUG BUSTER**: You must explicitly cast the `Object`, you, to a `Person` object. This can be done by changing line 9 to one of the following two lines of code:

```
me = you as Person;
```

or

```
me = (Person) you;
```

4. This exercise is on your own!

# Day 12 Answers

## Quiz

1. What method can be used to convert and format an integer data type to a string?

   The `ToString` method can be used. This is a method of the `Object` class, so all classes will have a `ToString` method.

2. What method within the `string` class can be used to format information into a new string?

   The `string` class has a static method called `Format` that can be used to format information.

3. What specifier can be used to indicate that a number should be formatted as currency?

   The `C` or `c` specifier formats currency.

4. What specifier can be used to indicate that a number should be formatted as a decimal number with commas and containing one decimal place (for example, 123,890.5)?

The format specifier that can be used is `N` or `n`. To format with the commas and decimal place, you use `N1`.

5. What will the following display be if `x` is equal to `123456789.876`?

```
Console.WriteLine("X is {0:'a value of '#,.#'.'}", x);
```

This displays `X is a value of 123,456,789.8.`

6. What would be the specifier used to format a number as a decimal with a minimum of five characters displayed if positive, a decimal with a minimum of eight characters displayed if negative, and the text `<empty>` if a value of zero?

The specifier could be `{0:D5;D8;<empty>}` where `D5;D8;<empty>` is the specifier.

7. How would you get today's date?

You can use the `DateTime` class with the `Today` static property.

8. What is the key difference between a string and a `StringBuilder` object?

A string cannot be modified. When methods manipulate a string, they must create a new object. `StringBuilder` objects hold string information that can be manipulated.

9. What special character is used for the string formatter, and what does this do to the string?

The string formatter character is `@`. This character tells the compiler to interpret a string literally rather then interpreting escape characters and so forth.

10. How can you get a numeric value out of a string?

One way is to use the `Convert` class in the `System` namespace.

## Exercise

1. Write the line of code to format a number so that it has at least three digits and two decimal places.

```
Nbr.ToString("000.00")
```

2. Write the code to display a date value written as day of the week, month, day, full year. (for example, Monday, January 1, 2002).

One possible answer is

```
Console.WriteLine("{0:D}", dt);
```

Where `dt` is a DateTime object.

3. The following is one possible answer:

```
// readln02.cs - Exercise 12.3
//-----------------------------------------------
using System;
```

```
using System.Text;

class myApp
{
  public static void Main()
  {
     StringBuilder Input = new StringBuilder();
     string buff;

     Console.WriteLine("Enter text. When done, press Ctrl+Z or enter a
➥blank line:");

     buff = Console.ReadLine();
     while ( (buff != "") && (buff != null) )
     {
        Input.Append(buff);
        Input.Append("\n");
        buff = Console.ReadLine();
     }
     Console.WriteLine("\n\n==========>\n");
     Console.Write( Input );
     Console.Write("\n\n");
  }
}
```

4. The following is one possible answer:

```
// conv_ex.cs - Exercise 12.4
// This listing will cut the front of the string
// off when it finds a space, comma, or period.
// Letters and other characters will still cause
// bad data.
//-----------------------------------------------
using System;
using System.Text;

class myApp
{
  public static void Main()
  {
     string buff;
     int age;
     // The following sets up an array of characters used
     // to find a break for the Split method.
     char[] delim = new char[] {' ',',','.'};
     // The following is an array of strings that will
     // be used to hold the split strings returned from
     // the split method.
     string[] nbuff = new string[4];

     Console.Write("Enter your age: ");

```

```
        buff = Console.ReadLine();

        // break string up if it is in multiple pieces.

        nbuff = buff.Split(delim, 2 );     // Exception handling not added

        // Now convert....

        try
        {
            age = Convert.ToInt32(nbuff[0]);

            if( age < 21 )
                Console.WriteLine("You are under 21.");
            else
                Console.Write("You are 21 or older.");
        }
        catch( ArgumentException)
        {
            Console.WriteLine("No value was entered... (equal to null)");
        }
        catch( OverflowException)
        {
            Console.WriteLine("You entered a number that is too big or too small.");
        }
        catch( FormatException)
        {
            Console.WriteLine("You didn't enter a valid number.");
        }
        catch( Exception e )
        {
            Console.WriteLine("Something went wrong with the conversion.");
            throw;
        }
    }
}
```

5. This exercise was on your own!

# Day 13 Answers

## Quiz

1. Are interfaces a reference type or a value type?

   Interfaces are a reference type similar to an abstract class.

2. What is the purpose of an interface?

   An interface defines what will be contained within a class that will be declared; however, an interface does not define the actual functionality.

3. Are members of an interface declared as `public`, `private`, or `protected`?

   Okay, this was a trick question. You don't use any of these modifiers!

4. What is the primary difference between an interface and a class?

   An interface does not implement any of the members. It only provides definitions.

5. What inheritance is available with structures?

   Structures cannot inherit. They can, however, implement interfaces.

6. What types can be included in an interface?

   Properties, events, virtual methods, and indexers.

7. How would you declare a public class called `AClass` that inherits from a class called `baseClass` and implements an interface called `IMyInterface`?

   ```
   public class AClass : baseClass, IMyInterface {...}
   ```

8. How many classes can be inherited from at one time?

   You can inherit from only one class at a time.

9. How many interfaces can be inherited (implemented) at one time?

   You can implement zero or more interfaces at a time.

10. How is an explicit interface implementation done?

    An explicit implementation is done by including the interface name with the member name when you define the member. You must also use casting to call the method.

## Exercises

1. The following is one possible answer:

   ```
   interface Iid
   {
      long ID
      {
         get;
         set;
      }
   }
   ```

2. The following is one possible answer:

   ```
   interface IPosition
   {
   ```

```
    bool Location(Point loc);
}
```

3. The code snippet does have an error. The interface tries to implement two data members (`Width` and `Height`). You cannot implement data members within an interface.

4. The following is one possible answer:

```
//  rect.cs - Exercise 13.4.
//-----------------------------------------------------------------

using System;

public interface IShape
{
   double Area();
   double Circumference();
   int    Sides();
}

public class Rectangle : IShape
{
   public int width;
   public int length;

   public double Area()
   {
      return (double) width * length;
   }

   public double Circumference()
   {
      return ((double) ((2 * width) + (2 * length)));
   }

   public int Sides()
   {
      return 4;
   }

   public Rectangle()
   {
      width = 0;
      length = 0;
   }
}

public class myApp
{
   public static void Main()
```

```
    {
        Rectangle rect = new Rectangle();
        rect.width = 11;
        rect.length = 4;

        Console.WriteLine("Displaying Rectangle information:");
        displayInfo(rect);
        Console.WriteLine("Width: {0}", rect.width);
        Console.WriteLine("Length: {0}", rect.length);

        for( int L = 0; L < rect.length; L++ )
        {
            Console.Write("\n");
            for( int w = 0; w < rect.width; w++ )
            {
                Console.Write("X");
            }
        }
        Console.WriteLine("\n");
    }

    static void displayInfo( IShape myShape )
    {
        Console.WriteLine("Area: {0}", myShape.Area());
        Console.WriteLine("Sides: {0}", myShape.Sides());
        Console.WriteLine("Circumference: {0}",
➥myShape.Circumference());
    }
}
```

# Day 14 Answers

## Quiz

1. You are in your living room and the phone rings. You get up and answer the phone. The ringing of the phone is best associated with which of the following concepts?

   a. Indexer

   b. Delegate

   c. Event

   d. Event handler

   e. Exception handler

   The ringing of the phone is best associated as an event.

2. Your answering the phone is best associated with which of the following concepts:

   a. Indexer

   b. Delegate

c. Event

d. Event handler

e. Exception handler

Your answering the phone will be equivalent to an event handler.

3. What is the point of an indexer?

   An indexer enables you to access information within a class/object using index notation.

4. When declaring an indexer, what keyword is used?

   An indexer is created similar to a property, with the `this` keyword being used instead of a property name.

5. An indexer definition is similar to which of the following:

   a. A class definition

   b. An object definition

   c. A property definition

   d. A delegate definition

   e. An event definition

   An indexer definition is similar to a property definition.

6. What are the different steps to creating and using an event?

   There are several steps to creating and using an event. This includes setting up the delegate for the event, creating a class to pass arguments for the event handlers, declaring the code for the event itself, creating code that should occur when the event happens (the handler), and finally causing the event to occur.

7. What operator is used to add an event handler?

   The += operator is used to add an event handler. The -= operator is used to remove an event handler.

8. What is it called when multiple event handlers are added to an event?

   Multicasting.

9. Which is true (note—none or both are possible answers):

   An event is an instantiation based on a delegate.

   A delegate is an instantiation based on an event.

   An event is an instantiation of a delegate. Don't let the word instantiation confuse you.

10. Where within a class can an event be instantiated?

    An event can be instantiated within either a property or a method.

## Exercises

1. The following is one possible answer:

```
//  indexer.cs - Using an indexer
//--------------------------------------------------------------------

using System;

public class SimpleClass
{
    int[] numbers;

    public SimpleClass(int size)
    {
       numbers = new int[size];         // declare size elements
       for ( int x = 0; x < size; x++ ) // initialize values to 0.
           numbers[x] = 0;
    }
// exception handling or programming logic should be added to the
// following to make sure the index is not out of range.
    public int this[int index]
    {
       get
       {
            return numbers[index];
       }
       set
       {
            numbers[index] = value;
       }
    }
}

public class TestApp
{
   public static void Main()
   {
      int size = 10;
      SimpleClass myObj = new SimpleClass(size);

      for ( int x = 0; x < size; x++ )
          myObj[x]= x * x;

      for ( int x = 0; x < size; x++ )
         Console.WriteLine("Ctr: {0}, Value {1}", x, myObj[x]);

   }
}
```

2. The following is one possible answer:

```
// indx2b.cs - Using an array instead of an indexer
//-----------------------------------------------------------------------

using System;

public class SpellingList
{
    public string[] words = new string[size];
    static public int size = 10;

    public SpellingList()
    {
        for (int x = 0; x < size; x++ )
            words[x] = String.Format("Word{0}", x);
    }
}

public class TestApp
{
   public static void Main()
   {
      SpellingList myList = new SpellingList();

      myList.words[3] = "=====";
      myList.words[4] = "Brad";
      myList.words[5] = "was";
      myList.words[6] = "Here!";
      myList.words[7] = "=====";

      for ( int x = 0; x < SpellingList.size; x++ )
          Console.WriteLine(myList.words[x]);
   }
}
```

3. This can be done by changing the `DoSort` method to `static`. The complete listing follows:

```
// deleg1b.cs - Using a delegate
//-----------------------------------------------------------------------

using System;

public class SortClass
{
    static public int val1;
    static public int val2;

    public delegate void Sort(ref int a, ref int b);

    static public void DoSort(Sort ar)
```

```
    {
       ar(ref val1, ref val2);
    }
}

public class SortProgram
{
   public static void Ascending( ref int first, ref int second )
   {
      if (first > second )
      {
         int tmp = first;
         first = second;
         second = tmp;
      }
   }

   public static void Descending( ref int first, ref int second )
   {
      if (first < second )
      {
         int tmp = first;
         first = second;
         second = tmp;
      }
   }

   public static void Main()
   {
      SortClass.Sort up = new SortClass.Sort(Ascending);
      SortClass.Sort down = new SortClass.Sort(Descending);

      SortClass.val1 = 310;
      SortClass.val2 = 220;

      Console.WriteLine("Before Sort: val1 = {0}, val2 = {1}",
                         SortClass.val1, SortClass.val2);
      SortClass.DoSort(up);

      Console.WriteLine("Before Sort: val1 = {0}, val2 = {1}",
                         SortClass.val1, SortClass.val2);
      SortClass.DoSort(down);

      Console.WriteLine("After Sort: val1 = {0}, val2 = {1}",
                         SortClass.val1, SortClass.val2);
   }
}
```

4. The following is one possible answer:

```
//  delegate.cs - Using a delegate
//------------------------------------------------------------------------

```

```
using System;

public class SortClass
{
   public static int [] vals = new int[10];
   public static Type arrType;

   public delegate void Sort( int[] vals );

   public void DoSort(Sort ar)
   {
      ar(vals);
   }
}

public class SortOption
{

  public static void Ascending( int[] vals )
  {
     int tmp;

     for (int first = 0; first < (vals.Length - 1); first++ )
     {
        for ( int second = 1 + first ; second < vals.Length; second++ )
        {
           if (vals[first] > vals[second] )
           {
              tmp = vals[first];
              vals[first] = vals[second];
              vals[second] = tmp;
              Console.Write("<.");
           }
        }
     }
  }

  public static void Descending( int[] vals )
  {
     int tmp;

     for (int first = 0; first < (vals.Length - 1); first++ )
     {
        for ( int second = 1 + first; second < vals.Length; second++ )
        {
           if (vals[first] < vals[second] )
           {
              tmp = vals[first];
              vals[first] = vals[second];
```

```
                    vals[second] = tmp;
                    Console.Write(">.");
                }
            }
        }
    }

    public static void Main()
    {
        SortClass.Sort up = new SortClass.Sort(Ascending);
        SortClass.Sort down = new SortClass.Sort(Descending);

        SortClass doIT = new SortClass();

        SortClass.vals[0] = 325;
        SortClass.vals[1] = 31;
        SortClass.vals[2] = 23;
        SortClass.vals[3] = 1234;
        SortClass.vals[4] = 12;
        SortClass.vals[5] = 91;
        SortClass.vals[6] = 100;
        SortClass.vals[7] = 3;
        SortClass.vals[8] = 2000;
        SortClass.vals[9] = 369;

        for ( int x = 0; x < 10; x++ )
            Console.WriteLine("Original value {0}: {1}", x,
➥SortClass.vals[x]);

        // A check here could be done to determine if the sort should
        // be ascending or descending. Based on the answer, you could
        // then declare either the up or the down object (instead of
        // declaring it above).

        Console.Write("\nSorting...");

        doIT.DoSort(up);

        Console.Write("\n\n");

        for ( int x = 0; x < 10; x++ )
           Console.WriteLine("Sorted value {0}: = {1}", x,
➥SortClass.vals[x]);
    }
}
```

The following is the output from this listing:

```
Original value 0: 325
Original value 1: 31
Original value 2: 23
```

A

```
Original value 3: 1234
Original value 4: 12
Original value 5: 91
Original value 6: 100
Original value 7: 3
Original value 8: 2000
Original value 9: 369

Sorting...<.<.<.<.<.<.<.<.<.<.<.<.<.<.<.<.<.<.<.<.<.<.

Sorted value 0: = 3
Sorted value 1: = 12
Sorted value 2: = 23
Sorted value 3: = 31
Sorted value 4: = 91
Sorted value 5: = 100
Sorted value 6: = 325
Sorted value 7: = 369
Sorted value 8: = 1234
Sorted value 9: = 2000
```

5. The following is one possibility for the code that is executed for the `ToUpperVowels` event.

```
static void ToUpperVowels(object source, CharEventArgs e)
{
    switch( e.CurrChar )
    {
        case 'a':   e.CurrChar = 'A';
                    break;
        case 'e':   e.CurrChar = 'E';
                    break;
        case 'i':   e.CurrChar = 'I';
                    break;
        case 'o':   e.CurrChar = 'O';
                    break;
        case 'u':   e.CurrChar = 'U';
                    break;
    }
}
```

To add this as an event, you could use the following line:

```
tester.TestChar += new CharEventHandler(ToUpperVowels);
```

# Day 15 Answers

## Quiz

1. How many ticks are needed to make a second?

   1,000 ticks equal a second.

2. Which of the following does a timer use?
   a. A delegate
   b. An event
   c. An orphomite
   d. An exception

   A timer kicks off an event. An event uses a delegate. This means that both a and b could be considered correct.

3. Which standards organization is standardizing C# and the Base Class Libraries?

   ECMA

4. What is the difference between using `Environment.GetCommandLineArgs` and `Main( String args[] )`?

   The `GetCommandLineArgs` returns the program name as the first argument.

5. When would you create an instance of the `Math` class (when would you create a `Math` object)?

   Never. The `Math` class contains all `static` members; therefore, you will never have the need to create a `Math` object.

6. What class or method can be used to determine whether a file actually exists?

   The `File.Exists` method can be used to determine whether a file exists. This enables you to determine which command should be used to open or create a file.

7. What is the difference between a file and a stream?

   A stream is simply a flow of information. It does not have to be associated with a file or be text.

8. Which `FileMode` value can be used to create a new file?

   `Append`, `Create`, `CreateNew`, or `OpenOrCreate`

9. What are some of the classes for working with XML?

   The System.XML namespace contains lots of classes for working with XML files and data. This includes `DataDocumentNavigator`, `DocumentNavigator`, `XmlAttribute`, `XmlAttributeCollection`, `XmlCDataSection`, `XmlCharacterData`, `XmlComment`, `XmlConvert`, `XmlDataDocument`, `XmlDeclaration`, `XmlDocument`, `XmlDocumentFragment`, `XmlDocumentType`, `XmlEditor`, `XmlElement`, `XmlEntity`, `XmlEntityReference`, `XmlException`, `XmlImplementation`, `XmlLinkedNode`, `XmlNamedNodeMap`, `XmlNamespaceManager`, `XmlNameTable`, `XmlNavigator`, `XmlNode`, `XmlNodeList`, `XmlNodeReader`, `XmlNotation`, `XmlParserContext`, `XmlProcessingInstruction`, `XmlQualifiedName`, `XmlReader`, `XmlResolver`,

XmlSignificantWhitespace, XmlText, XmlTextReader, XmlTextWriter, XmlUrlResolver, XmlValidatingReader, XmlWhitespace, and XmlWriter.

## Exercises

1. The following is one possible answer:

```
//  binWrite1.cs -
//  Exception handling left out to keep listing short.
//-----------------------------------------------------
using System;
using System.IO;


public struct Person
{
   public string FirstName;
   public string LastName;
   public int    Age;
   public bool   Member;
}

class MyStream
{
   public static void Main(String[] args)
   {
      if( args.Length < 1 )
      {
         Console.WriteLine("Must include file name.");
      }
      else
      {
         FileStream myFile = new FileStream(args[0],
➥FileMode.CreateNew);
         BinaryWriter bwFile = new BinaryWriter(myFile);

         Person client;

         client.FirstName = "Bradley";
         client.LastName = "Jones";
         client.Age = 21;
         client.Member = true;

         bwFile.Write( client.FirstName );
         bwFile.Write( client.LastName );
         bwFile.Write( client.Age );
         bwFile.Write( client.Member );

         bwFile.Close();
         myFile.Close();
      }
```

```
    }
}
```

2. The following is one possible answer:

```
//  math2.cs - Using a Math routine
//-----------------------------------------------
using System;

class myMathApp
{
   public static void Main()
   {
      int val;
      char disp;

      for (double ctr = 0.0; ctr <= 10; ctr += .2)
      {
         val = (int) Math.Round( ( 10 * Math.Cos(ctr))) ;
         for( int ctr2 = -10; ctr2 <= 10; ctr2++ )
         {
            if (ctr2 == val)
               disp = 'X';
            else
               disp = ' ';

            Console.Write("{0}", disp);
         }
         Console.WriteLine(" ");
      }
   }
}
```

3. The following is one possible answer. The user should enter a blank line to end input.

```
//  writing1.cs - Writing to a text file.
//  Exception handling left out to keep listing short.
//-----------------------------------------------------
using System;
using System.IO;

public class WritingApp
{
   public static void Main(String[] args)
   {
      if( args.Length < 1 )
      {
          Console.WriteLine("Must include file name.");
      }
      else
      {
```

```
            Console.WriteLine("Enter text to be stored in the file.");
            Console.WriteLine("Enter a blank line to end input.");

            StreamWriter myFile = File.CreateText(args[0]);
            string buffer;

            do
            {
               buffer = Console.ReadLine();
               myFile.WriteLine(buffer);

            } while ( buffer != "" );

            Console.WriteLine("Done Writing");

            myFile.Close();
        }
    }
}
```

4. **BUG BUSTER:** The files/streams need to be closed before ending the listing.

# Day 16 Answers

## Quiz

1. What is the name of the namespace where most of the windows controls are located?

   `System.Windows.Forms`

2. What method can be used to display a form?

   You can either pass a form to the `Application.Run` method, or you can call the `ShowDialog` method on a form instance.

3. What are the three steps involved in getting a control on a form?

   You need to create the control object, set the objects properties, and then add the control to the form.

4. What do you enter on the command line to compile the program xyz.cs as a windows program?

   You enter `csc /t:winexe xyz.cs` or `csc /target:winexe xyz.cs`.

5. If you want to include the assembly myAssmb.dll when you compile the program xyz.cs, what do you enter on the command line?

   You enter `csc /r:myAssmb.dll xyz.cs` or `csc /reference:myAssmb.dll xyz.cs`

6. What does the `Show()` method of the `Form` class do? What is the problem with using this method?

   This method displays a form and then moves to the next line of code. The problem is that the method doesn't wait for user input or anything else—it simply moves on.

7. Which of the following causes the `Application.Run` method to end?

   a. A method

   b. An event

   c. The last line of code in the program is reached

   d. It never ends

   e. None of the above

   A method within an event causes the `Application.Run` method to end.

8. What are the possible colors you can use for a form? What namespace needs to be included to use such colors?

   There is a wide variety of colors that can be used. These are available from the `System.Drawing` namespace. You can see the colors in Table 16.2. They range from `BlanchedAlmond` to `HotPink`! If you don't like the specific colors listed in the table, you can create your own colors using methods within the BCL.

9. What property can be used to assign a text value to a label?

   The `Text` property.

10. What is the difference between a text box and a label?

    A text box enables a user to enter data. A label is used to display data.

## Exercises

1. The following is one possible answer:

```
using System.Windows.Forms;

public class AnApp : Form {
    public static void Main( string[] args )    {
      Application.Run(new AnApp());
    }
}
```

2. The following is one possible answer:

```
// form3b.cs - Exercise 16.2
//---------------------------------------------------------------------------------------

using System.Windows.Forms;
```

```
using System.Drawing;

public class frmApp : Form
{
    public static void Main( string[] args )
    {
        frmApp myForm = new frmApp();
        myForm.Text = "Exercise 16.2";

        myForm.Width = 200;
        myForm.Height = 200;

        myForm.StartPosition = FormStartPosition.CenterScreen;

        Application.Run(myForm);
    }
}
```

3. The following is one possible answer. *Note:* Exception handling was included for the conversion from a string to an integer.

```
// Ex1603.cs
//-----------------------------------------------------------------

using System;
using System.Windows.Forms;
using System.Drawing;


 public class frmGetNumber : Form
{


   private Button btnOK;
   private Label  lblPrompt;
   private Label  lblResponse;
   private TextBox txtNbr;

   public frmGetNumber()
   {
      InitializeComponent();
   }

   private void InitializeComponent()
   {
       this.FormBorderStyle = FormBorderStyle.Fixed3D;
       this.Text = "One To Ten";
       this.StartPosition = FormStartPosition.CenterScreen;

       // Instantiate the controls...
       lblPrompt   = new Label();
```

```
          lblResponse = new Label();

          txtNbr = new TextBox();
          btnOK  = new Button();

          // Set properties

          lblPrompt.AutoSize = true;
          lblPrompt.Text     = "Enter a Number:";
          lblPrompt.Location = new Point( 20, 20);

          txtNbr.Width = 50;
          txtNbr.Location = new Point(140, 20);


          lblResponse.Width = 250;
          lblResponse.Height = 20;
          lblResponse.Text = "Enter a number from 0 to 1000.";
          lblResponse.TextAlign = ContentAlignment.MiddleCenter;
          lblResponse.Location =
              new Point(((this.Width/2) - (lblResponse.Width / 2 )),
➥140);

          this.Controls.Add(lblPrompt);    // Add label to form
          this.Controls.Add(lblResponse);
          this.Controls.Add(txtNbr);

          btnOK.Text = "Done";
          btnOK.BackColor = Color.LightGray;
          btnOK.Location = new Point(((this.Width/2) - (btnOK.Width /
➥2)),
                                          (this.Height - 75));

          this.Controls.Add(btnOK);  // Add button to form

          // Event handlers
          btnOK.Click += new System.EventHandler(this.btnOK_Click);
          txtNbr.TextChanged += new
➥System.EventHandler(this.txtChanged_Event);
      }

      protected void btnOK_Click( object sender, System.EventArgs e)
      {
         Application.Exit();
      }

      protected void txtChanged_Event( object sender, System.EventArgs e)
      {
         try
         {
            int iNbr = Convert.ToInt32(txtNbr.Text);
```

```

            if ( iNbr < 0 )
            {
               lblResponse.Text = "Number is less than zero";
            }
            else if (iNbr > 1000)
            {
               lblResponse.Text = "Number is greater than 1000";
            }
            else
            {
               lblResponse.Text = String.Format("Number is {0}",
➥txtNbr.Text);
            }
         }

         catch(ArgumentException)
         {
            lblResponse.Text = "No number.";
         }
         catch(FormatException)
         {
            lblResponse.Text = "Not a number.";
         }
         catch(OverflowException)
         {
            lblResponse.Text = "Number too big or too small.";
         }
      }

      public static void Main( string[] args )
      {
         Application.Run( new frmGetNumber() );
      }
}
```

4. **BUG BUSTER:** The following program uses the `Form.Show` method, which displays the form and then continues. This, unfortunately, reaches the end of the program before the form really has time to display. This causes the program to end before the user has a chance to really see the form, let alone do anything with it. The following is the application fixed:

```
using System.Windows.Forms;

public class frmHello : Form
{
     public static void Main( string[] args )
     {
        frmHello frmHelloApp = new frmHello();
        Application.Run(frmHelloApp);
     }
}
```

# Day 17 Answers

## Quiz

1. What class can be used to create a radio button control?

   `RadioButton`

2. What namespace contains controls such as radio buttons and list boxes?

   `System.Windows.Forms`

3. How do you set the tab order for a form's controls?

   To set the tab order, you set the `TabIndex` property on each control. The tab order will be determined sequentially, starting with zero, based on each control's `TabIndex` property.

4. What are the steps involved in adding items to a list box?

   Call `BeginUpdate`, add items using `Items.Add`, and call `EndUpdate`.

5. What is the difference between a `MainMenu` and a `ContextMenu` item?

   A `MainMenu` item is the menu attached to the top of a form. A `ContextMenu` item is a pop-up menu.

6. What is an easy way to display a dialog with a simple message in a simple dialog?

   Use the `MessageBox` class.

7. What are some of the preexisting dialogs you can use from the base class library?

   `ColorDialog`, `PrintPreviewDialog`, `FontDialog`, and `FileDialog`

8. If you want to display a form and not allow any other forms to be displayed or activated in the same application, what method should you use?

   The `ShowDialog` method displays a dialog modally.

9. How many forms can be displayed with the `Show` method at the same time?

   As many as you want.

## Exercises

1. Write the code to add two radio buttons called `butn1` and `butn2` to a group box called `grpbox`.

```
private GroupBox grpbox  = new GroupBox();
private RadioButton btn1 = new RadioButton();
private RadioButton brn2 = new RadioButton();

this.grpbox.Controls.Add(btn1);
this.grpbox.Controls.Add(btn2);
```

2. What code would you use to add a line to the MYMENU menu?

   MYMENU.MenuItems.Add("-");

3. The following is one possible answer:

```
// ex1703.cs - using the color dialogs
//-----------------------------------------------------------------

using System;
using System.Windows.Forms;
using System.Drawing;

public class ColorForm : Form
{
   private MainMenu myMainMenu;


   public ColorForm()
   {
      InitializeComponent();
   }

   private void InitializeComponent()
   {
      this.Text = "Exercise - Colors!";
      this.StartPosition = FormStartPosition.CenterScreen;
      this.FormBorderStyle = FormBorderStyle.Sizable;
      this.Width = 400;

      myMainMenu = new MainMenu();

      MenuItem menuitemFile = myMainMenu.MenuItems.Add("&File");
      menuitemFile.MenuItems.Add(new MenuItem("Color",
                      new EventHandler(this.Color_Selection)));

      menuitemFile.MenuItems.Add(new MenuItem("Exit",
                      new EventHandler(this.Exit_Selection)));
      this.Menu = myMainMenu;
   }

   protected void Exit_Selection( object sender, System.EventArgs e )
   {
      Application.Exit();
   }

   protected void Color_Selection( object sender, System.EventArgs e )
   {
      ColorDialog myColorDialog = new ColorDialog();

      if ( myColorDialog.ShowDialog() != DialogResult.Cancel )
      {
```

```
            this.BackColor = myColorDialog.Color;
         }
      }

      public static void Main( string[] args )
      {
         Application.Run( new ColorForm() );
      }
   }
```

4. **BUG BUSTER:** The program will compile and run. There is no real problem. The `Update Date` item has an indicator that Alt+D will work (the `&D`). The shortcut key, however, is defined as `Shortcut.CtrlH`. Although using two different values may be a little bit confusing, it is not wrong.
5. This exercise is on your own.
6. The following code can be added to the listing. The completed listing is available with the source code download (EX1706.cs).

   The following should be added into the current code within the listing:

```
      protected void FileAbout_Selection( object sender, System.EventArgs
➥e)
      {
         // display an about form
         frmAbout myAboutForm = new frmAbout();
         myAboutForm.ShowDialog();
      }
```

   The following should be added to the listing to create the actual dialog:

```
   public class frmAbout : Form
   {
      private Label Description;
      private Button btnOK;

   public frmAbout()
      {
         InitializeComponent();
      }

      private void InitializeComponent()
      {
           Description = new Label();      // Create label
           Description.Text = "My first about box";
           Description.AutoSize = true;
           Description.Location = new Point( 50, 40);
           Description.BackColor = this.BackColor;

           btnOK = new Button();
           btnOK.Text = "OK";
```

```
            btnOK.Width = 80;
            btnOK.Location = new Point( 60, 80);
            btnOK.Click += new System.EventHandler( this.OK_Selection );

            this.Controls.Add(btnOK);
            this.Controls.Add(Description);

            this.Text = "About STY Menus";
            this.Width = 200;
            this.Height = 140;
            this.StartPosition = FormStartPosition.CenterScreen;
            this.FormBorderStyle = FormBorderStyle.Fixed3D;
        }

        protected void OK_Selection( object sender, System.EventArgs e)
        {
           this.Close();
        }
    }
```

# Day 18 Answers

## Quiz

1. What is a Web service?

   It is a process that can be executed even though it might reside somewhere else on the Web.

2. What is the file called that helps a client application communicate with a Web service?

   A Web proxy

3. What program can be used to create the code to communicate with a Web server?

   WSDL.EXE

4. How can you tell a Web service from an ASP.NET page?

   A Web service has an .asmx extension, and an ASP.NET page has an .aspx extension.

5. How do you execute an ASP.NET page?

   You copy it to a Web server and then access the file using a browser.

6. What are the two types of controls used for Web forms?

   Server-side controls and HTML server controls

7. Does Listing 18.6 use HTML controls, HTML server controls, or Web server-controls?

They are Web server controls. You know this because they are preceded by `asp:`.

8. What is the difference between a standard HTML control and an HTML server control?

   An HTML server control executes on the Web server. A standard HTML control is executed by a browser. HTML server controls generally generate standard HTML controls.

9. What is the server equivalent of the standard HTML table tag?

   `HtmlTable`

10. How can you tell a server-side HTML control from a standard HTML control?

    The server-side control includes a `runat=server` attribute.

## Exercises

1. What is the first line of a C# program that will be used as a Web service? Assume the Web service class name is `DBInfo` and the first method is called `GetData`.

   ```
   <%@WebService Language="C#" Class="DBInfo"%>
   ```

2. What changes need to be made to a method to use it in a Web service?

   You must add `[WebMethod]` before the start of the method.

3. Add a `Multiply` and `Subtract` method to the `Calc` Web service.

```
<%@WebService Language="C#" Class="Calc"%>

//------------------------------------
// Ex-WebCalc.asmx
//------------------------------------

using System;
using System.Web.Services;

public class Calc : WebService
{
   [WebMethod]
   public int Add( int x, int y )
   {
      return x + y;
   }

   [WebMethod]
   public int Subtract( int x, int y )
   {
      return x - y;
   }

   [WebMethod]
```

```
    public int Multiply( int x, int y )
    {
       return x * y;
    }

    [WebMethod]
    public int Divide( int x, int y )
    {
       int answer;

       if ( y == 0 )
          answer = 0;
       else
          answer = x / y;

       return answer;
    }
}
```

4. Create a new client that uses the Multiply and Divide classes created in Exercise 3.

```
// Ex-webclient.cs
// Calling a Web service
//-----------------------------

using System;

public class myApp
{
   public static void Main()
   {
      Calc cSrv = new Calc();

      Console.WriteLine("cSrv.Add( 11, 33); = {0}",
                         cSrv.Add(33, 11));
      Console.WriteLine("cSrv.Subtract(33, 11); = {0}",
                         cSrv.Subtract(33,11));

      Console.WriteLine("cSrv.Multiply( 4, 11); = {0}",
                         cSrv.Multiply(4, 11));
      Console.WriteLine("cSrv.Divide(55, 11); = {0}",
                         cSrv.Divide(55,11));
      Console.WriteLine("cSrv.Divide(55, 0); = {0}",
                         cSrv.Divide(55,0));
   }
}
```

5. **ON YOUR OWN:** This exercise was on your own.
6. **ON YOUR OWN:** This exercise was on your own.

# Day 19 Answers

## Quiz

1. What is debugging?

   Debugging is the process of determining what a problem is in your listing and removing it.

2. Do preprocessing directives end with a semicolon?

   No. There is no semicolon in a preprocessing directive.

3. What bug is credited with forever associating the term *debugging* with computers?

   This was a million-dollar question on *Who Wants to Be a Millionaire*. The answer is a moth.

4. Which type of error will the compiler find?

   The compiler will find syntax errors. It won't find runtime or logic errors.

5. When doing a code walkthrough, which parts of a listing should you review?

   You should review all of a listing when doing a code walkthrough. You should read each line. One nice thing about using an object-oriented environment and object-oriented programming is that you can code classes in separate listings. This enables you to encapsulate their functionality. After you've walked through a class's code, you might not need to walk through its details every time you use it. Rather, you can make sure you call it correctly and that you accept the expected return types.

6. Which language has the fewest directives: C, C++, or C#?

   C# has the fewest. Many directives were removed to help prevent coding problems (bugs) that could be caused by overusing directives.

7. What are the directives for defining and undefining a symbol in your code listing?

   `#define` and `#undef`. Note that it is `#undef` and not `#undefined`!

8. What flag is used to define a symbol on the command line?

   You can use `/define:` or `/d:`.

9. What directive enables you to change the line numbers used by the compiler? What value can be used to change the line numbers back to the real line numbers?

   `#line` is the directive used. `#line default` would revert the lines following the directive to their original values.

10. What classes are provided in the base class libraries to help do debugging and other diagnostics?

    The `Systems.Diagnostics` namespace contains `Trace` and `Debug` classes that can be used.

## Exercises

1. What code would you use to define a symbol to be used for preprocessing? Call the symbol `SYMBOL`.

   You can either define the symbol in the command line using `/d:SYMBOL` or `/define:SYMBOL`, or you can define it using `#define SYMBOL`.

2. Write the code that you would need to add to your listing to have the line numbers start with 1000.

   ```
   #line 1000
   ```

3. The listing does work. It displays `"Hello Goofy World"`. The listing is equivalent to the following:

   ```
   //  fun2.cs - Same as the fun.cs listing...
   //-----------------------------------------------
   using System;
   #warning This listing is not practical...

   public class
   myApp { public static void
   Main(){Console.WriteLine(
    "Hello"
   + " Goofy "
   + "World"
   );}
   }
   ```

   This is the same as the following listing, which is formatted better:

   ```
   //  fun2.cs - Same as the fun.cs listing...
   //-----------------------------------------------
   using System;
   #warning This listing is not practical...

   public class myApp
   {
      public static void Main()
      {
         Console.WriteLine( "Hello" + " Goofy " + "World");
      }
   }
   ```

4. **BUG BUSTER:** You cannot undefine a symbol except at the beginning of the listing. You need to remove line 34.

   ```
   1:  //  bugbustd.cs -
   2:  //-----------------------------------------------
   3:
   4:  using System;
   5:
   ```

```
public class ReadingApp
{
    #if MYLINES
    #line 100
    #endif
    public static void Main(String[] args)
    {
        Console.WriteLine("In Main....");
        myMethod1();
        myMethod2();
        Console.WriteLine("Done with Main");
    }

    #if MYLINES
    #line 200
    #endif
    static void myMethod1()
    {
        Console.WriteLine("In Method 1");
    }

    #if MYLINES
    #line 300
    #endif
    static void myMethod2()
    {
        Console.WriteLine("in Method 2");
    }
}
```

5. This exercise was on your own.
6. This exercise was on your own.

# Day 20 Answers

## Quiz

1. How many times can a single operator be overloaded in a single class?

   An operator can be overloaded multiple times. See the answer to quiz question 2 for more details.

2. What determines how many times an operator can be overloaded?

   The unique signature of the overloaded operator method determines the number of times an operator can be overloaded. You can keep overloading an operator as long as each overload method is unique in its signature.

3. What method or methods must be overloaded to overload the equality operator (==)?

   If you want to overload the == operator, you must also overload the != operator, the `Equals()` method, and the `GetHashCode()` method.

4. Which of the following are good examples of using overloaded operators?
   a. Overloading the plus operator (+) to concatenate two string objects.
   b. Overloading the minus operator (-) to determine the distance between two `MapLocation` objects.
   c. Overloading the plus operator (+) to increment an amount once, and incrementing the ++ operator to increment the amount twice.

   Answer (a) is a great example of when to overload an operator. It makes sense that two strings added together would be the same as concatenating them. Answer (b) is probably okay because it would make sense that subtracting one `MapLocation` from another would equal the distance between them. Answer  is a bad overload option. Using the unary plus to increment might be okay; however, this generally isn't obvious. Using the increment operator to do a double add is goofy, so it definitely isn't a good overload example.

5. How do you overload the /= operator?

   Overloading the division operator (/)automatically causes the /= operator to be overloaded.

6. How do you overload the [] operator?

   You use indexers.

7. What relational operators can be overloaded?

   <, >, <=, and >=

8. What unary operators can be overloaded?

   +, -, ++, —, !, ~, `true`, and `false`

9. What binary operators can be overloaded?

   +, -, *, /, %, &, |, ^, <<, and >>

10. What operators cannot be overloaded?

    =, ., ?:, &&, ||, `new`, `is`, `sizeof`, and `typeof`

11. What modifiers are always used with overloaded operators?

    `static` and `public`

## Exercises

1. What would the method header be for the overloaded addition operator used to add two type XYZ objects together?

```
static public XYZ operator+ ( XYZ first, XYZ second)
```

2. Modify Listing 20.3. Add an additional subtraction overloaded method that takes two AChar values. The result should be the numerical difference between the character values stored in the two AChar objects.

```
//  Ex20-02.cs - Overloading an operator
//-----------------------------------------------

using System;

public class AChar
{
    private char CH;

    public AChar() { this.CH = ' '; }
    public AChar(char val) { this.CH = val; }

    public char ch
    {
       get{ return this.CH; }
       set{ this.CH = value; }
    }

    static public AChar operator+ ( AChar orig, int val )
    {
       AChar result = new AChar();
       result.ch = (char)(orig.ch + val);
       return result;
    }
    static public AChar operator- ( AChar orig, int val )
    {
       AChar result = new AChar();
       result.ch = (char)(orig.ch - val);
       return result;
    }
    // Following added for exercise:
    static public int operator- ( AChar first, AChar second )
    {
       int result;
       result = first.ch - second.ch;
       return result;
    }
}

public class myAppClass
```

```
{
    public static void Main(String[] args)
    {
       AChar aaa = new AChar('a');
       AChar bbb = new AChar('b');

       Console.WriteLine("Original value: {0}, {1}", aaa.ch, bbb.ch);
       Console.WriteLine("Difference between {0} and {1} is {2}",
                            aaa.ch, bbb.ch, (aaa - bbb));

       aaa = aaa + 25;
       bbb = bbb - 1;

       Console.WriteLine("Final values: {0}, {1}", aaa.ch, bbb.ch);
       Console.WriteLine("Difference between {0} and {1} is {2}",
                            aaa.ch, bbb.ch, (aaa - bbb));
    }
}
```

3. This snippet has a problem; however, it might not be the one you found. The obvious issue with the listing is that the overloaded method is for the greater than or equal to operator, and yet the check is for less than or equal to. This will actually not cause a problem in the compiling of the listing; however, the person using the overloaded method will most likely get a bit confused.

   The real error that you should be aware of is the return value. The overloaded relational operators need to return a Boolean value (type `bool`). This method uses and returns an integer. This is the real problem!

4. Modify Listing 20.7 to include a method that will compare a salary to an integer value. Also add a method to compare a salary to a long value.

```
//  Ex20-05.cs - Overloading
//-------------------------------------------------

using System;
using System.Text;

public class Salary
{
    private int AMT;

    public Salary() { this.amount = 0; }
    public Salary(int val) { this.amount = val; }

    public int amount
    {
       get{ return this.AMT; }
       set{ this.AMT = value; }
    }
```

```

    public override bool Equals(object val)
    {
       bool retval;

       if( ((Salary)val).amount == this.amount )
          retval = true;
       else
          retval = false;

       return retval;
    }

    public override int GetHashCode()
    {
       return this.ToString().GetHashCode();
    }

    static public bool operator == ( Salary first, Salary second )
    {
       bool retval;

       retval = first.Equals(second);

       return retval;
    }
    static public bool operator == ( Salary first, int second )
    {
       bool retval;

       if (first.amount == second)
          retval = true;
       else
          retval = false;

       return retval;
    }
    static public bool operator == ( Salary first, long second )
    {
       bool retval;

       if ((long)first.amount == second)
          retval = true;
       else
          retval = false;

       return retval;
    }

    static public bool operator != ( Salary first, Salary second )
    {
```

```
            bool retval;

            retval = !(first.Equals(second));

            return retval;
        }
        static public bool operator != ( Salary first, int second )
        {
            bool retval;

            if (first.amount != second)
                retval = true;
            else
                retval = false;

            return retval;
        }
        static public bool operator != ( Salary first, long second )
        {
            bool retval;

            if ((long)first.amount != second)
                retval = true;
            else
                retval = false;

            return retval;
        }

        public override string ToString()
         {
            return( this.amount.ToString() );
         }

     }

     public class myAppClass
     {
        public static void Main(String[] args)
        {
            string tmpstring;

            Salary mySalary   = new Salary(24000);
            Salary yourSalary = new Salary(24000);
            Salary PresSalary = new Salary(200000);
            int IntSalary  = 30000;
            int IntSalary2 = 24000;
            long LongSalary = 30000L;
            long LongSalary2 = 24000L;

            Console.WriteLine("Original values: {0}, {1}, {2}",
```

```
            mySalary, yourSalary, PresSalary);

      if (mySalary == IntSalary)
         tmpstring = "equals";
      else
         tmpstring = "does not equal";

      Console.WriteLine("\nMy salary ({0}) {1} IntSalary ({2})",
                   mySalary, tmpstring, IntSalary );

      if (mySalary == IntSalary2)
         tmpstring = "equals";
      else
         tmpstring = "does not equal";

      Console.WriteLine("\nMy salary ({0}) {1} IntSalary2 ({2})",
                   mySalary, tmpstring, IntSalary2 );

      if (mySalary == LongSalary)
         tmpstring = "equals";
      else
         tmpstring = "does not equal";

      Console.WriteLine("\nMy salary ({0}) {1} LongSalary ({2})",
                   mySalary, tmpstring, LongSalary );

      if (mySalary == LongSalary2)
         tmpstring = "equals";
      else
         tmpstring = "does not equal";

      Console.WriteLine("\nMy salary ({0}) {1} LongSalary2 ({2})",
                   mySalary, tmpstring, LongSalary2 );


   }
}
```

# Day 21 Answers

## Quiz

1. What can be used to get the type of an object, class, or other item?

   `typeof` can be used, as can `Type.GetType`.

2. What type can be used to hold a type value? What namespace is this type in?

   The `Type` type can be used. It is in the `System` namespace.

3. What concept provides information about a class at runtime?

   Reflection provides information.

4. What type would you use to get detailed information on a method's parameter(s)?

   The `ParameterInfo` type could be used.

5. What has been included in C# to help the language be expanded in the future or to help the language handle concepts not currently discovered?

   Attributes have been included.

6. Was the `WebMethod` tag you used in creating Web Services on Day 16 an example of reflection or an example of attributes?

   Actually, it is a bit of both; however, it is more indicative of attributes. `WebMethod` is an attribute; attributes are evaluated by using reflection.

7. Name three predefined attributes.

   There are a number of possible answers to this question. Four predefined attributes listed in today's lessons are `CLSCompliant`, `Conditional`, `Obsolete`, and `WebMethod`.

8. What are five things within a program that an attribute can be associated with?

   Attributes can be associated to an assembly, an event method, a field, a method, a program module, a parameter, a property, a return value, a class, or a structure.

9. What are the two types of parameters used with attributes? What is the difference between the two?

   Positional and named. Positional parameters appear first and are in a set location. Named parameters are optional and appear in any order after the positional parameters.

10. How can you limit what items an attribute can be assigned to?

    You can set `AttributeUsage` to an `AttributeUsage` target.

11. **BONUS:** What data types can an attribute parameter be?

    `bool`, `byte`, `char`, `short`, `int`, `long`, `float`, `double`, `string`, `System.Type`, or `enum`. The parameter can be an object or single-dimensional array; however, it must be one of the mentioned types.

## Exercises

1. Modify the Reflect.cs listing (Listing 21.1) to reflect on the `Object` class (`System.Object`).

```
using System;
using System.Reflection;
```

```

class Mymemberinfo
{
   public static int Main()
   {
      //Get the Type and MemberInfo.
      string testclass = "System.Object";

      Console.WriteLine ("\nFollowing is the member info for class:
➥{0}",
                                    testclass);

      Type MyType = Type.GetType(testclass);

      MemberInfo[] Mymemberinfoarray = MyType.GetMembers();

      //Get the MemberType method and display the elements

      Console.WriteLine("\nThere are {0} members in {1}",
              Mymemberinfoarray.GetLength(0),
              MyType.FullName);

      for ( int counter = 0;
            counter < Mymemberinfoarray.GetLength(0);
            counter++ )
      {
         Console.WriteLine( "{0}. {1} Member type - {2}",
                counter,
                Mymemberinfoarray[counter].Name,
                Mymemberinfoarray[counter].MemberType.ToString());
      }
      return 0;
   }
}
```

2. What methods are available in the `Object` class? Which methods in the `Object` type are also in the types you displayed in today's exercises?

   Remember that all objects inherit from `Object`. If you look at the output in today's listings (Listings 21.1 and 21.2), you should notice that all the methods indicated in this `Object` type are also present in those types. The output of the `Object` type reflection is

```
Following is the member info for class: System.Object

There are 7 members in System.Object
0. GetHashCode Member type - Method
1. Equals Member type - Method
2. ToString Member type - Method
3. Equals Member type - Method
4. ReferenceEquals Member type - Method
```

```
5. GetType Member type - Method
6. .ctor Member type - Constructor
```

3. Modify Listing 22.2 to use the `FieldInfo` type instead of the `MemberInfo`. Use this type to evaluate a listing for its field values.

```
// Ex2103.cs
//-----------------------------------
using System;
using System.Reflection;

namespace Reflect
{

 class Mymemberinfo
 {
    int MYVALUE;
    public  char efg = 'a';
    public  long hij = 10000L;

    public int myValue
    {
        set { MYVALUE = value; }
    }

    public static int Main()
    {
       //The following is the class being checked
       string testclass = "Reflect.Mymemberinfo";

       Console.WriteLine(
             "\nFollowing is the member info for class: {0}",
                                        testclass );

       Type MyType = Type.GetType(testclass);

       FieldInfo[] MymemberFieldarray = MyType.GetFields();

       //Get the MemberType method and display the elements

       Console.WriteLine("\nThere are {0} members in {1}",
               MymemberFieldarray.GetLength(0),
               MyType.FullName);

       for ( int counter = 0;
             counter < MymemberFieldarray.GetLength(0);
             counter++ )
       {
          Console.WriteLine( "{0}. {1} Member type - {2}",
                  counter,
                  MymemberFieldarray[counter].Name,
```

```
                        MymemberFieldarray[counter].MemberType.ToString());
         }
         return 0;
      }
   }
}
```

4. Modify the complete.cs listing to allow multiple attributes to be assigned to a single target. Assign two CodeStatus attributes to a single class.

   The following is one possible answer:

```
// Ex2104.cs -
//-----------------------------------------------------------------
using System;

[AttributeUsage(AttributeTargets.All, AllowMultiple=true)]
public class CodeStatusAttribute : System.Attribute
{
   private string STATUS;
   private string TESTER;
   private string CODER;

   public CodeStatusAttribute( string Status )
   {
      this.STATUS = Status;
   }

   public string Tester
   {
      set
      {
         TESTER = value;
      }
      get
      {
          return TESTER;
      }
   }

   public string Coder
   {
      set
      {
         CODER = value;
      }
      get
      {
         return CODER;
      }
   }
```

```

   public override string ToString()
   {
      return STATUS;
   }
}

// attrUsed.cs - using the CodeStatus attribute
//----------------------------------------------------

[CodeStatus("Final", Coder="Brad")]
[CodeStatus("First", Tester="Fred")]
public class Circle
{
    public Circle()
    {
        // Set up and build a circle class
    }
}

[CodeStatus("Final", Coder="Fred", Tester="John")]
[CodeStatus("Done")]
public class Square
{
    public Square()
    {
        // Set up and build a square class
    }
}

[CodeStatus("Alpha")]
public class Triangle
{
    public Triangle()
    {
        // Set up and build a triangle class
    }
}

[CodeStatus("Final", Coder="Bill")]
[CodeStatus("User Testing", Tester="Melissa")]
public class Rectangle
{
    public Rectangle()
    {
        // Set up and build a rectangle class
    }
}

class myApp
{
```

```
    public static void Main()
    {
        PrintAttributes(typeof(Circle));
        PrintAttributes(typeof(Triangle));
        PrintAttributes(typeof(Square));
        PrintAttributes(typeof(Rectangle));
    }

    public static void PrintAttributes( Type psdType )
     {
         Console.WriteLine("\nAttributes for: {0}", psdType.ToString());

         Attribute[] attribs = Attribute.GetCustomAttributes(psdType);
         foreach (Attribute attr in attribs)
         {
             CodeStatusAttribute item = (CodeStatusAttribute) attr;
             Console.WriteLine(
                 "Status is {0}. Coder is {1}. Tester is {2}.",
                 item.ToString(), item.Coder, item.Tester);
         }
     }
}
```

# APPENDIX B

# C# Keywords

Keywords have specific meanings and use, and are reserved in the C# language. The following are C# keywords:

## abstract

A modifier that can be used to indicate that a class is to be used only as a base class to another class.

## as

An operator used to perform conversions between compatible types. The value to the left of the operator is cast as the type on the right.

## base

A keyword that enables values and types in a base class to be accessed.

# bool

A logical data type that can be either `true` or `false`. `bool` is equivalent to `System.Boolean` in the .NET framework.

# break

A program flow keyword that enables program control to exit a loop or a conditional block (`switch` or `if`).

# byte

A data type that stores an unsigned integer in 1 byte—a value from `0` to `255`. `byte` is equivalent to `System.Byte` in the .NET framework.

# case

A program flow keyword that defines a logical condition within a `switch` statement.

# catch

Part of the `try-catch` error handling logic of a program. The `catch` blocks are used to specify exceptions to be handled and the code to be executed when such exceptions occur.

# char

A data type that stores a single Unicode character in 2 bytes. `char` is equivalent to `System.Char` in the .NET framework.

# checked

A program flow keyword that indicates that overflow-checking for integral-type arithmetic operations and conversions should occur.

# class

A reference data type that can contain both data and method definitions. A class can contain constructors, constants, fields, methods, properties, indexers, operators, and nested types.

# const

A modifier that is applied to a data member or variable. When used, the value of the data type is constant and therefore cannot be changed.

# continue

A program flow keyword that enables program control to automatically go to the next iteration of a loop.

# decimal

A data type that stores a floating-point number in 16 bytes. The precision of a `decimal` variable is better than that of the other floating-point types. This generally makes it better for storing financial values. The suffix `m` or `M` designates a decimal literal. `decimal` is equivalent to `System.Decimal` in the .NET framework.

# default

A label within a `switch` statement to which program flow goes when there is no matching `case` statement.

# delegate

A reference type that can receive a method based on a specified method signature. This signature of methods is based on the declaration of the delegate (similar to function pointers in languages such as C and C++).

# do

A looping program flow construct that causes execution of a statement or block of statements until a condition at the end of the block evaluates to false. Often called a `do...while` statement because the condition at the end of the block is contained with the `while` keyword.

# double

A data type that stores a floating-point number in 8 bytes. The suffix `d` or `D` designates a `double` literal. `double` is equivalent to `System.Double` in the .NET framework.

# else

A conditional program flow statement that contains a statement or block of statements that is executed when a preceding `if` statement evaluates to false.

# enum

A value data type that can store a number of predetermined constant values.

# event

A keyword used to specify an event. The `event` keyword enables a delegate to be specified that can be called when an "event" occurs in a program.

# explicit

A keyword used to declare an explicit conversion operator for a user-defined type.

# extern

A modifier that indicates that a method is external and thus outside the current C# code.

B

# false

A Boolean literal value. Can also be used as an operator that can be overloaded.

# finally

Part of a `try-catch` statement. The `finally` block executes after the `try` block's scope ends. It is generally used to clean up any resources allocated in the `try` block.

# fixed

A keyword used within unmanaged code to lock a reference type in memory so the garbage collector won't move it.

# float

A data type that stores a floating-point number in 4 bytes. The suffix `f` or `F` designates a `float` literal. `float` is equivalent to `System.Single` in the .NET framework.

# for

A program flow statement used for looping. This statement contains an initializer, a conditional, and an iterator. The statements within the `for` construct's block execute until the conditional evaluates to false. The initializer is executed at the start of the `for`. The iterator is executed after each execution of the `for` statement's statement block.

# foreach

An iterative program flow construct that enables you to loop through a collection or array.

# get

A special word used for creating an accessor that gets the value from a property. This is not a reserved word.

# goto

A program flow construct that jumps program flow from the current location to a labeled location elsewhere in the program.

# if

A program flow construct that executes a block of code when a condition evaluates to true.

# implicit

A keyword used to declare a user-defined type conversion operator that does not have to be specified (it will be called implicitly).

# in

A keyword used with the `foreach` keyword. The `in` keyword identifies the collection or array the `foreach` will loop through.

# int

A data type that stores a signed integer in 4 bytes. The range of possible values is from –2,147,483,648 to 2,147,483,647. `int` is equivalent to `System.Int32` in the .NET framework. Literal numbers with no suffix are of type `int` by default if the value fits within the given range for an `int`.

# interface

A keyword used to declare a reference type that defines a set of members but does not declare them.

# internal

An access modifier that enables a data type to be accessible only from within files in the same assembly.

# is

An operator used to determine at runtime whether an object is a specified type.

# lock

A keyword used to make a block of code critical. This section of code does not enable more than one thread to access it at a time.

# long

A data type that stores a signed integer in 8 bytes. The range of possible values is from –9,223,372,036,854,775,808 to 9,223,372,036,854,775,807. `long` is equivalent to `System.Int64` in the .NET framework. The suffix `l` or `L` designates a `long` literal.

# namespace

A keyword that enables you to organize a number of types into a group. Used to help prevent name collisions and to make it easier to reference types.

# new

An operator used to create an object. Also used as a modifier to hide a member inherited from a base class.

# null

A literal used to represent reference value points to nothing.

# object

A type based on the `System.Object` class in the .NET Framework. All other types are derived from `object`.

# operator

A keyword used to create or overload an operator's functionality in a class or structure.

# out

A parameter modifier that enables the parameter reference variable to be used to return a value from a method. The variable must be assigned a value in the method.

# override

A keyword used to provide a new implementation of a method or property, which replaces a base class's existing method or property with the same signature.

# params

A parameter modifier that indicates that a variable number of values can be contained in the parameter. This modifier can be used only with the final parameter in a method's parameter list.

B

# private

An access modifier that indicates that a method, property, or other member of a structure or class is accessible only within the same class or structure.

# protected

An access modifier that indicates that a method, property, or other member of a class is accessible only within the same class or within classes that are derived from this class.

# public

An access modifier that indicates that a method, property, or other member of a class or structure is accessible.

# readonly

A data member modifier that indicates that after the initial assignment—either at the time of declaration or within the constructor—the value within the data member cannot be changed.

# ref

A parameter modifier that indicates that changes to the parameter variable will also be reflected in the variable that was passed as the `ref` argument.

# return

A keyword used to return a value from a method. Process flow is changed back to the calling method upon execution of this keyword.

## sbyte

A data type that stores a signed integer in 1 byte. This is a value from –128 to 127. `sbyte` is equivalent to `System.SByte` in the .NET framework.

## sealed

A modifier for classes that prevents you from deriving from the class.

## set

A special word used for creating an accessor that sets the value in a property. This is not a reserved word.

## short

A data type that stores a signed integer in 2 bytes. The range of possible values is from –32,768 to 32,767. `short` is equivalent to `System.Int16` in the .NET framework.

## sizeof

An operator used to determine the size of a value type in bytes.

## stackalloc

A keyword used to allocate a block of memory on the stack. This block's size is determined by the data type and expression included with the keyword. This allocated memory is assigned to a pointer and is not subject to garbage collection.

## static

A modifier used to indicate that only a single value will be stored for the type. Used with fields, methods, properties, operators, and constructors.

# string

A data type that stores Unicode characters. `string` is an alias for `System.String` in the .NET Framework.

# struct

A value data type that can contain both data and method definitions. A structure can contain constructors, constants, fields, methods, properties, indexers, operators, and nested types.

# switch

A program flow construct that changes program flow based on a value of a variable. Flow can go to either a `case` statement or a `default` statement.

# this

A keyword used within a non-`static` method that associates a variable to the current instance of a class or structure.

# throw

A program flow statement that is used to throw an exception, which indicates that something abnormal has occurred. Used with `try` and `catch`.

# true

A Boolean literal value. Can also be used as an operator, which can be overloaded.

## try

The keyword used for exception handling. The `try` block contains the code that could potentially throw an exception. Used with `catch` and `finally`.

## typeof

An operator that returns the data type of an object. The type is returned as a .NET data type (a `System.Type` object).

## uint

A data type that stores an unsigned integer in 4 bytes. The range of possible values is from 0 to 4,294,967,295. `uint` is equivalent to `System.UInt32` in the .NET framework. A suffix of `u` or `U` designates an `uint` literal.

## ulong

A data type that stores an unsigned integer in 8 bytes. The range of possible values is from 0 to 18,446,744,073,709,551,615. `ulong` is equivalent to `System.UInt64` in the .NET framework. The suffix of `ul` (regardless of the case of the `U` and `L`) designates a `ulong` literal.

## unchecked

An operator or statement that can be used to indicate that overflow-checking on integer data types should be ignored.

## unsafe

A keyword used to identify code that is considered unsafe to execute in the managed environment. For example, `unsafe` should be used to wrap any code that uses pointers.

# ushort

A data type that stores an unsigned integer in 2 bytes. The range of possible values is from 0 to 65,535. `ushort` is equivalent to `System.UInt16` in the .NET framework.

# using

A keyword for creating an alias for a namespace. It can also be used to shortcut the need to use fully qualified names for types within a namespace.

# value

The name of the variable being set by a `set` property accessor. This is not a reserved word.

# virtual

A modifier used on a method or property to indicate that the method or property can be overridden.

# void

A keyword used in place of a type to indicate that no data type is used. In method declarations, `void` can be used to declare that no value is returned from the method.

# while

A looping program flow construct that causes execution of a statement or block of statements as long as a condition evaluates to true.

# APPENDIX C

# C# Command-Line Compiler Flags

You can set options with the C# command-line compiler. You can see the options by running the command-line compiler with the `/help` flag.

## Output

### `/out:<file>`

This flag indicates the name for the final output file. If this flag is not specified, the `out` name is based on the name of the first source file.

### `/target:<type>` or `/t:<type>`

This flag states the type of program that will be created. Possible values for `<type>` are

| *Type* | *Description* |
|---|---|
| `exe` | For a console executable (default) |
| `winexe` | To build a windows executable |
| `library` | To build a library |
| `module` | To build a module that can be added to an assembly |

### /define:<symbol list> or /d: <symbol list>

This flag is used to define symbols that can be used with the preprocessing directives. It is similar to using a `#define <symbol>` directive at the beginning of a source file.

### /doc:<file>

This flag specifies that XML documentation should be created. The XML documentation file will be named `<file>`.

## Input

### /recurse:<wildcard>

This flag indicates that all files in the current directory and subdirectories should be included according to the wildcard specifications.

### /reference:<file list> or /r:<file list>

This flag indicates that metadata should be referenced from the specified assembly files.

### /addmodule:<file list>

This flag links the specified modules into the current assembly.

## Resource

### /win32res:<file>

This flag specifies a Win32 resource file (.res).

### /win32icon:<file>

This flag indicates the icon that should be used for the output.

### **/resource:*<resinfo>* or /res:*<resinfo>***

This flag embeds the specified resource.

### **/linkresource:*<resinfo>* or /linkres:*<resinfo>***

This flag links the specified resource to this assembly.

## Code Generation

### **/debug[+|-]**

This flag indicates whether debugging information should be included (+) or omitted (-).

### **/debug:{full|pdbonly}**

This flag specifies the type of debugging where `full` enables attaching a debugger to a running program. `full` is the default.

### **/optimize[+|-] or /o[+|-]**

This flag specifies whether optimizations should occur (+) or not (-).

### **/incremental[+|-] or /incr[+|-]**

This flag indicates whether incremental compilation is enabled (+) or not (-).

## Errors and Warnings

### **/warnaserror[+|-]**

This flag causes warnings to be treated as errors. This means a final file won't be created if there are any warnings. + turns on, - leaves off (default).

### **/warn:*<n>* or /w*<n>***

This flag sets the warning level from `0` to `4`. Warnings each contain a severity level. Only warnings at or above the set level are displayed.

### **/nowarn:*<warning list>***

This flag disables specified warning messages.

C

# Programming Language

### /checked[+|-]

This flag generates overflow checks, if set to +, or ignores them, if set to -.

### /unsafe[+|-]

This flag allows "unsafe" code, if turned on (+), and doesn't, if turned off (-).

# Miscellaneous

### @<*file*>

This flag reads a response file (<*file*>) for more options.

### /help or /?

This flag displays help information similar to what is presented in this appendix.

### /nologo

This flag suppresses the compiler's copyright message.

### /noconfig

This flag prevents the CSC.RSP file from being automatically included.

# Advanced

### /baseaddress:<*address*>

This flag indicates the base address (<*address*>) for the library to be built.

### /bugreport:<*file*>

This flag creates a Bug Report file called <*file*>.

### /codepage:<*n*>

This flag specifies the codepage to use when opening source files.

### /utf8output

This flag causes compiler messages to be output in UTF-8 encoding.

## **/main:<*type*> or /m:<*type*>**

This flag specifies the type (class) that contains the entry point (generally a `Main` method). All other possible entry points are ignored.

## **/fullpaths**

This flag indicates that the compiler should generate fully qualified paths.

## **/filealign:<*n*>**

This flag specifies the alignment used for output file sections.

## **/nostdlib[+|-]**

This flag indicates that the standard library (mscorlib.dll) should not be referenced or used.



## **/lib:<*file list*>**

This flag specifies additional directories to search for references.

# APPENDIX D

# Understanding Different Number Systems

As a computer programmer, you might sometimes be required to work with numbers expressed in binary and hexadecimal notation. This appendix explains what these systems are and how they work. To help you understand, let's first review the common decimal number system.

## The Decimal Number System

The decimal system is the base-10 system that you use every day. A number in this system—for example, 342—is expressed as powers of 10. The first digit (counting from the right) gives 10 to the 0 power, the second digit gives 10 to the 1 power, and so on. Any number to the 0 power equals 1, and any number to the 1 power equals itself. Thus, continuing with the example of 342, you have:

| | |
|---|---|
| 3 | $3 \times 10^2 = 3 \times 100 = 300$ |
| 4 | $4 \times 10^1 = 4 \times 10 = 40$ |
| 2 | $2 \times 10^0 = 2 \times 1 = 2$ |
| | Sum = 342 |

The base-10 system requires 10 different digits, 0 through 9. The following rules apply to base 10 and to any other base number system:

- A number is represented as powers of the system's base.
- The system of base n requires n different digits.

Now let's look at the other number systems.

## The Binary System

The binary number system is base 2 and therefore requires only two digits, 0 and 1. The binary system is useful for computer programmers, because it can be used to represent the digital on/off method in which computer chips and memory work. Here's an example of a binary number and its representation in the decimal notation you're more familiar with, writing 1011 vertically:

| | |
|---|---|
| 1 | $1 \times 2^3 = 1 \times 8 = 8$ |
| 0 | $0 \times 2^2 = 0 \times 4 = 0$ |
| 1 | $1 \times 2^1 = 1 \times 2 = 2$ |
| 1 | $1 \times 2^0 = 1 \times 1 = 1$ |
| | Sum = 11 (decimal) |

Binary has one shortcoming: It's cumbersome for representing large numbers.

## The Hexadecimal System

The hexadecimal system is base 16. Therefore, it requires 16 digits. The digits 0 through 9 are used, along with the letters A through F, which represent the decimal values 10 through 15. Here is an example of a hexadecimal number, 2DA, and its decimal equivalent:

| | |
|---|---|
| 2 | $2 \times 16^2 = 2 \times 256 = 512$ |
| D | $13 \times 16^1 = 13 \times 16 = 208$ |
| A | $10 \times 16^0 = 10 \times 1 = 10$ |
| | Sum = 730 (decimal) |

The hexadecimal system (often called the hex system) is useful in computer work because it's based on powers of 2. Each digit in the hex system is equivalent to a four-digit binary number, and each two-digit hex number is equivalent to an eight-digit binary number. Table D.1 shows some hex/decimal/binary equivalents.

**TABLE D.1** Hexadecimal numbers and their decimal and binary equivalents.

| *Hexadecimal Digit* | *Decimal Equivalent* | *Binary Equivalent* |
|---|---|---|
| 0 | 0 | 0000 |
| 1 | 1 | 0001 |
| 2 | 2 | 0010 |
| 3 | 3 | 0011 |
| 4 | 4 | 0100 |
| 5 | 5 | 0101 |
| 6 | 6 | 0110 |
| 7 | 7 | 0111 |
| 8 | 8 | 1000 |
| 9 | 9 | 1001 |
| A | 10 | 1010 |
| B | 11 | 1011 |
| C | 12 | 1100 |
| D | 13 | 1101 |
| E | 14 | 1110 |
| F | 15 | 1111 |
| 10 | 16 | 00010000 |
| F0 | 240 | 11110000 |
| FF | 255 | 11111111 |

# INDEX

## A

## D



## E

## J-K



## L

## N

## R

## T



## U



## V



## W-X-Y-Z

# Notes